An Empire Teeters
Foray into Portugal's Fascism

**A Journalist Takes Notes in
Old Luso Colonial Africa –
Angola, Moçambique & Guiné Bissau
Summer & Fall 1963**

by

J. J. Hespeler-Boultbee

D1599450

CCB Publishing
British Columbia, Canada

An Empire Teeters – Foray into Portugal's Fascism:
A Journalist Takes Notes in Old Luso Colonial Africa –
Angola, Moçambique & Guiné Bissau Summer & Fall 1963

Copyright ©2020-2021 by J. J. Hespeler-Boultbee
ISBN-13   978-1-77143-414-0
First Edition, Revised

Library and Archives Canada Cataloguing in Publication
Title: An empire teeters foray into Portugal's fascism : a journalist takes notes in Old Luso Colonial Africa--
Angola, Moçambique & Guiné Bissau Summer & Fall 1963 / by J. J. Hespeler-Boultbee.
Names: Hespeler-Boultbee, J. J., 1935- author.
Identifiers: Canadiana (print) 20200261568 | Canadiana (ebook) 2020026172X
| ISBN 9781771434140 (softcover) | ISBN 9781771434157 (PDF)
Subjects: LCSH: Portugal—Colonies—Africa.
Classification: LCC DT36.7 .H47 2020 | DDC 325/.3469096—dc23

Cover artwork and design by J. J. Hespeler-Boultbee
Cover photo: Lisboa dockside: Portuguese pára-quedistas (paratroops) return to Lisbon from
Guiné-Bissau during the Carnation revolution of 1974/1975.

Photo credits: All photos and images contained herein are copyright J.J. Hespeler-Boultbee,
except the following:
1) Portuguese stamp of Antonio Salazar circa 1971 © Boris 15 | CanStockPhoto.com
2) Photo of Jonas Savimbi circa 1986 is in the Public Domain and is used herein without malice
3) Image of compass rose is in the Public Domain and is used herein without malice.

Text credits:
1) A quoted section from the poem "Jobson of the Star" written by Robert W. Service and published in the
book *Bar-Room Ballads* is reprinted herein with permission granted by the copyright holder, Mrs. Anne
Longépé.
2) A poem written by Joyce Gilchrist is reprinted herein with permission granted by the copyright holder,
Mrs. Joyce Gilchrist.
3) Text contributions by Ian Gilchrist are reprinted herein with permission granted by the copyright holder,
Dr. Ian Gilchrist.
4) Text contributions by Rev. Michael Solberg are reprinted herein with permission granted by the
copyright holder, Rev. Michael Solberg.
5) Text contributions by Dr. Chandar Sundaram are reprinted herein with permission granted by the
copyright holder, Dr. Chandar Sundaram.

Publisher: CCB Publishing
              British Columbia, Canada
              www.ccbpublishing.com

a honra é minha e dá me imenso prazer
dedicar este livro a dois dos meus maiores amigos portugueses:
Jorge Paes da Cunha Freire,
que me mostrou as ruelas e passeios de Lisboa
(e o que se esconde por baixo deles),
e o já falecido
Fernando Relvas,
historiador, contador de histórias
e um artista gráfico de talento excecional

Also by J. J. Hespeler-Boultbee

A Story in Stones:
Portugal's influence on culture and
architecture in the Highlands of Ethiopia
1493-1634
Foreword by Richard Pankhurst
©2011 – ISBN 9781926585987

Mrs. Queen's Chump:
Idi Amin, the Mau Mau, Communists,
and Other Silly Follies of the British Empire,
A Military Memoir
©2012 – ISBN 9781771430296

Somersaults:
Rovings, Tears & Absurdities -
A Memoir from the Fringe of Journalism
©2017 – ISBN 9781771432962

Acknowledgements

Jorge Freire, who shares a place in the dedication of this work, has been my friend and companion since almost the beginning of my association with Portugal and the Portuguese. It would be hard to outline the myriad ways in which he and his family have assisted me over the years – but in specific terms, and on more than one occasion, Jorge has acted as not just friend and sidekick, but as inspiration, commentator, translator, critic and more. We have spent many hours laughing together, and a few crying – all of them cherished memories.

While he lived and was my neighbour, Fernando Relvas (also a close friend to Jorge Freire) introduced me to an unusual and intense view of Portuguese history and culture – usually oblique, always rich, colourful and instructive. It was largely on account of his wide knowledge, incisive and humorous, that I came to look on the period of The Discoveries with such intrigue and interest, and so make of them an element of my own life. I feel greatly indebted to him, and hold my memories of him very close.

I wish to thank Joyce and Ian Gilchrist, Rev. Michael Solberg, Rev. Luís Samabundi and Jean Burgess, all of whom have enjoyed strong and enduring personal links to Angola. Alas, death has claimed all of my initial contacts from Moçambique, however I would like to acknowledge the current director of information for Gorongosa Game Park, Vasco Galante, who has been most active concerning the international restoration effort at the park after years of devastation and neglect owing to the Moçambique civil war in the final decades of the XX century. I would likewise wish to extend my gratitude, posthumously, to one of the last of the Governors of Portuguese Guiné, His Excellency Vasco António Martins Rodrigues – the unusually delightful informality of the occasion of our meeting being more memorable than his imprecise information ...

Eminent military historian Dr. Chandar Sundaram, most kindly reviewed the manuscript and offered particularly useful commentary and advice, for which I am grateful. Without his genial attentions and gimlet-eyed editing skills the manuscript would have lingered far too long and perhaps never have breathed itself into life the way it has. His essay on American involvement constitutes Appendix 12. A similar independent review was undertaken by my friend Rod Marsh, which has proven itself most timely and helpful.

Both the family of poet Robert Service and the United Nations Publications Office have most graciously granted permission for the inclusion of materials relevant to the text: the quotation from Service's *Bar-Room Ballads* on page 21, and Appendix #1 on page 465 which contains relevant portions of the 1964 UN working paper on Portugal's African colonies.

Anica Govedarica, Pedro Miguel Dias Duarte, Andrew Shore, Carmo de Castro, Alison Roberts, Luís Leotte de Rego, Alcina Monteiro, António Eloy Garcia, Teresa Loureiro, Luisa Valério, the van Zeller family, José Maria Machado and his wife, Teresa, as well as many, many others – all currently resident in Portugal – have proven to be the staunchest of friends over the years, and have provided welcome and vigorous support for the various tales I have spun them. I thank them for their unflagging generosity of spirit, and extend to each my warmest greetings and well-wishes.

Likewise, I am grateful for the encouragement and assistance of my neighbours and friends in Canada – among them my lifelong friend, the late Edmond Eberts Price who, along with the generous encouragement of his family, badgered me to begin this work. I finally got down to it in earnest brief months before Ed died. Great reassurance has been a constant from my friend and editor, Paul Rabinovitch. I wish to thank Susana Duarte for her monitoring of my fractured Portuguese. I am also most grateful for many and varied inspirational boosts from Munroe Archibald, John Azar, James Bowen, Marion Carroll, Shelley Coulombe, Pat Jamieson, Charles Joerin, Paulo Pereira, Maude Scott, Ramana Waldhaus, poet Paul Burnside and artists Carol Grenier, Jaroslaw Gwiazda, Charles du Vernet and Alain Vincent. I am much indebted to the professional crew at Gizmo's – Chris Benning, Jeff Robinson and Kelly Wagner – who kept me on track and keyboard functional despite my generational computer bewilderment.

On the occasional afternoon throughout the period of time it has taken to write and review the manuscript for this work, and in order to touch solid ground and come to grips with necessarily prosaic realities, I've taken to meeting with an acerbic and witty coterie of gentlemen, all my own age or older, who recount (sometimes over-and-over, admittedly) tales of their own more youthful exploits. They are funny and they are wise, and to a man they possess the capacity to squeeze – like toothpaste from a tube – the kernel of veracity from any and all encounters. They do this with an astutely bland and unvarnished bluntness I admire. Tongue-in-cheek, I tend to view them in much the way I consider that aggregation of rapscallions who beg to ride (bareback?) to Widecombe Fair atop Tom Pearce's over-burdened and swaybacked grey mare: a gleeful gang of aging pundits who, collectively, have offered me a generous measure of acuity and perk-up during the months when the writing of anything has been a chore. For their oblivious, always buoyant support, therefore, I wish to salute Gordy, Bud, Neville, James, Patrick, Maurice, Howie, two Bills and a Polish Michał … If they read this, they will know very well who they are.

I would like to acknowledge my family members: sons Timothy and Michael, daughters Teri Lee and Stephanie, my grandchildren and my great grandchildren. This work is offered as partial explanation of what I was up to that long summer and autumn in 1963.

Like all married men who blunder and blame, too often I am guilty of assuming I alone am champion of any of my day's positive achievements – if and when they happen. So here let me definitively admit this is foible at its most flagrant and fanciful. Too frequently exhibiting the grump of a gorilla, I hereby happily admit my indebtedness to my companion and wife, Alemie – for her patience, always, but more especially for the hundreds of small gestures she makes each day to assist me in everything I do.

Author's Note

Works of memoir are invariably set within the framework of history. The book you are now holding in your hands is *not* a history, but perhaps it could be a useful adjunct to commentary concerning this eventful period of Portugal's recent story – and no doubt Africa's, too.

Many place names have changed since the independence of Portugal's colonies. In general, and for the sake of consistency, I have continued use of names in vogue at the time of my visit – and with their Portuguese spellings. Thus the rendering of Portugal's capital city, Lisbon to speakers of English, is given as Lisboa; Mozambique is Moçambique, and so on. Current names of places used in the text, where applicable, are shown in parenthesis on the maps at the beginning of the work.

Conversations rendered in quotes are reconstructions from memory and notes, reconstitutions of speech from over fifty years ago. They should be accepted as basically accurate in their purpose of continuity of story, rather than verbatim – though in some cases they are, indeed, verbatim.

As the Portuguese refer to a *portugués* [m] or a *portuguesa* [f], so they refer to an *angolano* and *angolana*, or *moçambicano* and *moçambicana*, etc. – with the masculine applied in cases of mixed plurals. These general forms are adhered to throughout this work for the sake of overall consistency, but with deference to the adjectival use of capital letters in each case to conform with correct English-language presentation.

The names of many, but not all, individuals have been changed. This is intended as a conscientious effort to avoid personal injury, embarrassment – or possible litigation.

The author alone is responsible for all errors and omissions in this work.

Introduction

In modern times, the British, the French, the Spanish, the Dutch, the Belgians, the Italians, the Germans, the Japanese, the Russians and the Americans have all possessed colonies, and fought bitter wars with the people they have colonized and abused.

In every case the colonies have varied in form and texture. As is pointed out in this text, there was a time when it was thought noble to possess colonies. Great nations simply were not that great unless they could demonstrate their power over others. Colonies, by definition, are comprised of subjugated peoples, and subjugation is the kernel of power. Through colonization a powerful nation is able to gain land and its *usufruto* – the bounty of the land, be it agricultural or mineral – and is thus in a position to harness local populations to work as slaves, indentured or contract labour, or (in the words of George Bernard Shaw) as 'wage slaves.' To the victor went (and still go) the spoils, quite literally and, until very recent times, colonial history has been written by the victors – generally as propaganda to suit their own purposes.

Through a monumental misreading of history it would seem the British – her administrators and, following them like cattle to pasture, the people themselves – thought they could dominate forever places like India or Malaya or the colonies in Africa or the Caribbean. Certainly fortunes in national treasure were expended in shipping her armies and bureaucrats and settlers to every corner of her global empire, but the returns in booty and military manpower made it all worthwhile. Some hugely-favoured 'white' colonies broke away relatively early – the US completely, and New Zealand, Australia, Canada, South Africa becoming nation states within the lordly British Empire virtuously having attained the complete suppression, even annihilation, of indigenous peoples. There were strong bloodlines between these colonists and the Motherland ('Chips off the old block') so perhaps their breakaways, though resisted in Whitehall, were understandable. The Commonwealth of Nations is now a sometime-working body but was initially and quite hurriedly devised as Britain's face-saving legacy covering a vile system – a sort of 'Let's be friends' lickety-split paint job to tint over a former horrendously abusive system responsible for numerous wars and the deaths, misery and displacement of millions. Within the text (page 108) the reader will find the

Portuguese expression '*só para inglês ver,*' which translates 'only for the Englishman to see.' It is the cynical expression a Portuguese might employ to describe the lick of paint with which one might cover a patch of rust on an old car before selling it off to some unsuspecting sucker. A cover, a ruse, a little dishonesty that might not be discovered – the sort of thing an unwitting Englishman might fall for while visiting Portugal. It is an ironic *dito* – saying – in the instance of this discussion.

It is also ironic that, following their own independence, each former 'white' colony set about gradually re-stocking its population in the image of Motherland Britannia; the White Australia policy comes to mind, but other 'white' colonies had equally repulsive laws concerning racial minorities. The Canadian government incarcerated Canadians of Japanese extract, and confiscated their lands and livelihoods, at the outbreak of war with Japan in 1941; when population densities faltered, 'loyal' subjects were sought through immigration (with the imposition of a head tax for Chinese labour) – and, even now, the falsity of a revolting and meaningless oath of allegiance to the anchronism of the English monarchy. With all the jockeying about in the search for 'solutions,' someone got it right – or desperately wrong. Intentional or otherwise, the result has been the opening of an almost unstoppable floodgate of immigrants and refugees that has created nightmares for every government entity involved. If the status quo was ever the bedrock of domination, immigration both legal and illegal would appear to have snuggled a wad of explosives under it.

Britain was not the only culprit, of course; hers is simply the example the author has come to know best through personal experience. Where human movement and the dignity of human rights is concerned, all other colonizers have tumbled over one set of obstacles or another. The result has been that all concerned governments have been caught flat-footed. The chaos introduced by the abuses of colonization has been set loose on a global scale. Suddenly whole populations are on the move; whole nations are changing colour and learning how to turn formerly second-languages into first-languages. In this unrelenting process, thousands upon thousands of people have lost their lives – while the governments that have encouraged, created, permitted or tried to halt the turmoil of such mass movement offer little more than their tut-tuts of hypocritic horror. We are taught that communists and fascists alike refuse to listen to their people. Few observers are prepared to admit that democratic administrations are little better, that they also seldom risk listening closely to their people, let alone conducting government according to systems of universal reason, demand or fair play. 'National interest' covers a multitude of deceptions and deceits – just as 'competition' so often leads to cartels, the enrichment of the bosses, inflation and the misery (or enslavement) of the have-nots.

At the close of the First World War Woodrow Wilson, creator of the League of Nations, had argued for '... *a balance of power*' rather than '*a community of power.*' He had called for '*organized peace*' rather than '*organized rivalries*' – the 'competition' so diabolically nurtured by corporate greed to act as smoke screen to cover its enormous excesses at home and abroad, and subsequently refined as 'democracy' and 'free enterprise' – with all the scrumptious flavour of Mother's apple pie freedoms.

Several cases are mentioned in the text, so there is scant cause to create a list for this brief introduction. Because she is the protagonist of this study, however, Portugal's case needs to be the exception.

At the time of its demise in 1975, Portugal's empire was the oldest and most far-flung in the world. There were those enlightened and modern-minded Portuguese – great numbers of them – who opposed racism and abuse, and who genuinely wanted the nation's colonies to achieve peaceful transitions to self-government. At one time, before the wars of independence, that noble goal might have been possible. But there were those who, with almost religious fervour, believed in Portugal's historic aspiration – a 'civilizing mission' that required the nation to dig in her heels at all costs in order to achieve the greatness granted by God and so clearly enunciated in the epic poem presaged by the national poet Luís Vaz de Camões in his work, *Os Lusíadas*. These latter groups comprised the monied class that had lived off the wealth of the country's colonies for close to five hundred years, and whose status quo very well suited the fascist government and its highly efficient police forces. So entangled were the upper echelons of Portuguese society, the governor of the bank might well be the minister overseeing the family's fortunes in Angola, or the governor of a district in Moçambique was the nephew of a powerful vintner on the banks of the Douro. It was among this group in particular that was fostered the very worst of Portuguese racism – hangover from guilt of the long years of the nation's slave trade to Brasil – or mining in Angola, or transportation in Moçambique.

By 1975 (especially in America and certainly the tumultuous areas of black Africa – but also in Portugal) there was a worldwide abhorrence of racism of any kind. Racists ducked their heads to remain out of sight and await a later re-emergence. But for the moment the notion of the 'dumb black' was absolutely out-dated and had definitively and deservedly been kicked downstairs. However, while it had served the nation's fascists well up to that time, it was to become a particular stumbling block in the advancement of any useful relations possible between African indigenous, colonial settlers and the colonies' administrators and power brokers. The persistence of such well-defined racism – in which one's uniform was the pigmentation of his or her skin – gave added seasoning to a fascism that had arisen on the regal back of Divine Right. It made for one of the most horrendous of Africa's most ghastly wars, and in the end proved bitter medicine to the long-time governors of Portugal. At last they were obliged to acknowledge that the outraged majority of their own people hated them. That was the essence of Portugal's popular 'Carnation Revolution'[1] for nineteen months in 1974 and 1975. Initially a military coup, Portugal's armed forces, almost by accident, triggered a popular revolution. The fascists fled – many to the Americas – bringing Portuguese colonialism to its end and leaving behind an ecstatic population. Day and night, for weeks, the people of Portugal danced in the streets, honked their horns and cheered the thousands of military personnel patrolling the cities. What better way to show their delight than to pop red carnations into the spouts of the rifles touted by an equally happy and surprised soldiery, inviting all to join in the dance?

As may well be imagined, for nineteen months it was difficult to govern such a varied and euphoric populace, so the CIA arrived in the fall of 1975 to help bring everybody to their senses.

The world has taken several additional downward spirals since that time, but it might be useful to note here a capsule history of what preceded Salazar's route to power, and the ultimate demise of his *Estado Novo*:

On a single day in 1908 the Portuguese king, Dom Carlos, and his heir, Dom Luís Filipe, were both made victims of a successful assassination plot. Dom Carlos' eighteen-year-old second son thus came to the throne, ruling as Dom Manuel II, initially enjoying the sympathies of the population owing to his youth and the violent deaths of his father and older brother. But the prevailing mood of the country was republican; the monarchy was dissolved after Dom Manuel had been just two years on the throne, and Portugal was declared a Republic. The young king was forced into exile in Britain, where he died in 1932.

The Republic of 1910 was not a great success. Although it lasted until 1926, it saw the rise and collapse of no less than forty-five governments. Its instability and financial chaos ultimately gave rise to the *Estado Novo* of Dr. António de Oliveira Salazar who had been offered the position of economics

---

[1] *Carnation Revolution* – called thus because a jubilant population, unafraid of the military in the streets that had assisted the overthrow of an unpopular dictatorship, stuffed carnations into the muzzles of the soldiers' rifles and danced with them.

minister in 1926 with full control over the country's finances. He was named Prime Minister in 1932. Members of the National Assembly were chosen for their loyalty to the government, while Salazar himself selected his ministers and personally supervised their work. Political freedoms were hamstrung, and military police repressed any and all forms of opposition. It was in this climate that PIDE – the secret police – was formed, first as the PVDE (*Polícia de Vigiliância e de Defesa do Estado*). The force was re-named PIDE (*Polícia Internacional e de Defesa do Estado*) in 1945, DGS (*Direcção-Geral de Segurança*) in 1969 and then abolished altogether in 1974. A civilian organization of Portugal's intelligence services was set up in 1984, *Sistema de Informações da Republica Portuguesa* (SIRP).

Suffering a stroke, Salazar himself was removed from power in 1968 and died in 1970. He was succeeded by his protégé, Marcelo Caetano, who was deposed along with the entire dictatorial regime of the *Estado Novo*, by the *Carnation Revolution* on 25 April 1974.

JJH-B, Victoria, BC, Canada,
September 2020

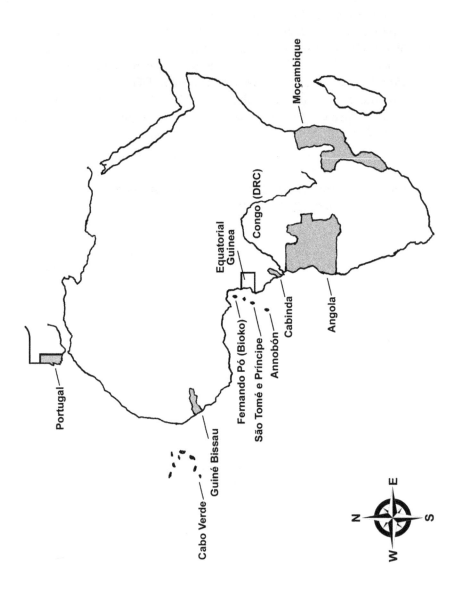

Portugal

Cabo Verde

Guiné Bissau

Equatorial
Guinea

Fernando Pó (Bioko)

São Tomé e Príncipe

Annobón

Congo (DRC)

Cabinda

Angola

Moçambique

N
E
S
W

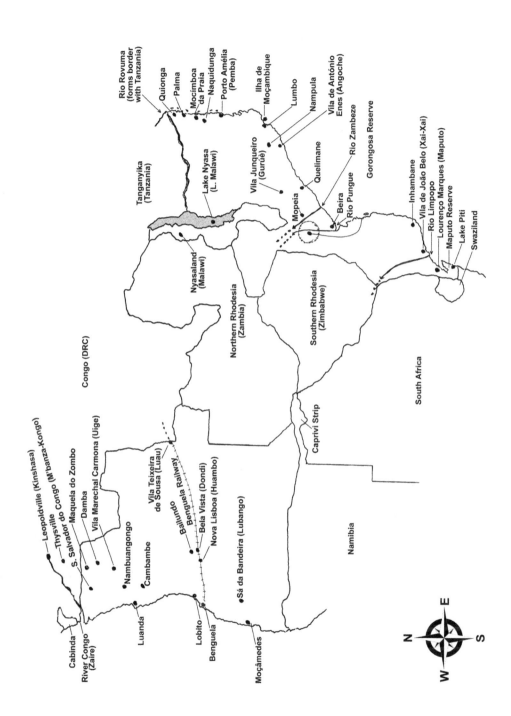

xvii

Place Names Listed on the Maps

Many place names in old Portuguese Africa have changed since independence. Pre-independence names/spellings are used throughout the work. New names, where they apply, are shown on the maps in brackets.

North
Portugal
Lisboa
Ceuta
Cabo Verde
Guiné Bissau

Guinea coast
Fernando Pó (Bioko)
São Tomé e Principe
Equatorial Guinea
Annobón
Cabinda
River Congo (Zaire)

Congo (DRC)
Leopoldville (Kinshasa)
Thysville
Fernando Pó (Bioko)
Equatorial Guinea
Annobón

Angola (North to South)
S. Salvador do Congo (M'banza Kongo)
Maquela do Zombo
Damba
Vila Marcchal Carmona (Uige)
Nambuangongo
Luanda
Cambambe
Lobito
Benguela
Benguela Railway
Nova Lisboa (Huambo)
Bela Vista (Dondi)
Bailundo
Vila Teixeira de Sousa (Luuau)

Sá da Bandeira (Lubango)
Moçâmedes

Surrounds
Northern Rhodesia (Zambia)
Southern Rhodesia (Zimbabwe)
Caprivi Strip
Namibia
South Africa
Swaziland
Nyasaland (Malawi)
Lake Nyasa (L. Malawi)
Tanganyika (Tanzania)

Moçambique (South to North)
Lake Piti
Maputo Reserve
Lourenço Marques (Maputo)
Rio Limpopo
Vila de Jõao Belo (Xai-Xai)
Inhambane
Gorongosa Reserve
Rio Pungue
Beira
Rio Zambeze
Quelimane
Mopeia
Vila Junqueiro (Gurúe)
Vila de António Enes (Angoche)
Nampula
Lumbo
Ilha de Moçambique
Porto Amélia (Pemba)
Naquidunga
Mocimboa da Praia
Palma
Quionga
Rio Rovuma

Contents

Part I – Portents 1

Part II – Angola 111

Part III – Congo (DRC) 217

Part IV – Moçambique 269

Part V – *Fim,* and Then Some 415

Part VI – Envoi 437

Appendixes 463

List of Acronyms, Some Unusual Words
    and Phrases 531

Confined inside his coop until he is killed,
the Rooster sings anthems to liberty ...

- Fernando Pessoa, writing as Bernardo Soares in *The Book of Disquiet* (#140)

PART I

Portents

Part I – Portents

Slaughter 3

Four Fascist Thugs 7

Colonial War 12

New Assignment 15

The Portuguese Consul 41

Doubts – The Birmingham Lesson 45

Deep Dig 52

Pink City 61

Others – and PIDE 79

Slaughter

In the first few months of 1961 the world's newspapers carried almost daily accounts of the fighting in the Congo. The peculiar turns and twists of events had moved so rapidly, and become so involved, that borders no longer seemed to mean very much, and one day's horror story was much like the one the day before, and the one the day before that. To those not familiar with the African scene, place names could mean very little. Whether what one read concerned Verwoerd's South Africa, Nkrumah's Ghana, Tshombe's Katanga, or the French in Algeria, almost everyone outside the troubled areas – the rest of the world – was aware only that Africa was in a hell of a mess. In the midst of all this, only one colonizing nation had apparently kept its nose clean – at least in terms of 'news' or propaganda – so silently 'clean,' in fact, that it came as a surprise when the world woke up to the fact that tiny Portugal possessed two of the largest colonies on the African continent, and several of its smallest; that she remained the last old-style colonial power in the world, and that her discontented subjects were now in full-scale revolt after nearly five hundred years of what the rebels claimed was stern and repressive domination.

Preoccupied with Cold War (1947-1991) problems, journalists everywhere seemed to have overlooked Portuguese Africa – an oversight that was forcefully and definitively corrected on March 15 and 16 of 1961, and in the months and years of war that followed. The Cold War had suddenly smashed its way into continental Africa – and it was there that it was about to come to a boil.

So far there had been faint murmurings at the United Nations about Portugal's colonial administration of Angola, Moçambique and Portuguese Guiné, the islands of Cabo Verde and tiny São Tomé e Príncipe, but the complaints had been muted. For a time Portugal had been able to point to the rest of troubled Africa and say: 'Look! They're in trouble, we're not!' and 'This is indication of the loyalty and satisfaction of *our* Africans.' One way or another, Portugal was able to play down her omnipresence in Africa, which was not so hard when so much attention was riveted on other regions of the continent. Few people were conscious of Portugal. No one seemed to know much detail of Portugal itself, let alone the Portuguese colonies or how they were administered. Few outsiders had ever visited them in depth. Worldwide, many had always assumed Portugal was some sort of adjunct to Spain … and some people still do. Few have ever really bothered to give Portugal much attention, and her empire, though now gone, still remains something of a mystery. The colonies were bypassed by most – except by America's petroleum barons who have long been mightily interested in the reserves of oil under the surface of Cabinda, the small enclave province to the north of Angola on the other side of the Congo River, and what lies under the surface of the waters of the Gulf of Guinea. This moneyed group's agitation involving Portugal's influence and control of the region was sparking the attention of the United Nations (and the Soviet Union) – but overall the events in Portugal's colonies played a weak second fiddle to what had been happening in the months and years immediately after the chaotic independence of the Democratic Republic of the Congo (DRC) in 1960.

An unexpected and sudden bloodbath in Luanda, Angola's capital, in January, 1961, had somehow not quite caught the full attention of the world's press; but then a far more widespread slaughter in the north of the territory was repeated with a vengeance on March 15 and 16. This time, once the scale and enormity of the atrocity was fully understood, the events managed to shove all other news to the inside pages. It took time for word to get out – and the word was that some three thousand people had been massacred over just those two days, and the killings were continuing.[2]

Up to this point Portugal had enjoyed relative anonymity; the colonies the Portuguese considered they 'owned' and had administered for so long were now hurled to the forefront of African affairs – and the government in Lisboa, desperately trying to rein in and control what had overnight become a problem, was now left tripping over itself in a desperate bid to hold onto the controls of a runaway rebellion.

From that time forward nothing of import could happen on the African continent without causing reverberations in Portugal, so entrenched were the involvements and interests of that little country throughout Africa. This has been Portugal's position since. Tempers have cooled in the intervening years, but from 1961 until independence was granted to all Portugal's African colonies in 1974/5, and even during the subsequent years of a tumultuous civil war that continued well into the new millennium, Portugal was obliged to settle into a very hot and uncomfortable seat at the international dinner table. African discontent was an integral part of the Cold War, forcing reverberations throughout the western world – especially in the case of Portugal's strategic position within the alliance of the North Atlantic Treaty

---

[2] See Heywood, Linda - *Contested Power in Angola*. Statistics vary greatly, and it is certain no one will ever know the correct number, but in this exhaustive study the Boston University professor estimates the Portuguese, both military and civilian vigilantes, may have killed as many as fifty thousand civilians in reprisals during the early days of 1961.

Organization (NATO). Each entity on the African continent was akin to the link of a chain; shake one and all of them jangled. There were few steps that Portugal could take without affecting her African colonies and, to an increasing degree, all other African nations. In Portugal what became known as the Overseas War was to rage almost simultaneously in each of the major Portuguese holdings on the continental mainland – Angola, then Guiné Bissau with Cabo Verde (1963) and, finally, Moçambique (1964).

In Angola there had been signs of discontent and random killings in the very first weeks of 1961, but the bloodbath launched by Angolano revolutionaries in the north of that territory on the Ides of March ensured there was no retreat from an all-out revolutionary war for Angola's independence. Perhaps the Portuguese administration might have preferred to play down their catastrophe in the colony, but it was immediately clear it would only be a matter of time before similar discontent would increase and spread throughout both Guiné Bissau and Moçambique – although there had been flare-ups and 'disturbances' in these latter two provinces going back over many years. Urgency insured there was no possibility of hiding what was going on. In Africa, Portugal was (still is) very much her brother's keeper. The only question that remained was whether the generally impoverished homeland would be able to cope with the dilemma tossed into her lap.

The ferocity of the revolution is now a matter of record. Its beginnings were graphically summed up in a lurid pamphlet, chiefly photographs, published by the Portuguese-American Committee on Foreign Affairs in Boston – an organization that worked in association with Selvage & Lee, the New York public relations firm hired to promote – justify – Portugal's deteriorating image abroad. Following the slaughters committed by the revolutionaries on March 15, groups of Portuguese vigilantes, with a bare minimum of military support available from the homeland, took to revenge killings the following day. In a land greater in size than all of Iberia, plus France (including Corsica) and four Sicilys, there were barely three battalions of soldiers either to guard the settlers and those Africans loyal to them or to combat the invaders. The African rebel force, the *União das Populações de Angola* (UPA) under the leadership of Holden Roberto, initially numbered some four or five thousand men.[3] Their weapon of choice on that first night had been the *catana* (*panga* or machete). As the confrontation continued weaponry was supplied to them – much of it sourced in America. Initially, about one thousand Portuguese settlers, scattered on isolated farms and in small villages, lost their lives. The pamphlet concentrates on the killings of

---

[3] See Appendix # 8, Holden Roberto.

the whites by the blacks, although in fact probably more blacks were killed; it has virtually nothing to say about the vigilante killings the next day when white Portuguese settler groups prowled the north of the territory and the capital seeking Africans and vengeance. In reprisal it is estimated they slaughtered possibly as many as six thousand indigenous over several days. (The figure of three thousand over the two-day period, a generally acknowledged figure, is in all likelihood a low estimate.) With limited air transportation for troops at its disposal, it was May before the Lisboa government was able to land the substantial reinforcements of a disciplined army in Angola. By that time the rebels were in firm control of most of the territory's vast northern border area, and sorties had been made against the capital itself.

Many of the troops serving with the permanent force in Angola had been Africans in colonial units, in much the same way as indigenous troops served with the British army in India and Africa, or with the French in Indo China and Algeria. Many of these soldiers, seeing little hope for Portugal's continued administration, and feeling none too sympathetic, deserted their units and took their weapons and military knowledge over to the rebel side.

The war was on, and the slaughter and reprisals continued. It dragged on in the three territories until the dictatorship in Lisboa was finally overthrown by the revolution of 1974. By that time nearly nine thousand Portuguese military had been killed in combat, some four thousand five hundred had died of disease or in accidents, and about thirty thousand had been wounded or in some way disabled. These were dreadful statistics for a country so small – a population just under ten million at the time. Over the course of the war, more than eight hundred thousand men were mobilized. Throughout the 1960s and into the 1970s the financial burden on the state ran between thirty to forty percent, bringing Portugal perilously close to financial collapse. Barely a family in Portugal remained untouched by the disaster.

On the side of the revolutionaries, an estimated sixty-five thousand combatants had been killed, along with a further fifty thousand civilian men, women and children. From the African point of view, each territory was fighting its individual war of independence; from the Portuguese perspective, a single ghastly war was being waged on three different fronts and it was only a matter of time before total exhaustion set in.

The fighting came to a fairly swift conclusion in Guiné Bissau, with independence being granted almost immediately once the dictatorship in Lisboa had collapsed. A one-year civil war (1998-1999) erupted following an attempted *coup d'état*; in which some seven hundred combatants were killed.

6

But in both Angola and Moçambique the conclusion of independence fighting marked the start of civil strife. Angola's civil war started up almost immediately, lasting (with short interludes) a total of twenty-seven years (over and above the fourteen-year war of independence). Uncounted thousands of troops and civilians were killed. In Moçambique the civil war started up in earnest in 1977 and continued until 1992 – a total of just over fifteen years (in addition to the eleven years of the independence war). Fighting and famine there killed an estimated one million people, combatants and civilians.

Four Fascist Thugs

Many ruffians prowled the halls of power in European capitals between the First and Second World Wars. Not including those who sprang out of the Russian Revolution of 1917 (Stalin most notably, but he was by no means alone) and those who acted on behalf of God's anointed crowned heads (all of whom toyed with dictatorship by virtue of their titles, and would not have considered it anything less than their Divine Right) the four big ones in Europe were Hitler in Germany, Mussolini in Italy, Franco in Spain and, lurking unobtrusively in the shadows where perhaps he thought his brutality was less noticeable, Salazar in Portugal.

Hitler and Mussolini both died trying to hold onto or re-create their empires. Germany had lost all her possessions following the First World War, some of which were colonies, others protectorates very much under Germany's full control. Prior to the war her reach within Europe had been very much greater than it is today. Outside Europe, German interests included extensive island holdings in the Pacific, known then as German New Guinea. On the African continent her territories included what are today Namibia, mainland Tanzania, Rwanda and Burundi, Cameroon and Togo/Ghana. She also had a toehold in northern South America, the Caribbean and Antarctica, China and Bear Island – a small Artic island north of Norway.

The Italy Mussolini 'inherited' in 1922, on the other hand, had fought on the side of the British in the First World War, so managed to maintain her overseas interests largely intact. This changed when Mussolini declared war on Britain and France in 1941, entering the fray on the side of the Nazis. By doing so he had hoped to increase the Italian Empire. (In fact, Mussolini's fascists had designs on Spanish Morocco, Spain itself, all the islands in the western Mediterranean – Corsica as well as Sardinia and Sicily – the Dalmatian coast, a huge swath of the Balkans and Greece). Prior to the war Mussolini also intended (and in large measure succeeded) in increasing the size of Italy's holdings in north Africa – Tunisia, all of Libya, the western half of Egypt, Eritrea, a strip of land along the Sudanese and Kenyan borders with Ethiopia, all of Ethiopia (which he invaded in 1935) and British Somaliland. Italian Somaliland had been under Italy's full control since 1920, but in fact Italy's interests had long pre-dated that. There had been strong trading agreements dating to the time of Ethiopia's Emperor Menelik, in conjunction with the authority of coastal sultans in the XIX century all along the coast of eastern Africa, stretching from the Sudan border on the Red Sea as far south as Zanzibar. Italy already held control over Libya, Eritrea and Somalia. Some historians consider Italy's invasion of Ethiopia to have been the opening salvo of the Second World War, for it was this act that finally demonstrated the ineptitude of the League of Nations, its powerlessness to apply the brakes to Mussolini's and Hitler's military aspirations. For the Italians, the whole conceptual bubble burst in 1943 with their defeat in north Africa by the combined armies of Britain, South Africa, Australia and New Zealand – and, within Ethiopia itself, by the armed forces of the Ethiopian Patriots and the British under the command of Col. Orde Wingate.

By establishing fascism in Spain, Francisco Franco had succeeded in exhausting his country beyond its realistic capacity to fight on. The Spanish Civil War, in which some two million people died, had brought Franco to power. The war had started in 1936 and ended only in 1939, pitting the left-leaning Republicans supporting the legally and popularly-elected Second Republic against the Nationalists – a coalition of Falangists, Carlists, Catholics and Spanish aristocrats led by Franco himself. Feelings were bitter on either side, and the devastation of the war was widespread, but apart from Spanish Morocco there was nothing much left of a Spanish Empire that Franco might have ruled even if he had had the opportunity. The countries of South America had broken away generations before. Instead, this wily dictator established a rigid dictatorship at home that relied anachronistically on modern weapons and Old-World pomp and privilege. 'Deterring communism' was the regime's *raison d'être* – but that was largely a cover for a police state that operated with much brutality and not too much oversight until Franco's death as an embittered old man in 1975. With almost his last breath, and with the pleas for mercy from practically every great man of the day ringing in his ears, he ordered the execution of two Basque freedom fighters and three members of the Revolutionary Antifascist Front. He died himself fifty-three days later and, under the constitution of 1978, capital punishment was abolished throughout the country.

Salazar's circumstances were very different. He inherited a ready-made empire that had had its beginnings on the African coast in the early years of the XV century – a span of years that, at the time of the empire's collapse, was approaching six centuries. When Salazar came to power, imperialism was already a done deal. If the possession of an empire is unacceptable today, it by no means indicates that was always the case. As noted above, there was a time when a great nation was not a great nation if it had no territorial possessions, or the power of slaves to maintain its machines and machinations in motion. Men in positions of power and authority change their minds slowly, and they are seldom blessed with foresight equal to pulling themselves out of the quagmires created by those who ruled before them. Men in power are not generally blessed with humility, and they hate to be backed into corners or forced to apologize. Almost certainly this was the situation Salazar was unable to see, let alone assess correctly. He was unable to gauge the immense variety of the empire he inherited; he could not gauge the levels of ethnicity, or the volatility of sentiments, the human yearnings for freedom or dignity, the basics necessary to live a life in peace and without hardship. Which leader of any nation has the vision or the stamina – or the funding – to correct the errors of his forefathers? Salazar most certainly did not. For all his intellectual and administrative abilities, he was as blinkered as any of the patriarchs who

sang the songs of Portuguese conquest. The dictatorship he launched lasted forty-eight years, yet he never ventured to visit his country's domains beyond mainland Portugal.

António de Oliveira Salazar died in 1970 at the age of eighty-one. He had been a brilliant law student and professor of economics at the University of Coimbra and had been appointed the country's Finance Minister in 1926 under the presidency of General Óscar Carmona. Since the mid-1890s the country had been sinking in debt, mismanagement and corruption. As a condition of accepting his appointment he had elicited from Gen. Carmona a *carte blanche*, a promise that he would be allowed total control over every department of governmental spending. Within one year he had balanced the books and set the country's finances straight. He persisted with his remorseless and austere budgeting, achieving such remarkable results year-after-year that, in 1932, Gen. Carmona appointed him Prime Minister.

His government, the *Estado Novo*, was ushered in under a new constitution, a form of government turning its back on Anglo-American style political parties in favour of a corporatism intended to ease the strain on Portugal's rural and urban impoverished. The system was anti-parliamentarian and authoritarian in nature; extremist groups of both left and right were forbidden. The most profound criticism of the system was that stability within the state could only be achieved by the heavy-handed abuse of human and civil rights – increasingly strong at home, but particularly so in the overseas provinces.

Salazar became incapacitated 1968 with a brain hemorrhage, his powers immediately assumed by his protégé, Marcelo Caetano. Although frail, he regained his lucidity, but intimates did not inform him he had been divested of his powers. Instead they allowed him to believe his 'rule' continued from within the privacy of his home – until the day he died. Caetano held the reins of the dictatorship and continued Portugal's colonial war right up to the eve of the *Carnation Revolution* – a highly popular uprising unleashed (almost accidentally) by the army's captains in April 1974. At first it was an attempted *coup* that transformed itself into a muddled effort to create something like 'democratic communism.' Instead it turned into a rambunctious form of governing that tumbled along chaotically for nineteen months – by which time the NATO allies, especially America, were totally alarmed. A CIA-organized intervention in November 1975 ultimately led to the creation of western-style democracy in elections the following year.

The thread that bound the lives of these four scoundrels to one another was fascism and its attendant brutality, and yet their differences were legion. An in-depth comparative study of them, placing each alongside the others, would make for a fascinating read, but certainly the cleverest – the best educated and the most devious – was Salazar. The names of Hitler and Mussolini survive as militaristic thugs. Each pinned his fortunes onto the back of a warhorse, and each fell into the rubble of the Second World War. Franco's thuggery also spiked in battle – the murderous Spanish Civil War that brought him to power. He survived the war and, as dictator, was widely feared and detested throughout his lifetime. His final battle was against the people of his own country. After a ruthless and terrifying forty-year dictatorship, Franco finally died in his own bed having kept his exhausted country out of the wider European conflagration.

Salazar, on the other hand, during the years of his rise to power, was revered – even loved – by many. He was the one who worked the miracle necessary to pull Portugal out of its prior forty-year period of fiscal turmoil. He had always shown a natural proclivity for subtlety, operating what, in the end, proved to be the world's most far-flung and longest-surviving empire from the shadows. By 1933, as he began consolidating his powers, the machine he kept in motion could hardly claim subtlety. Salazar, a silent and cunning mouse of a thug, managed to maintain Portugal's neutrality during the war. His position was delicate; if he overtly backed the Allies, Germany's geographical proximity and political rapport with Spain could have spelled disaster. Had he backed the Axis, it could have been equally disastrous, for it would have meant flouting a treaty signed with Britain in 1386 – the *Treaty of Windsor*, the oldest extant peace treaty in the world – and risking the collapse of Portugal's colonies everywhere, especially in Africa. In the end, Salazar compromised by selling tungsten to both the Allies and the Axis (Britain understanding Portugal's 'Hobson's choice,' and graciously looking the other way). Gathering momentum against those who opposed his *Estado Novo*, Salazar's police forces acted much as had the Gestapo in Nazi Germany.

At the end of the Second World War, not wishing to miss such a magnificent opportunity to crow self-congratulations while simultaneously reaping the benefits of a superb public relations gesture, and no doubt adding a smidgen of self-effacing modesty into the mix, Salazar gave his earnest blessing to the Episcopate of Portugal to erect a gargantuan statue of Cristo Rei – Christ the King – on the south side of the Rio Tejo, facing Lisboa. Arms outstretched in similar fashion to the Christ Redeemer figure dominating the skyline of Rio de Janeiro, the dictator's sympathizers and sycophants were happy to claim the statue had been commissioned by the Mothers of Portugal to express their gratitude to Salazar for keeping their sons out of the war. Only a dictator of Salazar's subdued brand of insensitivity would have felt comfortable basking in the sincerity of such heartfelt obsequiousness – but he carried it off.

Before visiting Iberia, most outsiders are convinced that Portugal and Spain are much of a muchness – see one and you will have a good idea of the other. The simplicity of this superficial thinking is as easy to accept as it is misleading. After all, the two countries share a common peninsula, their languages, not dissimilar, are both derived from Latin. Bull fights are fought on both sides of the extensive frontier that runs between them.

A more complex historical perspective, though, would require dividing Iberia into its numerous and separate ancient kingdoms and territories. Following the colonization of the Romans and the invasions of Vandals, Suevians and Visigoths, one begins to identify such historical names as Galicia, Asturias, Leon, Pais Basco, Navarra, Castile, Aragon, Catalonia, Extremadura, Andalucia, Granada. The divisions and boundaries throughout history appear to have been endless. Following the XII century, one begins to see the outline of Portugal as the kingdom that borders the Atlantic Ocean – and in fact the frontiers of its continental land mass have not greatly altered in almost nine hundred years. Portugal has the oldest frontiers of any country in Europe.

Which is precisely the point: while all Iberia juggled for position and unity, Portugal had remained pugnaciously independent and apart – and now, through the first half of the XX century, governed by a fashionably fascist cabal of intolerant thugs.

Colonial War

In March 1961 Portuguese settlers in Angola and the local government administration had found themselves, almost overnight, embroiled in an uprising of the African populace that rapidly transformed itself into a full-blown war of attrition. There had been serious trouble in Portuguese Guiné (Guiné Bissau) since 1956, and always the fear that it might infect Angola – which in turn might infect Moçambique. Yet no one had been sufficiently prepared for such a sudden and violent insurrection in Angola; nor for such a rapid increase in the existing problems in Portuguese Guiné. African liberationists had always called their fight in Portuguese Guiné a war of independence – for mainland Guiné and the islands of Cabo Verde; now, with the ignition of war in Angola, the overall independence struggle had become vastly augmented.

Guiné Bissau is a speck of a country, the small Portuguese and *mestiço* populations concentrated in the capital city of Bissau. But in Angola, a huge and wealthy expanse of territory, the immigrant and mixed blood settlement was extensive – not only in the many major cities on the coast, but also throughout the hinterland. Settlements, some well over a century old, were to be found on or near vast plantations of cotton, sisal, coffee, tea, palm, lumber and other major agricultural products. There were numerous extremely wealthy and productive mining communities.

One could not see into the future at the time, but this new front of the colonial war was destined to last thirteen years – until April 1974. Formal independence was granted to Angola on 11 November 1975. However, in 1963 the Portuguese throughout the colony, as well as at home, had come to accept the war would likely be long and bloody. The state of the alarm sounded two years previously had by no means subsided. The great fear now was that it would spread even further – as indeed it was already doing into other parts of the territory, and very quickly. Portuguese forces could hold their own for a time but were ill-equipped to deal effectively over the long-term with such a costly conflagration. For the moment Moçambique was in the clear, but within a year it, too, would be pulled in as a major third front. The government in Lisboa was reeling and desperate – not just because the war it was obliged to fight was a matter of national pride, but because the insurgents were receiving extensive munitions assistance from Russia, China, Algeria, Libya and Cuba – all of it being filtered in through neighbouring countries (Tanzania, Congo and the former French territories of west and north Africa). While Portugal was committed to NATO's position in the Cold War face-off, the indigenous population was digging-in for a long-haul conflict – the Cold War now warming up as it shifted to the African continent.

By standing up to communism in what it considered its national sphere (never mind personal and colonial motives) little Portugal felt it was doing a good turn for the western powers, and so was deeply offended by the intensity of the criticism it was receiving in the United Nations for what they themselves considered their enlightened brand of overseas administration.[4] The Portuguese, both people and government, were especially cut by the country she considered her number one ally: the United States of America.

In explaining himself to my new American friend, Dr. Ritto apparently had had a point, though the dignity and sense of panache he had felt bound to exhibit on behalf of his country forbade him to say it in so many words: Portugal was desperately in need of some good press, were it possible. No doubt he was hoping someone like his new reporter acquaintance could do the job for him ...?

My knowledge of communism, beyond the fact the Americans were

---

[4] Portugal's government made much of what it considered its special 'civilizing mission' in Africa – in territories she was now calling 'provinces' rather than 'colonies.'

convinced it was obnoxious, was close to zero. My knowledge of America had been rudely coloured by the rot I had witnessed that early summer in Alabama. Hardly an impartial referee, I found myself quite unable to come down convincingly on either the communist or US administration side in the confusing face-off between the two. At that stage of my life, just beginning to understand the extent of my lack of savvy, I felt like a political eunuch.

Stuck out on the extreme western reaches of the continental mainland, Portugal has always been distanced from the main routes of most adventurers' peregrinations through Europe. However, if for any reason in modern times this geographic location has been judged unfortunate, in times past the distance had proven a decided advantage, for it caused the Portuguese to turn their collective backs on the squabbles and manipulations of Europe's more cantankerous powers. She was small, so could never compete in the tribal wranglings for space and riches that for centuries had preoccupied both her near and more distant European neighbours. Instead, she looked the other way, built ships and went to sea. She was well in advance of Spain moving onto the world stage and may justly lay claim, for a spell at least, to having become the first global superpower. Portugal's historic days of dominance would run from the conquest of Ceuta in 1415 to the Battle of Alcácer Quibir and the disappearance of their king, Dom Sebastião, in 1578. Both Sebastião and his heir, the aged Cardinal Dom Henrique, died childless; there followed a period of sixty years – 1580 to 1640 – when three Spanish monarchs in a row (the Filipes I, II and III) were the closest in-line successors, and so sat as kings of both countries. This unpopular circumstance led to something of a general free-for-all involving Spain and Holland, then France and Britain, and finally Germany – all of them whittling away at chunks of the empire Portugal had earlier carved out, or merely eyed, for herself. It was a state of affairs that lasted up to the turn of the XX century.[5]

Over three hundred years after the restoration of the Portuguese monarchy Portugal, as she saw herself, consisted of not just the European metropolitan land mass, the borders of which had remained unchanged for close to nine centuries, but was master over possessions that belted the tropical and subtropical globe. Brasil had gone, having successfully achieved independence in 1822, but there continued a strong economic and cultural bond between the two countries that has lasted until this day. Although Goa

---

[5] During this period Spain effectively usurped much of Portugal's maritime dominance. Many Portuguese ships were commandeered by the famed Spanish Armada decimated by storm during its failed invasion of England in 1588. There followed the so-called *Restauração* in 1640 when a Portuguese king, Dom João IV, head of the House of Bragança, was finally able to mount the throne in Lisboa.

had been lost to India (1961) there was elsewhere still plenty of territory left to Portuguese administration by 1963. In fact, Portugal retained everything of the old empire that she had not lost centuries earlier to other colonizing sharks. Angola and Moçambique were the brightest diamonds, but there was also Guiné Bissau, Cabo Verde and tiny São Tomé e Príncipe, two islands in the Gulf of Guinea in front of Gabon. In the Far East, there was Timor-Leste, in the Indonesian archipelago, and Macau, a peninsula on the south coast of China, the two territories most distant from Lisboa's administrative centre. In 1963 all were still considered by the Portuguese to be 'Overseas Provinces,' coming under the aegis of the *Ministério de Ultramar* – which meant, in fact (details are moot) they were administered as colonies. Most were destined to receive their independence following the 'Captain's' or *Carnation Revolution* – but that was eleven years hence. Macau, leased to Portugal by China for a period of five hundred years in 1499, was returned to Chinese administration on time in 1999.

Additionally, there were the Madeira islands off northwest Africa, and the Açores islands farther out in the Atlantic Ocean – both of which have long been autonomous administrative regions of Portugal and remain so today. Numerous other territories – principally in Asia – had been lost over the centuries.[6]

Until I had set about a major reading blitz I could not have guessed at any of this. The only time Portugal had ever entered my consciousness was when my mother purchased some attractive *artesanato* place-mats for our summer dining room table. Printed on linen in bright colours were scenes of Nazaré fishing craft, all of them with decorative eyes painted on their prows, their barefoot sailors sporting rolled-up trousers and wearing nattily striped toques on their heads.

New Assignment

The events in Birmingham, Alabama, in the spring of 1963, informed the world at large – and in definitive terms – just how beautiful was Black. It was

---

[6] Throughout the sixty years a Spanish king sat on the Portuguese throne, there existed an agreement between the two nations that Portugal's overseas territories would not become Spanish but remain under a Portuguese administration. See also note 45, p.454.

not a new message, but it was a moment of awareness. The whole world was forced to sit up and start treating the concept much more seriously than ever before. This was the summer of Rev. Martin Luther King Junior.

King's drumbeat was so clear, so loud, so insistent it tended to blanket over all other orchestral pieces playing for a world audience that summer. North America was especially preoccupied with the Alabama noise in its own section. But if one was paying attention, there was an imperative rat-a-tat-tat emanating from other areas of the world, too – and rising to crescendo.

It was the summer in which stories in most of the world's newspapers appeared daily championing the idea of freedom for all oppressed peoples, reminding their readers that 'minorities,' taken as a whole, in actuality were a distinct majority. Largely because of King's movement, the benighted colonies of Africa, and people of colour everywhere – including those under South Africa's system of *apartheid* – were receiving special attention now that national freedoms had already been promised to so many. In the American union the fight was against the racism of the white population in the southern states. Despite gallons of condemnatory ink splashed onto news sheets, white racists everywhere in the south continued chanting their persistent hymn – that black was not only inferior and ugly but dangerous to boot. (The 'most dangerous' of all, the Black Panther movement, appeared only at the end of 1966.) For the most part, the world's press was now telling its readership the racist views of US whites were pure idiocy and were just as unchristian and inhumane as they would be anywhere else in the world. Racism was a stance inevitably on its way out, no longer to be tolerated or officially sanctioned, a sort of wind-chime ding-a-ling warning that indicated the 'winds' were not just changing, but that storms were brewing. Colonies, generally, already had – or were headed for – their independence. The US of A was behind the times.

Maybe due to complacency, the canker of racism appears to have re-grown, even managing to inoculate itself to a degree – but in the early 1960s there was a defiant hope that racists everywhere were finding themselves pushed into corners and suddenly alone.

This work concerns a journalist's modest observations of Portugal and her major African colonies in the summer of 1963. No one man, an outsider unfamiliar with the complex cultures involved and unable to speak the predominant languages, would be qualified to furnish a full and accurate report. But when large sections of real estate are locked up tight behind a barrier of weaponry, propaganda and the course of a five-hundred-year-long history, journalists come in handy to loosen-up compacted data, get the word out and perhaps, if they are lucky, to contribute a morsel of general knowledge to those trying to make relevant decisions in the wider world.

There can be little doubt that, at that time, the Portuguese were enduring a struggle far greater than a nation of such diminutive size could reasonably cope. The vagaries of history had dumped a large problem into Portugal's lap, so to speak, and those trying to deal with it were conspicuously unqualified.

There was a time before the wheel. There was a time when tribesmen looked to leaders to lead and would have spurned anyone unable – or, worse, refusing – to invite the head honcho's backscratchers to dinner. To be accepted as an aspiring leader would require enough power to put venison on the banquet table, an obligation to hold a firm grip on the economy. Money – and it was always short. An able leader would need to cast further and further afield – and when nations consider themselves leaders the result is colonialism – and fascism and communism. Democracy takes a hike. There was a time when no European nation could seriously consider itself a power unless it had colonies filled with the 'Great Unwashed' who did not look quite the same as 'us,' and were delighted to be 'protected' and serve the 'national interest' of a nation that was foreign to them – happily putting themselves and their families to work for starvation wages …

Britain had her literary heroes who championed empire; Rudyard Kipling wrote of Kim and Gunga Din and Mowgli, Rider Haggard's great hero was Alan Quartermain. All these fine fictional characters, scores of them, were conjured to appeal to the youth of Britain, whose loftiest aim was to seek adventure, fame and fortune in faraway lands ruled by a British monarch and protected by a British army. That way the local riff raff – the 'Great Unwashed' – could seethe and complain all it wanted (and they did) but remained essentially subdued while British fortunes were accumulated on their backs and by their sinew. Colonialism was always first and foremost a financial enterprise.

Portugal was a little different. Her empire, celebrated by Luís Vaz de Camões in his epic poem *Os Lusíadas*, featured a fictionalized real-life Vasco da Gama and his exploits in rounding the Cape of Good Hope, thus 'discovering' lands and seas all the way to India. His yarn was bolstered by a flesh-and-blood hero of his homeland's history. His exploits were a culmination, an end result, of an effort that had been started long before (by several hundreds of years) the British got going. Portuguese expansion had begun as early as 1415, with the capture of Ceuta; now, in 1499 the great sea captain da Gama had re-entered Lisboa in triumph with India behind him. Portuguese colonialism, as it developed, was no less bloody an enterprise than Britain's, but its motivations differed conspicuously. Portugal was the first country in recorded European history to set sail on the open seas and travel as far as they did. Their prime motivation was curiosity. Secondly, religious proselytizing. (Up to 1493 this religious motive could be expanded to locating the whereabouts of Prester John.) Thirdly, economic – finding the source of the spice trade.

In those early years something quite distinct was happening between the oppressors and the oppressed – namely miscegenation. For the late-coming British, even the thought of mixing the races was always considered unacceptable. It was the social attitude of the toffee-nosed British colonial classes who considered themselves superior to their subjects in every way imaginable – and it was carried through up to the time of the disintegration of the empire in the 1960s, and beyond. (Actually, miscegenation was much more common among the British than many of them cared to admit, but it was vehemently and actively – almost frenziedly – discouraged.) The concept of racial superiority among the Portuguese upper classes also existed, but in general miscegenation itself was accepted, widely practiced and considered a fact of life. Machismo among Latins – a man's fiery concept of himself as a super-specimen of virile *man*hood – coated with lashings of pride and an angry impulse to dominate – would, in broad terms, be less of a factor in the life of an Englishman than in that of a Portuguese.

A significant component of imperial historical timing created a difference in the acceptance of miscegenation. In 1500 there were very few Portuguese women who ventured to sea with their menfolk. Wherever it was they went (and the Portuguese went to many places on the surface of the globe) the menfolk were almost always without their women when they landed on far shores. By the time the British got around to travelling the seas as much as the Portuguese had been doing for several centuries, the ships were much improved, and the captains and senior military officers often took their families with them to far destinations. Military officers commonly travelled with their wives to places like India and Africa when the British Empire was at its peak, which was not the case among functionaries of the early days of Portuguese imperial expansion. A mixing with the local women was a natural factor in the Portuguese colonies. Settler Portuguese peasantry appears to have produced a mixed-race population earlier, faster and of greater proportion to local population statistics than was ever the case in the British colonies. One cannot deny racism is a major component of Brazilian life, even today, but one also cannot deny the country's extraordinary mixture of races – a force of nature which appears, belatedly, to be taking hold contemporarily among former predominantly white northern races. Another consideration: by the time British settlers were establishing themselves in their colonial outposts as functionaries and civil servants, they generally possessed superior education to that of their earlier Portuguese, and widely peasant class, counterparts.

By 1947 the choke-hold Britain had been using to maintain control over the Indian subcontinent (since 1600) was finally recognized for the rip-off it had been all along, but it was probably Kenya's Mau Mau rebellion, crushed by the British in 1961, that managed to skittle the clubs of colonialism everywhere and deliver a *coup de grâce* not just to British imperialism, but to the very idea of imperialism. All of Africa's subjugated peoples learned, just as fast as the message could be carried into the far corners of the continent's hinterland, that white mastery and its much heralded 'civilizing mission' had been exposed for the sham it was, its proponents themselves shown to be in dire need of civilizing. Furthermore, the lesson was clear: with military assistance from abroad the vulnerabilities of the ruling powers could be easily demonstrated. The oppressors could be beaten. Sudan, Tanganyika, the Rhodesias, Nyasaland – all of them rumbled, and scared the hell out of their surprised and over-extended British administrations. France, which had failed to pay attention to the cruel lesson of its ouster from Indochina in 1954, was forced to pay closer attention to an even more savage schooling in Algeria a few years later. Congo (DRC) had run away with Belgium's sword; the copper and gold of Katanga became the prize for throwing off the trappings of Catholic nunnery in Stanleyville. In old Lisboa the well-burnished stones that paved the streets of the Portuguese capital were fast losing their polish and had begun to rattle with the frantic comings and goings of military transport headed out to quell insurrection in the 'Overseas Provinces' – Angola (February 1961) and Moçambique (September 1964). Guiné Bissau, which had been bubbling since the mid-1950s, was in a state of open war by 1961, and considerably notched-up the violence in 1963. In 1961 the Indian Army had marched into Goa, Diu and Damão and put an end to what was left of Portugal's five hundred years of hegemony on the subcontinent, all to the cheers of populations around the world – except in Portugal.

The oppressed of Portugal's African colonies learned a useful lesson from all this action; more to the point, they chose not to fight their wars with *pangas*, as had the Mau Mau, but to arm themselves with the more effective modern weaponry and tactics now on offer by any number of sophisticated merchants of lethal hardware. Russia, China and the eastern bloc countries were only too eager to oblige. So, too, was the United States of America ... but (a forbidding tut-tut!) 'you must not use NATO weaponry to subdue your citizenry already in chains ...' (There must have been a 'wink-wink, nudge-nudge' in this admonition!) This was 'cold war.'

Returning to journalism in Canada after witnessing a small but significant portion of the desegregation struggle by the Afro-Americans in Alabama (itself an aspect of colonial subjugation) and forced to acknowledge how slim had been my own preparation for that southern assignment, frustration was leaving me with a nagging unease. Perhaps it was guilt, a wish that I had accomplished more in the time I had been there. Three weeks on the ground in Birmingham and now, back in Toronto, it seemed the journey had proven more pallid tourism than enlightened research – far too brief an exposure. In any field it is necessary to make a beginning, I would assure myself, and the beginning of anything often stutters. Once having set about the task of learning, though, it is a rare student who will care to admit he has had his head in the clouds – that even after a period of concentrated effort he simply may not have *understood* everything. Or anything.

Very often a journalist (reluctant to think of himself as a student) is no more than an exceptionally inquisitive – often arrogant and obnoxious – tourist. By definition he is the one who *almost knows* everything. Blandly he will accept the notion he is revered by all the great men of earth because, unlike the paparazzi he despises (they are mere snoopers with long lenses), he finds himself acceptable to the Greats, sits down with them in comfortable armchairs before television audiences, kibitzes and talks to them, sometimes every now and then, maybe, over a fine *tinto Alentejano*. He is convinced the Greats are convinced he maintains their greatness by inscribing their names into his newspaper. It is heady stuff. Always a student, a young journalist nevertheless cares not to hear he might be largely ignorant of what he is talking or writing about. (If he knew it all, he wouldn't be asking so many questions – which is the logic behind how the Greats convince themselves they have one-upped him/her. Great game, journalism.)

Though necessarily numbered, my days in Birmingham had been chock-full of activity. Later as a journalist about the only way to make amends for any poverty in the content of my writing was to regurgitate, again and again (feeble attempt to put a few pennies in the bank) the lessons that could be deduced from such limited firsthand view, to assess and re-assess how the experience had impressed and affected. Any Tom's body with his eyes open will naturally absorb, perhaps try to interpret, what he has witnessed in person – especially graphic images of hatred and violence in the streets. However, disseminating a comprehensible understanding will count for little if Tom is unable to call on a solid background knowledge – the *who, why, which, what, when, where* and *how* of the story he is writing.

My editors – and I liked them individually – were crafty and sharp-eyed foxes for detail, and ever suspicious of my information. They were pressed from above. As much as wanting to know every aspect of my assignment in Birmingham, they wanted to be sure I understood that being on site was itself minimal qualification for subsequent discourse concerning the broader aspects of Dr. Martin Luther King's unique freedom movement. Having been there (the superiors of my superiors let it be known) did not furnish me with the authority to present myself as one who knew the issues as profoundly as they would have preferred – or as they assumed they knew it themselves. This was blustering one-upmanship of the 'I'm important; you're not' sort. Yet I clearly detected these senior editors felt the weight of responsibility for absolute accuracy and had no intention of being snowed by an uppity young know-all. They used a bombastic reasoning to ensure I knew my place. In truth the font of greatest scepticism, for me, was not the African American community whose story I had been attempting to tell; it was the diffidence of the senior editors of the very paper for which I was writing. Facing them was more exacting than the assignment itself. I would exit their debriefing sessions convinced they judged me to be even younger and greener than I was. It was disheartening, and I might easily have curled up and accepted that I was of no more significance than they chose me to be: an impoverished and impressionable witness to one of the era's more exceptional events – representative of an important newspaper, but a greenhorn nonetheless. The teletype machines clattered on: the wire services were more reliable than an eyewitness.

However, I had a sound handle on my Robert Service. Though I said nothing and kept my head down, in the dark and secret recesses of my belligerent mind I managed to raise dissent:

> *... Now Jobson is a chum of mine, and in a dusty den,*
> *Within the street that's known as Fleet, he wields a wicked pen.*
> *And every night it's his delight, above the fleeting show,*
> *To castigate the living Great, and keep the lowly low.*
> *And all there is to know he knows, for unto him is spurred*
> *The knowledge of the knowledge of the Thing That Has Occurred.*
> *And all that is to hear he hears, for to his ear is whirled*
> *The echo of the echo of the Sound That Shocks The World.*
> *Let Revolutions rage and rend, and Kingdoms rise and fall,*
> *There Jobson sits and smokes and spits, and writes about it all.*

- Robert William Service, *Bar-Room Ballads*, "Jobson of the Star"

I have always imagined the poet must have known Jobson personally. By another name, perhaps, but the same man. However, although perhaps a smidgeon envious, he did not actually have a whole lot in common with the journalist he depicts nor, for that matter, much contact with him apart from the occasional beer in a pub off The Strand. That he knew journalists and journalism is evident. His depiction of Jobson's languorous arrogance is succinct; it flashes a wink at the man who wants everyone to think he has seen it all. But unknown to my senior editors, and even a bit of a surprise to myself, the experience of Birmingham had fortified me. I *had* been there, so I donned my thickest shell and wrote and wrote – long articles or brief comment, and for virtually any outlet that requested my 'expertise.' Perhaps the constant repetition of this exercise helped me to pinpoint a few of my own political ideas.

Confidence developed slowly. Additionally, and maybe more importantly, what emerged was *my* scepticism, *my* conviction, that many journalists not comprehending the depth of the events they witness, will skim the surface of what they nonchalantly term the *story* and, in the end, supply just that: a story – all too often the briefest of digests severely curtailed by the limitations of the reporter's personal involvement, background knowledge, character, bias. That says nothing about the interests of the journal's owners who, in the case of a vaunted 'Western Free Press,' first and foremost will sniff out the money, ever considerate of the sensitivities of their shareholders, and thus likely to view any detail of a story as merely adjunct to the sale of newspapers – a statistic to be shown to advertisers (whose sincere interest in the pith of any story would be questionable).

It was a difficult time. The seniority in years of many of my colleagues was very apparent to me; I was all too aware of my youth, its accompanying hesitancy (and often my over-reaction) to coping with the gruff terseness of people I rightly or wrongly considered bullies. I was adept at identifying within myself a naïve idealism and was capable of being almost painfully perceptive when it came to self-criticism. Even so, I suffered pangs of personal doubt when called upon to face down what justifiably seemed to be undisguised hypocrisy in the gathering and reporting of the day's happenings. It was the very devil of an inferiority complex, and it pushed me into pushing back – frequently too hard – standing my ground with admirable stamina, stoicism and cussedness, but limited rhetorical skill. I stammered, incapable of explaining myself or defending my arguments in depth. It was a defect with which I had had to wrestle since childhood. In the current instance – the context of Birmingham and Alabama – I had feelings a-plenty about what I had just experienced, but serious doubts as to the depth of my understanding and grasp of all the material presented to me in those three short weeks – this despite the certainty I was in possession of a dynamic concentration of data. Explaining myself was like dancing hippo-like in a shallow mud puddle: nothing elegant, constantly slipping and floundering as if trying to conceal that I had forgotten to don my tutu. Now returned to Toronto I had difficulty convincing myself as to just what it was I had absorbed and understood in Birmingham – and how well any of it had penetrated my consciousness, how much of it had stuck. It was necessary to answer to my editors; how well did they understand what I had understood of the data I was presenting to them?

Before leaving Toronto for the south I had been working during the days at the head office of a major bank, a nine-to-five routine in public relations. I hated it. Out of sheer boredom I had started moonlighting at two of the city's daily newspapers. At both I worked nights part-time – sometimes for different stories on both papers on the same night, and sometimes the same story for both papers on the same night. It was a harrowing game. Despite such zeal I was not taken on at either paper as a full-fledged member of editorial staff, and before heading south had decided to confine my efforts to just one of the papers. I was conscience-wracked, but unsure whether this was due to my duplicity or my stupidity. I handed in my notice at the bank as soon as I returned to the city and was now content to act as a stringer for the one paper I had represented in Birmingham.

There was constant work for me. Seldom did I finish up before two or three o'clock in the morning, sometimes closer to an early breakfast hour. The murky timetable suited me. A regular staff position would be offered in time, I was sure, but for the now I was content and earning good money. The work was high key and I was usually pepped-up when I left the downtown office, never quite ready to return home and go to bed. I loved the emptiness of the city's streets at that hour, and so would often drive into the Yorkville area where I was familiar with a number of the bars that remained open until the city's buses were fully operational for the day. One of my favourite haunts was an after-hours club operated by Clem Hambourg, a well-known jazz pianist, one of the originals of the famous House of Hambourg. He was thirty-five years my senior but we got along well and I enjoyed hanging out, sitting beside him at the piano and listening to him work out new riffs on the keyboard until long after the last of his patrons had left, sometimes not packing up until four o'clock. Many times after he had locked the doors to his establishment the two of us would go together to visit The Town Tavern on Queen Street East, the jazz club where Oscar Peterson was the feature artist for so many years. We would wait for Oscar to finish up, sometimes not until around five, and then the three of us, or sometimes a group of five or six or

23

more, would make our way over to an all-night diner on Jarvis Street to order up breakfasts of pancakes or ham and eggs. On one such occasion we were accompanied by two young Americans from their country's consular office, and in this way I came to meet Gerry Murphy, a fellow about my own age – jazz fan at night, aspiring diplomat during the day. We became friends and, when I told him about my recent foray to Alabama, his interest perked. He was envious, he said. Being hell-bent on a diplomatic career meant he had to forego the free and adventurous life he imagined I was having.

One day he called me and we arranged to meet for lunch. He had something special on his mind and wanted to talk about it.

"You've had this experience reporting from Alabama, and you've spent time in Africa ... Have you ever thought about going back to Africa ...?" he asked.

"Sure ... if I had the chance I'd go in a heartbeat!" I told him.

"Well," he replied, "one of my colleagues in the diplomatic corps here in Toronto is the consul for Portugal – Dr. Jorge Ritto. He's looking for a writer prepared to spend whatever time it takes to explore his country and the Portuguese colonies in Africa ... basically a public relations job for their government, I'd guess. Think you might like to take it on?"

"Why not? I don't know a whole lot about Portugal's colonies, but I'd happily give it a try ..."

Public relations job ...? I knew nothing about Portugal and its colonies. This sounded less like journalism and more like whitewash. Portuguese colonialism had been featured – and viciously criticized – in recent news stories. I had not paid it a whole lot of attention.

I had travelled widely in Europe and had spent a year with the British army in Africa. I barely knew where to look for Portugal on a map and, as to any of her African colonies, I was not even sure I could furnish their names.

But I was astute enough to realize the importance of not sounding too uninformed about it; I had had a similar experience – ignorance – prior to leaving for Alabama, so knew how to set about educating myself. I nodded my head, talked positively and asked what I thought might be a few pertinent questions. Right after lunch, in order to fill in the empty space in my brain box, I said goodbye to Gerry and raced off to a library to see what we had been talking about, and where these colonies were. I knew Portugal's capital was Lisbon – Lisboa – but not much more. Over the next few days I pursued an intriguing and in-depth study of the place; an encyclopædia assisted me locating the names of the principal Portuguese colonies in and around Africa.

Collectively, it was an area about which I knew nothing.

The landmasses of Angola and Moçambique, both enormous territories, straddled the southern portion of the continent. Looking at them on a map it seemed inconceivable I could have missed noting them. I must have had a vague notion they were there but had never had occasion to take a close look at either of them before. Portuguese Guiné, a tiny smudge of mainland surrounding a river estuary, together with a sprinkling of off-shore islands, was located on the gigantic western bulge of Atlantic Africa. Today it is known as Guiné Bissau. In addition, a variety of island groups formed separate colonies: Cabo (Cape) Verde in the Atlantic off the West African coast, in front and slightly north of Guiné Bissau; further south, tucked well inside the Gulf of Guinea towards the coast of Gabon and Equatorial Guinea, are tiny São Tomé and its sister island, Príncipe. Uninhabited at the time of their discovery by Portuguese navigators João de Santarém and Pêro Escobar around 1470, they are two peaks of a ridge of underwater mountains that, with the island of Fernando Pó (now Bioko), form a line running northeast into the centre of Cameroon, an extension of the Bambouto volcanic massif. The two islands constitute Africa's second smallest state after the Seychelles Islands. Madeira and the Açores, provinces of the homeland populated by the Portuguese since the XV century, are considerably further north in the Atlantic.

All this information was right there before my eyes, but for all my interest in Africana over the years I had never had occasion to encounter any of it. I spent several long and delightful sessions soaking up knowledge more readily equated with stories of Robinson Crusoe or Sinbad. There was a hint of incongruity as to how a sliver of a country like Portugal could govern such an extended empire, the very last of Europe's, or the world's, old-style empires.

Now I was reading additional reports about which I had known next to nothing: recent clippings in the morgues of the newspaper for which I was writing were describing instances of renewed violence in Portugal's bailiwick, and it was possible to start piecing together entire series of disasters. The loss of Goa on the west coast of the Indian subcontinent, in December 1961, had furnished a modest blip in Canada's newspapers at the time, but the trouble had not started at that point. By itself it seemed a rather ho-hum incident, not so terribly traumatic to anyone, though the action certainly pricked the egos of both the Indians and the Portuguese involved. Some sixty people had died during the flare-up. The incident had been loud and brutal and might have gone largely un-noticed in the English-language press but for the fact that both sides had hollered so vehemently. The event had been preceded earlier that same year when the Portuguese luxury liner, Santa Maria, was hijacked in the western Atlantic by a determined party of swashbuckling pirate-like *oposicionistas* to the dictatorship of António de Oliveira Salazar in Lisboa. What had been going on in these bucolic and secretive little corners of the tropical world? Reading the newspaper clippings, it now appeared the remainder of Portugal's once proud empire was in more turmoil than the rest of the world had been led to believe.

By the time Gerry and I got together for our next lunch meeting, this time with his friend, the Portuguese consul, I was moderately well-briefed.

As a has-been reporter there are now no longer any Big Stories I would particularly want to cover. It is not so much because I am tired, a fatigue that is the inevitable culmination of years lived. Until now I have been much blessed. Yet deep down, somewhere in the vicinity of my bowel, there has been growing a growling and restless cynicism at a corporate/capitalistic world (a shaky, almost indefinable concept) gone amok. Less than a fifth of the way into the XXI century, my worst fears bubble to the surface with the emergence of wildly irresponsible administration in the United States of America – coinciding as it does with a corrupt administration in Russia, and sundry other oligarchs, scalawags, cutthroats and bum boys whose selfishness and greed permit them to believe they own the right to govern every corner of this long-suffering world – the two percent who laud it over the rest of mankind and control the monies that pay for the armies and police enforcing their dictates. It is a timeless game, this anti-social routine, a mindset that runs hand-in-glove with the worst traits of mankind; the stakes are higher now that ungodly numbskulls have nuclear weapons to play with.

Though my fingers may twitch above the keyboard – no, there is no longer any immediate story I would especially care to report on except, perhaps, as witness to shed a shy beam of light on a distant portion of historic upheaval. It is a difficult story to tell when not crafting it as news, which it no longer is, so perhaps the whole take on it is better expressed (and more accurately) by resorting to memoir – 'historical journalism' – at its most personal and thoughtful. The format provides a small perk: it serves to relate a story intimately mulled for years, recounted until now informally only in random and cursory snippets, but which in fact is summary of a life's learning. Every man's story is unique. His viewpoint will likely be at sharp variance with that of another who had been right beside him viewing the same scene. Try for a moment to imagine the multiplicity, the weave, of yarns that might have been spun in the thousands of years that have passed since mankind first walked the surface of the earth trying to explain himself to others – the shawl with which each man and woman would be able to cover a most naked body. Were each story acted out, written down, or simply told at a campfire gathering, imagine the wealth of knowledge (and entertainment!) that could be made available to everyone present. It would be more than enough for everybody – and for an eternity. And yet we continue to tell our most fascinating stories ...

Immediately upon learning of the possibility of an assignment in Portugal, I dug into a mass of library reference material in a feverish attempt to catch up on a history I had neglected. In order to write the following section of this work, then, I make liberal use of far more material data and ideas than were available to me when Dr. Ritto issued his invitation – for at that moment of my life many, many political ideas were totally new to me, little more than words in a dictionary I may or may not have encountered or understood. It would be comforting to know my thinking processes have matured somewhat in the intervening years; in any event, it is now easier to cope with patterns of thought that fifty years ago would have provided a definition for jumble. In the years between then and now there have been events too numerous to count that have opened channels and given rise to revolutions in thinking. The process, for my own part, has been deeply transformative. In this I count myself little different from others – except that, for much of my life, I have been a journalist, an observer whose scatter-shot training ultimately spread somewhat beyond the limits of academia. In sum the resulting combination has lent itself reasonably well to journalistic hindsight – the assembly of memoir and autobiography.[7]

Most people fail to make careful note of whatever it is they see. They ignore their surroundings, take little trouble to observe and so pass on their way and quickly forget essentials. Like waking after a dream. Happily, there are those who write journals, and yet others who draw or paint. Some play notes on their pipes and strings, and others who try to capture a given moment in stone, perhaps fire their emotion into a porcelain cup or bowl, or a *terra cotta* sculpture that will outlast its creator by a thousand years. I have met people who drink holy water and are convinced they feel it seeping into the

---

[7] See Hespeler-Boultbee, J.J. – <u>*Somersaults* – *Rovings, Tears & Absurdities* – *A Memoir from the Fringe of Journalism*</u> – CCB Publishing, British Columbia, Canada, 2017.

very tips of their fingers and toes; others have joined me canoeing rivers that meander through bucolic countryside, or churn through ravines and gorges – and they are more than satisfied the God-given earth is before them revealed in its splendour for the very first time. I have motorcycled through morning mists settled over sleeping villages as obscure and forgotten and every bit as beautiful as a mysterious Brigadoon. There are people – a majority, perhaps – who would prefer to sleep in late. When they throw off the covers they stand and blink, turning circles in some form of self-activated but nonetheless automated dither, engines coughing to life, low revs. Many are non-participants in anything but the daily round, who refuse to look or feel; and yet they are prepared to defend a clear lack of empathetic observation by anything greater than the exertion required to fashion snide commentary or roaring stupidity. For them the rising and setting of the sun each day is already such a complexity they long ago tuned out and switched off whatever they considered their engines of enlightenment.

Penning the details of a personal story, even nuggets that merely hint at a passage through time and so, by all subtle measure, are incomplete, tends to force confrontation with certain agonies that are in no significant manner dissimilar from the sternest of punishments. The heebie-jeebies are real, whether they are to be found under a rock or under a bed, on the commuter train or in a portmanteau. Everyone has them and will frequently divulge the greatest of them only after squirming through the torment of a deep and personal examination. Bless them! There are also those who simply cannot endure the pain of the exercise.

So why even attempt to write memoir?

One answer for someone who *needs* to write – someone for whom writing is a creative obsession – is obvious: ease of access. A record. A visual artist wishes to express himself and may do so in any number of ways. He can choose pencil to draw his idea, or paint to colour it. He can choose to create landscape or portraits, or perhaps to paint in abstract. The range in any direction is infinite – he can choose realism if he so wishes, or abstract, cartoon and the creation of comic strip. Writing, like music or dance, is simply another form of artistic expression – words instead of images – and is likewise open to a limitless field of differing genres. Poetry and song-writing are closely linked. Prose can be fiction, advertising, history, factual or reportage, or whatever other genre one cares to tackle. A friend who retired as a professor of nuclear science once commented to me there is more material published annually, in his field alone, than he could possibly read and absorb in a single lifetime – and then there are all the other fields of endeavour and study and mere expression. Though by no means scant, one of the more concise areas of written expression would be memoir – not counting that portion of it that is camouflaged and re-issued as fiction.

Unadorned memoir is a genre unto itself. Very often it is the first form of writing a child will encounter when he pens for his language teacher an essay entitled 'How I spent my summer holiday,' or 'My dog, Spot.' It is a form that lends itself to ready access and can be a most useful tool when it is necessary to clarify thoughts and feelings or the deepest of spiritual tangles. It can prove itself a most intimate and cathartic form of personal examination, indulged for any number of reasons – to leave behind a personal history for one's descendants, to explain a history to which the writer has been uniquely privy, or to examine or explain an unusual viewpoint.

Every now and then I go for morning coffee at a popular house where I sometimes meet up with acquaintances – a coffee klatch of older men about town to whom I imagined, when we all first gathered, I would have been judged (and possibly correctly) by far the most fossilized. A good deal of banter and friendly insult goes on at these meetings, all of it generally well-meaning barb intended to incite a few morning chuckles. One of these men is a rough-cut hammer-and-planks sort of fellow with an easy gift of the gab and an incisive and prickly wit, who also happens to be creative and once made a living as a counselor – all the sorts of attributes and occupations one might imagine could be used most constructively to waltz his companions into spasms of incisive contemplation. But for some reason best explained by his own set of limitations and psychoses, this man appears to have decided – quite seriously – memoir is too self-indulgent to be undertaken by anyone save those whose lives have already been well-documented by the daily press. To me, of course, this spin is sad and a trifle chauvinistic coming from someone who takes pride in presenting himself as open and forthright, for if he stopped to think in rounder terms he might come to realize that without memoir, story itself would lack a most exciting ingredient – and leave no space for history. The poor man's singular bias differs little from the limited imaginations of those who consider history should concern only the lives and times of kings and despots, rather than as the broadly-woven tapestry of a much wider anthropology. With this last definition 'life and times' comes to depend heavily on the little guy who speaks up, contributes his voice no matter how frail to an on-going saga. No man should be afraid to smoke his own *chibouque;* memoir seen against the flourish of a broad history is nothing if not the up-close touch of what's going on.

The coffee in its cup on the table would chill and turn to mud in the time it would take to await a succinct review of A Coffee House Book of Quips & Guffawed Put-Downs – and other random orations sputtered into the morning air before the ignition switch had been engaged and the motor chugged itself into life. Being the great age I am, wrinkled, humourless and frequently at a loss to comprehend the day just started, it's quite possible I am missing the point of it all, anyway ...

With the gruel I ate every morning as a young man awakening to the world roundabout, there came the certainty that any fair political system can be at the peak of its functioning only by undergoing constant verification, correction and adjustment, that the words and actions of leaders and lawmakers are only as valuable as the means a society has at its disposal to hold them to account. This essential task falls to a vigorous, free, honest and informative press. There can hardly be a respectable politico alive who denies this reasonable dictum, yet throughout all the years of our lives democratic peoples everywhere have been obliged to accept – like sheep – something less than this high moral principal. Their loftiest dreams, ideals and efforts have been usurped by the corruption of the 'two percent.' The means of much of our communication have been assailed by thuggish narrow minds. Those who have perceived this attempted seizure (whether it had been surreptitious or overt) and who are convinced they do not have the power to counter it (the thugs will employ stealth when they wish to avoid provoking mass backlash) resort instead to the inevitable sad dictum: 'You should never believe all you read in the newspapers.'

'Fake news! Fake news!' shouts the loudest thug in the room, quick to perceive he has been provided with an excuse to grab the microphone and knee an uppity journalist in the groin.

Too right, you cannot always trust the press, and that is lamentable. In addition to some lazy and sloppy reporting (often, but not only, by young, inexperienced or easily intimidated and unworldly reporters who do not know how to ask questions) the readers of the daily press, the listeners and viewers of broadcast air, must be aware of – and allow for – news management with agendas. The same general rule of thumb applies across the board – print, radio, television, Internet, blogs, tweets, and any other means (some yet to be invented) – when seeking out accurate and truthful information.

Vigilance is essential, for in the vertiginous moment of the deadline mistakes will be made, sadly.

Vigilant, even critical, but not paranoid. The world has long been made aware that 'news' has often meant wading through a mix of stroked rumour and outright lies, coercions and deliberate misleadings. Some people eventually wise up. They even become clever and can assess how deception, often couched as worthy opinion, can and does play a major role in the dissemination of political knowledge. Hitler's henchman Joseph Goebbels, master of propaganda for the Nazis, taught the world that.

Much confusion is due to inexperienced news gathering, a reporter missing the point of what was meant or intended during an interview, or in the course of questioning. Careless editing too easily has the same effect as deliberate mischief. Sometimes the reports you read will arrive at your breakfast table as scrambled as the eggs, and it is a clever man indeed who can sift through it all to discover the valid from the loaded, the careless or the fraudulent. Unless you are very careful, attempting to inform yourself can result in extraordinary bamboozlement, a most cynical contortion of what somebody (anybody or everybody) is trying to say, and the message – any message, true or false – can lodge firmly in the mind of the unsuspecting, and the conspiracy theory is born. The *golpista* knows this well: to win hearts and minds he must first gain control of the enemy's television station and print media. So comes into play yet another dictum:

'The man who does not know the political slant of the news he reads is a damned fool.'

Two anecdotes might serve to address the matter of *know thy source*. The first:

In both 1977 and again in 1980 I was invited to return to Canada from my home in Portugal where I was engaged in teaching at the Universidade de Lisboa and simultaneously acting as unpaid correspondent for an outfit needing to brag it was Canada's principal (in fact only) international news magazine. The host of these two return trips to Canada, at the time the largest news organization in the country, had asked me to tour English-speaking campuses, thinking maybe I could direct a little extra light onto the impoverishment of the western news media's coverage of international affairs – particularly, in this case, the Portuguese *Carnation Revolution* that had triumphed over Salazar's vicious forty-year dictatorship.

At a time when the magazine I had been asked to represent was transforming itself from a monthly into a weekly publication (and now able to brag it had arrived in the Big League of news purveyors) management appears to have considered it would be a useful public relations gesture to list the names of correspondents in each issue – to impress its readership that their information was being responsibly written and collated by knowledgeable professionals strategically placed in the major capitals of the world.

That much was baloney. We were no more than glorified stringers. The paper's bite was toothless; printing the names of the correspondents right below the masthead was a transparent chicanery, its intent being to disguise a manifestly inconsequential but self-inflated hawker of gossip and lofty opinion that came very close to defining yellow journalism. The paper's content showed itself to be little more than an extension of the self-serving liberal egos of its directors and editors, who have traditionally kowtowed to the captains of coercive capitalistic commerce (lobbying, advertising) both locally and abroad. Possessing a resource-based economy, Canada has always shone in such international business circles as can be found in the production of oil, food and farm output, mining, timber, fishing, the manufacture of armaments, pharmaceuticals, and so on. Big money and powerful brokers have ever controlled the country's economy without too much genuine concern for a middle- and low-income (under-educated news-consuming) voter public, or the land's indigenous peoples. Above all these brokers of power have always desperately needed control over any flow of information that could possibly point to a serious disconnect between themselves and a world largely at odds with the privileges and comforts of those we have come to call the 'two percenters.'

Mainstream press has gone along with this because it is precisely Big Business that is the economic lifeblood of newspapers and the broadcast media through advertising – a fine example of the you-scratch-my-back-and-I'll-scratch-yours syndrome. Tell the advertising executive sitting behind his polished mahogany desk in his $1,500.00 duds that his ads exaggerate and tell lies, and he will vehemently tell you he is 'informing' the public, not bamboozling them, not brainwashing them – not even annoying them, really. 'Who are *you* to tell *me*, anyway?' and 'Are *you* someone special to whom I should listen?' and 'What's *your* nit-picking beef?' and 'Why do *you* choose to interrupt the course of *my* perfectly legal business?' and 'Are *you* a communist, or one of those dirty-necked and altogether distasteful socialists, or something?' There are yet other major factors that come into play: the assumed gullibility of the newspaper's readership, its lack of sophistication and worldly education …

In 1957 the newspaper for which I worked when I started in the profession, a major Canadian daily, consciously wrote its news columns to satisfy the comprehension level of a Grade IV student. While I was at the paper this level was raised to Grade VI. No kidding. No big words.

Gullibility works both ways, though. Dictators and oligarchs become complacent over time, overlooking the degree to which revolutionaries arm themselves with weaponry – especially the weapon of political smarts.

The subject of my address on both Canadian tours was *The Irresponsibility of the Western Free Press* in relation to the 1974 Portuguese revolution. By and large the talks were successful inasmuch as they initiated a degree of concerned discussion right across the country. The audience was not that mass of the voting public one would like to think could force government bodies to leap into urgent action. In a way my address was much like preaching to the already converted. Everyone seemed to *know* the nation's printed press was inadequate.

Much as revolution was called for in the fascist-led Portugal of the time, its most noteworthy aspect when it finally happened was a desperate lack of political sophistication, and the very clear absence of educational savvy and know-how of the long-oppressed within the country. The 'Great Unwashed' existed not only in the colonies, but at home as well. For all that one might legitimately have summoned considerable sympathy for them, they simply did not know the art of governing themselves when the immediacy of it was suddenly thrust upon them. Huge numbers of angry citizens found they could not live by slogans alone. The membership of unions and co-operatives, shouting from the floor, knew nothing of political or administrative organization. Prior to the revolution, and in the immediate aftermath, they were obliged to follow the dictates of fanatic usurpers whose principal skills lay in knowing how to shout louder than others, and to wield clout – occasionally physical – to enforce their will. 'News' was well-controlled; strict newspaper censorship, inadequate radio and television coverage. Thankfully, over the years, a dispossessed but clever *povo* had learned what was fair and what was unfair, and they knew they wanted to live in 'freedom.' Their greatest handicap was that they had no strong leaders to guide them in governance; they had no practical experience of the intricacies, the ins-and-outs of how to operate or manipulate their country day-to-day.

Rightly or wrongly, those in power in the west – chiefly America – failed to gauge the Portuguese in terms of their new independence, and they too quickly named this very just and mass revolution 'communism.' It is a trigger word, the one word that stirs vitriolic passions among those who aspire to riches: America's own wealthy but semi- and poorly-educated. Canada, of course, followed the US. Many of North America's loudest voices (not a few of them in senior government positions) were unable to differentiate, fine-tune or assess nuance. Among them were the strident voices of privilege who will forever remain convinced that a communist and a socialist are the same thing (because although not always the case, the lexicon of communists and socialists is frequently interchangeable – and anyway might as well be the same because both of them are seen as a threat to the current comforts and riches perceived to be the indicators of a functional democracy).

Portugal was (still is) a member of NATO – so how could it possibly be allowed to remain a member if run by 'communists' – the erstwhile enemy…?

The convolutions required to cope with the complexities of a new thinking were too confusing for a large rural Portuguese public so newly released and called upon to make its own bed, and it was too much for the broad understanding of Americans who have always been quick to rattle their sabres. It was too much for a news-reading public, and it was probably also too complicated for even intelligent journalists to assess consistently and accurately, to parse or write about coherently. Portugal's sudden and muscular sheer to the left had pushed the west's panic button. Frank Carlucci, Number Two man at the CIA under Stansfield Turner, was eventually dispatched (by President Gerald Ford) as ambassador to Lisboa with the specific task of collapsing Portugal's nineteen-month-old revolution and installing 'democracy.' (There was barely a mention of capitalism's interests in Portugal's former colonies in Africa: Cabinda's oil, Angola's mining of precious metals and diamonds, Moçambique's transportation systems into the southern African heartland.) Virtually none of this was ever intelligently reviewed in the western press – and certainly not in the slick Canadian tattler I was supposed to be representing.

I called the editor of my paper in Toronto to tell him there were sixteen political parties facing off in the coming election. More than half of them were *left* of the official Portuguese Communist Party, I told him …

"My God, man!" he interrupted. "Can't you try to keep it simple …?"

For newsmen covering the chaos let loose by the *Carnation Revolution* the political volte-face induced by Carlucci was distasteful and appeared demeaning for many Portuguese – a rump roar that rumbled across the delicate horizon of Lusitanian sensibilities. Nothing was simple. American-style razzmatazz and snake oil are antithetical to Portugal's small-c cultural conservatism, but there seemed little choice; revolutionary politicians were stopped dead and subjected to the will – political and military – of a far more aggressive street-corner scrapper. As in Britain during the Second World War ('Over-paid, over-sexed, and over here') *America vulgar* has never been held in high esteem in Portugal. At the end of his term as ambassador Carlucci had resumed his position at the CIA, and most Portuguese – tired, confused, numbed by centuries of oligarchy and the recent war in the colonies – resumed their prior assessment of America and Americans in general:

untrustworthy, gangsterish, crass – assessments that seemed not to faze the newly-delivered democratic government.

For a time it seemed every spiv and huckster in the country had been given licence to hawk the contraband nylon stockings he had filched from his wily grandmama. (Surreptitiously she had hoarded them in the bottom drawer of her dresser throughout the years of war and turmoil.) If Portugal was to abandon its colonies only in order to become a closer 'colony' of the Americans, then nothing was sacred anymore – and Portuguese culture and self-image had been dealt a savage and demeaning blow. Over the next half-century Portugal settled down and her harsh and most negative thoughts of America have softened somewhat. Perhaps America's intervention had been a necessary evil, after all. Portuguese may now wink and smile knowingly at one another even though, through the Trumping of America, there has been a certain legitimizing of what they suspected all along. In honouring their commitment to the west they must deal with duplicitous rascals.

This theme, and variations of it, were all written in the newspapers of the time.

The second anecdote is briefer, maybe pithier:

Long prior to the two Canada-wide tours described above, I well recall a conversation with the managing editor of Vancouver Island's Victoria Times. I was hired by the column-inch to write art criticism for the paper, but we were discussing in more general terms what constituted 'news.' At a certain point, perhaps with the notion I was imposing upon both his time and his patience (maybe he was merely trying to bring the conversation to a close) he blurted testily:

"If you think for one moment this newspaper exists for the benefit of its readers, you'd best be thinking again. Advertising, news, editorial content and every other damned thing concerning what's written in the pages of this newspaper exists in its entirety for the sole benefit of the paper's shareholders. Nothing else!"

Considering who said it, that comment should stand on its own.

Consumers of news, written or broadcast, are dealing with, and must remain on the lookout for:

a) A lack of background education on the part of even the most sophisticated individual journalists

b) Gullibility and the lack of education on the part of news consumers

c) Indifference, mendacity or arrogance on the part of news outlet proprietors

d) Profits and propaganda at the expense of truth

e) The lobbyist

These comments are deliberate. Accept them as cautionary – negative, possibly, in order to sound an alarm, yet simultaneously and hopefully to permit a contrary, even nobler, viewpoint to surface. Through years of association with members of the 'fourth estate,' the truth is that on many, many occasions – too many to number – I have felt astonished (even ennobled) by the dedication, knowledge, integrity and professionalism of numerous individual investigative journalists. Indeed, most people reading newspapers are more than satisfied these finer qualities of journalism shine abundantly in every edition of almost every newspaper. At one time or another in print, on the television screen, or at various sites on the Internet, we have all seen and had occasion to remark upon some of the very finest documentary film and reportage. There would be no point in attempting to knock down what is clearly fine, sometimes heroic, work. However, it is precisely because this abundant high standard of professionalism is so necessary and so anticipated, and that we are treated to examples of it as often as we are, that the instances of negative journalistic blunder are particularly noticeable. One goes to a newspaper in order to be informed, to search out and be educated as to the day's deeds and misdeeds. Clearly one must be intelligent about reading any newspaper, at least to have an idea of the paper's political stance. Fake news, warped news, misinformation – these do indeed occur, and far too frequently, and an unwary press can and does fall into the trap of institutional favouritism, wittingly or otherwise ministering to a variety of deceitful and dishonest people and their intentions – pushing propaganda. But when all is working as it should, and an alert society is being well-informed, one must admit that the press works wonders as society's protector. A free and independent press doing the job intended for it is the best guarantor of what we know as the 'free world.'

What is the difference, one might ask in the age of Trump, between a savvy assessment of what one is reading in the press and the corrosive broadsides of a dictatorial bully?

The answer to that query, as with all reasoned criticism, should be found in the relevant details being examined, not in a full-scale attack against those asking questions pertaining to the needs and concerns of an interested public.

Even in those instances in which there may exist the impression of willing competence on the part of the press, very often (and this is particularly the case in North America) a reporter's solid exposure to the real world (Life Experience) is frequently warped or absent altogether. This is a problem that starts in a home well-sheltered from the dangers of an open and often brutally abusive society – a condition exacerbated in the school room because of the trustees' fears of parental concerns, substantive and paranoiac. They want their pensions. Invariably these circumstances are tossed up in the face of those going out to discover origins and grapple with them. Being called to task and required to provide the detailed breakdown of an argument is no more than what might be expected of any journalist; it is the armature of his or her profession. If the information is sound there should be little reason not to go to press. News gathering, the various ways in which information is collected and disseminated regarding any happening or viewpoint, has altered drastically over the past fifty years and today bears little resemblance to the profession as I first encountered it. Although often (and often legitimately) claimed that the world's media outlets fail in their primary task of acting as watchdogs over the world's leaders, younger newsmen and women appear eager to throw themselves into the profession and take a stab at making their way in it. There is a certain idealism that comes with the exciting flush of one's first encounter with the newsroom. Overall, there has been an exceptional tenacity to XX century reporting – the kind of tenacity examined in detail, for instance, by an observer such as George Seldes[8], who spent his entire working life not only reporting on his times, but reporting on the reporters he encountered in the field. New generations have come forward. Reporters, who only a few years ago learned their profession in the school of hard knocks, are now being replaced by skilled computer technicians who have been processed through any number of journalism schools that are unwittingly, but constantly, threatening to douse much of the fire in a student's belly. The wishy-washy veneer of absenteeism that can so easily afflict much of today's press – lack of knowledge spells out a loud silence – is due in my understanding of things to inadequate preparation at a much earlier stage of schooling. Coddled at home by harassed parents, themselves all too often ill-equipped and culturally impoverished to understand or deal with a generation switched onto electronic information (true or false) of which neither generation has substantial or even meaningful comprehension, and to which neither has contributed, then coddled at school by teachers ill-prepared

---

[8] See Seldes, George – *Witness to a Century* – Ballantine Books, New York and Toronto, 1987. He became a reporter for the *Pittsburgh Leader* at nineteen and was an active journalist all his life. He died aged one hundred and four in 1995.

to accept responsibility for what these home fronts have produced and sent on to them, today's students are terrified of not being able to find, maintain or compete in order to stay abreast of a diminishing list of demanding jobs. They choose to learn from their iPhones or books before they dare to indulge solid experience. At all levels there is a 'know-nothing-been-nowhere-done-nothing' wall of ignorance about the world at large; history and geography are wrapped up under 'social sciences,' and budget cuts have pushed them into the broom closet at the end of the hallway. The same with 'the arts.' All these subject areas are basic, essential ingredients to an understanding of culture, the very glue that holds any nation together. They constitute the basis of good journalism, also, for if a newsman comes up short in this department he, or she, is going to make a mess of the story and prove a damned ass into the bargain. Yet in schools throughout North America these subjects receive a fraction of the attention and funding given the sciences and technologies – and it shows. With their eyes and hearts set on making a living for themselves at the conclusion of their studies, many young reporters fresh out of journalism schools (one can hear them prattling every day on television) have lost touch (if, indeed, they ever had it) with their backgrounds and cultures, and so tend to neglect the backgrounds, cultures and imperatives of those about whom they are reporting. The problem is general, and by no means the concern of journalism schools alone. With the barest knowledge of how the world works, or what it means to others beyond their borders, young men and women graduate from high school and are encouraged to continue immediately to college or university. To do this, they rack up huge student loans over a short period – so that by the time they finish their courses they are obliged to latch onto scarce employment almost immediately in order to make enough money to tidy up their debts. The system largely precludes grappling with Life at close quarters in the real world, and this in turn tends to favour the comforts of remaining close to home, close to the familiar, head down in a safe and earnest endeavor to 'forge ahead' on the job, or scouring the pages of a thick book in search of some 'other ...' Unfortunately, their teachers have also been through much the same process: out of high school directly into college, and then back into the classroom to teach and earn a living. In this they extend and perpetuate the same stagnant educational template.

Education: I comment briefly on how this was handled under Portugal's *Estado Novo* in the final chapter of this work, and much detail may be gleaned from a study of the UN report included in the final pages as Appendix #1. One point was stark: without a broad and inclusive knowledge of the world about him it would have been unreasonable to expect the average nine-to-five man-in-the-street (using only the tools of an internalized and parochial perspective, the same he likely encountered through his schooling) to avoid being lulled into the trap of agreeable (and largely self-centred) domestic insularity. This generality was much in evidence prior to the revolution of 1974. Judgement and emotion are easily confused, for no two judges will render precisely the same verdict. In such situation one's views can be seriously compromised. If the source of information is only a newspaper or the television news, how is it possible for the average man or woman to make a truly educated choice at the ballot box? How is the voter competent to assess facts, to decide what is propaganda and what is not? The democracy we like to talk about in the west, the loose elaboration of a set of rules by which our chaotic associations are governed, is a complex and dangerous *pântano*. One requires worldly 'smarts' to deal with the heavy lifting of the democratic process, and these were certainly not encouraged in the early education offered by the *Estado Novo*. It made for compliant workers in areas where they were needed; it also made for a willing soldiery when that was required. A poorly-educated peasant class was badly needed for the scrubby work.

The paramount exercise of 'fact checking' has always been a feature of a journalist's work patterns, and in many ways this has proven easier now that computers, digital phones and iPads have become so much a part of the game. (These gadgets also tend to make the task more treacherous; one must constantly be mindful that not everything on the Internet is factual.) However, one can admire the energy and dedication of today's younger generation of journalists, for all the warnings and criticism I deliberately level at them in these lines. Many attempt magnificent work on the job; when given the chance they do their utmost to report all the twists to all the stories and corruptions they come across; part of their often exceptional competence is due to their use of computers and the Internet to help them present their understanding of the world to a public eager to read about it, see or hear it. Whether or not their experience and educational backgrounds are able to keep pace is another matter; there are large differences between the best and the not-so-seasoned. One cannot help but admire the consummate professionals, especially those considerable numbers who place themselves in harm's way, who are persecuted or even killed for their integrity. Their dedication stands out; one can almost watch the transcendence of the best of them from obscure adventurers into concerned and mature seekers after solid fact and truth as they see it. They deserve nothing but the deepest sympathy and respect, for they are the single most reliable check on political power and fair governance.

Unseasoned journalists can be annoying, granted, and these are the ones we are more likely to encounter within a local milieu. Of far greater concern is his or her boss – or worse, the 'media mogul' – who, even should he attempt to downplay his role as boss, is nonetheless a person of almost immeasurable power and weight. This is someone whose position can be truly dangerous. If such a chief has a private or political agenda to push, manipulation is almost child's play for a capricious mind. It is easy for him to hide essential information in order to confuse a readership or clientele, to swing a vote or block a protest; it is called 'playing the news' – the choice of placing a story on the top half of the front page or inside, page eight at bottom left … It is possible to keep a people down by keeping them dumb, and no one knows this better than the editor-in-chief. Information is control; if this power is played straight and with honesty, all will be well. But an editor is dangerous when he countenances the camouflaging of facts or social movements. The bending of truth, the suppression of knowledge, becomes a Mephistophelean game. It is the reason, mentioned above, that the first target of a revolution must always be the source of information dissemination. Propaganda can never be undertaken lightly, and those who choose to indulge it for shameful purposes know this very well; the consequence of employing it carelessly is that truth eventually wriggles its way into daylight. Propagandists know they must maintain a tight hold on media.

The man who does not know the politics of the paper he reads is indeed a fool, for a news outlet will express a galaxy of opinion in any number of subtle ways. In addition to gleaning his knowledge of the day's political twists and turns from the skimpy content of the stories he reads or sees on his television screen, he would be best off having a clear understanding of the man who owns and controls the news outlet – his willing and influential investors, the chain of command he controls, his cronies.

Some men (the forty-fifth president of the United States of America is clearly one of them) seek confrontation with the press. If they can convince those who follow them that the press is a duplicitous enemy, they are satisfied they have placed themselves in a win-win situation. In this scenario, if a point is won, it is despite the criticisms of the press. If the point is lost, then it was the direct result of opposition by a dishonest press. Either way they find plenty of justification for screaming abuse at a vile and degraded press, ever the scapegoat for failure and inadequacy. A tyrant is not without a following of would-be tyrants, be he (or she) an airhead or a Caesar – and all are prepared to scream blue murder in their fanatic and lunatic support of the most outlandish hogwash.

The Portuguese Consul

Gerry met me at the restaurant entrance and, lowering his voice, kibitzed:

"He's a bit of a strange one, this guy, but I think you'll like him – conservative type. A bunch of us invited him to a beach party the other night. His idea of casual (most of us were in sneakers and cut-offs) was a four-button blazer in place of his usual three-piece suit, and a cravat instead of a tie. The scarlet handkerchief peeping out of his breast pocket is a permanent fixture, as are his patent leather shoes ..."

Entering the restaurant, I caught sight of the man immediately. He was not a large person by any means, but he stood out like a sedate windmill on the skyline, by far the best-dressed and coifed client among the lunchtime crowd. He wore a natty European-cut business suit with, as Gerry had whispered, a scarlet handkerchief in his breast pocket that appeared to be his stylish 'uniform.' He spotted us approaching, rose from behind a table set against the back wall and bowed with a ritual courtesy (I think I heard him click the heels of his patent leather shoes) before shaking Gerry's hand.

"And you are the journalist!" he said, turning to me with another gracious bow. "It is a great pleasure to me that we meet ... I have read your reports from Alabama."

Dr. Jorge Ritto spoke with greatly exaggerated formality, as if welcoming me to the halls of some august society of XIX century geographic explorers. He had been most impressed by my succinct journalistic style, he said – encouraging, and even convincing me (at least for that moment) that he meant it and that I was important to him. His eyelids fluttered half-closed as he lifted his head, a movement of lofty aristocracy that permitted me to see straight up his nostrils. His syntax was a little squiff, but it might have been no more than his accent. I had never met a Portuguese before.

The epitome of confidence, he waved us to our places. We proceeded to order our meal, and over the next hour or so I came to be acquainted with Portugal's trade representative in Toronto.

He delivered an encapsulated rundown of matters Portuguese, for the country had been catching much negative attention over the past year and it was now his mission to set a cockeyed record straight. I made as if to

41

understand both his references and his humour, but in fact I didn't. For starters, I was having difficulty with his allusions to the benign dictatorship of Dr. António de Oliveira Salazar; Ritto spoke of his country's dictator as a warm grandfatherly sort of character, leading me to visualize Santa Claus' jolly cousin. This didn't quite jibe with the information drummed into me from grade school on – that dictators are generally repugnant fellows with bad breath and steel-cold eyes, thus deserving the bullet that eventually cuts them down. Saying nothing, I waited for him to continue. Perhaps I would be able to pick up the thread as we went along. Rhetoric concerning his impoverished little country on the rump end of Europe had been building to a crescendo throughout the past several months, said Ritto, pulling a wry face. There had been much criticism, even insults hurled about at high levels. Clearly his delicate personal sensitivities had been assailed.

All of Africa was burning for its freedoms and independence, he said. There was no trouble in my understanding of his reference here, for only a few short years before I had been involved with the Mau Mau uprising in Kenya – arguably the first contemporary, and the loudest, of Africa's anti-colonial freedom movements to date, and now that country was soon to be granted her independence. I had kept abreast of what the British and French had been doing in Africa. There had been the Suez confrontation with Egypt. I had been in South Africa; I knew the Congo (DRC) was in such a hopeless tangle that it could take generations for the place to sort itself out. But Portuguese Africa? That was even remoter, more unsung, even, than Italian Africa ...

Other powers have colonies, but not Portugal, said the consul – as though he himself not only understood his government's instructions but believed its definitions. What others called Portugal's colonies were in fact indivisible portions of Portugal itself – 'provinces,' not 'colonies.' Portugal's was a case apart that outsiders had never understood. Criticism was misguided; there was no reason whatsoever for the Portuguese (or others, for that matter) to pay attention to adverse criticism. All of Portugal's territories were already free; there was no portion of the country that needed additional freedoms. Portugal *was* Africa, he told me – an African country with the seat of its government just across the water in Europe. No country in the world knew Africa better than Portugal ...

Ritto sounded utterly convincing, and I began to realize it would require a dedicated insider to comprehend the concept or details of his argument. He knew his country's story well, and his government's line even better no doubt.

Despite the racial events tearing up its own south, the United States administration serving President John F. Kennedy had been particularly aggressive in sessions at the United Nations in its condemnation of Salazar's dictatorial fascist government in Portugal – the *Estado Novo*. Such an abusive and inept colonial power, the Americans avowed, had no business shoving its weight about in Africa, warring on the African people it called its own citizens and whose only crime was their aspiration for freedom and independence. Portugal, said the Americans, was a racist state – a brother in NATO, but an unruly little brother requiring constant admonishment.

In Portugal, surely the original land of dry humour, there was a current one-liner, the consul said – a pithy observation concerning America's struggle with racism:

"In America the people are such democrats they can even choose to be racists if they so wish …"

Ritto was immensely pleased with his joke.

Faced with extraordinary problems in Africa, Portugal took the appraisal of American criticism with a pinch of pepper. Portuguese humour was quick to pick up on what was widely seen as American hypocrisy, duplicity and self-serving do-goodism. UN General Assembly speeches, all that talk of brotherhood and democracy intended as pointed castigation of Portuguese policies in Africa, was considered the thinnest veneer of hypocritical self-righteousness.

The commentary cut deep in Lisboa, however, for the fascists really felt they had been in sync with their American counterparts in the fight against communism – where, in fact, they were being out-maneuvered. And, oh yes, there was oil in Cabinda …

Racism was measurable, Ritto assured us. In America, even today, a fair-skinned child born to a mixed-race union would be considered 'black.' In Portugal, regardless of the hue of the skin, the child would be Portuguese.

He meant, in other words, a mite better than black. That, I pointed out, was not the reverse of racism, but simply the reverse *face* of racism – the other side of the same coin. My observation did not seem to register with him.

I looked over at Gerry Murphy, the American who had brought this meeting about. He looked about the same age as Ritto and me, and the Portuguese had let slip that he was my age at the time – twenty-seven. He had rosy cheeks with a light dusting of bum fluff on them, like a peach, and he spoke in heavily accented but precise, almost pedantic English. He possessed the typical Portuguese inability to pronounce correctly the final "d" of virtually any English word or syllable; it came out something like 'd'th.' (I was to discover much later that only the most accomplished of Portuguese using English as a second language can cope with the final 'd' of an English word, so that a sentence like, 'He had had a hard-headed Dad,' coupled with the silence of the Portuguese letter 'h,' could prove an elocutionary obstacle of almost insurmountable proportions.)

Ritto wanted me to travel to Portugal and 'tell the truth' about his much-maligned country.

"I want you to have a completely free licence, to go to all parts of the country, see it for yourself ... This is something that's not available to just anyone, so we will assist you – permissions, letters, introductions, visas ... We can facilitate bookings. You will be free to travel within the country, anywhere you wish."

I was cagey.

"Ah, but what am I going to learn of the way you treat your African provinces by travelling about Portugal ...?" I asked him.

He hooded his eyes, fluttering the lids, partly contemptuous and partly hurt by my ignorance. With care and the sweetest reason, he explained:

"As I told you, Moçambique and Angola are provinces of Portugal, just as are the Algarve and Minho. So are São Tomé, Guiné and Cabo Verde. I can arrange for you to have our permission to travel to all parts of the country – and I urge you to do so ..."

As anyone knowing the system of the press throughout North America would note in an instant 'freebees,' though useful, are suspect. Journalists are not supposed to pay for their stories, nor are they to accept favours. Years of treating virtually everything with the mean edge of cynicism has taught most journalists it is rare for someone to offer up something for nothing.

"You will not deny you want me to do a public relations job for you," I told him. "But understand, I am a journalist. I have wide latitude and there are many things I can do, but also many things I simply cannot do. One certainty is that I could not use any newspaper to paint over the excesses of your country's government were I to find them. I could only accept your offer of a journey like this if I have your complete assurance I will be able to call it as I see it."

"Absolutely!" he replied. "I can assure you the Portuguese government has nothing to hide, nothing at all. I will furnish you with a letter, if you like, stating that you are a free agent – most definitely a free agent. You may show it to your editor."

His country's administrators spoke not propaganda; only the truth ...

First rate diplomat, Ritto.

"We stand to gain nothing if we merely see you safely from one public relations gesture to another," he said most reasonably. "Anything else, it would show in your writings. No, you must be totally free to write as you wish, to report. My only stipulation – because I am convinced of Portuguese correctness – is that you write the truth. Always the truth."

Doubts – The Birmingham Lesson

Re-nestled comfortably in my Toronto digs, I was all too aware of many self-doubts. Somehow I felt it would have been safer to wait, to resist moving outwards again too soon in order to discover and write about any new dimensions to my world. Fear was a check. I was afraid to sally out untested and uninformed, perhaps into yet another situation akin to Alabama in which I would feel out of my depth. Besides, if I waited, there was a chance I could be taken on full-time staff at the newspaper. It would be a significant career move. To take off right now on what could be little more than a chancy freelance junket might collide with these aspirations. I needed to talk to someone, to background myself much more thoroughly than I had prior to Birmingham – and so I chose to express my hesitations to one of the newspaper's senior anointed, an older senior reporter I had befriended, and whose opinions I respected.

"Don't beat yourself up!" he scolded me. "You'll get it right! You can't reasonably expect to have the experience until you step out from under your shell – but then, you do actually have the experience. Move yourself and deal with it. You've done it all before. It seems to me you have been blessed considerably more than most of us ..."

On several occasions we had sat over flagons of after-hours beer, and he knew something of my background with the British colonial military in Kenya and Malaya, and that I had been a reporter for several years in western Canada. He had read what I had to say about the Alabama excursion.

"I suppose it's natural to query your own abilities, your own level of understanding, your take on responsibility. More power to you if you can do that objectively. But don't go public with your personal heebie-jeebies ...! Keep your self-doubts in your pocket. Don't pull them out for anyone to see."

It is hard to measure yourself when you're alone on a story and the only yardstick to go by is a cynical editor back in Toronto, he lectured me. Many of the guys sitting at the editorial desk picking apart the stories reporters had written, have little choice but to examine the world from a static position – under bright lights, but indoors and behind a desk. Just as it is a reporter's job to poke holes in the frontline material he digs up, so it is the editor's job to poke holes in whatever story the reporter brings back to the news desk. It is no more than what an editor is supposed to do. Some of them, he assured me – which was something I had myself noted from time to time – are gnarled-up and bitter gaffers, aged and jaded prematurely, who take pleasure in downgrading and trampling anyone simply because it is in their power to do so. Often they will consider some young buck half their age should be taken down a peg or two. It goes with the territory – every young reporter encounters something of the kind, the bitter envy the older man feels for the youngster he sees moving onto his patch, taking over his old hunting ground.

"You've accomplished something many have not, you silly bugger. You've been out there. You shouldn't be baring yourself to me about your jitters. You are one of the lucky ones ...!"

Paraphrased, perhaps, but about the way I recall it. Not for the first time in my life I was fortunate in finding a colleague prepared to stand firm right beside me at a crucial point, damp my doubts, confirm my scatty rationalizations and thus help propel me to a decision.

Despite tangible insecurities, the trip to Birmingham had been a rollicking adventure. When I had left Toronto earlier that spring – a bit heady, dead set on getting out from under my dismal job working in public relations for a bank, re-establishing myself as a journalist and digging my teeth into a good story – my motivation had barely risen above acknowledging I desperately wanted a change. Returning to the city three weeks later I was very much aware I had been on a mind-bending escapade, though I do not suppose I was yet able to calculate – fully – to what degree my nous had been stirred. One doesn't learn maturity from books, or necessarily from wild car rides to wild places; nor is it certain to appear when absent a qualified instructor who will observe and correct one's work, awarding either a gold star or a thrashing. On my own, and faced with the routine of earning a daily living, it was difficult to judge the impact on my psyche of an experience like Birmingham. One doesn't always understand nous in the moment the switch is flicked on, to know for certain when or if the juices are flowing correctly. Sometimes a delayed reaction takes over, occasionally it's even deliberate – a deviant way to stimulate reaction and thus better assess it. When my marriage was crumbling and I was sure my life was going to hell, I regaled a much older friend with my woes. A Scot and a strong Presbyterian, he heard me out twitching his shaggy eyebrows and uttering barely a word.

"Aye, that's the way of the Lord!" he had said at last. "Such a pity it is that He doesn't deliver His punishment for our wickedness in the instant we go astray. A swift boot to the backside now and then might give us pause to stop and think – help us gain insight into our stupidity before we demonstrate it!"

Hindsight is no substitute for acumen. My return to Toronto was at the precise moment in US history when, between the brutality of Birmingham and the March on Washington, the country had seemed to pause ever so briefly to catch at its breath and count its horrors. I was not entirely convinced I had participated in an especially significant news event. Not one with legs, as the pundits say. In faulty anticipation that the momentum of the events I had been covering would die down, I wondered what the next story would be – and perhaps that is why I did not bother to transpose my scribbled notes into more comprehensible form. I was not adroit enough to consider that journalism, in this as in so many cases, constituted frontline recording of history, that fifty years on the story might yet remain incomplete. Right now I was *here*, but the story was brewing over *there*.

Thank God idiocy is only one ingredient in the process of awakening. I have always slept soundly; more's the pity that at the time of my entry into Alabama I was not yet fully awake, a state of incorrigibility that might have proven far worse but for my fortuitous meeting with the English journalist, Harry Pinsway[9] who, with barely a word, brought me to my senses. Yes, there is a story here … write it down.

America had seemed unstoppable following her victories in the Second World War. It had been the only nation in the world to come away from that catastrophe strong enough to stand on its own and at the same time initiate the Marshall Plan, ultimately hauling a shattered Europe back onto its feet. In the US during the late '40s and '50s there had been a burst in industry almost

---

[9] See Hespeler-Boultbee, J.J. – *Somersaults* – *Rovings, Tears & Absurdities – A Memoir from the Fringe of Journalism* – CCB Publishing, British Columbia, Canada, 2017 – Harry Pinsway, journalistic counsellor, friend and companion – the 'story' being the extraordinary black desegregation movement of Dr. Martin Luther King Jr. in Birmingham, Alabama, in early summer, 1963.

equal to (in some ways even surpassing) the country's herculean efforts during the war. Returning GIs could go to college and learn new trades and professions; cities grew, and there was a boom in the housing industry, new roads and bridges were built throughout the land. For the first time the masses of the middle class could own their own homes, with an electric refrigerator in the kitchen in place of an ice box; the stores were full of newly designed and manufactured goods, and Detroit was working three shifts a day in an effort to put a new automobile onto every driveway so its owner could travel coast-to-coast on a network of brand new interstate highways. America was booming, able to take on anything – the Korean War, as well as numerous other foreign incursions to halt the 'relentless spread of communism ...' In the early '60s no one doubted President Kennedy when he said he was going to put a man on the moon within the decade. The Beatles came over from Britain to perform on *The Ed Sullivan Show* and suddenly an unfettered and uninhibited middle class was transforming the cultural undercurrent of an entire Western liberal landscape – new freedoms of expression, new freedoms of drugs and sexual mores.

But something was cooking in the southern United States; the word there was 'freedom,' too – albeit in a totally different context. By the early summer of 1963 people were talking about *'Freedom Summer'* – and the cook pot, now black and scalding, finally blew its lid that May. With considerable discomfort, and after many white-on-black confrontations in the south (almost invariably that way around – whites ganging-up on blacks, lynchings and terrors committed by the Ku Klux Klan), Americans coast-to-coast had been forced to acknowledge there was something rotten in a racial mix that white America had more-or-less accepted for generations – strictly on *white* terms. But white America really did not seem to know what to do about it, and the rolling of the good times permitted a camouflage to be thrown over the deepest of the nation's social ills. Up to the time Birmingham erupted, it had appeared impossible to judge the situation clearly or in its entirety. Explosive social reactions in the streets and any number of inflammatory speeches were major distractions in local districts, but on their own perhaps they proved to be so startling they only blurred one's vision of distance and extremity. They were not just happening locally; they were happening haphazardly all over the country.

Even when walking the streets of Birmingham with Harry Pinsway it was almost impossible to gauge the impact of what was going on around us, or to judge the scope of what was in fact a national crisis. While Harry was an invaluable assist in helping me structure my personal journalistic abilities, I very much doubt even his knowledge and shrewdness would have been broad enough or sharp enough to evaluate the overall picture. Both of us earlier – he in Britain, myself and others in Canada – were no guiltier than anyone else in our failure to pay a great deal more attention to the catastrophe before it happened. Although shortly we were to be right there in one of the main trouble spots, I very much doubt any conscientious journalist would have been able to assess the complexity of an event that was spreading so rapidly throughout the nation. Once Harry and I had met up and were moving among the crowds in the streets of Birmingham, it seemed we were far too close to the action to draw an accurate or realistic perspective of the entire movement. A general state of mesmerized confusion appeared like a contagion to lie over all of North America, lasting right up to the night of the television coverage of the police response to the children's crusade – children being kicked, beaten, hosed down and arrested – and then the penny dropped on the national psyche. With a thud. The country – the entire world – was horrified by the images, and Americans could not ignore their problem any longer.

My days with Harry in Birmingham had been full and exciting, and although he had not posed as my mentor, there is no denying the fact: I could have had no better companion on that special assignment, nor learned more from anyone else. Martin Luther King had been released from prison only a few weeks before either of us came on the scene. His famous *Letter from Birmingham Jail* had been an attempt to call immediate attention to the violence and injustice being unleashed against the Afro-American communities throughout the south – though the world at large was slow to pay attention. The letter was the written warning, and not everybody could digest it immediately. The action that summer was in Birmingham, in the streets of the city, in its churches and classrooms. The actors were those shortly to be incarcerated in the city's jail by Bull Connor, the city's 'security chief.' The newness of television's national coverage was at last playing a part in disseminating the details, and a nation just awakening from a decade of plenty, the certainty of America's rightful place in the world and its self-satisfying comforts, was being obliged to acknowledge all was far from well with a significant segment of its population. Ordinary people were being forced to question their values and morality, and to take sides. Harry had a clear (though incomplete) perspective, and I was close enough to him that his vision stimulated my own.

By August a slumbering America had been jolted into wakefulness, and so marched on Washington – one million people and the largest political rally in the history of the country to that time, converging on the capital to demand equal status for all Americans of whatever race. This was when Rev. Martin Luther King made his famous 'I have a dream' speech that seared the nation's conscience. Just three months later President Kennedy was assassinated – and, not long after that, in the summer of 1964, the horrifying Ku Klux Klan slaughter of three civil rights workers in Mississippi in which local police and civic leaders had been implicated. It was this last well-publicized event that spurred President Johnson's Civil Rights Bill through Congress in July 1964. It was all too much for the people to absorb in anything but short gasps – and then, in early August, came the Gulf of Tonkin incident. It was the foil that prompted President Johnson to re-think a military assistance programme to the south Vietnamese, and so to escalate tensions into a full-blown war – and to weather the accusation of doing all this merely to disguise his incompetence back in Washington.

By now the American kettle was percolating …

"It's up to you," Dr. Jorge Ritto had said. "The offer exists for the moment; I have no idea if it will be the same a few months from now …"

The editor at my newspaper furnished me with a letter of credential, as he had for my assignment in Birmingham, but with a cocked eyebrow and a caution:

"Those bastard Portuguese fascists are killing people in Africa. They're suckering their own impoverished peasant farm boys into doing the job for them – boys who are no more than cannon fodder, and they are being killed in significant numbers. Make no mistake, Salazar is a fascist, not a whole lot different than Hitler, Mussolini and Franco and a dozen other sons-of-bitches buying western arms to hold their own people in check. Few individuals from here have ever been able to get into Moçambique or Angola, so for you to go there could be useful for us. But you'd best observe well, write about what you see and treat what you're told with the greatest caution. Your stories will come through me and if for one moment I suspect you're just accepting the Portuguese line, I'll junk 'em."

My final meeting with Ritto was particularly inspirational. Again we met for lunch. I had thought it would just be the two of us, but he brought someone with him – a man I judged to be some fifteen or twenty years senior to either one of us.

"I have wanted the two of you to meet. I think you will find you have much in common, much to talk about …" said Ritto, by way of introduction.

The man's name was Ronald Lawrence. He was a journalist with the *Toronto Telegram*, and had only recently returned from an extended foray into central Africa – Angola and Moçambique being among the many countries he had visited.

"You will like it, no question. Fascinating lands, both of them. So, too, is mainland Portugal," Lawrence told me, but beyond that gave the distinct impression he was holding something back. Before lunch was over, however, he had given me his card and asked me to be sure to call him before leaving the city.

The two of us met up a day or so later. It was not a lengthy meeting. He handed me a slip of paper on which he had written a short list of names and telephone numbers.

"Be careful over there," he warned. "You will most certainly come across the Portuguese political police, PIDE. They are everywhere, and they are nasties. Try to remember the names and numbers on this list, then destroy it. Do not allow it to come into the hands of the Portuguese police. Everyone on the list is a worthwhile contact for you, some pro-fascist, others anti. I am sure all of them will be useful to you – but better by far that you keep all of them to yourself. Memorize the list – don't take it to Portugal with you. The police have a way of making anyone's life a misery, you'll see – and they love lists ..."

It was not a long list, and I did as he suggested, committing both names and numbers to memory. I never saw Lawrence again. By the time I arrived back from Africa, he had gone back deep into the Ontario wilderness he loved and called home. I did not know it at the time, but it had been a fortuitous encounter. The name Ronald Lawrence has become synonymous with the study of the environment and wildlife, and the man was already famous throughout Canada and many other parts of the world. He wrote several well-received books concerning his adventurous life and his encounters with the wild. Many times he was honoured by both governments and naturalist societies.

By the end of that July I was in Lisboa. I thought I might have to stay for a week to orient myself, inform officials at the various ministries which parts of the empire I would like to visit, and to allow for them to arrange papers, bookings and transport.

Important or otherwise, all the officials I met had smiles for me: 'Do feel free to ask if there is anything at all you might need. We are most anxious to assist ...'

Hm-m-m ...

As it turned out, I was obliged to remain in Lisboa three weeks in order to prepare for the trip to the African territories.

Deep Dig

On the verge of setting out I rolled up my sleeves in a concerted attempt to dig deeper into the background of the areas I was about to visit, but I kept sidetracking myself in an effort to gather loose ends together. The more I dug, the more I seemed to find there was to dig, and the loose ends just kept coming. It was like picking nits. There was no Internet in those days, so it meant going back over newspaper morgue stories, then delving into obscure bibliographical reference material. Often pulled off onto some delightful tangent, so acquainting myself with strands of history I had never heard about and would never think to use in any practical way, I began to discover something of the Portuguese claim to the littoral of Africa – the most gripping yarns of tropical sea voyages, sagas of castaways and survivals, the alliances that Portuguese envoys made with African kings, the expeditions of their military into the hinterland of an unknown continent, the building of railways and the stories surrounding the spice trade, and any number of mining concessions and enterprises. Steeped as I had been on British and North American histories, it was refreshing to unlock a Pandora's box of information that every now and then appears to have added a morsel of tangential intrigue to our busy-busy list of worldly concerns – all with a Latin twist, and much of it kernel to values we hold within our own Anglo-western cultures.

There was a massive quantity of ground to be examined. Strange to me at the time, I found much of it stretched well beyond the bounds of that part of Africa controlled by Portugal. Money and armaments were useful trails to follow, I thought, and this particular form of investigation took me all over the shop. Guiné Bissau which, under the leadership of Amílcar Cabral and his PAIGC (Guiné Bissau and Cabo Verde independence movement), had been causing the Portuguese trouble since 1956, had ramped-up its activities with the aid of the communist bloc countries. Cabral had established contact with the leaders of the liberation movement in Angola – the one thing the government in Lisboa feared most.

It was less than seven years since I had been released from a two-year stint of obligatory National Service with the British army.[10] Although a Canadian national, I had been sent to boarding school in England and had been caught in the military web immediately upon leaving. All foreign residents of the United Kingdom were liable to serve and there seemed no harm in it at the time. All my school chums were in line for their service; it was the next big adventure on the cards. As I have written elsewhere, not serving was not an option. The empire was still out there, and beckoning. None of us yet knew how, or had the moxie, to stand up and say 'no,' or to burn our draft cards. In my own case, one could augment that list by adding my youthful naïvety, discussed above.

Dissecting that two-year period, I spent one-and-a-half years on active service, or travelling between one theatre and another, and found myself fighting in precisely the kinds of situations the Portuguese army was in now – jungle warfare. My enemy had been chosen for me: in Kenya I was sent to augment the slaughter of Africans (Mau Mau) who were annoying the British; in Malaya I was sent to help in the slaughter of Chinese Malays ('Communist Terrorists' or 'CT's') who were annoying the British. My enemy's motivation was no different than it was for the Africans in Portuguese Guiné and Angola (and a year later in Moçambique): a search for freedom, independence and self-determination - and a longing to avoid continued inhumane abuse.

I knew that in the case of the Mau Mau there had been no exterior echelon of support for those who opposed the British, as there was now for the liberationists in the Portuguese colonies. The Mau Mau had virtually no political base, lived lives of almost total deprivation in the forests where the British army had encircled them; they fought with *pangas* and homemade firearms, and yet they had kept the British on the hop for nine years – this despite their main strategy, towards the end, being one of personal survival, and to avoid contact with the British at all costs. The case was different with the Chinese in Malaya, for their senior elements had been trained by the British to fight in the jungles against the Japanese during the Second World War; they had received not only excellent jungle warfare training, but during the conflict had had the foresight to abscond with a mass of British weaponry and hide it in secluded jungle caches. They had also had time to establish links with support groups both inside and outside the country. Because of a far better organization than the Mau Mau had ever been able to develop, the Chinese CT's on the Malay Peninsula were able to extend their hostilities for

---

[10] See Hespeler-Boultbee, J.J. – *Mrs. Queen's Chump – Idi Amin, the Mau Mau, Communists, and Other Silly Follies of the British Empire – a Military Memoir* – CCB Publishing, British Columbia, Canada, 2012 – stories from military National Service in the British colonies.

a total of thirteen years. Despite the ultimate *military* defeat of each of these 'terrorist' groups, in the end both Kenya and Malaya were able to negotiate their full independence once the fighting had stopped. The Africans lined up to fight the Portuguese were in far stronger position.

So much I had learned from my own limited experience. What else was going on?

It seemed to me at the time, and it has become increasingly apparent ever since, that there is a background and a pattern to the events of the late XX century about which many of our leaders, both democratic and dictatorial, have deliberately chosen to remain blind and hapless. It would be well to back up for a moment, avoid picking on any one event and devote a moment to examining a much broader canvas. Doing so will furnish a more coherent perspective, help tint in bolder colours a few murky portions of a global picture – as it did for me when I finally got around to querying what was really happening in the world. Whether in Canada, the USA, Europe or Africa, I was beginning to understand the world I wanted to patrol and write about could not be examined piecemeal, but demanded research that encompassed all of it – a confrontation incorporating globalization some years before the term became commonplace. The exercise got me started delving into research, history and a level of news gathering that has occupied me ever since. Just by trying to understand the narrative of global strategies it appeared my geographical and cultural interests were being markedly expanded.

Immediately challenging and complex, this search led away on the wildest of tangents – seemingly far wide of the target in the important research so necessary prior to my departure for Africa. For some reason – more than just whim – it made sense to be tugged clear of the subject of Portugal alone. To my entrapped western (and northern) mindset, Portugal remained extraordinarily distant and unknown, so poorly understood that I could only guess at its problems by trying to compare them to forms of colonialism as practiced by Britain, France – and the United States of America. Consequently, I found myself digging into areas I had never really considered before: the political pendulum that swung inexorably all the way from fascism through to communism, to see how each worked – or failed to work – and the denominators common to both. Though on the surface so different one from the other, for the life of me, when I moved in close the two extremes, as practiced, appeared about equally unscrupulous and vile. In cases it was difficult to tell them readily apart.

Between one and the other – an unsavoury sandwich of political vacillation and cowardice, an area where political nabobs danced what they insisted was a perpetual democratic jig atop a bed of red-hot political coals – metaphorical fornicators and bum-holers at each extreme were quite ready to sell themselves for practically any price. One came across as the extreme of selfish capitalistic excess – a vertical concept in which much-vaunted trickle-down economics simply did not function as it was supposed to because those who possessed the knowhow and the wherewithal that was meant to trickle down hung onto their assets and did not give a tinker's cuss for the unfortunates on any lower economic level. The alternate came across as a horizontal concept, the much-vaunted social equalizer hidebound by its inept bureaucracies, leadership jealousies, corruption and dishonesty – and above all, in its more liberal guise, its utter blandness.

I tried to confront the juggling and jockeying of the Cold War's alliances – in particular NATO and how, for instance, the United Nations could coerce a country like Canada to participate in the aftermath of the Congo Republic's independence. Likewise, I read up what I could find on the Spanish civil war and how that sad event proved such a useful training ground for fascism, as well as a showcase for communist duplicity. My efforts were made in order to tie down and clarify, for the sake of my own curiosity, an overall historical picture of the first half of the XX century with (I thought) a mind to a better comprehension of the second half. All of it seemed to me to have a strong bearing on what was happening in Lisboa just then, and beyond it in Portuguese Africa. From a North American standpoint, aside from the 'clear confusion' that Portugal was in some way linked to Spain, what little was *known* of Portugal was additionally and hopelessly tied to what little was understood of Brasil. Without fully comprehending why, all that amounted to little more than the knowledge that the three countries spoke off-shoots of Latin. Perhaps there was even a general acceptance Portugal and Brasil retained close cultural ties – though without much grasp of what those might be. Both countries had agreed to Brasil's independence as early as 1822 – so clearly Portuguese colonialism differed in detail from whatever forms of administration were thought to have been the traditional practice of other and more widely-known European colonial powers ...

About this time I had a conversation with a man somewhat older and more experienced than myself, a man I thought could express his superior general knowledge to my advantage. He was a photographer at one of the city's major dailies and was quite used to covering and photographing the world's most memorable personalities and events.

"Ah!" he exclaimed, as those who know everything are wont to do. "The

Portuguese! That rabble are the very worst colonialists of them all ...!'"

They were not, I was subsequently to learn for myself, but it was a pronouncement I was to hear time-and-again from people who 'know' about such things – and I kept hearing it until the time I became convinced *all* colonialism is 'the worst.' No exceptions. Certainly inefficient, it was impossible to compare Portugal's administration of her colonies to the callous and barbaric brutality of the British or French – or the Belgians, or the Americans. They were all dreadful – which was a detail beyond my capacity to assess at the time. Unfortunately I harkened with interest to the opinion of the photographer – and in moments was hopelessly sidetracked.

Writing about this period of research, this very deliberate period of attempting to garner a specific knowledge – and doing so more than fifty years after the fact – remains as clear to me now as if it were still a most present goal. With hindsight, the events of the time and the bells they set a-jangling in my head have become ever clearer; in addition to witnessing the events I describe in these pages I became also a protagonist. The first of these protagonist roles had come as a soldier in the British army, as both fly-on-the-wall witness and participant in the collapse of the British Empire. The second had come as a journalist in Alabama at the beginning of the summer of 1963, close-up observer to the un-picking of the two hundred-year-old social fabric of the American south. I could see, but I could not assess. But in either case I was insufficiently astute to be able to gauge what was happening *historically*. Similarly, now, I was facing the conundrum of Portugal and Portuguese Africa. There was no way I could have had a broad comprehension of what was shortly to follow; in 1963 it was not a case of any deliberate career-path planning on my part. If anything, it was merely a haphazard snatch at random opportunity, an adventure. I was a freelance reporter eager to find a good story, and perhaps would be lucky enough to use it to carve a niche for myself, little more. Opportunistic, not the least altruistic. Africa again! I was able to see the exciting adventure of it, the opportunity it was opening for me. But I was not yet able to assess the disintegration of empire – the last and most far-flung of the world's old-style empires. It was teetering on the brink of collapse, but I had no idea – perhaps not even until I had been long back among the comforts of my home in Toronto. It was only later it dawned on me I had been invited to witness the opening scene in a slow-motion saga – the demolition of some giant five hundred-year-old edifice, a relic in concrete, stone, timber, fabric, flesh, blood, agonies of culture and history. It had been chosen for obliteration to make way for some new development; I was to have a front row seat, but the whole show was to be in a foreign language. Apart from my recent studies, I really had no clue as to what I was to be watching.

A wise man will look to history in order to comprehend his today. Glancing over what is written in these next pages, the reader must accept as a given that the world all of us have come to know is what it is because of what it was made – in large part, over the last couple of centuries, by the English-speaking peoples. There is no intent here to manufacture history; one event leads to another and at any point we can look back and think we lay claim to an historical viewpoint – though in fact we are looking at a *tableau*, a series of events as if they were stamped on a ribbon, or on a film we have already seen, and which is now lying on the cutting room floor ready to be pieced together by some enterprising clairvoyant calling himself an historian – or an arrogant politico who tells you he knows what's going to happen next. Most assuredly, much of what could be revealed would be little more than long portions of this account – left to lie on the cutting room floor. The larger, perhaps more generous view is that we are all directors, and thus pretty sure we know what we have witnessed. 'I was there; you weren't!' – the very reason we may not care to re-examine or re-hash what has already happened, although we do most dearly wish our version of the story be told. So we up the ante a little bit, ramp it so that our (by now grossly exaggerated) view of the story is sufficiently sensational we can be sure *this* version is the one people will believe – and pay to hear or read ...!) In fact much of what was happening globally had come about, at least in the modern era, largely as a result of events initiated by Britain's colonial salad-mixing of the world and its peoples, her creation of a template for the Americans who, in attempting to build a global economic empire for herself, diligently reproduced British arrogance without quite mastering the finer points of British finesse, or French *savoir faire*. (American reproach of the British and French for their invasion of Suez in 1956 is a useful case in point.) Continuing much the same pattern of whine-and-shove, they were keen to lecture the British, and anyone else who might have been listening, concerning the Rights of Man and the disgrace of possessing colonies in the last half of the XX century, as if to say their own simultaneous actions worldwide have never been significantly different. Few would argue today that the American concept of globalization has brought into being a wider brand of fiscal colonization – cumbersome, corrupt and virtually unmanageable.

How green has been the valley of my imaginings! Britain and America and most other countries in the western bloc have been little more than foils – all of them having lived loudly and chaotically through the many traumas of the XX century. But Portugal, hunkered in the silence and secrecy of its isolation, had had the stopper ripped off its lamp and there was no way to fit the genie back inside. The wick had been lit, so to say; everyone could at last see plainly. The country was ill-prepared to cope with what was coming.

Not totally disconnected from consideration regarding my upcoming venture into the Portuguese world, and with a nod to thoughts of arrogance (history does not so much repeat itself as provide parallels), one of the cornier nuggets that both amused and startled me (because I had never learned about it as a schoolboy) concerned the 1494 *Treaty of Tordesilhas*.[11] It, too, has had a strange and concrete effect on the way our wonky world has been carved up.

At Tordesilhas was signed a treaty between Portugal and Spain (sanctioned and blessed in 1506 by Pope Julius II) that divided the world between the two of them. An imaginary line was drawn from the North Pole to the South Pole down through the Atlantic Ocean, then another up through the Pacific Ocean from the south to the north. Negotiations and adjustments continued over several centuries but, in essence, Spain considered herself entitled to everything west of the Atlantic line, Portugal to everything east of it – right around the world as far as the Pacific line – and the two countries generally honoured the agreement. (The Dutch, British and French, naturally, ignored it willy-nilly.)

The lines through both oceans were considerably bent. The Atlantic line's northern sector was not of too much interest to the Spanish who were unconcerned by Portugal's annual crossing of it in order to reach their fishing grounds off Newfoundland and up the Labrador coast as far as Baffin Island. Further south the line veered deep into the Amazon area of South America. Portugal came away with by far the lion's share in this arrangement; by jigging the Atlantic line to the west in order to embrace most of Amazonia, she succeeded in laying claim to all of what is today Brasil on South America's eastern side. On the opposite side of the Atlantic, Portugal laid claim to virtually all the Atlantic islands and the entire coastline of Africa from Ceuta, east of the entrance to the Mediterranean, west around the great bump of western Africa, into and around the massive continental concave of the Gulf of Guinea, and so south to the Cape of Good Hope, then up the Indian Ocean side of the continent to the Strait of Bab el Mandeb (they were

---

[11] See Boxer, C.R. – *The Portuguese Seaborne Empire 1415-1825*, Hutchinson & Co., London, 1969. The *Treaty of Tordesilhas*, 1494, divided the globe between Portugal and Spain.

never able to unseat the Turks or Egyptians from the Red Sea's west coast), the Yemeni coast, the Persian Gulf, almost the entire coastline of India, about half of the island of Ceylon (Sri Lanka) including its entire west coast from Matara in the south to Jaffna in the north, the coasts of Bangladesh, Burma, Malacca, Indonesia and the Spice Islands, the south Malay peninsula, and north to posts in Japan and China. Spain claimed the coasts of western South America, Mexico and the western coast of North America, most of the islands of the Caribbean, all the salt water of the Pacific Ocean, and the Philippine Islands. It is due to this extraordinary treaty that one speaks Portuguese today in Brasil, and Spanish in Chile, the Central Americas and, even today (in ever-decreasing numbers) the Philippine Islands. Australia was not discussed in any Portuguese navigational history that survived the great Lisboa earthquake of 1755; however, there is considerable evidence to show the Portuguese had circumnavigated the continent, and none to show they had ever told the Spanish about it. Australia was reckoned to be, for the most part, on the Spanish side of the Tordesilhas line.[12]

Another morsel of like arrogance was displayed by Portugal in 1662 on the occasion of the marriage of Princess Catherine of Bragança to Charles II, King of England. Catherine's mother, Luisa, had assumed the role of Regent of the Kingdom of Portugal upon the death of her husband, Dom João IV, in 1656 – a position she held until her eldest son, Afonso VI, reached his majority and was able to mount the throne in 1662. Luisa was an intelligent and highly competent diplomat, and saw it as her responsibility to oversee the solidification of a new alliance Portugal had agreed with Britain – a part of which was in the form of a dowry to be offered to King Charles at the time of his marriage to her daughter. As the Kings of Portugal were the de facto lords over great stretches of the Gujarat and Malabar coastlines of the Indian subcontinent, it was decided that a portion of the dowry on offer to Charles should be the group of islands and malarial swamp on which today sits the city of Mumbai – Bombay, as it was known for several centuries. The British had already launched the East India Company (1600), but there is no doubt the gift secured Britain's greater interest in what India had to offer.

Major powers churned their various paths across the surface of the globe with little regard for the smaller nations tossed about in their wake – nations like Portugal, which had been a major Mediterranean Renaissance player, had been obliged to wrestle with her own special set of entrenched problems.

---

[12] See McIntyre, Kenneth G. – *The Secret Discovery of Australia – Portuguese Ventures 200 Years Before Captain Cook*, Souvenir Press Ltd., London, 1977. The author presents evidence the Portuguese 'discovered' the continent some two hundred years before Capt. James Cook.

Portugal had to work out solutions for these, one of which was how to man the largest navy plying the world's seas of those early days in full view of a highly critical international audience.

There was no way of knowing at the start of this research that eventually I would be spending the best part of my working life in Portugal; with that experience and the hindsight of the years that have passed since, it is not reasonable to look on any of the foregoing commentary as irrelevant. Over recent years Portugal has been forced to abandon the Ruritanian mindset it had nursed throughout the centuries of a quaintly antique pastoral past – the onset of most of her growing pains coming in the years since her 1974 *Carnation Revolution*. The world's super power for a brief long-ago (1415 to 1600), Portugal's leap into the modernity of the XXI century has required a degree of enlightenment it had previously possessed in sparse quantity – and it has been obliged to perform this while simultaneously struggling under the imposition of a heavy load of Big Power baggage.

Over the years there has appeared no good reason to cease the broad scope of these research readings, nor in any way curtail what has so clearly proven itself to be the broad background of an essentially schizophrenic story – for that was the distressing condition into which Portugal was nudged by its western associates following its revolution a decade after my initial visit. There had never been logical limitation to the discoveries I was making for myself; the patterns of bullying and coercion anyone could outline in broad terms has proven itself a global continuum, it is sad to say. A long list would provide only the briefest summary of Big Brother behaviour. The English-speaking powers and their allies that play what the British have cynically called '*The Great Game*' have, over time, expanded their base catalogue of transgressions to encompass smaller nations, like Portugal, and sweep them along despite whatever is in the minds and hearts of the local population involved. The process is strictly political; culture, always resilient, is nonetheless forced to bend somewhat in face of degradation, humiliation or even, in an extreme case, to the fear of annihilation.

All of this was the substance of the world I was feeling cocky enough to step out and conquer in 1963. I read the newspapers intelligently and had a fair grasp of the background of what was appearing in the mass media; I was becoming better than averagely aware of global jostling. Yet reviewing that period now, and with a more developed sense of geopolitics, I would have to admit my cognizance amounted to a thin stream; nothing to brag about. I had not the least idea of the extent to which black Africa and black America might have been watching one another – for years and throughout long periods of global mayhem. I was a young, green and gung-ho journalist looking for action anywhere I could gobble it up. The wider dynamics and machinations of the world did not present on the menu any delicacy for which I had hitherto developed a virtuoso taste.

My Kenya and later Alabama sojourns had constituted a great awakening to Afro-culture, but in the end they only signalled the start of a long journey, and I had yet to grasp a more comprehensive understanding of the world about me than what I was reading in books and newspapers. Canada was where I had earlier chosen to pitch my tent, but I was fast coming to realize that for me, personally, my homeland was not where I needed to be.

It would be tempting to label much of what I've written here, stretching both forwards and backwards in time, as 'red herring' – but there is purpose to its inclusion. It is intended to illustrate a developing and delicate political climate at the very moment this rather green reporter was preparing to leave for Portugal. It was a climate that enveloped Portugal and her colonies, and very much pinpointed the inevitable manner in which her affairs would later unfold ... As had been the case with my assignment in Alabama, my view of it all was to be limited – but it was more than enough to get the picture.[13] I was learning to read the residue tea leaves.

Pink City

The Toronto-Lisboa flight landed briefly at the international airport on Ilha de Santa Maria in the Açores. There is another airport in the Açores, the American NATO air base at Lajes on the island of Terceira – the same strip made famous in the summer of 2001 when the engines of a Canadian Air Transat flight shut down due to a faulty fuel feed. The pilot managed to save the lives of the more than three hundred people aboard by gliding his stricken plane for nineteen minutes over a total of one hundred and twenty kilometres, to make a 'hard landing' on the tarmac of the military air base.

An archipelago of nine inhabited volcanic islands some one thousand four hundred kilometres west of the European mainland, the Açores have been an

---

[13] See Hespeler-Boultbee, J.J. – *Somersaults – Rovings, Tears & Absurdities – A Memoir from the Fringe of Journalism* – CCB Publishing, British Columbia, Canada, 2017.

integral self-governing region of Portugal since they were first settled in the 1430s. Many islanders have chosen to migrate to the United States and Canada, and there is a particularly numerous population of them in the Toronto area. Many of those aboard the flight I was on were visiting their island families; others would be boarding to continue to Lisboa. I was hearing Portuguese spoken for the first time. It sounded like Russian to my untrained ear ... I walked across the tarmac to a café in the terminal.

"*Staff-chá!*" someone said to me when I tried opening the locked door.

I had no idea what the man was saying, but clearly I was not about to be served anything. Back on the plane I asked one of my fellow passengers the meaning of *staff-chá*.

Está fechado – it is closed. My first lesson in spoken Portuguese – in which I learned the colloquial linguistic penchant for swallowing the first and last letters of just about every word in a sentence – *(e)sta – f – (e)sha – (do)*. It was to cause no end of consternation when finally I settled down to learn the language – and discovered, by-the-by, it had nothing in common with Russian.

The plane flew right over the capital, by which time the passenger who had taught me to say *staff-chá* had also taught me how to call his city Lisboa – pronouncing it *Lizh-bo̅-a*. It was a morning of brilliant summer sunshine, the first thing to impress being the exceptional quality of the light, its clarity and brilliance bouncing up off thousands of whitewashed houses that spread blanket-like up the hillsides from the bank of the wide Rio Tejo estuary. From the air the roofs of the houses presented a mass of brick-coloured terracotta tiles. I was excited, certain I had never before laid eyes on such a stunning urban panorama. The scene was a wash of pink.

"People have called it the Pink City," my companion told me.

I stayed at a comfortable small hotel on the Avenida Duque de Loulé, and that first morning in the city took a walk down the full length of nearby Avenida de Liberdade – from Marques de Pombal to Restauradores. I counted three cars. Eight lanes wide and with a double boulevard, the avenida was then – and still is – the city's main thoroughfare. The most charming – and incongruous – sight was to watch a shepherd lead his flock up the avenida's full length to put them to graze on the lawns of Parque Eduardo VII. Within a few years the shepherd was gone, never to return. By the mid-1970s automobiles had arrived in quantities sufficient to choke the city's main thoroughfare from end-to-end. Maneuvering a motorcycle or bicycle to where it might fit into the stream of traffic has since become an undertaking for the brave and those with lightning-swift reactions. Lisboa then, Lisboa now: one city, two faces – like a child grown to maturity.

I had been summoned to appear for an interview before a functionary of the *Ministério de Ultramar*, misjudged the distance to the palace in which his offices were located, and so found myself in a hurry to keep the appointed hour. Hopelessly lost on that first morning among the corridors and casements of the ancient ministry building, I knew I was running late. I had the official's telephone number but was unsure where to find the correct office in such a large building with so many corridors and doors. As I was running up the wide marble staircase from street level to the floor above, a young cavalry officer hove into view at the top of the stairs and started a slow and stately descent. I stopped him to ask where there might be a telephone so I could make my excuses, explain my tardiness.

I spoke no Portuguese, so used the one word, 'telephone!' – the word and its pronunciation virtually the same in Portuguese, *telefone*.

The young officer, head high to give him a clear line of vision from below the peak of his cap, his back ramrod straight, was a couple of steps above me. He looked down on this scatty and disorganized civilian *estrangeiro* with an air of haughty annoyance at being stopped from going about his business. For a long moment the officer stood and regarded the interruption, one eyebrow raised. His uniform was a lightweight grey in colour, offset by a veritable bouquet of braided lanyard bursting from under the epaulette of his shoulder. His collar dogs and buttons were gleaming and a ceremonial dress sword flashed along the side of his left leg, its silver scabbard shone impeccably. He wore jodhpurs tucked into the tops of highly-polished brown riding boots. Slowly he pulled a pair of close-fitting white gloves onto his hands, snugging each digit finger-by-finger.

"Do you know where I might find a *telephone*, please?" I asked, a tone of just enough urgency in my voice to indicate a need for help. I smiled in what I thought was a friendly fashion and made the gesture of a telephone receiver with one hand, holding it up to my ear so there could be little doubt as to what I needed.

"Telephone," I repeated deliberately, clearly.

The cavalryman raised his chin imperceptibly so that his gaze ran down either side of his austere nose, causing him to hood his eyes ever so slightly.

"I do not speak English," he said, in flawless English.

"Telephone!" I was a little desperate – because of the time, but also because of his haughty stupidity. A Russian would have understood my needs.

"I do not speak English," the officer, scowling, enunciated a second time – again in flawless English.

Saluting with a casual but studied politeness, stiff enough to brook no further response, the young officer stepped around me and marched down the staircase about as slowly and as carefully as he had been pulling on his gloves.

I had no idea why I had been summoned to the ministry but assumed it must be something to do with my forthcoming departure for Angola. The appointment had been specific, and eventually I arrived within a minute or two of the required time, but I was nonetheless kept waiting nearly an hour in a sparse antechamber of the palace (all Portuguese government ministries appear to be housed in ancient palaces) before being ushered into the presence of an undersecretary for public relations. I was shown into a long heavily-paneled chamber with floor-to-ceiling windows on one side and large XVIII century tapestries on the other. A narrow scarlet carpet ran the entire length of the room from its doorway to the base of an ornately-carved desk at the far end, and there sat a bald-headed little man in a dark suit with nothing on the tableau in front of him except a single dossier. As I approached he appeared more clearly – as unkempt a personage as I had ever seen occupying a seat behind a desk in an office. I looked closer. He wore rimless glasses. He had a long neck, thin and with a two-finger gap between his skin and the edge of a rumpled collar. His tie, of non-descript colour, might once have been used to support his trousers; it was likewise thin and with a greasy sheen that suited the scrawniness of what looked to be an unwashed neck. There was no chair available for me to sit on, so I approached, feeling like a small schoolboy hailed to stand before his schoolmaster.

Obnoxious little man, he knew there was someone standing before him but kept his head and eyes down. After a long pause, and still without looking up, he opened the dossier and started reading loud enough for me to hear:

"John Jeremy Hespeler-Boultbee ..." he pronounced my name in the same accents and intonation I had heard from Jorge Ritto in Toronto.

"We (it was an imperial 'we') see that you were born in Vancouver, Canada, the son of J – and S – ..."

He named my father and mother and intoned my correct date of birth.

"... Your mother took you and your older brother to Australia in 1938, and your parents were divorced shortly thereafter. You attended primary schooling in Australia, Canada, the United States of America and Great Britain, and the latter is where you finished your senior schooling – at

Malvern College …"

"You were summoned for two years of active military service in the British army in 1954, with postings to both Kenya and Malaya …"

He went on for several minutes, recounting in precise but heavily accented English details of my personal history that I can only assume he must have obtained from some source of personal records in both Britain and Canada. I was surprised and perplexed, and not a little angry. It seemed to me this impersonal rendering of my résumé was intended as a humiliating strip down – maybe even a threat.

At last he looked up, peering at me for the first time. He closed the dossier, a cold and unfeeling examination of my person through thick lenses. More than the stern schoolmaster, he now resembled the darkest and most unsympathetic of bureaucrats – reptilian in every sense I could imagine. I might have laughed had I not been so infuriated.

"What was all that about?" I wanted to know.

"We would not want you to think that we Latins are inefficient," he squeezed out from between his tight red-brown lips. He was making an attempt at a smile, but it was neither amusing nor convincing.

"From what paranoia does your government suffer that you would assume I think you inefficient? That's utter nonsense. And a most peculiar way to invite me into your country …"

He stared without expression.

"Good day, Mr. Hespeler-Boultbee. You will find your way out is precisely the way you came in."

And so the interview, if it could be described as such, was concluded. I was summarily dismissed. Angry, I hurried out of the palace and hailed a taxi to take me back to my hotel. Efficient, maybe, and that much was certainly surprising; but I could not imagine why such a theatrical performance unless it had been especially designed to intimidate. Why would any official of this pot-boiled little corruption of a country go to the trouble of digging so thoroughly into my past? My first reaction was a feeling of utter disgust, but behind it I felt uneasy and fearful.

In the end I was kept waiting nearly three weeks in Lisboa while my travel documents were being sorted out – something that might have been undertaken by Ritto prior to my departure from Toronto. I was assigned a 'minder,' a cheerful young fellow who told me he worked for the 'ministry' and wanted nothing more than to ensure my welcome and well-being.

I hinted that perhaps I could be left on my own.

"Oh!" he exclaimed expansively. "Of course I can leave you on your own if you wish. There is no shortage of other work to keep me busy, you may be sure. But I have been assigned to take care of you, and if you send me away my boss will just find me some other work to do. I won't have nearly as much fun as I will if we spend the time together. Besides, I can show you many things about Portugal – and I would love to hear what you can tell me about Canada ..."

Winning fellow, and of course we laughed.

"You are a government officer, and I am a journalist. Do you think I cannot understand that you simply want to keep an eye on me ...?"

"That's true," he admitted, smiling. The Portuguese are nothing if not disarming.

"But you are here, and if you don't have me as a guide, then you will certainly have someone else – and you may not have as much fun with another as you will have with me. I have a job to do, and I need to show my boss that I am doing my work adequately. On the other hand, you have to remain here for however long it takes to arrange your papers before you go overseas, and in that time I can show you many things that will give you a useful background concerning Portugal. I can organize a car, we can go to see different places, and I can tell you many things about the country and our culture that you will probably want to know about. Another minder might not choose to do all that. He might just get in your way ..."

My minder's name was João Serrano and, as it appeared I would have no choice but to accept him or someone else, going along with his suggestion seemed the best I could do. It helped that I quite liked him; perhaps there would appear the opportunity for me to steer him from affable minder into becoming an affable fixer. We could mind each other.

"Fine!" I agreed, and promptly invited him to dinner.

Serrano worked for an organization that went by the acronym SNI – *Secretariado Nacional da Informação* – a 'welcome-to-Portugal' and information service providing courteous assistance to visitors like me and, by-the-by (as an arm of government) acting as informant for the nation's political police.

The unpleasant skulduggery and snooping of any clandestine police force aside, the arrangement proved to be most fortuitous – for Serrano liked his dinners, I was to discover. He displayed considerable skill at selecting both the right restaurant and the right wine to go with the meals we were to have together. There is an almost infinite selection of fine eateries in tucked-away corners, and all up and down the cobbled and narrow streets of old Lisboa. We sampled a good number of them – in Bairro Alto, Alfama, Cais do Sodre and further west along the river towards the Palácio de Belém and Estoril. We had use of a government car, so took drives into the countryside as far as Cascais, Sintra, Costa da Caparica and Belas – even to Fátima and Alcobaça considerably further to the north. Thus I found myself each day looking forward to my outings with this young spy – who was nothing if not forthright about what his job entailed.

For the remainder of my stay Serrano and I got together every morning. He had a job to do, snooping on all my comings and goings; and I had little to do and nowhere to go before all my travel papers were in order. Minder and car (plus driver) were decidedly useful in that they provided me with a welcome mobility, and an opportunity to learn about Portugal. As I had been assigned to his care anyway it would only have caused trouble had I attempted to flee his attentions, so I knuckled under and made most liberal use of both him and the car. We each appeared to look forward to our meetings, in fact. He was an upbeat fellow, and would come to the hotel enthusiastically about seven o'clock every morning, when we would sit at breakfast in the roof restaurant, mulling over maps and deciding on the day's programme. Younger than I was at the time, he had a humour I liked and was no doubt destined in life for greater things, but for the moment comfortably nestled into his job for the dictatorial central government so that he, like me, could not easily alter our circumstances. There was nothing furtive or suspicious about him. He gave the impression he took his job seriously only insofar as he was required to be conscientious – thorough enough to keep a good thing going for himself, and so remain in my good graces. The job paid him a fair salary – a necessity, he said, because he was also a student at university, and yet a loose enough arrangement that he did not feel pressed to play the heavy-handed bureaucrat. His boss wanted him to be friendly, and he was.

I was content to play foil, tourist to Serrano's guide – and he winked and smiled. We performed our roles with sufficient candour it was easy for me to form a comprehensive knowledge of the city core, something of the country and a smattering of its history. It was necessary, and he knew it, that I should broach numerous awkward questions concerning Portugal's social and political circumstances. He never attempted to dodge my queries. It gave me a feeling of confidence in him, although it seemed prudent to hold myself back and express minimum commentary of my own – on anything that might indicate I was other than a totally impartial observer. Often he was the one to open a subject, leaving conversational fissures by which I could pry further and discover significantly more information about the regime that governed him and was currently waging a bitter war on two (soon to be three) major fronts in Africa.

"Yes, we're a dictatorship," he answered candidly to one of my queries. "But we must accept the arrangement, try to demonstrate our placid acceptance of it. As you can imagine, to do otherwise could cause substantial discomfort. Many people are in opposition to the government. They are disorganized and by themselves in no position to govern. Portugal has been a dictatorship since the time our last king was assassinated. That was in 1910. Prior to that we were an absolutist monarchy – which is just dictatorship by another name. We have never known the kind of democracy you have in Canada. Do you think the *povo*, the people, of a country as poor and backward and unsophisticated as Portugal could possibly know how to govern an empire as large as ours? I doubt it. We need dictatorship …"

"Who constitutes the opposition?" I asked.

"Communists, mostly. Anarchists. There is an independence movement of sorts in each of our major colonies, but back here in the *Metropole* independence is something we are told we already have, so I don't really know who is in opposition. I've never encountered an opposition ..."

I laughed.

"That's because they have all fled abroad – to places like Canada! Were you never told that?"

He laughed with me and his eyes grew big as he raised his hands in the air, an attitude of one who has abandoned himself to Fate.

"… And you'll find us in France, and the Netherlands, and Luxemburg," he added gleefully. "Like mice, there are Portuguese everywhere."

"Exactly!" I responded. "A whole diaspora of insistent and demanding critters. They have chosen to live abroad because they'd be arrested if they remained within the country, right?"

"Well, of course! If they don't like what is happening here, they must go abroad. It's natural."

His open matter-of-factness both amused and puzzled me.

"Who keeps an eye on oppositionists? How do the people in charge know who to arrest?" I asked.

"Well – we have a police force for that …"

I nodded my head towards a dishevelled policeman in the street. The fellow was leaning aimlessly against a wall, smoking a cigarette. He looked as though he had been partying all night and was still drunk.

"Do you mean to tell me if you went up to that policeman over there and told him you were a member of the opposition, or a communist, he would arrest you on the spot?"

Serrano chuckled.

"Well, that particular one doesn't look as though he would be very effective, so I'd probably not bother to approach him. He might not know what to do with the information, and if he thought you were a threat he could just take it into his head to beat you about the ears with his truncheon. But if he's capable of doing his job, yes, he'd probably arrest you. I don't know anyone so stupid as to want to speak to him. He's a policeman. No one wants to speak to policemen."

"I guess that's my point. You would not be free to say what you want – assuming you wanted to."

Serrano was not a foolish man, and it was not difficult to see the direction my questions were taking.

"No, no!" he corrected himself. "That policeman is a silly fellow doing the silly job he is told to do because he knows nothing else. He only wants to fill his belly and bed his ugly wife, and he will only spring into action when he is so scolded by his superiors he realizes that by not following orders he will lose his job. He is a policeman who attends to matters of traffic and petty street crime or making sure shop doors are properly locked at night. We have other police who look after the more serious matters of security and control."

I had the suspicion I had already encountered them and said so.

"Exactly that," my companion concurred. "PIDE – the *Polícia Internacional e de Defesa do Estado*. They are the ones who would have informed the ministry about your background and your arrival in Portugal, for instance. Every country has a police force like them ... and from what you have to say it sounds as though there has been a connection between PIDE and your police forces in Canada."

"PIDE?" I repeated.

"Yes. Nobody really knows who they are, and nobody likes them. They have a uniform but seldom dress up in it, so you cannot recognize them when you see them in the street. There are thousands of them, and they are everywhere. They are very good at what they do ..."

"And what do they do?" I asked.

Serrano smiled. We were sitting at a café table, and he playfully nodded his head towards a man reading a newspaper at a nearby table.

"He could be one – assigned to watch over the two of us. Or it could be our waiter, or the man who polishes your shoes. They are not all policemen; they are informers – little men who make extra money by bringing information to their police handlers ..."

"Like Gestapo?"

"Exactly! Gestapo. Not officers exactly, but very much like Gestapo ... informers." agreed Serrano.

Old Lisboa looks and smells its age. Although one may have difficulty counting them now because the area is so built-up, the city is spread out across a range of small hills – seven is the number sited, as with the tradition in the case of Italy's ancient capital. Nooks, alcoves and hideaways – *becos* – are concealed around many corners; narrow cobbled alleys lead to the feet of obscure stairways and the low doorways that have secured the homes of Lisboa's residents for generations.[14] It is an enchanting city, filled with surprising delights in the way of stonework, statuary and fountains. Through wrought iron gateways one will catch glimpses of verdure, tiny urban flower gardens – and a few big ones. In unsuspecting places there are flamboyant bushels of bougainvillea hanging languorously over old stone walls into brilliant sunlit streets, each an indication of some refreshing secret bower somewhere out of sight on the other side of the masonry. After sundown, some streets bare the almost overpowering scent of night-blooming jasmine, *dama-da-noite*, so intense it can easily waft up heady images of Paradise. Close to the Rio Tejo, in the vicinity of the Casa dos Bicos on the edge of the Alfama district, the scent is of coffee – warehouses full of it imported from Angola and Brasil, and other exotic places the world over. This is an area of the old waterfront associated for hundreds of years with the unloading of the river's traditional barges, *fragatas* and *varinos* – huge heavy-timbered lateen-sailed craft, their hulls lovingly decorated in bright colours by their owners. They are gone now; in the days of my first encounter with the city these

---

[14] A resident of Lisboa, born and raised, bears the nickname *alfacinha* – 'little lettuce head' – an ancient appellation likely coined in the early days of class rivalry by the market gardeners whose cultivated fields surrounded the city's walls. It no longer has any particular pejorative meaning. However, a pejorative sense was definitely intended by the snooty *alfacinhas* in naming their produce suppliers – and the district in which they worked – as *saloio*. The word conjures a country bumpkin, a lout, or a clever trickster. Nowadays the references hardly apply, and both groups tend to accept these old nicknames with good humour.

elegant sailboats still crowded the docks of Terreiro do Paço and Cais do Sodré.

Serrano walked me back and forth over most of the city centre – from the gardens of Parque Eduardo VII to Rato (Mouse Square), and from there along Rua da Escola Politécnica to the gardens of Principe Real with its thirty-metre wide *Cedro do Bussaco* – a cedar tree with such a wide and sprawling canopy it has to be surrounded and supported unobtrusively by an extensive metal cribbing. Serrano told me how his grandmother used to bring him to this same place when he was a child wearing a little sailor suit, a white cap on his head, a red tassel hanging from the back of it. She told him that once her own Grandmother had brought her there to play under the spread of this same tree's wide canopy. A little further on, from the Miradouro de São Pedro de Alcântara, there is a panoramic view right across the central downtown portion of the city to the Castelo de São Jorge, the major defence of the city erected by the Moors nearly one thousand years ago. Underneath its great pile there lie the stones of other defensive structures that archaeologists have dated to six hundred years before the birth of Christ, and there are others even older below them. Indeed, the site of Lisboa has been occupied by humans since pre-Paleolithic times.[15] The city's name is derived from the word Olisipo – Ulysses. Ancient Latin geographers wrote it 'Ulyssippo,' but it was a name that existed among early Greek and Phoenician traders long pre-dating the historic period when the city might have anchored the western extremity of the Roman Empire.

One morning we walked down the steep hill of Rua do Alecrim to the train station at Cais do Sodré, then caught the tram that runs along the river. We got down at Belém – and spent most of the rest of the day visiting the *Museu Nacional de Arqueologia* that had been attached to the same structure as the *Mosteiro dos Jerónimos*, the *Museu de Marinha*, just around the corner, and the *Museu Nacional dos Coches,* a block or so east of Jerónimos. All four of these locations are within easy walking distance of one another, but it was a tall order to give each its due in a single session even considering the leisurely break we had taken over lunch. I confess an ulterior motive for insisting

---

[15] Visiting Barcarena, one of Lisboa's dormitory communities a short distance north of Caxias, the archaeologist in charge of excavations at a recently-discovered Paleolithic site handed me a blackened shard – a ten-centimetre section of the lip of a ceramic pot. One could see the potter had attempted to decorate the work by notching its rim, removing tiny scallop-shaped pieces of clay with the flick of a thumb nail, a charming detail that had survived the intervening years. Just that small personal feature somehow closed the 5,000-year gap in time, particularly so when I noticed by its imprint that each little scallop clearly showed the artisan's thumb nail had a small v-shaped nick broken from its tip.

Serrano take me to each in turn, one after another. My silly intent was to test him.

Serrano had been in every way a gracious and most accommodating host to me, but I had not quite arrived at the point of fully understanding or trusting him. Fringing my more familiar normal, I was worried – concerned almost to the point of paranoia – that operatives within this police state would try to bamboozle me, to withhold information, set me on some fool's errand by pushing me in a direction I did not want to go. The worst scenario would be that, through my own carelessness, I might be tricked into some indiscretion, and that because of it good people in opposition to the regime would be picked up and maltreated – or worse.

So I resolved on this Belém excursion to give my minder, my new friend, the test of as heavy a load to carry as possible, to oblige him to slog around these various sites with me so that I could attempt to calculate the true level of his interest. My thinking was that if he was not much interested in me or my enthusiasm, he would in some way show it – giving me a hint of his impatience, his intolerance and possibly whether or not he viewed me as a fellow traveller or as just a useful means of his continued doubtful career as informant for the political police. It appeared to have been a very good test indeed. As it turned out, Serrano's enthusiasm built alongside mine. I was very much interested in everything we were seeing at these museums. Since childhood I have been more than casually interested in boats of all kinds, and particularly in the construction of models. At the maritime museum, one of the very finest I have ever seen, were hundreds of the most exquisite models of every type of craft ever manned by Portuguese seamen. Seeing the displays in this museum was one of the finest treats anyone could possibly have offered me. I must have shown it, and Serrano turned out to be totally taken up by my interest, delighted with himself for having brought me here. After the maritime museum, we headed into the archeological museum right next door – and this, too, enthralled me. Some of the most fascinating readings I had ever undertaken had been in anthropology and history – and here was a museum created precisely to show off the thousands of artifacts in witness to these fields of study, back to before the beginnings of Iberian civilization. A part of the same building, a matter of only a few steps further along the street, was the late Gothic monastery and church of Jerónimos. Begun in 1501, this World Heritage structure is often held up as a prime example of Portuguese architecture of its genre, stonemasonry in the highly decorative Manueline style. We must have spent fully an hour inside, examining the intricacies of what I can only describe as stonework filigree – in the nave, the apse and especially in the silence of the covered two-storey cloister.

I was speechless. Traipsing around museums is always exhausting, and we had knocked down two of them before lunch; not only that, Jerónimos was the equivalent of a third. In England, in Canada, in Italy and France, I had closely studied art and architectural history – and here I was in one of Europe's finest capital cities (few others escaped the destruction of wars over the past century; Lisboa is a notable exception) surrounded on every side by the very objects that had always intrigued me the most. Right at that moment I was as dog-tired as I had been hoping to make my minder, but entranced and in a fog – a happy sightseeing overload.

"There are some fine restaurants in this vicinity. Let's stop for something to eat, and perhaps a bottle of wine ..."

Affable, Serrano. My minder was reading my mind; the doubts of trust evaporated at the first scent of delicious Portuguese cuisine as we approached the door of the establishment he selected.

From the restaurant's front patio I could look to the southwest and see a gigantic *padrão,* the monolithic plinth that rises by the side of the river like a stone hand, with its out-sized representations of the 'Discoverers' clambering along its sides. Work on the monument started in 1940. It was a homage to that host of hardy Portuguese souls who had braved the unknown, gone to sea to establish the nation's worldwide empire and open sea lanes to lands few Europeans yet knew existed – all of it in ships that, for the most part, were no bigger than the lifeboats of modern cruise ships. These merchant seamen brought wealth to their city, their country, their king – and broke the Oriental spice trade stranglehold Venice had hitherto held over all of Europe. A little further along the embankment the Torre de Belém, a tiny XVI century Manueline fort, marked the location of Vasco da Gama's embarkation for India in July 1497. He landed at the same point when he returned from his successful voyage in August 1499.

"One more important museum ..." said Serrano as we settled into a repast of bread, sardines and delicious green peppers.

Perhaps I had had the notion to try to draw Serrano out, maybe even expose him, by pushing him to the point of collapse so that he would reveal to me something of his own biases. But my stoutest effort failed. He was working for the political police, true, and perhaps not directly as a policeman himself; I did not feel altogether happy about his stated obligation to report my thoughts or actions to his superiors. But here he was, calling me on the very game I had devised to play on him, and I could not help but be amused by the situation. Relaxing over lunch I realized he was prepared to tackle any challenge I threw at him. Perhaps he was even trying to push *me* to the point of exhaustion – but if that was his objective I was not blind to it; he was doing what he was doing because he was enjoying himself, and he wanted to. Perhaps the fellow liked me enough to enjoy my company, wanted to show me his Portugal. No quarrel on that score – I was having fun!

However, love of museums is ultimately limited by stamina.

"Which museum is that?" I asked him.

"The coach museum," he replied triumphantly. "It's almost next door to the restaurant here ..."

"Good idea!" I chuckled into my wine glass. "My aching feet tell me: let's do one more museum before we call it a day ..."

The Museu Nacional dos Coches is housed today in a state-of-the-art building erected specifically for its purpose and was opened in 2015. However, when I visited Belém with Serrano in 1963 the museum was located in the old horse-riding arena of Palácio de Belém, itself once a part of a royal residence but today the formal home of the President of the Republic. The old arena building, a delightfully ornate example of early XVIII century neo-classical structure and decoration, is just across the street from the new museum, and it still possesses a few examples of the former display. Originally the arena had been designed as a riding school and was used for the exhibition of equestrian shows; it measured some fifty metres long by seventeen metres wide, and had low balconies running the full length of the interior that permitted the royal family to watch events being performed on the sawdust-covered floor just below them. The decoration of the hall – murals, sculptures and panels of *azulejos*[16] – added immeasurably to the impact of the coach exhibit when the arena was first converted into a museum at the behest of Queen Amélia. That was in 1905. Right from the outset it proved to be a popular public attraction, but the space was altogether too small to be able to house and exhibit the full collection of royal coaches – a lack now corrected (some fifty years after my visit there) by the opening of the new hall and museum facility.

Some of the decorated coaches housed within the museum date back to the late XVI century. It might be considered a strange motif around which to create an entire museum, but if one stops for a moment to realize there are

---

[16] *Azulejos* – *azul* = blue. Glazed tiles, early examples of which were often predominantly blue in colour, are a feature of Portuguese decoration dating to earliest times. There is debate as to whether the form is Dutch in origin, or perhaps a Portuguese genre introduced to the makers of *delftware*. Moorish tiles – also '*azulejos*' – have existed in Portugal since long before the rebellion of the Visigoths (Battle of Covadonga, 722) and the onset of the *Reconquista*, late IX century.

elaborate car museums and aero museums (and only earlier that morning we had been in a maritime museum) – why not a coach museum? Step inside and it is very plain to see Queen Amélia was a far-sighted lady and had lit on a fine idea. With more than seventy examples of royal coaches to support her project, she knew how to appeal to her public. The result is one of the most original and charming museums in the world. Quite incidentally it is also an excellent educational facility concerning transport in the long-ago days before the internal combustion engine, and additionally gives an insight into how royalty wore the dog without getting their feet dirty as they travelled about the countryside in the exercise of their long list of official duties (in order to secure their other long list of Divine Rights).

Nudging my suspicions and paranoia aside, and calling up whatever it is within me that tries to deal with empathy and gratitude, I had to admit I was gradually coming to like my minder, to understand that he was quite openly prepared to give me the benefit of any doubts he might have had concerning my enquiries – and probably expected no less forthrightness in return. And yet the niggling suspicions persisted – there was always that annoying rationale: he was 'only doing his job.' My bad: I could not figure out why an operative for the Portuguese fascists was going to such lengths to show me around and keep me happy. Government representatives, and Serrano himself, must have known I was going to try to look far beyond any favours being shown to me while I was kept waiting in the capital. I had given everyone plenty of warning. No one would have been so naïve as to assume I would not call out my findings as best I could judge them, whether positive or negative. I had accepted Jorge Ritto's invitation on behalf of his government, but I was also mindful of my editor's warning – that he would trash any reportage he felt was merely toeing the Portuguese line.

On the other hand, here was a most willing guide, with car and driver – an open-ended offering. We were free to use it to go anywhere we pleased by day. Within the city we could manage quite well without a car, and at night it was somehow easier to prowl the local nightspots and bars on foot. Usually by nightfall we were spent and ready to give tourism a rest. However, it was good to have the car available to us if we wanted it.

But we did very well in the days before I set out for Africa; I saw a great deal of Lisboa and environs, I learned much about the Portuguese themselves and had every good reason to be immensely satisfied.

One day we drove out beyond Belém, west along the riverside road known as the Marginal. Its curves and the speed at which its users drive have given this stretch of blacktop the unforgiving reputation as the most precarious road in Europe. True or false, it is without doubt a hair-raising roadway. At speed, it's dangerous; and if you slow down, the speedsters flying past will create plenty of danger anyway. The thirty-five-kilometre strip runs from the city's Cais do Sodré station, parallel to the commuter railway line that ends at Cascais, a stop or two beyond Estoril. It is a forty-minute trip by rail – and not a great deal shorter even if driving at breakneck speed, for one has to negotiate drivers of the Marginal who are convinced the stretch is a racetrack. Beyond Cascais the road rounds a wide curve to the north leading to the desolate and windswept spread of Praia Grande do Guincho, in summer a pan of golden hot sands that draw the crowds despite a surprisingly vigorous and chilly surf. The hillside town of Malveira da Serra rises a few kilometres behind this favoured beach, and from there a road leads on to Cabo da Roca, the westernmost point of the European mainland. 'Here the land ends and the sea commences ...' wrote national poet Luís Vaz de Camões somewhat obviously, for it is the point where the mountain of the Sintra range tumbles vertically over a cliff, one hundred metres to the rocks that edge a constantly roaring Atlantic. A Scottish wag once lamented, there was 'nothing beyond ... except America' – but before the 'nothing beyond' is a desolation of heaving ocean, broken only by the islands of the Açores. There, poking themselves out of the deep in a straggly east-west line, about one thousand four hundred kilometres clear of the Portuguese mainland (two thousand kilometres short of a Florida or a Manhattan landfall) they have formed an independent region of Portugal. They are a happy circumstance. In the first half of the XV century they were settled by hardy Portuguese adventurers – sailors and their women whose descendants have lived there and fished the surrounding waters ever since.

An alternate turn-off from Malveira is the lonely road that wends its way northeast through cool forests of pine and cedar, following the spine of the Serra de Sintra for twelve kilometres to the old royal town of Sintra, with its several castles and a score or more of ornate palaces. From Cabo da Roca the land rises quickly close to two thousand feet above the surrounding countryside and is noticeable from a considerable distance round about. Lord Byron waxed poetic about Sintra in his epic work, *Childe Harold's Pilgrimage*. He visited throughout the district, a quiet, cool and restful retreat for the nation's royal family who in summer were anxious to escape the heat and bustle of the capital city. Byron was there during the period of the Peninsula War against France (1807 to 1814) and was well-received by the Portuguese, allies of the British. During the latter portion of the war in Iberia, the Portuguese forces were commanded by a British general – Napoleon Bonaparte's nemeses, Sir Arthur Wellesley, better known later on as the Duke of Wellington. Byron befriended and stayed with numbers of the royal household and other aristocrats who had not fled the country at the start of the French invasion. Many of them had built homes for themselves around the royal palaces of Sintra in their efforts to curry favour with their monarch.

At first sight it is tempting to evaluate the overall impression of Sintra and its palaces against the exotic mountain buffoonery of King Ludwig's Bavarian fairylands and their tragically Wagnerian haunts of sad and dark tales. But bleak views and hastily-concocted castle follies are easily set aside: Sintra's outlandishness is far more obliging – even humorous. There is a fey quality to the place, true, but the overarching feeling is the idea that Portugal's aristocrats must have been mightily enjoying themselves among their stony outcrops and leafy green forests, whereas poor Ludvig was beset by any number of warrior gods thundering across the ceilings of his staterooms to drive him out of his mind. Not quite Wagner, Sintra is more like Moody Blues in bare feet and sunshine – even when the fog sweeps in off the Atlantic.

There is a tram that clatters from Sintra to the seaside town of Praia das Maçãs. The line was first opened in 1904, abandoned around the time of the revolution in 1974, but then restored and expanded in 1980. It leads to (among other charming sites) Casa de Búzio, one of the finest seafood restaurants along the southern portion of Portugal's Atlantic coast. I did not know it at the time Serrano first took me there for lunch, but the Sintra area was to become my home for fifteen of the twenty-five years I was eventually to spend in Portugal. The gardens of Monsanto, the Convento dos Capuchos, the magnificent beaches of Adraga, Grande, Maçãs and Azenhas do Mar – these and so many other locales were to become as familiar to me as the pepper trees in my garden at Almoçageme.

There were other excursions on other occasions during those first few weeks before departing for Angola. One morning we drove to the ornate (and unfinished) XIV century Manueline monastery of Batalha, not far from Alcobaça and Fatima, then returned to Lisboa via Caldas da Rainha, one of the principal centres for Portuguese ceramics, with visits in passing to the jewel-like walled town of Óbidos and the Palácio Nacional de Mafra. This last was completed in 1755, its construction so exorbitant it almost destroyed the Portuguese economy. Mafra was so big it would easily have contained an entire regiment of monarchs plus their flunkies – and even then, one crowned head might have missed another in its warren of passageways – and its one thousand two hundred rooms. The façade of the palace is over two hundred metres across.

One day I asked if we might visit the quarries and marble-cutting centres of Pêro Pinheiro, which Serrano thought was a superlative idea – so we went. On the edge of town is an entire marble pillar. It fell off an XVIII century truck, so to speak, and has lain where it landed ever since. No one ever troubled to pick it up – and would likely not have known how to, anyway. It must weigh many tons; if anyone would have been able to pick it up, where would they have put it? Much better as a curiosity, lying where it tumbled, right beside the roadway.

On another occasion Serrano organized a motor launch so we could venture out to the centre of the Rio Tejo, there to watch as the first pilings were being sunk to take the roadway across one of the longest suspension bridges in the world. When it was complete it was named Ponte Salazar in honour of the dictator. After his *Estado Novo* was pitched out in the revolution of 1974 it was re-named Ponte 25 de Abril – the date of the dictatorship's demise.

All of these excursions were enjoyable, and I learned much from them. Serrano was a knowledgeable and entertaining companion, but I fretted North Americanly because it seemed to be taking far too much time to prepare documentation and make the necessary arrangements that would have allowed me to be on my way to Africa. No hurries, no worries, my minder chirped. Yes, the relevant government entities had received ample notice of my travel plans, but this is a Latin country, you see, and things run on Portuguese time in Portugal, my minder explained patiently. Dead slow. Dead stop. Whatever!

"You are too North American. If you race a little slower you will come to know us better – and possibly even quicker ..." my minder somersaulted.

I settled in to wait and managed to make a creative time of it. The hours we spent walking or driving in the government-supplied car certainly filled many an hour when I might otherwise be kept anxiously twiddling my thumbs as the visas and air tickets failed to materialize. There were days when Serrano would swoop me up with his bright smile and a well-planned outing – on one occasion to Lagos in the Algarve or, on another, when I found myself examining one of the largest dams in Europe just then under construction in southern Alentejo at Santa Clara-a-Velha on the Rio Mira.

The days sauntered by. Sometimes, for short periods, I would be left on my own to explore and take photographs of the city. More than once I walked throughout the Alfama district, a venerable quarter that survived, unscathed by the Lisboa earthquake of 1755. I rode the trams that clattered along the city's numerous streets, broad and narrow; I took photographs of intricately-designed *azulejos* – the colourful ceramic wall tiles that could be found sheathing the walls of both private and public buildings in every quarter.

Likewise, I took delight in capturing the myriad mosaics decorating most of the city's sidewalks – *calçada portuguesa.* These are made of approximately eight-centimetre cubes cut from basalt or limestone laid down un-grouted on top of a fine sand, unique labour-intensive black and white designs that somehow add immense pleasure to urban ambles. To this day it remains a feature gracing almost every town in the Portuguese-speaking world.

An acquaintance told me a story concerning the siege of the city's castle of São Jorge, along with the naming of the community of Carcavelos a short distance further downriver.

According to this story, in 1147 Afonso Henriques was busy laying siege to the city from a defended position outside the castle walls. He heard a voice calling to him from the ramparts. It was none other than Carca, the Moorish defender himself:

'Dom Henriques – you have no *colhões* (balls) for this fight!'

Dom Henriques raised his sword as a challenge, then turned around and dropped his drawers, presenting his bare arse and his testicles to the cheeky Moor.

'Carca! Vé-los!' – or 'Carca, take a look at them!'

From that day forward, goes the tale, Dom Henriques' camp outside the walls was known as Carcavelos – one of the dormitory communities on the *linha de Cascais* just west of Lisboa.

Others – and PIDE

Saying nothing to Serrano, I contacted several people whose numbers I had remembered from Ronald Lawrence's list – people I wanted to see without risking a minder looking over my shoulder. As a matter of routine, I had called the Canadian Embassy, and thus came to meet the embassy's Art Blanchette and Clifford Smith.

Over the years since this journey in 1963 I have learned a few futile lessons about talking to officers at Canada's embassies abroad. Travellers to out-of-the-way places often feel the need to let people know where they are, or intend to go, as a precaution in case of unforeseen troubles, and indeed

Canada's embassies encourage their citizens to do just that. Embassies actively seek Canadian travellers to report in to their overseas representatives. It would seem a useful and intelligent step to take, and there's no denigrating the idea. However once checked-in, the air changes; the official attitude tends to become: 'Now, bugger off – and don't you dare get yourself into any sort of a pickle that will require our attention.' These paperwork entities – embassies – have been set up, it would seem, to ease trade and immigration deals on the one hand, and on the other to make matters so complicated for the individual that he will happily keep his distance. They are a lofty breed, diplomats. With a working trade deal, they can brag to the Foreign Affairs Minister they are bringing home the bacon; an individual's personal problems might interrupt a golf tourney or a cocktail party – or heaven forbid, cause an embarrassing scandal. Those unlucky enough to run into trouble of any kind are distinctly unpopular with embassy staff, and forthcoming assistance is likely to be rendered slowly and grudgingly, as if a penalty must be paid to the nation as a whole, and especially its embassy operatives – 'an inconvenience to you for the inconvenience to us.' Immigration is even more sinister. Applying from Africa for admittance to Canada (or from anywhere, actually) one is instructed to '*apply online.*' This simple demand wrinkles the brows of thousands of Africans anxious to make a new life in the New World – for the average African does not have a computer of his own so that he might be able to sit and carefully read the application's online instructions; nor do printing machines abound in such reliable quantities that applications, questions or instructions can easily be printed out. It is very likely that in an applicant's area there are frustrating delays in getting online at all, or that anything like the broadband or WIFI required exists. In addition, there are almost assuredly language problems. The run-around is like a cruel game in frustration, invariably playing out to the advantage of the immigration department. Despite its rhetoric to the contrary, immigration is ever looking for useful ways to express the hypocritical all-Canadian 'sorry, but I don't make the rules' – or to offer an outright 'no.' Its application is selective – and is widely judged to be racist. Nothing could be viler to an anxious and harried would-be African immigrant than the totally reasonable and smiling well-fed Canadian shrugging his shoulders and saying how he regrets saying what he has been instructed to say. My experience has been that Africans will smile and spread their hands in acceptance, but they well-know Canada's hypocrisy.

Silence works, sometimes. Very often it is the only approach to getting something accomplished. Commentary of any sort tends to create a vindictive balking, which can make matters worse. On this occasion, green, and unaware of the difficulties outlined above, I duly trotted over to the Canadian embassy to present my credentials.

Art Blanchette took me aside and with seemingly great concern for a young Canadian citizen about to step into a cow pat, advised me not to pry too closely into the affairs of an unruly – nay, anarchistic and thoroughly irresponsible – opposition to a government that was 'doing the best it can under the circumstances.' Uncomfortable and embarrassed, he was trying to balance a willingness to accept that Portugal (like Canada) is a member of NATO with the sure fact that its leader was a ruthless and much-loathed fascist dictator who, to curry favour with the western powers and pull in a chunk of foreign currency, rented out space for a mid-Atlantic US air base on one of the Açores islands – and probably also purchased armaments manufactured in Canada.

How extraordinarily diplomatic, I thought. How very Canadian – perpetually (and always so awkwardly) *entre a espada e a parede* – caught between the sword and the wall.

Maybe he did not comprehend that *contention* and *problem* are the very fodder of journalists and journalism, but he would have seen the quizzical look that crossed my brow, so perhaps it prompted the lame reply:

"At least for the moment. If they don't like what you're doing, or even the questions you ask, it could throw off the rest of your visit here. You may even find your trip curtailed. You are a guest ..."

As if to appease me, he bought me a coffee, offered me the use of the embassy car and driver to make a site-seeing visit to Castelo de São Jorge (on this occasion I collected Serrano and we visited the castle together) and left me feeling *gauche*, puzzled. Before parting he handed me a slip of paper with the name José Shercliff written on it – along with a telephone number. It was a name and number I had already memorized. He said I would do well to call on her, which had been my intent anyway.

Beyond that slip of paper Art Blanchette's well-intended kindness was not helpful. It was painfully clear that in the stormy waters of an alien sea, he did not want some hot-shot reporter rocking his diplomatic boat. My immediate and unjustifiably angry perspective railed at what I judged to be the sanctimonious wishy-washiness of a Canadian bureaucrat. I have encountered what I have considered diplomatic sogginess on numerous occasions since this Lisboa encounter with the Canadian embassy. I tense for it, expecting it, a prelude to dreadful disappointment. With the encroachment of age and, hopefully, a reduction in the level of youthful bile (toleration easing the weight of heavy limbs) perhaps it is better to admit that what has irked most has always been the lower rung of the diplomatic ladder itself. After all, if an insensitive gung-ho scrum-bum thinks he can recognize sanctimoniousness, surely those on whom it is daily lathered in thick doses must be able to notice it as well – and not take kindly to its incessant application. The exercise of an insincere diplomacy at the wrong moment, no matter how kind the intent, can surely contribute to failure as well as success.

It was just a passing thought.

Likewise, my meeting with Clifford Smith tended to disappoint. He, too, was kindly, attentive and interested in my journey, even invited me to his home for dinner and to meet with his wife and young family. Although connected to the embassy, Cliff was actually a representative of Canada's immigration staff. During the afternoon we took a trip together to Sintra, then ambled through the Cascais fish market to pick up some specialty for dinner that evening. From conversation at the family dinner table I learned that none of the Smiths were too taken with Portugal, that all of them desperately wanted to return to Canada. This runt little country was too old, too set in its ways, they claimed, the culture too bound by old traditions and the heavy emphasis the Portuguese themselves placed upon their history and claims to worldly and geographic importance – the era of The Discoveries …

It prompted me to speak up – none too diplomatically:

"How is it possible to understand Portugal and the Portuguese if you cannot bring yourselves to the point of knowing or acknowledging their history and culture, demonstrating – to them – your admiration for them? Surely to be successful in giving, it is incumbent upon you to accept them unconditionally …"

"I don't think we're trying to give them anything …" Cliff began.

"Then I fail to understand!" I interrupted. "As an immigration officer I thought you were offering to give them Canada …?"

The fish was delicious, but we had arrived at a conversational impasse and I was soon on the commuter train headed back to the city and my hotel room.

There were some six to eight names on my list. The first and, by my reckoning, by far the most significant was José Shercliff.

Erudite, a no-nonsense journalist with a well-deserved reputation for speaking and writing her mind, José Shercliff was an amiable English lady renowned among the ex-pat community for her altruism. This showed itself especially towards those who had forsaken their own homes and countries because of the Second World War and, becoming refugees, had trekked all the way across Europe in the hope of reaching the safety of Lisboa. From here it was possible to board regular trans-Atlantic flights to the Americas. She talked of her prior work among the war refugees before she lit onto anything in the way of Portuguese politics.

Immediately upon graduating from Oxford a couple of years prior to the outbreak of the war, she had decided she wanted to live and work in Paris and was able to arrange a job with the American library there. This served her well and she simultaneously began stringing for London's *Daily Herald* – but in June 1940 she was forced to flee the country when France fell to the Nazi invasion. Her editor had intended to send her to the United States, which would have entailed travelling from London to Lisboa in order to catch one of the regular flights out of occupied Europe – a most efficient flying boat service much used for ferrying refugees across the Atlantic. Providing one could get to Lisboa, the service was considered the safest method of escaping the continent during war-time. Her travel plans were delayed due to the extraordinary number of refugees trying to get onto the flights, so at this point she decided to become involved in refugee relief – which eventually led to working for the British Special Operations Executive. She never made it to America. The SOE was a British espionage consortium formed in 1940. It was linked to MI-6 but was virtually unknown beyond those who served the secretive organization. It had operatives in all parts of Europe and was somewhat affectionately known as the 'Baker Street Irregulars' (a reference to the location of its headquarters in London, and the fictional home of Sherlock Holmes). Occasionally it was also known as the 'Ministry of Ungentlemanly Warfare.' Apart from agents before and behind the lines, and in addition to reconnaissance and sabotage throughout war-torn Europe, SOE was responsible for keeping an eye on the networks of spies (both Allied and Axis) that were operating more or less at will in neutral Portugal.

José resumed her interest in journalism after the war, remaining in Lisboa and signing on with *The Times* in 1961. I reached her by telephone, and she invited me for lunch at her home in Estoril. At her instruction, I took the commuter train and then a taxi, about thirty kilometres west of the capital. She lived comfortably alone, and over a simple meal she welcomed me to Portugal with down-to-earth political commentary on how the place seemed to work, and the areas in which it appeared to be failing. Up to that time, she had lived more than twenty years in the country, spoke the language and considered she knew the place well.

"Salazar was in charge when I came here, and he is still in charge – as is Franco, in Spain. Salazar calls himself Prime Minister, which is his official position – but make no bones about it, he is a fascist dictator of precisely the same stripe as his neighbour in Spain – and, for that matter, as both Hitler and Mussolini," she told me.

She went on to explain that she knew she was recognized and only marginally tolerated in Portugal, despite occasionally expressing her contrary views. This, she felt, was largely because the Portuguese have a certain reverence for England and the English, and because they did not wish in any way to upset their oldest ally and its Number One newspaper. The Portuguese took pride in the non-aggression treaty they had signed with Britain in 1386, and they honour it today as fastidiously as do the English. But for all that José had been given licence to write news from Lisboa, she very much understood she had not been given permission to write editorial comment about (and certainly not against) the regime. She was careful about what she reported in her newspaper; verbally, and in company she felt could be trusted, she expressed her views more openly.

Several times she had been interviewed by the political police, she said.

"PIDE – *Policía Internacional e de Defesa do Estado*. They are a clandestine political police force, trained initially by Scotland Yard and thereafter by the Gestapo just prior to and during the war. They have a reputation for one of the most thorough secret police services in the world ... Have you encountered them yet?" she asked.

"Yes, I think I had a brush with them," I said, and I related the account of my meeting with the unpleasant bureaucrat at the ministry the day after I arrived.

"Well, he probably wasn't a member of PIDE himself, but no doubt he had availed himself of their services. They are extremely capable at what they do – cruel but very capable. They have never done me harm, but you don't want to get too close to them if you can help it," she said.

José had met Ronald Lawrence and remembered him from his visit the year before. She had been impressed with his knowledge of both Spain and Portugal, and it was she who told me that Lawrence had fought with the Republicans during the Spanish Civil War.

"He was able to give me a list of names …"

"If he gave you names, and you have written them down – you be careful with it. PIDE loves to have lists of names, and you can be sure if they find it they will seek everyone whose name is on it and pay them a visit," she warned.

"Tell me about PIDE," I asked her.

José repeated to me much of what Serrano had said about PIDE, but her description was wider and more objective. She said, for instance, that this police organization consisted of literally thousands of operatives nestled into every niche and cleft throughout Portugal and the colonies. Additionally, there were hundreds more spread throughout the extensive Portuguese diaspora – Brasil, all the major countries of Europe, and both the United States and Canada. She claimed PIDE was the gum that had held such a monstrous dictatorship together for so long. Octopus-like, the organization was widely acknowledged to be one of the most well-informed and ruthless secret service operations anywhere.

"It was the principal model for Israel's Mossad intelligence service," she informed me matter-of-factly.

The precursor to PIDE came into being in 1933, shortly after the launching of the right-wing *Estado Novo* by Salazar and his backers. Initially drawn from the border and international police forces, it was first known by its acronym PVDE (*Polícia de Vigilância e de Defesa do Estado*), and came under the direction of a police captain who, before and during the war, had worked closely with British Intelligence Services, Scotland Yard and MI-6. In 1956 this highly accomplished policeman, Agostinho Lourenço, had been promoted to head the international police force, Interpol.

However, just before the Second World War, and even during Portugal's war-time neutrality, agents of the Gestapo had become active in the country, infiltrated the service and trained Portuguese agents in how to spread terror, to disseminate propaganda, and use torture most effectively. It was the PVDE that had set up the political prison camp at Tarrafal in the Portuguese colony of Cabo Verde. The place was known to the population at large, and quickly became notorious for the disappearance of its inmates and for a variety of barbarous tortures carried out there. Communism and the Communist Party of Portugal became targets of the force at the outbreak of the Spanish Civil War; the PVDE moved fast and with considerable vigour against groups of anarchists held to blame for the 1937 attempt on Salazar's life. The force was disbanded at the end of the Second World War but was immediately replaced by (basically just re-named) as PIDE.

After the death of Salazar in 1970, and for several years after the events described in this work, the force was again re-named – becoming the *Direcção-Geral de Segurança*, or DGS, but known (and loathed) throughout the country as PIDE/DGS. Ultimately it also was disbanded at the time of the *Carnation Revolution* that finally dumped the dictatorship in April 1974. For a full decade there was no security service operating within the country at all but, in 1984, after several international and local incidents, the government established the *Sistema de Informações da República Portuguesa*, or SIRP.

"They are diabolical," José commented of PIDE, as it was still known at the time. "They are ubiquitous and answer only to Salazar. Any opposition to him is quickly crushed. They control the press, the radio and television. Mail is regularly opened, and telephone conversations – even yours asking if it would be alright for you to visit with me today – are tapped and recorded. Informers are everywhere, and people under suspicion are watched continuously ..."

José was the first to tell me about the popular General Humberto Delgado, candidate for President of the Republic who, in 1958, ran against arch-conservative Américo Tomás and lost by a wide margin – probably due to large-scale ballot box stuffing by operatives of the *Estado Novo* and PIDE. Immediately following the election, Delgado was expelled from the military and was chased into exile.

At first a strong supporter of Salazar and the dictator's 1932 replacement of the Republic that had made a mockery of governments ever since the assassination of King Carlos I in 1908, Delgado had been an early admirer of Adolf Hitler. He had even written a book in which he castigated democracy, labelling monarchs as gangsters, and the former Republic as the plaything of a cabal of bandits. After a posting to Washington as war-time air attaché he modified his views considerably and switched his sympathies to the Allies. By 1958, as candidate for a democratic opposition expected to carry the election easily, he had become Salazar's sworn enemy.

He was still in exile – first in Brasil, later in Rome – at the time of my visit with José in Estoril. In the year following my visit to Portugal and this conversation with her, Gen. Delgado was to establish, from his Roman headquarters, the Portuguese National Liberation Front. He and his secretary attempted to return to Portugal in 1965 – but both were assassinated by PIDE after being ambushed on the Spanish side of the Portuguese/Spanish frontier.

Another of José Shercliff's romantic political heroes was Henrique

Galvão, a military man and a former deputy who had represented Angola in the Portuguese National Assembly.

As a deputy in the 1940s, Galvão had sharply criticized the *Estado Novo* for its 'shameful' reliance on forced labour in the colonies. His criticisms were ignored at first, but his words were barbed and altogether too strong for the regime to tolerate. By 1952 his continued attacks were severe enough that he was arrested and spent time in jail, later being forced into retirement from the military. In 1959 he fled Portugal for Venezuela and then, in 1961, he became the leader of a group of some twenty-four like-minded *oposicionistas* in what became known as *Operação Dulcinea* – the hijacking of the Portuguese luxury cruise ship *Santa Maria* at sea off the Venezuelan coast. The attackers shut down all normal communications but sent out regular broadcasts telling the world at large they considered Salazar's regime in Lisboa a fascist dictatorship; they demanded independence for Angola. For twelve days the group, by now labelled terrorists and pirates, remained undetected in the seas off northeastern Brasil. They eluded the combined British and American navies throughout this time, and finally docked safely at Recife where they were granted political asylum. Galvão then admitted it had been his intention to sail on to Angola and there declare the former overseas province an independent nation.

It was the kind of story that grabbed the romantic imaginations of every Portuguese opponent to Salazar's *Estado Novo* regime and gave them hope. But Galvão remained in exile in Brasil and never attempted to return to Portugal.

"One of my very favourite people," José told me at the time. "His actions were piracy, but a sort of Robin Hood kind of piracy. He's getting on in years now, so I think he has probably served his purpose in life; some people really admire what he did, but he's not short of enemies. Many Portuguese were alarmed and consider him a traitor, so I am sure he will be killed if ever he tries to return. But he certainly doesn't lack for courage, and what he did alerted the entire world to the shortcomings of Salazar's regime."

A writer of great eloquence, Galvão penned several books, the English language edition of one of which, published at New York in 1961, is *Santa Maria: My Crusade for Portugal*.[17] It is his own version of the events that led to the hijacking. He died in Belo Horizonte, Brasil, in 1970.

---

[17] See Galvão, Henrique – *Santa Maria: My Crusade for Portugal*, New York, 1961.

One of the names on Ronald Lawrence's list was a journalist by the name of Raul Rêgo.

"First rate fellow," Lawrence had told me. "An *oposicionista* as sincere and straight as an arrow. If he's out of jail, you should certainly try to meet with him."

There was no way of telling whether his telephone number was located in his home or his office, but I tried it anyway and he came on the line almost immediately. He gave me the name of a café in the Chiado, and told me to meet him there in an hour.

"I have a thin face, wear glasses and a beret – and I'll be reading *Diário de Lisboa*," he told me.

He was easy to spot sitting at a table; we picked each other out simultaneously as I entered the café. He smiled warmly as I approached, removing his beret and standing to greet me. He was perhaps fifty years old at the time, bald across the top of his pate, his spectacles austere rimless lenses suspended from a beam of dark compound plastic that ran parallel to his brows and cast a shadow across his eyes. From this deep recess his gaze penetrated every corner of the café as he took note of everything around him. To me he was every inch the journalist – someone I might have spotted as a journalist had he just passed me by in the street. His aspect was serious, his honest face lined by the cares of what I could only imagine was a disciplined and almost deliberately difficult life, a scornful but tolerant acceptance of all the lies he had been told. His reputation as a severe critic of Salazar's dictatorial regime was well-known, which is doubtless why he had spent so much time in jail.

Raul Rêgo instantly impressed. I told him about my encounter with Ronald Lawrence back in Toronto and was taken by his response.

"Ronald is an extraordinary man. I have the deepest respect for him."

I had not really made much of an assessment of Lawrence, so was unsure what to say in reply. I told Rêgo that Lawrence had only been introduced to me as another reporter, and that I had not enquired into his background.

"Ah!" exclaimed Rêgo. "Lawrence is not one to talk too loudly of himself, but I am sure you would come to recognize the man as a national treasure if you knew him better."

I was intrigued. It seemed strange that I should have come all the way from Toronto to Lisboa to learn about a man described to me as a Canadian national treasure – especially from the lips of a man who might well have been described in those same terms by his own people.

"Do you know him well?" I asked.

"It seems I know him better than you do. His father was an Englishman, his mother a Spaniard. Ronald himself was born a Spaniard. For two years he fought for the Republicans when he was just a boy in his teens – and he also fought in the British army throughout the Second World War."

I knew none of this. It had not occurred to me the man I had met was anything else but a senior reporter for *The Telegram* in Toronto, and that he had travelled to Angola in the year prior to my own trip out there.

Rêgo smiled.

"No – he's done much more than just that. He is one of Canada's leading naturalists – has written something like twenty-five books about wildlife. He is a reporter when he needs to top up his bank balance, but far more importantly he is an accomplished writer about the conservation of wild animals and their habitat. As a reporter, true, he has been everywhere, but his home is somewhere in the wilds of Ontario. I've read a couple of his books, and they are extremely well done. I met him when he was here a few years ago, and then again last year after his journey through Angola."

"He told me you had been in jail here …?" I ventured.

"Yes," said Rêgo with a shrug. "It is hard to be an honest journalist in Portugal. I'm currently out of jail on bail of six thousand escudos. My newspaper salary is not very high, so I am trying not to forfeit it – but it is very difficult to be a good journalist, to tell what one believes is the truth, without running foul of the government. If political parties were permitted in Portugal, I guess you'd call me a socialist – but even that is denied here, so sooner or later I expect to lose my bail monies and be returned to prison. As things are, I am known as a liberal … my first interest is the freedom of the Portuguese press."

"How many times have you been arrested?" I asked him.

The first time, he said, was in 1945, when he had been working as press adviser to General Norton de Matos, who had been named head of the MUD (*Movimento de Unidade Democrática*) and had set his sights on becoming President of the Republic. That year the MUD had been re-organized into a political party from a group that had been formed two years previously calling itself MUNAF (*Movimento de Unidade Nacional Antifacista*). The election, which came in 1949, was so clearly rigged in favour of the dictatorship of Salazar, that Norton de Matos withdrew his name.

Later Rêgo also acted as press secretary to General Humberto Delgado. On this occasion the general was preparing to enter another rigged race for the presidency in 1958. Rêgo continued to thump a socialist drum on behalf of Delgado and was arrested and thrown into prison for the second time in 1961. He had written several books which were severely censored, as was much of his journalistic writing.

"It's a price we have to be prepared to pay if we want to see free elections in Portugal – to say nothing of the colonies."

"You mean the Overseas Provinces ...?"

"No. I mean colonies. The wealth of Portugal has been sucked out of Angola and Moçambique for five hundred years. They are colonies, *sem duvida*!"

"What may I expect when I get to Angola?" I prodded.

"You will be considered a guest, so unless you do something outrageous you will come to no harm. Even so, PIDE will be watching you, so you must take care. They are clever fellows. They'll want to know who you are talking to."

Raul Rêgo had been sent to jail in 1961 and, as I subsequently learned, was returned there yet again in 1968. Following the revolution of 1974 deposing the dictatorship, he was elected to the Constituent Assembly and the Assembly of the Republic as a member of the Socialist Party. He was appointed Minister of Social Communication in the first Provisional Government following the revolution. He died in 2002.

I had the name of Dr. Luís Lupi on my list. At the time of my visit he was the head of the Lusitânia News Agency. Serrano wanted to come with me; he thought meeting Lupi might one day prove to be useful should he be in need of a job. No, I told him. I had work to do, and I did not want to have to 'share' my interview. Lupi was one of Portugal's more strident journalists, head of the country's major news agency. I was sure Lupi would have nothing to say to me that he would not be happy to share with my young minder, but I just did not want Serrano tagging along. There were – there still are – times when interaction with someone who might have information garnered in interview is sacrosanct. There are also means of enquiry that may invite the same question to be asked at several varied layers, so that both questions and answers can be smothered in subtle inuendo. Body language and tone come into play. I had the notion – and it was probably correct – that having a minder peeping over my shoulder could be a distraction.

The exterior of Dr. Lupi's office was unassuming. I had great difficulty in finding it. One had to enter the building from an open square and step around a cluster of shoeshine boys perched on stools in the doorway. I was expecting the chief of Lusitânia News to be equally unassuming, in keeping with the surroundings – a quiet, efficient editor-type who absorbed what he saw in silence and spoke only in print.

I was ushered into a drawing room next to his office, and the atmosphere was like the lull between the last chords of the overture and the opening of the first scene …

The curtain went up with a bang.

The double doors to the inner office were abruptly thrown wide and Dr. Lupi stood there with arms outstretched to greet me. Magnificent entry, had it been staged. Maybe it was. I thought to applaud him.

As it turned out, Dr. Lupi was tough meat. He was a difficult man with whom to relax or from whom it was possible to pump information. He was altogether too busy telling me about himself to be fully conscious of any questions I might have had. He seemed incapable of answering anything directly. He had an academic standing that clearly meant a lot to him and appeared to require constant defending. His status and reputation as director of one of the nation's major news outlets showed itself, clearly indicated by his essay-length answers to the simplest questions I squeaked into the gaps of his breathless monologue. He held viewpoints both political and social of which he was totally convinced, informing me they were correct and well thought out, and things would straighten themselves out just as soon as the world started paying attention to him. Others tended to get things wrong, he wanted to tell me – the government, the western press, the opposition; anyone, in fact, who chanced risking the expression of a viewpoint. Such a catastrophe that others weren't listening to him, he seemed to be saying – ineffectual people who simply failed to comprehend …

I tried to take notes, but after a time my eyes began to glaze over at the incessant pummeling of his voice, and it became imperative to seek a way out. I was sure there was nothing he was saying to me that would not eventually show up of its own accord in my personal searches. If it did not, then perhaps it had not been worth my while noting in the first place.

He was a small man, dapper and sporty, with an impeccably-trimmed Van Dyke beard.

"Welcome! Welcome!" he shouted at me. "Come in and tell me all about Canada!"

There were no introductions. It hardly seemed necessary, and he guided me to a chair. I had but a moment to gather my wits, blink and take stock of myself.

"Another foreign journalist, eh …! Come to have a look at this miserable Portuguese dictatorship … Ha! Ha! And maybe you already have some ideas, heh …? What do they say in Canada, heh?"

He liked to dominate, so I had to let him, and tried to pay attention to his talk rather than make specific notes from the gush of his words. He pointed, waved his arms, thumped one hand with the fist of the other, and strutted back and forth in front of me like a campaign general, one moment shouting, the next dropping his voice to a dramatic whisper. His enthusiasm may have been genuine enough, but I found him mulish and rude. I sat; he stood and paced back and forth.

Occasionally he would lurch to his desk and fling himself into a chair, look at me in silence to be sure he had driven some dramatic point home. And as soon as he was satisfied that he had, or he had seen me take a breath in order to ask a question, he would pop up again like a geyser and then stalk the floor some more. Occasionally I'd punch a question through to him, but he had a tiresome trick of answering it before I'd finished asking it, and it usually took him off on some tangent with long-winded explanations. One could easily weary of this man, he appeared to be telling me.

Dr. Lupi at first surprised me by slamming the Salazar regime. I hadn't expected that. He was far from satisfied with it himself, he declared, and assured me he had spoken out against it on numerous occasions – and to the dictator himself …

Dictatorship?

Yes, it was that; but the word itself was overblown, had a bad reputation. He would hardly call it dictatorship. Elections were held in Portugal from time to time. The people wanted Salazar in. That much was abundantly clear, he said. Perhaps as Prime Minister he had been in power too long – perhaps that was one of his failings. Perhaps there was not enough emphasis on the bright young future, the dynamic modern age. Perhaps Salazar was even a little backward in his politics, a little too fond of the past, and of Portugal's great history. Perhaps he had rested too long on the laurels of this history, not long enough on the demands of a future governed by science and a liberally sophisticated society. He was an elderly man, after all.

Yes – Salazar had faults. Everyone has faults …

Criticism is the price a leader must pay, a chance he must take, Dr. Lupi shouted at me … The roads were bad, yes. The country's schooling left much to be desired, that was also true. There were many things wrong with Portugal – just as there are many things wrong with the American way of life, the French, the British … even the Canadian.

Hadn't the Canadians treated the country's original inhabitants rather poorly? Dr. Lupi asked.

As to the overseas territories, wasn't it a shame they were chiefly located in Africa? Perhaps, had they not been, the ferment of independence might not be quite so noticeable … Africa is so very much in the news these days. Oh dear! Oh dear …!

But with Portugal's overseas territories things were different than elsewhere. They were not just colonies, nor had they ever been, although they had been called that, once. They were integral parts of the homeland. Look at America – had she not overseas territories just the same, Hawaii and Alaska? Where was the difference?

No, Angola and Moçambique and the rest – they were all parts of Portugal, just as if they were physically, geographically, attached.

Independence?

Why? Had these territories themselves not elected to remain part of the Portuguese nation?

One day, perhaps, the people of Angola and Moçambique would ask to be granted their independence. Maybe. And then it would surely be given. Was not Portugal a democracy in fact? Was not the homeland's love and esteem for the people of these territories of such a magnitude that they would be granted such a request if it were made? Of course! Why would the Portuguese government want to hold anybody against their expressed will?

Dr. Lupi had a dream.

He begged me to consider the case of Brasil, a huge territory – by itself almost a continent – to which Portugal had granted independence in 1822. (And was this not just an example of how amenable the Portuguese can be with the people of her territories?)

Brasil was a fine case in point, for here the Portuguese 'mission' had undoubtedly succeeded – a nation of black, white and Amer-Indian peoples had been knitted together there on the South American continent – a fine example of Portuguese tolerance and her far-sighted racial attitudes. Here was a nation in which one's race was of insignificance, for all who lived there were Brasilians – and with the fine traditions and heritage of Portugal to back them up ...

What better example, he asked, could be shown the people of Africa, the people of all the world, than two territories on the African mainland itself, where black, white and coloureds could live harmoniously together? Two Brasils straddling Africa south of the Sahara – Angola and Moçamnbique. The concept appealed to Dr. Lupi. Surely it would appeal to anyone of intelligence ...?

I did not argue with him. If one could believe, or accept, that such a Brasilianization was, in truth, what the people of Angola and Moçambique wanted, there could be little argument. Even so, the idea seemed far-fetched to me.

Lupi exhausted me. When I left his office my brain was like sludge. I was at odds with emotions churning about in my head: a strong dislike for the man, coupled with the feeling that somewhere, in all his non-stop harangue was a certain wacky logic born of a nationalistic tunnel vision. I could not help but wonder if the people of Portuguese Africa had any idea at all of Brasil, what it was, or if they wanted anything like a Brasilian destiny. Had anybody ever thought to ask them? Most of them would never have heard of the place. And I wondered if it would not more likely be the Portuguese government itself that would impose Brasils on either side of Africa, whether the Africans wanted it or not ...

Dr. Lupi had a theory – but who might be even remotely interested? Lupi's loopy idea, I reckoned.

One thing was clear to me: here was a journalist who appeared to have been co-opted throughout his journalistic life – a journalist who had been prepared to play ball with the fascists and had made quite a comfortable living at it.

António – I was never to discover his real or family name – was a very different sort of person.

As I was to find with most *oposicionistas* I met, he was only too ready to talk and to answer as best he could all the questions that a nosy reporter could put to him.

He was an elderly man, a former journalist with twenty-five years of experience behind him. He was nervous, like a rabbit with his eyes fixed on approaching bright headlamps. Meeting with him was not an easy matter. I had had to make several contacts by telephone first, arranging to meet various intermediaries, and only much later in the day was I able to join him. Arranging to meet one of the intermediaries in a downtown café, we drove about in taxis for nearly an hour before we kept the rendezvous in some remote section of Lisboa it would have been impossible for me to locate again.

I was disappointed in my meeting with António. I had no qualms about the sincerity of his opposing political views, but I was singularly unimpressed with the melodramatic staging of our meeting.

A small ratty-faced man, António appeared to crave anonymity by sitting in the darkest corner of the room. There was a telephone, and I noticed when it rang once that he became quite visibly agitated, signaling to the others in the room to maintain silence.

I sat on an unforgivingly hard wooden chair, resting my notepad on a shaky table.

"You will not to use my name …?" António instructed.

Considering the effort I had made to reach him, the question seemed ludicrous. In any case, I did not know his name, beyond António – and even that probably was not his.

We had no translator. My Portuguese was non-existent, and his spoken English was weak, so I was finding it difficult to piece together the various segments of information he raised during the course of our conversation. In a general way I gathered that he had once been in jail, severely beaten and maltreated, that he was presently out on bail for his political activities, and that he had deliberately refrained from joining any political party.

I asked him what his own work in the opposition entailed.

"My first concern is for the freedom of the press – to abolish censorship and to allow the newspapers to publish criticism of the government – openly," he said.

It would be well for me to try to visit a newspaper office to see for myself the manner and extent of censorship, he told me.

"Not one newspaper in all Portugal is permitted to print what it likes," he said.

Then I asked him to tell me in detail about his confinement in prison.

He found it difficult to talk at first, indicating the subject was distasteful for him, but with a little prompting he then spouted forth most detailed descriptions of mediaeval dungeons and torture. Regarding one confinement (I was never able to determine how many times he had been arrested and thrown in jail) he said:

"Two years ago I spent a month confined in Aljube prison for signing my name to an opposition programme. For ten days of that month I was kept in solitary confinement in semi-darkness, in a cell that measured maybe one metre by two metres. I was beaten frequently by members of PIDE, made to stand almost naked in cold water, to face strong lights."

"What would happen to you if you were discovered to be talking to me?" I asked.

He shrugged.

"It would not go well for me. And maybe it would not go well for you, either."

"I suppose you are considered to be a communist?" I asked him.

He found the idea amusing, and he turned to speak to some of the other people gathered in the room.

Someone else answered for him:

"No, he is not a communist."

Then, as if to parrot what Raul Rêgo had told me, the man who had answered my previous query said:

"If political parties were allowed in this country, he would probably be identified as a socialist. In the current Portuguese political lexicon, the words 'liberal,' 'socialist' and 'communist' are considered the same."

"What is the extent of the opposition in Portugal?" I asked. "What are your aims? What do you hope to achieve?'"

António answered:

"The opposition is much fragmented. There are many groups. What unites us right now is knowing very well what we don't want," he said rather pathetically. "We have the common idea of a democratic government, but as a broken opposition we all come to it by different roads."

Though fractured, the opposition was extensive, he said. Without publications or other means of measuring its size, the force of the opposition was almost impossible to ascertain.

"It is not that the opposition is a legal entity, you see. There is an official opposition to government – on paper – but it is not effective at all. It has no teeth. Would you not be surprised to learn it is appointed by the government itself? This is no exaggeration!"

António was like a beaten man. I might have felt sorry for him, for it was plain that he had suffered a great deal. Time and again during our discussion I sought in him some spark of fervor or determination, something solid to go on. But I fancied what I saw was stubbornness in place of strength, disorganization where I had hoped to find a semblance of unity. There was a bland nothingness about the man, a vapidity. No matter what side a person might champion, one hates to see a man licked. The temptation is strong to offer some form of encouragement to anyone in this situation. But what was so depressing about this meeting with António was my inability to summon the least will to offer sincere encouragement. I suspected those who had thrown him into jail were looking forward to doing it again – and then again.

If this is the opposition, I thought, then Portugal had best continue for the time being with its awful dictatorship – for surely there was nothing on which to build in this camp.

I left him as I had arrived – in elaborate and probably quite unnecessary stealth.

Coming as they did in such quick succession, this pre-Africa series of meetings and interviews unfolded for me like a sequence of rapid-fire stage skits, each one quite startlingly different from the others. Meeting Manuel

Rino at the office of the *Secretariado Naçional da Informação* (SNI) was like running into an elderly and absent-minded school headmaster, such a foggy sort of encounter I was only dimly aware of him until I managed to snap out of my mindlessness just moments before I was ushered out of his presence. It had not been my intent to meet him, but it became necessary for some reason best known to himself when I showed up at the SNI office looking for Serrano, whom he appeared not to know.

During my talk with Dr. Caldeira Coelho at the information office of the Foreign Ministry[18] shortly after my arrival in Lisboa, I had expressed an interest in looking into Portugal's educational system. Various articles I had read in Toronto had referred to Portugal's lamentable reputation in offering schooling to the mass of the country's poorer classes. It had been described as inadequate in the extreme, and deliberately so. Education was a particular interest of mine, I explained to Coelho, and I would like the opportunity to explore it in some detail with a view to writing a comparative study between the system I knew in Canada and the one in Portugal. Coelho, I could see, was a little taken aback. He had expected to be questioned on matters relating to policy and politics, not education, but he said he would see what he could do.

Setting up a meeting with someone at the Education Ministry was impossible at the time I talked to Coelho – at least on this leg of my trip – so I was asked to set my questions down on paper and present them at SNI – which I did. This list of queries had been taken away, and so now, stepping into the general office, I was suddenly summoned before Manuel Rino and introduced to him as the organization's director of foreign press.

He was an enormous man – bland-faced and unsmiling. My list of educational questions was before him on his desk.

"I have been asked to speak to you about education, and was given this list of questions, but what am I to do with it?" he asked. "Many, many questions," he mused, turning the document over and waving it over his head.

He offered me a seat in front of his desk.

"Yes," I said. "Education is a broad subject."

He was agitated. "Quite!" he agreed. "*Pois!*"

He asked me why I was so interested in Portugal's educational system.

"Don't you think the level of education is a base indicator of almost any

---

[18] The *Ministério dos Negócios Estrangeiros*, the Foreign Ministry, should not be confused with the *Ministério de Ultramar*, the Overseas Ministry. The former deals with all foreign countries; the latter dealt strictly with Portugal's overseas provinces.

society?" I suggested. "Your system of education is surely of some importance to the overall impression visitors must gather of your country. It's at the foundation of your society, I'm sure you'll agree, so naturally I have an interest in it."

"Of course, it is … yes," he agreed, his voice trailing off.

But he was still far from satisfied, and it occurred to me perhaps the only thing that might meet with his approval would be for me to withdraw the questions and drop the subject altogether. It was plain both of us were running into difficulties. I could see it was not quite his area of expertise, that he himself did not have the answers to so many questions and really did not wish to be bothered answering them.

I got up to go.

"It would be really good to have that information," I told him. "How soon might I expect it?"

Perhaps a little bullying at this stage could do no harm.

"Oh, very soon, very soon," he said, flustered.

"I'd like to have them before I leave for Angola. Perhaps you could have them tidied up in a day or so? They are rather important …"

Rino blustered some more.

"Certainly, *senhor*. Certainly …!"

I knew, absolutely, that if ever he was to get around to answering these queries, he for one would be in no hurry. His advantage: he would know when I would be leaving for Angola, and all he had to do was procrastinate till then.

Sucking in my breath, I left his office muttering. So gracious, he was. So clearly determined to grant his attentions, he seemed to want me to understand – but later. His terms, his timing - not mine.[19]

Dr. Ribeiro da Cunha, spokesman for the Portuguese Overseas Ministry, had been one of the first Portuguese officials I had met after my arrival in

---

[19] See Appendix #1 – United Nations working paper – section on education; also author's commentary in Scholarly Afterthought, p. 432.

Portugal some days before. Prior to going to his office I had stopped at a sidewalk café on the boulevard of Avenida de Liberdade for a cup of coffee. I remember it only because a small boy, recognizing me as a foreigner, approached with a packet in his hand and offered me some – wink-wink – 'dirty pictures.' Arresting sales pitch. He was no more than nine years old.

Dr. da Cunha spoke to me of the Africans I would shortly be encountering, calling them his 'brothers' – but refraining from going as far as Dr. Lupi in advocating a mass racial mix. It was impossible for the Africans to live without the whites, he told me.

"It is unthinkable that Africa can survive without the whites. The accusation is that Portugal had milked the cow – but not fed the cow. This is just not the case," he said.

He told me the uprising in Portuguese Guiné was not because it was of economic significance to anyone, but as a protest that 'we are there.'

He expressed the opinion that the Africans in all the Portuguese territories would have to learn to get along with the whites generally, and especially with Portugal and the Portuguese.

"I challenge any country in Africa to show me as good services as those we have established for our Africans in Guiné, Angola and Moçambique."

Da Cunha talked down to me, irritating me by indicating he was very much irritated by my questioning – and no doubt also by me personally. He was not prepared to recognize my job required I ask him questions, and at one point I felt obliged to remind him that I did not have access to the same pat answers he did – but that I needed them. Though spokesman for his ministry, I wondered how often he had to deal with members of the foreign press.

Instead of answering my queries directly, he would reach to a shelf behind his desk for any one of scores of colourful pamphlets – beautiful Portugal basking under perpetual sunshine.

"Here! I could answer your questions, but you might as well read the official government viewpoint on the matter ..." he would say, flicking a booklet at me. By the time I left his office I was carrying a sizable armload of them.

In the end da Cunha escorted me to the main door of the building where we ran into a young Englishman by the name of Michael Teague. Da Cunha introduced him as the representative of a New York advertising and public relations firm – and I happened to have heard earlier that same day the company had been hired specially to promote and polish the Portuguese government image abroad. More of a PR specialist trying to cope with a major series of Portuguese governmental problems than a useful liaison with the foreign press, it was clear this Englishman was the kind of outside operative with whom da Cunha preferred to deal. Being bombarded with nosey journalistic-type questioning was not his strong point. Journalists pumping him for information appeared to wrinkle the smooth operating style of his dinosaur ministry, which just then was trying so hard to remain in full charge of running a Portuguese Empire in imminent danger of disintegration.

Teague and I met later at my hotel over a drink. I told him about my meeting with da Cunha and suggested it might have been a better public relations gesture had this particular official given me straight answers rather than throw a bunch of pamphlets at me.

Teague laughed.

"Understand, this is not your ordinary western democratic government. Officers here are not well practiced in the art of Public Relations. Maybe he just didn't like your questions," he said.

"The way to get along with Portuguese officialdom is to agree with it. You will learn that as you stay longer in the country. Start bucking them, or backing them into corners with difficult questions, and invariably you will set them on their guard. Hoods will drop down over their eyes – and their faces will become blank. I know the routine well."

He also happened to mention he was looking for another job.

It was late and I had had a basinful of Portuguese politics for one day, along with those who would drum their labyrinthine ideas into my ear. A nightcap was in order, so I made my way to the refuge of the *boite* on the top floor of my hotel.

I was glad I did. It afforded a chance to meet one of the more delightful characters so far during this tarriance in Lisboa – a man who, in his way, managed to tell me as much as any of the others about life in his delightfully confusing little country.

Manuel Viegas sauntered over to my table from the music dais and struck up a conversation – in English, happily. He was a chirpy fellow and liked to talk. Dipping his forefinger in his whisky glass, he wrote his Christian name in large wet letters on the polished surface of the table.

"Man-u-el," he said slowly, as though he knew how dim-witted foreigners can be.

"I not speaking English too good, but I getting better all time, huh?"

Manuel was the leader of the dance combo in the club. The place was a regular haunt for air crews from all parts of Europe and North America, as well as for off-duty members of the staff of the American embassy just down the street. Lots of opportunity for Manuel to improve his language skills.

He was not afraid to promote his own genius, and so told me quite matter-of-factly that, at the age of thirty-three, he was considered one of the city's most recognized and talented musicians. Four of his original songs had made top of the charts locally in recent years, and the success established him as something of a senior among Portuguese composers of ballads.

"What instrument do you play?" I asked him.

"Music! Anything you show me!" was his boisterous answer.

He had studied at Lisboa's conservatory for two years but gave it up when he found the strict life and discipline prohibited him from playing what he liked when he liked. From watching him, I was able to satisfy myself that he had mastered the piano, the vibes, accordion, bass and drums – and that he could sing passably well. Manuel Viegas was a dreamer, though possibly he had a better excuse for dreaming than most. Two years prior to my meeting with him, Walt Disney had come to Lisboa to make a film. A straggly-haired mutt called 'Hector' was the film's main character. Apart from being the charming tale of a dog's life in Lisboa, the film showed off some of the city's high points and gave an intricate visual description of a romanticized Latin pace of life.

Manuel was asked to write music for those parts of the story that required a particularly Latin theme.

"Now I spend much of my time dreaming. I dream for my boy," Manuel confided passionately.

At the time, he was drawing an income of just under $100.00 per month. While his efforts as a musician were based largely on personal ambition, Manuel was also anxious to buy a decent education for his son, Tiago. The lad was due to start school that year – with only the first four years of education being provided by the state. (The following year the state raised the limit of compulsory schooling to six years.) After that Manuel knew he would have to pay for Tiago's education out of his own pocket, and he knew, too, it would cost a fortune if the young fellow was ever to go as far as university.

"What are Tiago's ambitions?" I asked Manuel.

"I think he want to be engineer. But he's a little boy. He not know what he want. If he don't want to be engineer, he want be something else – and he need school to be whatever he want."

Clearly this is what kept Manuel working every night at the *boite* – his own greater ambitions brutally trimmed. He wrote music and he played music, for it was all he knew.

"Sometimes I wish I'd stayed at conservatory, but it was no good for me. I had to write music. I had to live what I felt ..."

No easy matter on less than $100.00 a month, even in 1963 ...

He was a skilled and dedicated artist. In the mornings, before the city awoke, he would put away his flashy night club clothes and go to work in earnest. He would already have put in more than five hours of hard playing in the club – and he would have enjoyed it, too. But the wee hours were his. The last of the nighthawks would have moved on and, when all was still, Manuel would find himself a quiet spot by a window overlooking the lights of Lisboa and the distant Rio Tejo, and out would come pen and paper.

Words and music were an all-consuming activity for him. The two pieces he had written for the Walt Disney movie were accomplished in just such a way, and in just such a mood, he said. Music and lyrics came to him immediately; the only work required was putting it all down on paper.

Lisboa lua e noite was written within the space of an hour in a sidewalk café; *Alegria bailando* is a dance, and the musician was inclined to discard it with a shrug as inferior and unimportant.

"I was told how to write it. It was a necessary piece for the film. But *Lisboa*, this is a piece of me. The words, the music, the everything!"

Manuel's effervescence might have given the impression he liked to play at playing, but anyone with the intent of getting to know him would see through his playfulness in a moment. He was a worker. He faced his considerable odds with determination, absolutely convinced his efforts would pay off for little Tiago one day. But his manner was happy-go-lucky. An optimist if ever there was.

"When I come to North America, I come because I want to – not because I have to. Many of my friends have go America, and they are happy. But I have work to do here first, and it takes many escudos to buy a ticket to

America. But I will come! One day you will see this name in big lights!"

And he tapped with his finger in the splash of whisky he had spilled out on the counter, and re-wrote the capital M of his name, over and over ...

Of all these people, da Cunha and António were to fade into a sea of hundreds of featureless faces; I was not to meet either one of them again. I saw Lupi briefly in Luanda when he accompanied President Américo Tomaz on an official visit to Angola, but I had no wish whatsoever to dally with him. Back in Lisboa months later, I was to meet once more with Rino – who produced a list of answers to my queries about education. Viegas I was pleased to see again, still putting in his hours every night in the club on the top floor of the hotel, still writing lyrics to his songs and dreaming of the day Walt Disney would call ...

And Raul Rêgo ... and José Shercliff ...

Meeting people and talking to them was, still is, a fundamental of journalism, no less a basic than is close personal observation. At once it is the very stuff of a news-gatherer's source of bread and butter, and the bane of his existence. It is a test of endurance, and an arduous work, to weigh that which is valid in an amateur philosopher's thinking against a superabundance of much wooly-headed and loquacious explanation. Portugal's domains, at least in 1963, appeared to be full of amateur philosophers – and historians. Throughout the trip I attempted to discover the names of practically everyone I encountered and, if someone of special interest or of captivating opinion, I would attempt to make a special note. I was left with many points to ponder. Everything I saw and heard was new and somehow immensely significant.

In Portugal one breathes history. I think it no exaggeration to say I have never visited a country where the history of the nation is so starkly intertwined with their daily lives. Alongside the country's creative ceramics and stonework, 'history' in all its contortions, confusions and entanglements was – and will doubtless always remain – the single quality that radiates through every aspect of the Portuguese psyche. Many people go to Portugal for a holiday. If they want to make solid contact with the Portuguese and their culture, accomplish more than simply spending their tourist dollars on Portuguese sunshine, they would do well to read the history of the place before going. There is bountiful material. This could be said of anywhere, but it is particularly true of this extraordinarily ancient and homogenous nation.

It was a warm evening. The sun had fallen behind the rooftops, but it was still light. The trees on the boulevards cast long shadows into the streets. People had quit work and were going downtown to the bars, theatres and restaurants. Lisboa's night was about to come to life – my early impression that much of what went on in the city happened after dark and under the sidewalks.

I bought stamps from the clerk at the hotel desk, gummed them to the backs of a stack of postcards, and handed them back to the receptionist for mailing. Then I crossed the lobby and stood for a moment in the main doorway watching the passing traffic and people outside on the street.

The doorman, dressed in green livery and peaked cap, asked if I wanted a taxi.

"No thanks," I told him. My intention was to return to my room in a minute or so and spend an hour before dinner catching up on the writing of my notes.

The doorman smiled. He had seen me coming and going over the past few days, recognized me as a guest and so thought he would get a little closer. He was a chubby fellow and his uniform did not fit him too well. His colouring was swarthy, but he had unbelievably pink cheeks – like Belisha beacons.

He said something in Portuguese that I did not understand, then came over to where I was standing. He was smiling and winking. With furtive familiarity he used an elbow to nudge me in the ribs.

"Eh?"

He fumbled in his back trouser pocket and pulled out a scrubby little notebook. Flipping it open, he pushed it up under my nose to show off a handful of tatty-edged photographs – young women in what he clearly took to be sexy poses and various stages of undress. There was a handwritten list of names followed by what looked like telephone numbers.

I was somewhat surprised and not quite sure how to react. It appeared he had gone to considerable effort to draw up this catalogue of his 'stable.'

Scores of pictures and names – how could one man have tabs on so many! The book's smudged pages had been copiously thumbed through and perused aplenty.

It was hard to imagine this surreptitious pimping seriously augmented the income of the city's nine-year-olds and hotel doormen, I thought – a sort of moonlighting before the hour of moonlight.

"Girlie?" the fellow queried in possibly the only English word he knew. His wink was not quite a winner. He nudged me some more, jerking his hands and flicking through page after page.

"Thanks, but no thanks …!" I told him, holding up my hand in the internationally accepted signal for STOP! I wanted to laugh.

My rejection penetrated, but he was unfazed. I am sure he did not understand one word I said, but it mattered nothing. He grinned a little stupidly, shrugged, then moved off to the far side of the doorway to hail a cab for a small group of guests who had stepped from the hotel lobby behind me. Behind his back his chubby hand pushed and poked the dog-eared notebook into his hip pocket, where he knew he could readily find it again when it was required.

Instantly his posture rearranged itself to become the ingratiating doorman with his hand out and ready to receive a tip – a hustler, okay, rather than a sleazy pimp, and I returned to my room to write the eternal moment into my notebook.

Antero had been a young Portuguese immigrant to Canada six years prior to my arrival in Lisboa. He had returned to Portugal only recently. His mother had become ill and he felt it his duty to return to look after her.

He had departed Lisboa under a cloud in 1957. He had seen his friends arrested and was himself a strong opponent of the dictatorial regime of Salazar. He might have been arrested, too, had he not bolted the country and gone to Canada. After six years it is unlikely anything would befall him as a Canadian once back in Lisboa, but it would have been foolish to think his activities of six years earlier would go unnoticed by the Portuguese authorities. I never came to know Antero well, but I was aware he knew PIDE was watching his every move in the event he might lead the way to others of similar political recalcitrance.

The casual visitor to Portugal invariably finds the place enchanting. But if one stopped to take a closer look at it with more intensity than one might as a tourist, one would see other things. There were facets of this police state that were amusing – quaint, even. But there were others that would have been incomprehensible, insidious. The vistas of pink roofs and tiled walls were like a finger in the eye to anyone who also observed the *bairros de lata* – the filthy open-sewer and rat-infested clap-board shanty towns that had sprung up in virtually every district of the city.

I was taken aback one day when Antero informed me I could be fined for proffering a light to a lady struggling to fire up her own cigarette. I did not have a licence to carry and use a cigarette lighter, he explained. It was a form of tax in a country that had no income tax. In any case, the government owned the match factory, so arresting the owner of an unlicenced lighter protected a government monopoly.

Petty?

The law would have appeared to be just that – in the pettiest of ways minimizing and attacking a people who showed an enormous zest for life and innovation, a deep sense of the æsthetic and refined. The lowliest of Portuguese citizens would have had a keen sense of his nation's long history of heroic achievement. He would be aware the world still owes his people a more robust recognition, that his forefathers had earned the right to the national pride he expressed. Such a mean and petty law, and so many others like it, cut the Portuguese down somehow, reduced the poorest of them.

The scope of such minimalist thinking was insidiously narrow, like the inane rules and drills one might encounter in an exaggerated and highly regulated penal system, where vindictive punishment is more the intent and true reform a joke left at the institution's gate. There seemed to be many sinister aspects of life in this little country. It was the imposition of conditions that was insidious, of course, not the people; not the country as a chunk of real estate.

When a schoolboy does well at his lessons, he is doing no more than what is expected of him. He might bask in the praise or flattery given him by his teacher for his efforts, but his greatest reward (although he may not recognize it at the time) is the satisfaction of his own self-improvement. When he does badly, he can expect to be criticized, even punished; anyone who has ever been a student knows full well how frequently too much emphasis can be placed on shortcomings; it is disheartening when good qualities and earnest endeavour are overlooked. There is always the possibility this underlying philosophy is behind a great deal of 'democratic' newspaper criticism and castigation; perhaps the international media felt – still feels – it possesses every right and good reason to lean heavily on regimes it sees as oppressive, regimes that would appear to go out of their way to display insidious aspects of themselves. Regimes like Salazar Portugal.

Visitors were encouraged to seek after Portugal's history, her landmarks, her achievements in redevelopment or the beauties and amenities they had come to the country to enjoy. But let the curious visitor enquire tenaciously into matters of politics or social structure, or go into such matters as education and illiteracy, or slums and housing, or seek answers to questions involving government structure, opposition, health care, colonial policy – even press censorship ... Ah! This would be a different matter. The Portuguese are a proud people, the enquirer may be told, and clearly have no wish to be embarrassed by such in-depth enquiries.

The cynical Portuguese expression, 'só *para inglês ver*' – 'only for the Englishman to see' – goes back to around 1805 and the time of the Portuguese/Brasilian slave trade. The British Royal Navy had been assigned to assist abolition by intercepting slave ships on the high seas before they reached port and unloaded their wretched cargo. All manner of concealments and tricks were played by the slavers to avoid detection by the British – and these constituted leaving in the open whatever could be inspected by unwelcome attention. Modern use of the expression might be equated with 'pulling the wool over one's eyes.'

There was much about Salazar's *Estado Novo* that was held in concealment – most definitely *not* for the Englishman – or anyone – to see. Take a good look around, but anyone seeking too ardently for insight into what made Portugal tick in the era of the *Estado Novo* would have been liable to come face-to-face with that which was most invidious about this little Latin land. Every country has secrets, some many more than others, and there are the secrets that may be revealed only to conceal those that may not.

I had an example of this demonstrated one day when Antero took me to see an acquaintance who was the Lisboa correspondent for a large London newspaper. The telephone rang as we entered his office. He said:

"Listen-in to this ...!"

There was a long and silent pause, then the caller spoke in Portuguese. So did the journalist. But they had no sooner begun than there came on the line an audible clicking sound.

"PIDE," explained Antero when the call was complete. "But they don't bother hiding their action – they just come on the line and listen-in to anything they wish."

The correspondent commented:

"My home is not secure, either. Bit of a nuisance, but I'm used to it. When I have calls to make that I don't want others to hear, I have to go to a call box – or phone from a friend's place."

Much later during my stay in Lisboa this same journalist introduced me to a friend of his, a former newspaper editor from one of the Lisboa dailies. The three of us talked for a couple of hours – and during that time I learned of the editor's personal harassments by PIDE. He had spent several years in Lisboa's Aljube jail, an establishment generally reserved at the time for political offenders.

His treatment was rough for a middle-aged man. He had been beaten repeatedly at one stage of his confinement; he had been forced to stand for hours on end in frigid water; he had been kept for weeks in a darkened cell, only to be taken out and questioned for hour after hour under bright spotlights.

What were his political views? I asked him.

"I am just an *oposicionista*," he replied. "We are numerous, but we are disorganized. We know not so much what we want as what we don't want. It's pathetic, but we find it difficult to organize the way we want to, need to ..."

It was almost impossible to gauge the extent of opposition to the Salazar regime. Labour unions were controlled; the ballots of opposition members in the House of Deputies were counted by government-chosen returning officers; where large organizations were permitted, they were well-infiltrated by members of PIDE. Demonstrations were forbidden; the press was heavily censored.

I was able to see press censorship in practice when I was in the capital, but the system was the same in Portugal's colonies, and I saw it – a well-practiced routine brought from the homeland – when I was in Beira, Moçambique. In Lisboa I was aided by an opposition reporter who sneaked me through the back door into his newspaper's editorial room one weekend night when the plant was shut down. We spent considerable time going through the files of news stories and photographs.

There is extraordinary complexity in the publication of any newspaper, but when daily operation and deadlines are circumscribed by censorship and threats of prison, or worse, the system becomes nightmarish, 'news' takes second place, and deadlines tend to go by the board. Every single story in any and every edition of the paper had to be set in type, proofs run off, and copies sent to the local censor for his approval, temporary suspension or outright rejection. The North American model of a newspaper – rush to print, then out on the street for sale before any competitors – was impossible in Salazar's Portugal. A story that made its way into print without considerable alteration was most definitely a triumph, a feather in the cap of the journalist who worked on it …

PART II

Angola

Part II – Angola

Luanda Minders 113

Arms and Anti-Americanism 121

Cambambe Safari 124

South to Lobito 130

Black, White and the Mix 140

Mountains, Sea, Desert 145

Benguela Railway 160

Missionairies 165

Spirit Dance 176

War Zone 197

Luanda Minders

The plane – a three-tailed, humped-back propeller-driven Constellation (its silhouette resembled a porpoise) – left Lisboa late at night, and we had crossed the coast of the north African continent within twenty minutes. We headed for Kano in northern Nigeria where the craft was re-fuelled, and the passengers disembarked for breakfast in the terminal building. Africa again; it was a thrill to return – but, wonder of design though it was, and workhorse of so many airlines, the Constellation was neither the swiftest nor most comfortable means of air transport. The TAP (*Transportes Aéreos Portugueses*) staff had not yet learned to be as surly and unaccommodating as personnel of many North American airlines – and perhaps they still haven't. They did a first-rate job of feeding us well and making us comfortable, reducing the tension of a long and noisy flight – which today is a joy to think back on. Nowadays we have become used to sardine packing – bigger planes, more people, less space, same discomfort, and dreadful food. Though today's airlines generally convey us at greater speed, crowds and line-ups can slow down the here-to-there process. Snarls and the impersonal barbarity of many airline crews – as well as the expressed entitlements of clients themselves – make it clear the traveller is worth no more than the price of his ticket. There are a few chintzy extras – old films, sometimes broadband – and the ads tell us we are being treated with some sophistication, which seldom pertains to meals; the quality of these universally deteriorated over a period of years – and on some carriers has become either non-existent, or virtually inedible pre-packaged muck. There! That should make me feel better for the next time I have to fly.

On this occasion the flight took us direct from Kano to Luanda, the capital of Angola – fifteen hours in all from Lisbon – and I was met by Lieutenant Joaquim Gonçalves, about whom Ronald Lawrence had cautioned me back in Toronto.

Quim, as he suggested I call him, was a cavalry officer, and quite the oldest lieutenant I had ever encountered. He announced he would accompany me to my hotel in the capital's downtown centre, then leave me to rest.

"Total gentleman, total Lothario, total scalawag," was Lawrence's description of the man who was to be my principal 'minder' for the duration of my stay in Luanda.

"He's a government man, and you mustn't forget it," he had said. "He is a gallant, and presents himself as a gentleman. He will show you exaggerated respect – but don't be fooled. You may be sure he will pass on to his seniors any information you might give him. It's his job, so be careful."

I was frankly taken aback by Joaquim's age. Despite his craggy face and jowls, and the white hair that usually denotes a sage, a man of encroaching old age, and possibly wisdom – he possessed the devilish good looks of a *bon vivant* and the erect baring of a soldier half his age. Even so, I judged him certainly old enough to have been my father. He had a full head of snow-white hair which contrasted starkly with the deep tan of his handsome face. His appearance did not compute with my preconceived notion concerning the age of junior officers. Lieutenants are usually in their early twenties; Quim would have been in his late fifties.

His daily attire consisted of a simple and well-tailored tropical military uniform. He wore an open-neck short-sleeve khaki shirt, pressed impeccably, exposing more of his tanned chest so that one could tell in a trice he had spent many long years in service under a tropical sun. Regimental insignia had been sewn onto his shirtsleeves, and colourful ribbons adorned his left breast above the flap of the pocket. Spotlessly clean jodhpurs of an off-white twill were tucked into well-polished brown riding boots that rose to just below the knee. On his head he wore a white military-style peaked cap.

That first day my minder was thoughtful enough to leave me alone for several hours after the long trip south. The hotel was located on the fringe of the city's central business district, but many of the rooms – my own included – were on the long rear side of the building overlooking the outdoor dining patio and the main beach that swept for several kilometres along the seafront. Some enthusiast, out of sight but not out of hearing range, decided his motorcycle engine required revving at long intervals throughout the afternoon and into the night, but exhaustion finally laid her soft hand on my shoulder and by the time I awoke the next day's sun was already high and the day warm. I took a late breakfast in the hotel dining room, and Joaquim joined me there. He suggested we spend an hour or so making a promenade of the city's centre and waterfront.

In the downtown area of the city, the Portuguese architectural influence was very much in evidence. Along the front there were enough high-rise buildings to give the impression of a dynamic and modern seaside metropolis; interspersed between them were numbers of stately old homes that gave the whole seafront an aspect of staid control and continuity. Only a few blocks behind them, however, one very soon encountered the familiar impoverishment of Africa. These were the mud and wattle huts, the *dukas* and *shebeens* that, with minor variations, are a feature of African townships the continent over, from the Cape to the Mediterranean.

I needed a few small items from a pharmacy so, as we were concluding our morning tour and returning to my hotel, I asked Joaquim to tell me where I could find such a store.

Telling me was not enough; he had to escort me. We entered a small establishment that had the word *farmácia* in blue lettering over its door. There was very little on the shelves, but it was plain the sale of medications was the store's principal business and that I might find there the various items I needed. Behind the counter an appealingly self-possessed Portuguese girl, like myself probably in her late twenties, greeted my minder with a broad smile of recognition. Joaquim likewise greeted her effusively, then went on to explain why we had called on her. A conversation inevitably followed, all of which left me completely outside the picture. We were in one of those situations where, had I spoken up for myself, circling a finger around a petty wound or uttering the words 'band aid,' I am positive I would have been well understood and served in a moment. As it was, speaking no Portuguese, there was little question of being permitted the prerogative of trying to explain for myself. Aside from whatever he felt were his necessary attentions to me, the responsibilities of Joaquim's task were considerably eased by the fun he was having in conversation with this most agreeable shopkeeper. It was clear my minder and the pretty attendant knew one another. Time passed easily.

In the process of negotiating a purchase on my behalf Joaquim informed me the lady's name was Maria Esmeralda Magalhães, that she had graduated in pharmacy just a few years before at university in Lisboa, and had returned to her home in Luanda to open this business and live with her aging mother. Her father and her brother were fighting in the north of the country against the 'bandits.'

Joaquim held his hand up to indicate the girl, and crinkled his brow at me – the sort of gesture an ostler might make indicating the rear end of a horse:

"Is she not a beautiful lady?" he asked, with a teasing sideways glance at the shop girl.

"Of course!" I agreed instantly, and most Canadian-ly uncomfortable. We are a tediously polite people.

"Would you not like to take her out to dinner?"

The lady herself was now smiling. I would have been most surprised had she not been attuned to Joaquim's manoeuvrings and manipulations, and I suspected she knew a thing or two about his reputation with the ladies. The two of them were now having a bit of sport at my expense.

115

"I'd love to take her to dinner, Joaquim, but then I fancy you would, too. Why don't we all go to dinner together …?"

He turned to say something to Esmeralda in Portuguese. I suspected it was to inform her I was willing to take her to dinner, but then there appeared to be some sort of game going on that involved my participation – except I was not quite sure how to play. Esmeralda made it plain by coming around the counter to stand beside me and slide her arm through mine. She posed coquettishly as though waiting for me to escort her out the door.

"… What do you suppose we might talk about, if just the two of us?" I asked my minder.

"Ah, Jeremias!" expostulated Quim. "Surely I don't have to answer that question for you! You're a strong man, she's a beautiful woman, no? What more do you need to know …! You mustn't let a trifling absence of language skills impede your clear duty …!"

"Thank you, Joaquim, but I'd be curious to know what Esmeralda would have to say about what you call my 'duty.' Surely she should be consulted…?"

"Of course, she must be consulted!" Joaquim burst enthusiastically, whereupon he turned to the lady herself and (I could not be sure) issued her our combined invitation for dinner that evening. Esmeralda went along with the game, but I couldn't keep up. I did not know these people, and I did not care much for Joaquim's manner, or what I thought he was saying. The play seemed off, a teasing sort of irritation – jocular bullying, which I've always found conniving, almost cowardly. Esmeralda, it was evident, was perfectly able to handle herself. Playful, as if she understood she had to be, in front of the lieutenant, she nonetheless displayed a maturity that I felt was absent in him. I was surprised and embarrassed, and she sensed it. This was the moment, recalling Lawrence's warning, when I could discern clearly that I must not get too close to this man, give him a little extra space and not to overly trust him.

Smiling, feigning no commitment, Esmeralda looked me up and down, then turned to Joaquim and scrunched her nose. With gestures, a comic facial nuance and flick of her wrist, she pretended only limited satisfaction with what she saw. That much of her body language came across without words, a clever pantomime that sailed well over any language barrier.

"Well, it appears I am the odd man out," the gallant returned. "Tell you what – lunch comes before dinner, so why don't we all go back to your hotel for some lunch – and we can talk about dinner. I will translate. When you both know one another a little better I shall leave you on your own so that I can get on with some other work I must attend to this afternoon."

All I had wanted was a box of band aids and some other small items, but it looked as though I was not going to get them without a certain degree of gamesmanship. The store was not stocked with everything I needed just then, Esmeralda told Joaquim, but she could have everything ready a little later in the afternoon. She would deliver them to me at my hotel.

With that and our collective decision to lunch, Esmeralda ushered us back into the street, locked the door of her shop behind her and, each of us stepping on our own shadows in the heat of that noon hour, we walked through the few narrow streets back to my hotel to sit at a dining table on the beachside patio. Before us was a wide and empty stretch of yellow sand, a rippling surf running its length into the distance, and a breeze that wafted in from the South Atlantic to kiss our cheeks and play gently with the fringe around the brightly-coloured umbrella that sprouted from its stalk in the centre of our table. The timeless ocean stretched its impersonal calm before us; a scorched and ancient land was at our backs as we sat on the edge of Africa.

"Are you a racist?"

Joaquim's question thudded like a brick tossed into my soup. It was direct, completely at odds with the peaceful setting of our lunch table. In Africa racism is a subject everyone must consider at some point, but the last question one might expect.

"No. I am not," I replied. "Why do you ask?"

"Well, one has to ask. Portuguese in all our territories have been accused of racism. By and large the Portuguese are not racists. For all our problems and cultural quirks, that is not a major one. We have lived with Africans for as long as the nation has existed – the Moors of the Maghreb, the days of slavery. In the XVI century close to a third of Portugal's mainland population comprised black people – slaves and freed slaves. They became close members of our communities and families, and today in Portugal you may be sure there is not a single family that does not have African antecedents somewhere in their line. The accusation of racism is recent. It was the concoction of our enemies, and for political reasons ... Americans, who *are* racists ..."

"Why did you ask me such a question? Do you think if I was a racist I would tell you such a thing? Most racists, surely, would go to great lengths to deny it, don't you think? If I was racist I'd do my best to keep it from you. I can't see it as the sort of thing I'd want to publicize."

Joaquim smiled.

"Possibly you, not. But that has never been my experience," Joaquim told me seriously. "Most racists I've encountered have told me their preference right away – not necessarily of their own volition, or with words. They may be thinking they're fooling people, but their actions, their gestures, their faces – these will tell me. Within minutes these will tell me. Racists cannot conceal their hatreds, and they don't feel well in the company of non-racists."

Esmeralda sat quietly watching Joaquim and me while this conversation was in progress. She did not speak enough English to allow her to join in, I thought, but it was clear she understood the subject of discussion. Now and then Joaquim would turn and say something to her, creating space for her, and her commentary would come back as short two- or three-word interjections of query or confirmation. We ordered our meal and, while waiting for it, Joaquim leaned in to widen his discussion.

"I do not for a moment take you for a racist, Jeremy, but it's important to let you know how the very concept of racism has been forced upon the psyche of the Portuguese, and the effect this force has had on us as a nation.

"Racism and xenophobia exist all over the world, and you'll see as much of it here in Africa, between African-and-African or white-and-African, as you will find anywhere else. So, in Portugal, too, there is racism, of course – just as I am sure there is racism in Canada. But I want you to understand that it does not exist among the Portuguese in a cultural way, the way it does in South Africa, for instance – or in America. Sure, the Portuguese instituted the slave trade across the Atlantic and, in the past, we carried out the most brutal activities within our colonies. But vile slavery was good business and racism was incidental. It has existed for much longer than Portugal has been a nation. Since man first walked the earth. Later, within the span of recorded European history, no nation was taken seriously unless it had domination over lesser groups. Colonization, in fact.

"The suppression carried out against the Africans by the Portuguese, here in Angola, for instance, as well as in all other parts of the Portuguese-speaking world, has been driven by commerce almost exclusively – not, as in South Africa and America, because white people have an innate aversion to black people, or think they are superior. That is not our way. We have a very strong sense of *class* in Portugal, but the class differences between Portuguese these days – and it has been largely this way for several hundreds of years – is based on money, not colour or racial background. Any class difference is abhorrent, but it would be a grave injustice were you to write in your newspaper that the Portuguese class system is fundamentally based on racism, or that strong class differences are to be found here. They are not."

I listened carefully to this, even managing to write down a few notes. Esmeralda, I saw, was listening carefully, too. Then she surprised me by saying in English:

"I am *mestiça*."

"Exactly!" Joaquim reacted by lifting his hands and looking at me, his point confirmed.

I did not know the term; I looked from one of them to the other, confused. Esmeralda laughed, shrugging her shoulders and unable to say more. Joaquim was the one to explain.

"Esmeralda is telling you she is of mixed parentage. She is part African, part European Portuguese ..."

"You could have fooled me," I replied. Esmeralda's skin colouring was darker than mine, a healthy tan I put down to her Latin origin and continued life in the tropics. She held out the paler undersides of her forearms, making light of the comparison between them and the blanched colouring of the upper arms showing below the cuffs of my own short-sleeve shirt.

"Many Portuguese are what you call half-caste," explained Joaquim. "The colour of the skin and the facial features are the usual indicators, but not always. Much depends on how far back in time the mixture occurred. When the mix was several generations ago, it can be difficult to tell – as in Esmeralda's case ..."

He spoke a few words to her and waited for a response.

"Yes," he said when she had finished answering him. "She's more-or-less confirming what I was saying. Her great-grandfather was Ovimbundu – the largest tribe in southern Angola. But as you can see, she's no less Portuguese than I am ..."

He sat back with a broad smile on his face.

"Esmeralda is *mestiça* – and certainly proud of it," Joaquim said.

"You see even a subtle difference between *mestiça* and African – but you are not racist ...?" I was fishing.

"No," said Joaquim. "I see the difference, certainly, but then so do you. That alone does not make either of us racists. More important, Esmeralda is Portuguese ..."

Shades of difference. He was explaining something to me I had never had great cause to consider before. He waited for my reaction, but I did not feel competent to give him one.

"Well!" Joaquim could see his lesson had probably confused me, so decided to conclude it.

"Esmeralda is *mistiça*. More to the point, and like so many of our Portuguese girls, do you not find her a most beautiful lady?"

That fact was not in dispute. Esmeralda was enjoying the embarrassment of my reasonable and all-Canadian effort to appear correct. I was very much aware that what she saw in me was really a most discombobulated self-consciousness. Unlike Africans, Canadian Caucasians can manage a ruby-hued blush on occasion. The real picture of my confusion must have shown itself as a self-criticism for not having had the wit to see (until I was told) she was part-African. But even having been informed, I was having difficulty in seeing her as anything but a pleasingly handsome and confident girl. Men make few excuses. They will see what they want to see if a woman interests them ...

We passed an hour talking and laughing, the sun beating down on our necks. It and the bottle of fine wine we demolished with our meal had made me sleepy. We all rose to go – Joaquim to his office, Esmeralda to her shop. I was still a little jet-lagged.

"Esmeralda will bring your things over for you later in the afternoon," Quim said.

"Thank you. Does she require I pay for them now?"

I leaned forward to take the wallet from my hip pocket, but Esmeralda put a hand to my chest and wagged the forefinger of her other hand under my nose.

"No pay now. *Ma'logo* ..."

"Don't give her money now. She's not sure of the cost. Let her gather the items together and you can pay her when she gives them to you," Joaquim translated.

When the two of them had left I moved to a rattan *chaise longue* that had been placed in a shady corner of the patio, next to a door into the hotel lounge. Good place for a nap, I thought. The food, the wine, the sun, the air – I stretched out and slept till quite late in the afternoon.

The evening was coming on fast; by the time I awoke the sun was sliding well down the slope of its daily journey to the western horizon. A second chaise longue had been pulled up alongside mine and Maria Esmeralda, sound asleep, was stretched out the full length of it. I lay quietly and watched her.

On the floor under her head was a small package of light green wrapping paper, its edges held in place by transparent tape. I didn't want to open it for fear of making a noise and disturbing her, but I was sure it contained the items I had ordered earlier in the day.

Arms and Anti-Americanism

Anti-American feeling was strong in Portugal, but it appeared to come as a surprise to those who noted it – Americans as well as Portuguese. The two countries had long been close friends and allies. In 1942, during the height of the Second World War, both Britain and the United States had signed an agreement with the Portuguese to use the island air base of Lajes in the Açores in order to protect Atlantic shipping. Following the war, the Americans expressed a desire to renew their contract and continue to use the strip and its facilities.

Apart from the Cold War, and the utility to which the field at Lajes was put during this time in order to face off against the Soviets, post-war 'freedom movements' in the colonies of those nations who possessed them had picked up in intensity all over the world. The American voice of support for them was strong and persistent. Particularly following the Suez Crisis of 1956 Americans felt an obligation to champion the underdogs in all colonial disestablishment situations, and suddenly little Portugal was made closely aware that, friendship or no, the Americans were not going to back down in their efforts to up-stage the Soviet bloc where 'democracy' was concerned. The Cold War was on, but the Portuguese, particularly those who had settled in the colonies, read this as an alarming and unnecessarily unfriendly gesture by the Americans. The anti-American sentiment was especially strong in Angola. It was an antipathy more notable and of far greater complexity than any threats from the communist bloc, or the Congolese who were kicking up such a stink right next door. The Americans, with whom the Portuguese were supposed to be on friendly relations through NATO membership, were considered duplicitous, the 'Enemy Number One' that kept the Portuguese army on its toes all along the three thousand-kilometre frontier Angola shared with the Congolese Republic. The Americans were blamed for supplying arms, money and moral support to both the anti-communist Congolese, as well as the membership of the pro-west rebel Angolano movements headquartered in Leopoldville. The Portuguese administration occasionally expressed doubts and its 'serious concerns' about the validity of American 'friendship,' but there was no doubt at all in the minds of most Portuguese to whom I spoke on an everyday basis – the soldiers, the plantation owners, the businessmen in the towns. In these areas there was an alarming and almost universal mistrust of anything the Americans said or did; to many Portuguese in the streets and countryside, and certainly in the colonies, the Americans were just playing a Cold War game that ultimately would be most beneficial to themselves. More than once I heard the opinion expressed that if only the Americans would back off and leave Portugal's colonial problems to be solved by the Portuguese themselves, matters would then stabilize. The Portuguese had heard the British Prime Minister's dour warning about the 'winds of change' blowing across Africa; they had 'got the message.' Those to whom I spoke claimed they understood the western viewpoint but added that they themselves were perfectly capable of complying with, and overseeing, the broader demands for independence. Portugal could manage very well, thank you, if America would simply refrain from goading the antagonists. A cynical suggestion was discussed quite openly among the Portuguese – that if the Americans continued prodding, the Portuguese administration would eventually be persuaded to succumb to US demands for concessional rights over Cabinda's oil, which was all they really wanted anyway. Not a particularly friendly face-off.[20]

When one heard of a Portuguese casualty in the fighting, it was common to hear the Portuguese blame the Americans. It was 'their' ordinance that had been used. During the time of my visit the main trouble area was in the vicinity of Nambuangongo, between Luanda and Carmona – a small community less than two hundred kilometres from Luanda and a good three hundred kilometres south of the Congo frontier. But one did not hear of casualties very often. The Portuguese preferred to keep that sort of thing quiet. Not only would such news have been bad for morale, but the Portuguese themselves would have wanted it to be known they had the matter of fighting their war well in hand – that they had already won the war and it was now mostly a simple matter of mopping up. (The war was most assuredly a long way from being 'won,' and in fact never was; but in the face of propaganda necessity, that is what the Portuguese administration wanted the

---

[20] There were at least two sides to this consideration – yet the fact remains: with a few short breaks for negotiations, American financial support permitted Jonas Savimbi to perpetuate his war in Angola a total of 41 years. The war ceased almost immediately after Savimbi had been killed, so there is a measure of relevance to this argument.

world to think.)

The Portuguese claimed they had isolated terrorism into pockets, the chief of which was Nambuangongo. There was enough evidence to show they had achieved something of that order. But the question arose: how were arms being shipped to the terrorists in these pockets?

Regardless of the aid the Americans may or may not have been giving to the rebels, either directly or indirectly, there were also many tales (whispered around Luanda coffee houses and bars, or shrugged off in casual conversation) of Portuguese sharpies themselves selling arms to the rebels in northern Angola. Some people appeared to be making a fair living at it.

I mentioned these rumours to a young army officer. He was on leave in Luanda prior to returning to the Nambuangongo area, and his reaction was immediate.

"Do you know who could be doing it?"

I did not, but he followed up my negative answer with the tidbit of information that the last terrorists his men had captured in the Nambuangongo area had been carrying weapons marked with Portuguese serial numbers. In addition, some of the prisoners were carrying receipts for their weapons – bearing Angolano stamps and cancelled in Luanda. American collusion was suspected – perhaps a consortium of both American and Portuguese making handsome profits – Portuguese arms, American shipping and transport. In fact, looking at a strategic map of the fighting areas it seemed unlikely arms shipped from the Congo would be able to get as far south as Nambuangongo. The place is a long way from the Congo frontier. It was in an isolated pocket of land and, outside that pocket, the countryside was honeycombed with Portuguese roadblocks, inspection posts and patrols. Moreover, it would have been difficult for any arms shipments to reach Nambuangongo from the coast. In Luanda Joaquim had told me that in any twenty-four-hour period Angola's entire coast was being patrolled by six frigates of the Portuguese navy, and by radar-equipped aircraft. 'Russian fishing vessels' had been sighted within coastal waters, he told me, and Portuguese authorities had become afraid their enemies might be trying to land weaponry. I took the information with a pinch of salt. That standard of efficiency, that level of organized surveillance, seemed a little far-fetched by my reckoning.

It was in this same conversation that Joaquim had informed me rebel chief Holden Roberto, leader of the National Liberation Front of Angola (FNLA), was not Portuguese. When I checked later, I was to learn Roberto had been a descendent of the monarchs of the Kongo Kingdom, had been born in São

Salvador, Angola, but had moved with his family to Congo (DRC) when he was two. To my thinking this made him about as legitimate as anyone to fight for an Angolano cause.

Despite Portuguese military precautions there was still the possibility arms were being filtered-in from the north. A constant watch on the Angola/Congo border was impossible due to the terrain: rugged hills, thick bush, jungle. But, due to these same physical features, and the abundance of military security, it would have been extraordinarily difficult to transport even small quantities of light armaments overland as far south as Nambuangongo. On the other hand, it would have been quite reasonable to move arms in quantity to the Nambuangongo vicinity from points *inside* Angola – to the south of the fighting zone, for instance, around Luanda, or further east.

Both private and military planes flew into and out of Luanda on irregular daily schedules, as well as into and out of small airfields at other locations, and they could have achieved this with minimal or no control. Road checkpoints south of the trouble zone were not all that difficult to circumvent. I travelled on one small road to the north of Luanda, and the only checkpoint encountered consisted of a couple of African soldiers who looked as though they had had little better to do than wave at passing cars. In any case I was not stopped, let alone searched.

If some shady foreign operatives were indeed shipping loads of arms to the rebels, it also remained highly likely they would have been reliant on Portuguese assistance. If that was the case – possible, for there was no shortage of Portuguese, military or settler, who detested the Lisboa dictatorship – it is very possible there were individual Portuguese who would have been pleased to change sides in order to confound their own government. Authority was lax – security blankets were riddled with holes. And, of course, there was always the factor of unscrupulous corruption that accompanies any military action ...

Cambambe Safari

One of Africa's largest dams is located at Cambambe, and a small party of us gathered together at my Luanda hotel for a day's outing to visit it. Setting off, our excursion had all the outward appearances of a safari. Boxes of camera equipment, along with bags and boxes of supplies urgently required by the dam's administrators – all carefully wrapped in dirty tarpaulins – were loaded onto the roof rack. It was an open vehicle. Great vacant spaces, 'windows' without glass, gaped wide to allow for the entry of dust, grime and bugs. By the time we had cleared the city's outskirts we were already coated in a dry red powder and could taste the grit of Africa's fine topsoil in our teeth. We presented a sorry crew on our way out; by the time our journey was less than half-over we looked as though we had been slogging through the bush for a month.

Cambambe is a mere two hundred kilometres southeast of Luanda, but to get there one had to travel one of the worst highways south of the Sahara. Two hundred kilometres (about one hundred and twenty-five miles) is not a particularly awesome day's drive by Canadian standards. But then Canada's roads (bar, perhaps, stretches of the Yukon Highway in spring) are no match for Angola's when it comes to sheer discomfort. Not only was the road in terrible condition; we were making the trip in this Grade A bone-shaker of a safari wagon.

We comprised an eclectic contingent. Our driver was an ex-buck private in the Portuguese army who had recently received a painful injury to his right (accelerator) foot – the one he rested with unvarying and excessive pressure on the gas pedal. He brought a loquacious young friend to sit up in the front between himself and Joaquim, who pretended to be our guide and knew several of those who ran the dam operation. The young fellow – his name was Henrique – was Quim's equal in loquacious blather; he did his best at keeping up a running commentary for most of the journey. Proclaiming himself the auxiliary driver, this irksome blowhard remained turned towards the rear seat for almost the entire trip. He carried a rifle with him 'in case we run into an elephant.' Several times I found him catching at his breath as if about to launch into something truly intriguing when Joaquim would raise a hand to indicate nothing doing, and the boy would clam up before he got rolling. It seemed Joaquim's hand was the only thing that could stop him.

For all that, Joaquim was quite a wearisome gasbag himself. He started the day so fastidiously turned out in his military duds that he looked for all the world as if dressed for a role in the opera. At first it was strange the road dust did not dare to cling to him. His stories managed to impress Henrique, who was too consumed with himself to realize he was being upstaged by the lieutenant. The younger man, wide-eyed and attentive, seemed to egg on the old warrior – who then proceeded to prove himself just as wearisome. In some

125

way encouraged, Joaquim happily spun us yarns of his cavalry days, relating how he used to train the very finest of Europe's horses and riders for gymkhanas and shows in all parts of Europe. Being the unbridled Lothario described to me by Ronald Lawrence, he tended to use equestrian terminology to describe the women he admired, and likewise the various attributes of female anatomy to describe his horses. It was startling to hear him refer to the fine line of a lady's neckline as her 'withers,' her hair as a 'mane,' or the curvature of a well-formed leg as a 'fetlock.' Lady or steed, when he attempted to portray a 'mount,' it was difficult to know whether he was using the word as a verb or a noun. Ladies were 'beauteous beasts,' he soliloquized, and it was not a great stretch to imagine what he and his liaison of some romantic moment were up to when he took her for a 'gallop.' Throughout the day he gave us a somewhat curtailed demonstration of his prowess and form, riding the front seat of our clapped-out vehicle with the precision and straight-backed rigour of the finest horsemanship. As the day wore on, and despite his dandy attire he soon became (like the rest of us, we were happy to note) as dirty and bedraggled as the most disreputable traveller on a taxing road trip.

Riding in the back, bouncing like basketballs on a hard and unforgiving leather-covered bench, two Belgians and myself made up the balance of our party. Ours was a largely silent back seat participation – silent but for the occasional expostulation at the violence with which we were being thrown about, at times in danger of toppling from the vehicle. One of the Belgians, a hydrologist from the University of Ghent who had his own special reasons for visiting the dam, spoke reasonably fluent English; the second, an educationalist, spoke only French, and I had no capacity to say anything reasonably intelligent to him. My French has been known to make Frenchmen wince – as it still does. My back-bench companions and I were reduced to smiling a lot, more out of a reassuring sympathy than actual joy, making gestures and shouting monosyllabic gibberish at one another over the roar of the engine and the grinding of gears. Under my breath I muttered curses, grumbling mightily every time we hit a bump, so was readily disposed to convincing myself the shock and pain were personally intended. It was a pain exacerbated by the horrendous realization that later that very afternoon we would have to travel the length of this damned road a second time if ever we hoped to return to Luanda. By the close of the day the two Belgians and I were obliged to acknowledge a grudging envy for Joaquim's exceptional 'cavalier' capacities, both physical and spiritual; he rode the wagon with the ease of the horseman he described in his stories.

Hearing these complaints from the rear, Joaquim explained the road had suffered especially heavy damage through the constant stream of construction vehicles that had travelled to and from the dam site.

"Yes, but that was four years ago," wailed the Belgian who could wail in English.

"And we are repairing it," was the reply.

The driver swerved to avoid collision with a large African lady, straight-backed and proud, carrying a basket of fish on her head.

"The man who built this road is in jail now," Joaquim volunteered matter-of-factly.

"What did he do?" someone queried.

"He built this road!" replied Joaquim.

"So – he was a dishonest contractor who cheated the government. What happened to him ...?"

We were all interested to know more about this dishonest contractor, so the driver applied the brakes to pitch us all forward far enough to catch the rest of our guide's story. Someone said, "Thank you," and our driver grinned.

"Well, if you look – and you don't have to look too closely – you will see that the contractor was very sloppy. He laid the tarmac right over the top of the soil. See? No aggregate base, no rocks," Joaquim replied.

The rest of us were dumbfounded. How on earth could the fellow ever get away with such a thing!

Joaquim's answer was a shrug.

"Well, he didn't, did he? He's in jail."

The journey to Cambambe took a shade under four hours – exceptionally good timing considering the number of bends, swerves around potholes (large enough to bath in) and herds of goats we encountered. Not one of us was in a right frame of mind to be hugely impressed by Africa's second-largest dam when we finally got to it. One of the Belgians, seeing the immensity of the thing, enquired if perchance the contractor for this job was also behind bars...?

But the Portuguese staff at Cambambe were, of course, extremely proud of their dam. Every school year squads of children would make the same excursion we did. Bundled into and onto army trucks (sturdy vehicles) the youngsters would sally out to the dam like pilgrims to witness this magnificent achievement of Portuguese engineering skill – albeit the Portuguese who made the darned thing were a darker shade of brown than their fellow countrymen. It was an education for the children, even though getting there would have qualified as extreme and unjust punishment.

When they showed up, the children were told, as were we, that the hydro potential of the dam will one day be enough to service all of Angola with power – all with just four mammoth turbines. Right then only one was in operation, but it was sufficient to supply electricity to the entire city of Luanda and the township of nearby Dondo. And the one turbine, we were told, was currently working at a fraction of its capacity.

Work on the dam had started four years earlier. Today, and at the time of my visit, the concrete half-moon of the structure rises to a height of more than four hundred feet above the bed of the Rio Quanza. The barrier holds back a lake seven kilometres in length. Of the five hundred people employed at the site, three hundred were African (Cape Verde islanders were considered better workers than the locals). The two hundred Portuguese who worked at the site were all specialists.

Living conditions, Joaquim explained, were 'exceptionally fine.' No doubt this was why he was so anxious to make the trip to show them to us. A government man through and through, he wanted to impress upon us how the Portuguese were making an honest attempt to improve the lot of the territory's inhabitants. There was a distinct lack of the familiar mud-and-wattle huts so many Africans have lived in for generations; instead, row upon row of little brightly-coloured concrete homes dotted the hillside to the north of the river - which might very well have passed as encomium to Pete Seeger's colourful little boxes made of ticky-tacky.

The Portuguese rolled out the red carpet for their foreign guests. Over lunch we made polite conversation as we sat on the high balcony of the senior officials' clubhouse. Below us we could see the reservoir, the dam and the Quanza. In the distance the sunbaked African bush stretched away to the south.

"We must make an early start back after lunch," said Joaquim, a clear reference to the state of the road.

One of the Belgians looked up at him slowly, grimacing.

"Are there any plans for building a landing strip nearby?" he enquired.

Joaquim shrugged. His conversation was all splayed-out hands and the lifting of shoulders.

Receiving no reply, the Belgian drew a deep breath and commented with dry reserve:

"I am sure you will agree with me that the contractor of the road that led us here deserves to be in jail, *senhor*."

The poor fellow really did not want to face the only road back to Luanda.

We requested more rest-and-stretch stops en route, and at one of these we pulled to the top of a small rise to step out and watch a buffalo in the distance. We were just getting back into the car when there was a crashing in the bushes next to me. I spun just in time to see a flash of brown disappear from under my feet into the bushes.

"What was that?" I asked Joaquim.

"A bambi," he said – a duiker, the smallest of antelopes.

Henrique was prowling around the car holding his rifle at the ready, as though to defend us against some hideous jungle creature.

The Portuguese call the species a *bambi* because the animal in some way resembles the Walt Disney cartoon creation – a small buck, not more than two-and-a-half feet in height, long-legged and light brown in colour. There were small lighter patches on its back spilling over its flanks to its belly.

The sun had sunk below the horizon and the light was fading quickly.

"Spotlight!" Henrique whispered urgently.

But I had already turned it on. Quietly opening the car door on my side, I stood on the running-board to examine the creature. It could not have been more than fifty paces from me.

As though hypnotized by the light, the animal remained almost motionless in the bush, its delicate head held high to sniff the night air. It was quivering as it looked at me unsure, perhaps, as to whether to be curious or afraid. I should have spoken up or clapped my hands loudly.

I ducked my head back into the car to speak to the two Belgians, offering them use of the spotlight.

"Can you see it?" I asked.

They both craned their necks in an effort to see the animal, and both nodded their heads with enthusiastic delight. It was, indeed, a beautiful little creature.

Then the rifle cracked.

I had not been expecting that. Henrique had mentioned earlier he might want to do some hunting, but I had rather supposed he would prefer to set his sights on something more substantial than a *bambi*.

The light was not quite powerful enough to give Henrique a clear target image. Opening his door as quietly as I had done mine, he had used the hood of the car to steady his aim.

129

By any standard it was a poor shot.

He hit the duiker at an angle that shattered its backbone. It fell to the ground, crying like a child, and thrashed about in the roadside grass. Then it stopped thrashing and lay quivering on its side, only its eyes casting about in terror.

Both Belgians broke into a torrent of French-language outrage.

For a moment I was too taken aback to do or say anything. I watched as Henrique approached it with his rifle. Taking the weapon by the barrel, he made as if to club the *bambi's* head. But then it wriggled, and his blow went wild.

I ran up to him.

"Shoot it, man!"

"I don't want to waste a bullet," he whined.

Snatching the rifle from him, I put a round into the duiker's heart. The whole incident must have taken no more than a couple of minutes, but it coloured the rest of our journey to Luanda. Nobody spoke. Feeling in a way humiliated, or upstaged, once back in the car Henrique expressed anger at being deprived of whatever satisfaction he might have received from the act of the kill. He glowered sulkily like a child whose bicycle had just been confiscated. He knew what he had done, and needed to have his action justified.

All of us were angry with him for his insensitivity, his banal non-stop prattle – even for his abysmal aim. Before handing the rifle back to him I removed the clip so he would not be tempted to shoot anything else.

South to Lobito

On the morning I was due to catch a small four-seat aircraft flying south to the coastal port of Lobito, Joaquim sent a messenger to my room asking me to come to his office. There was someone there he wanted me to meet.

"I'd like to present to you a fellow traveller – another Joaquim," he said.

"Two Joaquims – that makes a team ..."

"There are lots of us!" said the new Joaquim. "*Muito gosto* – my name is Lemos. You may call me by the diminutive, Quim, if you like. It might help you to tell us apart … I'll be going to a number of communities in Angola, and I understand you'll be travelling, too. Perhaps we shall meet up along the way …?"

He spoke excellent English.

"He also has business to attend to in Lobito, so he will be sharing your flight south. As you can see, he speaks your language quite well, so he might be able to assist you from time-to-time. It's a fine morning. You should have a very pleasant flight down the coast," said my minder, lieutenant Joaquim.

Once airborne, we climbed to about three thousand feet and levelled off over the top of the coastal cliffs. Below us were spread some of the loneliest beaches in the world. We covered the four hundred-kilometre distance in something under two hours. With the South Atlantic Ocean to starboard and the expanse of Africa on our landward side, we had a clear mid-morning view along the entire route – an opaque heat-mist in the far distance of the hinterland, but not a cloud anywhere close enough to impair a perfect wide-angle panorama.

Off the port wing was a wide expanse of yellows and ochres, dark browns, greens and blues, and a perplexing kaleidoscope of shadow patterns. Borrowing binoculars from the pilot, I spent several minutes scouring for signs of life on the ground above the shoreline and along the length of several of the beaches. In the muddy waters verging the estuary of a small river I imagined I caught a glimpse of a crocodile, only noting him because of his quick movement; but the more I studied the scene the less I could make out. I tried to convince myself, then decided there was nothing there. Nothing at all that looked alive – not a person, not an animal; just a vast and starkly empty landscape. Hot and jagged, it all had the appearance of a diorama created by an angry god on a yesterday that must have lasted a full forty million years. The scorched earth had been thrown down like a counterpane, carelessly rumpled by unearthly upheavals or heavenly negligence. Gazing over this sunburned scene out of the plane's window was hypnotic, like looking into a bonfire on a night so dark the eyes are stayed and can see naught else but the flames.

"It looks so absent of any signs of life, so empty …!" I shouted to Lemos over the sound of our engine.

"Maybe from up here, but I can assure you it's not! Right down there we have examples of every animal in Africa – and a substantial human population as well. Six or seven millions …"

(That demographic was a figure I came to review with considerable surprise when I knuckled under to the writing of what you are this minute reading. By the end of 2017 Angola's population had increased to just under thirty million – more than a four-fold increase in fifty-five years. This despite the hundreds of thousands killed in over forty years of one of Africa's bloodiest wars.)

"If you can't see any sign of life on the left, take a look out your right side …"

My companion was laughing at me, so I did as I was bid. At first the expanse of the South Atlantic spread into the haze of the distance and looked even emptier than the view on the other side of the plane. But then I looked down into the shallows closer to the coast. In some places the waters were almost pitch black, but in others the continental shelf was much lighter and so transparent I could easily see the seabed, its yellow sands sliding gradually out into the deep until I could no longer distinguish anything but the solid mass of black ocean waters.

Silhouetted against the uniform light of the shallows, ghost-like and slow-moving as if their batteries were losing charge, hammerhead sharks – hundreds and hundreds of them – turned lazy circles as if part of an outsized computer screen-saver. No other species appeared; just a teeming mass of these strangest of sea creatures, with their peculiarly-shaped heads and offset eyeballs.

In some way it was as if the plane was flying the length of a fulcrum that lay along the African coast – on one side the extended mass of an inhospitable burned-out landscape, devoid of any signs of life; on the other the broad ocean shallows full of fearsome life and activity. Although it makes perfect sense, I have never been especially partial to the concept of the food-chain and have not generally felt kindly towards those beasts interested only in devouring me for lunch. I looked down into these coastal waters and saw there a horrifying danger. I read somewhere there are nine different species of hammerheads and learned that only three of them would be interested in eating me. Comforting. Which ones were below me now? I was happy not having to enquire too closely, but the mere thought of being in the water with these animals gave me the willies. I do not care for crocodiles any more than I care for sharks, and would prefer not to become too intimate with either, but I recall how the thought occurred to me just then: if I was required to leap left or right from the safety of my present seat, I would have chosen to go to the left – in the hope that if I managed to get my feet onto dry land again, there just might be a fighting chance of avoiding the crocodile I fancied had been there a few minutes ago. Strong swimmer though I was, were I to land in the sea I would be entirely out of my element and without a ghost of a chance of negotiating with unfriendly hammerheads ...

Motivated by such paranoias, I lifted my gaze and looked out the front windscreen instead, over the pilot's shoulder. The coast and the beaches and the cliffs stretched out for kilometres before us without sign of town or habitation. All was empty, and we were heading for a zone known globally as the Skeleton Coast. An alarming name, but it was a relief not to have to look down on the hammerheads. The crocodiles, too, were not quite so close, nor so numerous ...

Oh dear! The world is so filled with nasties.

Lobito was a seedy, emaciated little town in those days, so Lemos and I not only found ourselves staying at the same hotel but that evening connected again over a sundown supper in the hotel dining room. He told me about his business ventures, how he had come to Angola as representative of a shoe manufacturer in Lourenço Marques, Moçambique's capital – the city he called home. He was in partnership with his brother and a friend and was now travel-

The baobab tree – meeting place on the outskirts of Lobito

ling across the continent on his first extended business trip in an effort to set up outlets for the company's lines of footwear in Angola's primary towns. It all sounded perfectly plausible, and I soon found I quite took to this new acquaintance. He had about him an easy curiosity and zest for life. Although quite a bit older than myself he came across as a much younger man, someone on the brink of a profitable breakthrough in his life – a display of the sort of infectious and up-beat personality that easily draws people to his table.

That first evening together the two of us laughed a lot over our meal. One of his merrier conversational sorties was his explanation of the word 'Canada.'

"The Portuguese were everywhere," he told me. "They gave names to places all over the world – your own country, for instance …"

"Oh …?"

The Portuguese had been fishing off the Atlantic coast of Canada for centuries, he said. They had been emigrating there for a long time, too, settling mostly in little shelters and communities they had built for themselves along the shores of Newfoundland. One must assume they would know something about the place, he insisted seriously. He was aware Canadians themselves have several curious stories concerning the name of their country – some accurate, others tongue-in-cheek – so he felt there could be no harm in adding yet another to the list. It was the sort of basic knowledge a patriot should have concerning his country, but doesn't always, don't you think …?

Dogmatically, with wrinkled brow and mock seriousness, he set about cracking this nut for me, setting me straight on a most obscure tidbit of my homeland's trivia: the origin of the name Canada.

It was Portuguese, he assured me.

"Really …?"

I played sceptic, listened without interruption …

"Sure, it is! The name is taken straight from the Portuguese – '*cá*' meaning here, and '*nada*' meaning nothing. 'CA-NADA: here is nothing.' It was the first impression of ancient Portuguese mariners when they sighted the ice-bound coastline of your country …"

He watched my face, noting my doubt.

"Do you mean to tell me you don't know the origin of the name of your own country?" he chided, insistent and laughing triumphantly. He wriggled with satisfaction at his victory over me, although I was sure even he must have had some doubts as to his story's accuracy. I laughed, too, but not for the same reason …

I cannot be sure where I learned this most significant piece of information, but from infancy I had always known the word Canada was derived from the First Nations peoples of Stadacona village – the place that is now Québec City. The story as I had it concerned the French explorer Jacques Cartier who took a group of Iroquois back to France with him, and noticed they referred to 'kanata,' a Huron-Iroquois word, when speaking of their homeland.

A young fellow who had joined us at the table chimed in, assuring us how well suited to Canada were Portugal's earliest settlers there.

"Why would you say that?" ignorance prompting my foolishness, and vice versa.

"Because we Portuguese have been drinking alcohol for so long, since we were very small, and have so much of it in our bodies ..."

"Huh?" I couldn't believe my ears, but his earnestness drew my attention.

It turned out he had a brother living in Canada. One night when it was very cold – several degrees below zero, it seems – this brother collapsed by the side of the road as he was walking home. He was found by neighbours the following morning – alive, I was assured, "because the alcohol in his blood wouldn't freeze."

On the un-tested assumption that further nonsense might be avoided by merely going along with his story, I succeeded in closing him down by nodding seriously and feigning astonishment. How could one rationally do otherwise?

Lemos, seeing no dissension on my part, chose to acknowledge the fellow.

"See...?" he said to me pointedly, as if my silence indicated I had had a revelation.

The young man who had come to our table uninvited was named Dino. He was the drummer in a small combo playing that evening at a local *boite*.

"I want to invite you both to come to the club tonight and hear my group playing. I think you will enjoy it – the whole town will be there ..."

We agreed to go. Dino was a chirpy, chatty fellow. On the surface he might have come across as naïve, even frivolous and something of an annoyance, but there could be no denying his taut-sprung intensity. This showed itself clearly enough when he spoke of his music; at our table he spoke of little else. It was the clearest evidence of his greatest confidence, the one thing he knew best. When he spoke of his music, he became animated, enthusiastic as though he had only recently come upon it himself and was now adequately liberated to proceed claiming it his most prized attribute. In a positive way it helped him face the realities of his existence in this remote corner of remotest Africa. A man as dedicated to classical opera as Dino was to his invigorating dance music might have had a decidedly difficult time in Lobito; so, too, would a ballerina, or a Shakespearean actor, or a graduate of the Paris Beaux-Arts. But Dino gave out the distinct impression he was in Lobito to stay, that the accumulated cultural content of this place (plus its sun and beach) was more than satisfactory for his purpose until well into the future – and perhaps forever. Lobito was his kind of town. Here he would make his mark. What he most needed to do at this stage of his life was persist with his rhythms and catchy funk, the harmonies he so dearly loved. In time Lobito would grow around him like a cloak, nestle him in the comforts a casual visitor might not see, furnish him with purpose and everything any man would require to fulfill his needs – which would of course include fame and riches …

He had to go off for a rehearsal right away, so could not take us there himself, but he explained just where the club was located, and we all agreed to meet up there within the hour.

Considering Dino's build-up, the *Boîte Exótica* was something of a surprise when we finally found it – a little out of the centre of town tucked in among a cluster of high palms on the edge of the beach. Its setting on the sands at sundown proved a mystic scene – a couple of low wattage light bulbs being the only illumination of its exterior. The place looked charming in the low light of evening. The interior was moderately better lit, yet despite the illumination a few moments of concerted eye-strain were required in order to be able to see wall-to-wall across the club; its deliberate dimness was greatly exacerbated by the smoking habits of patrons and staff. The floor was of poured concrete, but the rest of the place – walls, roof, ceiling – appeared to be hammered together out of driftwood, large gaps being covered by weathered planking, rotting plywood and strips of torn-open burlap coffee sacks, plantation names yet visibly stencilled in black, red and green inks. The place was wide and spacious, thus requiring two rows of interior support posts for the ceiling and tin lid above it – the posts also of undressed wooden poles that had likely been scrounged off the beach. There was a stage at one end standing only one shallow step higher than the 'dance floor.' Beside it there was a bar and small smoke-blackened kitchen. Perhaps twenty cheap metal tables and their accompanying paint-chipped and clanky metal chairs were scattered higgledy-piggledy around the edge of the club. Inside, *Boîte Exótica* was not charming. It would have required a raucus band of loud trumpeters and a crowd of two hundred howling-drunk patrons who'd have given not a pirate's damn what the place looked like as long as the booze was flowing to qualify for that adjective.

There was none of that the night we dropped by.

A big black mutt dog with sway back and splay legs loped over to slobber a welcome as Joaquim and I entered at the door. The dog's master, who turned out to be the owner of the club, ran behind the animal hopelessly trying to stop it from jumping up on the guests. The fellow was too clumsy, too slow – and three sheets to the wind, besides. The mutt had already collided with my companion – not so much a jump; it was an old dog, and the condition of his legs would not permit more than an ungainly lurch. It crashed into Lemos who stepped backwards in order not to fall over but, in doing so, upset one of the steel tables and sent it clattering to the floor. The owner himself was of no assistance. His eyeballs rolled and he burped whisky, a cocktail of bilious stomach acids mixed with a cheap alcohol, the stench of rancid sweat given off by a long-unwashed body. He advanced hand extended. Before he could get his words out, though – greetings for us, curses for the dog – he somehow managed to get one of his rubbery limbs tangled around the metal leg of a lone chair. The contortions required to maintain his balance caused him to step onto one of the dog's paws, and this brought on a solo canine performance of ear-splitting yelps – which then set off a chorus of bellowing from the kitchen and the angry entry onto the scene of the owner's wife. Cursing her husband in a loud shrill voice, she took the mutt by the collar and dragged him across the dance floor into the blackness of the kitchen.

The owner would have fallen except that by now he had hold of my hand and I was able to stabilize him, keep him upright. His half-closed eyes did not quite connect with mine, but his mouth formed a grin.

"Zhou're velcome!" he slurred. "Zhou're ze forin dignity zat graces my *palais de dance* – and I am honoured …"

Quim and I were shown to a table at the edge of the dance floor, and a bottle of some obnoxious liquor (perhaps the same gaseous brew that soured the owner's breath) was plonked down before us so we could sour ours, too. Dino and his fellow musicians had just finished a set. He ran over to us, big smile, as he angled for compliments.

For my taste the group was unsynchronized, cacophonic; it was a painful intrusion to my inner ear, and drowned out any possibility of conversation that might have been worth conducting. I looked across at Joaquim and he was smiling beatifically, busily searching for words to praise the artistry of the drummer and his rag-tag group of virtuoso wizards. I told myself it was going to be a long evening, and when Dino finally returned to the stage I turned in dreadful disconcertion to my table companion. Before I could launch a single word, however, he shouted above the din:

"Aren't they fantastic!"

I was instantly choked silent. Grinning at Joaquim like a fool, it seemed the best thing I could do would be to remain silent and permit him to enjoy himself. I looked desperately about the room to see what reaction was emanating from other patrons, but in truth there were too few of them, and they were scattered about at such a distance from our table, that I could see none of their faces through the thickness of the atmosphere, let alone tell what was in the mind of the person behind each mask. Much better to shut-up and meditate.

But conditions in the club and in my head were hardly conducive to meditation. Many of the tables were empty; Dino's estimate of audience concentration – 'the whole town' – was far from accurate. The tables and chairs might have accommodated one hundred people, but I counted those who were clearly clientele rather than staff or band. They numbered eight.

This proprietor was a Greek named Titos. He was dark complexioned, short and with a paunch, and wore at least three days of growth on his jowls. For a shirt he wore a singlet, and his trousers looked as though he had been working in the oil pit under his car. Thongs served as footwear. Before the next set, he took a microphone and looking straight at me, announced:

"To honour the noble guest from Canada ..."

He waved a hairy arm vaguely in our direction, giving us a clear view of his faded mermaid tattoo. The amplifier screeched so loudly we could barely distinguish his words:

"...Lola, special import exotic dancer of Paris ... will dance for zhor delight – ze famous dance of ze *Legend of India* ...!"

His voice lifted with an exclamation mark – *Boîte Exótica*, indeed!

At the very next table to ours, lying across it like a slab of fish about to slide off its market counter, a woman – late thirties to mid-forties – had failed to move so much as a muscle since we had entered and sat down. I had taken her to be asleep, although she was still clasping in the hand of one outstretched arm a tumbler half-full of a yellowish liquid. I could smell it but could not be sure whether its perfume emanated from her glass or the pores of her skin. I suspected it to be the same brand of rotgut Titos had been consuming, only that she had likely been into it the entire afternoon prior to our arrival. It was a fluid that served to float her to the halls of oblivion, but she looked as though her barge had been towed into place by the tousled black locks covering that portion of tabletop not occupied by her out-flung arms and motionless torso. She was bare-legged, wore no shoes of any kind and, though

I presumed she must have been wearing panties, she clearly wore no brassiere under a slip so skimpy she might as well have been stretched out starkers.

As Titos made his announcement, Dino began a long and expectant roll on his drums ...

To my mind, and perhaps Lola's as well, there was a matter of uncertainty as to whether this was her theatrical cue. Upon hearing her name Lola raised her head and languidly looked about the room. Slowly her eyes came to focus on Joaquim and me, then she tucked in her chin, drew herself up – and rose unsteadily from the table beside us. Watching her – a slow-motion film clip of a car crash passed before my mind's eye – moment of fascination at something so fast moving so slowly. I recalled once being a participant in a disaster in which the car I was riding slammed into a solidly-planted tree. The cessation of speed proved a sudden factor, but the mind registering the instant of impact, interestingly, seemed capable of recreating the drama in an endless loop of stills ...

Once perpendicular, Lola hurtled pell-mell around a dance floor that had recently seen neither broom nor mop, with the result that her bare feet were soon the same dirty grey colour as the unforgiving concrete. Her face was a study in concerted determination, and this had the effect of puckering her lips into what would have been a terrifying kiss had she attempted to plant it. Her eyes had rolled back under their heavy lids so she would not possibly have been able to see the object of such a fearsome act of passion. Likewise, she would have been unable to distinguish clear space from posts and metal tables and chairs – a factor that became evident as she collided with several of each. At one point she stubbed a grubby bare toe against someone else's booted foot carelessly left in the path of her maelstrom. She thumped into one of the waiters serving a tray of drinks. She knocked over a chair. She staggered and spun, then spun and staggered – now and again beaming along her arms to locate the expressive sweep of the occasional lost or stray hand. The motion had the added advantage of helping her recover her balance. Determination personified, was Lola. Both Joaquim and I were wide-eyed and muttering – he with his acute embarrassment for her (I think he thought she was giving me a poor image of his homeland and its people); myself in prayer because I wanted nothing less than for the lady to conclude her performance as soon as possible and sit down.

It happened quicker than I had imagined.

For an instant something had distracted me, and it was only out of the corner of my eye that I saw Lola winding herself up like the spring of a jack-in-the-box. By the time I had turned my full attention back to her again it was altogether too late for Joaquim or myself to attempt anything like an intervention. At full charge, and with her eyeballs rolled back to view whatever she possessed for a brain, she propelled herself like a rocket across the open space of the dance floor. Right in front of our table, giving us a front row display of the cellulite layering her upper thighs in dimpled white blotches, she performed a mid-air-splits – and passed out a full metre above the level of the concrete floor. She fell as would a wet fish cast alone and forlorn onto dockside from the hold of a grubby trawler – the day's take, splat – and moved nary a muscle. For some seconds she lay flattened and inert, spread-eagled like a starfish when the tide has gone out.

Snorting and snuffling as though he had just found his dinner bowl, Titos' black mutt loped over and pushed his mutton-fat muzzle into Lola's crotch. There were shouts from band members on stage and Titos, tottering like a brick wall in the instant of its collapse, appeared above his special import guest from Paris, grabbed her under an armpit, and dragged her away to the darkness of the kitchen in much the same way his wife had earlier dragged away the dog.

"The show appears to be over," Joaquim announced, and Dino was still beating his drum.

Black, White and the Mix

Everywhere I went in Angola I saw African youngsters scratching a living for themselves in the towns and cities – peddling newspapers on street corners, selling lottery tickets or toting around shoe-cleaning outfits in the hope of drumming up a two-cent shine.

They were invariably dressed in tattered rags. Often it was their mothers who sent them into the streets, and they had better have something useful in hand when they returned home. These children were never seen as store clerks, waiters, or hotel bellhops. These sorts of jobs went to older white or *mulato* children. There was no official racial segregation in Angola, but there was indeed a brand of discrimination. It was a distinction born of financial ability. Most poor people were African, and it was they who formed by far the larger share of the bull-low class, priced-out every time. A built-in segregation.

The Portuguese were proud of claiming there was no racial segregation here. "Everybody's as good as the next man – within his class," I was told –

not once, but many times.

The truth was that one group had very little in common with the other. While the whites to whom I spoke claimed they were more than willing to assist and work with the Africans any way they could, it appeared interests, occupations and lifestyles worked against them – on all sides. Lobito was small, dynamic and go-ahead, and it was clear the Portuguese who lived in the town were there on some kind of specific mission that kept each of them so busy with his own individual life he had no spare time or energy for anything or anyone else. Jobs tended to be technical, yet there were few if any technical training facilities yet developed, and the apprentice system was haphazard at best, useful for some, perhaps, but leaving behind the greater population of those who might otherwise have been included as viable workers. While spoken intentions were commendable, anything beyond the expression of them that might have entailed earnest action tended to bring forth negative attitudes amounting to little more than a critique of the plight of 'our' poverty-stricken Africans. Explanations of 'why,' and at best the enquirer would be met by an overwhelming sigh of well meaning but useless compassion. White concerns exhibited a surfeit of pride in personal achievements and acquired status; it was easier, perhaps, for the whites to put to one side the problems the Africans had to face every day. I thought I detected something like the admission: 'The poor devil's drowning, true, but I'll wait to see if he surfaces – then give him a hand ashore …'

By and large the Africans (those not baring arms in the northern jungles) appeared to have learned the severe lesson of knowing their place. When one passed groups of them walking by the sides of the roads in the country round about, they would stand back and doff their hats. When you passed through a doorway very often you would find an African stepping forward to hold the door open – and he'd sometimes bow as you passed. When you stopped an African in the street to talk to him, to ask directions, perhaps, he would remove his hat and stand to attention – then twist the hat awkwardly in his hands, not knowing quite how to look you in the eye because you were a "white *senhor*."

There was certainly a racial barrier here – a sort of in-bred discrimination born of subservience that had no recognition on paper.

But it existed.

One day I was sitting in a restaurant having lunch when an African boy came in, trying to sell lottery tickets. The only clients who could afford to eat there were Portuguese whites, or *mulatos*. The boy approached each table in turn, trying to catch people's eyes and offer them an easy win. It would have been a simple matter to notice him, to turn to him and say 'no thank you' – to look at him at least.

But that is not what happened.

The kid stood there, sheepish and ignored, waiting for someone to look up, not daring to interrupt the flow of talk or whatever was passing between the white people at the table. He would just stand, in silence, right beside a table of restaurant clients, and the people seated would ignore the boy, talk around him or through him as though he did not exist.

Finally, acutely embarrassed, the youngster would give up and move to the next table – where precisely the same thing would happen all over again.

It was an agony to watch.

There was a young fellow in Lobito, African, who was quite unable to use his legs. They were stunted, thin and warped. I saw him on several occasions crawling through town – and his hands and stumpy legs bore a hundred callouses from years of getting about that way. I watched one day as he was trying to cross a busy street. He would wait for the traffic, looking for an opening, then painfully strike out between the lines of cars.

At one point he misjudged, and the car had to come to an abrupt halt to avoid hitting him. The lad was terrified – and the driver blatted hard and long on his horn, screamed an abuse, and passersby gathered around – not to assist in any way, but to tell the boy in the gruffest possible way to go back to the side of the road and wait until traffic had passed.

Perhaps the most pitiful incident of all (what is the cause, and to what degree, does one man wince at the pain of another?) was on the occasion when I was walking out of a hotel in Benguela. I had just bought a packet of cigarettes at the bar and was using the bar exit onto the street – an open doorway, a patio of mostly empty tables at that particular hour of the day, and then a long ramp down onto the sidewalk.

In the doorway I passed an African on his way in. He was dressed in a tattered and soiled army jerkin, with the remains of an old blanket thrown about his shoulders. He had no shoes, and his feet were clubbed and calloused.

He was blind, tap-tapping his way forward across the hard ramp surface with a whitened stick.

The fellow had evidently lost his bearings and, with the ramp leading directly into the building, he was unable to tell that he had wandered up off the sidewalk and was entering the hotel bar.

I passed by but turned when I heard the angry shouts of several of the Portuguese waiters and the bartender.

Ejected: this blind old man failed to meet Benguela hotel dress code

Bewildered and now flustered, not knowing which way to turn, the blind man was forcibly turned around and pushed back to the street ramp in the roughest and most aggressive way.

When I enquired of the waiters why they had been so unpleasant to the fellow, I was curtly informed:

"He was wearing neither shoes nor necktie, and that is against the house dress code."

There was an open-air cinema in Lobito that was a major attraction. A very large screen had been built of whitened masonry, the wide pit area in front of it being an open and informal bar-cum-ice cream parlour with interspersed and irregular concrete furnishings. Large slabs of masonry were intended as tables, smaller ones were spread about to act as seating, with liberal spacing all around to allow for easy access and walkway space. It was like a small park, and both young and old enjoyed visiting during the afternoons. A film would be shown once the sun had gone down.

On my last evening in Lobito, Lemos and I decided to visit this unusual social facility to see what was playing. It was within easy walking distance of the hotel, so we ambled over to the place well before sundown.

"Where are you headed tomorrow?" Joaquim enquired.

South, I told him, to the inland city of Sá da Bandeira, and from there to Moçâmedes, a port and rail terminus not far from the Namibian frontier.

"Ah-ha! You'll be going into the mountains of Sá da Bandeira, and the desert at Moçâmedes – so you will be seeing a variety of landscapes, perhaps animals, too … you are going to have a great trip!"

We arrived at the outdoor cinema and ordered beer at the bar counter. Standing there, travel companions and friends clearly supportive of one another, were two exceedingly Arian-looking young men, both with striking blonde hair, sun-bleached to the point of near whiteness, their athletic bodies tanned and vigorous. Arian gods, both. They were dressed in almost uniform bush shirts and sturdy ankle boots, one in khaki shorts the other in lederhosen. The shirtsleeves of both men were rolled up to exhibit athletic biceps. They addressed us in English, and I was not surprised to hear their speech carried the heavy guttural overlay of strong German accents. They had sampled the beer an hour or so before our arrival, so now both were in good spirits, bright-eyed, laughing and joking. We quickly learned they had immigrated together from Germany to Namibia, where they were living in Windhoek – one working as a builder, the other as a mechanic. They were now on holiday, having driven north across the Namib desert in a specially-equipped four-wheel-drive vehicle. They had been two or three days in Lobito and would shortly be heading north to Luanda.

We drank with them and enjoyed the stories they told of the trip north and then, just as the sun was going down, the light fading, and everyone was getting ready to watch the film, there was a sudden hush that came over the assembly around the bar. Heads turned.

A young lady, clearly of mixed race, had stepped into the dim electric halo of the bar's light, coming up behind the two Germans, tall and in a faded tan cotton dress that caught every puff of the evening's zephyrs. Her long black hair was pulled up on top of her head to reveal the curve of her neck, her bare arms seemed to float at her sides. In every aspect she exhibited the soft and total confidence of a woman who knew and understood her exceptional beauty.

Joaquim leaned towards me. Under his breath, whispered in my ear:

"Here in Lobito – would you ever expect …?"

Stunned and suddenly short of breath – perhaps assisted by the unlikelihood of the locale and the surprise at seeing such a graceful vision just there, just then – I do not believe I have ever encountered a woman who embodied so completely everyman's concept of such female perfection.

In turn, I commented to the two Germans:

"What a fabulous-looking girl ...!"

As if connected at both hip and shoulder, the two German boys turned in unison to see what had attracted everyone's attention – then quickly, again like synchronized clockwork, both turned back towards me, flustered and embarrassed. Both of them buried their noses in their beer glasses.

Then one of them, in a low conspiratorial tone so his voice would not carry too far, said to me:

"She doesn't look quite white to me ..."

Lemos heard the comment. He looked at me in puzzlement, jaw dropped. It was an extraordinary thing to hear said. Unreasoned racism was not new to me. I had encountered it before, but on this occasion there were no words that could accurately describe how the German had said what be said, with German accent and guttural phlegm.

My companion covered his eyes with one hand and gently shook his head in disbelief. We took our beer to one of the concrete tables set to one side, and prepared to watch the movie. The Germans did not join us, and we did not see them again.

Mountains, Sea, Desert

After breakfast the following morning, Joaquim Lemos shook me by the hand and wished me a pleasant journey.

"Thank you, Quim," I told him. "It's been good to know you. You have been a good companion for me here in Lobito."

"Well – we do not have to say goodbye just yet. We are both going to be a few more weeks in Angola, and it's very possible we shall meet again in one town or another."

We parted company at the hotel, and I set off for the Lobito airport to meet up with my pilot.

Sá da Bandeira is almost directly south of Lobito, but this portion of

Angola's coast lurches so far out into the Atlantic that, just a few minutes clear of Lobito's airport, ocean waters are soon at no point visible. Sá da Bandeira is close to two hundred kilometres inland from the coast. Below us at first was a broad coastal strip of green and arable land, but very soon we passed, on our starboard side, the gigantic mass of a lone mountain cluster – the Serra da Neve – that sat solidly between our line of southerly advance and the coast. We were flying at a height of about seven thousand feet, just a little lower than the highest peaks of the mountain. At that time of the morning, several hours before the sun reached its zenith at this longitude, the entire eastern face of the rugged mountain was tinted a brilliant brown-gold, painted those fantastic and mysterious colours as the day was rising from the heart of a land already well-scorched across its full continental width. Directly in front of us, looming and showing a dark countenance as yet untinted by the coming day, we could see the upcoming Chilengue – a rugged mountain chain that lies diagonally across the southwestern section of Angola, an extended arm of the country's core massif that pushes itself towards the coast in the extreme south of the country. The city of Sá da Bandeira is close to the tip of this arm at a height of five-and-a-half thousand feet.

I was met at the local airport by an objectionable minder named Rodrigues, who ham-sandwiched himself within the bounds of my personal periphery the instant I alighted from the plane. With a torrent of words, he immediately found reason to whisk me away in his car for an early and not altogether pleasant lunchtime grilling. His questions were incessant, and at first obnoxiously intimate, followed by a string of auxiliary sorties concerning the answers to matters of which I had no knowledge whatsoever, or that required the expression of opinions he himself would have been better able to address. Lunch amounted to one intense fishing expedition – to which, in my pique, I contributed as little as possible. Once he had decided I was a clueless imbecile (it did not take him long) he then turned table on me, and began to spout off on numerous matters that were of no concern to me at all, all the while breathlessly announcing (different words, but repetitious theme) he was enamoured of the great work being undertaken in Lisboa by the dictatorship – and what did I think ...? Absurd little man, he alone was prepared to save the province of Angola – and, in due course, the entire nation – a country that, thanks to men of his own sterling ilk, was just now rising from the ashes of centuries of poor leadership and governance – and would soon be showing the world at large, as Portugal's gallant navigators and discoverers had done in the XV century, how mankind should really take charge of its responsibilities to all nations and peoples and the general run of history itself ... Western Alliance, nothing! Portugal would show the way. Clutching his fork with a slice of beet impaled upon its points, he raised his fist under my nose to emphasize an unflagging and pompous patriotism, thereby obliging me to use an intervening hand to redirect his unsteady offering so that I could pop a morsel of lunch into my own mouth.

"Here in this region of the Serra do Chilengue the natives are particularly colourful," he announced, as though describing a flock of multi-hued birds in an aviary.

"The women go about bare-breasted, which would be shocking – except they make up for it by adorning themselves with beautiful silver costume jewellery ... If you are clever, you can buy it from them for very little money…"

Wink – wink.

"Gives a man a good excuse for studying these lovelies in detail. Ha! Ha! Ha!"

He talked so much and laughed so hard at his own witticisms he was quite unable to hear his own voice or register its shade of dark crudity.

After independence in 1975, the city of Sá da Bandeira was to be renamed Lubango. It was, and remains, the capital of Huila province, which takes its name from the principal ethnic group that lives on the high Huila plateau, the proud nomadic Mwila people. My crass minder, in mocking so lasciviously the womenfolk of the tribe, was referring to a relatively small caste that has steadfastly resisted the encroachment of colonial settlers or, for almost the entire period of the Portuguese occupation, refrained from living in or even entering the city itself. The women do, indeed, traditionally go bare-breasted in the countryside, and many of them still prefer to dress in the most colourful and flamboyant traditional manner. Their personal ornamentation, mainly silver jewellery and beadwork augmented with colourful raffias and fabrics, is nothing short of spectacular. They, and their menfolk also, often like to 'sculpt' their hair, styling it into solid shapes by caking their scalps with a thick brown mud and then letting it dry.

After lunch Rodrigues collected two other visitors to the city (perhaps he was their minder, as well) and the four of us drove into the wild mountain country that surrounds Sá da Bandeira – a dramatic landscape that, for a time managed to silence him and his infernal chatter. Within minutes we were clear of the city and driving through a terrain that had not changed in any substantial way since mankind first walked this way and hunted for his dinner in these bushlands. They were not the highest mountains I had seen, but they remain some of the most dramatic – deep jungle-filled chasms, the rivers of which had scoured their courses between sheer rock cliffs. Here and there these cuttings widened into broad valleys, their floors frequently carpeted by an impenetrable haze. In places the road we were travelling wound its way to heights from which we could look back and down onto the entirety of the city we had left behind.

Eventually we came across a small gathering of dilapidated mud and wattle houses, not even enough of them to call a village, and there were two girls squatting together by the side of the dusty road. They watched us as we approached up a slight incline and passed close beside them, coming to a stop between them and their view of what were clearly their homes and shelter. Rodrigues turned off the engine, and the girls did not move.

Mwila girls

"I told you we'd find some bare-breasted girls up here. Ha! Ha! I keep my promise ...!"

Uneasy, I had expected the girls to get up and run to the shelter of the houses. Although we had not seen anyone, it seemed a fair assumption they had family members inside or close by. But they remained rooted to the ground on which they sat. Our sudden arrival had been an intrusion, trapping them by coming between them and a bee-line they might have felt inclined to use. I had seen them glance at one another, but neither moved to get up or move away. If our sudden appearance bothered them greatly, they had simultaneously declined to show it. Instead they gave the impression they knew the safety of their home was a mere call away. They squatted in silence, and I could read on their faces a look of poise – a comforting – each must have felt to have her companion near. Rodrigues got out of the car and haughtily ambled his way over to speak to them, the swagger of a bully. From inside the vehicle we could see the scene clearly, Rodrigues standing with his hands on his hips, leaning forward slightly, patronizingly, the two girls looking up at him and responding to whatever it was he had to say. One of the girls lifted an arm and waved it in the direction of the houses as if telling her inquisitor where she lived.

Rodrigues returned.

"If you give them a few coins, you can take a picture of them," he said.

This brought to the surface an extraordinary confusion of feelings in me. I felt embarrassed, and my first instinct was to say that I did not wish to photograph them – that, indeed, I would have felt uncomfortable taking their picture. That would have been a lie; I very much wanted to snap this image of a timeless and chance encounter, knowing instinctively it was an image of history, and that in a year or two or three it could never again be recreated so perfectly, so naturally, as it was just then. One of the fellows in the car with me, maybe a somewhat less sentient journalist than I was, and making no bones about wanting the picture, climbed out of the back seat, walked over to the girls and snapped a few photographs. He spoke to the girls quite easily, squatted down beside them to examine more closely the intricate silver and leather ornaments each had about their necks and arms, and made offer to buy one of the girls' coil bracelets. She demurred, and a lengthy bout of haggling followed. He wanted the ornaments; she wanted more of his money. She was clever, held up a hand and shook her head. I watched. A good photo-journalist is like this guy, I tried to tell myself – move right in, say nothing, get the picture … It was a strong lesson for me.

"How much do you think they want for a photograph?" I asked Rodrigues.

"Nothing - or give her five escudos if you want. That's plenty," he replied.

At first I could not bring myself to take the photo, but instead took a twenty-escudo note from my pocket and was about to give it to one of the girls, when Rodrigues jumped at me.

"Take your photograph first, and don't give her so much!" he commanded, sheltering my hand and the money from the girls' vision.

"Give to her too generously, and the price will go up for the next man who wants to take a picture of her. She will come to expect that sort of money from everyone. Five escudos, that's enough!"

The girls did not miss a beat. They understood everything.

Five escudos, twenty escudos, it hardly mattered. Either sum was an insult, considering the extent of our heavy-handed invasion – but I had not yet quite figured out how to tell this damned minder to go to hell. He was eyeing me carefully to see I gave only what he had suggested, so I gave each girl five escudos, and clutched a fistful of coins in a hand in my pocket, prepared to drop them like Hansel and Gretel's breadcrumbs as I walked away from them.

Rodrigues glared. He had noticed I had not yet taken a photograph.

A tall man had appeared in the doorway of one of the houses, his wife at his side; parents of one of the girls, as it turned out, and aunt and uncle to the other. Rodrigues called to them and started to walk over, giving me the chance to place the coins I was holding in my hand onto the ground in front of the girls. They both smiled, and one of them quickly put her foot on top of the little pile. I winked at her and she looked back at me deadpan. Her companion reminded me of a conspiratorial Mona Lisa, and I hurried after my minder.

Mwila man and wife outside their home

We spent fifteen or twenty minutes passing the time with the older couple in the doorway of their home, and I was not hesitant to take a photograph of them. But walking back to the car with the journalist who had taken a few shots of the two girls, he asked:

"Why did you not take a photo of the girls? You paid them generously enough ..."

"It seemed a bit invasive," I told him, excusing my timidity and laughing unconvincingly.

Then I said: "Maybe you could just give me one of yours ..."

"No, no, no ...!" he replied instantly. "You'll get no better chance than the one you have right now to record something so unusual ... They're still sitting out there. Go talk to them. They'll let you take their photo."

His advice made me realize the uniqueness of where we were, gave me a jolt of renewed resolve. Of course, talk to them ... Their agreement would make all the difference.

"You were speaking to them in Portuguese? Would you translate for me, then?" I asked.

We approached the two girls, and the journalist again spoke to them. His manner with them was easy and informal. He shrugged his shoulders and smiled, a few hand gestures. Clearly he was speaking about me, and the two girls giggled.

"Take your shot," he said.

In the instant I clicked my shutter something distracted both girls, one squatting the other seated on the ground, and they started to look away. It was the only photograph I took of them, but it turned out to be a good one. Ignoring Rodrigues, I gave them an additional fifty-escudo note.

We returned to the car, and by nightfall the city.

I should have remained longer in Sá da Bandeira. It was a picturesque town, and I would have loved to have spent more time hiking in the *serra*. But the aircraft was costing money, and the next morning I was due in Moçâmedes. I had been told of a Canadian missionary headquartered in Sá da Bandeira, so determined to find him. That evening I enquired of the name at the hotel reception – Lutes – and learned he was well-known in the city.

"Ah!" shouted Rodrigues, who had come up behind me, listening-in. "I know him. I'll take you there!"

"I think I'd prefer to go on my own," I told him.

"Why? You think I smell bad – Ha! Ha!"

To me he did, but his stench was not just from his unwashed armpits. His was a slinky-stinky personality, and I did not like him. I very much wanted to get away from the man. Mistakenly I thought he would be sensitive enough to permit me to visit alone with a fellow countryman. I tried something else.

"Really, I just want to visit a minister ... perhaps make my confession," I straight-faced.

"Of course! Of course!" the bugger responded. "Protestants – you no doubt both have confessions to make to one another ... I've got the car. I'll take you there. You'll never find him by yourself."

And so I came to meet Rev. Donald Lutes at the Missão Evangélico. My minder drove me there, then tagged along behind me as I approached the missionary's front door. When Lutes opened it my minder stepped around me, and thrust his cheeky hand out for the minister to grasp. In an instant I could see by Lutes' eyes he was not pleased to see Rodrigues. His face was an expression of consternation, silently asking why I had brought this creature to his doorstep.

"My name is Jeremy ..." I started to say to Lutes over my minder's shoulder, but Rodrigues interrupted.

"I've brought you one of your countrymen for a visit. It seems he has something to confess – Ha! Ha! And how about you, reverend minister? Do you also have something to confess? Ha! Ha! You both go ahead. Don't pay any attention to me ..."

And with that he moved inside, past Lutes.

The minister was chagrined, that much was obvious to me; but he was too much a gentleman to comment about what I could see so clearly in his eyes. And, for sure, whatever was going on in Lutes' mind would have been a mystery to a man as boneheaded as Rodrigues. We were invited in and shown into a spacious living room. A lady I took to be Mrs. Lutes diplomatically left for the kitchen to put the kettle on for tea.

It was not until we were comfortably seated that Rodrigues finally thought to ask if he was welcome, or if perchance we wanted him to leave. It was clever timing, and barefaced. Good manners obliged Lutes to say he was more than welcome to stay; it would have been difficult for him to say otherwise. More than merely bad manners, a 'please go' would have indicated we had matters to discuss that we wished to keep secret from a man so palpably an agent for the political police – and that alone might easily have brought on a bout of vindictiveness. A 'please stay' was licence to listen-in to whatever passed between the minister and myself, opening a situation both Lutes and I might have felt an instinctive urge to defend – but only with the greatest difficulty, now, because the wretched minder had already been granted permission to remain.

Aside from the uncomfortable little game we appeared to be playing, I detected that Lutes had his own well-honed sense of grace and fatalistic good humour, and that this passed clean over the head of the idiotic but sinister minder he was obliged to host. A simple smile from the Canadian served to remind me he well understood the role of a man like Rodrigues, and how he presented a clear danger to the missionary, his family and their work in Sá da Bandeira – and even to myself. Then he openly and ever-so-graciously explained it:

"And *Senhor* Rodrigues would be the first to inform you of the difficulties facing us as a family were we, for instance, to return to Toronto on leave. Our visas to live and work in Angola are in fine shape for the present, but if we want to return after our sabbatical we would have to re-apply for new visas. With the war on it's by no means a certainty they would be granted, am I not right *Senhor* Rodrigues? We are Protestant missionaries, you see," this explanation was intended for me. "... Not missionaries of the preferred Church of Rome, and not Portuguese, so our motives are, you might say, somewhat suspect. Earning the full trust of the local administration has had its share of difficulties ..."

He beamed a kindly smile at my minder. Besides, he went on to explain, there was so much work to be done at the mission that he was frightened to be gone from it for too long a period.

"If I took a couple of months off, I'd never again get caught up with the paperwork ..."

Rodrigues, taking it all in, sat silent. He smiled back at our host, but not with his eyes. As Lutes very well understood, Rodrigues despised and mistrusted Protestants.

I was petrified and angry, and regretted I had brought about this encounter.

A small boy was following me across one of the town's central compounds. Barefoot and dressed in a ragged shirt and shorts, he was a happy lad with a fun smile. He had a rubber ball which he would throw in the air and catch, or else butt with his forehead and play across his shoulders, or sometimes trap with his nimble feet. Here was a man, *estrangeiro*, who wanted to take his photograph, so he put on a show of his prowess – twirling and dancing with his ball or turning somersaults. He dropped the ball onto the ground between his toes, urinated over it, then fell on his knees to scoop the dampened earth into a mound over the top of it.

Small boy and his ball

He must have seen I was startled, quizzical – so he jumped into the air, turned a full circle, and faced me again, hands on his knees and now holding the ball. He laughed, then turned and ran away across the compound.

Joaquim Lemos was the first person to greet me when I arrived at Moçâmedes airport.

"Hello, my friend!" he called across the arrival concourse. "I just now arrived from Lobito. Do we have time to sit over a morning coffee?"

We did not. I was happy to see his cheerful face again, and I had much I would have liked to talk to him about, but the local minder was already on my case and insisting we leave at once for my hotel.

"I have arranged for you to visit the prison farm at São Nicolau. It's a short flight there and back, so I suggest you change into comfortable old clothes and leave your suitcase at the hotel. You'll be back in Moçâmedes before nightfall."

In Lisboa at the start of this journey I had made a special request to visit São Nicolau. I had heard good things about it, unusual things: an oasis prison farm with a difference. I had been told the detainees had all been captured in the course of the fighting in the north of the country, but that some had been shipped down from the war in Guiné Bissau. To the Portuguese they were 'terrorists,' or 'bandits,' but with a confident eye to a future halt in military actions, apparently the Portuguese government was willing to take a stab at rehabilitation. São Nicolau was set up as an 'open village' surrounded by a broad and forbidding desert in place of guards, cells and bars. There was not the least chance to escape from such a place, for the desert at this location swept right into the sea, much as it did along the Skeleton Coast just across the southern frontier in Namibia. The idea was to make conditions at the camp so enticing and so humane that no prisoner in his right mind would want to flee. It was to be an experiment in re-engineering the nearly fallen. Just in case the thought of escaping did enter a prisoner's mind, however, inmates were informed of the vastness of the forbidding desert, that the few streams crossing it were filled with crocodiles, and the off-shore seas were swarming with hungry hammerheads. São Nicolau was supervised, I was informed, by a well-trained staff. Under this supervision the prisoners were given the material and equipment to build their own houses, plots of land were laid out for them to cultivate their own crops. A primary school and a health clinic had been established, wives and children were encouraged to join their menfolk, and every effort was made to create a social structure that put captives and guards on an almost equal footing.

It sounded almost paradisiacal – but I needed to confirm.

We circled the area before levelling off for a landing. São Nicolau was an oasis. From above it was easy to make out several hectares of green fields – cane and rice cultivation, sturdy palm and fruit trees. Teams of men were working in lines on ploughed lands and were easily spotted from the air. A broad beach separated the community from the sea, and otherwise the place

155

was surrounded by the sands and scrub of the Namibe Desert – which disappeared into the distant horizon. There was a scrubby-looking water course that failed to look as though it could produce so much as a single cup clean enough to drink, but apparently it was sufficient to produce ample sweet water for the area's extensive cultivation.

Worker/prisoners at São Nicolau

On landing, we were greeted by the prison warden, Gaspar Pegado, a great bluff fellow dressed in peaked cap, jodhpurs, boots and carrying a riding crop. He had a booming voice and a laugh that sounded like the explosion of quarry dynamite.

"Do you ride?" he asked, almost before my feet had touched the ground.

"Yes ..."

"Com'on, then! I've got your mount for you right here ..."

There was no time to check the girth strap or shorten stirrups. Two rather small horses were leathered-up and ready to go, and Pegado was in his saddle almost before I could pass off my jacket and briefcase to the plane's pilot. As I swung myself onto the back of the remaining mount, Pegado wheeled away and set off for the cane fields at a full gallop. There was barely time to toe my feet into the stirrups before my own mount started up in hot pursuit.

It was a memorable and exhilarating ride. We went flat-out for at least a kilometre before I could see Pegado begin to rein-in his little thoroughbred.

"Good run, no?"

"It certainly was!" I concurred, drawing up to him out of breath. "Do you do this sort of thing on a daily basis?"

"We try. It's good exercise for me, and good exercise for the horses. I have four in all, but it would be good to have more. We have races from time to time …"

"Races?"

"Oh, yes. Some of the staff ride quite well, and so, too, some of the inmates. We have a lot of fun."

Pegado could see the question in my expression and laughed.

"No worry! No worry! There is no way for the prisoners to escape, even if they wanted to – which they don't. They are all very happy here. You know, we constructed a prison block just beyond the houses over there, steel door, bars on the windows … and it's never been occupied. The inmates are happy here. They have work, they have their families. There is nowhere for them to go. We use the prison to store our vegetables …

"If for some reason one of them decided to take one of the horses and make a run for it, he wouldn't get very far. He would be dead before nightfall trying to cross the desert – and so, also, the horse – in which case that prisoner, if he still happened to be alive, would have to deal with me!"

Pegado took great pleasure in showing me about. On horseback, he led me to fields where straw-hatted men – prisoners – were working under a broiling sun, using hoes and shovels to prepare a series of irrigation ditches for several recently-ploughed fields. They were singing and, at least to my eyes, appeared content.

"Here we are planting turnips and cabbages. There are potatoes in that next field, over there … and beyond that we're experimenting with olive trees … Everything we need can be grown here … we are completely self-supporting. Soon we hope to market our produce in Lobito."

Pineapples were in abundance there. Coconut palms had been planted close to the main administrative area, and along a wide avenue leading off towards the cultivated fields. Fruit trees abounded, and there were fields of sweet potatoes, yams and beans. Pulled-up on the beach were several small metal-hulled boats used for fishing just off the coast; on shore were racks and shelves and several small thatched huts, all necessary for drying, storing and packaging an abundant catch.

I saw no restraining walls, barbed wire, pill boxes or guard towers. There was the small jail block but, as Pegado had explained, it was used for storing vegetables.

Seeing my expression of curiosity and surprise, Pegado shrugged his shoulders and laughed.

In the centre of the compound – it was laid out like a small village – there was a communal wash house where the wives of the prisoners could beat out their laundry and hang it all out to dry on adjacent lines strung between posts. The women smiled and sounded quite happy; in the fields their menfolk, too, sang and chanted, calling out to one another all day long … There was a chapel, and a school. As we approached, the teachers escorted their students outside the schoolhouse to present us a cheerfully discordant song of welcome.[21]

Impressive: at the time of my visit, São Nicolau was 'home' to three hundred and forty-four prisoners, all (I was told) former combatants, seventy-five of their wives and one hundred and fifty-three children – eighty-two of whom were students in the local school. These were Pegado's figures.

The plane returned to collect me at about 4:30 in the afternoon. I think the pilot had had a good lunch. We taxied out onto the dirt runway and, after the wheels left the ground, the fellow did a full throttle climb, then swooped around and dove straight at Gaspar Pedago on his horse. As we pulled up and levelled off just feet from the ground, the warden, laughing, raised his peaked cap and started his horse into a gallop beside us, racing the plane towards the central compound. The little game lasted only a few seconds before we had to pull up again to avoid the palm trees in the centre of the community. My stomach rose somewhere up near the back of my tongue, and my eyes must have popped open like two startled fried eggs.

At least my pilot got a laugh out of it. I needed to plant my feet back on the ground in Moçâmedes before I could join in the fun.

That evening there was a 'spontaneous' political rally in the centre of the town to show support and gratitude for the Salazar dictatorship in faraway Lisboa. It seemed an incongruity to me, so I paid attention from the sidelines. As was my habit throughout the journey, I wrote out a short description of

---

[21] See Appendixes #6 – Song, and #9 – Jonas Savimbi.

what I had seen and mailed it back to the newspaper in Toronto. By now I had learned about keeping notes – and duplicates of everything. I had absolutely no idea how efficient the postal services might have been – from Portugal, let alone from some dot on the map of Portuguese Africa. For all I knew whatever stories I sent out might have been lying at the bottom of a pile of papers in some nondescript propaganda office in Luanda, or Lisboa, or used as a combustible to boil the water for some clerk's afternoon cup of *chá*. It was to be months before I finally discovered how incredibly competent and reliable the Portuguese postal service really is – and the exceptional pride in it held by virtually everyone in the country. After many years of association with Portugal's *CTT (Correios, Telégrafos e Telefones)* I feel obliged to pronounce it one of the finest services I have ever encountered. (I was also to learn the country's first postal service was initiated by Dom Manuel I in 1520.)

It was not until I had arrived back in Canada at the conclusion of the trip that I discovered the headline writers had given my São Nicolau story from Moçâmedes the most perfunctory of titles:

Rally

More than 3,000 people, Africans and whites, packed along the streets and sidewalks in front of the Administration Building in this small Angola town – some of them obviously keen Salazar supporters, others just present to be entertained by a little first-class Portuguese propaganda.

It was a golden opportunity for pressmen to take photographs so that, the following day, the world at large could be shown how pro-Salazar the people of Angola are.

I watched the performance with a growing sense of alarm, as truckloads of Africans, obviously straight from the settlements and reserves, were wheeled in and told where to stand in front of the speakers' rostrum. They all looked starry-eyed and bewildered and, as the evening progressed, I'm sure many of them had no idea what was going on, or what was being said – or the significance of it.

Martial music, and people scattered among the crowd to shout 'Viva Salazar!' at the right moment, gave the whole performance such a bogus effect that I couldn't help mentioning it to one of the Portuguese officials present.

"Every country has to have something of the kind," he told me, smiling.

One of the first speakers was an old man who claimed to have lived in Angola more than 50 years. He always considered himself Portuguese, he told his audience, and Angola was his home. He addressed the crowd in a high-pitched, emotional voice, waving his arms, and thumping his point home with shouts of 'Viva Portugal!' that were picked up and chanted by his audience.

The shouting seemed to come from the front of the crowd where groups of youngsters, youth groups and football teams, stood on the steps of the Administration Building just under the speakers' rostrum, waving banners and shouting. I wandered to the back of the crowd and watched from there – and what I saw was a good deal more impressive than all the shouting and speech-making from up front.

Groups of people stood about silently – both Africans and whites. There was hardly a word from them – not a sign of the emotion that was so apparent under the rostrum. These people, the vast majority of the crowd by a long shot, were not in the least impressed by the show. I got the feeling that they had heard all this before; that the constant high pressure, and rather crude Portuguese propaganda-machine was losing some of its effect. Their indifference was incredible – but their pictures appeared in the following day's paper nonetheless.

Benguela Railway

For many of the first years of the XX century the Benguela Railway was the easiest way of shipping cargo – ore and passengers – from the Katanga copper mining area of Congo (DRC) to the Atlantic. Travelling in the contrary direction, heading east from the coast towards the interior of the continent, the line extends from Lobito and Benguela on the coast to Vila Teixeira de Sousa (now Luau) on the Congolese border, a distance of nearly one thousand three hundred kilometres. It cuts Angola into two almost equal halves. From Vila Teixeira de Sousa there was a rail link into the copper belts of Katanga and Zambia. Opened in 1903, the line was to suffer virtual destruction during Angola's colonial and civil wars between 1961 and 2002 and was completely abandoned in 1984. Colossal Chinese assistance has greatly modernized the rail links throughout Central Africa in recent years; they began repairs to the

Benguela Railway in 2006, and the full connection through to Luau was inaugurated in 2015.

However, in the early 1960s there was still a regular service in operation from the coast to all the interior stops along the line – over sixty of them. Nova Lisboa was my next destination; I hopped aboard the train in Benguela at 6:00 in the evening, sought out the club car, and passed an enjoyable evening with my fellow passengers until climbing into the bed in my cabin at ten o'clock. We were scheduled to arrive at our destination late in the morning of the following day.

It was as rickety an old train as I have ever ridden, only modestly more sophisticated, it occurred to me, than the famous narrow-gauge slate quarry Talyllyn Railway in southern Snowdonia. The engine was a steam locomotive that might have been a prop for a First World War movie (*The African Queen* comes readily to mind). Most of the coachwork appeared to have been part of the original early XX century assembly – decidedly Edwardian-colonial in aspect. The slat-seating and cabin partitions were structured in wood and covered with layers of a thick varnish that had suffered lamentably under the tropical sun, all of it now well-tarnished by decades of oil splash and coal and wood smoke[22], rain-season mud and dry-season dust. Seats of the bar car and day coach were upholstered and well-worn, but there was an old-world and ongoing effort to maintain a high standard of cleanliness and organization for passengers riding inside the coaches, and a semblance of well-mannered and attentive service by the African or *mestiço* stewards and attendants. Despite an undeniable charm, though, there was no escape from the strong odours of grease blended with burned eucalyptus fuel and the culinary aromas that emanated from the on-board galley. An inescapable pungent fragrance wafted throughout the train, permeating everything so that one simply had to get used to it. Opening windows helped; if smoke happened to billow in, elsewhere in the coach it could be persuaded to billow out.

For me, the movement and clatter of trains, the rhythmic tickety-tick of steel wheels passing over track-joints in the stilled darkness of a sultry African night engendered the deep sleep of something close to hypnosis. In the morning I awoke at first light to the shrill chatter and giggling of a bevy of Portuguese ladies hanging over the rail of the last car's tiny rear balcony. I pulled on a pair of pants and a t-shirt, and ambled aft to see what all the commotion was about.

The train was not moving very fast. These ladies – they were not

---

[22] Sparks causing track-side fires commonly caused havoc along the right of way.

youngsters, but mothers and grandmothers – had engaged in an early raid of the restaurant car and had made off with several loaves of bread and some cookies. They were breaking the baked goods into small morsels and throwing them over the balcony rail – to a host of small children who were running beside and behind the last carriage, doing their best to keep up with the train.

"*Olha aquele puto!*" – "Look at that kid!"

The dame who uttered that exclamation broke a bun in half and tossed the two pieces to one of the little boys racing over the sleepers. He failed to catch either of them, and they fell to the ground. Scrambling at the edge of the track to prevent any of the other children from getting to the pieces first, the little fellow used his football acumen by moving his legs and body around to guard what he felt was rightfully his. Then he snatched the bits off the grubby ground and crammed them into his mouth. Yet another boy broke past him and ran forward, holding out his hands and looking up, calling imploringly for the ladies to throw something to him, too. One of the women pitched a whole bun at him, then laughed delightedly when it hit him on the head and fell between the tracks.

"What are you doing …?" I demanded.

I had not seen any of these women on the train the night before and had no reason to know who any of them were. Likewise, they could have had no idea who I was, and possibly did not even understand the words I addressed to them now. But they could not have mistaken my tone.

One attempted to respond to me in English.

"They have no bread …" she said haughtily, then giggled stupidly with her companions. Her unspoken comment: as a foreigner in these parts, who was I to question them? I had no business asking questions that too easily could be taken as rebuke.

"Nor cake?" my sarcasm, echo of French revolutionary propaganda, flew past her.

Unable to express any clear reason for feeling reprehension at what they were doing, or even having a clear understanding of it myself, I backed away and started to return to my cabin. *This was my quarrel; this was not my quarrel.* Several other passengers – strangely all of them female – were leaning from their windows, likewise pitching food and small coins onto the right of way, watching and clapping as the children tussled one another to gather up the largesse.

162

A boy begs for food, running beside the track of the Benguela Railway

Then I took a couple of photographs of the kids as they raced after us. They ran their hearts out, trying their best to keep up with the train as it gradually picked up speed.

Snapping shots of them felt like feeding ducks at the park – not so different from the women I'd scorned.

For me it had never been easy to point a camera at someone for a candid shot, yet the ability to do so is a fundamental requirement for a photo-journalist – witness these children, and the girls at Sá da Bandeira. It has taken hindsight to realize how glad I am to have taken those shots – and others. The journalist must take the shot, then ask the question. There is no better way to take a worthwhile news photograph of people than to be bold – thoroughly intrusive. By its very nature a camera is an in-your-face instrument. It does not lie. It cannot edit, revise, control, audit or censure. The original image is right there. Any alterations must come later and be made deliberately. In general, the closer the lens to its subject the more detail it will see; back away and close detail vanishes, giving way to the generality of panorama.

Over the years I developed a rule of thumb – in two parts – that served to convince me I was making the subtle distinction between a journalist and a *paparazzo*:

First, was the photograph intended to augment a news story? If it was, then news is news, intrusion would be total, as brute and in-your-face as was allowable (or safe) – and there would be no payment on offer for any number of shots.

Second, if the photograph augmented a feature – an explanatory story not qualifying as news – then permission would be sought, apologies would be made for intrusion, and a modest fee might be on offer (even if not always demanded).

The techniques of photography have changed mightily since the introduction of electronic digital imaging. The use of film (some purist photographers fervently believe there is no substitute for it) can be restrictive – not least is the fact that the length of a celluloid film roll in its cassette must be limited, thus restricting the number of shots that can be taken before re-loading. A long roll of 35-mm film will contain space for perhaps thirty or thirty-six shots. On this journey I used, almost exclusively, a small Japanese twin-lens reflex camera with an excellent lens. The negative was a respectable four-centimetres square; the rolls permitted no more than twelve exposures.

Press photographers would happily use up metres of film at any one time – the assumption being if one shot does not work out, the next one might. But when one is carrying limited quantities of film into areas where replacements cannot be purchased, there is a tendency to become more selective with each shot, a perspective that was only reinforced when it became necessary to feed another roll into place – in my case, after every twelve shots.

Colour film was in short supply at that time, so most of my work on this trip was in black and white – which made it imperative to seek out light source and pay close attention to shadow. It was a challenge in a land of strong sunlight and dark skin tones. I failed as often as I got it right. However, I became very good at the fluid motion required for changing rolls of film without lowering the camera's quick-action sight from the level of my eye. On two special occasions, one in Angola, the other later in Moçambique, it was necessary to catch fast action sequences of dancers – and to this day I am convinced the only way I might have improved on the results would have been to use a movie or video camera, both items beyond my capacity at the time.

Missionaries

Back in Toronto it was Arnold Edinborough, editor of the monthly general interest magazine, *Saturday Night*, who tipped me off to the group of Canadians working for many years as staff at the Protestant mission headquarters of Dondi at Bela Vista – a small dot on the map one hundred kilometres northeast of Nova Lisboa. Some of the mission staff had been there since the 1930s. Edinborough was a friend to one of them, Doctor William Sidney Gilchrist of Nova Scotia. He had not been in touch with his friend for several years, he said, and he could not even be sure whether Gilchrist and his family were still in Angola. The physician was well known as a champion of African rights, Edinborough informed me, and along with many other foreign missionary personnel had worked in accordance with the Portuguese colonial administration. But now the work and sympathies the missionaries held for their African congregation was perceived as little more than the unwelcome meddling of foreigners, a political threat that was too often running foul of the aims of the Portuguese fascist regime. In view of the present upheavals little, if any, news of missionary welfare and activity in Angola was getting out; none in several years.[23]

"It's quite a worry," Edinborough said. "News of them has always been sporadic, and now there is nothing at all. It would be good if you would try to locate Gilchrist and his companions, perhaps just pass along messages of

---

[23] Missionaries had to follow strict conditions to secure their residency and work status. Going on leave was tricky, some missionaries – particularly Protestants – running the risk of being denied re-entry. In terms of unified health agendas, missionary programmes were generally acknowledged to be considerably more numerous and effective than their counterpart Portuguese government health programmes. See also Appendix #7 – Portuguese toleration of Protestants.

goodwill."

He found Bela Vista and Dondi on a map and pointed them out to me.

"All of them will have had a wide experience of Angola, so it will be worth your while to meet up with them if you can, pick their brains for what's going on ... Any one of them would prove to be a most useful contact for you..."

So I had written ahead, and while in Lisboa had made a special effort to have Nova Lisboa, Bela Vista and the Dondi mission included on my itinerary. Unfortunately, I arrived in Nova Lisboa two days ahead of schedule and had thereby thrown the office of the local district administrator into a flap. He met with me briefly at his office but said he expected to be tied up for the next couple of days and would therefore not be able to spend time with me.

"How would it be if I put you in direct contact with someone from the mission staff ...?"

"Perfect!" I replied, and his secretary was immediately on hand to shuffle me around to the home of Rev. Dr. Murray MacInnes and his wife Innes, thus loading the problem I represented into the laps of a most accommodating Canadian couple.

It was a fortuitous move. Without any warning these good people just moved over, changed their own plans for the following days and claimed to be delighted to take me in tow. Murray himself would drive me out to the mission the following day, after which he had to continue south to collect his

children from another mission outpost. It looked as though, for a few days at least, I was to be relieved of a constant Portuguese minder.

Dondi Mission

166

The Protestant mission of Dondi at Bela Vista was no small operation. Today, as this work goes to print, it is being developed into a university with a view to it one day becoming one of the country's foremost centres of learning.[24] The mission complex when I visited comprised input from several different Protestant denominations – United Church of Canada, the US United Church of Christ, the South Africa General Mission, the Plymouth Brethren, all the partners of the Evangelical Alliance as well as the indigenous Angolan Protestant Church and the Portuguese Protestant Church. One churchman compared the variety of the Christian faith in Angola to a wide river that had spawned a variety of currents: Roman Catholic, Protestant, Pentecostal, apostolic and messianic. Dondi had become the major centre for Protestant mission activity spread widely throughout southern Angola. Many of these mission stations, not all, were strung out close to the route of the Benguela Railway. They came into being largely as a result of the pioneer work of the Canadian cleric, Rev. Dr. Walter Currie, at the turn of the XX century, who maintained close co-operation with American and British Protestant churches.

The first clusters of the Dondi complex, founded in 1903, were up and running by 1914, and were intended to follow on the ideals and zealous work begun by the Scottish missionary, Dr. David Livingstone in the 1880s, in what was later to become Nyasaland (still later Malawi). At the time of my visit the operation at Bela Vista came under the direction of a highly dedicated team of ministers, teachers and medical personnel from several different denominations. The name I heard most was the United Church of Canada, but responsibilities appeared to have been shared around equally by members of all groups. Dr. Gilchrist, I had been told, was now one of a highly dedicated group of medical officers working within an enormous complex of missions, the operations of which spread among stations large and small located throughout the provinces of Namibe, Huila, Huambo, and Bié. Although Dondi appears to have been the fruit of a variety of different supporting mission organizations, some more intent in proselytizing than others, all seem to have been equally involved with the teaching of a way of life. There was, of course, recognition among the foreign Protestants that they shared the same fundamental Christian faith with the Portuguese Roman Catholics, but they suspected the Portuguese dictatorship was appropriating the Roman church as

---

[24] Both the United Church of Christ (USA) and the United Church of Canada sprang originally from the Congregational Churches in their respective countries, the Canadian Congregationalists joining Methodists and Presbyterians in 1925 to form the United Church of Canada. The union of churches in the USA occurred several years later, but it was the cross-border Congregational commonality of the late XIX century that led Canadian Rev. Dr. Walter Currie and his American counterparts to establish jointly the Angola missions in that century.

an instrument of control and oppression.

Murray and Innes made their home in Nova Lisboa where he had taken on the responsibility of overseeing a residence for high school students coming in from remoter towns. He gave me a rundown of mission activities as we drove out the following day to the Bela Vista station. In addition to the residence, the mission supported a hospital consisting of a leprosarium (currently treating fifty patients), a sanitorium (treating one hundred and thirty patients), a maternity (twelve patients at the time of my visit), a children's ward (able to treat thirty patients at any one time), and a men's and women's ward (at the time treating fifty-five patients). In addition, there was an operating theatre, a public health clinic, outpatient facilities for fifty or sixty patients (in private accommodation) and a nursing school.

I was dumbfounded to learn that just three mission staff, all from Toronto, oversaw this entire hospital complex – nurses Lillian Taylor and Jean Walker, and Dr. George Burgess, the latter being the director of the hospital as well as fourteen outlying village dispensaries.

"It's a lot, but we really couldn't do it without the Africans themselves," Nurse Lillian told me. "Right now we have twelve of them, most trained here at Dondi, who act as auxiliary nurses and laboratory technicians. None of this would be possible without their input. I have so much faith in them."

In addition to the hospital, the mission housed and ran several learning centres. Nurse Lillian acted as my guide and took me on the rounds of each of these facilities. Escorting me from point to point, she could see I was amazed at the load of work they had taken on at the hospital, so I think she quite enjoyed laying it all out for me.

The first, the Currie Institute for boys, was basically an agricultural school, its principal was Dr. Allen Knight of Bracebridge, Ontario. The institute catered to some two hundred boys, all boarders, and was divided into two sections: a technical school which provided the first two years of vocational high school, and then the institute proper which offered a three-year vocational training course in agriculture and teacher training.

With an eye to food security, the agriculture programme was concentrated on a trade base, with strong emphasis on leadership in rural areas. The teacher training was highly specialized and was run separately, and there was a strong emphasis on leadership here, also. Dr. Knight had a staff consisting of both Portuguese and Africans. The director of teacher training was himself Angolano, Rev. Teodoro Chitunda, who had completed his studies in rural teacher training in Lisboa and had just graduated from the mission's seminary.

In addition to the institute, there were some four hundred rural schools scattered throughout the mission area – part of a linkage of some two thousand four hundred mission schools operating in the southern provinces of the country under the leadership of such entities as the United Church of Canada, the United Church of Christ (USA) and the United Church of USA. Students from these rural schools were frequently sent on to the Dondi complex at Bela Vista, as they qualified and as room for them became available. Nurse Lillian told me the Methodists had much the same sort of programme operating at Malanje, in the rural countryside east of Luanda. The Baptists had been doing the same at São Salvador near the Congolese frontier, but had been forced by the fighting to close and disband. Many of their missionaries were now to be found in Congo (DRC), she told me.

Having absorbed what I could of all of that, Nurse Lillian then introduced me to the Means School for girls, directed by Dr. Burgess' Montreal-born wife, Phyllis. This school catered to one hundred and seventy girls, all of them boarders. For academic subjects and in preparation for entering the lyceum at Nova Lisboa, the girls mixed with the boys from Currie, but additionally studied their own special subject areas – teacher training and home economics. There was a kindergarten available to children of mission staff and families from nearby villages which was operated as a training opportunity for the girls of Means School. In addition to the director and two Portuguese, there was a staff of nineteen teachers.

The girls studying their academic subjects walked to class at the Currie Institute each day, but they were discouraged from socializing too closely with the boys. Any sort of social mixing was generally limited to religious services on Sundays. I wanted to know how this arrangement could be monitored efficiently but refrained from enquiring too minutely. It seemed to me there must have been a well-implanted form of personnel supervision, likely coupled with the discipline of cultural taboo in which family and community obligations had yet to be met. It was something sufficiently pervasive and so personal I felt discouraged from asking awkward questions of people whose religious feelings might have been offended. Convincing or otherwise, I felt sure I would have received only bromidic answers to soothe me. My hang-up, not theirs.

Yet another institute of learning at Dondi was perhaps the most enlightening – the Emmanuel Seminary. It was described to me as a 'union seminary,' operated jointly by the United Church of Canada, the Methodists, the United Church of Christ (USA)[25] and with the input of several non-

---

[25] See Appendix #10 – comment by Rev. Michael Solberg.

denominational Angolan churches.

In all, sixteen students had graduated from this seminary the year before my visit, and sights were set for an additional twenty in the current year. All of them were boarders; about half married and living in on-campus quarters.

Emmanuel Seminary provided a three-year course in religious studies: the Old and New Testaments, theology, church history, homiletics, liturgy, the more general problems of churches operating in rural areas, and a short course in sociology. The dean of students, himself a minister, explained the need for a honed-down curriculum. Whereas in western countries religious teaching might employ familiar stories and knowledge as a part of its principal base of religious instruction, at Dondi a student's earlier schooling had almost invariably, and of necessity, been drastically limited to the most basic academic essentials. In many instances the Christian story might have been completely unknown. With such limited grounding, typically consisting of only two years of high school, it could prove difficult to grasp the fundamentals of seminary teachings.

"We try not to set our sights too high at the outset," the minister explained. He looked at me as though hoping I could understand (and maybe forgive) that which he himself might have considered a top-down pre-condition to tackling a complicated area of study. He spoke humbly and thoughtfully.

Christian concepts may be easily understood by someone emerging from a western and generally Christian-oriented society, he explained, but they were not always so easily understood by rural Africans who often sprang from pantheistic backgrounds.

"Our teachings must be inclusive of those who have been grounded since childhood in such belief systems. Our instruction needs to be carefully tailored, understandable and practical – at least initially – so that a totally new idea can take hold," he said.

The conversation raised certain troubling (for me) theological questions to which the founders of the seminary had most certainly devoted considerable attention when the idea of religious teaching must first have occurred to them. As had been the case in my earlier conversation concerning the boys and girls of Means and Curry getting together, I was intimidated now by my ignorance; I was curious, of course, but I hardly knew how to phrase intelligent questions concerning religious instruction, let alone did I feel confident enough to discuss such things with someone I supposed was of the highest moral rectitude. Religious schooling was something I could comprehend; the mores of 'tailoring' that teaching to accommodate prior social behaviour left me on shakier ground. I decided it was a subject area I would not query too aggressively. Full of my oats and confident in certain fields, there were also times – too many for comfort – when I saw myself as a very inexperienced lug-head, and a questionable journalist. Man of the world in tight and timid shoes. Overall, I was trying to grasp both the *fait accompli* of the here-and-now as well as the logistical how of setting up such a school in such a place, so I contented myself to accept the guided tour and listen to the minister's explanations with neither question nor comment. He informed me, for instance, that the building housing the seminary had been completed ten years previously, but that the seminary itself had been operating at the mission since 1936. I think I managed to raise an eyebrow.

But then, as luck would have it, two English-speaking African seminarians came forward and we were able to engage in a free conversation. Both men proffered the sort of information that might well have interested my Toronto newspaper contacts.

One of them was Rev. Teodoro Chitunda, a man slightly older than me, a recent graduate of the Emmanuel Seminary currently living at the mission with his wife, Amélia, and their small daughter, Eufrasia. I took a liking to him right away. He was intelligent, had studied abroad, so came across to me as a man who knew the road he wanted to travel. The second student was Figueiredo Paulo, aged twenty-one, who was on the point of leaving the mission to teach primary school at Chilesso mission, about one hundred kilometres north of Nova Lisboa. He, too, was confident and clearly wanted to make a useful contribution to his people.

Both men had strong opinions to express:

"Officially, I am Portuguese," Chitunda told me. "The Portuguese government has told me I am Portuguese – but if I go to Portugal, I will just be another negro. I think it is better for us to have our own country, where all races can live in harmony. I like to live with the Portuguese, but I am an African – my natural home is Angola. Here we do not like Salazar's politics, and there are plenty of white people who feel the same."

Paulo chimed in:

"The Portuguese government likes neither the Protestant nor Roman Catholic missions to be teaching in schools. They believe the missions are training us to fight them. Our people are poor. They live off agriculture. When Africans are educated, they begin to understand how things really are, and it is not hard for us to see which is the better way of life – the old or the new.

We are part of a new world. Our elders agree with schooling, and they try to encourage us to go to school because they have found that when a son is educated he can be of more help at home. It's simple, but in this way we are able to understand education is a good thing – more money and better life."

He went on to explain that in Angola the largest and best organized missions are Protestant, not Roman Catholic. The Portuguese can control the Roman Catholic missions with greater facility because the leaders of those missions, and the entire staff of them, are compliant Portuguese fearful of what their government might do to them personally. This is not the case with the Protestants, who come from Canada, the United States of America and Great Britain. This is why the Portuguese authorities dislike the Protestants, he said, and why, when a Protestant goes to his homeland on furlough, he is under threat of being denied re-entry to Angola – and the threat of being denied the continuation of his work in his mission is about the only punishment the Portuguese can hand out to him as a means of control. A Portuguese national might suffer far worse consequences.

Chitunda continued:

"Officially there is no discrimination here in Angola – at least not on paper. But there is. We see it more in the rural areas, where the whites own little shops. They don't consider the Africans, and they treat them very badly. It is hard for Africans to get jobs with such people. In the big cities it is quite different. There we simply have no money, so the discrimination is economic."

Paulo:

"The badly-educated whites do discriminate against Africans ... I spent eight days in prison in eastern Angola. One day we did not eat for twelve hours. No washing, nothing to drink. We had no clean clothes to change into. I was made to lie on ice for thirty minutes. The border authorities beat me the first day. I had permission to cross the border (into Congo) but the soldiers at the frontier thought I was lying and would not let me cross. I was afraid. I thought I was going to be killed.

"They gave my name to PIDE and released me only when they discovered I had done nothing wrong. At the same time, they told me one day I might be called to be judged. That was over a year ago, but I've not yet been called. I live in fear of being called ...

"Only Africans are unable to make any progress in industry and education. It is a form of discrimination."

Chitunda:

"Just after the violence of March 1961, PIDE was paying five hundred escudos for each name turned into them – by anyone. It was an easy way for some Africans to make money. They just turned in any name – and what did they care that innocents were being arrested?

"Holden Roberto seems to be a good man, but I do not agree with his 'Africans only' policy. We are going to need the whites here for many years to come, to help us build the country. We do not want another Congo. We need the good Portuguese – and good people of other nations, too. Many of us feel that if the Portuguese want to stay here, they should be allowed to. We want freedom without bloodshed – and the Portuguese government does not help in this way. Who knows, maybe it will be different after Salazar goes …"

Rev. Murray MacInnes had joined my tour through the seminary, and entered the conversation:

"It is hard for me to know the Roman Catholic standpoint, but for two years – from 1961 until now – it has been hard to convince the Portuguese (authorities) that Protestant work has a future here. The anti-Protestant propaganda against us has been so strong that people's feelings have become terribly agitated among the ordinary Africans living in the villages. I see it where our missions operate. They (the populace) were ready to march in here and set on fire all we have built over the years. People were frightened, and it was dangerous for us. We could have been picked up. The place could have been closed down or burned down overnight."

Murray was then the chairman of the seminary board of directors, and they had always made a point of electing their officers democratically. It was considered a useful and practical civic lesson for the Africans, both at the mission and in the surrounding villages, so as often as possible – and in everything – the Africans were given rein to choose for themselves. It was a useful lesson in democracy, Murray explained, and they liked it.

"But the Portuguese officials frown on democracy of any type," he explained. "They look on missionaries as instigators of rebellion."

Murray was a straightforward man who calculated his words carefully and left little doubt about his thinking. In no way did I receive the impression he was indulging the Africans he contacted through his mission work. He talked sincerely of their dignity and spoke matter-of-factly of the suspicions and seeming conflict of interests held by Portuguese officialdom concerning the work of the missions.

"The Portuguese know perfectly well we are trying our best to give the Africans a schooling, that we have been in the field of education for many years and have a pretty good idea how to go about it. We are organized, have access to funds through our churches back home – and I think, overall, the Portuguese even have a grudging appreciation for what we are trying to do. In fact, we are doing a lot of their work for them. As long as we are providing educational services, they don't have to. It saves them a great deal of money. At the same time, though, by teaching our students how to reason for themselves, we are adding to the Portuguese headache. The Africans who have been living in this region for hundreds of years are not merely bush animals – they are thinking, reasoning, highly intelligent human beings, and they know that by getting themselves an education they can eventually better themselves and the lives of their families. They are not fools and they value the education we can give them.

"From the Portuguese point of view there is a downside: that we are instructing the Africans in the ways of independence – and I suppose, in one very narrow sense, they are correct. A man or woman who has an education is someone whose feet are planted firmly on the ground and understands their rights as human beings. From our point of view, we have many more successes than failures. These people are learning they do not need the Portuguese ..."

There were numerous other educationalists linked to the Dondi mission network. Millicent Howse, of Newfoundland, was a seminary teacher and looked after the all-important work of Umbundu translation requirements. Marie Crosby, who came from Toronto, was in charge of the Dondi press and its network of literary and distribution services. Margaret Neuman, a US citizen, taught at the school set up for missionary children. Dr. Knight's wife, Eleanor, taught music at the same facility.

The mission's Etta Snow acted as principal of Lutamo, a girls' vocational boarding school, which had one hundred and forty-two students at the time of my visit. She also headed a co-educational primary school catering to one hundred and twenty boys and one hundred and forty-seven girls. In addition, there were some day students who came in from the local villages to attend classes. The primary school curriculum took students through to grade four. Students could remain in class anywhere from two to six years and, following Lutamo may then have gone on to either Means or Currie.

Seminary

Basketry – a quiet moment

We stayed for lunch with Etta. Afterwards, Innes needed to get back to Nova Lisboa, and managed to get a ride with one of the seminarians who was going there. Murray was charged with picking up his children who had been visiting friends at the mission in Bunjei. The cross-country road south was untried, he explained, and might be something of an adventure. He thought the distance would be about one hundred and twenty kilometres. Would I care to keep him company?

Spirit Dance

No one was better placed than Murray MacInnes to give me a run-down on what was going on in the country, I reckoned. It was still my intent to make my way to the areas of fighting in Angola's north – but for now I was in the central south, so wanted to make the most of it. Tensions in the country were evident, but at the time I was none too aware of the displacement that war inevitably causes; the fight had not as yet been carried into the south, so almost by chance I had an ideal opportunity to get a good look at the lay of the land – before the chaos set in.

For several weeks I had been hearing a concerted argument from almost every Portuguese official with whom I had had contact – basically the line that the Africans in both Angola and Moçambique were more than happy with their dictator in Lisboa and were proud to call themselves Portuguese. It was a point of view that ran counter to what Chitunda had been telling me, but I suppose I was not entirely convinced. The Portuguese had been in Angola, for instance, since the XV century. Surely this counted for something, no? No, Murray reminded me; the Portuguese had been on the littoral of Angola for five hundred years; they did not penetrate the interior of the country in any great numbers until the 'Scramble for Africa' of the late XIX century.

Murray had served in Angola the best part of ten years and spoke both Portuguese and Umbundu fluently – the latter being the language of the Africans with whom he had to work everyday. Living as he did in Nova Lisboa, he was able to see how the city had been constructed architecturally along typical Portuguese lines, its African citizens thus going about their daily lives inside a Portuguese mould.

Everyone in Angola expressed an opinion one way or another concerning the delicate point of the Africans' Portuguese-ness – and Murray and I continued discussing it as we drove south in his mission truck from Bela Vista to Bunjei. The visit to the station at Dondi had intensified my questions and our deliberations. It occurred to me that if, in fact, the Africans in this vast territory ever considered themselves so well-indoctrinated by a close five hundred-year association with a Latin heritage, or in any way related to a whole conglomeration of imposed Latin values (beyond using Portuguese as a lingua franca) then perhaps the Portuguese could have a smidgen of claim to Angola as an 'overseas province' of Portugal. The local inhabitants might even then withhold their revulsion at being branded 'colonial.' If they could only be truly content ...

But they were not, and therein lay the kernel of the controversy. No amount of wishful thinking on the part of a tyrant or his henchmen could ever hope to instill contentment in a people who clamoured so fervently for their independence, resisting being painted with a Latin brush. The concept is idiocy. In the north of the country the Angolanos were prepared to fight for their release from Portugal. Perhaps (as actually transpired) it would be only a matter of time before that discontent spread to the south ...

Murray was anxious to get to Bunjei. We would be spending the night there, so if we wanted a supper we should try to arrive before darkness fell at six o'clock. He was not worried about the safety of his children being so far from their home; he was, however, concerned that three rambunctious children might well have outstayed their initial welcome. We were headed along a new and untried road that would add a score or so kilometres to the overall length of the trip but would bring us out on a paved highway that, hopefully, would cut down on our running time.

As it turned out, though, our short-cut was a wild road and longer than we had anticipated – a weaving bare lane of ruts and potholes and choking red dust that hung in the air long after our vehicle had passed. It was a sweltering afternoon and though we were hurrying as fast as we could, the going was both agonizing and slow. Every bump, every pothole, threw us about inside the cab like unwanted toys being cast into the play-box. Murray at least had the steering wheel to hold onto; I had to make do with grabbing under the edge of my seat with one hand and fending off against the cab roof with the other. The base of my spine was taking a pounding.

For hours we wound our way through African bushland. We had no map, so were navigating blind and by guesswork. Now and then we would pass a school house or a church, rudimentary structures that Murray seemed to recognize, and claimed were within his parish. Small villages of mud and wattle huts would pop up out of the boondocks, far from other habitation; sometimes we would pass a tidy little farm on which a Portuguese farmer-settler would have set up with his African wife and a scattering of their offspring – all of them eking out a bare living from the stubborn red earth. The bush would give way here and there to open plain, and then suddenly we would be deep in bush again – and everywhere the dust from the road was carried on the wind, sucked up by our backdraft and thrown up by the wheels into our cab. We could taste the stuff in our throats, our teeth gritted on it, and it floated down on our hair and clung there with our sweat like a cradle cap.

I had dozed into a tense muscle-supported sleep when suddenly Murray shook me awake again.

"You'll want to get pictures of this," he told me.

He stopped the truck and I peered off into the bush. Far away on the right the houses of an Ovimbundu village were clustered among the wattle trees, and across an open space to the left of the road I could see a horde of villagers standing around the edges of a second clearing in the bush.

"They must be spirit dancers," Murray explained tersely, pointing. "I've heard about them, but I've never actually seen them before."

It was only then I noticed a strange figure prancing through the trees like a gazelle, pausing every now and then to jump high in the air. At first glance the man looked as though he was wearing a lion's mane on top of his head. Another one appeared, and then another – and way down the road we could see more people dressed in this extraordinary way, strange in their raffia-like garb.

He seemed to be floating ...

… and ran like a gazelle

"Get your camera. I'll see if they'll talk to us," Murray said as I climbed out of the car.

He called to the men softly, trying to entice them over.

They would have none of it and they darted off through the grass and bush, wheezing and puffing in a rhythm, like locomotives, dancing and leaping as if on stage, resembling an excited flock of ostentatious cranes trying to look over one another's shoulders out of a cage constructed of the dense bush. Each had a long stick he waved in the air, more in greeting than as threat. Their faces were hidden behind masks of grass and reed netting, and the same netting was pulled over their legs like stockings. Their bodies were covered with brightly-coloured cloths and strips of animal hides – gazelle, leopard, monkey and crocodile skins.

"They're quite drunk, of course," explained Murray, more to himself than to me.

Or else, as I have been told, they were using powerful hallucinatory drugs – possibly combined with alcohol.

Again he called to them in Umbundu, asking if they would allow me to take their photographs. But as soon as I approached them they would float away out of range, darting and prancing elegantly into the air, then landing softly on the balls of their feet and vibrating every muscle in their bodies as though an electric dynamo was at work inside each one of them. It was quite impossible to take their photographs, so Murray slipped the car into gear and we started to move off.

We were just picking up speed, the bushes on either side of the track brushing against the sides of the vehicle, when we passed a man dressed, like his companions, in nets and raffia and wearing an enormous headdress. We almost clipped him as we passed, for his dress made him virtually invisible. Murray failed to see him even when I pointed him out.

The man was a good half-metre off the ground, as if suspended – levitating – not moving his limbs excessively but vibrating his entire body in the same way as the others we had seen, fast as a tuning fork.

"Hey! Murray! Stop! Did you see that?"

Murray slammed on the brakes, and I leaped out of the cab with my camera, levelling it at the fellow on the side of the track. He turned and ran through the bush. *Paparazzo*, I could snap only three shots of him as he sped off – two as he stood by the track, one as he fled my intrusive lens. I was fleet of foot in those days, but he stayed well ahead of me and clearly knew his way through the bush and where he was headed. No sound. He didn't crack a twig, but ran gazelle-like, his movement seeming to be suspended in slow motion. I estimated each of his paces was three of mine – perhaps three metres in length. Silence. The only noise was my puffing.

My still shots do not show his levitation, or the incredible length of his strides. Nor do they indicate in any way his phenomenal speed. I was so absorbed by what I was seeing that I hared on after him, trying to keep up and draw abreast of him - but there was not the remotest chance of overtaking him. Presently I broke out of the bush onto a wide clearing, perhaps the size of a couple of football fields. Hundreds of men milled about, dozens of them in similar mystic garb. Strong arms reached out and grabbed me, holding me fast.

There was great excitement – angry shouting I well comprehended, but in words that meant nothing. Murray came at a run, heaving up behind me out of breath.

"Be careful, Jeremy! Be calm. They are drunk – or drugged. There is far too much excitement here ..."

He turned then and spoke to some of the men in Umbundu. Towards me they had appeared menacing, but now they listened to the minister. Murray translating for me, it turned out I had trampled onto soil that was sacred to them. They wanted me to step back, clear of a large patch of open circular ground. With Murray's help everyone settled down, and it was accepted that I meant no harm – only wanted to take a few photographs.

"You should have asked ..." Murray was saying.

"When was there time to ask ...?" I answered gasping for air, and sheepishly. "Hell, Murray! I can't miss taking pictures of all this ...!"

Murray translated, shrugging his shoulders in apology to the men gathered about us.

An old man approached, an elder of the village we had passed, and Murray started explaining our position. He pointed at my camera, everyone now smiling that they understood I only wanted photographs, and the elder readily agreed that I could take more – as long as I did not step on the sacred ground.

"There's a fee ..." Murray explained to me. "He wants two cigarettes."

This was absurd – I offered him the entire pack of a local brand. The old fellow refused. He only wanted two. So I took two from the package I had in my breast pocket and handed them over. He accepted my payment gleefully, clapping his hands twice and patting me on my shoulder. He refused my offer of a flame, instead stuffing one cigarette behind each of his ears. I was perplexed and turned to Murray for some explanation.

"He doesn't smoke ..." Murray smiled.

All the while he had been looking around, studying faces in the crowd, and then I saw him greeting people he apparently recognized.

"You know some of these people ...?" I queried.

"Oh yes, I recognize quite a number of them. This one's a parishioner of mine ... and that one, over there ... good Christians, they are, so I wonder about their attendance at a pagan spirit dance ..."

Murray tried to hide from me his self-evident mortification. If I felt sorry for him, it was also hard not to smile.

The old chief laughed a lot, too, when I drew attention to the cigarettes behind his ears. He was dressed in an ancient and tattered surplus US Army jacket, a khaki yachting cap on his head (anchor on the front) and rubber gumboots on his feet. Other men gathered about as I attempted to foster goodwill, passing out cigarettes until I had no more to give.

The chief swept his arms around the open field, pointing at my camera and indicating I was free to take as many photographs as I wished. There would, however, be an additional fee, he said to Murray. For a few moments the two haggled over an additional fee. Two cigarettes, I agreed, was woefully inadequate – so I was prepared (within reason) to cough up some hard cash. Bartering went back and forth for several minutes, and eventually Murray announced:

"Give him an additional one hundred *escudos*," he said.

"Surely not ...?" I replied – for it was a paltry sum, and I was more than prepared to pay more.

"No – one hundred *escudos*, and not a *centavo* more," Murry said earnestly. "I've had to argue hard on your behalf. If you pay him more he will ask for more next time – and there will come other photographers after you're long gone, you may be sure."

I had heard this argument a few days ago in the Huila district ...

With the business negotiations done, the elder now explained we would have to wait a little while for the menfolk to re-gather. It seemed that our vehicle sweeping up in the cloud of dust we had created had frightened off quite a few people. Seeing us coming, they had quickly disappeared into the bush, thinking we might have been Portuguese officials arriving to put a stop to their rites. Or, worse, to conscript them for manual labour.

While we were waiting, men quietly trooped back to the sacred enclosure in their ones and twos, I asked Murray to explain what the ceremony was all about. What was the occasion for the gathering?

A sight like this was rare, he told me, and our receiving permission to take photographs was an even rarer privilege. This particular dance was undertaken only once in several years and was aimed to appease the spirits, and to increase the village's fortunes at a troublesome time by scaring off evil djinn. The dance had been preceded by a feast, and much drinking of home brew beer. The word went around quickly that Murray and I were guests, and so in place of the initial suspicion that we had come to put an end to the village's special event, we were treated with the utmost courtesy and no small amount of curiosity. Even so, my camera appeared to register doubtfully with both viewers and viewed. My subjects did not understand what a camera was, why it was used or how it worked. That I could make pictures – of each of them – was an unintelligible mystery to them, and it was virtually impossible to explain simply. When Murray told them I was creating a picture of their activity, they frowned quizzically. Why? Did I wish to *capture* them? To do them some harm? What would I do with the pictures of them?

Murray went to his truck and returned with an old newspaper. Speaking slowly and carefully, he opened it up on the ground and gave some of the elders a lesson by pointing out random photographs on its pages. The little machine I held in my hand, he explained, was used to make pictures such as these. It helped that my camera had twin reflex lenses. With great difficulty I managed to keep their curious fingers from mauling the machine and smudging its lenses, but was able to point out how its horizontal window sight could frame a photograph. (The digital photography that was to come along many years later would have clarified the mystery of this lesson in seconds.)

Although the dance was known by reputation, Murray told me it had seldom, if ever, been witnessed by outsiders, and he was not aware that anyone had ever photographed it. My 'news nose' twitching, I was eager to capture such unusual images, and so was encouraged to abandon the last dregs of my conceited righteousness about the consideration and concerns I should have had for sticking my camera into other people's privacy. The villagers prepared the clearing for their dancers, and I went to work for posterity – or so I thought.[26]

Sweeping the 'dance floor' back and forth with brooms of long grasses and leaves, the dancers and their assistants then drew a large round circle in the dust – about half the area of a football field in the centre of a much larger space – and I was told that this was to be the limit of my movement. The sacred ground was now prepared, and under no circumstance was I to bulldoze across their line. I did note, however, that some of the men were so drunk they stumbled right across the centre of the encircled space and no one appeared to object too strenuously – but then they were a part of the gig, so I guess they were excused.

This was a 'men only' occasion. The women, Murray told me, were either terrified of the dancers' powers, or they feigned terror, fully knowing that for this occasion at any rate the performers were not even human. The men and the boys, some two hundred of them, gathered on and around the dance floor, while the women watched, assembled two hundred metres distant on the slope of a small hill, their daughters close by. Hollow log drums covered with hides were brought up, and soon everyone had caught onto the rhythms, clapping their hands, stomping their feet, and moving their bodies in time.

Murray and I mingled with the menfolk.

"If Innes and the children were here, they would have to join the women up there on the hill," he remarked.

---

[26] Journalists love to be 'first' – but as it turned out, I was not the first person to capture photographs of this spirit dance. That honour goes, I understand, to Dr. Sid Gilchrist.

On the central dance floor

Masked male dancer,
dressed as woman,
nurses wooden doll 'child'

A small boy holds the drum

A full hour had passed before we took our leave and turned our attention to collecting the children. On our way back to the truck Murray complained to me he had seen at least several of his parishioners among the inebriated dancers – all of them good Christians who greeted their pastor with respectful cheerfulness. Now he chuckled, agreeing that in the moment perhaps a little animist ambiguity was not necessarily an indication of his total failure as a Christian minister.

"No," I agreed. "In addition, looking at it from their point of view, perhaps a tidbit of animist ambiguity might stand a better chance of pleasing all possible gods …"

We were in some rush to get to Bunjei, but between the pagan dance floor and our destination I fell to musing once again about who qualified as 'Portuguese.' For sure there did not seem to be so much as a dram of Latin culture expressed by the participants of that spirit dance in the bush. There were a lot of their kind in Angola – Africans all, no matter how their Portuguese political masters might have tried to colour the matter.

I asked Murray to explain something of the background of the people we had just encountered. As with most Europeans entering any African territory for the first time I felt confused by the names of the various tribal groups I was hearing about, and was generally unable to distinguish between one ethnic group and any other. In Europe the delineation between cultural entities is generally dictated by a national boundary. Cross any border and one will encounter a totally new set of cultural mores and language. However, it was not such a clear-cut case on the continent of Africa. As of the late XIX

185

century, a variety of colonial masters had drawn up maps according to their own whims and dictates, crossing local cultural frontiers at random without so much as a wink of regard for the indigenous peoples who had lived in those areas for generations. Over the centuries the Africans had managed to achieve their own cultural mixes and territorial enclaves all by themselves; after the entry of the various colonial powers, what might have existed as the groupings of various homogenous nations and kingdoms became instead an aggressively confused tossed salad. The result, looking down at a colonial era map of the south-central portion of the continent – Angola somewhere about the centre of focus – it becomes clear that the tribes and nations of the territory's north also bulldozed across an artificial Belgian border into Congo; the peoples of Angola's eastern regions had more in common with Katanga and the lands that eventually became English-dominated Zambia and Malawi. In the south, Angolano peoples spread across a German frontier into northern Namibia, and vice versa.

The Ovimbundu, today amounting to a little less than forty percent of Angola's total population, are believed to have completed their migration into the highlands of the central and southern areas of the country from lands much further to the northeast around the XVII century. They displaced the indigenous cattle herders who had occupied the highlands before them and became, over time, by far the largest of all the ethnic and linguistic groups within what is now Angola. They lived according to a system whereby the inheritance of lands was patrilineal, while all household and moveable goods were passed on matrilineally. They were skilled agriculturalists, the women cultivating corn and beans, and tending small herds of sheep, goats and cattle, while the menfolk were hunters and competent traders that set up lines of communication with other tribes and peoples. Beeswax was one of their staple trade goods.

The Portuguese explorer Diogo Cão arrived at the mouth of the Congo River in 1483, establishing a first contact with the Kingdom of Kongo and the Bakongo and Lunda-Chokwe tribes to be found in the regions south of the Congo estuary. Their early trade with coastal tribal groups proved fruitful and they were not rebuffed in their early attempts to introduce Christianity, despite several wars being fought between them and the rapid growth of the slave trade in that region. Moving southwards along Angola's Atlantic lands during their XV and XVI century period of global discovery, the Portuguese quickly established themselves on a wide strip of coast that ran from Luanda south to Lobito and Benguela. As they moved into the southern interior of the land, they encountered the Ovimbundu who themselves had begun their migrations into the interior of this enormous and fertile country. By the XVII century

Portugal's burgeoning trans-Atlantic slave trade came into full swing. They had first established the trade on the Guiné coast, gradually moving around the great western bulge of the continent to all of the coastal lands of the Gulf of Guinea. Among the peoples they encountered, and in the interior among the Ovimbundu, they were to discover willing participants as facilitators in the capture and trade of various tribal groups inhabiting the interior of the continent.[27]

In the late XIX century it was the Ovimbundu who made the strongest contact with the North American Protestant missionary movements that were just getting started in southern Angola at the time. In some parts of the country the Protestants arrived even before the colonial Portuguese Roman Catholic missionaries, and there is little doubt that they were considerably better organized and funded. The United Church of Canada and its prior affiliates were instrumental in setting up churches, schools, clinics and hospitals throughout the southern reaches of Angola – and so spread their knowledge over a very wide area. It was precisely because of this that, after the uprising against Portuguese colonial rule in 1961, the presence of all Protestant organizations came under suspicion. Agostinho Neto, who led the MPLA (Popular Movement for the Liberation of Angola), and who ultimately became the independent nation's first president, had been schooled by the Methodists. Holden Roberto, who founded and led the FNLA (National Liberation Front of Angola), and had established the Revolutionary Government of Angola in Exile (GRAE), had been the leader of the uprising in 1961. He had been raised and taught in a Baptist mission. Jonas Savimbi[28], an Ovimbundu, had initially joined Roberto as GRAE's Foreign Minister. In 1964 he split away from the FNLA and Roberto and, after a trip to China, created UNITA (National Union for the Total Independence of Angola) two years later. As a child, he had been schooled as a Congregationalist.

It is possibly with some notion of reason, then, that in the collective mind of the suspicious Portuguese fascist dictatorship there should be a straight line between the teachings of Protestantism and the violent revolution that had thrown sleepy little Portugal into utter chaos, threatening the loss of enormously rich territories and the very existence of the world's last colonial empire. Protestants had thus become an easy and useful target for Portuguese blame and criticism.

---

[27] See Appendix #2 – Ethnic Appellations.
[28] See Appendix #9 – Jonas Savimbi.

The MacInnes children were no longer at the Bunjei mission when we finally arrived. The three of them had managed to scrounge a ride back to Nova Lisboa with one of the local mission staff. Murray was concerned but expressed some relief his offspring would be travelling the main road to the regional capital, not the horrendous bush track we had followed earlier in the day.

Both of us were exhausted and filthy after our travel. It had been a long, hot and sweaty trip, and a considerable quantity of the dust we had churned-up on the road leading to the mission now stuck to us like the pie on Coco's face. Betty Gilchrist, a Canadian, and Ki Henderson, an American, who were mission staffers and had not gone with the children to Nova Lisboa, were on hand to make us welcome and issue whatever good-natured comments seemed most appropriate to raise our spirits and make us comfortable.

All of us sat until late into the night discussing the high costs of schooling for those with children living in the surrounding villages. Life seemed full of unfairness and unnecessary hardship. Betty recounted the sad tale of a local chief, an old man who had been thrown in jail for failing to collect his people's taxes. And only a little earlier in the day there had been a group of contract workers – forced labour – working on one of the nearby roads. They had suddenly been whisked away in trucks, presumably because their Portuguese overseer had noticed our arrival in the vicinity.

"Contract labour is always hidden away when visitors are in the neighbourhood," Betty said. "The Portuguese don't like to admit such a cruel system exists."

She related how the local administrator levied taxes on some people, and not on others.

"He behaves like a potentate, does as he pleases. The locals don't like him…"

Murray spoke about education and poverty in both the colonies and Portugal itself. Officials were most eloquent in their descriptions of education facilities, welfare institutions, hospitals and first aid posts, housing developments and so on – but it was a different picture when making a close examination of how things were in reality – the despicable and numbing poverty of the masses in the colonies, the squalor to be found in the outskirts of any city in Metropolitan Portugal itself – the infamous *bairros da lata.*

Where was the money coming from to rectify all this? Where, after the Portuguese authorities had finished their grandiose trumpeting, were the results on the ground? There were big promises for improvement almost immediately after the outbreak of the revolt two years previously – belated motive for change – but no sign yet, even in the bigger centres, of any serious effort to tackle colossal problems allowed to percolate through close to five hundred years of abuse.

"Ah …!" most government-paid operatives would exclaim – and then would follow the usual lame excuses, the blame thrust upon others, the curses and the laments, the detailed, tedious explanations of how and why and why not …

Racism …?

That, explained Murray, was the brain teaser question for which every visitor to Portuguese Africa tried to find an answer. It was ambiguous …

Racism, yes. Discrimination, yes. But segregation – generally, no. There's not much on paper that could prove the point one way or another. A few poor whites lived in the African quarters of Luanda … Throughout the country, particularly in rural areas, white children in government schools, although few in number, could be found sharing the same classroom facilities as African children. They were, for the most part, the sons and daughters of Portuguese settlers – themselves often relocated impoverished peasantry.[29]

"We do not keep statistics for schools – who is white, and who is black…" I had been informed in Luanda – and was later given the same information in Lisboa. Segregation, I was told, generally followed along financial lines – and these were universal: if one had a sizeable quantity of money, one was able to socialize freely; those without money (and in Angola that was the majority of the black population, and poor whites) were not.

"Some Portuguese officials go to great lengths to be genuinely fair," was Murray's comment. "There are others, though, who most definitely do not. And fair or not, all Portuguese in Angola are frightened."[30]

"The Protestant missions in Angola are facing a very difficult task," Betty said. "The Portuguese are suspicious. They do not trust us, and yet they are obliged to acknowledge we have been working in vital areas, trying to do the

---

[29] See Appendix #3 – Racism.
[30] See Appendix #4 – Forced Labour.

work that they themselves have been unable to do, or have neglected for so long ..."

If memory serves me correctly, in 1963 the exchange rate was approximately twenty-eight Portuguese escudos to the American dollar. To register to go to school, the parents of a child of ten had to be able to produce a birth certificate at a cost of sixty-five escudos. The certificate would be considered out of date after three months so that if registration was not completed promptly, it would cost another sixty-five escudos. To collect the certificate from the administrator, the would-be student (or parent) would sometimes have to travel a considerable distance. This could easily run to two hundred escudos over and above the cost of the registration certificate. In the Bunjei area, a child could be declared indigent by the administrator's office – but then to obtain a certificate to that effect he/she would have to 'open' a signature with a notary public at a base fee of twenty-four escudos. The application to do this would cost seven escudos, and to have it stamped as official yet another six escudos – in all, thirty-seven escudos to the notary in order to be registered as having no money.

None of these figures are substantial sums to a North American, nor were they in 1963, but for an African student such amounts were prohibitive. The list goes on:

Throughout the year students were expected to fork out more money. They were obliged to join their school's '*caixa escolar*,' a form of academic society. In addition, in the colonies, white children and *assimilados* (African and mixed-race children thought to have attained an acceptable level of civilization) between the ages of seven and fourteen were obliged to join the Portuguese Youth, *Mocidade Portuguesa*.[31] Invariably costs for these could run to one hundred and twenty or one hundred and fifty escudos per year.

Notebooks and textbooks, when they were available, could cost one hundred and fifty escudos a year. Taking a 'third-class' exam might cost thirty

---

[31] *Mocidade Portuguesa* - established in 1936, this movement was modelled on the *Opera Nazionale Balilia* of fascist Italy and the Nazi Hitler Youth. At the end of the Second World War, this organization abandoned its paramilitary format and was re-moulded into a sort of Roman Catholic youth, or scout movement that existed until 1974.

escudos and, upon completing the exam, there would be an additional twenty-escudo cost for the diploma just earned. A student would require this diploma in order to progress to the next academic level. A fourth-class exam (over the age of eighteen) required a student to make a declaration of necessity to take the exam (thirteen escudos for the declaration, plus a one hundred-escudo revenue tax stamp affixed to the application), and then pay an additional thirteen-and-a-half escudos to get on the exam list. If the student had studied on his/her own and was not attending regular classes, there would be an additional two hundred escudos to pay.

I learned of one case in which a young African student had written his exam, but there had been a re-zoning of his home district so that his diploma was incorrect when he received it. It indicated he was 'Mr. X of Y village, Z district' when he was by now 'Mr. X of Y village, W district.' Because of this error on his diploma (which would have been his passport into the next class) he was forced to sit the exam again, come up with all the requisite expenses – and then be set back a full year.

Murray listed even further expenses for students writing government-set exams. There was a general tax that amounted to two hundred and fifty escudos a year. There was a tax of ten escudos per year for drums and dancing, and a further twenty escudos for distilling. In addition, at tax time each year, everyone – students included – had to pay twenty escudos to see a propaganda film, the money being paid to the local administrator to cover the cost of screening the film. Some more honest administrators saw it for the racket it was, and so refused showing the film or taking any money for it.

Betty told me something of her family story. The name Gilchrist in southern Angola carried with it a certain cachet. Her father, Dr. William Sidney Gilchrist, was born in Nova Scotia in 1901, and spent a total of thirty-eight years as a medical missionary in Angola. He married Frances, her mother, two years prior to completing his medical studies in Halifax, and the two of them volunteered to go abroad immediately. They were appointed to Angola by the Board of Overseas Missions of the United Church of Canada in 1928, but first spent a year in Portugal learning the language and acquiring a degree in tropical medicine. They arrived in Angola in 1930.

Dr. Gilchrist's first station was at Camundongo where, in addition to his routine clinical work, he set up a leprosy clinic. He spent the World War II years as a medical officer with the Canadian army, first in Britain, then later in North Africa and Italy. He returned to Angola in 1947, setting up his practice in the mission hospital at Dondi, and later moving to facilities – largely self-created – at Bailundo.

The Protestant presence among the Ovimbundu of Angola was large and, after the outbreak of the colonial war in 1961, it was held in great suspicion by Portuguese authorities. Roman Catholic missions and schools, which had been operating in the north of the country as early as the XV century, derived their staff principally from Portugal and from the local Portuguese-speaking population; they were relatively easy for the authorities to monitor and control. But the Protestant missions were different. They were an offshoot of work being carried out by British and North American missionaries in central southern Africa and were treated – particularly during the colonial war – as interfering foreigners. Their broad success among the Ovimbundu owed much to the Christian zeal of early missionaries in the region – and especially to the input of North American funding. Most notable among the earliest Protestants was Rev. Dr. Walter Currie. He and his wife were sent to Angola in 1885 by the American Congregational Mission Society in Africa. In 1914 this group, aided by congregations in Canada and the US, purchased nine thousand hectares of land from the Portuguese just outside the town of Bela Vista, in the centre south of the country – not far east of Nova Lisboa along the Benguela Railway, construction of which had been started in 1902. The missionaries established a central mission station on their new lands – plus a high school for boys, a school for girls, and sufficient acreage left over for the building and equipping of a major hospital complex. Dondi, as it became known, very quickly found itself a major training centre serving multiple Protestant mission stations in the south of the country; Murray told me it was hoped eventually the whole complex might evolve as the core of a future university.

The Gilchrist family thought of Africa as their home. It was particularly difficult to return to Canada on furlough, for there was an ever-present danger of not being permitted to re-enter the territory. Betty was unable to tell me the whereabouts of her mother and father at the time of my visit, only that her father had felt it expedient to absent himself and his wife and to remain difficult to find for various periods of time during the early portion of the colonial upheaval. In fact, although he moved from mission to mission quite frequently, he was never out of touch with his colleagues, and I am now inclined to think Betty, not really knowing who I was, decided she would not put me in touch with her father. It has never really entered my mind that I might have resembled a PIDE agent – but the bastards were milking information from every possible source, and there was always the danger that I might inadvertently lead the police to their quarry. In the suspicious climate of the times it was impossible to blame Betty's caution. As I was discovering for myself, PIDE agents came in all unlikely shapes and sizes.

It was not until I began writing about this portion of this present work that I learned a more detailed account of Dr. Gilchrist's departure from Angola – which, of course, occurred after my conversation with his daughter at Bunjei.

Twelve of the doctor's Angolano health colleagues were arrested and taken, it is believed, to São Nicolau. They were tortured. Some confessed to PIDE that the physician had attempted to assist them by getting word of their plight, and the chaotic conditions facing the missions in Angola, to the United Nations.[32] Shortly after this, Gilchrist was summoned to appear at the Bailundo police station where the officer in charge advised him he had received orders for his arrest. Apparently among the police there was considerable sympathy and affection for the doctor. The police chief told him that if he and his wife left the country immediately, he would hide his directive until they were gone. To remain would undoubtedly have meant the arrest and possible torture of others in order to enable the state's case, so Dr. and Frances Gilchrist caught the train into Zambia. At that point the doctor suffered a heart attack and was duly flown back to Canada. After a considerable period of convalescence, the Church Mission Board permitted him to return to Africa – to southern Congo, an area receiving large numbers of Angolano refugees. He worked there through 1968 until 1970, returning to Canada shortly afterwards.

I told Betty of my intention of heading to the war zone in the north of the country the moment the Portuguese would grant me permission. She was encouraging, and told me that her brother, Ian – also a physician – had felt pressure to leave the territory, and was presently somewhere in the northern area, or perhaps even in Congo (DRC). He had chosen to work with the rebels against the Portuguese, she said, and believed he had established a clinic to assist refugees and wounded rebels who were able to make it over the frontier to safety.

"I'll find him," I told her – and, indeed, finding Ian Gilchrist, or his father, became one of the chief motivations for me to remain in Angola. I was heading north, so it seemed I would be seeking Ian first.

---

[32] See Appendix #5 – Torture.

Up to that time I had been embarked upon a pleasantly exciting and enlightening tour, but my principal object had hardly yet been attained: to make an intelligent assessment of Angola's struggle for independence from Portuguese colonial domination, and I wanted to dig a little deeper into the subject – try to understand it better and write a few good yarns about it. There were two objective comparisons I could draw on from my own background: the independence efforts of the Mau Mau, in Kenya, and the war against the communist Chinese takeover of Malaya and Singapore. These two military engagements, in my limited capacity to understand such things, were much different one from the other. In Kenya, the Mau Mau were largely on the run from the very start of their rebellion. They had virtually no weaponry, save the *panga* – machete. They had a variety of simple homemade guns (I saw some made of hollow curtain rods, with elastic bands to snap a crude bolt). There was nothing like the highly sophisticated ordnance brought to bear by the British troops and the loyal African colonial regiments that fought alongside the British. There were no pitched battles. The Chinese communists, on the other hand, were another matter. They were dedicated, uniformed, well armed, well organized, and had fought in the Malay jungles since the time of the Japanese occupation during the Second World War. They certainly fought numbers of pitched battles and managed to tie the British into knots for thirteen years before they were finally defeated and forced to the bargaining table. The war against the Mau Mau was totally different; but even though the Africans were so poorly armed and trained, and had virtually no organization whatsoever, they kept the British fully occupied for nine years.

With this reality in mind, I wondered how the Portuguese would fare (on three separate fronts, as it ultimately turned out) against infuriated African nationalists who were now being armed with highly sophisticated weapons, and had the sympathy of the world behind them …?

A sad postscript to the Gilchrist story: Dr. Sid Gilchrist, his wife and their daughter, Betty, all managed to return to Canada on furlough in 1970. Dr. Gilchrist himself was about to embark on a speaking tour to promote a newly-established scholarship fund he had just recently succeeded in setting up through his United Church contacts. The three of them were travelling in a car near Red Deer, Alberta, when they were involved in an horrendous car accident. All three died.

I have thought so many and so many times of the events described in the above chapter; events that have stayed with me, separating the 'then' and the 'now,' but somehow ever assisting in the general coalescence creating the man I have become. One of life's sterling lessons, thumped home and, for *carimbo*, a golden locket.

If I close my eyes, I can take in great wafts of the dust and the bush, and feel how it fills the pores under the knuckles of my fingers; if I block my ears and concentrate, the phantom shapes and aberrant movements of the spirits as they dance on their sacred ground become for me so vivid my vision is blurred by my tears. The memory of the drums throbbing the course of my spine can make my teeth chatter, bring the taste of the dried-out shrubbery to the tip of my tongue; I can feel it in my neck and across my shoulders. The sensations can cause my fingers to twitch as if I was working once again the shutter release and roll-on mechanism of my camera, and I both see and sense far more than I could ever hope to photograph.

But the strongest impression of all is my chase through the long grasses, between and around the spine trunks and whip-like branches of the bush-trees, and the phenomenal speed with which this spirit sped nimbly away in front of me, like a gazelle out front and gaining distance all the while.

Two men, not at all alike.

There was no means for me to know anything of the man I chased; I could have had no idea who he was, or what might have been flashing through his mind as he ran; for sure he could have had no correct notion as to who I was – some white apparition in strange factory-made clothing leaping from a fast car, a shiny chrome gadget in hand to use (as his superstitions, or his training, or his gods might have informed him) to work some harm on him.

He would certainly have heard any number of stories about the Portuguese police and military raiding parties that descended on villages like his – how they would arrive in fast cars and trucks, just as Murray's mission vehicle had done, and how they would sweep the lanes with drawn weapons, entering houses at random to single out men – or women – and take them away. Knowledge of the end result would eventually filter down to the families of the villagers left behind – or maybe it never would. Everyone would have come to hear about the incarcerations, the beatings, the hard labour. It would have lasted for days, or weeks, or months. Sometimes the incarceration would have been far away, and sometimes those who had been taken away would never return.

Such stories would have been the salient sum of any 'knowledge' the fugitive spirit could have had concerning the man who was chasing him through the bush.

And my knowledge?

Nothing at all. Even his name would not have mattered in the least. I 'knew' only that his raffia dress was so outlandish, so unusual, it spiked my intense curiosity. I had seen his levitation, hadn't I? Whatever it was I 'knew' amounted to nothing beyond my occupation: I was a photo-journalist and bounding away in front of me was a story I had never before encountered. My *raison d'être* at that very moment was to bring that story forward, to lay it before my ever-so-rational world. Chasing that man was my work.

Now I was not shy about poking my invasive camera into someone's face, as had been the case just days before in Sá da Bandeira, when I had had my doubts about photographing the Mwila girls. The 'right now' immediacy of the chase nullified my doubts, for some reason. On the contrary, the 'right now' gave me reason.

Villager from a straw hut – wife, children, perhaps some chickens, a donkey for carting firewood; if he was wealthy maybe he would even possess a bullock for ploughing ...

Our worlds collided at that chase through the bush and, by any measure, what a fantastic collision! The vitality of my intense curiosity was equalled by the vitality of his reaction – inasmuch as he understood (as I did not) that white men in fast cars can spell calamity for black men in bondage. Most earnestly, I am sure of it, did I wish him no harm by such callous and thoughtless intrusion; in calmer hindsight our sudden arrival, followed by the chase, must have frightened him out of his wits.

Excusable? No, not at all.

Explainable? In philosophical terms, and the crassest of human terms, yes.

One of the fundamentals of our humanity, perhaps the greatest, is our curiosity. All space is 'out there.' We have convinced ourselves we need to know about it, so we spend billions of dollars firing off spaceships and telescopic equipment to gather information – and we will never stop.

Mankind 'knows' his curiosity is noble, sacrosanct, and that his greatest heroism is to put himself on the line, so he listens to space knowing one day he will go there.

We have other 'certainties.'

Every religion in the world assures us God is 'out there,' and for centuries our greatest thinkers and leaders – pontiffs and priests, rapscallions and outrageous liars – have been assuring anyone who will listen that they have a secure handle on knowledge of the unknowable. And those who believe them – millions – spend hours on their knees, their hands beseeching a sign in the air somewhere in the vicinity above their heads.

Wars have been fought, millions have died, cartloads of bullion have been looted and spent or squandered in this great quest for God – a never-ending effort to satisfy our curiosity.

Hang a bauble before a child, and he will reach for it.

Curiosity – considering the irony of the ephemeral Portuguese hospitality on offer in my case – was the very impetus behind the era of Portuguese navigational discoveries. It was the more prosaic curiosity of Portugal's kings five hundred years ago that had summoned these people to these very lands in southern Africa, and that had brought about the eventual establishment of the extraordinary empire now teetering in its throes and on the cusp of collapse.

In the frenzy of the chase I had no clear understanding of why that swift and spirited man was so desperate to run from my camera. Having thought about him so many and so many times since, and in the solitude of my years, I think I have come to a conclusion:

I wanted to catch him and pin him to a display board like a butterfly. He wanted none of it. He had yet some colourful flying in mind. I wanted capture. He wanted escape.

War Zone

I had stayed at the Grande Hotel Univérso when I first arrived in Luanda, so headed there when my plane arrived back in the capital from Nova Lisboa. Almost the first person I saw as I crossed the lobby to the reception desk was my former acquaintance, Joaquim Lemos. It was not an unanticipated encounter. I had had a hunch he would show up again once I re-entered the course of my more formalized tour.

"*Senhor* Jeremias!" he called out, and for an instant I thought he was faking surprise. "We all thought we had lost you! I haven't seen you for weeks ..."

I was tired, and I had a pile of notes on scraps of paper, plus my diary entries, and I wanted to get to my room and review everything. I had not had a great deal of time to myself in the past few weeks, and right then I could not have felt less like socializing. I tried to make my excuses.

"Come on!" he said. "The night is young, yet, and surely you have time for a quick visit to the bar before we go in to supper. I want to hear all about your explorations ..."

There was no dodging him, so I agreed to meet him within the hour, then fled to my room for a cold shower and to organize my notes so I could work on them after supper. I laid everything out on top of my bed in some sort of order, at the same time tucking several rolls of film into the toe of one of my spare shoes and placing the pair of them under the chair at the writing desk. There were never good places to hide my personal notes and photos, but I had taken to poking rolls of film into the toes of my shoes and then making it look as though I had just kicked them off. The shoe with the film I carefully placed onto its side, sole outwards, the opening for the foot turned away from immediate easy scrutiny. I was not terribly worried about my notes; they were handwritten in a form of self-developed speed-writing that I was quite sure no one could possibly decipher – a series of dots and dashes and squiggles, a highly personalized form of calligraphy in chicken-scratch. If someone came into the room they might well have been tempted to leave the notes alone; they looked like gibberish and, had they been taken away for laboratory analysis, they would have remained gibberish until I decided to translate them and treat them otherwise. There was always the possibility of someone just gathering them up and tossing them out, but I took the trouble to re-write much of this scrawl into small notebooks which I burrowed into the depths of my kit. If destruction had been some unseen enemy's serious intent there would not have been a whole lot I could have done about it. It was the same with film; a cluster of little canisters was bulky, and could have been found easily with minor perseverance. I realized that tucking them into the toes of my shoes was a feeble effort at concealment, but I went through the ritual anyway.

I was being paranoid. I had this urge to hide things, yet who was likely to come into my room? Why would they have wanted to? What might they have expected to find? Innocuous notes, and a bunch of exposed film showing little but tourist images ...? I simply could not hide the notebooks, so tucked them into the deepest recesses of my travel bags, and hoped for the best ...

Joaquim was waiting in the bar. We had a beer a-piece, then headed into the dining room.

All through the meal I was thinking of my notes and my rolls of film. Worry-wart, and I tried to shrug such nonsense out of my head. Anyone wanting to snoop might have chuckled at my stupidity, my amateurish efforts at concealment ...

I had created something in my head and was working myself into a lather. I had this certainty ...

Tired, I finally made my excuses to Quim, left him and went up to my room.

Sure enough – someone had been in there while I had been in the dining room. The papers on the bed had been picked up and put down again – carefully, but in a slightly different order. And my shoes! I turned to them hurriedly; they had not been moved from the position in which I had left them. The film was still crammed into the toe of one of them. Someone had been inquisitive about the papers but had not thought to look inside the shoe. Nothing had been taken. Notebooks were in place in my kit.

My first instinct was to seek company. Alone in the room I had felt violated, peculiarly vulnerable – even a little afraid. Taking the rolls of film from the shoe, I stuffed them into my trousers pockets and quickly left the room, locking the door behind me. Joaquim might still be in the dining room; I'll talk to him, I thought.

A mirror in the foyer reflected the corner of the dining room where we had been sitting at the table, and Joaquim was indeed still there. But there was someone else with him ...

Maria Esmeralda – the girl from the pharmacy – she must have arrived in the dining room at almost the same moment I had left the table. I had been upstairs in my room for only the briefest time before turning about and coming down again.

She was perched on the edge of her seat talking earnestly to the shoe salesman, her hand on his arm, and looking as though about to get up. I watched in the mirror; she stood up to conclude whatever she was saying, then took her leave of Joaquim and headed for the doorway I was about to enter. I did not want her to see me, so stepped quickly behind a pillar and watched her leave the hotel. It seemed such an unlikely sort of encounter, but I did not have time to assess what might have been going on. There was no particular reason why the two of them should not have known one another; after all, they both knew the other Joaquim, the cavalry lieutenant. What I had seen in the mirror might have passed for intimacy, but it was not quite that; something was going on between them. It did not look like a romance. My uneasiness was hardly abated, but now I was very curious.

Joaquim was still seated at the table. I decided to tell him about my room but avoid mentioning Maria Esmeralda, just to see what reaction might be forthcoming.

"Shit!" I exclaimed as I approached. "Some nosy parker was rummaging about in my room while we were having dinner."

Joaquim looked alarmed.

"That can't be!" he said. "Are you sure?"

"Certain. I left some papers on my bed, and they're all out of order now. I don't think any are missing, but someone has certainly taken a look at them."

Joaquim got up out of his chair.

"We must notify the hotel management ..."

"What good would that do? Yes, we can tell someone at the front desk, but whoever was in my room is long gone by now. Telling the hotel staff would be protocol, no doubt, but I don't think it will inform us any better."

I sat down at the table again.

"Perhaps I'll have another cup of coffee ..."

Joaquim sat beside me looking concerned. I did not mention to him that the notes on my bed were in chicken-scratch speed writing that only I would have been able to understand. I did not mention to him that I was headed to the north of the territory early the following morning. I did not mention that I had at that moment several rolls of unexposed film in my pockets. And I did not mention that I had seen him talking with Maria Esmeralda – and neither did he.

Finishing my coffee, I again bid Joaquim a goodnight and headed back up to my room. My mind was in turmoil, and I needed time to figure things out.

There was absolutely nothing, either in my notes or on film, that would have been of the least interest to the Portuguese – nothing at all except doubts or suspicions, or perhaps the origin of some paranoia. At all times, these same Portuguese authorities would have known where I was, and with minimum effort they could probably have found out very easily who I had been seeing. The only blank space for them would have been the days I had spent at the Protestant mission. Were they really all that suspicious of a collection of altruistic mostly Canadian Christians operating a mission complex (admittedly of considerable size) way off in the southern mountains? They could have asked me who I had been seeing, and I would have informed them quite happily.

There was nothing to hide, so it was difficult to comprehend how my visit to the missions at Dondi, or Bunjei, could possibly have been of the least interest to anyone. So far I had learned a few details concerning the local politics, but there was no way I felt myself qualified to write very much more about this journey than an expansive, perhaps exotic, travel piece. There were no skeletons in hiding – not yet, anyway.

The little plane headed out at first light for the military airfield at Maquela do Zombo, a small operational town almost within spitting distance of the Congolese frontier. On the way north, somewhat short of halfway between Luanda and our destination, the pilot told me he would fly low over Nambuangongo to give me a bird's eye view of the worst of the original trouble area.

"You won't like what you are going to see," he cautioned.

But in truth it was hard to recognize very much of anything at all. The early armed conflict around Nambuangongo and the surrounding villages and plantations, the extensive killings of both settlers and indigenous, had been two years previously. In the intervening time the bush and jungle had run rampant over deserted plantations of coffee and palm, so there was little indication of anything more than rapacious nature creeping into what had once been habitable. We buzzed a couple of plantation homes, blackened and gutted by fire – destruction and indication of interrupted life and industry, but hardly a sight that by itself would cause me to shudder in fear. The application of a little imagination, however, brought home the isolation of these farms, and maybe something close to the horror that must have been felt by the families facing imminent slaughter. Even from the plane I could feel the silence of the place. We circled a few times over the remains of several of the farm complexes. Nothing moved on the ground. Normally a plane circling low over roof-tops would bring out curious onlookers by the hundreds. In this case, nobody. I saw no living things at all – no people, no animals. There was no life whatsoever down below us; as far as I could see to all points of the compass, a great and silent emptiness.

The pilot registered the question on my furrowed brow and guessed what I was thinking.

"No one," he said. "This used to be one of the most heavily populated rural districts in Angola – some of the best coffee-growing country in the world. Look at it now!"

For perhaps ten minutes we coursed back and forth over a wide area above Nambuangongo. The town itself, clearly still operating as a town – people, shops and livestock – nonetheless looked more like an open and very active military barracks. Soldiers and military vehicles were everywhere, all of them nestled into the confines of this dusty nondescript country town. But from above we could plainly see the hinterland around this small centre was devoid of normal activity. Roads leading off into the countryside were bereft of traffic except, here and there at key points, the inevitable robustly armed military roadblocks. What had once been outlying villages now lay in ruins, little more than heaps of brush where once there had been a house, here and there, an open space of pounded earth – perhaps once an open-air village market now bereft of all signs of life and gradually returning to jungle.

There was an airfield and we could have landed at Nambuangongo, but instead we picked up on our original intent and headed northeast towards Maquela do Zombo. From the air we could pick out military posts dotting the countryside near this northern Angola centre, some within disused farms, others in abandoned houses in the valleys and hills, tucked away but sandwiched between the town and nearby thick jungle.

Maquela do Zombo itself, when finally we landed and drove into its centre, was at that time quite the most degraded urban cesspit into which I have ever wallowed. I cannot think of one any worse. After more than half-a-century, and with vivid memories of the place, that maxim still holds in my mind. The plane arrived a little before noon, and I was met by a representative from the local administrator's office, who took me by car to a no-name hotel in the centre of the town. It was such a ramshackle flea-infested doss-house I was immediately persuaded almost anything – a flower perhaps, or a coloured sign – might have elevated its decrepit down-at-heel image. I dubbed the establishment The Grande Hotel de Maquela do Zombo. If that was its name, perhaps I would be able to stay there. It suited the cynic in me, a mean sentiment to maintain my own wobbly sense of humour and perhaps enhance the most dismal of failures.

Overall Maquela do Zombo's most striking feature: the silence of the place. The people mute, who moved about. Civilians in rags looked like zombies risen from a corrupted turf; soldiers in the streets, like predator animals, eyed the locals askance and in chary fear. Rebel with *catanga*? Prostitute with clap? Soldiers held back their customary banter with black civilians. Soldiers held close their trust and their loaded weapons. The silence was heavy. Motors of passing vehicles sounded muffled.

My diary entry of first impressions is brief:

A dog is taking a crap in the middle of the road just outside my room. Good for him. Seems he has the savvy to express himself succinctly. This place is the shits.

I winced painfully watching a legless beggar, filthy as though he had just crawled from the swamp, hump his way along the street – the lower extremity of his trunk tucked into a leather sack-like pouch, a kind of body sock that protected his butt from abrasions and slivers. It was attached by a pair of leather braces over his shoulders. In his hands he held two pieces of wood about the size of large shoe-polish brushes. These had handles attached to them so that, by 'walking' with them as if they had been shoes, and manipulating his strong arms, he could lift and propel himself forward across the ground with some dexterity. It was an awkward locomotion, but evidently he had been powering through life this way for a number of years, levering himself along the town's dusty byways like a cumbersome sack of spuds.

I desperately needed to clean up, so sign-signalled a man swishing a mop down the hotel corridor to discover where I could find a bathroom.

He directed me to what might once have been a public wash house behind the hotel – concrete laundry tubs and a couple of lose-hinged doors to adjoining toilets (take-aim holes in the floor) boldly marked *'Senhors'* and *'Senhoras.'*

I pushed open one of the doors and was bombarded by an almost impenetrable swarm of flies and a stench that caused me to step back a pace. There was no question of my entering that fetid little chamber. I walked around the back of the building and relieved myself against a rear wall.

The diary entry, a flagging humour:

My room is a hoot. I can see I'm going to have to get drunk tonight ... I'll have to bed down in the dark – a good thing: I won't be able to see the other creatures sharing the covers with me ...

The room was built like the stall of a barn. The window was an open square hole in the wall, glass never installed, but with warped wooden shutters that failed to close properly. The bedroom door opened in two halves, top and bottom, as it might in the home of a goat, but they also did not synchronize the way they should have. The room's side walls did not reach the ceiling; they were thin wooden partitions that divided the space from that of its neighbours on either side, in effect partitioning, but leaving open, the interior of the building end-to-end. Any idea of privacy had disappeared through wide crevasses and bad joinery. Above the bed there was no ceiling, but the joists of a roof covered with corrugated iron *chapas*. The blankets looked unsoiled in the half-light, but smelled of mildew – dank and probably hiding hundreds of creepy-crawlies with teeth. The well-flattened straw mattress was so thin my buttocks could feel the pattern of the bedsprings.

Strange, horrid little community, Maquela do Zombo. There were people – civilians – but an emptiness about the place that was more than mere isolation; it was a social vacancy with an air of threat to it. Portuguese troops were everywhere in the town, giving the place the ambient of a barracks. The civilian population was there but scurried about barely seen. What the soldiers termed the 'African quarter' was sparse and in a shallow hollow over to one edge of the community, away from the main collection of houses. The whole town had looked pathetically small from the air. In the countryside round about there were no Africans roaming freely as they do in the south of Angola, or in other urban portions of the continent. Here one could drive the rutted dirt roads for kilometre after kilometre and never see a soul. On either side the rich greens and browns and deep purples of the land rolled away like a carpet over the hills and into the valleys – but there was no cultivation; no one to cultivate. The walls of old farm houses stood stark and roofless, decaying and crumbling, left to the encroachment of the bush. Some were burned out. Their owners had left them in 1961 at the outbreak of the terror that had afflicted the vicinity, and they had not yet returned.

Platoon officer
with troops,
Maquela do Zombo

Letters from home

Mascot

José António Luz de Almeida, a captain overseeing operations at the town's headquarters garrison, explained two types of military activity being carried out in the area: the first was to patrol the border with Congo some thirty kilometres to the north; the second was to cope with the growing refugee problem.

Maquela do Zombo itself had come under attack by the rebels in 1961. They had been driven off by settler vigilantes and the military, but were never far away. The population in the surrounding countryside had suffered dreadfully. Whole villages and plantation settlements were wiped out, burned to the ground. In the first wave of blood-letting, scores of white settlers had been butchered; in the 'white terror' that followed, Africans were killed indiscriminately – not only by the enraged white settlers and farmers, but also by the rebels themselves. Panic stricken, the population fled – to other safer areas in the south, or into the larger towns, or north across the Congolese border.

During the two years prior to my visit the Portuguese army had managed to regain some of the military initiative in the zone, pushing most of rebel cadres back into the jungles to the southwest or over the Congolese frontier – this latter a grand mix of rebels and refugees so that no one knew who was who. Gradually a kind of order had been restored locally, at least for the now. But the insurgency could reappear any time ...

Refugee townsfolk had returned, first in ones and twos – later in greater numbers – but there were no houses for them, either in Maquela do Zombo or in the nearby villages. All around the town farms and crops had been deserted or destroyed, and almost every building in every surrounding community had been wrecked. Co-operating with what civilian authority they could find, the Portuguese troops were even now trying to set up new habitations in the area. Building anew was a less traumatic alternative than trying to rebuild what had been so thoroughly wiped out, but it was not always the most practical solution. It was proving a huge and complex task. Some old buildings could be restored; new houses had to be built – but all of it quickly and, for safety, as close as possible to the larger community. New crops had to be sown and as they were growing, the population had to be fed and clothed. Simultaneously more and more refugees were returning home – not to farm their old lands in the open countryside, where there was always the scare of being attacked again, but to find new livelihoods in the comparative security of community life in the garrisoned town, protected by their own numbers as much as by the Portuguese army stationed in the town and its nearby villages. Families and individuals needed to be close together. New cultivation was hesitant around the settlement – and in between one settlement and the next kilometres of open fertile land had necessarily been left to the encroachment of the tropical bush.

All of this was offered up in conversations with Luz de Almeida and his junior officers – their freely volunteered information and opinions confirming what had been so apparent from the air. We took beer and a late lunch at the officers' mess, and these remarkably jovial young men, with the confidence of soldiery everywhere who had no immediate battle to fight but a conviction they were winning anyway, filled me in about what else was happening in their jurisdiction. There had been a lull in the fighting, they said. Pitched battles between soldiers and rebels appeared to be in decline for the moment, but patrols were active and necessary along the frontier. Ambushes were not uncommon.

We rode in a jeep loaded with well-armed Portuguese soldiers and headed north to a border post about thirty kilometres away. A second jeepload of soldiers followed behind us, all of them likewise armed with automatic weapons and bandoliers across their chests. It was a bad road all the way, but we took it fast and soon came across a monstrous bush fire which I was told had been set by the army so that they could see better. It was illegal, but a common practice. In the vicinity several fires were burning, and near one of them we came across a junior platoon officer and some of his men. I queried the fire.

"Everybody does it," was the response. Armies don't always follow regulations – not even their own.

Clearing the bush between the trees made for better visibility, creating fewer possibilities for concealment to those fighting against the soldiers and lessening the likelihood of an ambush. It did not always work, I was told. Sometimes, when the revolutionaries were patrolling in strength, the concealment offered by brush and grasses counted for little. The junior officer who had just joined us gave a crucial example:

"A month ago I was on a patrol with about twelve of my men over land that was essentially open and free of undergrowth. It seemed the way forward was clear, but there was a slight fold on the surface of the land in front of us that was more than enough to offer cover to the enemy. We were easily out-numbered. The only thing that permitted our survival was that we had superior fire power. There must have been about forty of them, and they just rose from the ground as if they had been hiding in burrows. We didn't see them until they were firing at us ..."

"What was the outcome?" I asked.

"We had three light machineguns; they had rifles and machetes. They wounded one of ours; we killed thirty-two of them, and a few of them managed to get away along gullies and into bush. We were very lucky. Their training is usually much better than what they displayed on that occasion ..."

Were they fighters? Perhaps refugees?

They were fighters, I was told. Part of the reason for military patrols was to prevent the movement of refugees out of the area. Civilians were needed to start the farms again, but they desperately wanted to get away; if they stayed on the land sooner or later the rebels would make demands of them even if the Portuguese did not. They were easy targets from both sides of the quarrel.

"You bivouac out here?"

"Units from the company take turns. I bring the platoon from the barracks at Maquela, and we come out into the bush for a week at a time. We live in the open but move every night. If we stayed longer the residents of any locale in the area could betray us. The rebels would soon discover us and we'd come under attack ..."

"And you always have the better weaponry ...?"

"Till now, yes. But somebody's supplying them. We have captured weapons from America, some from Czechoslovakia. And they're getting better at using them, too ..."

The young officer spoke with the youthful confidence of someone who does not yet have all the facts; he gave the impression the Portuguese army was handily bringing the rebellion under control. That was in the summer of 1963; but talking later that evening to others in this forward unit it was hard for them to disguise the more palpable realization of what was likely as time wore on. Time was on the side of the rebels. As it turned out, these were only the early days of a bitter colonial war that was to persist for another eleven years. It would be followed by a civil war that would last until 2002 – a total of over forty years of fighting lay ahead. This early portion of conflict was draining Portugal's resources and bringing untold miseries to thousands of Portuguese and Africans alike. God alone knows what it was doing to people's psyches.

We returned to Maquela do Zombo, and I was able to take a shower at the officers' mess.

"I want to be clean for whatever creatures are to share my bed with me tonight," I joked.

My companions roared with laughter that I should have chosen to turn down a room at their officers' mess in favour of a room at the Grande Hotel de Maquela do Zombo. They knew very well what a shabby little bug-pit it was.

"O Senhor Jeremias escolheu foder com as pulgas em vez das putas ...!"

Imagine my surprise when, arriving late at the hotel, tired but well-fed and drunken, I discovered Joaquim Lemos, the shoe salesman, seated on a wicker chair and waiting for me in the dark of the hotel's front porch.

By now I had become clued-in to the constant presence of minders – people selected from various walks of life, it seemed, just to keep an eye on my wanderings. There had been Serrano in Lisboa, then Lieutenant Joaquim Gonçalves in Luanda, and that nasty little man, Rodrigues, in Sá da Bandeira; I had suspected another, a businessman from South Africa on the train up to Nova Lisboa, his accent had been none too convincing. He had probably been Portuguese, I reckoned. And Esmeralda ...?

And now here was Joaquim Lemos, waiting for me at my hotel. We sat side-by-side on the porch.

"Come off it, Joaquim!" I upbraided him. "How many pairs of dainty Italian shoes do you suppose you're going to sell in Maquela do Zombo?"

It was dark, but I could see enough of his body language to realize I had embarrassed him.

In Moçâmedes the climate and sandy terrain had warranted little more than bare feet, or thongs. In Maquela do Zombo military-style corps boots, or gumboots, would have been a better suit.

"Friends by now we ought to be," I told him. "We've been travelling together for over a month. "Maybe you really are trying to set up a network to take orders for your line of shoes, but I reckon you have also been assigned to keep an eye on me ... no?"

He looked sheepish.

"Well, yes, I am a shoe salesman, of course. It is a part of my business in Lourenço Marques – just a part. I have many business concerns there, my fishing company probably the most important of them. But to be honest with you, this extra activity isn't quite what you think it is. I get paid for it, true, but it provides very little money, and that is not the reason I do it. Neither does it indicate my political bias. But it really is not an activity I can refuse. Things would go very badly for me if I give excuses and turn down a request from our authorities. You know about PIDE – they co-opt anybody and everybody they can. They knew I was coming to Angola on business, and I was asked to befriend you – so that I could make reports to them, who you are seeing, and so on. It's not exactly hard work. They pay my travel here and there, and I appreciate the way in which you've been leading me into parts of this country I would never have visited just selling shoes ..." he admitted.

"Look," he said, sweet reason itself. "We've come to know each other, and I like you. Yes, you could say we are friends by now. It has been a pleasure for me to know you, and I can assure you there is nothing in my reports to PIDE they could not find out for themselves by some other means. However, if I refused to report to them, if I made excuses, then I could be in serious trouble myself. Licences would be denied me, my own business would come under scrutiny, I wouldn't be able to travel with as much facility. They'd get nasty with me, tell me I'm refusing to do my part for my country, and so on. Much easier to say 'yes' to them ..."

I laughed, and not unkindly. His was an entirely likely explanation. The fascists had decided he could be useful to them, and they had put him on the spot.

"Do you agree with what your colonial authorities are doing?" I asked him.

"No. Of course not. But that's beside the point. If they didn't select me to follow on your heels, they'd find someone else. Believe me, you are far better off with me following you about. And I'm even enjoying myself ..."

Serrano had said pretty much the same thing when we were together in Lisboa.

"It won't be me on your tail when you come to Moçambique, so let's just keep it friendly – between you and me and no one else. I think we've enjoyed each other's company, no? Much better if we can keep it like that. In a week or two I shall be returning to Lourenço Marques, and someone else will be assigned to you there. I'd really like it if you'd come to visit with me when you get to Moçambique ..."

"What do you suppose happened in Luanda, after dinner the other night? Someone had entered my room and rifled through my papers, and it couldn't have been you ... Was it Maria Esmeralda?"

"I should let her tell you that herself," he replied. "But yes, it was. She is in precisely the same situation as I am. You say she didn't actually take anything?"

"Not as far as I know. I don't know what she could have done with it if she had, other than maybe set fire to it. No one would have been able to read my scrawl ..."

"She's a pharmacist," he said. "I'm convinced she is not the least interested in knowing what you are writing in your notes. Moving the papers around on your bed was probably just her way of warning you to be careful. She told me she likes you, so I'm sure she meant no harm.

"All the same," he added. "You should be careful with any papers like that. These PIDE people can be vindictive. If they suspected you were writing unpleasant things about them for your newspaper, they probably wouldn't try to read your notes. They could take them, perhaps burn them just to cause you an inconvenience ..."

Joaquim and I talked on into the night, and I gradually sobered up. I had horrors of climbing into the bed in the room, so had been happy to sit outside. But eventually we parted company.

"Where are you staying?" I asked him.

"At the officers' quarters," he said. "I gather they offered you the bed they've now offered me. They told me you didn't want it ..."

I was itching ferociously even before I climbed into bed with the bugs. The conviction of a poor night's rest had been firmly implanted, so I had a miserable night of it. But I had a sense of relief at my conversation with Joaquim. There was no question but that I would look him up once I arrived in Lourenço Marques. Unlikely, perhaps, but as things eventually turned out we formed a pretty warm relationship that lasted from then until Joaquim died a successful businessman in Lisboa some twenty-five years later.

From Maquela do Zombo I flew south via Damba to Carmona, arriving in the early evening. The plane was met by an official of the local governor's office, José de Mello, who escorted me to the Grande Hotel do Uige with instructions to freshen up and be ready for supper at 8:30 sharp. That was not such an imposition for me, but perhaps it was for him. He finally showed up at 9:30. We dined at the hotel. The rains had come. There had been a downpour just prior to my arrival in the town, everything sparkling and smelling deliciously fresh with the special scent that emanates from damped-down road dust mixed with the gratefully regenerated greenery of the hedges and boulevards.

Mello brought along a flabby little man whose name I never noted and now quite escapes me, but whom I remember principally for his atrocious manners at the dinner table. He would fill his face with food, then attempt to talk Portuguese politics with such voluble energy that the stuff he was trying to chew would squish out at the corners of his mouth and dribble down his poorly-shaven chops onto his chin. From time to time little specks of food would explode from his mouth across the table disappearing, presumably, onto the plates of his dining companions – or into the wine goblets. He waved his arms over the table as he guzzled down his food and drink and shouted out his viewpoints, then he would use the backs of both his hands and forearms to wipe away whatever excess food and spittle might have escaped his scarfing. The overall effect of what I am sure he intended as erudite discourse owed less to the information he was attempting to impart than to the sense of utter fascination I could not help but feel at its machine-gun delivery. Mello himself remained withdrawn throughout the meal, although I developed through the evening a distinct impression he had organized this little event with some cunning purpose in mind. More minders.

After eating we took coffee on the hotel veranda and discussed the merits of a film then showing at the local theatre – an Italian production with Portuguese subtitles that, when we finally decided to go and see it, was for me impossible to follow. On the screen was depicted a particularly oily Latin spiv who, at least in my imagination, might have been our loquacious dinner companion's cousin.

"It was a bit difficult for me to understand. Might have been easier if I had been able to speak Italian – or Portuguese ..." I told Mello afterwards, though I had quite enjoyed using my imagination to create a storyboard in my head.

"It was a simple story of Latin slothfulness," he quipped. "I'm sure you were able to get that much out of it, no?"

"Not really," I replied. "I thought the greasy little guy instinctively knew when to run and where to hide ..."

"No! No! You've got it all wrong. The greasy little guy was the bad guy – he survived, but all along he deserved to die ..."

"Oh! Indeed, I did get it wrong! I thought the bad guy was the general with his arm out ..." I mocked the straight-arm fascist salute, and Mello smiled.

"Not a memorable movie, it would appear, but you play the part well ..." he commented.

It was late, and Mello decided he would accompany me on the walk back to the hotel. It was necessary to seep a long time in the Portuguese culture if one wanted to gain a deep knowledge of the people, he told me. Portugal's was a noble history, and the Portuguese a noble people – possibly the most homogenized of all the European tribes. As a people, they had been pushed into the far southern corner of the continent where, in comparison with all of Europe's other nations, they had largely been left alone and spared the greater part of the traumatic round of conflicts that had been tearing other countries into pieces for generations. They had fought well and bravely during the First World War, he said – on the European front as well as in the defence of Angola and Moçambique. Many different peoples had moved through the country over the centuries – Phoenicians, Celts, Romans, Visigoths, Moors from the Maghreb – but by and large they had stayed and become a part of the fabric of what was now Portugal. Mello loved his country dearly, but he spoke of it with sadness in his voice.

"We made friends with the English and war on the French during Napoleon's time, but by and large the only people we fought over and over, so that we could secure our land and call those attacking us 'enemies,' were our neighbours from inside Iberia – the Spanish. We fought many actions against them, and they never conquered us. In the end, all the kingdoms of Iberia amalgamated into what is now Spain – except Portugal. Of all of them, we were the first – and the only ones to stand alone. By the time Spain was formed as a nation, we were already an homogenous people. In that way, in all of Europe, we are quite special; we have not had to contend with the backwards and forwards of invaders coming and going. Our borders today are pretty well the way they were drawn up over eight hundred years ago ..."

The two of us sat on the empty patio of the hotel, and for an hour or more Mello instructed me on the finer points of his people – and why they were here in Africa. Our loquacious dinner companion had gone to his home and bed.

"Who was he?" I asked.

"He's a friend. His wife died a couple of years ago, and we find we rather lean on one another ..." His voice trailed off and he sat quietly for several minutes, alone with his thoughts. Then he broke his silence and returned to our history lesson.

"You know, we have had this extraordinary history," he said. "Think of it: we are right on the edge of Europe with nowhere to go but out to sea. And we were very much a part of the new thinking at the time of the early Renaissance. Our ships were sailing off the coasts of Africa – in the

Mediterranean, the Atlantic and the Indian Ocean – in the 1400s. We were inventing ways to cross the seas long before the other nations of Europe. When they were timidly sailing within sight of their coasts, we were headed for the horizons. That's how we were able to gain such a head start in movement and trade – and discovery. We had developed specially-designed ships, specially-designed sails and rigging, specially-designed navigational equipment; we made maps and kept records, and we had an abiding curiosity about what was beyond our shores. We took the spice trade away from Venice, and overnight we were rich – a super-power. It was our time, our great time. We were on the fringes of Africa from those earliest days, and it didn't take us too long to begin moving into Africa's interior. We've been centuries in Angola. This war we are now being forced to fight – it has come upon us as a great and painful surprise.

"We had our days of real glory many centuries ago. You could say our imperial greatness lasted from the conquest of Ceuta in 1415 until the Battle of Alcácer Quibir in 1578, and the death of the country's boy king, Dom Sebastião.

"That's one hundred and sixty-three years that we were dominant, able to hold our own against the Hollanders then, in succession, Spain, Britain and France," said Mello, concluding his capsule history lesson.

"During that whole time our population never exceeded one-and-a-half million people. Against such odds, we were quite unable to regain our position of former glory – but we didn't do so badly. Not bad at all, if you think about it …!"

At this very moment, he told me, Portugal could rightfully claim to be the last of the world's old empires.

I wanted to bring him back to the present.

"You've been living in Carmona since before the present uprising. What happened right here?" I asked him.

His response was sobering. A cloud seemed to cover his brow, and for a few moments he just sat in thoughtful silence. Tears welled in the corners of his eyes and he nodded his head.

"Ah! Yes, of course, that's why you're here, and you are right to ask. This is where it began just over two years ago – here in Carmona, and at many other centres near here: Damba, Maquela do Zombo, Salvador, Santo António do Zaire, even as far south as Camabatela and Nambuangongo. There were attacks in and around all of them, and in all Angola we had perhaps two thousand soldiers to contain it all.

"That first night thirteen Portuguese were killed at Zalala, twenty-three at Kuitexa, seven at Mucaba, and so on. There were killings all over. About twenty were killed just on the district roads around here. Not so many right here in Carmona itself. My son was one of them ..."

Had I heard him correctly?

"Your son, Mello? Your own son was killed?"

He had been my minder until that moment, but now I saw him as a lonely old man forced to recall all over again that his only son had died in this mean, vicious little war. Perhaps he thought he had come to grips with it, but no man comes to grips with the loss of a son. His body was crumpled; his worn and off-white cotton jacket hung on his shoulders like a shroud. He pulled his tobacco and matches from a side pocket, and just held them in his hand. Mello was considerably older than me, and his tropical life had burned and lined his sad face, reddened his eyes and attacked his lower eyelids so that they sagged. Until this moment, I had quietly amused myself, thinking he resembled a Basset hound. Now, quite suddenly, I could not see it anymore; his was the face of a capitulation, a loss so profound, so immensely heart-rending I could feel his hollowness within my own breast.

"Yes," he said. "The attacks started in the district on March 15, and my son was one of those who died, here in Carmona, a few days later. I was right here, on the veranda of this hotel, when the first attack came at about 2:30 in the morning. I went immediately to my home and defended it with my wife and my son, and two others, but we were not attacked on the north side of the town, where my home is. We learned there was a force of about six hundred attackers, but they didn't come that first night to our place, thank God. Carmona itself came under attack the following night, so we had some warning ... but the rebel forces were never able to capture and hold it ... Two platoons of paratroopers dropped into Carmona within the first forty-eight hours of the start of the trouble, and we saw no replacements until May. Very quickly we formed civilian vigilante groups and so were able to fight back ..."

Overnight there were hundreds of refugees both in the urban centres and wandering about the countryside. Every town in the north of Angola was facing something of the same sort of situation. There was widespread panic, and no one seemed to know where to go or what to do. Mello soon found himself assigned to refugee problems.

"People were nervous, as you can imagine. Trigger-happy. My son had gone to help at the local barracks. There were only twenty-three soldiers there; four were Portuguese officers, the rest were Africans. My son was alone on the road when he was shot, so no one ever discovered exactly what had happened, or who did it ..."

PART III
Congo (DRC)

Part III – Congo (DRC)

Leopoldville 219

Antagonists – A Colonial Survey 245

Luanda *Ciao* 265

Leopoldville

The Democratic Republic of the Congo (DRC), as it is known today, received its independence from Belgium at the end of June 1960. Patrice Lumumba, leader of the *Mouvement National Congolais* (MNC), served as the country's newly elected first Prime Minister, overseeing the transition from Belgian colony to independent nation. Almost immediately following a hurried and chaotic hand-over, the Congolese army, the *Force Publique*, mutinied. A leftover from the large punitive colonial force raised by King Leopold II in 1885 to enslave and suppress the territory's impoverished population, it was commanded by Belgian General Émile Janssens, with an officer corps of white Belgians. He and his fellow officers had little faith in the ability of the new African leadership to control such a vast country; the discontented African rank and file felt necessary changes in the military structure would be too slow if the force was to continue to be led by Belgian officers.

Although Lumumba was exceptionally popular throughout most of the country, this was not so among the military, nor among the general population in the eastern provinces where western capitalists were keeping greedy eyes on the enormous mining wealth of the area. The mutiny was widely supported by the co-opted and secessionist-minded leaders of these provinces – South Kasai and Katanga – with the none-too-covert blessings of Belgium and the United States.

Lumumba had applied to Belgium and the United States – and the United Nations – for assistance in bringing the ensuing chaos under control, but his entreaties were denied. In a sense, his predicament was not unlike Fidel Castro's in Cuba a couple of years earlier: his leadership was socialistic – and nationalistic – political perfidy in the face of aggressive capitalist posturing with an agenda already in mind – and gung-ho to snip off the budding of any recreant upstart. When Lumumba turned for help to the Soviet Union he was immediately branded a 'communist' by his adversaries. This was sufficient excuse for the secretive political forces of Belgium and the United States to persuade the country's new president, Joseph Kasavubu, to dismiss him. He was turned over to the Katangan army barely two months after being named Prime Minister. One of the leaders of the *Force Publique* that had opposed Lumumba from the very beginning was Joseph-Désiré Mobutu who, as Army Chief of Staff, had staged a *coup d'état* earlier the same day Lumumba had been arrested. Lumumba was held in captivity in eastern Congo until January 1961 then, with the connivance of America's CIA and the Belgians, he was tortured and executed. In 1965 Mobutu staged a second coup, installed himself as dictator, re-named himself Mobutu Sese Seko, and proceeded to exploit his own people, stripping his country to enrich himself, in the process becoming one of the wealthiest men in the world. His overt corruption largely and conveniently overlooked, he remained America's corporate darling until his death in 1997, thirty-two years later.

Mobutu was useful to the west. Katanga is one of the richest patches of real estate in the world. It produces cobalt, high grade copper, tin, radium, uranium, gold and vies with Angola and Russia as one of the world's leaders in the production of diamonds. To this day mining interests, particularly from the United States and Canada – as well as the country's old colonizer, Belgium – have been a constant in destabilizing the Congo. Initially this was accomplished remarkably easily by supporting Katangan separatist aspirations and by contributing to a prodigious propaganda campaign. It is easy to exploit the confused, and to keep the confused confused. It is not difficult to mix bogus altruism with propaganda to create turmoil and disorientation – not unlike administering a powerful sedative drug to facilitate an act of rape. The more unstable the country, the more corrupt its leader(s), the easier it becomes to rip off the local population. International instability has been the most useful tool of western corporate democracies for generations; propaganda – hard-sell advertising – has become the staple of free enterprise.

Portugal's elites had been living off the fat of their African colonies for centuries; the wealth of Angola is in every way comparable to that of Katanga – plus there is the addition of Cabinda's oil. My interest in visiting Congo (DRC) had been to try to understand and report on the colonial situation next door, particularly as it seemed to be falling apart. Had I been snowed by the sweet reason of the Portuguese 'line' I am sure I might have become their darling. However, once it was detected that my questioning tended to be combative, my (I thought) quite reasonable tack was that of any western journalist: that, most likely unimpressed by Portuguese propaganda, my best tack would be to assess as quickly as possible the various impediments crudely strewn in my way. These would have been set in place specifically to sway my judgement, plant doubts in my mind, or even in an attempt to assume control over my output and so contain any damage inflicted through unwanted journalistic enlightenment. My Portuguese hosts were stubbornly unimaginative in trying to employ a range of devises to curb journalists like me, to prevent us from seeing and presenting to the world too much bad press, or of revealing too much of the misery existing among the African populations of the colonies. In my own case, once invited it would have been difficult to impose a blanket censorship, but a variety of minders had been doing their best to prevent me from seeing what I really needed to see to get a clear picture. Despite the annoyance of this, an image was filtering through in any case. I felt it was now an imperative to visit the centres of action – the front, if there was one – and it was clear, even to my hosts, the only practical way this could be tackled would be an approach from the other side. I made up my mind to enter the Congo, meet up with the rebels operating from there, if possible, then try to re-enter Angola's war-torn region from the north.

It was no longer possible for me to rely on the gracious guidance of the Portuguese. I needed their permission to leave the country, and to re-enter it when I was done; they would not have cared to admit such a thing, but their controls over me were such that they had me well-cuffed. I could not do very much without their say-so, the watchful gaze of PIDE and the constant presence of their minders. They did it in the nicest way, of course, and with smiles and open hands and slaps on my back – and many shrugs. No gentleman is so suave as a Latin gentleman. This is the side of them I was encouraged to see, and I think if I had learned anything at all from my hosts, it was to try to be as genial with them as they were with me. By the same token, few cruelties can be quite so dispassionately meted out as Latin cruelties – and this, to be sure, was the side most colonized African knew best – the side of them I was discouraged from examining.

A visit to the Congo would have been most useful. I put in my request through Lieutenant Joaquim Gonçalves, who treated it charitably enough – but with just a smidgen of suspicion. He agreed to ask his superiors. In the end I was permitted a ten-day absence, otherwise I would not be allowed re-entry to Angola, and that would mean the end of my entire travel programme, In addition, I would have to agree to a thorough debriefing by the Portuguese military when I returned.

Ah-ha! The cuffs were tightened. They proved a limitation indeed.

It seemed drastic, but I put on my most cheerful countenance, and willingly went along with their demands. Once I had initiated the idea as forcefully as I had, expressing a cooperative geniality was really the only thing I could do to avoid antagonizing my hosts and creating a mountain of needless suspicion. If everything worked out the way both the Portuguese and I wanted it to, I'd get my story, and they stood to learn something useful from the debriefing – some benefit in the scheme for both of us …

Not much has gone very right in the Democratic Republic of the Congo since the early days of independence and the assassination of Patrice Lumumba. By paying colossal kickbacks to Mobutu, mining concerns principally from Belgium, the United States and Canada, had been well-positioned to plunder the country of its riches, giving back as little as possible to the Africans who lived at the entrances to the mine shafts and did the work. These mining companies succeeded in large part by deliberately fostering division along the lines of Britain's ruthless XIX century concept of 'divide and rule' – taking advantage of the inevitable conflict that too easily flares between the numerous ethnic groups within and across the country's borders. It is an astonishing figure, but as I write these sentences I have become aware of statistics indicating more people have suffered premature death – by all causes – in the Democratic Republic of the Congo in the past near-sixty years since independence than were killed in the front line fighting of both World Wars I and II combined. The nation's civil war, plus its off-shoots and retaliations, which have raged on-and-off since 1961, are collectively (military and civilian) second only to the Second World War in claiming the most human life of any war in history.

It is not the purpose of this work and I am not in a position to examine these awful statistics in detail. Suffice it to say the numbers would be alarmingly high even if only a percentage of them were accurate. The point is that in the summer of 1963, just three years following independence, the DRC (the country has gone through several name-changes) was an ungodly mess. Because of Cold War tensions extant between the Soviet bloc and the west, it was difficult to travel between fascist-controlled Luanda and Leopoldville.[33] Visas and permissions were difficult to obtain; flights were irregular. On the day I was able to make the trip to the capital of this unruly nationalistic oligarchy-in-the-making, I flew as one of only two passengers on board an airliner with seating capacity for thirty-six passengers.

Descending from the plane at Leopoldville's international airport, I was

---

[33] Both blocs shamelessly faced off for favoured influence over the riches that seemed up for grabs in eastern Congo. The Soviets were anxious to obtain a foothold in such a newly-liberated and wealthy part of the African continent. The United States, in leading the west and hypocritically warning of the dangers of letting the Congo 'go communist,' was equally as dishonest as the Soviets in their befriending and supporting a thug like Mobutu – their venal eyes all the while on both the wealth of eastern Congo and the oil of Cabinda. In a land so desperately in need of assistance, funds flooded into the coffers of Mobutu (his overseas bank deposits are still a matter of conjecture) – along with lavish quantities of arms for the repressive regime's military and police forces. Nearly sixty years on, no one has ever come to grips with the problems that beset DRC.

met by an untidy and drunken Congolese soldier who shoved a sub-machinegun into my belly at the foot of the stair and demanded my portable typewriter.

I smiled and attempted to explain in my halting French that I was a journalist who had come to report on his beautiful country for my newspaper, and that I needed my typewriter to accomplish the job.

He nodded understandingly, then made aggressive motions for the camera slung about my neck.

"But I need that, too ...!" I protested, nervously eying his finger on the trigger of his weapon.

At that moment the sole fellow passenger on my flight, by now standing behind me on the stair, chimed in with a most effusive stream of sweet French language reasoning, and in English he suggested I open my arms and hands benevolently and smile.

He in turn smiled at the red-eyed souse of a soldier, explaining in very simple terms that he was an Italian member of a United Nations team come to the country to assist in welcoming the Congo into the great family of nations, and that this miserable little fellow threatening my life had a major part to play in the proceedings ...

"...Just like this journalist gentleman," he said. "And if you take away the tools with which he has come to assist, he will be unable to work – unable to assist ..."

At first the soldier had difficulty paying attention. His gaze flitted angrily from my camera bag to my typewriter to my face. I tried to smile as instructed by the UN officer, but found it hard to take my eyes off the fellow's sub-machinegun. It seemed dangerous to make eye contact, but at last the Italian's words began to penetrate whatever it was the soldier might have used to acknowledge the world around him, and he turned his gaze to the man behind me on the stairs. He moved his head ever so slightly, a sort of lowering of the brows that indicated he was attempting to hear what was being said to him and, to my great relief, shifted the muzzle of his sub-machinegun away from my navel. Almost courteously, with words I could not understand but gestures that are surely universal, the fellow opened an arm in my direction to motion me forward, wafting the full complement of passengers forward off the stairway on which the two of us had been held captive for several long minutes.

Crossing his hands on his breast, the Italian bobbed his head several times in obsequious gratitude, whispering sideways for me to do the same. As we walked purposefully across the tarmac into the terminal building he said to me out of the corner of his mouth:

"Do not turn around ... Do not look back ... Keep walking and we'll be alright ... He knows if he opens fire he'll be shooting at all those officers standing by the terminal door ..."

Welcome to Leopoldville.

The Portuguese had allowed me ten days; the Congolese granted a visa for eight. My kind UN assistant at the airport was named Guiseppe Gallai, a representative of the United Nations Educational, Scientific and Cultural Organization (UNESCO). He was met by a car and driver, and willingly escorted me through a labyrinth of tumultuously busy and filthy streets to a contingent of the Canadian army that was billeted in quarters near the centre of the city. That first night I was offered a warm welcome – a shower, a hot meal and a bed – at the officers' mess of the Royal Canadian Corps of Signals (57 Canadian Signal Unit). It was the French language arm of the regiment under the command of Colonel D.G. Green. The unit had been chosen to work with United Nations forces in setting up communications throughout the country during the first years of utter chaos that had followed independence in 1960. The soldiers were doing outstanding work, but in the short time I visited with them it became apparent they were battling uphill.

I was a persistent smoker in those days and, during that morning as I was walking back into town from the officers' mess, I passed a young boy in the street carrying a wide selection of cigarettes on a tray supported at waist-height in front of him by a strap around his neck. I was especially surprised to see him carrying a few packets of my own preferred Canadian brand in their distinctive packaging – Export-A. I stopped him and asked to buy one, for which he charged me eighty Congolese francs. Translated into Canadian funds, it was a sum somewhat less than I might have paid for the same packet in Toronto, so I felt I had struck a bargain.

Later that same evening, though, socializing with my countrymen in the lounge of the officers' mess, I realized the pack of cigarettes I had bought earlier was now almost empty, so I rose from the table where I was seated and approached the bar. The steward was a young corporal from Québec. In addition to a display of various alcoholic beverages there was also a small array of the various cigarette brands he was offering for sale – among them I could see several identical packs to the one I had purchased from the boy in the street that morning.

"Export-A? Certainly – that'll be three francs, please, sir," the barman said.

"Three francs! Good god, man! – I paid eighty francs for the same thing on the street earlier today. How come you are asking only three …?"

"That doesn't surprise me at all," the steward replied. "All equipment destined for the Canadian UN military contingent here, including everything you see on display behind the bar, is brought in from Canada by RCAF air transport. It is landed at Leopoldville airport – but it is unloaded and moved to the UN warehouse by a unit of the Pakistani army. They rob us blind. The kicker is that I must pay for these cigarettes at the Pakistani-supervised warehouse – close to eighty francs a pack, as you did on the street. But our government insists I sell them to you over this counter at the regulation price of just three francs. Crazy, huh?"

Crazy, indeed, but only a small peek at the level of corruption I was to learn about that evening (accompanied by the cynical laughter of experience) from the Canadian officers who had been serving in the Congo since independence.

"I'll tell you a story," one of the senior officers offered up. "We're supposed to oversee the establishment of communications throughout the entire country, and we've been working pretty hard at it. A few months ago we heard from one of our teams, way off in the boonies up-river, that as our boys were uncoiling huge wheels of copper wiring, and laying it down over long distances, some enterprising gang of thieves was hard at work behind them, rolling the stuff up again and selling it off on the black market. While they were at it, they also walked off with an enormous transformer we had just installed. God alone knows what they wanted that for …"

More jaded laughter.

"How about the train? Tell him about the train," one of the officers chuckled into his beer.

It was hard to piece the story together, the men were laughing so hard, but the almost unbelievable gist of it was that an entire train, engine-to-caboose, had gone missing somewhere between its departure in Katanga and its destination at the coast west of Leopoldville.

"The whole bloody train?"

"Yeah. It happened a year or so ago. A full train, several rail cars loaded to the brim with ore, left Kalemie, on the west side of Lake Tanganyika – or somewhere in Katanga – headed for Leopoldville, and eventually the coastal port of Matadi. It started out, but never arrived. For a journey like that, the train first travels on track, then the cars are loaded onto barges, to be transported by river – then they are put back on rails, and then off again onto barges. It's a hell of a rigmarole, entailing no less than eight transfers from barge-to-rail and back again. Somewhere along the way the whole goddamn train managed to vanish into thin air. It now lies at the bottom of a river, somewhere, or else it was diverted off into the bush to be used as chicken coops ... We've been told they're looking for it, but no one's yet been able to find it ..."

Several other people dropped in at the mess that evening. Two of them were diplomats from the Canadian Embassy – Lyon Weidman and Christopher Anstis. They, along with the senior Signals officers, were curious about what I might have seen during my rounds in Angola. I saw no reason to hold back telling them what I could, but what surprised me was that the Canadian military men appeared to know so little; one of them even asked me where Angola was – 'exactly.'

Later in the evening, the kindly Italian who had helped prevent me from being machinegunned at the airport, Guiseppe Gallai, made his informal appearance. Happy to see him again, I told him I had come to Leopoldville to try to find two people: Dr. Ian Gilchrist, the son of the missionary doctor Sid Gilchrist, whom I had failed to meet during my visit to Nova Lisboa and Dondi, and Holden Roberto, leader of the revolutionary *União das Populacões de Angola* (UPA) – the organization that had initiated the northern Angolano slaughter in March, 1961 – an action which, by the end of that year, had not only led to the deaths of thousands of people in the north of the country, but created a massive influx of refugees into the DRC.

The group of us sat in the mess and talked until late in the evening. Guiseppe knew his way about the city and appeared to be well-connected with local goings-on and who it was that could pull strings to help get things done. Whether you wanted to build a house or park a car, or sell your vegetables in the market, someone had to be paid off.

"No one can achieve anything at all if he goes at it by himself," he said. "Everyone is on the take, no matter how big or how petty. To get into a government office to speak to an official, you must pass through a veritable army of little thugs and thieves and fixers, and they all want whatever might jangle or crinkle in your pockets. It's a little different for UN personnel and the military but, even then, it is virtually impossible to get anything done in a hurry – or even in a timely fashion. Or at all. This is the land of slow calculation and exquisitely overt corruption – and some of the worst offenders, it can be said, are the Belgians. Not surprising, really. They've had a hundred years of experience out here."

Great fun! This comment got everyone laughing.

"No, really!" Guiseppe emphasized cheerfully. "The entire Congo basin is a vipers' nest. Angola is at war, but in terms of corruption it is nothing like the Congo, and its utterly chaotic twitching, during this moment of peace. People are trigger happy, only they haven't opened fire everywhere – yet ..."

The Portuguese were colonizers, he admitted, but their domination over the Africans under their rule had been a benevolence compared to the sheer brutality of the Belgians' behaviour, and the ways they found to abuse every level of the Congolese population.

Just two short years before my arrival in Leopoldville, Holden Roberto's UPA had amalgamated with the *Parti Democratique Angolaise* (PDA) to form the *Frente Nacional de Libertação de Angola* (FNLA) – and unleashed his horrendous assault on northern Angola.

"Fifty thousand dead on both sides, Angolano and Portuguese – and in less than a month?" I queried. "It would seem to me the Belgians don't have a monopoly on brutality ..."

"Well, I suppose we shouldn't be too surprised by whoever it is who removes the cork from the bottle of poison. After all, Holden Roberto is supported quite openly by the United States of America ..."

Hearing that comment, I could not help but notice how the Canadian officers fell silent.

"You shouldn't have any trouble finding the person you need," Guiseppe said to me as he dropped me near the centre of the city. He knew the UPA/FNLA compound and had agreed to pick me up and take me there on this morning.

"There!" he said, pointing to a seedy-looking house that, except for its greater size, looked little different from any of the others on the street; old colonial structure, sun-blistered paint of undetermined dark colour on its walls (blue? green? grey?) – topped by a tin roof. "Dr. Gilchrist is assisting the Angolanos and that's his clinic, so someone will be able to help you."

I walked up to the open front door and was met by a very attractive young

Caucasian lady coming out.

"I'm trying to get in touch with Holden Roberto, the leader of the UPA/FNLA ..." I told her hesitantly, thinking maybe I should have attempted to address her in my appallingly inadequate French.

Holden Roberto

"He might be in the office," she replied in familiar and perfect English. "Come inside and we'll see if he's there ..."

He wasn't.

She reached out and took a small blonde-haired boy from the arms of a young woman I assumed was his Congolese nanny. There was yet another little white boy hanging back in the shadows.

"It appears he'll return later this afternoon," the young white lady told me. She fondled the small child and kissed him.

Mother.

"I could wait," I told her. "I've come up from Angola to try to meet with him. There's someone else I'd like to see, as well. A medical doctor from Dondi by the name of Ian Gilchrist, son of Dr. Sidney Gilchrist ..."

"Ian is not here, either," she smiled. "I know that for a fact. He's down in Thysville. I'm his wife – Joyce Gilchrist ... This little fellow is our son, Sean. That one, hiding over there, is Erin ... And Dr. Sid is not here ... If he is in the Congo I think we would have heard about it by now ..."

Dr. Ian Gilchrist

She was delighted and expressed gratitude that I had recently seen her sister-in-law, and was able to say, in addition to the news of my visit to Dondi, that all had seemed well with her. I told Joyce it had been Betty who informed me where to look for her brother; that if I could find Ian I would surely find Roberto – and vice versa. Holden Roberto, as leader of his northern Angolano troops, used this very house as a portion of his headquarters operation. The UPA/FNLA soldiers were encamped in the military installation at Thysville, conveniently located halfway between Leopoldville and the Angola frontier.

For the time being this house was also home to Joyce and Ian and their small family. It did not appear to be the principal UPA/FNLA headquarters, but rather part of a compound in which Holden Roberto maintained several offices and working facilities. I had the impression his organization retained the use of several properties in the vicinity and that this particular building housed Dr. Ian's miniscule clinic in addition to being living space for the doctor's family. Dr. Ian's principal activity was to serve the hundreds of exhausted refugees who had fled the fighting in Angola, as well as injured rebel personnel. The clinic doors were open to any Angolanos in need of medical attention – and, by nightfall, to any requiring a stretch of floorspace and a roof over their heads. Stacked up the walls, and in corners, the interior of the house was in use for storage – sacks of rice and grains and all manner of other foodstuffs. In the tiny dispensary space was being used for hundreds of sealed boxes of medical supplies. Opened boxes, jars and bottles lined the shelves that had been put up against all the walls; they were even piled under a simple examination couch.

"It's a little crowded, as you can see," Joyce said with surprising good humour. "Sometimes we have as many as thirty people crammed in here overnight. Especially when the rains come."

Anyone might have been favourably impressed by this young mother's stoic dedication trying to raise a family in such crowded conditions, and in face of such a heap of other people's miseries. Yet she must have known what she was getting into when she elected to follow her doctor husband into the heart of an awakening Africa. She was twenty-seven years old. She had been born in Ingomar, Nova Scotia, daughter of a United Church minister. After her schooling in Maritime Canada, she majored in psychology at Mount Allison University in Sackville, New Brunswick, and met her future husband one summer when she was working as a nurse's aide at a Toronto mental hospital. Ian was there attending a pre-medical course. They were married on the day Joyce graduated from Mount Allison – the marriage at noon, the graduation ceremony at 2:00 PM.

"From the time Ian and I planned our marriage, I knew I would be coming to Angola," she told me as we sat and chatted in her Leopoldville kitchen – but it was not to happen immediately. Both of them went on to further studies at Dalhousie University. Joyce took a degree in education, while Ian knuckled down to his first year of medical studies.

He had been born in Halifax but spent his first few years in Angola where his father was physician for the complex of Protestant missions and schools in the south of the country. As a child he learned to speak Umbundu fluently. The family remained in Angola until the outbreak of the Second World War, returning to Canada in 1940. Dr. Sid Gilchrist joined the ranks of the North Nova Scotia Highlanders, serving out the war in England, North Africa and Italy. Following the war, he specialized in public health at the University of Toronto, then returned to Angola with the family in 1947 to serve at the mission station of Dondi.

Dr. Ian completed high school in Canada moving on to university and, in time, taking medical studies in Nova Scotia. He returned to Angola in 1961 after the uprising against the Portuguese had started. He took his small family with him, but they were able to remain only a short time before visas expired and were not renewed. They were obliged to leave the country. From Luanda they flew via Brazzaville, then on to Freetown in Sierra Leone, where their second son was born, and Ian was able to work in a local hospital.

"It was a blessing – an immense relief that at last I was able to communicate with people in English …" Joyce said.

They had been in Freetown a matter of only a few weeks when Ian received a request to assist as a volunteer at the American missionary hospital in Leopoldville to work under Angolano Dr. José Liahuca – who in turn answered to the rebel leader, Holden Roberto. Joyce returned to Canada with the children, and only after Ian was settled in his Leopoldville post was she able to join him there. It was in this way that Ian came to work with the refugees fleeing into the Congo from northern Angola, and so come to know Roberto.

For two years Holden Roberto's UPA, though based in Leopoldville, had been operating in considerable disruption and confusion. One of the most pressing matters related to where soldiers could be billeted, and more adequately armed and trained. There were thousands of Angolano refugees flooding into the city, many of them volunteering for the fight against the Portuguese, but some of these newcomers favoured the political motivations of the UPA while others were quite vehemently opposed to it – political differences generally running along ethnic/tribal lines. Although new recruits were needed, individual volunteers had to be carefully screened and monitored. For the longest time, shelter being at a premium in a city burgeoning with refugees, Roberto did not have a proper headquarters or an office from which to run his government in exile. This was the position Ian found when he initially came to the city.

As for myself, I had so little time available in Leopoldville I was never able to meet with Dr. Ian. I learned the essentials of his story from his wife when I met her that day after being dropped off by Guiseppe Gallai. After I had left the Congo I developed a correspondence with Dr. Ian that continued off and on over a number of years.

When the small family had initially come to Angola in 1961, Joyce was able to assist Ian's mother, Frances, with bookkeeping at the mission hospital.

"In a way I found Angola much as I'd expected it," said Joyce. "Ian had talked about it a great deal. I was taken with the un-tropical nature of the place – the two feet of deep dust on the road to Bailundo. The cities impressed me, they were so modern and colourful, and I was fascinated by the mosaic work on the sidewalks ...[34]

"It has been just about impossible to find anywhere to live in Leo," she told me. "The UPA really need the space we occupy as a storage area. But here we are – in Leo – and I like it. There are so many people I am never alone, and there is never a shortage of things to do, to say nothing of trying to look after my own two children. I am not a linguist, but am trying to cope with French, because we are living in a French-speaking country, and I am seriously trying to learn Portuguese, as well as Umbundu, the language of our mission district. It's not easy."

Ian worked with Dr. Liahuka in the compound of Roberto's government in exile. Periodically the two physicians would be absent together for extended periods, and Joyce would not know where they were.

"I suppose there is a certain degree of danger, but I don't think Ian has yet crossed back into Angola. I'm not too worried for the present," she told me.

When she had spare time she taught English to a few of the male nurses – one hour, five days a week, if she was not called elsewhere.

Joyce said she had always been a pacifist and had earlier found herself at loggerheads with Ian's view that the time had come to fight. Opposition to Portuguese colonial rule had been much of her husband's life, she said; her own views were somewhat less passionate.

"But I switched my tune when I arrived in Angola and saw the conditions there. Now I am sure fighting is the only way to change things. Ian has had to live most of his life with these frustrations. It's hardly surprising he feels stronger about it than I do."

At least on the local level, which she could more accurately assess when she was at the mission station, the Portuguese administration of the towns had seemed exceptionally poor, exceptionally callous. Perhaps egalitarian laws existed on the books, she said – or at least the Portuguese always insisted they did – but they were not being applied conscientiously in areas located far from the watchful eyes, or sympathies, of any central governing power. People suffered because of incompetence and corruption – and those who suffered the most, of course, had brown skin.

Talking about Holden Roberto, Joyce considered him a fine man, a good leader of his men and of his cause. She saw great similarity in the political views of both Roberto and her husband; perhaps that was why the two of

---

[34] Decorative mosaic sidewalks have been a feature of Portuguese cities for centuries, both at home and in their colonies.

them got along as well as they did.

"Ian has strong feelings that justice must prevail. He has a genuine affection for the Angolano people and is outraged they have been so badly treated. Some people might call him a fanatic. I don't, of course. I see him as dedicated, and I can understand it because I have a certain knowledge myself, now. He writes quite a bit – for Africa Today, and the Canadian Broadcasting Corporation ..."

It was extraordinary to me to find this seemingly all-Canadian girl, so incredibly alone in this teeming city with her two small children, gamely forging ahead with her everyday chores as she waited for her man to return – and all of it in the utter silence imposed by her admitted inability to cope with any local language.

She laughed.

"I'm never alone," she waved at the horde of refugees both inside the house and outside in what passed for a garden.

"I'm never without lots to do. And, as to language – well, of course I would like to be able to speak to everyone with greater facility – but that is coming, and for the moment there are other far bigger handicaps. When we first came here, food was difficult to come by, for instance, but we are managing. We eat quite well now. There is a lot of variety in the market, although the prices are high by Congolese standards. Both kids had measles, and that threw us a bit. But we're really very comfortable. As a matter of fact, I even feel a bit guilty about sleeping in a bed. Everyone else, as you can see, must sleep on the ground. They're all around us – so I don't feel lonely. Mind you, with all these sacks of flour stacked in the house, the mice are dreadful. I pity the poor people on the floor. The other night a mouse ran across my bed, which was a little annoying. But mice don't bother me now the way they used to ..."

She had a houseboy, Mauricio, who cooked and helped with the children, and kept the place as clean as he could.

"Ian and I both find we can do quite well on very little. We could live anywhere. I suppose I'm a bit that way – restless, content with few things that others might insist are necessary. Really, I am happy here."

We talked about money. The regular exchange rate at the time ran at sixty-four francs to the US dollar; the black-market rate was three hundred and fifty francs to the US dollar.

As to the house: in addition to kitchen and UPA office, there was a clinic and a room where surgeries were undertaken. There was one bedroom, and an upstairs guest room, a storage room and a front room that doubled as living room and extra storage space. The refrigerator stood against one wall in the living room area.

Outside in the garden, refugees lit fires every evening so they could do their cooking, using the smoke to keep the bugs at bay. Perhaps not the life of choice for many North American housewives, but Joyce Gilchrist seemed to be sailing through it all with an immensely cordial spirit.

My first appointment with Holden Roberto fell through. He was a busy man, trying to co-ordinate the training of an army at Thysville; maintain control over an army active in the fields and jungles of northern Angola; politicking for acceptance as a very active and militant guest of what passed for a government in exile in Congo (DRC) – without drawing down on the head of the government in Leopoldville the wrath of an angry Portuguese army. In addition, he had to send emissaries to explain the rebel cause to such entities as the United Nations and the newly-formed Organization of African Unity, and he was trying to create a coalition with other nationalist entities facing off against the Portuguese. He was also busy cozying-up to the USA in the hope of garnering further funding. (The UPA was sponsored as a government in exile by the American Committee on Africa through its Emergency Relief Fund for Angola). Much as such a man-on-the-go might have needed publicity for his cause, Roberto had to call a halt to his schedule at some point of any given day, if only to snatch a few hours of sleep.

I had been able to take a couple of pictures of him in the afternoon, while it was still daylight, but then he said:

"Let us meet this evening," in the office at Joyce's home. "There is a guest room at the house, with two beds. One of my men will be staying the night there, but you are welcome to take the extra bed. That way you could spend the night with us and it would give us an opportunity to relax. We could talk until the early-morning hours ..."

It seemed the best solution, so I returned to the Signals' mess to collect my gear and thank the Canadians for their hospitality, appearing after sundown at the UPA headquarters to enjoy a late supper with Joyce.

Holden Roberto showed up at about 10:00 PM. He entered the building with another man, a large and bearded individual whom he introduced as the UPA's Foreign Minister, Jonas Savimbi.

Both men wore tinted glasses, even though it was dark outside, and their ability to see in the dimness of the city's unlit streets must have been hampered. Savimbi took his impenetrable green glasses off, revealing alert eyes and an intelligent face. Roberto did not; he wore glasses that had been tinted yellow, which seemed to temper his eyes and give his countenance a sinister appearance. His eyes were like hard brown glass marbles, and his face had a set, almost malevolent, aspect – considerably more threatening than his companion's, I thought. Joyce excused herself to attend to her children, leaving me alone with the two men in the small UPA office.

Savimbi sipped from a bottle of fruit juice and said nothing. He remained about an hour, allowing Roberto to do most of the talking, then he excused himself to go to bed. Holden Roberto settled back in his chair and we talked informally for several more hours about the situation in northern Angola.

"… And we are increasingly active there. The whole area is up in arms. Savimbi, the man who was just here, is from the southern region. He wants to carry the fight into the south …"

Roberto said he wanted me to take a week and travel with him to the training camp at Thysville. It was impossible. My visa to remain in DRC was limited to eight days – now almost expired; even if I could extend it, I was limited by the Portuguese to just ten days – and if I over-stayed that, then I would be in danger of not being permitted back into Angola and having the rest of my trip cancelled. I knew, moreover, that if something like that were to happen, and the Portuguese got as nasty with me as I was told they could be, then my finances would not suffice for me to travel on alone.

"That's too bad. I think you would be impressed with the quality of the troops …"

"I'm sure I would be," I told him. "But I have seen soldiers in training before, so am not unfamiliar with the process. If I changed my plans to over-stay my time away, the Portuguese would surely deny me re-entry to Angola…"

He understood the point.

"The only thing that might make that a risk worth taking would be if I could cross the border with your men, see some of the action for myself – and then return here with them …" I told him.

"The Thysville camp might be a useful experience for you, even though you say you have seen soldiers in training before. But it could take you the better part of a week to get down there, see the place and get back," said Roberto.

"As for entering Angola with our troops, that would be dangerous ... You could very easily be mistaken for a Portuguese, and I would not be able to guarantee your protection. You might become the target of either side. Dangerous for you, dangerous for us. So, no – anything like that is out of the question."

Roberto was thirty-eight years old at the time of our meeting. He referred to himself as the president of the Angolano Government in Exile. He was born on the Angola side of the border, in São Salvador do Congo in 1923, but left for Leopoldville with his parents when he was two. He was a descendent of the royal family of the ancient Kingdom of Kongo whose lands were bordered in the west by the Atlantic Ocean, and in the north crossed over onto the right bank of the Congo River. It was a land that stretched eastwards some nine hundred kilometres from the coast in its northern section, narrowing to approximately five hundred kilometres from the coast in the south. North-to-south, the kingdom extended from the riverbank lands on the northern side of the Congo River, south to the Kwanza River in the latitude of Luanda, Angola's modern capital. As a kingdom it lasted (with much interference from Portuguese, Belgians and others) from approximately 1390 until 1914, with its capital at M'banza-Kongo – which the Portuguese had named São Salvador do Congo (it reverted to its original name after independence in 1975). The Bakongo are a sophisticated coastal and inland people who had signed trade treaties with the Portuguese as early as the XV century. Christianity was successfully introduced as early as 1485 with the conversion of King Nzinga a Nkuwu.[35]

Roberto claimed his political awareness dated from the time in 1954 when he returned to Angola for a visit and saw Portuguese officials maltreating an old man. It was an incident that stimulated strong political views, and eventually led him into forming the FNLA – *Frente Nacional de Libertação de Angola*. Within a short space of time this group would join with others and transform itself into the UPA – *União dos Povos de Angola*. In 1958 Roberto

---

[35] A small stone Roman Catholic church was erected at M'banza-Kongo in 1491 and is said to be the oldest church in Africa south of the Sahara Desert. It suffered extensive damage in successive conflicts, but was repaired and was consecrated as a cathedral in 1590. Now known as the Cathedral of the Holy Saviour of the Congo, its revered ruins still stand today. See also note 40, below, and Ilha de Moçambique, p.338

travelled to Ghana for the All-Africa Peoples Congress and, while there, met with such other African political luminaries as Kwame Nkrumah, Patrice Lumumba, Tom Mboya and Kenneth Kaunda. He met Jonas Savimbi, an Ocimbundu from southern Angola – the man who had just gone up to bed – in 1960 when the latter was a scholarship student at the University of Freiburg. The following year the two of them united their efforts to combat the Portuguese.

"We are against oppression, not against whites," Roberto told me. "If the whites understand this, they may certainly stay in Angola. We would like to be free – not against anybody. Every country in Africa is against oppression; there is not one that is against the whites. However, if our victory over oppression is military, then yes – the whites will have to go ..."

We were talking about land reform when he added:

"The whites seized their farms here by force, so we will return these farms to the Africans. Really, it only amounts to those very large lands owned by Europeans living in Europe ..."

I listened attentively, for in a single assertive sentence he seemed to be saying the whites would be welcome, yet altogether unwelcome if Angola's victory over the (white) Portuguese would be military. Taking away the larger farms controlled by rich absentee-Europeans, while understandable – maybe even deserved in many instances – also struck me as more threatening than welcoming and could have the effect of up-ending know-how in areas of production, trade and export. With no insight as to the details or trade-offs involved in any such action, and basically disconnected from any emotions involved, what I really picked up from this conversation was a piquancy of the ominous. There was no inkling of quarter, of negotiation that might be absent indignation or blind revenge. In a confrontation in which the uniform of one's team is the colour of skin I sensed both threat and fear.

We spoke at length about the war he was currently waging against the Portuguese. In Thysville there were three thousand seven hundred men undergoing training, he said. The officers were being trained by Algerians. His forces were receiving arms from Algeria, Tunisia, Congo (DRC). "... None at all from outside Africa."

He admitted that in March 1961 "... We attacked certain settlements in the north of Angola." In turn the Portuguese attacked African villages and wiped out many.

"Our troops have fought only the whites and those Africans under their command – but when there is war, everyone suffers. The innocent in Angola

237

have certainly suffered."

He considerably understated this horrific event. In fact, he had led a force of some four to five thousand UPA guerilla insurgents on a killing spree in northern Angola. Men, women, children – black, white or *mestiço* – and animals were hacked to death or shot. Whole villages and outlying plantations were burned to the ground. Within a day or two, more than one thousand Portuguese settlers had been slaughtered, and an even greater number of Africans who had been loyal to them or had simply got in the way. The action had taken the Portuguese by surprise and initiated equally ferocious local Portuguese vigilantism. The ensuing bloodbath continued for weeks and from the outset brought on the displacement of more than one hundred and fifty thousand Bakongo refugees. There had been a UPA uprising in Luanda the previous month, but it was really this terrible event in March that triggered Angola's thirteen-year War of Independence.

Asked about his personal life, Roberto told me he had finished high school in Congo (DRC), then became a civil servant for several years – up until 1957. He travelled to Accra, Ghana, working for two years in the Ghanaian Foreign Affairs Ministry. He visited America as one of Ghana's representatives to the United Nations, only returning to Congo in 1960 – with the express purpose of organizing the UPA. He said his organization continued to broadcast to Angola twice a week in seven different languages.

"The dry season is bad for us. The wet season is to our advantage. We managed to send about one thousand five hundred soldiers into Angola last wet season, and they are fighting there now. They operate in small groups of ten or twelve men at a time, and they are doing well. You will see – we will increase our drive ..."

It was well past three o'clock by the time I went up to bed myself.

I slept that night on the spare bed in the same room as Jonas Savimbi. He was asleep when I entered the room and remained silent and inert the entire night. He was up before me at first light, but we had a good opportunity to talk over breakfast in the kitchen downstairs, and then outside in the yard.

Jonas Malheiro Savimbi was born in 1934 at Munhango, a whistle-stop on the Benguela Railway somewhat east of the line's mid-point where his father was the local station master. He attended missionary schools in southern Angola, in the same Protestant system of which the mission at Dondi was such an important part, as well as at schools operated by the Roman Catholics under the direction of the Portuguese government. He did well and was granted a scholarship to study medicine at the *Universidade de Lisboa*, but that was not quite how things worked out.

Jonas Savimbi

At the university Savimbi met with Agostinho Neto, who was also studying medicine there and was destined to become the first Prime Minister of an independent Angola. He also associated with many other young students anxious to see independence in the colonies and an end to Salazar's dictatorial *Estado Novo*. PIDE, ever alert to the first whiff of rebelliousness, began to take an interest in Savimbi and his political awakening so, with the help of French and Portuguese communists, he fled to France and then on to Switzerland. At Lausanne a group of American missionaries was able to provide funding for him to study political science. He received his doctorate at the University of Freiburg – where he chanced to meet Holden Roberto.

Roberto and Savimbi differed considerably in both age and temperament. Roberto was more than a decade older than Savimbi. Roberto, shrewd and with friends in high places, had been politically active for longer. He appears to have been better-connected than his Foreign Minister, and was well-known to other African leaders. He knew many powerful players in Washington and at the United Nations. Savimbi was not just an impressively large and well-built man. One could tell in an instant he was intelligent and calculating, giving out the impression his tendency to silence was because he saw the need to watch, and store away for some future use, any useful information about the people he met, their ideas and what they thought. The common goal both men articulated was their determination to rid Angola of Portuguese colonialism, but I recall having distinct thoughts concerning how each of them might go about it. I saw Roberto as ruthlessly vicious and cerebral, one who appeared not to have shied away from slaughter on a large scale to get what he wanted. Savimbi, while powerful and determined, came across to me as a dark brooder, but somehow 'friendlier' – better able to sit down, listen, negotiate and then move with decision and ruthless determination. Roberto was my size; I could have taken him in a fight – but he might have sent his boys to deal with me later. A fight with Savimbi would have been very different – one to be avoided at all costs. Negotiation would have got me only so far before he would have picked me up and hurled me against the nearest wall, breaking every bone in my body. It is interesting for me, nearly sixty years on, to recall how I had assessed them at the time I met them, and to compare what I thought then with what happened to each of them later.

Savimbi told me the MPLA (*Movimento Popular de Libertação de Angola*, led by Agostinho Neto) 'no longer existed,' and that the movement had no soldiers fighting in Angola. He claimed only the UPA was legally and well-established, and had fighting men in the field. This was a boastful exaggeration, but I accepted his word at the time because I did not want to interrupt the flow of his conversation. I was taking notes. It had been difficult to get him going, but now I wanted him to keep talking. Crossing or interrupting him might have closed down his dark brows, stifling or diverting a proud man, perhaps turning him off altogether.

He agreed with Roberto that the UPA was not seeking a 'black Angola,' that the movement was going to form a co-operative government of all races; and yet he confided to me that he personally wanted no Portuguese in any future government of Angola.

"We will increase our fight," he declared confidently. "Next month we will start our efforts in the south and from Katanga – and we will keep going until Portugal agrees with the principle of self-determination."

He offered the information that there were some twenty thousand trained

UPA nationalists currently fighting in Angola – a highly-inflated figure, I suspected, and one that did not jibe with what Holden Roberto had told me. I found this Foreign Minister pleasant enough, but pugnaciously rash, tending to overconfidence, and not a little naïve. He was sincere in his manner of talking, knowing precisely what he wanted and needed to say, but he brooked no discussion, and even scoffed at some of the questions I asked him. Why, for instance, when he was a representative of the largest of his country's southern tribes, had he not already attempted to recruit them into the fight?

"I will go there. I will go there!" he said. "They know me, and they are with us. I have only to give the word and I shall have a whole army of the Ovimbundu people ..."

I began to wonder why he had abandoned his medical studies, and it dawned on me that perhaps he could not make the grade. Scholastically, perhaps, but temperamentally ill-suited to dedicating himself to the altruistic pursuits of a physician. There was something edgy and almost unstable about his manner in talking to me. I saw him as Messianic. I asked him where he and Roberto obtained the funding to continue his fight; was it from the communist bloc of countries ...?

Ha! That's the talk of an ignorant and sensationalist-seeking journalist! I did not know what I was talking about. Neither he nor Roberto were in the least sympathetic to communism, he said.

"There is no danger of communism in Angola. None! If ever they show their faces, we will fight them, too. We are prepared to fight anyone who stands in the way of our self-determination, and we are prepared to fight for a long time, if necessary ..."

Both Roberto and Savimbi unsettled me – Roberto cold, calculating, polite; Savimbi brash, dangerous, a moroseness about him – and not a little dismissive. When I met Roberto, I was already aware of what his organization had done – that he had masterminded the attack in northern Angola initiating this war and been responsible for the gruesome deaths of so many thousands of people. I fancied I could see the blood in his eyes behind his tinted spectacles, and I did not feel he was a man I would want to trust. Savimbi was different, but with him I felt my distrust was based on his bombastic pronouncements, a bluff know-all manner, and that moroseness which, to me, indicated diffidence and possible brutality when opposed.

It was an unusual coincidence that I should have met these two men, and particularly at the time I did. They were destined, shortly, to quarrel with one another, Savimbi stomping off to rally his southern tribesmen and build them into a formidable force, Roberto to continue as before with his northerners at the head of his exiled government – and ultimately the two of them to commence fighting one another.

The Americans had a field day. From very early on they had given financial assistance to both Roberto and Savimbi in their fight against the Portuguese. The Americans, as always interested in 'influence,' power and profit – 'national interests' – said they were only guarding against the 'expansion of communism.' At the same time, on the same pretext, they desperately wanted Portugal to remain within the structure of NATO, and were alarmed in case they let go of Angola and, in doing so, allowed the Soviets to gather in the highly valuable pickings. (By the time the Portuguese *Carnation Revolution* rolled around in 1974, the Americans were highly alarmed that Portugal itself might topple into the 'communist camp.') All along, and quite schizophrenically, the US was supplying two revolutionary armies with weaponry and logistics while decrying Portugal's use of NATO weaponry in fighting their colonial war. The Americans did little to hide their drooling over Angola's Cabinda oil, and the quantities of diamonds and other precious and semi-precious stones and ores to be found in the country. Many promising mining opportunities were to be found in the country's eastern regions. Canadian mining concerns were also licking their chops. To numerous such western corporate entities it did not matter which of the two organizations, FNLA or UNITA, rose to the top in the confrontation with Portugal so long as whatever resources were in the country could be extracted profitably – and withheld from the Soviets.

It is hard to make an accurate assessment of a man based upon a mere few hours of journalistic question-and-answer – but now, looking back, I think my initial feelings about Roberto and Savimbi were substantially correct. Although both are revered today as 'fathers' of their nation, both also showed themselves to be determined, cunning and ruthless, self-serving to an extraordinary degree – they would have said 'necessary' – their alliances questionable. Tenacious warriors, both ultimately failed in their efforts to expand their individual bases beyond the narrow interests of their tribal origins, both became instigators of disunity – and both, to put it succinctly, were killers. Political unity is a sometime thing throughout the African continent; in Angola, Agostinho Neto and his MPLA – also ruthless, but with the sophisticated military assistance of Cuba – succeeded better than his rivals. As the man who finally filtered to the top in this extraordinary conflict, it would have been fascinating to have met him also.

The colonial war – Angola's War for Independence – was fought over a period of more than thirteen years, March 1961 until the cease fire of April 1974. Skirmishing and flare-ups continued between the different factions until the outbreak in earnest of the Angolano Civil War in November 1975, which lasted until April 2002 – another twenty-six years, making a total of some forty years of warfare. The United States was not the only country interested in defeating communism in Africa, but the Americans, in putting up the bulk of the funds that kept this war of attrition going, were undoubtedly the greatest enabler, denying for so long the stability essential for dialogue to take root and flourish. With an eye to the riches Angola had to offer, the blood was being shed by others, so all the US had to do was keep the money and arms flowing until one side or another rose to power. The Cubans knew this, so threw their effort into support for '*o povo*' – the people the western powers called 'communists.' It worked. The Cubans, supporting Agostinho Neto's 'communist' MPLA were instrumental in the defeat of both Holden Roberto and Jonas Savimbi.

It might be helpful to take a quick look at each of the three main groups that had emerged to fight the Portuguese, and later one another during the country's civil war. Acronyms and initials indicating alliances in movements (which very often amalgamate or disintegrate) can be confusing, and this is particularly the case when trying to conduct even a truncated survey of such a complex and extended period of warfare.[36]

The principal rebel groups:

UPA/FNLA and GRAE – The *União dos Povos do Norte de Angola* – UPNA – (Union of the People of Northern Angola) had initially been founded by Holden Roberto in 1954. As this original movement expanded its base, incorporating several smaller freedom groups, its name was transformed again, after 1959, into the *União dos Povos de Angola* – UPA – (Union of the People of Angola). Still later, by joining with groups from a wider range of ethnic bodies, it became the *Frente Nacional de Libertação de Angola* – FNLA – (National Liberation Front of Angola) in 1961. (Throughout the time

---

[36] In an article in the July 1962 issue of *The New African*, 'Mistimed Angolan Quarrels,' David Baad estimated 'at least eight different Angolano nationalist organizations are now operating in Leopoldville.' Most of these groups had Portuguese titles. When each was reduced to its initials, the list could add up to a veritable alphabet soup of confusion.

of my brief visit to Congo in the summer of 1963, both Roberto and Savimbi in conversations with me referred to the amalgamated rebel forces as the 'UPA,' the broader appellation, I assumed, not quite yet in vogue.) The UPA was generously funded by the United States upon its formation, and this continued when the movement later expanded and the name changed to the FNLA. The FNLA was additionally (and intermittently) funded by Ghana, Israel, France, West Germany, South Africa and China as well as a number of African countries, notably Zaire (Congo (DRC)). Weaponry was in short supply at the very beginning but supplies greatly increased and became more sophisticated as the war progressed. In addition to being the figurehead of the FNLA, Roberto had also been successful in pulling together an umbrella government, the *Governo Revolutionário de Angola no Exílio* – GRAE – (Revolutionary Government of Angola in Exile) with its headquarters in Leopoldville under himself. It was formed in 1962, was given recognition by the Organization of African Unity, its forces fighting mainly in the northern forests of Angola. Ultimately this dissatisfied Jonas Savimbi, who insisted on a swifter and more robust incorporation of the southern tribes, and expansion of the war into all of Angola. Roberto's hesitation brought about Savimbi's resignation as FNLA Foreign Minister in 1966, and he set about the establishment of his own movement – UNITA. As Roberto started to lose more and more ground and credibility the US gradually withdrew its aid and began to grant more support to Savimbi and his UNITA – so that Roberto was finally obliged to drop out.

UNITA – *União Nacional para a Independência Total de Angola* (National Union for the Total Independence of Angola) – was founded by Jonas Savimbi in 1966. He had become disillusioned with his former colleague when Holden Roberto hesitated to move into the southern regions of the country where most of Savimbi's tribe lived (about one third of the country's total population). After the 1974 revolution toppling Portugal's dictatorship, UNITA was drawing the greater part of its support from South Africa and the United States in confronting the communist-backed MPLA under Agostinho Neto. Neto's summoning of massive backing from Cuba's military and air force prompted Roberto to withdraw the UPA/FNLA from the fight. Internal divisions and general disarray sundered UNITA's ability to cope militarily or win electorally. Savimbi, tenacious and unbending, kept on fighting, however. He was killed in February 2002, which gave rise to an agreement to end hostilities two months later. The movement transformed itself into a political entity in 2003 under the leadership of Isaias Samakuva, receiving twenty-seven percent of the popular vote in elections held in 2017.

MPLA – *Movimento Popular de Libertação de Angola* (Popular Liberation Movement of Angola) led by communist supported Agostinho Neto – ultimately rose to the fore and provided the Angolano population its first taste of independent government. The movement was formed in 1956, and at first drew on the Ovimbundu peoples of southern Angola for the greater part of its manpower. It was assisted by the Soviet Union and, later, by significant numbers of both troops and *matériel* from Cuba. Considerable but somewhat lesser support came from Romania, East Germany, Yugoslavia and a select group of African countries. After Angola's independence in 1975, and during the civil war that followed closely on its heels, weighty elements of the Portuguese army – some twenty thousand men – continued the fight on the side of Neto's MPLA and their Cuban allies against western-backed Roberto's UPA/FNLA until its collapse, after which Neto then was able to turn his full force against UNITA. Agostinho Neto was not only independent Angola's first president, but his homeland's pre-eminent poet. He died in a Moscow hospital of pancreatic cancer and chronic hepatitis in 1979 at the age of fifty-six, and was succeeded by José Eduardo dos Santos.

Today all thee leaders – Holden Roberto, Jonas Savimbi and Agostinho Neto – are considered highly respected founders of modern Angola.

Antagonists – A Colonial Survey

Many years passed in which I had no contact with Ian and Joyce Gilchrist. Up to this point in the writing of the story you hold in your hands, I had no idea where they might have gone, or even if either of them was still alive. The Fates prevailed. Quite by chance I happened to locate them – fifty-five years on! – living in the sub-Arctic regions of northern Canada, and still very much involved with a multiplicity of their African interests and contacts. After Angola and the Congo there were projects that took the two of them to Cameroon, Tunisia, Burundi and Senegal – in all these places they left their individual and indelible marks as surely as they themselves had been marked.

There is a hackneyed romantic saying (banal, but significant) that those who have been to Africa recognize and know well:

A man may leave Africa, but Africa will never leave him.

"We still have contacts and lasting relationships with Angolanos, Sierra Leoneans and Cameroonians, and with the Angola Scholarship Fund, and an Angola reunion group," Ian writes. "Last year I got out a book on an early American missionary artist and her paintings. There is a surfeit of archival/historical projects in the works. So, yes ... the continent remains in our blood."

My meetings with both Holden Roberto and Jonas Savimbi were necessarily brief, and any assessment I could make based on information gleaned from my Congo interviews with them would be decidedly limited in scope. But I was aware Ian and Joyce had worked closely with both men concerning the flood of refugees moving north into the Congo. They knew them well. The four of them had lived in close proximity, worked together, each befriending the other. A war that, by its close, had lasted some forty years had enveloped all of them towards the close of the XX century. It had been one of the longest wars in living memory, and this young Canadian couple had been with Roberto and Savimbi at the very start of it. Each would have seen the other as a protagonist in an extraordinary drama. With a background in Angola's Protestant movement that had for years been mistrusted and in confrontation with the fascist regime governing the territory, witnessing officialdom's abuses and listening to the harsh tales of their friends and parishioners, it should hardly come as a surprise that strong opinions and a deep recognition, of each other, should have developed between them all.

I was merely a journalist trying to gather information. It is the way of newspapering: get in, grab 'the story,' tell it. By no means did I possess the details of the complete story and its background, and certainly not the kind of detail that Ian and Joyce could have told. It was clear they would have a viewpoint totally different from anything to be gleaned from the newspapers of the day.

"What did you know of Roberto and Savimbi?" I asked my old friends when it came time to write down this portion of this work.

Dr. Ian Gilchrist's answer lends a fascinating slant to a story widely unknown, and just as widely misunderstood by many. Closing the years, and a wide gap in my personal awareness, we launched into a most interesting correspondence. Edited portions of this – marked 'IG' – may be found included in appendixes at the end of this work.[37]

The assignment in Angola, fascinating in every way imaginable, had not permitted a front line look at this most bitter war of independence. There was no 'front line.' Cajole as I might with local authorities, civilian and military, the Portuguese were not about to grant any foreign journalist permission to visit such a fluid zone. Nor was the rebel leader going to let me accompany his troops. Limited by time on both my Angola and Congo visas, it was clear remaining on the Congo side of the border was no longer a useful option. My time was up. Moçambique was next on my list, and now I wanted to get there quickly.

Before leaving Leopoldville I was contacted by an American, the military attaché at the US Embassy, Col. Knut Raudstein, a man who appeared to have considerable experience at doing his government's bidding in many parts of the world. His specialty for the moment was central Africa. He insisted on treating me to lunch and was most solicitous: of course, an experienced journalist "such as yourself, sir," could understand why his own country's representatives were unable to operate in Angola, he smiled reasonably, muttering the usual platitudes about respecting sovereignty …

"Even in a land like Portugal, where everybody is watching everybody else, it is hard for us Americans to obtain information," he said jokingly. "We can operate all over the continent, but not in the Portuguese colonies. No one appears to want us around … Ha! Ha! Ha!"

The CIA has a name people recognize, I thought. They *know*.

He said he was dismayed, oh indeed, sir, so very dismayed, by the terrible things the Portuguese had been doing there. Lord-ee, civilized countries like Canada and the US could do little but suffer bucketloads of angst over such uncivilized behaviour, tut, tut, tut … But if'n y'git the chance to compromise your journalistic integrity – jes a li'l ole bit, not so's you'd be noticed, y'unnerstand – pr'aps you would be good enough to send your lunchtime buddy a report or two on whatever military activity the Portuguese were getting up to … Lists of military hardware would always be most useful …

---

[37] See Appendixes #6 – Song, #8 – Holden Roberto and #9 – Jonas Savimbi.

The good colonel pumped me for as much information as he thought he could get, but – my-o-my – he must have been disappointed. I had made virtually no headway at all with those kindly Portuguese military men, I told him. They had been open, treated me with the greatest cordiality and respect, listened intently to my queries, even taken me to dinner – but they had given me nothing more than warm Latin shrugs and smiles for answers. I could probably have learned more by talking to the Canadian Signals in Leopoldville. Perhaps the colonel could try that ...?

And Raudstein ... well he knew nothing at all, really – *no, sir, nuttin'ad'awl* ...

It did occur to me (Oh, my goodness me, what disappointment!) this ever-so-friendly colonel was just trying to tickle information out of me – use me, as it were. He was not in the least interested in treating me to a good luncheon. He wanted nothing more of me than to check me out. I could sniff the unsavoriness of it all. The mendacity was mortifying ...

No doubt he had heard some western journalist was hanging about Leopoldville asking questions, so needed to be sure who I was. It only cost him a lunch.

Minders everywhere! My-o-my, agin. How the inquisitive do quiz ...!

Holden Roberto and Jonas Savimbi had both been generously funded by the United States. This funding was granted (first and foremost, it was claimed) because of their courageous fight to win Angolano independence from the Portuguese. This transparent little heroic was not true. By far the greater motive for funding them was that both men were anti-communist and, as is well-known, the Americans have always been gung-ho to 'stem the tide of communism' – and use these warring adversaries of the Portuguese (and each other) as proxies to do a good turn for the USA. Behind that – not voiced aloud and denied when it was – lay a most sinister corporate motive. There was then, and there still is, a sizeable commercial motive for American involvement in Angola – one of the richest pieces of real estate in the world. The American administration, along with their free-wheeling corporate darlings, had little to lose by funding both Roberto and Savimbi. It made not a scrap of difference which one of the two of them came out on top in the end. In either case the benefits to the Americans further down the road would be the treasure chest of Angola's riches. It mattered little to the Americans that two expendable African warlords were quarrelling with a third, the communist-supported Agostinho Neto. Neither did the Americans give much of a damn about Portuguese sensibilities, for they knew that Portugal would eventually have to capitulate to one nationalist or another, and in any case were tied into knots by their obligations to NATO and the western allies. No matter whose blood spattered on the ground, Americans (ably assisted by their corrupt puppet, Congolese President Mobutu Sese Seko) would be on hand to dip greedy hands into the oil barrels of Cabinda and the bucketloads of Africa's notorious blood diamonds from northeastern Angola and eastern Congo.

Saving the world from 'communist domination' and, one day, the big payoff: that was why Col. Knut Raudstein was in Africa – and the flavour of my lunch.

And had the Americans, perchance, been funding any of the units fighting in Angola, I queried the good colonel, sort of by-the-by …?

"Oh no, no, no!" he assured me. "Just looking around – though we wouldn't want the communists gathering too many rosebuds, now, would we…?"

When studying Portugal prior to my visit I had attempted, in vain, to stay on track. Without intent, I kept wandering off-course and bumping into a strain of geo-political nuance that kept insinuating itself into almost everything I was reading: America – with one strong arm of control dug deep into the hairy mane of the British imperial lion …

I pondered much at that point. Meditative, inquisitive. I was never quite knowledgeable enough to come to grips with what was gnawing away at me. The Africa I remembered from the time I served there in the British army seemed so raw, so basic, when I first encountered it. I would be looking at it anew, with a Portuguese overlay. It was difficult to comprehend why everything had to be so complex. In the intervening years though, between the then and the now I have lived and learned a great deal more about the intricacies of that extraordinary continent, examined in some detail the forces that have borne down on every square metre of its landmass. But knowing more does not necessarily bestow wisdom. It's as if the more you know the more you realize you don't know, so the pondering has to go on …

America! I could comprehend the idea of a global policeman, even the possible need for one – thinking all along that was precisely the role the United Nations was supposed to be carrying out. And then, in an attempt to be a little broader in the acceptance of international realism, it was perhaps not beyond reason to imagine something might come up that the UN couldn't handle – a situation in which intelligent discourse had suddenly collapsed and now there might be a need for more and bigger guns. The concept of calling in the western powers as a global policeman just might have had a certain *raison d'être*. No one would like it, but perhaps the world could be made to understand ...

For the life of me I could not see a man like Col. Knut Raudstein as a 'global policeman.' Big man with big stick, a thug with licence, possibly – enforcer – but never policeman. It was people like Raudstein, and I met numbers of them, who helped me in the rapid development of my biases.

No one seemed to like communists very much, at least not the white man from the western camp. As I saw it, communists were just human beings with a fairly simplistic notion of spreading the wealth around – an almost Christian concept in which, like most humans in most of their undertakings, they tended to fail. Yet, as the cold war progressed, we were being taught to hate these people more and more until, at some trip-point, there was absolutely nothing good about them at all – not even their humanity – and so everybody armed themselves with nuclear weapons. The loudest voice promoting this indoctrination – always – was American, or an American acolyte, the pedlar of propaganda in the service of the man with the money and the big stick. The Korean war – was that not an overt attempt to exterminate all communists? We tried, but there were just too many of them ...

Ever since the end of the Second World War the colonial dominoes had been toppling everywhere – and with particular rapidity, and noise, on the African continent. While there was a crying need for order and some serious policing, once a semblance of order was restored the first people to be seen racing across the continent were in civilian clothes and carrying briefcases – the representatives of western corporate carpetbaggers, hot contracts in their hot hands all ready to be signed. I was sure I could see the hand of the American State Department in all of it. What was it really: the 'communism' that was so abhorrent or the orphaned goods and chattels that, even before abandonment in the face of violence, appeared ripe for plunder and looting?

Raudstein may have looked like a soldier; he sported a uniform and had brass on his hat. But was he not, beneath his impeccably-starched safari shirt, one of the Central Intelligence Agency's Pillagers-in-Chief? The new colonizer?

'Restless natives' were nothing new. Colonialism was something I had experienced and understood. There had been numerous colonial upheavals in the years leading up to the two world wars. In North Africa, the French had been in control of Algeria since 1830. There had been a variety of uprisings in French-controlled desert domains. In large part these were tribal affairs, but because of colonial attitudes of the period these oppressed lands were liable to garner more notions of romance than expressions of sympathy. The French Foreign Legion – Beau Geste on desert patrol – was paramount in every schoolboy's library of adventurous comic books. France maintained a tight control over 'her' part of the world until well after the Second World War – and her influence in Africa is a factor to this day.

In 1888 Sultan Yusuf Ali Kenadid had signed a treaty of protection with the Italians – over an East African territory later known as Italian Somaliland. His move had been made, however, with an eye to personal aggrandizement and preserving control over his sultanate rather than seeking independence for a land the Italians soon came to look upon as their own. On the continent's Mediterranean coast, just across from Italy, the idea of independence was very much on the mind of Omar Al-Mukhtar as early as 1912. Courageous and wily guerrilla fighter of the Libyan desert, he opposed the Italian occupation of Cyrenaica until his capture and execution by Italian Governor Rudolfo Graziani in 1931 – the same scoundrel who within a few short years would gas Ethiopia and lay the ancient country to waste.

Kwame Nkrumah dated his political awakening to the Italian invasion of Ethiopia in 1935, becoming politically active in his homeland Gold Coast (later Ghana), in 1948. He led his country to independence from Britain in 1957.

Apart from the special case of Liberia on the continent's west coast, which had been settled in 1820 by American freed slaves (black colonists!) anxious to reclaim an African homeland, Ethiopia remains the only country in Africa that has never been colonized. Independence was a given for Ethiopians. The Italians invaded twice – in 1896, when their army was virtually annihilated at the Battle of Adwa, and then again at the end of 1935 when Benito Mussolini's vengeful forces arrived with tanks and aircraft and cannisters of poison gas. On this latter occasion the invaders were able to chase Haile Selassie into exile for most of the six years of their conquest and occupation. Although thick on the ground and ruthless in their efforts to control the population, the Italians were harried continuously by the Ethiopian Partisans, and were permitted barely a moment of peace. A combination of Ethiopian and British forces defeated the Italians in Ethiopia in 1941 – an action that ultimately led to Italy's capitulation in the Second World War (October 1943).

251

Léopold Senghor's *Bloc démocratique sénégalais* – BDS – and Patrice Lumumba's *Mouvement national congolais* – MNC – were both founded in 1948. Senghor served as president of Senegal from the country's independence from France in 1960 until his resignation in 1980. Lumumba, an immensely popular first prime minister of the Republic of the Congo (DRC), helped to lead his country to its independence from Belgium at the end of June 1960. The provinces of Katanga and South Kasai in eastern Congo announced their secession two weeks later. In the countrywide chaos and civil war that followed Lumumba was deposed, arrested, imprisoned, tortured and finally shot in January the following year. The assassination was planned and co-ordinated by the American CIA and carried out by Belgian operatives. It paved the way for Joseph Mobutu Sese Seko, a corrupt pro-American strongman, to assume power for the next thirty-two years as his backers helped themselves to the vast mineral riches of eastern DRC.

In South Africa, racial segregation had been a part of the political and social landscape ever since the arrival of white settlers in the XVII century. The system of *apartheid* was officially declared in 1948. Largely viewed with sympathy by white racists in the southern states of USA, it was possibly the one word that best linked the freedom movement of South Africa with the desegregation struggle in America. Black America had been fighting racial inequality since long before the official abolition of slavery in 1865, and a century later this fight was not entirely lost on black Africa. Following President Lyndon Johnson's Civil Rights Act of 1964, African American leaders voiced the strongest condemnation of *apartheid* – and maintained their criticism right up to the time when it was dismantled and the figurehead of South Africa's resistance, Nelson Mandela (jailed since 1962), was finally released from prison in 1990.

Although there had been periodic risings in numerous parts of Africa, slavery and a vice-like colonial grip kept the entire continent firmly under heel until the end of the First World War. This had been ensured through partition of the continent by the European powers in 1881 (ratified by the Berlin Conference of 1884). From that point on there was not the remotest possibility of discussion concerning 'equality,' let alone 'independence,' until after the Second World War. The privileges of colonialism rendered any serious question of the kind unthinkable – even treasonous.

Of the European nations involved in colonialism Britain was by far the most noticeable, unavoidable since she lauded it over the greatest number of territories – approximately one quarter of the world's landmass. At the height of empire this would have been a mark of pride. After all, in the years when she acquired most of her colonies no nation was taken terribly seriously if it did not have 'subject peoples' – an empire. Since the beginning of the XX century Britain's armed forces departed the shores of the 'Sceptred Isle,' bound on foreign interventions, on more than thirty occasions – not including the two world wars – in order to bully, suppress or 'protect' her 'national interests.' The colonies, reasoned Madam Britannia with majestic arrogance, were hers. After 1945, however, possessing colonies became an embarrassing and expensive encumbrance.

The list of British interventions is both tragic and fascinating. There have been more than twenty of them involving their military just since the close of the Second World War. A partial list, in no special order, follows.

The first of these post-war interventions was the British-Zionist confrontation with the Palestinians, 1945 to 1948, which overlapped with the Greek civil war, 1946 to 1949, in which she also played a major role. The British did not have an easy time of it in Palestine: a cynic slogan I remember from my teen years: 'Join Her Majesty's Royal Navy and see the world; join the Palestine Police ... and see the next.'

At about the same time, chastened and embarrassed to the very tips of the feathers on their plumed helmets, the curtain was about to be lowered on the pantomime of Britain's involvement with India. It was a military involvement only insofar as it was a mammoth military stand-down. Having used extensively both the Indian homeland and the Indian Army during the Second World War, a rash of promises made before and during the war finally had to be honoured. There was no longer any reasonable excuse to hold onto this so-called 'jewel' in the British crown, and it was snatched away with devastating rapidity in 1947.

A stunning example of Britain's arrogance and stupidity (there were many but this one was particularly ripe) was the attempt by British military colonizers at the close of the Second World War to put on trial by courts-martial some of the leaders of the Indian National Army (INA) who had purposely and (from their political standpoint) patriotically joined with the Japanese after the fall of Singapore in an attempt to rid the subcontinent of continued and unwanted British colonial occupation. These infamous 'Red Fort Trials' in Delhi – which included charges of treason, and triggered mutinies within the Indian forces upon whom the British relied for the security of the Raj – were an utter fiasco. They were called for November 1945 and were cancelled in red-faced embarrassment in May 1946.

Perhaps the Cold War, 1947 to 1991, may not be classed as an intervention *per se*, but it was certainly a period of high tension, interference and manipulation. Fear and propaganda had reduced whole populations in the 'free' west to states of utter paranoia – a situation that had existed in one place or another, and in one form or another, ever since the Russian Revolution of 1917.

Fear of communism had driven the Korean War, 1950 to 1953. The same fear was also behind the Malayan (peninsular) insurgency, 1948 to 1961. Even the Mau Mau rebellion, 1952 to 1961, was (incongruously) blamed on 'communists' by terrified settlers. The Suez Crisis, 1956, was instigated by fiercely nationalistic and socialistic Egyptian President Gamal Abdel Nasser who, apart from taking over the Suez Canal, was held to be a closet communist and in any case far too close to the Soviet Union. The Dhofar Rebellion, 1962 to 1975, brought the British in on the side of the sultan against 'communist rebels.'

Starting long before the 1947 partition of India and Pakistan, there had been the huge shake-up within the empire that involved the ultimate independence of those two nations and eventually (after another war) Bangladesh in 1971. These did not involve British military actions, but they certainly involved a large and disruptive rearrangement of military personnel, property and posts. The Indonesian-Malaysian confrontation, 1963 to 1966, though not considered a war as such (it was never declared) nonetheless involved considerable hostility – Britain on the side of Malaysia within its then colony of North Borneo and its protectorate of Sarawak. China and the Soviets backed Indonesia.

The Cyprus Emergency ran from 1955 to 1959 and was a particularly vicious episode. The Brunei Revolt, considered one of the first actions of the Indonesian-Malaysian confrontation, was in December 1962. The Northern Ireland 'Troubles,' though simmering in the mid-1950s, picked up in intensity in 1969 and continued into the mid-1990s. In 1999 a company of Gurkha special forces serving the British was deployed to East Timor. There had been a Royal Navy intervention in the Sierra Leone civil war in 1999, followed by a more robust ground troop intervention in May of the following year. The action was wrapped up by September of that year, although 'training teams' were left on the ground.

A number of nasty bullying confrontations in the seas around Iceland came to be known collectively as the 'Cod Wars,' the first of which was in 1958. They continued off and on until 1976, only ending when Britain was finally forced to accept Iceland's insistence of a two hundred mile fishing limit around her shores.

Aden, which had been steaming with resentment since the mid-1950s, occasionally flaring into conflict, finally developed its very own full-blown emergency – which ran from 1963 to 1967. As I write these words, Yemen has once again been fanned into a major war of attrition – this time with the participation of the west's disreputable quasi-ally Saudi Arabia using largely American and Canadian armaments – (a most successful business deal).

The Iranian Embassy Siege in 1980 was hardly an 'overseas incursion' – it occurred in the heart of London – but it involved an action lasting six days, had been launched against an Arab-Iranian group of invaders, and resulted in the deaths of seven people – two hostages and five invaders. A number of awards were meted out to police and the British army's Special Air Service (SAS) personnel. This action was followed in 1982 by Britain's extraordinarily vicious ten-week brawl with Argentina over two territories in the South Atlantic, the Falkland Islands (the Malvinas to the Argentinians) and South Georgia and South Sandwich Islands. More than nine hundred people lost their lives in the conflict which, although the Argentinians surrendered, to this day remains a bone of contention between the two countries.

Not yet mentioned, but certainly a subject for scrutiny, is the matter of the Indian Ocean island of Diego Garcia, where the local inhabitants (talk about the 'Little Man!') had the extraordinary audacity to be living happily among their palm trees and fishing huts. Many years before someone in London decided the island actually 'belonged' to Britain. The mostly barefoot and ill-represented native islanders (they only numbered about two thousand) conflicted with Britain's broader strategic interests – so they could be, should be, and were, removed from the island between 1968 and 1973, before too many questions could be asked of the inhabitants or by human rights organizations. The place was then 'out of bounds' to all comers, the world was subsequently informed. Gifted (leased) to Britain's very good friend and ally, the United States of America, mid-ocean Diego Garcia is currently one of the west's prime military air bases in Asia. British (and, by extension, American) actions in regard to the island, and the forced removal of its people, have been condemned by the International Court of Justice, the judgements of which have been non-binding and, to date, ignored.

The arrogance and infamy of power is a library of incomplete books. The shameful behaviour of Britain and the United States over Diego Garcia and its adjacent islands is reminiscent of an earlier age – the age of out-and-out piracy. About this episode very little has been written or said. After all, who has it in him (or her) to make a difference? The highest court in Britain described the British action as 'repugnant' – which it was and still is, but who's listening? 'Protection' was the handy euphemistic mantra initially chanted for the islanders, who were left to wonder if they really needed it. Then the mantra mysteriously morphed itself into a fear of 'terrorism' or 'communism' – or perhaps by now 'national interest.' Is it any wonder that people subjugated and abused so brazenly choose to fight back if they can? And for that matter at what point does mere bullying itself become 'terror?'

Diego Garcia is not the only tiny place that has been bullied into submission by overwhelming western power, and this incident demonstrates military might is not always necessary. The tiny (seven square miles) volcanic island of Annobón in the Gulf of Guinea south of São Tomé e Príncipe, a semi-autonomous province of distant Equatorial Guinea, has a population (Portuguese/Angolano mix) of just over five thousand impoverished souls whose distant government has encouraged European and American companies to bury large quantities of dangerous garbage on the island for years. A well-documented outrage, these western interests pay off the country's brutally corrupt dictator-president, Teodoro Obiang Nguema Mbasogo, two hundred million dollars a year. The garbage: ten million tons of toxic sludge and seven million tons of radioactive waste. Recent reports, meanwhile, indicate the island's ecosystem is on the point of collapse, and local inhabitants are becoming sick because of the dumping.

Many unconscionable Britons flutter their eyes and claim Britain is not the only guilty party. Maybe the claim makes them feel cleaner. Others, through harsh experience, have been obliged to consider a much-changed world; the Netherlanders were close on Britain's heels in the Far East at the end of the Second World War. After the collapse of Japan's occupation of Indonesia, the Netherlanders fought a losing battle against the Indonesians themselves in a vain attempt to re-establish their colony. For a time they had eyed the British from a distance, perhaps hoping for assistance in regaining their lost empire, but when it came to fighting it was with neither heart nor conviction. They were obliged to grant Indonesians their full independence in 1949. (In any case, Bung 'Karno' Sukarno had already declared the nation's independence on 17 August 1945, just two days after the unconditional surrender of the Japanese.) Wisely, and with a degree of sensitivity (if not exactly to the Indonesians, then at least to themselves) the Dutch realized it was cheaper, and more could be gained, by making friends of the Indonesians rather than enemies. Historically the Dutch have always been most able handlers of their money, so were pragmatic when 'empire' proved such a jingoistic factor of their national pride. Even so, it is a curiosity that more Netherlanders lost their lives in fighting the Indonesians between 1945 and 1949 than had died throughout the entire duration of the Japanese occupation of their colony during the Second World War. The trauma and severity of that statistic alone appears to have taught them a live-and-let-live lesson.

The so-called Arab Spring – a failure, but which at first had filled many millions of hearts with hope – began in the winter of 2010, but proved to be the catalyst for chaos in both Egypt and Libya, and an excuse for Syria to ramp up its civil war at the onset of the following spring. By September of 2011 both the British and Americans, excusing their actions under the guise of 'national' and 'humanitarian' interests, and with the blessing of NATO, now became heavily involved. This gave licence to the Russians and the Turks, the Kurds and the Iranians, plus a host of other politico-military interests, likewise to step forward and throw their hats into the mêlée. 'Terrorism' – largely blamed on the Islamic State of Iraq and Syria (ISIS), as well as such organizations as Al Qaeda in the Middle East, Al Shabaab in East Africa and Boko Haram in West Africa – have managed to contort themselves into something infinitely worse than anyone might have thought possible – the result, one might say, of years of abuse, betrayal, humiliation and lies by the western powers. Col. T.E. Lawrence (of Arabia fame) described it all masterfully in his book, *Seven Pillars of Wisdom* – one of the finest pieces of war literature ever written in any language.

Ever since the war fought between the Soviet Union and Afghanistan, 1979-1989, which gave rise to the Mujahedeen, 'terrorism' appeared to be adopting a quasi-Islamic countenance. It became harder to blame the old bogey of 'communism' as being at the root of it all; it was also hard to blame 'colonialism' directly, possibly because such an unsavoury word in this instance was not accompanied by an English- or French-speaking face. However, the Afghans seem to have had no problem defining their war as a fight against a colonial takeover by Russia, and there was also little love lost between the Afghans and the British and Americans who had flown to their assistance. Terror tactics as they are perceived had been building in tempo, and the definition of just what they are now has altered to such an extent that no one can help but wonder to what degree earlier actions identified as 'terrorism' had been, in reality, gentler forms of apprenticeship. The Iraq War and the Iraqi insurgency ran from 2003 to 2009, followed by the Libyan Civil War – all of which helped to put paid to the inappropriately-named 'Arab Spring.'

It is not hard to see how by far the greater portion of these actions involved western military forces beyond the bounds of their home turf. Most of them had little or nothing to do with the comforts the British or Americans customarily enjoyed within their own living rooms – beyond the fact that someone somewhere was rattling the cage of 'imperialism' – and thereby threatening financial mischief.

Euphemisms are always useful: 'emergency,' 'police action,' 'detention,' 'troubles,' and so many others – even 'national interest,' 'corporate necessity' and 'imperialism' – are catch words or phrases that, at least initially, have specific meaning. Over time they can be – and are – tossed willy-nilly into a mix to create a thorough propagandistic obfuscation. No government today would be safe without its euphemisms and slogans, so there are hundreds of them. Governments rise and fall on them. 'Make America Great Again,' 'Brexit' or 'Sunny Days' are slogans with definitive purpose – but they are, as well, euphemisms designed to disguise everything from utter bilge to bouquets, to obfuscate and avoid awkward unpleasantries. Such catchy words and phrases are employed to express fairness and justice in situations where these qualities do not exist. However, though he may be slow on the uptake, the Little Man is smart and hogwash seldom convinces him for long. Eventually he is able to see through the fallibility of the words, and very well judge the legitimacy of those trampling his rights and freedoms. In many cases it was precisely such euphemisms that encouraged him to pick up his cudgel to defend what he perceived were his rights – and so occasionally discover along the way he had the ability to fight his oppressors on more-or-less equal terms. It has only been a matter of time before 'terrorism' itself has become an overworked but useful euphemism – especially (and for decades) as applied to leaders prepared to sow chaos and tell their followers – and everyone else – they 'will not talk to terrorists.' Sounds tough, so numbskull leaders believe this gives them the right to strike hard. Few of these so-called leaders have stopped to rationalize that if one does not talk to terrorists it becomes impossible to discover precisely why they have turned to terrorism – but perhaps that is the point. They are not interested in talking or even knowing; they need to *win*. Careless toughness, cruelty – and especially greed – feature large in the wielding of numbskullism.

The unique national temperament of the French, meanwhile, not only permitted the world at large to see how Gallic pride had been assailed, but howled about it bitterly, and immediately busied herself – vainly but ever so heroically – in trying to re-establish colonial control over Indochina at the conclusion of the Second World War. After some seven hundred thousand people had been laid in their graves, the French eventually handed their mess over to the Americans in 1954 – whose motive was anti-communism rather than France's pro-colonialism. (As history has recorded, the Americans talked brashly of victory – until more than fifty-eight thousand of them had been killed by the time of their defeat and pull-out in 1973.)

By 1954 the Algerians were forced into confrontation with France for their freedom and independence – a war that, by its conclusion, had claimed an estimated one-and-a-half million lives. With tears, much *élan* and nationalistic flag-waving, the French fought a bitter war to maintain their control – but President Charles de Gaulle finally called a halt to the slaughter and granted the country's independence in 1962. Later reprisals in the Algerian countryside and in France itself claimed a further fifty thousand lives. It was hardly an epoch of Gallic *gloire.*

Belgium's King Leopold II established his control over the massive Congo basin in 1884, maintaining it as his personal playground and fiefdom until his death in 1908 – at which time it became a Belgian colony. This benighted land celebrated its independence in a bloodbath in 1960 and, since that time, its inhabitants have rarely been free from cycles of sectarian and political massacres. Incomplete statistics indicate millions of Congolese have lost their lives in fractional fighting since the country's independence. The consequent destabilization has been of immense benefit to the foreign financial and mining interests (much of it Canadian) that continue to eye the country greedily, jostling one another for control of its enormous and varied resources. In all of this, an exceptionally weak Belgium, almost immediately after granting the colony its independence, assisted in both the election and assassination of Patrice Lumumba, the fledgling country's first Prime Minister. After five years of internal strife, and with the assistance of the United States of America, the country fell into the hands of dictator Mobutu Sese Seko who ruled ruthlessly for thirty-two years, slaughtering any and all opposition. He changed the country's name to Zaire, imported arms on a large scale from the west and used his formidable army and police forces to reduce its people to the worst extremes of poverty to be found anywhere in the world. Always a friend to the western powers who supported and benefitted from his dishonesty, Mobutu finally died as one of the richest men in the world in 1997. In the meanwhile, as the millions of Congolese lives had been lost, so many more millions suffered the most abominable levels of poverty, misery and human degradation.

So far a survey such as this blows only feebly against the dense fog that has obscured the machinations of the modern world for over a century; it is admittedly somewhat raw in that one of its requirements for these pages is brevity. It will serve, however, as introduction to an even foggier sequence – a look at one of the greatest and biggest bruisers of them all. The war in Viet Nam, the major portion of French Indochina, had consumed all of France's administrative and military energies between the end of the Second World War and their ignominious defeat at Dien Bien Phu in 1954 – at which time the Americans decided they were better equipped to handle the problem; they were confident they were the ones to prevent the 'domino effect' of a communist takeover. The major segment of America's war in the region raged throughout the 1960s and 1970s, the British being exceptionally censorious of American involvement – only toning down their criticism when they themselves became seriously embroiled in the 'Troubles' of Northern Ireland.

The Gulf War ran from 1990 to 1991. The Bosnian War was fought from 1992 to 1996 and was followed by Operation Desert Fox against Iraq in 1998. The Kosovo War, the closing convulsion of the conflict inside a disintegrating Yugoslavia, came in 1999. The so-called 'War on Terror' started in 2001 and has continued to the present time involving combat in Syria, Iraq, Afghanistan, both east and west Africa, and elsewhere. The Iraq portion came to some form of conclusion with the pull-out of British troops in 2013 – but half-a-dozen years later the country is still an unpleasantly dangerous place, and western 'advisors' have returned. Afghanistan and its Taliban continues to seethe against the chiefly American presence.

Communism and terrorism in their varied forms became, and remain, the Big Bad Bogeymen. The terrorism has been undeniable; no one can mislabel it, or miscalculate it when they can see it. But 'communism' is still trundled out when an excuse has been needed – for any reason. *It* (whatever 'it' happens to be) has been all because of the communists. Even when not specifically named, 'communism' has been lurking in the background. Today the word is that communism has been defeated – yet the current US president, pilloried for any number of high crimes – even impeached – is above all held in contempt for his cozy relationship to Russian oligarchs – who were communists only yesterday. That's too close; the implications of Trump's *amizade* with Putin alarms most Americans. 'Communism,' 'oligarchs,' 'treason' – big no-no words like these find their way into the commentary pages daily. Awareness is slow, but only now, approaching the conclusion of century XXI's first quarter are the pundits finally drawing a parallel between Russian corruptions and American corruptions ... Corruption is corruption, and it is rampant – and having a devastating global impact.

During the Second World War, and picking up velocity in the late 1940s and early 1950s, then continuing through the second half of the XX century into the first years of the XXI century, the bellowing of America has consistently warned of 'communist takeovers' and 'falling dominoes' in every corner of the world – such a veritable paranoia concerning the raising of communism's ugly head that one almost inevitably feels inclined to search elsewhere for motivation. Big America being the land of history's greatest capitalist experiment, one must turn to the structure of its financial families to see what all the fuss is about, and here one will encounter such a wall of privilege and corruption that practically any survey would amount to little more than a cursory dabbling. And the condition will remain for as long as the mass of aggrieved Americans resist the notion, let alone the need, for a total rewrite of the rules – call it revolution – within the administration of their own governmental and corporate institutions. And then there is the proliferation of guns …

No wonder America has armed itself to the teeth and murders itself at a greater rate than any other developed nation on earth (close to sixteen thousand gun deaths in 2015). Everyone seems afraid of everyone else, but the general instability brought on by fear of the other (foreign or domestic) appears to pile up at the feet of those who are 'making a killing' – the money-making two percent who block more equitable distribution of the wealth. In the end it is hard to divorce the corruption of foreign policy from the corruption of the boardroom. No wonder America, the wealthiest nation in the world, is the only developed country that has struggled time and again to institute universal health care for all its citizens – and failed. The country is literally held back by the myopic introversion, selfishness and resistance of that segment of society wealthy enough to allow it to happen, ably assisted by the uneducated and bamboozled masses who have been totally confused by the word 'socialism' – and, lately, 'terrorism.'

Propaganda. It's not difficult …

Armageddon, the populace is warned, is nigh upon us all – which, to the abject mentality of the schoolyard bully, is why America needs to arm itself and take charge.

Consider:

Although America was involved in a three-year military incursion into Russia almost immediately following the 1917 Bolshevik Revolution (in concert with the armies of sixteen western allied countries) and spent the following two decades propagandizing against the flaws and terrors of 'reds' and 'communism' and 'socialism,' the first significant communist confrontation with which the world had to deal following the Iron Curtain partition of Europe at the end of the Second World War was the Berlin blockade and air lift of 1948-49. Then came the Korean war – a major conflict that pitted the 'free world' under the banner of the United Nations (loudly championed and led by the Americans and British) which lasted from the summer of 1950 until the 'cessation of hostilities' brought the carnage to a halt in the summer of 1953. In that three-year period more than three million people lost their lives (thirty-six thousand five hundred Americans). The communism the west was fighting in Korea has altered considerably; so far there have been three generations of a sordid dictatorship which today offers little in relation to the communist tiger the west took on back in 1950. The country's leader, Kim Jong Un, is a dangerous dictator who is not yet going through his mid-life crisis, but who, since 2011, has delighted in pulling down Uncle Sam's breeches. By threatening America with nuclear attack, Kim has managed to raise the North Korean brand of 'communism' to surreal new heights as a curiously overriding enemy of the west. Korean hatreds and suspicions continue sixty years on, with troops massed on either side of the border – and, of course, an enormous American military presence in South Korea. As this essay goes to press no internationally recognized peace treaty has ever been signed between North Korea and the west, although President Trump, who took many strange turns during his first term in office, aimed to correct that oversight by writing 'love letters' to his counterpart, Kim Jong Un. The full scenario has yet to be played out.

The industrial might of the United States was robust enough to shore up and rebuild Europe after the Second World War, at the same time providing the required muscle to police a smashed Germany and Japan and keep the Soviet Union both on edge and at bay. However, the USA permitted more than just a thimbleful of licence to their old friends and comrades-in-arms as they emerged from the Second World War and the Korean conflict. They were left with sufficient grip on their colonies to permit them a false omnipotence. But the meaning of 'war' was being redefined, guerilla and clandestine actions were becoming more common, weapons were more readily available to the disenchanted and 'police actions' were proving necessary in any number of places to ensure 'stability.' This tended to have a contrary outcome, heavy-handedness inflaming the disenfranchised – yet still the various satellite empires blundered on. The Americans had had the good sense to reduce their substantial presence in the Philippines relatively soon after the conclusion of hostilities in the Pacific in 1945, and before post-war internal struggles in that benighted archipelago picked up steam. Even so, they have maintained a significant military presence in the Philippines, as well as in Korea and Japan. Their friendly presence has hardly disguised their voraciously capitalistic motivations globally. Within the same frame of time that Britain had mobilized her forces to chalk up the bulk of the above mentioned thirty-plus hostile incursions, the USA (a Johnny-come-lately when it came to wielding colonial power) could lay claim to a far longer list of geographical locations where there was either outright military action, or the exercise of considerable and coercive military muscle – almost all of it in the name of 'security' and 'national interest.'

First communism and then terrorism; both buzz-words have created such a level of screaming hysteria throughout the USA that simple people have become frightened out of their wits. These initial fears have been easily fanned into breath-stopping anxieties often by government, often by racketeers, often by free-market entities with the wide assurance they are operating within the law – 'just doing good business.' A worried but rampant political right has found reason to trample worldwide social obligations. Seen in this light, the rise of a man of like Trump is understandable even when a comfortable majority considers it nonsense.

Consider where the Americans have wielded their might – (thousands of American soldiers would have difficulty finding some of these places on a map). The list is alphabetical, dates indicate initial involvement; many of the incursions have been recurrent:

Afghanistan (1979), Albania (1949), Algeria (1958), Angola (1975), Australia (1973) Bolivia ((1964), Bosnia (1992), Brasil (1961), British Guiana (1953), Bulgaria (1990), Cambodia (1955), Chile (1964), China (1945), Colombia (continual involvement from 1903 to present), Congo (1960), Costa Rica (1953), Cuba (1959), Diego Garcia (1981), Dominican Republic (1960), East Timor (1975), Ecuador (1960), Egypt (1956), El Salvador (1980), Ghana (1966), Greece (1947), Grenada (1979), Guatemala (1953), Guiné-Bissau (1975), Haiti (1959), Honduras (1980), Indonesia (1957), Italy (1947), Iran (1953), Iraq (1956), Israel (1948), Jamaica (1976), Jordan (1948), Korea (1945), Kosovo (1999), Kuwait (1956), Laos (1957), Lebanon (1956), Libya (1981), Mali (2018), Morocco (1983), Nicaragua (1953), Pakistan (1978), Panama (continual involvement dating from 1850 until the present), Peru (1960), Philippines (1945), Saudi Arabia (1957), Serbia (1999), Somalia (1993), Sudan (1998), Syria (1956), Thailand (1955), Viet Nam (1950), Yemen (2018), Zaire (1975).

Heavy scowling and friendly finger-wagging has kept an extended list more or less within bounds:

Central African Republic, Chad, Côte d'Ivoire, Djibouti, Eritrea, Ethiopia, Gabon, Georgia, Kenya, Liberia, Macedonia, Mexico, Nigeria, Senegal, Sierra Leone, South Ossetia, Tanzania, Turkey, Uganda.

It is telling, perhaps, that Equatorial Guinea, one of the world's most corrupt regimes, makes neither list – an absence explained, perhaps, by the fact that the tiny country is one of the largest oil producers in Africa south of the Sahara, with revenues deriving from more than four hundred thousand barrels per day. Eighty percent of the country's oil is controlled by a Texas-based oil company.

Going back to 1900, and not including the two world wars, United States forces have left their barracks and travelled overseas to 'protect US interests,' or otherwise assert themselves, on more than seventy occasions. Since the Russian Revolution of 1917, the United States has proven itself most energetic in intervening globally to 'stem the tide of communism.' In fact, this policing, far from being the altruistic concern the US government claims to harbour for the well-being of its fellow man, has instead shown itself to be an extreme protectionism in order to safeguard and expand the profit margins of American companies and their shareholders, and others who share the values of American-style capitalism.

On 20 October 2017, news anchor Chris Hayes of New York's MSNBC television network, did a quick round-up of current military deployments by US forces. In numbers that varied from single digits through to full fighting units, the American military was ensconced in one hundred and seventy-six locations worldwide – outside the USA in an estimated nine hundred military bases. Africa has been only one global region of intense US military interest. The US, operating out of twenty different African countries, conducted six hundred and seventeen military operations in various parts of the continent in 2014.

Closer to the truth, expressed by America's definitions of itself, there are surely more fascistic criminals, loose and throwing their weight about (and likely armed) than in any other country in the world. But beware! One could be shot for expressing the idea too fervently. The reach of fascism is wide and varied – intrusive, intolerant, grasping, arrogant, heartless. The talk and the action: these are certainly arrogance. With the shrug of indifference habitually proffered to the Little Man, corporate fascists would prefer the world's population be grateful for their *altruism* rather than critical of their barbarism. Somewhere deep within the deliberately concocted topsy-turvy confusion of this milieu lies the identifiable heart of global corporate greed and corruption – and today it expresses itself most frequently in English.

It is amusing, for a reflective moment, to consider how the sages have thought about 'greed' throughout the ages. A charming old Italian proverb translates well into English:

'Big mouthfuls often choke.'

Just musing, Col. Raudstein. It occurs to me there are eight billion souls presently walking the surface of our planet, with the possible 'sustainable limit' extended to nine billion (give or take a billion; who's calculating?) If mankind's social obligation is to feed, take care of and improve the lot of such a huge number, might it not take something like 'socialism' – hopefully a cleaned-up corruption-free version of it – to do the job ...? When comes the crunch, the eight billion (and for sure the nine!) will not be counting on the largesse of oligarchs or the world's wealthy – or even the most reasonable of market practices. Communists and socialists and terrorists have hitherto proven most useful scapegoats, but one cannot forever present them as the root cause of all the world's ills.

Thank you, Col. Raudstein. You set my juices flowing. It has been a long and bizarre ponder. Now – about Portugal and her African colonies ...

Luanda *Ciao*

There had been little more to accomplish in Leopoldville in the brief time left on my visa, so I bid Joyce farewell and returned to Luanda to prepare for my trip to Moçambique. It would entail further irksome confrontation with Portuguese minders, and some military, but by now most of them had faces familiar to me. It seemed best to treat them with humour. They were a fact of life for the moment. In the first flush of brilliant tropical sunlight I had not seen them but, once I knew of PIDE's existence it was possible to discover a Pink Pantherish skulking about them – and in a whimsical frame of mind I could see humour in it. Now the rains had come, perhaps they would be wearing hats and mackintoshes; they could pull the brims of their fedoras down to hide their shifty eyes and turn up their coat collars to guard against the seasonal mosquitoes that bit their scrawny red necks. Their gumshoe footfalls would never be heard against the pitter-patter of the rain ... These were the guys who had been trained by the Gestapo, and who in turn trained elements of Mossad. Wow!

I would love to have met once again with Joaquim Lemos before leaving Angola, but he had returned to Moçambique by the time I arrived back in Luanda, and I was confronted instead by Lieutenant Joaquim Gonçalves, the cavalry officer – and the beautiful Maria Esmeralda. They both had macintoshes.

The two of them came to my hotel at supper hour – she to say hello; he, in most casual fashion, to ask a few questions regarding everything I might have seen and heard while being entertained by Portugal's enemies in Congo. There was not a whole lot of interest I could have said to him. I made no effort to hold back – there was simply nothing to tell Joaquim right then – or his commanding officer when we met the following day for a more vigorous questioning. Altogether, there was little about my trip that would have been of any use to the Portuguese military effort. Even revealing my talks with Holden Roberto and Jonas Savimbi received shrugs of apparent disinterest; rebel belligerence was well understood and invoked little response. However, I did take some delight in revealing the name of Col. Knut Raudstein. No one professed to recognize the name. Lieutenant Joaquim had noted it down when we talked in the hotel, saying he would pass it along to his superiors. The officers who spoke to me the following day made considerably more fuss over it. Who was this man? Why had he gone to the trouble of taking me to lunch? Having an idea of the paranoid mindset of these senior military men, it was entertaining to hear their harrumphing at one another – presumably over the meddlesome and unwelcome probing into Portugal's affairs of an American military spook. Undiplomatic and most irregular! Inadvertently I had induced some small consternation at the Luanda HQ.

But that evening at the hotel, after my arrival, Maria Esmeralda sat between us looking most fetching in a white tropical outfit. She had thrown her rain gear over the back of a chair, and shaken out her hair. She looked from one of us to the other, saying not a word until, finally, the dashing Lieutenant Joaquim stood up and declared he had work to keep him busy in his office late into the night.

"Perhaps the two of you can manage without me for a while? Think things through and if you have anything more to tell me, we can get together, perhaps at breakfast tomorrow …?"

When he had gone, I looked at Esmeralda. There was nothing particularly useful we could say to one another, but I reckoned I knew who she was, so spoke my piece anyway. I was angry.

"You disappoint me, Esmeralda. You were rummaging about in my hotel room when I was staying here before – before I went up into the Congo … you were going through my belongings. I don't imagine you are a thief, but you've been spying on me for the fascists, and that's unpleasant enough. You don't understand what I'm saying to you, so I can't see any harm in telling you I think you're one sneaky bitch …"

She had been looking at me cow-eyed, not quite a smile on her face. Now she had a surprise for me.

"Bitch?"

Her brow furrowed. Her eyes hardened. She knew the word. She pronounced it 'beech.'

"No, Jeremy, I am not beech …!"

She understood the word. Someone must have used it on her before. I could feel my lip curling, my nostrils flaring, and I think I sniggered at her.

"No, Jeremy," she said. "Not beech. Just girl with PIDE on top of me – so I cooperate but not make even leetle money. I get pay to go into your room – no choice. Everyone is pay, leetle bit … nothing!"

She shrugged her shoulders contemptuously.

"If we say no, then PIDE comes and makes big problems. You are lucky it was me, because I am honest and did not take something from your room. I moved papers here or there to let you know. But I not read, and I not take – and in report I was made talk about you, I say I think you are honest man …"

"You speak English …?"

"Yes – I speak. Nobody use English here, so I don't tell that I speak it. If Gonçalves know I speak English he obliges me for more work. I don't want it, but it is not easy to tell him no."

I said I would be leaving in a couple of days for Lourenço Marques.

"That is good. Someone else will be behind you there, to watch you, to spy you – so be careful. You perhaps see Joaquim Lemos again. Greet him for me. I think he is good person, too, but caught in trap like me, like everyone."

And that was the end of it. She left shortly, kissing me on both cheeks.

"*Ciao*, Jeremy," she said. "There is no war in Moçambique. Not yet, war."

Two days later I flew to Lourenço Marques. I tried calling on Esmeralda at the pharmacy before leaving for the airport, but her place was shuttered and I never saw her again.

PART IV

Moçambique

Part IV – Moçambique

Lourençco Marques 271

The Great Grey-Green, Greasy Limpopo River 282

The Zavala Dancers 288

Fish and Elephants 295

Mocímboa da Praia 307

Jungle Justice 323

Palma and Rio Rovuma 326

Ilha de Moçambique 338

Road to Nampula 353

Mopeia Highland Whisky 357

Guerillas and Green Tea 368

Beira and the Spanish Catamaran 380

Gorongosa 388

Censorship and Arrest 401

Lourenço Marques

No, there was not yet war in Moçambique. The plane from Luanda to Lourenço Marques, the Moçambicano capital, flew in via Beira, from which point on there was a palpable lack of tension, an air of sunny, laid back Indian Ocean seaside bustle and affability. The tensions encountered in Angola, offshoot of anxiety brought on by such appalling war in the north that had given every sign of moving south, were non-existent. Arriving in the early hours of a bright morning, this city seemed open, free of secrets. No war, no PIDE.

Children make music in streets of Lourenço Marques

It was wishful thinking, needless to say. PIDE was always everywhere in Portugal and the Portuguese territories. The fact I was unaware of it and as yet had no conscious contact with it did not mean it was not present. However, in the first hours after my arrival I entertained the heady feeling of a welcoming and jubilant city, one of the most important centres of commerce and transport on the East African coast. From the plane there had been an opportunity to scan our approach over a sparkling, well organized city – avenues, tall buildings, greenery and a bustling port complex.

It had been a long flight, with time to spare to write in my diary of my last moments in Luanda:

... A late afternoon walk through city streets before leaving ... run

into two people I know ... a student from her school in Lisboa, a young girl named Maria Elsa, nicknamed Navy by her school fellows ... met first in Carmona at informal gathering organized by José de Mello, spend most of an evening together because she could speak excellent English ... breath of air for me, and she needs to demonstrate her prowess ... vivacious and funny girl, bubbly bright and innocent conversation ... on a Luanda street I'm headed in a few hours to Moçambique and she departs any moment in the opposite direction ... Lisboa and her studies ... our conversation is abbreviated, clipped, filled with the best intent, yet the coming distance already established ... both of us feel exhilaration and anxiety at being on the move. Now there is little to say except for the exchange of contact addresses and promises (surely to be broken) to get together ...

Then ... Dr. Luís Lupi of Luso News Agency in Lisboa – awkward surprise for us both ... says he will contact again before my flight leaves Luanda tonight, but I rather hope he will not ... He makes a great show of noting my hotel and room number. There is every indication of disagreement, a stiff argument ... and I cannot be bothered. I heard his views before coming to Angola, so forcefully expressed I am now unable to see how or why he could possibly have altered or improved on them in any way – or, for that matter, have found any renewed interest in whatever I might have to say. I found him a bore in Lisboa and have every reason to suspect he would still be a bore in Luanda ... (Hooray! He does not show at my hotel room.)

At the Luanda Continental Hotel I managed a last minute meeting with friend Jorge Rodrigues and his father, both of whom I met on my initial swing through this city. They showed up with university student Alexandra Pera, and were clever enough to note my interest in her ... so the kindly older man defensively informed me she had a boyfriend in Lisboa ... Indeed, I would have been much surprised had such a beautiful girl not had a boyfriend or two lurking somewhere in the wings of her recent past ... stunning blonde, so fair I was quite taken aback. I have not seen a blonde since Toronto ... this one ably chaperoned by Jorge and his father.

The elder Rodrigues pushed me hard on considering matters of Portuguese 'freedom.'

"All Portuguese are already free – and so are these people," he said, waving his arm around Africa, condemning my naïvety in championing the African trend toward self-determination – or even rule by a majority. He was well able to draw the difference between the Portuguese and 'these people.' His debate was thoughtful and articulate – but not new to me ... variations on his viewpoint had been voiced in many quarters during the past weeks. I had heard them many, many times:

"... Angolanos are like children who need care and guidance ..."

"Sure ..." I concurred, trying to avoid extending the argument. He smiled as though I, too, was little more than a child.

The diary indicates I was sorry to leave Angola ... concerned about the opinions collected from others and now churning themselves over in my mind ... outside pressures were hard to combat ... irksome heated discussions were avoidable only if I fell in line with what's being claimed ... that all African countries are bound to be backward for generations to come ... but then there was this distinct and most incredible optimism in my mind concerning the people and their abilities ... so determined, so upright, so expectant, so worthy under the weight of imposed shortcomings. They stood accused and guilty and imprisoned all at once – and they had not given their full answer yet ...

It was a ten hour flight from Luanda to Lourenço Marques. We had stopped in Lusaka on the way into Beira, then south ... Met by government representative (another minder!) Fausto Ferreira – journalist by night – who took me to the Polana Hotel and introduced me to Margarida Lopes de Almeida, Brasilian poetess, who had been on my flight from Luanda, though her fame was unknown to me. A large and most imposing lady, hair dyed bright orange, which contrasted poorly with her strip-joint scarlet lipstick and nail polish. A 'dame' in the most reverential sense, she exuded 'character' and 'presence,' and loads of a muted other worldly theatrical carriage. The word was that she had written extensively on Angola and Moçambique. I was dazzled, totally charmed. Latin lady with pizzazz, and she didn't have to move a muscle.

Minder Fausto Ferreira made a point of telling me he did not know my minder from Luanda, Joaquim Lemos, which I immediately took as an alert not to mention names. He and his driver helped me to my room, and I threw my bags onto the bed. Then he offered a government car to drive me wherever I needed to go in the city. It was ten o'clock in the morning. I was out of money, I told Fausto, and needed to visit the British consulate. There should be mail waiting for me there – perhaps even a cheque.

Sure enough there was a note from Arnold Edinborough of *Saturday Night* magazine, enclosing his personal cheque for a substantial piece I had mailed him from Angola – sufficient Canadian dollars, if I could get hold of them, to see me on my way through Moçambique.

How to cash a sizeable personal cheque drawn against a Canadian bank account while passing through Lourenço Marques ...?

The world lived by different criteria in 1963. Trust and necessity, combined with courtesy and good humour, had meaning in that recent but fast dimming age.

"Give me your cheque – I'll happily honour it for you," the consul had said.

A telephone call to a local bank, some quick calculating – and I left the British representative's office inside an hour, my pockets stuffed with Moçambicano *escudos* to the value of the cheque's Canadian dollars – more than enough to put my mind at rest for the remainder of my journey.

"Now," said my minder, "how about that quick tour through Lourenço Marques, and then some lunch?"

I was hungry. Fausto did not appear to be an aggressive person, so for a short while I was determined to enjoy a superficial association with PIDE's representative.

Later he had his driver return me to the hotel. There was a welcoming swimming pool, but an even more welcoming shower and comfortable bed. I needed to relax and take a nap after the tension of the flight, the whirlwind tour of the city and a very full and delicious seafood lunch. My room had a view over the Indian Ocean, and a warm breeze tinged by the distinct fragrance of beach salt and seaweed wafted up to me bearing the sounds of distant city traffic. It was late afternoon by the time I awoke. I took a second shower, spruced myself up, then went downstairs to see what goodies the Polana Hotel might have on offer at the bar.

I had only the vaguest plans for my journey through Moçambique, so sat at a table to peruse tourist pamphlets and go over notes I had made in conversations with travellers I had met in Angola and Portugal. I also had Joaquim Lemos' telephone number, so countenanced the idea of getting together with him – later perhaps ...

"Mister Jeremias ...?" A query at my elbow. I looked up.

It was a small man in his mid-forties, his brown skin clearly denoting mixed race, dishevelled in a well-worn khaki tropical suit, a tie about his neck holding together the unbuttoned corners of his shirt collar looked like a dirty hank of rope hanging from a gibbet. He was Andrade, the driver of the car in which Fausto had collected me from the airport, and later driven us to the restaurant where we had taken lunch.

"Yes, Andrade …?" At first I had not recognized him. The man was on his own, so I peeked past him expecting to see Fausto close behind. He wasn't.

"*Senhor* Fausto asked me to see if you wanted the car …?" he said.

No, I did not really want the car at this hour. Had he been waiting for me in the hotel lobby …? I was a little puzzled. Perhaps Fausto and Andrade were taking it in turns to keep an eye on me.

"Where is *Senhor* Fausto?"

"He's not working now, but he asked me to come and see if you needed the car?"

It had been my intent to call Joaquim, and there was no point in turning down an opportunity for transportation if it was readily available.

"Maybe – can you wait just a moment while I make a telephone call, Andrade?"

Using the hotel exchange, I telephoned Joaquim's home number from the reception desk. His wife answered, then called him to come on the line. He was pleased to hear from me, asked what time my plane had arrived.

"It came in this morning, and I was immediately swept up by my local minder …"

I heard a chuckle on the end of the line.

"… He's gone now, but his driver is here at the Polana asking if I need the car this evening, so I'm mobile. Can we get together for a drink, maybe?"

Yes, said Joaquim – in about an hour. Perhaps the driver knows the Rua do Major Tavares …? I put Andrade on the line so the two of them could co-ordinate time and locale, after which the driver passed the handpiece back to me.

"The driver knows the street," Joaquim said. "I've given him the name of a club down there, so he'll take you – and I'll join you in about an hour …"

I had brought with me from Angola a few rolls of film un-processed, so asked Andrade to take me to a photography shop to have them developed and printed. It turned out to be an overnight process. Then I turned my attention to

Rua do Major Tavares – a section of town, Andrade warned me darkly, in which a respectable gentleman should not be seen – let alone recognized. The more he did not wish to take me there, the greater my wish to make up my own mind. He balked. I insisted. He buckled.

The whole area of Rua do Major Tavares – the street itself and several of the side streets – formed a grotty red light district, each seedy front displaying a paint box of illuminations of varied intensity, and each depending upon the level of its proprietor's ability to pay his electrical bill. The ritzier joints displayed chintzy neon – red, blue, yellow primary flashes; the lower dives no more than dim-wattage light bulbs. Andrade registered horror that I should be so intrigued, refusing to escort me into the murkiness at the end of the road where there was only candle power – and red, at that. He insisted he take me immediately to the restaurant Joaquim had indicated. Apparently he knew it.

He parked the car and we walked a couple of blocks on broken sidewalk. I let him lead the way. We passed by several places where we might have stopped for a beer, and pleasant enough places they appeared to be, but he hurried me on, finally settling for a grubby-looking little hole-in-the-wall on one side of a square, not far from a bazaar and the restaurant picked out by Joaquim.

"We stop for a beer here. This is where your friend told me to bring you. Not clean place. Maybe we move when he arrives," he said.

Down-at-heel sort of hole-in-the-wall but enticing.

"You don't like this place?" I enquired.

"This is nasty quarter of town. I cannot understand your friend inviting you to come here," he said, prudishly.

"I guess he suggested it because he knows I would want to see it," I attempted to reason.

"There are pretty places in this city. Why seek filth?"

This little man was getting on my nerves, and I did not feel I needed him to set me straight. He himself was no one to judge, I thought. In his threadbare suit with food stains down its front, its collar darkened by unwashed hands and oily hair, his trousers shiny-bottomed and baggy-kneed – he was himself the very ambassador of filth. Perhaps he reasoned his own squalid appearance better qualified him to identify squalor.

A mixture of people, differing races and colours, sat at tables both inside the café and outside, where a pocket-sized sidewalk patio was set up to impede pedestrians or snare them for the small change in their pockets. There was a handful of whites, whose accents and boisterous voices indicated they were tourists from South Africa; among the others there was almost every shade of darker skin and facial structure – from exceptionally dark, almost blue-black, to those who might have been Portuguese with suntans, Indians or coastal traders from just about anywhere in the mid-east. There was even one young fellow with Negroid features whose white skin and red-rimmed eyes clearly indicated albino. He sat with others and joined in the animated conversation at his table – in him not a hint of the stigma I had noted elsewhere on the rare occasions I encountered an albino. It was the stigma that hid him from public view. I saw no Asians in the crowd, but in all it was a notable mix – one I had never seen before in Africa – and certainly not in the southern United States. Hovering on the fringes was the inevitable troupe of African shoeshine boys dressed in drab khaki shirts and torn shorts.

Andrade indicated a table outside and sat in one of its chairs, morose, glaring and uncomfortable. We ordered beer, and the waiter brought two bottles. Furrowing his brow, my companion turned quickly and signaled for the waiter to return. He said something in Portuguese, and the waiter scurried away to fetch a couple of glasses. I looked at my watch and noted we had half-an-hour before Joaquim would arrive. I did not wish to spend more time than necessary with this querulous fellow.

He spoke a fairly clear English, and I also discovered he had a slight knowledge of Swahili. I tried him out with it, but he was embarrassed, and did not want to pursue a conversation in it.

Trying to figure out what was eating him, I concluded he did not think it kosher to be seen hobnobbing with a client – an exaggerated sense of social mores that appeared to leave him unable to explain himself to himself. He was a snob, I reckoned, an embarrassed bottom-feeder unable to raise himself out of the level of life he detested but had come to assume was his. His hairline in front receded so far he was unable to pull a forelock; it occurred to me he had so markedly learned his lowly status he felt it his place to correct those who might encourage him to escape it, even momentarily. He visibly squirmed. There was no kicking back and relaxing with a beer, in his case. It was strange – without even trying (and I wasn't trying!) I discovered it was possible to assault this man in the area that hurt him most grievously – in his warped sense of dignity and correctness. I wondered how many times in his life he had sat drinking beer with his boss, or someone else whom Fate had decided was in need of his anonymous services – and hated being where he was. I might have felt sorry for him but realized there was no point; no amount of effort on my part would permit this man to loosen up either with me or himself.

He eyed the South African group angrily.

"It is against their law to sleep with a black woman," he said contemptuously. "So they come to Moçambique to sully our black women, then go home and tell each other stories about it."

"Are you married, Andrade?" I asked.

"Yes," he replied.

"Is your wife a black lady?"

"I don't know what you mean. I have never spoken to her of her colour – or mine ..." he added, glowering. He was suddenly defensive – probably did not like me any more than I was liking him.

To an outsider Andrade might have gone unnoticed in that café, with its chattering kaleidoscope of humanity. Pitiful little man, he did not see himself as one of them, but as someone apart, a superior among inferiors. He knew he was a servant of men and hated it. Consciously making the effort to see himself as a cut above others, he also recognized the trappings of his insignificance, his need to revert to his miserable self when he is called to work or has to take an order. His snobbery was a camouflage, a defence. There was a sadness that surrounded a man so unable to square himself to himself, but there was no way I could feel sorry for him. I saw him as a curiosity for sure; never had I identified so coherent a pattern of it. A dangerous man, for all that.

More of this and I would have become frantic. Then I saw Joaquim making his way along the street. I greeted him like an old friend. Behind him walked Fausto Ferreira with a broad grin on his face. From the corner of my eye I saw Andrade leap to his feet and stand to attention.

"I understood you two did not know one another ...?" I said to Fausto.

"We don't – but then we do. I lied," he replied grinning.

Andrade fell behind us into shadows and returned to his most ignominious self. I had no idea what he was thinking and did not care an awful lot. I was happy to be with Joaquim again, and even if Fausto was my minder, at least he was a jovial character – not morose and withdrawn like this bloody driver. Yet the man stuck around. While the three of us made merry at a couple of bars and clubs, Andrade strung along behind us – fourth leg to a wobbly table. We were not using the car but Andrade, who refused to drink with us, had the keys in his pocket and let it be known he considered it his personal responsibility to see me safely back to my hotel.

"Actually, that won't be necessary," Joaquim said. "I've got my car, so really we have no need for the government vehicle. You'd best go home to your family …"

Joaquim spoke in English rather than Portuguese, and Andrade understood perfectly well. He responded in Portuguese. It appeared he would take his orders from Fausto – not from Joaquim. It looked as though he would not take orders from me, either.

Fortunately, Fausto saw the acute level of discomfort Joaquim and I had felt from the very moment we had all come together, and he was no doubt feeling himself – that Andrade was more spare wheel than fourth leg. He chose his moment, then spoke to the driver in Portuguese. Andrade looked hang-dog and beaten – dismissed. He listened to what Fausto had to say, glowered angrily and muttered a response. Then he turned and slunk away into the night.

"What on earth did you say to him?" I asked.

Fausto looked sheepishly at Joaquim, smiled but said nothing.

"He didn't want to be with us, but he didn't want to be told to leave, either," Joaquim said to me. "Not a very pleasant fellow …!"

"Difficult!" Fausto commented. "I'll be hearing about this from my boss tomorrow."

I was up and about at an early hour the following morning, but the sun had been even earlier and was already warming the sweet air where I had decided to take my breakfast on the patio of the Polana Hotel. Aromas of greenery and flowers and fresh-turned garden beds rose from the kitchen vegetable patch just out of sight around the edge of the hotel. The fringe of the crisp white linen spread across the table-top was tickled by a breeze off the Indian Ocean but was secured firmly in place by four shiny steel clips. The setting of monogrammed tableware and cutlery signalled the illustrious name of one of southern Africa's finest hostelries. Just below where I was seated was a large swimming pool. Beyond that, over the balustrade that marked the limits of the hotel's grounds, some of the city's upscale residences nestled comfortably into a riotous quarrel of green, colourful rhododendrons, bougainvillea and tall palms. The walls of the houses were obscured, but I could see many of their pink tiled roofs. The sounds of the day's activity were still a little sleepy but were carried up to where I was seated. I could hear children laughing, the rise and fall of a hawker's call as he wound his way among the streets below, shouting out whatever it was he had to sell. Someone rang a bicycle bell and, way off in the distance, so far it was a curiosity rather than a serious distraction, the hammering of a pneumatic drill. About a half-kilometre off, running parallel to the front of the hotel's breakfast terrace, was the line of the coast and its beaches – and beyond that the wide expanse of the Indian Ocean. Although I could feel the sea breeze up on the terrace, there appeared to be not so much as a ripple to cross the entire silver blue sweep of the water's surface. The unique purpose of such an apparent aquatic stillness, as far as I could make out, was to reflect – all the way to the distant horizon – the exhilarating perfection of a cloudless sky.

I signalled for a waiter to bring me the menu, and flicked a starched white napkin across my knees.

An exceptionally tall and dark man, immaculately liveried as a waiter, and sporting a pair of spotless white linen gloves, hurried to my table. His smile was as bright as the day, his teeth an unbelievably even and gleaming whiteness.

"How may I help you, *Master*?" he said, placing a menu on the table.

I was so stunned I thought I could feel my mouth falling open, and for a long moment I could not think what to say.

"What did you call me?" I asked.

Only a short time before this I had been covering the racial problems in Birmingham, Alabama, and had seen aspects of American racism so horrible, so cruel, that whatever had existed as rationality or normality in my mind was in serious peril of erasure. The 'slaves' had turned on their '*Masters*.' The words of insult and hatred, abject servitude and heartless domination, were in everyone's ears – if not actually on their lips. The sordid system of South Africa's ghastly *apartheid* government, with which the turmoil in Birmingham, Alabama was being compared, was a freak show known to everyone, its abysmal details appearing in the newspapers day after day. '*Master*' had been a word applied to me as a small boy in boarding school, but it had nothing to do with the context in which this waiter, in all innocence, had just addressed me. Somewhere along the way someone had taught this poor fellow that '*Master*' – you down there, me up here – was a correct form of address, and one couldn't help but wonder whether he had been even peripherally aware of how it would clang in the ears of someone attuned to the vocabulary of human rights.

The man looked quizzical.

"You do speak English, right?" I asked him.

"Yes, *Master*!"

"Where are you from?"

"I from Lourenço Marques, *Master*."

'*Master*' – '*Master*' – '*Master*' – his repetition of the word was shattering. Instantly, of course, I was aware that the word was one he had been instructed to use – probably since his childhood. At some point in this man's training some boss, likely some *mordomo* anxious to please (or elevate) hotel guests, had decided this was the way to do it, that this was a correct and acceptable form of addressing someone. To me the word instantly conjured images of subservience, cane field slavery and the whip. But then, that was the fruit of my ecumenical Canadian-ness. I would not have been surprised had he used the word 'sir.' We articulate the word so frequently it is virtually meaningless. I would have known how to reply to that. But '*Master*' – in this setting it was a word with wallop. It was an *apartheid* word. *Bwana*. It clashed so loudly in my ears that later, when I again heard it being used in the hotel lobby, I looked up and was quite alarmed to note it appeared to be quite acceptable among the other guests milling about with their luggage at the reception desk.

"Please," I began to address the server at my table – and still I did not know what to say. Only that I did not want to be addressed as '*Master*.'

"Please do not address me as *Master*," I pleaded. "I am not your *Master*."

He looked confused.

"No, *Master*," he replied.

There was little else I could say to him. He did not know it, but right there in front of him I had run into a wall. Perhaps, had I been staying longer at the hotel, there would have been the opportunity to instruct him in the intricacies of my sensibilities, but then I realized it would have meant tackling the entire training format and staff of the hotel – and their enculturation behind that – and in the end everyone would most likely have chosen to ignore me. I would have been bucking a training deeper than I could possibly dig.

That one word, used in that context, told a story – a monstrously cruel saga.

The Great Grey-Green, Greasy Limpopo River

Joaquim wanted to take me to his fishing operation at Lake Piti in the very south of the country – but Fausto said he had already organized a tour for me to go north to Xai-Xai and Zandamela to see the Zavala dancers, and on the way to stop by the Limpopo settlement project. This last was important – something the Portuguese had not managed to install so successfully in Angola: the confiscation of indigenous lands to make way for Portuguese peasant settlement. Apparently the project on the Limpopo was well advanced.

A carload of us set out with Fausto at six o'clock in the morning – Fausto, his young wife, and a Flemish music professor – Dr. Edgar Willems. A blessing for me: someone else was driving. Andrade had been left behind.

It was to be my first sighting of the 'Great grey-green, greasy Limpopo River' of Rudyard Kipling fame – many crocodiles …! Maps indicated a highway bridge, but it must have been the wishful thinking of the cartographer. There was no bridge. Either it did not exist – or else it existed in a place where we were not looking for it when the road we were on reached the riverbank. To get where we were going, we needed to cross this famous river and it was very wide at this point. None of us could have guessed what had become of the bridge – but as it turned out, it did not matter … Right where the road ended in front of us, the sluggish flow of the waterway carrying a massive amount of silt downstream, there was a barge onto which we could load our vehicle. This conveyance was operated by a small group of happy young men who had found a most engaging way to pass the time and make a living for themselves – hauling their barge across the Limpopo by their calloused hands, using a steel cable that had been anchored into solid concrete abutments on each bank of the river. This cable had been run through a series of pulleys that had been secured in place on the deck of the barge. The going was slow and hard work, but that did not seem to faze these fellows. They laughed and sang and danced and mimicked each other as little by little, they pulled their ungainly raft into the middle of the stream. Not for a moment did they let up on their clownish antics – and they were genuinely happy doing it. They were clever – we were a captive audience, and we were going to have to pay for this little entertainment.

There were six men in all, three of them required to make up a team that ran up-and-down the length of the barge's deck, pulling the cable as they made their way to the stern of the craft – where they would turn around and dance their way forward again. Sometimes they would circle our vehicle as they moved back into position to repeat the hauling process. They would take turns at this, but never once did they lose the rhythm in the change-overs. Theirs was such a happy dance that we joined in, clapping and keeping the rhythm going. Caught by the current halfway across, the barge swung into a wide downstream arc that would have placed immense strain on the cable's anchors, and for at least half of the journey the men had to fight against the water's enormous pressure pushing against them. As we closed on the far bank, the group assured us they wanted nothing extra for either their considerable labours or their antics – just the price of the crossing. Their bill was so modest, their work attitude so merry and cooperative, that we gave them a handsome tip anyway. Smiles all around. We never received adequate explanation for the absence of the bridge; perhaps the cartographer, after gazing into a crystal ball and thinking with wishful imagination, decided crossing the river by barge was a far more colourful way to overcome the obstruction of the Limpopo.

The barge team watched us as we started up and continued on our way. They sat back down on the deck of the barge and waved at us, keeping up their singing and prancing about until we could no longer see them. Traffic was meagre that day; no matter – one team of jolly ferrymen seemed to know very well how to pass the time usefully, and they were still there at the end of our excursion when we were obliged to return the way we had come.

We were met at the settlement project by forestry engineer Nuno Menano, who told us the scheme had been operative for about ten years and was intended for people of all races – black, white and *mulato*. The project comprised an enormous area of farmland. Three settlement towns had been completed already, with two more currently under construction – basic housing for the settlers, some of whom had been in place for several seasons, others just starting to arrive and take over their small farm allotments. More families would be brought in from Portugal over time, we were told, and more such settlements were under consideration for other regions of Moçambique.

From here to the north the topography tended to be low and seasonal swampland – *pântano* – but when irrigated (rather than inundated) it was considered some of the richest and most arable farmland in the country. This physical feature – the exceptionally large district of Inhambane – stretched up behind and beyond a string of coastal towns, the city of Inhambane being the largest and most prominent among them. The area was criss-crossed by scores of streams and rivers, particularly in the southern section, while a fragile coastal strip of low-lying dunes and sandy rises formed the only barrier between this interior landmass and the Indian Ocean. At the time of my visit to the region, the entire area was sun-baked and dry, but it will long be remembered as the main region of severe flooding – aggravated by Cyclone Eline – that crippled Moçambique in the year 2000 and was considered the worst catastrophe to strike the area in more than a century. The Rio Limpopo rose to twice its normal height, the farms of the entire settlement scheme were wrecked, hundreds of people died and thousands more were displaced from their homes. The devastation spread all the way up the coast as far as Beira and beyond to Quelimane. It was a devastation that left behind a secondary devastation for everyone; during the civil war (at the time of my visit it was still far into the future) the area had been liberally sprinkled with land mines – so many that, by 2000, thousands of them were still buried and lethal. The flooding shuffled much of this superficially-buried ordnance around, so that military maps that might have indicated where to search for them were often of little value. Clearing the land of mines continues apace in various parts of Moçambique even today.[38]

My impression of the homes being constructed in the new towns of Freixel and Guija was that they were far too small and cheaply-built. It looked like accommodation to pass muster with a peasant underclass – convenient and decorative public relations being the criteria rather than anything substantial and solid, or even comfortable. My thinking: more of a show project than an honest-to-God effort to raise living standards above a minimum level. It seemed that for very little extra – and perhaps to demonstrate serious good intent – it would have been possible to create housing communities substantially more worthwhile. Perhaps the real intent was to import peasantry with little or no attempt to provide more than a workforce to farm the land ...

I realized I had seen this before – in Benguela, Lobito and Carmona: a conscious effort to build to a minimum, the lowest possible standard, that may yet claim to be the best possible ...

Churches, schools, all public buildings and state-funded housing – everything that was new was inferior, deliberately low cost.

Why?

No one told me the answer, but by the time our small group had looked over the settlement scheme at the Rio Limpopo, I reckoned I had the answer:

It seemed to me the entire effort was to put bodies on the ground – to mix

---

[38] Climate change, storms and cyclones in this area of East Africa appear to be growing more severe. Another devastating flooding occurred in early 2019.

races deliberately, and to start the project with people who would cause least trouble: impoverished Portuguese peasantry who would be content to farm a patch of their own land far from Fascist Central, alongside poor African and *mulato* peasantry, all of whom would be content they were at last being granted something by a government that till now had never really given them anything more than a damn. Besides, as noted above, Lisboa would have considered other advantages to the scheme: it would enable control of both people and agricultural production; boost the Portuguese presence in Moçambique; and provide the *Estado Novo* with a ready comeback when accused of colonial occupation and exploitation:

The intended message, both spoken and unspoken: 'These are Portuguese lands, farmed by Portuguese of all colours … We are not racists …'

We were shown a network of irrigation canals, and then treated to lunch at a special hotel reserved for government guests (no peasantry permitted) at the site of a small dam. During lunch I got into an argument with *Engenheiro* Nuno Menano who, as he did not have an American to pick on, decided to pick on a Canadian instead. He hated Americans, he told me venomously. They were materialists, generally gullible and simple-minded, lacked foresight and gave Portugal 'nothing.' Americans only had eyes for what they could take from Africa and were indifferent (unlike the Portuguese) to the plight of the Africans. They had no understanding at all of Portugal's great 'historic mission' in Africa.

"All I have ever received from America," he laughed, "is this Coca-Cola…" (he raised it before me in mock toast) "… chewing gum … the belt that is holding up my trousers – and lessons in hypocrisy."

Acknowledging his talk, answering his queries, seemed to goad him on. He was offensive, so it occurred to me the best way to put an end to his ranting would be for me to shut up. Perhaps it was not my prerogative to be offended. I ate the balance of my lunch in silence, only managing to get in the occasional lick in response – still more to tantalize than to contribute to any cogent discussion. His mind was already made up, so discussion would have been a fruitless drill. He flung his arms wide with impressive and magnanimous gesture. The Portuguese were only trying to help the people of Moçambique, he assured me. When all was said and done, it was Portugal's responsibility – historic (messianic) mission or white man's burden – for the entire territory was a legitimate province of the one nation …

"Your attempt to help is in all likelihood insufficient, *Senhor Engenheiro*," I told him, "… and the Limpopo project is a case in point. It would seem to me that here on the Limpopo you are offering too little, and far too late – and to the wrong people."

Within a few years, war had ensured the project's demise – and the floods of 2000 had shuffled around so many hundreds of thousands of landmines, scattering them throughout the area, that wide swathes of the district of Inhambane were soon returned to fallow. De-mining this area is an ongoing nightmare even as I write these words. But in 1963 there was no sign of war in Moçambique. It was coming, but its approach was delayed; it did not arrive until November 1964.

A man as blinded by his convictions as *Engenheiro* Menano could have had not the slightest idea of what was soon to rise up and crap all over his precious Limpopo project.

We stayed over in João Belo at the Xai-Xai Hotel, dining that night with the local district governor. Professor Willems nodded his head and smiled; he could not have been less interested in the politics of all we had seen. Throughout the day, as our small party had been escorted about, he had padded along with short steps, a beatific smile on his face, and listened attentively to everything being said to him – now and then nodding his head and raising an eyebrow. His mind, I could imagine, was full of musical notes. He spent a great deal of his time humming to himself – a bit like Pooh Bear searching for the honey pot, I thought. I had been the one to take the political bait, both asking and answering so many questions that by suppertime I was tired and more confused than ever. As our meal dragged on and came to an end, I sat at the table nursing a brandy in company with Fausto and his wife, trying for the life of me to pay attention to the governor's incessant stream of talk and explanation, propaganda couched as reasonable discourse. Out of the corner of my eye I watched Fausto's wide-eyed and energetic enthusiasm, and listened to his platitudinous asides. Attentive, was the minder on my tail, but I thought I detected in him just a smidge of amusement – or was it doubt? As a North American, the governor was telling me, it would be asking almost too much for me to understand the magnanimous mindset of the Portuguese. Much too much; the Portuguese were working wonders in Moçambique, the governor enthused; it was something they had been doing for centuries. It was their mission. Few could understand it – really only a Portuguese would be capable of full understanding … Colonialism? No, sir, not at all. Try brotherly love – multi-cultural comrades standing arm-in-arm, shoulder-to-shoulder, together with their African brothers and cousins looking boldly into the bright sunlight of a new epoch … mid-morning of a great day ...

Fausto yawned. I think his wife kicked him under the table.

Fitful slumber in my hotel bed that night, and up early to discover the handle of the door to my room was broken so that I could not get out. There was a telephone with which I could call the front desk, but it did not work. My window looked over a terrace where a few guests were already at breakfast, so I signalled to them (language did not work either) – but they called a waiter, who in turn called a receptionist, who in turn fetched a maintenance man who came to my door and fiddled with it for fifteen minutes. Finally he kicked it open and I was free.

"Orange juice, scrambled eggs and coffee, please …"

Fausto and I took a walk, just the two of us, along the beach at Xai-Xai. We passed a nun giving lessons to a class of young students seated in a semi-circle around her on the sand. The bluest sky, the calmest sea, a beach that rolled away before us – so many hundreds of hectares of the purest golden sand – and a semi-circle of little school children sitting for a morning lesson from their teacher …

"Let's not talk politics," I pleaded with Fausto. "Everyone wants to explain to me the Portuguese mission in Africa, and I'm tired of listening to it. They all use different words, but the theme is tediously the same – un-ending repetition."

"Good. I do not wish to talk politics either," Fausto told me. "But I want to say one thing to you: I am obligated by PIDE to watch over you here in southern Moçambique. You need not worry on my account, but while you are in Lourenço Marques you must be careful of the driver, Andrade, who was with us when you first arrived. He is dangerous, and you must not trust him. I don't know anything about the driver we have for this journey. He's new. But Andrade I know; I am his superior, and I know him. Be wary of him …

"However, I do know your friend Joaquim. He is my friend, too. We've known each other for several years, and like me he also has to work for PIDE from time-to-time. We do what we are obliged to do – but that does not mean we agree with them, or their methods. Be careful, that's all I want to say to you about politics this morning …"

We kicked off our shoes and walked northwards on the soft sands. Now and again we would pass an outcrop of rocks, but there was nothing else and no one else on this sandy beach that stretched for kilometre after kilometre.

We rejoined Fausto's wife and Professor Willems in time for a lunch on the hotel terrace, and in the early afternoon our driver was ready with the car for the hour-long journey north to Zandamela. This part of our expedition would be for the professor's benefit – an appointment with a special group of African musicians.

The Zavala Dancers

We drove northeast along the coastal road towards Quissico and, after about one hundred kilometres, came to the tiny village of Zandamela, which came within the jurisdiction of a Portuguese administrator named Saul Dias Rafael. We were expected, and he met us when we pulled into the village.

Giving us a quick survey, Rafael explained how the local tribe in this area numbered about one hundred and twenty thousand souls. They called themselves Chopi and had as their tribal grand chief a man by the name of Zavala – who in turn gave his name to the district and the paramount group of musicians and dancers in that area.

Rafael smiled. "There is nothing like this from Cape Town to the equator," he told us, and he proceeded to introduce us to both the musicians and the dancers.

We were excited, of course, and so prepared ourselves for some thrilling entertainment. However, I cannot believe that any one of us was prepared for the programme Rafael had arranged.

In this village, the Zavala dancers comprised a large troupe of both dancers and musicians, but for today's demonstration, especially organized for the benefit of Professor Willems, the administrator had been able to assemble some twenty dancers and a small 'orchestra' of perhaps twelve instrumentalists. There were, he said, ten such bands – one for each of the grand chiefs in the district. The unique instrument they played was known as a '*timbila*' – a locally-built type of xylophone, or set of vibes, made from indigenous woods specially chosen for the purpose and bound together with strands of a local vine. Under each slat, or sounding board, there was tied a gourd to act as resonator.

Zavala dancer

Timbila

The deep copper and gold and ore mines across the border in South Africa drew many skilled underground workers from the Inhambane district. It had created a vast movement of people back and forth across the frontier, Rafael explained, and so the music of this area – and the dance – had been carried by them over to the mining areas. In this way both music and dance had become known well beyond the Inhambane district. As an example, he mentioned the famous 'gumboot' dance of the Johannesburg mines; because of the transient nature of the miners' work, this particular music and their various dances had become well-known throughout southern Africa.

Professor Edgar Willems had brought with him a wooden box, the exterior aspect of which might have resembled an ancient suitcase – except that it was nothing of the kind. It was, in fact, an electronic machine that could be placed on the ground on a set of fold-out legs, and then connected by cord to our car's battery. I thought this machine appeared very much like a portable version of something I had seen years before in the studios of a radio station, but as I was not (and still am not) a technically-minded person, its precise name and use have always been a mystery to me. What I noted, however, was some kind of recording device capable of spitting out a paper ribbon on which was printed a graph – a printout of musical cadence and rhythms picked up by a microphone. In attempting to write this paragraph I turned to scholars in the audio department of the music faculty at the University of Victoria – and, in an exercise of most imaginative description (not unlike trying to explain a spiral staircase with your hands in your pockets) I was informed I had most likely been looking at an older version of an electro-magnetic oscillograph.

It took Dr. Willems a few minutes to hook up his equipment, running an extra long extension cord to the car battery, the vehicle itself parked as far away as possible so the sound of its running motor generating the required power would be muted. A microphone was set on a tripod right in front of the *timbilas*. And then the show began.

Not for the first time in travelling through Africa was I astonished by what I saw and heard – but this encounter with the Zavala dancers surely ranks as one of the most exceptional. Nowadays it is possible to use easily transportable sound and video equipment – gadgets that can fit comfortably into a vest pocket. This has brought on a surge in our ability to catch and record the moment – and then to play it back. Instant recall, accuracy, long-term memory – all of these have been impacted and were generally unavailable at the time we visited Zavala. As a result, huge changes have come about over the past fifty years – exceptionally rapid when measured against the span of Africa's timeless line of history. Prior to the appearance of these digital gadgets there was plenty to assist our memory, but few instruments that could play back incident visually and aurally in anything like real time and thus permit something more than thin recall. For a hundred years or so there have been bulky cameras and sound systems, but few people could lug that weighty stuff around easily, carrying it into pockets of Africa's hinterlands, and perhaps even fewer who could afford to acquire such equipment in the first place. Prior to that, in an effort to cope with its multitudinous images, the world at large was obliged to recall its sounds and images by writing about them or perhaps producing drawings and etchings. Movements and sounds were non-existent. In the case of dance and other strains of physical cultural expression, restrictions on technical equipment – electricity! – would frequently put the kybosh to intelligent explanation. In the past this had the adverse effect of aiding an abundance of exaggeration and falsehood. Who would know? 'Darkest Africa' made pots of money for corrupt people only too willing to exploit what others, in the conscience of genuine knowledge, have denounced as bunk or outright lies. Such behaviour has sewn great confusion in the minds of those who have never visited Africa, and created almost irreparable damage to the Africans themselves – as the objects of every sort of exploitation. Now I had been invited to a dance, an occasion of fun and entertainment – and learning. Exploitation was the farthest thing from my mind. This was an expression of their history as well as their culture.

Only in Africa have I witnessed the full effect of African dance and rhythm. There have been stage productions in North America and Europe where Africana is presented as spectacle; and almost always it has been of the most incredible quality. What's missing, though, is the bush – the spontaneity of locale that works in perfect harmony with inspiration. That is something that can never be recreated on stage – smells, dust, dirt, Mother Earth and the celebration of Life itself. However, I did the best I could with my twelve-shot twin-lens reflex camera. The results, while pleasing, present nonetheless a truncated idea of what I was so privileged to witness that day.

Dance is a recipe of movement best explained by the dance itself, but permit just a few inadequate lines to detail what these Zavala dancers dished up for us that afternoon:

Imagine, if you will, how the human body vibrates and shivers in reaction to exceptional cold – the tension and simple speed with which it moves. Now remove the brutality of temperature and imagine the body shivering by itself. Add liberal quantities of heat and sweat but maintain the vibration – and mix in the easier mechanical movement of body, limbs, neck, head and facial expression. Rev to high speed – to a point beyond which you are convinced no human body could possibly move itself faster. Add pin-point control over the whole shebang – and allow the percussion to hammer its way into your brain at the fastest tempo you have ever heard.

Memory transports me! Indeed, this is possibly more difficult than trying to describe a spiral staircase ...

The troupe performed for us three numbers that afternoon. The first was a war dance, *The Dance of the Swords*; next came a dance of homage to the governor general of Moçambique, which was called *Chibudo*. The last number was called a *Medano* – a spontaneous dance of 'criticism and honesty,' accompanied by song. Rafael explained to us this last number was performed to encourage local tribesmen to report 'the unusual' to the authorities – a concept that fell in step with what I believed the Portuguese powers might have approved, and in which I was sure they had no small a hand. This type of performance would, for instance, light on some action that should have been reported, but had not been, leaving someone to suffer because of the oversight. One performance of *Medano*, Rafael gave as an example, concerned a group of Africans who had found a war-time mine washed-up on the seashore. They should have reported it, but failed to do so, and several men were injured when the device exploded. The song and its accompanying dance was intended as a criticism of the men's 'dishonesty' in not reporting the mine, and an object lesson to those in the audience who heard it.

"Such performances have immense power over the local villagers ..." Rafael told me.

"I'm sure they do; but tell me, are these dances from the wellspring of their own culture, or are they in some way coerced – encouraged – by the Portuguese authorities ...?" Dr. Willems asked the question for me.

Rafael smiled. He understood very well the political nuance to the question.

"Both, really," he replied. "These kinds of performances were a part of their own cultural schooling, back-up for their own safety facing enemies in the bush – animal or human – and out on the sea, where some of them make a living by fishing. Various Portuguese administrators, and perhaps myself included, have seen the benefit of this type of bush learning. It is helpful in a variety of ways ..."

Professor Willems had been paying close attention to the performances, and he now summoned us over to where he had set up his apparatus.

He was intrigued by the dance, but his attention was focussed especially on the progression of the music – and the graphs that his machine was producing. He told us that he did not have on hand the sophisticated equipment necessary for recording the music itself, but that the oscillograph was able to give him a detailed 'picture' of it. None of us was a musician, and while his graphs made sense when he explained them, they really were not all that sexy.

"Think of it like this," the professor explained. "In our western cultural tradition, we are pretty much restricted, in musical terms, to a two-four rhythmic pattern. These performers, on the other hand, have a much wider selection ..."

He laid out a strip of graph paper, about a foot in length, on which there was shown a random pattern of ink lines zig-zagging up and down. They represented, he said, an extended phrase of music, and we could see they were anything but regular. The section was taken from a pattern of music occurring near the beginning of the piece he was recording. He then took a second strip of paper of the same length, recorded later in the same piece, and likewise marked by graph lines. He placed it over the first and held the strips up to the sunlight. The lines on one strip – all of them – matched exactly those on the corresponding strip.

"Perhaps this does not mean very much to you," he told us. "But this complexity of lines indicates something I have never seen before. I have travelled the world over listening to the finest orchestras in existence, and without the least hesitation I can say that in my life I have not encountered orchestration as fine, as complex or as sophisticated as what we have heard here today."

At the close of the day the kindly Professor Willems called together all the musicians and dancers to deliver an adjudication. Everyone listened carefully to what he was saying.

"It is difficult to explain my emotion," he told them, Rafael interpreting. "Your work is full of life and personal improvisations – and you work together with incredible precision, every individual element as in a clock. I am impressed by your sincerity, and how your artistic expression is so close to nature. It is pleasing – you are so clever, and I am sure that your powers of perception are entirely due to your music. You are like a gathering of poets – all of you quick and sensitive ..."

To Saul Rafael the professor said:

"Your attitude towards your people is outstanding. You say you know nothing of music, and yet you have been able to realize the importance to them of their phenomenal abilities. This is something wonderful, something vital to them – but also to you, who holds their beautiful culture in your hands. You are a fortunate man. Let them soar, my friend. Allow them to find their wings and be proud that they invite you to fly with them. This is a gift to you, and they in turn are most fortunate you have received it so well from them."

Because of the exceptional all around us in the modern western world, we have become blasé about exceptionalism – and especially about that which is often most original and notable. We tend to acknowledge the high level of technical sophistication which we are able to impose over something basic and God-given. In the early '60s Africa was very much more of a remote and mysterious place than it is today, closer to Burton's *First Footsteps in East Africa* (1859) which, in turn, was not so very far removed from Bruce's *Travels to Discover the Source of the Nile* (1768-73) – or even earlier writings – all of it describing what was, until about the 1960s, still seen and described as 'Darkest Africa.' The greater part of the entire continent remained substantially unchanged from remotest antiquity right up into our own lifetimes. 'Modern' Africa – the Africa with which we wish to relate as brothers today because we, too, have grown and no longer want to be associated with the disparagement the entire continent suffered during that time of ignorance and colonialism – is a recent phenomenon. Sensitive contemporary thinkers may even consider that comment disparaging, but belittlement and insult is the farthest thing from my mind. Quite the contrary, for the point is that a colonial mindset was still very much in vogue in the early '60s, and it was the colonial mindset that, for generations, so deliberately held Africa down. The dramatic changes (never complete) that have overtaken societies in all parts of the world in more recent times are perhaps nowhere better identified than they are today in Africa. That does not, and cannot, in the least subtract from the surprise and delight felt by a traveller from the privileged and developed west who might be guilty of packing his insensitive ignorance along with his Big Adventure Safari kit. Africa is a colossus on the move, make no mistake.

One of the regrets nibbling at the edges of my consciousness even today, more than fifty years after that memorable excursion, is that I had no video camera, no sound recorder and no colour film – as had also been the case when I encountered the Umbundu festival of spirit dancers in southern Angola. It was necessary to make do with what I had – and perhaps I did not do too badly, after all. The colours and sounds that leap off my black-and-white stills are vivid among my memories, and my octogenarian imagination is still quite capable of reassembling that entire day – in blazing full colour. Certain events in life will grab a man by the scruff of his neck and shake him like a leaf in a cyclone so that he will never forget the experience. I have witnessed a few memorable cyclones, and that day with the Zavala dancers was surely one of them.

Fish and Elephants

Joaquim Lemos was laughing.

"For three days you escaped your minders ..."

"No, I did not!" I expostulated, my eyes on Fausto. All of us were sitting in the living room comfort of the mid-town home Joaquim shared with his wife, Ramira.

"We were together in the car all the way up into Inhambane – we stayed in the same hotel, walked the same beach and listened to the same music. And he's still on my ass!"

Fausto also laughed. Everyone was aware Fausto had been appointed my minder in Lourenço Marques, as Quim had been in Luanda and elsewhere. The two of them had a good laugh about it.

"Never mind, Jeremy, I'll write for you such a good report that our dictatorship will award you a medal!" Fausto said.

Ramira entered the conversation at that point:

"Don't make fun of this! Don't make light of it – otherwise your guard will fall down, and it will not go well for you – or for him."

She glanced over at me, a serious look on her face.

"You must maintain your role, Fausto. You must! And you must be careful, too, Quim."

She was right, and all of us knew it very well. Joaquim and Fausto ceased their laughter and looked somewhat sheepish in face of her forewarning. PIDE posed a constant danger. Both men had been assigned to me as minders, the one in Angola, the other in Lourenço Marques. Although neither of them was committed to Portugal's fascist regime, they both knew they had been compromised and used by PIDE. It was a laughable situation from only a careless viewpoint – but most assuredly it would not have gone well for any of us if the authorities would have been able to hear our laughter. It was unlikely anything much would happen to me other than the prompt curtailment of my odyssey. I did not want that to happen, but at least if it did I would likely have been able to claim the assistance of my government – or, in a pinch, the British. But if the opposition mindset of either of these two men came under the least suspicion, they would most certainly be headed to prison – and very possibly worse.

"You'll be having minders all the way, Jeremy, so know about it and be alert," Fausto had forewarned me. "Be careful who you trust. That driver – Andrade – for instance ..."

"He was not such a sympathetic character that I'd have felt like trusting him, anyway ..." I told Fausto. "He showed himself to me quickly, so I never seriously entertained doubts about him. I could see right away something I didn't like. When you met me at the airport, I assumed you must be working for PIDE also ..."

"And I still do, as you know. I told you when we walked on the beach at Xai-Xai; here among friends we can be open about it. I think you know you can trust us – but you mustn't trust everybody. Many, many people are in opposition to our government, but it is not something anyone is at liberty to admit."

For now it was possible the government of Portugal was unaware of their spies' contrary political feelings, or of my own rapidly developing sympathies, and so preparation of the paperwork required for me to continue my trip through Moçambique was currently being reviewed at the governor's office. I had discussed my full itinerary with Fausto, and he in turn had handed it over for the approval and signatures of the powers-that-be. It would all take a few days – an ideal time to take off on a short trip to the southern border area and take Quim up on his offer to visit his fishing concession at Lagoa Piti. We had decided to take the next three days to visit with Joaquim's permanent on-site fishing crew.

That evening Fausto helped us pack our gear into Joaquim's company Land Rover, all of it necessary to establish a comfortable camp at the lagoon. Both Fausto and Ramira would have to remain at their respective jobs in Lourenço Marques while Quim and I travelled south. I stayed at the apartment that night so we could make an early start the following morning. Joaquim had two partners in the business – one being his brother, the other a man named Alfredo Sarmento who would drive down in the company truck a little later in the day.

Lagoa Piti was about one hundred kilometres south of Lourenço Marques. It would take us an hour-and-a-half to get there. Our first stop was at a produce market in the city to stock up on provisions for the camp. This was to be a provisioning run to serve the entire complement of permanent workers at the camp. It meant loading the basic food requirements for some thirty men and women, intended to last them for at least a couple of weeks. Into the back of our vehicle we loaded sacks of rice, yams and sweet potatoes, flour, corn and biltong, cans of cooking oil. Then we headed for the fish market to inform the purchasing agent we were in operation and would be back in two or three days well-stocked with boxes of freshly caught lagoon fish. We stopped a third time at what must have been the last service station on the road out of the city to fill several jerry cans with gasoline for the vehicles.

There was a good packed-earth road all the way to Bela Vista, then a road of somewhat lesser quality that took us down to a little town called Salamanga. Here there was a bridge crossing the Rio Maputo, from which point we headed east into the heart of the low-lying scrub and forest lands of the famous Maputo Elephant Reserve. We were going to drive directly through to the lagoon but chanced on a herd of elephants and I insisted on stopping to take a few photographs.

The animals were well hidden from view at first. We had slowed to a crawl as we skirted a watering hole, and I was looking for crocodiles, but on the other side of the car there was a tremendous noise emanating from some low bushes – animals fighting. We stopped, and I saw two male warthogs tearing viciously at one another. I wanted to get out of the car and take a closer look – whereupon Joaquim said:

"Better not get out just here ..." and he nodded his head towards something in the bush.

Standing quietly against the trees, partially concealed by their own silent shadows just the other side of the warring warthogs, was a family of three elephants – father, mother and juvenile. This 'baby' was the size of any full-grown elephant I had ever seen before. The mother was massive, and the father a monster I would not have believed had I not seen it so clearly. As we pulled to a stop, the warthogs ceased their quarrelling.

"Quickly – take your shot. They're close, so we'd better get out of here...!"

Joaquim already had the car in gear. I had his camera in my hands, loaded with colour film. I leaned across him, shooting from the driver's side window. All three elephants had started to flap and spread their ears – signs of the alarm that could have preceded a charge. The two warthogs scampered off from close in front of them.

I clicked the shutter …

"Gotta go!" Quim grunted, and the car shot forward at speed on the dirt track, out of the range of any inquisitive pachyderms.

My photograph turned out to be a fair shot. It was the equal (I dare to laud myself!) of another taken the following day at a watering hole – an immense lone bull come down for a drink, and to give himself a bath.

Old bull comes for his bath, Maputo elephant reserve

This Maputo reserve was renowned at the time as an integral part of Moçambique's 'Elephant Coast' – later known as the Maputo Special Reserve. It was home to a herd of well over one thousand of the largest elephant sub-species in Africa, migrants up and down the coast between this reserve and their other favoured haunts in the Kwa-Zulu area of Natal. During Moçambique's civil war (1977 to 1992) the herd was reduced –slaughtered for food, victims of mines, ivory poached to pay for the war – to fewer than one hundred and twenty animals. Today wildlife conservationists from Maputo's reserve and the Moçambique wildlife protection agency, in cooperation with two other bordering reserves in South Africa and Swaziland, together forming the Lubombo Transfrontier Reserve, have coaxed elephant numbers back up to close to seven hundred – and the numbers are mounting annually. Other wildlife that had suffered almost total decimation (for the lions it was a complete wipeout) are being reintroduced, and there is a conscious effort to restore the whole area to its original natural state.

The Maputo section of the park was originally formed in 1932 and has been expanded over the years to more that one thousand square kilometres of grasslands, wetland swamps, mangroves, forests and numbers of lakes and coastal lagoons. Since 2010 more than four thousand animals have been relocated into the park from other reserves – gazelles, warthogs and zebras have all been returned. Now there are plans to bring in rhinos, lions, leopards and cheetahs. In the swamplands and lakes there exist hippos and crocodiles – and throughout the park an exceptional abundance of colourful bird species.

Lagoa Piti, lying right alongside an Indian Ocean beach, does not have any opening to the sea. It is the largest of a series of small lakes within the Maputu Reserve, which incorporates almost the entire Machangulo Peninsula – all of it on the very edge of the Indian Ocean and separated from it by only a few metres of the narrowest of rocky banks and sand dunes. This coastal barrier, though, rises to over fifty metres along various stretches. The land surrounding the lakes lies at close to sea level, in places even lower, so that brackish waters seep through the sandy-bottom of the line of coastal banks. This feature, and the presence of small local fresh water courses, ensure the lakes are topped up. But for a few small hills, the entire reserve comprises low-lying flats, so that much of the area is swamp and wetland covered by mangrove and coarse grasses that grow high between wide stands of forest. Much of the growth tends to be yellowed by a strong sun in the dry season.

The fishing at the time of my visit with Joaquim Lemos was plentiful and lucrative. His employees had set up a camp on the west shore of the lake, and operations were moving right along when we arrived fairly late in the morning.

Fishing camp at Lake Piti

Laying net in the water

Gathering net with fish

Packing fish boxes

The method of catching the fish was by deploying a single large dragnet. The net would be carried straight out over the lagoon waters at a right angle to the beach by a slow-moving outboard engine boat. It would have two lines attached to it; the out-going line, well-anchored ashore, would be fed out to its full length as the boat moved into deeper water. Once the line was completely extended, the boat would be turned to run parallel with the beach and drop its wide net; it would then return to shore with the second line. Two teams of perhaps ten men each would then work both lines simultaneously, hauling in the net. It was heavy going; hundreds of fish of all types would be swept up and pulled into the shallows of the beach, all of them thrashing the water in their attempt to escape. A team of men would hold the net above the surface of the water, while others would wade in among the fish and start throwing them up onto the beach, there to be sorted and selected and tossed into large wooden boxes. These would have been brought down to the water's edge – each box containing fish of a like species.

The fish boxes were large – and very heavy once filled. The cry would go out, "Four-four!" – and teams of four men each would take up on the corners of each container, carrying it further back up the beach to the sorting, gutting and salting area. By this time Alfredo Sarmento had arrived with his truck, and at the end of the day the catch was sent off to the market in Lourenço Marques.

The survival instinct of one prodigious type of fish amazed me. It was a catfish, full-grown about forty-five to fifty centimetres in length, some big ones up to sixty or seventy centimetres, robust and as ugly as a warty old grandmother with straggly whiskers on her chops. The fish's mouth wore a perpetual grin much like the Cheshire cat's. The fishermen would pull in great numbers of them, but these critters were fighters, and did not submit without a supreme struggle both in the shallows and on the beach. Because they put up such a determined fight for life the fishermen would throw their catches of catfish onto the sand, well-clear of the edge of the surf. They were easier to handle once they had baked for a time in the hot sun. If they were thrown into the boxes too soon, they would often retain enough fight in them to throw themselves out again, and it became a scramble to pick them up off the ground still wriggling in the fish-packing area.

"Watch this!" Quim said – and he picked up one of the many catfish that had been lying on the beach for at least an hour.

Grabbing it behind its head and by the tail, Joaquim carried it to the edge of the water. The fish began to squirm and thrash its whole body in an effort to escape. Joaquim then tossed it back into the lake, whereupon it flicked its

tail and flashed out of sight.

"That creature has been lying for an hour in the baking sun. Any other species would be dead by now ..." he said.

Alfredo had been watching, and now he walked over to us nodding his head.

"And that's not all," he said. "Take a look at this!"

Grabbing a very strong sample of the species that had likewise been lying in the sun waiting to be thrown into one of the boxes, Alfredo took his fish knife and deftly opened its belly. It wriggled, but then lay inert as he disemboweled it. With the fish's guts lying on the sand, he carried its body to the edge of the surf, and placed it in a transparent ankle-deep section of water right at our feet. As soon as it felt itself free in its customary habitat, it flicked its tail and headed instantly out into the deep.

"It will die out there, of course – probably to be eaten by some predator. But that fish still wants to fight!"

Joaquim and I returned to the city after two days beside the lake. We had pitched a tent, but it was no sanctuary from the bug life of the swamp, so I was happy to leave when we did. Those bugs had teeth, and I was happy to close the door of my memory against them. Not so with the Maputo elephants; they were the biggest creatures I have seen before or since, in any part of Africa, most notable and memorable animals.

The colonial war with Portugal was to break out the year after I left Moçambique, and although it concluded with the *Carnation Revolution* in Portugal itself, resulting in independence for all of Portugal's colonies in 1975, the destruction and fighting did not let up until 1992 when the civil war, abetted by *apartheid* South Africa and Ian Smith's racist Rhodesia (ostensibly to 'defeat communism') finally fizzled out. Both these murderous outside regimes were merciless in their random destruction. More than one million people were killed, and one cannot help but wonder whether the figure would have been quite so high if the two sides in the Moçambicano conflict had been left to their own devices – to battle it out minus the 'assistance' of eastern and western superpowers. These outsiders time-and-again showed they cared not a damn for the indigenous people or their casualty numbers.

In addition to such figures of personal tragedy, the country's animal population also suffered. The famed parks – notably Maputo and Gorongosa – were blitzed, bombed and mined to such an extent that virtually all species were affected, some wiped out almost entirely. Unimaginable numbers of animals in every category were annihilated – target practice, bush meat or wanton destruction – and it is only now, some thirty years after the cessation of the fighting, that some progress in restoration can be calibrated. Recovery efforts have been little short of heroic. A de-mining programme has been in operation since the end of hostilities and will likely be a factor in the country's progress for several decades to come. Animals are being brought onto the reserves from elsewhere in Africa. There is a conscious effort to combat illegal poaching and instruct the local population in the very real benefits of animal husbandry.

Arranging the travel documents took longer than I had supposed and, in the end, I remained about a week in Lourenço Marques, keeping my room at the Polana, taking my meals in the dining room and using the swimming pool. But I also saw a lot of my minder, Fausto, who would show up and take me on excursions about the city – usually accompanied by Andrade the Abominable as our unsmiling silent driver.

Having been warned about Andrade, I took care not to engage him too frequently in conversation, and then only in the most cursory manner. He was shifty-eyed and morose, addressing me in grunts and single syllables, and only when he could see I was alone and unattended. At other times he would fall silent the instant Fausto swept back onto the scene with a bright smile and some cheery remark. He resented his lowly status as driver while Fausto had the greater responsibility of being the senior representative of his ministry –

and thus favoured by his operatives at PIDE. The miserable fellow, who always appeared wearing the same rumpled shirt as he wore yesterday, was made even more miserable because, I think, he could see Fausto and I were laughing and enjoying our conversations with one another. It was envy, pure and simple – certainly not (at least at first) because we viewed him as a low-ranked driver that we preferred not to talk to the fellow. On the few occasions when we went for outings, using the services of other drivers, we could relate to them perfectly well, including them in our lunches and table talk. But Andrade was special. He was ominous, sullenly disrespectful. He neither liked nor trusted Fausto. It was not his choice alone that he remained his skulking distance from us, for it was clear Fausto did not like him, either. Once or twice we had attempted to include him; at a beach-side restaurant, for instance, he insisted on proving himself such a morose and unpleasant figure that Fausto finally suggested he take his meal separate from us – which he did, at once resenting and preferring it that way.

The man unnerved me, nevertheless. It was Fausto who had recognized Andrade as dangerous, and the reasoning for this assessment became clearer to me the more I saw of the fellow. Simply, Fausto was playing – maybe carelessly – two sides of a game, dead earnest but with humour and humanity. His driver, also, was always in dead earnest, but he was a true believer in his adherence to the fascist idea of the *Estado Novo.* He was totally unable to smile with us, or otherwise break the fetters that had him so locked-in and blinkered. A fanatic for the hard steel edges of his box – and so dangerous indeed.

Fausto and I had just finished dinner in a pleasant downtown restaurant one evening, and were waiting for Joaquim and Ramira to join us for coffee, when I again brought up the subject of Andrade's treachery and all-too-apparent sordid personal torments. The man had been dismissed after he had delivered us to the establishment, and there was no mistaking the dark look in his eyes as he dropped us off.

"You told me not to trust him," I said. "I don't – but I'm curious to know why you feel so strongly about him ...?"

Fausto made a wry face.

As a journalist, he explained, he was a member of a select breed, all too many of whom had been co-opted by PIDE to do their nefarious bidding. Much as he would love to denounce, in a newspaper, the scurrilous little rats like Andrade – lots of them, too – whose lives were only made complete by the degree to which they could cause suffering for others, journalists were not at liberty to write what they wanted to write, or what they felt they ought to write about all aspects of the current political climate in Portugal and its colonies. It was boring to have to churn out the garbage the government wanted journalists to write. Fausto would write a story the way he saw it, he told me, and the censor would come along and cut it to pieces. If, by chance, a journalist ever happened to gain a reputation for being one who was continually censored, PIDE would begin to take notice – and start to make life hell for him. PIDE loved to put journalists in jail – and a low-ranked man like Andrade would not hesitate to report on anything he saw that roused his suspicious.

So Fausto had decided to do PIDE's bidding willingly – and to work against them from within – a strategy that, so far, was working for him. He was careful, he said, and they trusted him. He was intelligent, resourceful, had an education, and above all had made himself useful to them, doing the sort of work I had seen him doing – basic public relations for his government. The catch was that he had to write reports – but he was good at it. And the same criteria was applicable to Joaquim Lemos – both he and Ramira, working clandestinely, were most effective *oposicionistas*.

"But Andrade," Fausto concluded, "… he's an ignorant little brute. He has a family and needs to feed them. He thinks that by ingratiating himself with PIDE they'll eventually take notice of him, promote him, pay him a better wage. Money. I know what he is doing, and the treachery he would employ to be noticed and promoted. It's the way he works – for money, and a pat on the shoulder. He thinks he's being patriotic."

His contempt for his driver was evident.

"PIDE knows what he is … they are not stupid. They can see immediately he had no ability to meet and deal with people – that he has become envious and embittered, and so he doesn't move. But a bitter man can be a dangerous man, which is why I cautioned you to be careful of him. He's an ignorant man, and only a driver – but he can easily cause a lot of trouble, and would probably love to do it …"

On the other hand, PIDE would not likely be bothering Joaquim or Ramira very much because they knew he had a business to run – and besides, Ramira was working for the state, Fausto told me. The organization had given Joaquim a tryout in Angola, following me about. He was a businessman and, if they were sure of his loyalty, it was because they would have known he would be wanting to guard his business above all.

Fausto thought it unlikely PIDE would call on Quim again any time soon, unless by doing so they could use his business to disguise their own odious activity. The police would have checked him out, no doubt, and decided he was good for the kind of low-key assignment he had been asked to conduct, watching me in Angola, but they would have respected his status as a businessman. The reports he fed them about me had probably been quite sufficient. The police were evidently satisfied he could handle that level of work for them, Fausto said. By comparison, working as a trusted stenographer for the government, Ramira had already been cleared by the police, and was totally trusted by them as being 'on the inside.' (Arcane experience with secret service flatfeet has left me with the conclusion they are not easily taken by imaginative or abstract thinking, and might thus be inclined to start from the simplest given. Rigorous vetting might take second place to loyalty or sycophancy.) As a consequence, Ramira was especially useful to the opposition movement. She was tough, but under no illusions. She knew very well how hard she would fall if ever her true sentiments were discovered.

"I appreciate your telling me all this, Fausto, but all the same, allow me to turn the warning back to you," I told him. "You laugh easily, but nothing is more suspicious to a warped and twisted mind as laughter … So it is *you* who must be on your guard. I believe you when you say a man like Andrade is a threat – I'm sure he is, but he is of far greater danger to you than he could ever be to me. Were Andrade to get nasty with me, as a final resort I would likely have the resources of the Government of Canada arrayed behind me. Were he to get nasty with you, you'd have the resources of the Government of Portugal and its police right on top of you."

He laughed. We both laughed. However, when I met up with Ramira in Lisboa some years later, after the collapse of the dictatorship, I asked her for news of Fausto. She told me he had run afoul of PIDE and been picked up.

And when I finally met with Quim again, he said much the same thing:

"They came for him one night and took him away. I made several attempts to locate him, but it was difficult to ask questions without implicating myself. We never heard more of him. I think he must be dead."

There was never any proof, of course, but I have always assumed Andrade had had a hand in it.

Fausto's last words to me before I left Louranço Marques had been a caution:

"Be careful of your minders, Jeremy. Some, like Andrade, are obvious bastards, and would turn you in just for the thrill of doing PIDE's bidding. It's their only opportunity to exercise their little power. Please don't look on all Portuguese as being as bad as some you are likely to meet – but take care not to be too quick to treat us all as friends. Politics is involved in everything now, and politics can be nasty. Joaquim and me, I think you know, are your friends; others may not be so kind. Be careful of your trust."

Mocímboa da Praia

From Lourenço Marques I flew north to Mocímboa da Praia, a very small coastal town about sixty kilometres south of the Tanzanian frontier. Here I felt I was back in somewhat familiar territory, inasmuch as Swahili was a local lingua franca; I had studied the language only a few years earlier. While by no means fluent, I could manage to carry on or understand a simple conversation in the language. It boosted my confidence, and I like to think it gave me a small edge.

Moçambique is a long country, south-to-north, and while I was not able to touch down in every district, I did travel the full length of it. The flight north was no simple affair, inasmuch as I had to change planes at Beira. From that point on to Nampula I found myself seated next to a beautiful young lady by the name of Fernanda de Sousa, who worked in Beira in the accounting department of Moçambique Railways. She had a boyfriend in Nampula and was flying up to spend a few days with him and his family. She was charming and vivacious, so we talked a lot – and the time passed quickly. We flew over the delta of the Rio Zambezi to Quelimane – the port city on the Rio dos Bons Sinais – the 'River of Good Signs' – which legend says was named by Vasco da Gama himself, and the point from which the famous explorer-missionary-teacher, David Livingstone, embarked for home after crossing the continent, Luanda to Quelimane, in 1856.

Following the usual perfunctory how-do-you-do's, it took Miss Fernanda about thirty seconds to launch into her political view of Portugal's colonial affairs. She took a surprisingly strong *oposicionista* stance – a bold, even reckless, opener with someone she had only just met. Her come-on came with smiles and frowns, and many personal questions, which rather gave her show away. She was just a mite too glib, and it immediately set me on my guard. For whatever end – now, how could I possibly be sure? – she was pumping me for my own views.

"I love Moçambique," she said passionately. "I was born here. This is my land, and I am a proud Moçambicana. My family has been here for generations, so we know our Africans. They are our brothers ... Really, I do not know how our government cannot accept them as our equals ..."

So I twigged immediately. 'Our' Africans? Right, Miss Fernanda, I know who *you* are!

The rest of our conversation was a game. She pumped, I huffed and queried her – question-for-question – and was careful to say nothing derogatory about the *Estado Novo*. Better to be wide open, I reckoned, expressing only surprise and joyous wonder at the way the Portuguese maintained such a far-away country, all of it running so smoothly. My only opinions were the expression of total wonderment – the beaches, the climate, the friendliness, everyone's sunny smiles, and everything so very much more superior to the way I had seen life in other African countries ... How could I possibly not voice my admiration for such a far-sighted and generous administration? She warmed to me because she could see I 'understood;' she was happy in that I could so easily concur with her views, how my expressions of praise richly amplified the pride she so abundantly (and deservedly) felt at the way her fascist masters were running her country. Very quickly, I am sure, she forgot she had a job to do. Dazzling like a snake ...

I wondered how she had been recruited. A telephone call, perhaps, from Mr. Government Big in Lourenço Marques to his good friend, Mr. Railway Big in Beira. Easy, but it brought home the caution issued only hours earlier by Fausto.

At Nampula Fernanda de Sousa kissed me on both cheeks, wishing me farewell. She was happy that she had fulfilled her obligation to PIDE, but she did not say that. Her happiness was because the two of us had had such a pleasant journey after all; because my consistent questions and expressions of delighted surprise at her answers had in no way forced her to think or – God forbid! – argue. She had worked her magic. I had been sure, from the moment we sat down side-by-side, that she had been carefully instructed to take careful note of any contrary views I might have expressed – and so was delighted that I had not caused her some unpleasant (perhaps offensive) confrontation. I had to change planes, and no sooner had I bid farewell to the bedazzled Fernanda than I was tapped on the shoulder by José Garcia Soares, the administrator for Nampula District, who made it clear he knew my itinerary.

Of course, he did – and I never had need to connect with Fernanda de Sousa again ...

My onward flight was not due to depart for a couple of hours, which left just enough time for me to squeeze in an hour or so with the local administrator for a debriefing and an earful of propaganda over lunch in the airport cafeteria. My intent, once in the north, was to work my way south again, point-by-point, and so eventually arrive back in Lourenço Marques to catch my flight to Lisboa at the conclusion of this escapade. For the present, a smaller local airline ferried me southeast to the coastal city of António Enes, then up the coast to Lumbo, Porto Amélia – and finally, ten hours after leaving the capital, my arrival at Mocímboa da Praia, a full hour before nightfall, to be met by this district's administrator, Francisco Chaves.

In 1959 Mocímboa da Praia had been on the receiving end of a major tropical tempest that had virtually wiped it out. At the time of my visit the population was about twelve thousand. Today it is three times that, still not a big city but important as a northern port and contact terminus for the movement of people and goods to and from southern Tanzania. The devastation of the storm in 1959 had been so widespread, so severe, that the Portuguese government had sought out an energetic achiever to go north, take command of the situation, rebuild and revitalize the town and get the local industries humming again. Fishing was one of the town's principal occupations; another important business was the export of tropical hard woods; the man chosen for this daunting undertaking was Francisco Chaves. By the time I met him he had had close to five years to establish himself and his will in Mocímboa da Praia, and almost immediately I became aware he was considered the town's chief potentate. He told me so.

Francisco was a power pack – a one-man whirlwind to beat back the ravages of the storm that had destroyed the town five years earlier. When I arrived, all the debris had long been cleared away, of course, houses had been rebuilt, and yet others were under construction. Boats had been repaired and the fishing industry re-established; timber exports, though clearly lacking sufficient infrastructure, had been resumed and had become a major activity on the town's waterfront, where barges laden with jumbo-sized hard wood logs were being loaded by hand, back-breaking muscle – and the flimsiest of cantilevers and ropes.

Chaves wore the uniform of his office – white shorts, short-sleeved white shirt, and a military-style peaked cap, white but for its black peak and so rumpled it looked as though it had been baked in a bread oven. He was a sturdily-built fellow, not tall, but strong and exuding bags of confidence. He walked briskly, issuing orders left and right as he progressed through the streets. He seemed to know everybody, and every detail of the town's workings – what buildings were going up, who had just dug a well or installed a pump, how the electricity had been installed that was intended to service the entire population. Down at what passed for a dock area he slapped the fishermen on their backs, encouraged the men working on their boats, and stopped to talk with a group of men heaving gargantuan logs onto a barge for shipment up into Tanganyika. Everyone we met, black or white, responded to him with cordial informality.

The evening I arrived Francisco's wife, Graça, cooked up a fine supper for her family, and I was invited to participate as one of them – which meant clearing the table and washing the dirty dishes afterwards.

"Normally we have our houseboy do all this, but tonight we have to be quick if we're going to see the film ..." Francisco commented, hustling his kids into their pajamas so all their sitter had to do was give them a snack and tell them their bedtime story.

The film was to be shown at the local club – a sort of tropical version of the Portuguese *sociedade* that exists in virtually every village in Portugal. Generally these establishments are a cross between a pub and a recreation centre, the facilities of which are open to just about anyone with a coin in his pocket and a yen for informal company. I had never seen anything quite like them in Canada, but found I quite liked the idea behind them – a dispensing of all class and clan differences in a congenial and unconstrained setting that permits mixture – even encourages it. In Portugal many years later, I always found the village *sociedade* to be a unique leveller – a place where an underling could really square up to his superior, employee-to-boss, and almost always be assured of a supportive crowd to out-number any big shot. The English pub comes fairly close but does not quite fill the same function as the Portuguese *sociedade*. On this evening, a once-a-week treat for the townspeople, the featured film was a showing of the 1958 Hollywood technicolour production, *Queen of Outer Space*, presenting the ambrosial Zsa Zsa Gabor in the role of the heroine. It was not quite my preferred genre, but I got an immense kick out of the audience – who clapped and shouted and jeered and whistled – precisely the behaviour demanded for a creation of this special camp. My diary informs that the audience in Mocímboa da Praia that evening seemed to enjoy the movie in about equal measure to my enjoyment of their reception of it; not a cinematic production to be remembered for its content so much as by the setting and the boisterous manner in which it was received. *Sociedade* with a liberal twist of African bush.

The homes of the general population of Mocímboa da Praia were designed by a Portuguese engineer who, within certain parameters, worked around each family's specified needs. Mortgages were available, so that within a ten- or twenty-year span each homeowner would have clear title. I liked this idea better than the 'cookie-cutter' homes I saw being built for the Limpopo development. There was a touch more individuality about them. However, I was astonished to see the way in which they were being built. Every timber in every house was being individually cut to size. The work was pleasing to look at, but slow. If I was trying to rebuild a community from scratch after it had been knocked sideways by a storm, I would have opted for some form of standard wood-sizing so as to put up adequate shelter for as many people as possible – as rapidly as possible. There was no two-by-four sizing in these houses. No quarrel with the carpenters, but it seemed to take them hours to trim each plank and then fiddle it into place. I mentioned this to Francisco, and he shrugged.

"These people like their individualism," was his comment.

"How about an electric saw?" I suggested. It occurred to me that if the timbers were pre-cut to a pre-set size, there would be a saving in both time and labour, and houses would go up at a much faster rate.

Francisco pooh-poohed the idea.

"Too standard," he said.

This was the point at which he informed me all the carpenters and builders were under contract to him personally. He was receiving funds from the government, calculated on a daily basis. The longer he could keep the men working, the longer the funds would filter in to him – and presumably he was taking a cut somewhere along the line.

After watching him for a couple of days I began to feel a certain antipathy. He 'uncled' the Africans in talking to them, I thought – talked to them, but through them, only superficially mollifying one, it appeared, before quickly moving onto the next. I did not like the way the Africans felt constrained to play up to him, sycophantic sucking-up in order to receive that jovial pat on the back. I did not much care for his bluffness, the way he spoke down to certain people while his hand was on their shoulder. I noted that even with his wife and children he displayed a sort of lord-of-the-castle attitude. His words were not necessarily unkind – just easily thrown out, and too often over his shoulder. He was gracious enough to me personally, but he clearly thought his own viewpoints were of far greater import than anything others expressed – and I was only a visiting foreigner.

As administrator, Francisco Chaves wore a number of hats: he was the town's mayor, the chief of town planning, the chief of police, and the chief (and sole) magistrate. Within his district, his was the last word in matters of education, health, justice, social amenities, and the water and electrical services. With all the air of authority he could muster, it seemed this busy man bore the brunt of responsibility for pretty well everything that happened in Mocímboa da Praia – even to the choice of the movie we had seen in the club the previous evening. Without delegating authority, it seemed to me little wonder things slipped now and then, much energy expended – but also much wastage in failing to accomplish simple things. The cutting of timbers for housing was only one example of what I considered inefficiency.

I learned there were some two hundred soldiers garrisoning the local barracks, that their officers and sergeants were all white Portuguese. The military medical post also took care of the local populace, working in close harmony with the town's fifty-bed hospital. Chaves introduced me to the hospital director, Dr. José Julio Xavier Barreto, a soft-spoken and eloquent Goan. He had a staff of three other physicians, and a whole cadre of medically-trained African orderlies. He was a quiet man, a collector of stamps, so put in his order for a collection of Canadian stamps once I had returned home. Understandably, he refrained from criticism of the Portuguese administration of Moçambique, and in fact went out of his way to offer praise of them, with profuse expressions of thanks for their generosity in permitting him to carry on his profession among them.

"You see, I consider myself Portuguese – as Portuguese as any of them, but of a different racial origin, you see. Goa and Portugal have been linked for centuries. For two years now Goa has been a part of the new India, and that is as it should be. But I am Portuguese now and am honoured to be working in this wonderful part of Portugal."

Dr. Barreto spent much of his time working in clinics set up throughout the district. When absent from Mocímboa da Praia the daily work of the hospital was entrusted to other medical personnel that had been trained under his administration.

"We couldn't manage without them," he said of the orderlies. The chief complaints among the general population were yaws, venereal disease, leprosy, sleeping sickness – and the greatest scourge of them all, tuberculosis.

"That's the bad one, the *really* bad one – but, you know, Africans tend to leave their treatment until it is too late, so there are many complications with their overall health – and a totally avoidable extension in their period of treatment."

I remembered how back at Dondi, Lilian Taylor had complained that the rural hospitals in the Portuguese overseas provinces were too slap-dash. She was talking about how things were in Angola, but it was easy to see the same problem existed in Moçambique. Patients showing positive response were permitted to leave hospital care too early so that treatment was often curtailed, or dropped altogether once there appeared to be an improvement. Lilian had told me that at the Dondi hospital patients were obliged to take the full treatment under hospital care and observation. Here, in Mocímboa da Praia it seemed when an African patient felt an improvement, little effort was made to stop him from leaving. His bed would soon be occupied by someone else in dire need.

"If things go badly for him, he may decide to return to the hospital – or possibly he'll just crawl off into the bush and die," Dr. Barreto said. "We try to stop them, but it is beyond our power to hold them."

Conditions inside the hospital were horrendous. The beds had no linen, and very often only a slab board in place of a mattress. Many of the patients were filthy when they arrived; some might be given a bath, but sanitation was a sometime thing, depending upon the work overload and who was on duty.

I queried these things with the good doctor. He shrugged, spreading the palms of his hands.

"Of course, you are right. I give orders to the staff, as do the other doctors, but we are all extremely busy, and I by myself cannot police the hospital here too efficiently if I am off in the district clinics. I need help, but I cannot do everything myself, and I cannot force issues," he said.

By this I understood his meaning to be that his work was overseen by the district administrator – and that he was generally fighting an uphill battle for supplies and medications. As chief of hospital administration, and overseer of health issues throughout the district, Chaves was in charge – and it was Chaves' responsibility, not the doctor's, when matters of health were permitted to slide due to a lack of oversight or funding. The general absence of communication between Chaves and his chief medical officer was conspicuous. There was no proper delegation of the many responsibilities, and thus too much rested on the shoulders of just the one man. Dr. Barreto was plainly outgunned.

Now and then I was able to avoid minders and commitments seemingly designed to keep me chasing my tail. When this happened, I was able to sidestep the perceptible stress of feeling monitored, and enjoy walking out on my own – on this occasion through the African residential quarter of Mocímboa da Praia. For brief periods I could be alone to enjoy creating a personal interaction with the people I met. I was staying in Chaves' house, and he made sure I was fully occupied most of the time – which was a form of minding, I suppose. Perhaps it was ungracious of me, even inaccurate, to tag him as my minder; it was possible he did not really give a damn. He was a busy individual, and I knew he was anxious that I should depart his town with only the best of impressions of what he was attempting to do there. But then a trap is a trap, no matter who sets it, and escaping for even a short time to go solo gave me an immense sense of relief. Chaves had told me both the Macua and the Makonde – particularly the Makonde – had long been noted for their artistic abilities. I had heard this before, so poked about on a half-hearted mission to scout for wood carvings and artwork. I particularly wanted to find one or two outstanding pieces of ebony sculpture, although I was aware there were numerous other types of hardwoods in the country – rosewoods and *makulas*.

Ebony carver shows his works

I did not speak any Portuguese at all at the time, which was the lingua franca throughout Moçambique, but in the north of the country Swahili is spoken by many, and I was able to employ that in a most fractured and limited way. Linguistically it is related to both Macua and Makonde which, although

314

Portuguese is considered the lingua franca, are the two largest local languages. It was not unusual for people to mix-and-match and come to something of an understanding in Swahili – a primary language across the Rio Rovuma in Tanganyika, and an important secondary language in the region of Cabo Delgado. On this one precious occasion I found myself, camera in hand, exploring a part of the town I had not been in before. On a narrow street I came across a silversmith and his wife outside their house. He was squatting on his haunches on the dusty ground, working at a crucible over a small brazier. His wife was operating a hand bellows at his direction, blowing a charcoal fire into a fierce heat. Their actions pricked my curiosity, so I was content to stop and watch as the two of them worked. I wound up sitting with them for well over an hour, and we were able to start up a rudimentary conversation in Swahili. None of us spoke it very well, but it was enough for him to explain what he was doing.

Silversmith makes a chain bracelet

He had melted down old South African coinage that had been minted in almost pure silver. When it was liquid, he poured it from the crucible into a mould he had made from clay – a single line scoured into a flat surface, so that when it cooled he had made himself a length of silver wire. He repeated the process several times. This done, he hammered the wires flat and cut them into short lengths of about one centimetre. Working deftly and quickly, and using his hammer, pliers and a set of special tools, he soldered each tiny piece into an oval, connecting each link both lengthwise and widthwise to form a chain about four centimetres and several links wide, and perhaps sixteen or seventeen centimetres in overall length. Of the same material, he then formed a simple clasp mechanism for each end of the chain – and after an hour or so held up for my critical approval a plain but exceptionally lovely articulated bracelet.

I was astonished by his dexterity – his nimble fingers and air of absolute confidence. He possessed a rare virtuosity with both tools and metal – a master of his special *artesanato*. It was his confidence and surety that appealed so highly, even before I had taken a close look at the perfection of the bracelet itself. He burnished it with a rag, then passed it up to me for examination. Still warm from the firing, it had not the finished precision of a piece I might have found at Birks, or at any other fine jewellery store back in Toronto. I doubted that a trained professional jeweller would have made a similar wristband – nor one to equal such unique and delightful appearance. It was a one-off, a hand-crafted piece that no one else could possibly have copied or reproduced. Instinctively I knew that if ever I was offered the choice, the gift of a jewel I had witnessed coming to life in the hands of its maker, comparable to the one I was looking at – or another, in which the craft of its maker was so expertly concealed it would be impossible to detect the deftness of the artisan's personal skill – I would hands-down prefer the former.

"*Maridadi! Maridadi sana!*" I told him. I was delighted and knew no better way to express my sense of joy at his triumph.

He smiled broadly, contented that he had pleased me so well.

I held the bracelet out to him, intending to put it back into his hand. Instead he closed his fingers around my own hand so I could not let go the piece, pushing it towards me and making signs that he did not want it back.

It was embarrassing. I did not have enough money on me to make the purchase there and then and supposed he would want more than I could afford. I turned my trouser pocket inside-out to indicate I had no cash with me, instead using my limited Swahili to inform him I would return with funds. How much did he want for the piece, I tried to ask.

He shook his head.

With that, his wife stood up. Looking me straight in the eye, she snatched the piece from my hand and thrust it into my empty shirt pocket, patting the pocket when the piece was deep inside.

Her husband clapped his hands and grinned broadly, showing me all his teeth.

"Tomorrow morning we go to Naquidunga," Chaves announced. "There is a big festival there, and I have notified the chief I shall be bringing a distinguished guest with me."

"Who's the guest?" I asked innocently.

"You!" he exclaimed, and he let out a loud burst of laughter.

"What does 'distinguished guest' entail?" I asked again, sceptically.

"Oh, nothing at all, really. The villagers always like an excuse to celebrate, so tomorrow you will be the focus of their attentions. Not anything for you to worry about. You don't have to wear a frock coat or a crown. You might be expected to give satisfactory entertainment to a young lady in the darkness of her chambers, but if that is about to happen I'll try to give you warning in advance …!"

Seeing my quizzical expression, he laughed.

"There's nothing to be alarmed about. You're going to have a good time. If you stay close to me, I'll be able to explain what's going on. I try to go to all the villages in my district at least once a year, and they always like to turn the occasion into a *festa*. It's an opportunity for me to meet with the various chiefs, to hear their requests and complaints. It will be fun, you'll see. They'll make a fuss over you, but it's nothing – you'll enjoy yourself!"

Naquidunga was a small village, something more than a widening in the road less than an hour by jeep from Mocímboa da Praia. As we approached it, Chaves driving, I saw about one hundred metres in front, a high arch of tropical shrubbery and grasses and flowers, all of it woven into an armature of interlaced sticks that spanned the full width of the entry road into the village.

"Ye Gods …!" What an extraordinary structure! Someone – a whole regiment of elves with flowers in their hair – must have taken a month to build such a thing.

The arch rose to a height of about six metres, and was solidly-built. It was made basket-like, a weave of bamboos – the base of its support on either side of the road much like the houses one will see built of woven sticks and plastered with mud and cow dung. In this case, though, there was no mud plastering. Instead, the openings between the bamboos were interlaced with still green shrubbery and a mass of flowers of every colour. The substantial bases soared upwards, tower-like, then as the structure thinned-out, they were made to lean towards one another to meet at the top, completing the arch right over the centre of the road. It looked as if it was intended as a permanent structure, but Chaves assured me it was not.

"It will be up there for a few days, perhaps, but then they will have to dismantle it – before it falls into the roadway."

I thought to photograph it, and probably would have done so had we stopped thirty metres in front of it so that I could have fitted the whole thing within my camera frame. But we were rolling forward, and there was a commotion up front – a distraction that caused Chaves to slip the gear into low, slowing the car to a crawl. Shot in black and white, I realized the scene in front of us would not have made such a great impression as it did in full screaming colour – and I could tell there were going to be many great shots to be taken that day. I needed to conserve film.

Chaves roared his loud laugh, then turned to me.

"They have decided to make this a very special occasion, I see ..."

He looked me up and down, inspecting my most informal bush attire.

"We should at least have dressed you up. An admiral's uniform wouldn't have been out-of-place!"

Twenty metres before passing under the archway, two lines of perhaps fifteen young girls each came charging out from the village, through the archway and straight towards our vehicle, their phalanx filling the dirt road.

Some greeting party! They were ululating; the noise they created as they advanced was deafening – first in front of us, then right beside our ears as they passed the car and surrounded us,.

They were barefoot, topless and dressed in grass skirts, each girl wearing bracelets of woven grass around their arms and ankles. Flowers were woven into the hair of their heads, and with their arms they pumped the air and waved them as if they were the limbs of trees in a high wind. Turning their heads from side-to-side, they came onto us swiftly, clapping their hands, ululating and shouting in high-pitched voices, dancing as they approached – all of them smiling and laughing as they kicked up the dust of the roadway. Chaves applied the brakes and slowed the open jeep till it was barely moving. The look on my face must have shown how startled I felt. One of the girls mimicked me from ten centimetres in front of my nose, then she reached out and stroked my cheek with the backs of her fingers. In an instant she was gone, and there was another girl in her place, handing me a flower she had plucked from her head. I glanced at Francisco and saw him receiving the same treatment on his side of the car.

Just as we were passing under the arch, our little procession now swollen a hundred-fold, was halted by two outlandish-looking individuals, shoeless and bare but for green cloth wrapped around their waists like kilts and tied in place by coloured cords. There were daubs of white on their brown bodies. The Makonde, both men and women, frequently followed an ancient beautifying technique by passing a 'nail' – copper, iron, silver – through the upper lip to stand upright in front of the nose, rhino-like; one of the two men was utilizing this decorative feature. But instead of passing the nail through his own upper lip, he imitated the procedure, the nail piercing a wooden replica of his lip. It was attached to the lower portion of his face like a mask; both men had bound these imitation upper lips in place over their own natural features, using strings knotted at the back of each of their heads to secure the devices in place. From these wooden facsimile lips were suspended long false beards, which they occasionally stroked. They both wore sunglasses – one of them neglecting to remove the price tag – and each wore a long-feathered wreath on his head, like a crown, which he would snatch off in salutation, then replace, all with the abrupt movements of a barnyard cockerel.

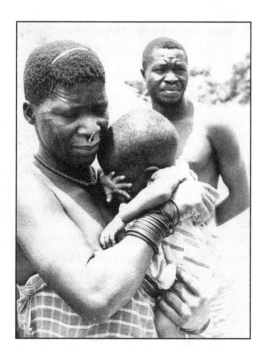

Makonde family
(note scarring and lip 'nail')

319

Naquidunga greeting

Somewhere at the back of the throng, off the road into the village, there was a consistent drumming, and the girls who had first welcomed us and handed us on to be greeted by the two cockerels could now be seen beyond some houses and trees a little way off, still dancing and gyrating. We gravitated that way, now on foot. Everywhere there was movement and excitement, and hordes of little children. A kind of bandshell had been rigged up, made of bamboos and grasses, and this was soon to be the centre of some sort of ceremony. But first we had to be shown a full programme of entertainments, all of which involved costumed and masked dancers.

There was even a fiddle-playing 'fire walker,' except that he was not walking, as such, and nor was he playing a recognizable fiddle. I was pulled into a circle of spectators gathered about the musician who pranced and danced as he sawed away at the string of a one-string fiddle. The instrument's sound box resembled a small drum attached to a one-metre long neck, from the end of which the tautened thin string connected the far end of the neck to the drum. He played the instrument as one would a violin, by drawing a crudely fashioned bow across the string to make a sound – a tone he could alter by applying pressure at the end of the neck. Assistants had placed a shovelful of red-hot embers on the ground and, without stopping his fiddling, the young fellow walked backwards onto the top of them, then sat himself immediately in front of them and inched his bum backwards until he was seated right on top of the glowing coals. He was wearing a grass skirt, and this began to smoke, some of the grasses actually catching fire. His headdress fell away from him as he lay down, the hot coals now under his buttocks and lower back – and he continued playing. After a minute or two, and still sawing

320

away at his fiddle, he leaped up and came towards me to present himself unscathed. His skin was hot, but there was no indication he had been burned in any way.

| Fiddling as he backs onto red hot coals | … and he lies down on them |

An hour or so passed before we were finally ushered into the bandshell. Three tall-backed wickerwork seats, like thrones, had been set out on the dais – for the administrator, the chief and myself; other dignitaries gathered about, standing on either side of us. The chief and the district administrator were important men and, as guest of honour, it appears I was also. However, it was Francisco Chaves who really called the shots with the people of Naquidunga, so all I had to do was sit back and watch. He would be the decision-maker for whatever business was enacted – infrastructure and housing, food and water distribution, defence against wild animals. He smiled and waved, leaning over to talk to the chief in Portuguese, and then to me to give me a rough translation of what was going on. I took a few notes and was scribbling onto a pad of paper when, about a half-hour into the proceedings, I became aware of a man in the front rank of the audience who was addressing the chief in Swahili. I listened carefully.

"Please ask the administrator to issue us guns," he was saying. "You could tell him about the leopard that has snatched away several people in recent evenings, down by the river … We need guns to protect ourselves …"

I had conversed in the language on several occasions in Mocímboa da Praia, but I had not let it be generally known I could cope with it. I certainly

321

had not informed Francisco Chaves. So, assuming I could not understand a word of what had been said, he leaned towards me and said, in English:

"They are speaking in their own language – and I don't understand it very well. I can speak Makonde, and some Macua – but the language they are using now … I don't know it …"

Then he turned quite angrily to the chief and snapped at him in Portuguese.

The chief then turned to the man in the audience, addressing him in Swahili.

"The *effendi* does not like that you speak in a language he does not understand. Can you not make your request in Portuguese?"

The man in the audience replied in Swahili that no, he spoke no Portuguese because he was just visiting from Tanzania, the far side of the border formed by the Rio Rovuma, and did not speak Portuguese. He was Macua, he said, and did not speak Makonde very well, either. Perhaps the chief would be good enough to translate the request for him …?

The chief glanced sideways at Chaves, holding up his hand indicating he needed to speak further to the man – but in Swahili.

"The man is speaking in Swahili, *effendi*, so permit me to find out precisely what he wants."

Then he turned to the man in the audience and reprimanded him:

"If you speak in Swahili, the administrator will understand that you do not speak the same language as we do, and that therefore you do not come from here. You must be careful …!"

The Tanzanian smiled.

"I understand," he said. "But it is the administrator who needs to be careful! It would be useful if the Portuguese could issue us with some guns…"

The chief replied, again in Swahili:

"I cannot ask him for guns just now; it is premature. But I will tell him about the leopard …"

Now the chief turned and had quite a long conversation with Francisco Chaves, this time in Portuguese. I listened but could understand nary a word of what was being said. However, after they had finished talking the administrator turned to me with a smile and gave me an improvised English language translation.

"It seems there has been a leopard prowling about that has attacked a couple of their women down by the river. It could be true, it could be untrue – but I know what they want. They want me to give them guns. I rather suspect it's just a ruse so that they can get a weapon or two issued to them legally. But you know, I am not a fool – and I am not about to arm these Africans with anything like a rifle. It would be only a short time before they would turn it on me!

"So I told him: we have no guns to give to them to fight the leopards – but that I would be happy to have a team from our game department come and stay a few days at the village. Perhaps they will be able to track down the leopard, if it exists in fact. Somehow I doubt it – I think they want guns ..."

It was an insightful altercation for me to hear, and I never did inform Chaves that I could comprehend an important aspect of it that he could not. Quite distinctly I had picked up the message between the two Africans that they were attempting to collect weapons and, like Chaves, I could well imagine the purpose for which they required them. There was 'not yet war in Moçambique,' as Esmeralda had told me some weeks before as I was leaving Angola. But there was war, most definitely, elsewhere in the Portuguese colonies, and it was not difficult to imagine it coming to this peaceful land, in due course – when people like the ones I met that day in Naquidunga were ready for it.

Jungle Justice

The sun had passed its zenith and was casting its heat back to earth with the force of a god angered by the imperative of having to waste energy on such a burned-out landscape. The ground was khaki and ochre and brown. Fine dust had been churned into the air by the traffic that moved along the town's pitted roads under a monotonous blue sky. Nights, sultry, suffocating, failed to dip the thermometer by more than a point or two, and in any case made no difference to the quantity of matter that rose from the roads and settled onto the sparse vegetation that struggled for survival within the confines of the urban area, clothing it in khaki, ochre, brown – only here and there an undergarment of green. The back of my hand brushed along the fender of the administrator's Land Rover as I turned in at his gate. The intense heat of the metal body scorched me as though I had laid the back of my hand into a fry pan.

Everything stood on its own shadow. Flies swarmed about my head. They loved the sweat on the back of my neck. It was mid-afternoon. I had already taken two showers and was wearing my second shirt of the day. The sensation of rancid sweat-smelling tropical clothes is an acquired discomfort. One has to become used to it – corrugated iron roofs, dust, sweat, flies. Soggy clothes. These were the invariables in that miserable little town in that season.

But the administrator wore white. He always wore white. White shoes, white knee socks, white shorts, white shirt – and his crumpled white hat with its black peak. Administrators in Portuguese Africa looked a lot like sea captains. But if they ran their districts like ships, they were not always tight ones.

Francisco Chaves had arranged for a car to take me to the northern frontier a little later in the afternoon, and I wondered if the vehicle was yet ready. Dark descends at six o'clock at that latitude, so I was anxious to make as early a start as possible. I called in at the administrator's office to speak to him about it.

People were moving about inside the small building. Lunch was just over for most people. The meal, the heat, the hour of the day – movement had a lazy somnolence to it. Nobody wanted to be in a hurry to do anything except seek out a chair or stool on which to set. From the outer office I could look through a half-open door into the administrator's private chamber. There he was seated behind a large brown desk, while around him were numbers of clerks shuffling papers.

"Come in! Come in!" he shouted, spotting me through the doorway.

He lifted himself out of his chair and waved at me to enter. Everyone turned.

"Sit here!" he commanded, indicating a place right beside him. "You might find this very interesting …"

So, I sat.

"What's going on?" I whispered.

An African woman was standing off to one side, almost behind the door. She was talking, but no one appeared to be listening.

"We're holding court," the administrator said, with no attempt at lowering his voice.

The woman continued to talk.

"She is giving evidence," the administrator said.

He settled back and looked at his watch, yawned and smiled at me. He lit a cigarette. The woman prattled on.

Then he said:

"I'm the judge here. I'm the judge, jury, chief of police and jailer. And administrator, of course. An administrator has many jobs to do. I'm the chief town planner, chief of education, and chief agriculturalist for the district ..."

As he talked the woman kept up her continuous flow of evidence.

Suddenly Chaves leaned forward to address me again.

"Have you met my assistant?" he enquired.

I had not, so he introduced us, raising his voice just enough that it would carry into all corners of the room above the woman's evidence. She did not let up for an instant. Then he introduced me to the other men in the room, and each stepped forward in turn with a greeting and an outstretched hand. We exchanged cordialities.

I was worried. The woman's evidence was simply not being heard.

Then the telephone rang. It was the administrator's wife. They talked for a few moments and then he hung up. The African woman talked on.

"That was my wife," said the administrator. "Your car will be here about five o'clock. That's not too late for you, is it?"

It was a little, but I shook my head, no.

"The road to the north is very bad, very bad ..."

We fell silent for a few moments and listened to the woman's evidence. Her eyes were fixed on a pen-stand on the administrator's desk, and she stared at it intently as she spouted forth, determined to voice her full story. For the first time I could hear what she was saying. She was talking a native language. Although I could neither speak it nor understand it, I could pick out the occasional word here and there ...

"Do you understand what she is saying?" I whispered to Chaves.

He seemed to be sitting on my shoulder, reading my mind.

"Yes, I can understand quite well ..." he said.

I hope so, I thought, though I doubted him.

"She is talking Macua. It's similar to Swahili. You can probably understand a few words if you listen carefully ..."

325

I nodded.

"I speak many languages," he told me proudly. "I can speak French better than English ... and the nine dialects of my district. They're all different languages, really. And Portuguese, of course ..."

"How about Swahili?" I asked.

"No – Swahili is related to many of the languages around here. It's a preferred common language for some of them, but I don't speak it myself. It would be useful – but then, as I speak all the local tribal languages I probably don't really need it ..."

I gave up trying to listen to the woman and turned my chair towards the administrator's desk so I could devote my full attention to him.

"Do you want me to tell you what this is all about ...?" he asked.

"Please do."

So he did, and the woman talked on ...

Two Africans standing before the administrator's desk were accused of breaking into the woman's house and assaulting her small daughter. The girl's screams had awoken the mother, and she had come on the scene just in time to see the two men running away.

"But that's a serious charge," I said.

"Oh, yes. It certainly is," the administrator acknowledged.

"But you've hardly heard any of the evidence ..."

The telephone rang. The administrator answered it. Talked. Hung up.

"Oh! I've heard the story before. People here tell me everything. All of this is really only a formality ..." he assured me. "The men are guilty, no question ..."

Palma and Rio Rovuma

One day the administrator of Palma, Henrique Galha, same rank as Francisco but considerably younger in years, had come through Mocímboa da

Praia on his way north to his own district. Calling in on Francisco and his family, he appealed to me as a friendly and easy going fellow. When he had offered to show me the Rio Rovuma, Moçambique's northern frontier with Tanganyika, I accepted happily. I was enjoying my stay in Mocímboa da Praia, but Francisco was a busy man and there were moments of tension when I felt I was in his way. The timing was right, so Henrique and I set a day for him to pick me up. He, his wife and family had a spacious house in Palma. Plenty of room for guests to stay over.

It was almost nightfall when we set out, and pitch dark by the time we arrived. The roads were the worst imaginable and, although the distance was not that great, it took us over three hours of painful bouncing about in a hard-sprung four-wheel-drive military vehicle to get there. I'm blessed with a long neck; it suffered such excruciating whiplash I had to wrap it in a towel to prevent even further serious injury. We saw a hyena on the road, quite clearly, though at first we thought it was a leopard. Their coats are much the same colour under a car's headlights.

Arriving exhausted, Henrique presented me to his wife, Maria João, and explained that the rest of the household had already turned in for the night. We downed a quick supper, following which, we enjoyed an hour of quiet relaxation over a brandy in the living room before heading off to bed ourselves.

Palma was a city of three thousand souls at the time I visited. It is located in the very top right-hand corner of Moçambique. Almost next to it, the tiny settlement of Quionga sat on the bank of the Rio Rovuma and, on a bluff high above it, there was the customs post at Litumba. This consisted of a couple of grass shacks and a corrugated iron throw-together pill-box overlooking what was, at the time, a sluggish stream meandering between islets of sand and high banks of bush and scrubland – Tanganyika just across the way. In charge of the post in this remotest corner of the Portuguese Empire was a much-under-worked Portuguese official who seemed to while away his time at a chess board, perhaps teaching the game to an African girl who hung back and frowned – in shyness, I imagined, or perhaps anger at our interruption. I did not ask many questions of my host, but it did occur to me there would have been remarkably little to occupy a man at Litumba: the girl, the chess, the bush and the river. The place was eight kilometres inland from the coast, so one could not actually see the ocean or its beaches; there was a track that wound its way down to the river. There was a very gentle movement of air and, although we were a few kilometres distant from the coast, I could smell water, seaweed and waterborne vegetation carried up the estuary. I stood and gazed at the flank of Tanganyika. Very soon the air would be warmed and stilled and silenced, and there would be an oppressive heat haze, even before mid-morning. From the bluff we could look into the dark waters that were tidal for several more kilometres up-stream. At one point I thought I heard something like a lion roaring – once – and then all was quiet again. Later some sounds of splashing, and then the grunt or bark of some unseen wildlife.

"All before you on the other side is Tanganyika!" Henrique laughed. "No fences necessary. The frontier is well-guarded ...!"

To avoid the heat we had left the house before breakfast to make this short excursion. I had said I wanted to see the river, maybe even cross into Tanganyika. (The country was to merge with Zanzibar and become Tanzania a year later.) We moved closer to the edge of the bluff so I could see a broader expanse of the river, its banks and a few sandy mid-stream sandbanks.

There were no guards to be seen, no wall nor fencing of any kind to mark a frontier. Just the ragged line of the river waters. They were continuous, but low, and now from the higher ground it was possible to make out numbers of hippos wallowing in the shallows and along the beaches.

"And where there are hippos, there are usually crocodiles nearby – at least in this river," Henrique was positively chipper.

I looked more carefully along the banks of both sides and on the sands of the islands – and then I could see them. Huge and terrifying animals lay like logs sunning themselves, occasionally slithering into the waters to cool off. As far as I could see up and down the river, dozens of silent crocodiles. It was impossible to tear my eyes away for the longest time, as though I had been hypnotized by my revulsion of them.

"Let's get out of here ..."

Henrique laughed. The fellow manning the pill-box grinned lecherously and pulled the African girl into his side. She giggled when he put his hand on her bum.

"You don't want to walk across into Tanganyika ...?"

"Not today, thank you!"

We drove back to Palma where Maria João had made us a breakfast. She introduced me to her sister, Maria de Fatima, and two bumptious young African pre-teens, João and Joana, who had been adopted and come with the family from Henrique's previous posting. I reckoned Henrique to be in his mid- to late-thirties; his wife and her sister were considerably younger, and very probably several years younger than myself. In the instant before introductions the previous evening I had imagined Maria João to be Henrique's daughter …

Henrique had set his usual morning schedule aside to play host to me, so through the morning we sat quietly over coffee. Conversation, as might have been expected, followed political lines, and I quickly received the impression my host in Palma was notably more liberal in his thinking than my host in Mocímboa da Praia. His whole manner was more lenient and tolerant towards the Africans under his charge. He told mc how he and Maria João had started a creche so the mothers of the children could be free to set up their own little businesses. He also told me, for instance, he had tried to establish contact with his counterparts on the Tanganyika side of the frontier, local district administrators and commissioners, so that locals could establish lines of communication with relatives on the other side of the river – maybe stimulate small enterprises. In this he had had little success with aloof British authorities. He was a quiet and thoughtful man – efficient, deliberate and considerate of others. His laugh was spontaneous and genuine.

"There is so much to be done – and I could do all of it if only I had the means," he said. "But this is a large country to control, and there is never sufficient funding. Here in Palma we are too far away to be noticed by our central government."

We passed the afternoon walking through the town, and it was difficult not to make the comparison between the reception Henrique received from those we met in the streets, and those I had seen interacting with Francisco in Mocímboa da Praia. In Palma people were more informal and easygoing, not so anxious to please their administrator, his family and the senior officials who worked with him.

In the evening we all went to the *boite* – one of my more delightful experiences on this trip. It turned out to be an enlightening venture.

The *boite* was an open-air dance in the lower section of the town, down the hill from the residential centre, at the edge of a small park where there was a bandstand and picnic tables. Fifty or sixty of the local townspeople were on hand when we arrived, and more appeared as the evening progressed. The drums were beating out an insistent rhythm as we appeared, and they did not stop until long after I had found my way back to bed and closed my eyes for the night. A Portuguese army officer serving in the area a year or so before had taught some young school pupils a selection of his country's catchier folk songs, and they had caught on so well that many of the town's residents now knew them by heart. An impromptu concert did not take much organizing; a couple of people started up the singing, and in no time everyone who knew the words – it seemed like everyone did, except me – gleefully took up the strain. Then came a few of their own favourites, to their own incredible rhythms. It was a delightful contrast, and it was amusing to see how the youngsters enjoyed dancing in couples, European-style. They giggled a lot, possibly embarrassment at being watched by Europeans, but their self-consciousness (if that's what caused the giggling) did not prevent them from letting rip. It was unusual to see them enjoy dancing in this unaccustomed manner, but they were good at it.

To ask a girl to dance, a young swain would present himself immediately in front of his selected partner, stand to attention and throw her his version of a military-style salute with his right hand. It was meant to be crisply and smartly offered, as a junior would salute his commander, but left to the untrained handling of embarrassed youth it usually came across as a somewhat rag-tag spoof which some girls clearly considered ridiculous. To me it was a strange procedure until I realized Palma was a semi-military town, and local children saluting their intended partners could well be no more than an attempted carryover of observed and well-ingrained Portuguese military courtesy. Once a young swain had greeted his hoped-for partner in this way, and been recognized by her, he would then have to wait to see what happened next – whether she would welcome his invitation or perhaps just giggle. Sometimes the girl would be so excited to dance she would leap to her feet by way of acceptance, and off the two would go in a swirl of dust. Occasionally a young man's advance would be crushingly refused. The girl would turn haughtily away, leaving the poor cavalier to stand there with his hand still at his forehead in salute. Being thus spurned, I noted on several occasions, the poor fellow would shuffle his feet in consternation. Then, instead of completing the salute, he would transform it into a self-conscious scratching of his head. As a lesson in universal human nature, it was difficult to refrain from smiling. But the boys were always courageously unfailing, their request for their partner always accompanied by the salute.

But those who danced! What an exhibition of amazing and subtle footwork – and often coupled with incredible gymnastics! I watched their gyrating hips, their somersaults and backflips. Were I to attempt such movement, it surely would so dislodge every osseous chunk of my wobbly spine, I would suffer a permanent kink to the scruffy neck that holds my head in place. Bad road to Palma, nothing! Different music, different beat, different rhythms, and a far younger crowd – but in its way this was almost as exciting as my encounter with the Zavala dancers.

The most popular dance was the 'twist,' and these youngsters were experts at it. Little João and Goana, the two kids Henrique and Maria João had been raising, held the floor. They had plainly spent many hours practising together but, no denying it, they were incredible dancers. Their mastery of the twist lifted the dance to a new height of sophistication. I had seen couples on dance floors in North America, but it was nothing that could be compared to what these little kids could do tucked away in this obscure corner of the African bush. The youngsters told me their friends had introduced the dance from Tanganyika after they had been up there on holiday, and all they had had to do was improvise the rest …!

At one point I wandered off to sit by an enormous fire, and a group of African children joined me there. We spoke for a long time in Swahili, and they assured me my language passed muster. Gradually more and more of them came over to join us. They were curious because this 'Englishman' was able to speak to them in something like their own language – most unusual for a white man, they said. They were used to being addressed in Portuguese whenever they were addressed at all by whites.

Later we all returned to the dance, and my little friends put on a special record for '*Senhor Inglês*'. A twist, of course. I danced with Maria Fatima for this one, and the youngsters cheered us on as if they had been watching a football match. Compared to the children, though, our effort was probably lacklustre at best.

Diary note:

We pass many Africans walking on the road on their way into Palma… Henrique says they are mostly Islamic, and I remind him how his colleague, Francisco, had told me that, in the interior of Cabo Delgado Province, most Africans are Roman Catholic, but that they change to Islam when they come to the coast. It was a matter of convenience, he had said. On returning to the interior these same people become Roman Catholics again.

"They change their religion as we change our shirt …" he had said.

Henrique comments:

"I doubt that. It would be relatively easy for a Roman Catholic to declare himself for Islam, but never the other way around. Islamic law forbids apostasy under pain of death."

I sat with Henrique, Maria João and Maria de Fatima after lunch, and we talked for a couple of hours while João and Joana played outside with a group of their friends. I commented at how pleased the children had been the night before to see Maria João dancing with her husband. Henrique nodded. He loved the simplicity of life here, he said, but he feared for the future of the people whose lives were rooted in Palma.

"I want to remain Portuguese, and I also want to be able to remain in Portuguese Africa. I'm fearful of being forced to make a choice. We cannot go on living day-by-day like this, never quite knowing what may happen in the future. I feel within a year there will be a substantial difference here – good or bad I cannot tell, but I'm afraid. We cannot continue to drift ..."

Before the end of the year he was due to go on leave to Lisboa and would spend a year there. He said he wanted a leisurely trip home, a long sea voyage with his family. He did not expect to be re-assigned to the Palma District where his job, until now, had always depended on the state of the roads.

"I've not had a holiday from bad roads for ten years, so I am looking forward to a respite!"

The electricity failed throughout Palma just as we were about to leave to return to Mocímboa da Praia. The town's generator needed a new drive belt. It would have to be shipped up from Lourenço Marques. No planes into Palma, and no boat delivery either. The belt would need to be flown into Mocímboa da Praia, then be picked up by car ...

"That's how we live ...! Lisboa will be a big change from Palma's forever bush, but I'll miss this place!"

In all I spent three days in Palma with Henrique and his family. It was a restful time. Henrique's personality was more laid back than that of Francisco. I felt no tension and even if I was in some way being monitored (it seemed unlikely) there could have been no possible harm done. I did not go anywhere, meet anyone, talk politics with anyone – so there would have been nothing to report. Henrique went about his daily chores, but was always close to his home, always in a good humour and ready to chat. He had an easy way of communicating with everyone, seemed to like having me around and enjoyed talking playfully with his wife and her young sister – nothing of the tension I had felt in Francisco's frenetic company. Henrique was especially good with João and Joana. Our conversations almost always included an expression of his concerns for their future. When I was not talking to Fatima or playing with the children (the three of them were like a rambunctious team, and I delighted in being invited to join in their games) I would spend the time going for walks, reading or working on my notes. But eventually I had to return to Chaves' place in Mocímboa da Praia in order to continue my journey south. I was fearful of the road we would have to travel, so we set off in Henrique's vehicle early in the afternoon. At least we would be able to see the potholes we had to negotiate, and those stretches of the road washed away by the rains and not yet repaired.

An intimation of the strain I had felt during my stay with Francisco Chaves surfaced the very morning after my return to Mocimboa da Praia. I had left the bathroom door slightly ajar while I was shaving, and at one point had the uneasy sensation someone was standing on the other side of it. Unseen, I reached over and quickly flicked the door wide open – then was surprised to find Francisco standing there in his pajamas. He also was surprised, but instantly flashed a broad smile and extended his closed hand towards me – an offering of something secret.

"Do you like pearls?" he asked, matter-of-factly.

"Yes," I replied, curious.

He stepped across the threshold into the bathroom and poured a small handful of exquisite seed pearls into the plastic soap dish I used when travelling. He explained how some of the local fishermen found such things regularly.

"I have to go back down to the fish dock after lunch," he explained. "Come with me and you'll get a chance to meet the people who find these things."

Later in the day the two of us went down to the dock area of the town. Chaves walked with me for a time, but then declared he had other business he had to attend to. He introduced me to a group of fishermen and dockside workers, then left me alone with them.

I watched a crew of men manhandling large and heavily dense logs – amazed by their combined brute strength and horrified by the total absence of workplace safety precautions. No hard hats, no boots – just bare feet and muscle. The logs lay where they had been beached, and now they were being rolled – manually – up a flimsy plank structure onto the deck of a transportation barge, a height of about two-and-a-half metres. Tattered ropes were used to assist. Now and then a log would slip, and it seemed only by the Grace of God that it did not roll back down the angled planks and crush the men on the ground. They huffed and puffed and heaved – and when the log was finally settled in its place on the deck of the barge, the men would give a cheer, clap their hands and congratulate one another. One giant hardwood log at a time.

Loading hardwood logs

Elsewhere on the beach some of the fishermen were caulking the seams of their boats, ready to head out to sea as soon as the fishing season started.

Walking about freely, I was able to pass more than two hours with these men. I drank *pombe* with them – a home-brew millet beer. We sat in their dockside shanty and talked in a mutilated sort of Swahili accompanied by lots of pantomime. At first their wives and children hung back in the shadows and watched the meeting of their menfolk with this *estrangeiro*, but it was easy to laugh at our linguistic antics and it was not long before they, too, joined in the conversation. I like to think this foreign interloper appeared to them as a mite friendlier than most of the white men they came across in their lives. It was easy to glean the impression there was not a great deal of contact between the local whites and the local blacks – perhaps some between the menfolk of both races; none at all between whites generally and the women and children (unless the woman was a house servant or a prostitute).

A fisherman caulks his boat

"You come from a distant country," pronounced one of the fishermen who seemed to be the most loquacious of the group. Then the others hung about behind him, listening intently in silence.

"Yes," I replied. "It's on the other side of the world. There we don't have oysters to create such beautiful pearls for us."

I showed him the seed pearls – five of them – that Chaves had given me earlier. I had put the lid on the soap dish, and was carrying them in my pocket.

The fisherman looked at the tiny pearls, frowning and distracted. Then he raised his head and looked into my eyes, the lines on his brow deepening noticeably.

"But do you have Portuguese in your country?" he asked.

"We have many Portuguese there," I said. "As with all of you, they are good people, kind people. They work hard and love their families and communities. We like them."

The fisherman's eyes narrowed.

"You like them? Don't they take your fish? Don't they take your trees and your food? Don't they keep you in poverty? Don't they take everything away from you? Your children, your women, your young men ...?"

I laughed, not unkindly. No, I explained, it was not so. On the other side of the world the Portuguese were as everyone else – just men, women and children like all men and women and children. They took nothing especially unto themselves; nothing that all men were not free to take. They would work, earn money and then buy their needs ...

"Why should they take from us and not from you?" the fisherman wanted to know, and for a time he fell silent.

There was little I could say that would adequately explain how things really were on the other side of the world, but I still held the soap dish in my hand and so I opened it again to reveal the pearls.

"The administrator gave me these this morning," I told him. "He said he received them from you. Did he take them from you, or did you give them to him?"

"We gave them to him. We give him lots of them. They have no special value for us."

"Then how can you say the Portuguese take things from you, when in fact you give things to them?"

"But if we didn't give them to him, he would come and ask for them – or just take them anyway," the fisherman said. "So, we choose to give them. That way he cannot say that we take things from him or hide things from him. No! That way he will think we are his friends – but we are not his friends. One day someone he thinks is a friend will come close enough to kill him. We have many problems here, and the biggest is that we are not free from the Portuguese. Soon there must be war. Then Moçambique will be our uniform, we will use our boats to block the entrance to our harbour – and we will fight the Portuguese. We must be patient."

"I am sorry," I said to him. "I have seen war. It feeds on hatred. It is a terrible thing to see such a vengeful monster come out of the sea ..."

"Keep the pearls with you," said the fisherman. "They are of no importance to us, but they will be a keepsake for you. Remember us when you are on the other side of the world."

I embraced the fisherman, took his children on my knee, but soon went on my way. They had spoken to me of an impending cataclysm, and I felt a deep and heavy sympathy for what seemed to be in wait for everyone involved.

It was not quite a year following this meeting, when I was back in Toronto, safe on the other side of the world and had had the pearls set into a hand-crafted broach, that I learned revolution had finally swept into northern Moçambique's province of Cabo Delgado – a local rising at first, with ample support and assistance in *matériel* from across the border in Tanzania. Someone, no doubt a newspaperman with the usual journalistic assurance of his firsthand information, informed me the administrator of Mocímboa da Praia, his wife and every member of his household had been slaughtered in the initial days of the bloody uprising.

Not true. Many years later I was able to discover that no such massacre befell that family. Francisco Chaves returned with his family to Portugal, and there he became a respected university teacher.

However, I have never been able to find out what became of Henrique Galha, his wife Maria João, and their two delightful little children, João and Joana. Likewise, I've never discovered any trace of Maria João's beautiful young sister, Fatima. Henrique was looking forward to an extended period of leave …

There is a contemporary and sad and alarming post-script to be added to the story of Moçambique's northern Cabo Delgado province:

Three police stations in Moçimboa da Praia were attacked in a pre-dawn raid on the morning of 5 October 2017. Some thirty attackers killed seventeen people. Fourteen of the perpetrators were captured, and from them it was learned the gang consisted of Islamist militants calling themselves *Ansar al-Sunna*. It differs from, but is associated with, *al-Shabaab* in Somalia – which in turn has been strongly linked to *al-Qaeda*. The Islamist objective appears to be the establishment of a caliphate on the African mainland and some, or all, of the off-shore islands.

Since 2017 scores of similar raids have been conducted, on the coast and in all parts of Cabo Delgado. Thousands of people have been killed in most brutal and terrifying ways. A terrorizing weapon of choice is the machete, which has been widely used in beheadings – of those who refuse to join the insurgent ranks, of women and even children. The insurgents appear to be mainly locals but are supported by operatives from Tanzania and Somalia. Some appear to have been trained in camps abroad. They are sophisticated, well-trained and well-armed, know the land and speak the local languages.

The government of Moçambique maintains its own army in the province, paratroopers and specialists from the south of the country, but to little avail. The government initially brought in mercenaries from Russia, but these proved unequal to the task and in 2020 were withdrawn to their base near Beira complaining the local terrain and conditions were too difficult. Some of their losses were due to disorientation in the jungles, to attacks by wild animals, and loss of morale in fighting an intransigent enemy on his home turf. The area has plentiful numbers of lions and leopards, which have made bush patrolling hazardous. In addition, all local waterways are teeming with crocodiles.

The situation is on-going.

Ilha de Moçambique

Having reached the northern extremity of the country it was now time to turn south again and, in a series of zig-zag leaps by air and car, I managed to visit several of the exotic points I had flown over (or near) short weeks earlier: Porto Amélia, Lumbo, Moçambique Island, Nampula, Vila Junqueiro, Luabo and Mopeia on the Rio Zambezi. Last on the list were Quelimane, and south from there to Beira and the fabulous national game park of Gorongosa.

One of the things I remember most clearly about this journey south through the northern half of Moçambique, was the extent to which I found it necessary to defend myself from a persistent and tedious onslaught of Portuguese propaganda. This issued mostly from men in uniform – military, or civil administrators. In all of the places named in the above paragraph I was beset by men who took umbrage at my quaint Canadian ideas of human rights and dignities, and so took it as their responsibility to straighten me out. Their basic argument was always the same: 'Portugal was older and had travelled further, so knew best.'

Well, frankly, Portugal did not know best. To my simplistic way of thinking this was so abundantly clear I found myself growing impatient hearing over and over again the same sheep-like bleat for an 'understanding' of why it was so imperative for the Portuguese boot to remain firmly on the African neck. I'm no economist, but it surely was not very difficult to comprehend how the rationale for whatever ailed everybody was as much economic as it was racial. Selfishness and greed bred intolerance; intolerance fostered selfishness. Circle.

I had had a close-up view of British behaviour in their colonies. I had been obliged to participate in 'wars' – military actions – in four of those colonies[39], and in expanded hindsight had decided I would probably have fought more enthusiastically in each instance for the other side. More recently I had immersed myself in the race hate problems of Alabama, in which the physical and verbal abuse brought about by arrogance and convictions of entitlement, leading to intolerance, appeared to have few limitations. Lesson: xenophobia is arrogance, and arrogance in any disguise is a monstrous depravity – as well as an economic stupidity.

However disguised – usually couched in florid terms of cultural imperative – the arguments of racists are invariably simplistic:

"We're alone in the world, but we fight together. I will kill Niggers as brutally as they killed in Angola if they try to kick me out of Africa!"

So said one of our supper companions one evening in Mocímboa da Praia, an obnoxious little man, an air force major who was the second in command of the air base at Nampula. He lit into me over the supper table like a yapping canine. Other guests who had arrived with him, also like hounds in chase, could see the game was on, and they came after me in a pack. I could hardly open my mouth before being shouted down – which didn't make for good argument. It was more in the style of a Hyde Park Corner harangue. It occurred to me the force and tone of their tongue-lashing was augmented by the perceived need to impress their commanding officer.

I had heard it before. On this occasion I had had the temerity to comment that I would have been a deal more impressed if the Portuguese could show me as much as they tell me. They talked of 'all' they had given the Africans. The response: fine, let's examine the 'all' they claimed to have donated …

What impressed me most about the pack (and I guess in so many words and half-sentences I had said as much) was their complete inability to listen to

---

[39] Kenya, Aden, Malaya, Singapore.

another argument – and in this case how alike the white racists in the Southern United States to whom I had spoken when I was there. An inability to acknowledge the existence of another people, or another point of view. But maybe they dared not, for fear of losing their courage, their 'ground' – or their argument. And most of all, what it would cost – in money – to correct five hundred years of wrongs.

My table companions were attempting to rationalize their very presence here in Africa.

On the one hand they talked of standing and fighting (or at least the Little Major did) and on the other they claimed they were at one with the Africans – who 'are born Portuguese.'

They talked incessantly of trouble coming 'from outside' their region (or province or country) as though, by coming from outside it absolved them of all implication and responsibility for the racial problem brought on and exacerbated by the inhuman economy of their own colonization.

'White-think' as opposed to 'black-think' – and it was all them (outside), not us (inside).

Sitting in their uniforms nursing their after-dinner brandies, everyone at the table thought himself in some way superior to those he commanded, or those who were beating their drums down in the town centre. The idea that what he thought was his 'right,' his due, was unacceptable to most of the civilized world, and in particular to every black man in Africa who wasn't already in jail or a looney bin, simply did not occur to him. Blacks were not human beings – yet, insisted my dinner companions, they were somehow 'our Portuguese brothers.' They could not understand why such an insistent argument fell short of good sense to me. Not one among the guests was able to understand this sort of resistance-belief was neither controlled nor confined by boundaries. Not one of them possessed the mental agility to permit the idea they were confronting an all-Africa mindset, and that all any individual could ever possibly hope to do about it would be to fight a delaying and ultimately losing action. These warriors spoke a universal claptrap they could not understand themselves: messages well-comprehended, and denied, by every African across every boundary on the continent, as well as by men of vision far beyond. I found then, I find now, idiot dogmatism unpalatable medicine for the resolution of any problem.

But the Little Major was beside himself. He yapped on:

"And when it comes down to it, yes, we Portuguese are vitally in need of the wealth in Angola and Moçambique, and we shall fight to keep it. The whole thing is a matter of economics so – so much for your theories on human rights ...! There is no human rights problem. Just economics!"

Ah-ha! Finally, he says it. Getting to him was like a taste of maple syrup. There was no delight in what he said, but there was modest delight in his admission. For that alone I wanted him to stick around a bit longer, so I could jab it to him once again ...

At another dinner, this time in Nampula, the provincial governor arrived so late we could not sit down until ten o'clock, by which time I was dog tired and about ready for bed. It was painful to have him prod me with his nauseating propaganda, imperative that I could see everything through his eyes – my travels had brought me so far, after all, that now I '*must* report the TRUTH!' – shouted for emphasis.

My response – by now parrot-like – was that I was aware of the Portuguese argument, and I would be better able to put faith in what I could see than in what I was being told.

Through a translator the governor told me he always received a most regal reception wherever he went in his province, so I asked if he felt that, in itself, was sufficient proof of the warm feelings between the Africans and himself...?

His reply was yes, he was more concerned with dealing with the present – not too concerned about the future. I asked him why – and was left with the impression present problems are burden enough without worrying about the future. I expressed surprise at this.

"If there is trouble in the future ..." he was about to spout something I had heard before ... "I am certain it will come from *outside* Mozambique – not from inside."

Yes – I had heard it before. It was an obvious answer, in a way. The Portuguese boot was on the African neck so hard that if help was to come from anywhere at all, it would have to be from sympathizers 'outside.'

"You must tell the truth about what you see on your travels, and try your best to correct a wrong impression held about Portugal throughout North America ..."

It was Portugal's national day, Republic Day, the Fifth of October. Nationalism shone brilliantly, so we parted the best of friends while he turned to attend a small flag ceremony and reception in honour of this special occasion.

Long lines of townspeople had formed in order to shake hands with him, but most noticeable was that the majority, by far, were women, old men and children. There were few younger men in the line, if any, and I wondered what they were thinking.

Unlike the governor, I was much inclined, and obstinately, to dwell on what might happen next ...

My 'wrong' impression: I saw lower-ranked Portuguese leaders who were scared out of their wits by what might be ahead of them in the not-too-distant future. It would take more than a flag ceremony to convince me all was well in Moçambique.

It would have pleased the governor immensely had I taken his picture: Governor Colonel Basilio Pina de Oliveira Seguro.

But I did not take a photograph of him. Nothing too *seguro* about Seguro, I thought.

The conversation with these Portuguese military Pooh-Bahs at Nampula had ticked me off. No one would have enjoyed being treated with the condescension they employed on me as their captive lunch guest, but I have since tried to see it more from their perspective – and with a smattering of humour. At the time, though, I was left with the wide assumption (since I was only asking questions) that their spitting at me was simply their way of fulfilling some sort of psychological need. And what did they say as they spat? America? It varied little – but America? Almost all the senior officers to whom I spoke referred to the duplicity of America's friendship – and I suppose they shovelled it on top of me because I hailed from the country next door. They mostly spoke in the past tense, with something of the bewilderment of a jilted lover. To a man they admired America and its people but (also to a man) expressed outrage at what they saw as a lack of depth, the superficiality of libertines. One spoke, elegantly, of the 'veneer' of American friendship as something particularly despicable to a people so rooted in the passionate loyalties of the Latin cultural family.

Once again, as after my unpleasant encounter with the American attaché in the Congo, I had found myself perplexed by what part the United States of America had to play in the mess the Portuguese had created for themselves, but the subject came up too often to be a matter of chance. Time and again I was hearing variations on the same theme – American chicanery, American double-dealing. In an African context, 'containing communism' simply didn't wash. That much was as plain to me as it was to my military hosts. Alabama had taught me something that stank: false solicitude. Could it have been the same stench, emanating from the USA, that these Portuguese officers were smelling?

My imagination is overloaded. There is a malaise that sits on America's shoulders like a great black toad. It is likely this has been the case for many, many years – a discontent that casts a shadow of mildew across American exceptionalism. It is political, social and economic. It is certainly religious, inasmuch as such a quantity of their chromium-plated and self-indulgent holy-roller appeals to schmaltz and the dollar bill ever won them a genuine blessing. (Imagine the white god of the supremacists driving around in a gold-plated limousine.) And it is educational – for many millions of her children have certainly been 'left behind.' It is a malaise that has contaminated every plane of the nation's psyche. As if the predominantly negative gun-car-and-violence prone movie cultures were alone insufficient degradation, there is the mistrust and antipathy bred by archaic and xenophobic concepts of racial 'purity;' and the most of it not born of outright selfishness springs from an impoverishment of basic education and social ideas. 'Freedom' has come to mean liberal me-ism, licencing the individual to 'express himself' by breaking with not only the requisites of a functioning and just society, but even the mores of those who might in all other social circumstances be considered his peers. It is the sort of frightening science-fictional chaos depicted in any number of Hollywood productions in which the heroes and gods are equal representatives of a space everyone wants to occupy, tries to occupy, but has so far failed to make not the least effort to know deeply or comprehend universally. Explosions and gaudy visual affects stand in for convincing penetrative thought. A variety of gung-ho entrepreneurs – gangsters and con-men – have been trying since the early days of snake oil hucksters and Buffalo Bill to fleece a living from these iffy social phenomena, so the junk concepts have been widely exported – and the madness augmented to global proportions. People who have little or nothing at all, who go nowhere and produce nothing but that which suffices for themselves alone, fancy they now have a newly-burnished understanding of how the world totters along. America. It is so sad we make a joke of it.

There is much in Africa the rest of the world needs. What these Portuguese military men appear to have concluded, at least to some degree correctly, is that America wants Portugal gone so that, on the pretext of 'ridding the world of communism,' American corporatism can scramble in and sign the contracts – before Russia or China. (Canada will 'register' the mines.)

It was difficult to summon support for what the Portuguese military was clearly prepared to do in order to secure her old territories. It was painful to listen to the excuses and explanations of how Portugal had managed to screw it all up so badly. And it was painful to listen to these senior officers squeal about how America was playing such a double game when, if they had had the minutest dram of innate worldly wisdom, they should have known that deceit is America's concept of good business and her historic forte. In vain did I inform them I was not an American but a Canadian. What's that, you say? There's little to choose between them? They are basically the same thing? Hm-m-m ...

Thus have I mused in the years since that summer in Africa. Looming out of the wings of this tragic theatre, like the low rumble of off-stage thunder, it was impossible not to deduce the sinister presence of a lurking America, rubbing her hands in greedy glee. But it would have been unseemly for America herself to have appeared before the on-lookers. Portugal may have been the guilt-ridden historical protagonist battling under the footlights. America wrote the script, acted as prompter and fixer – and, *finalmente*, was ready at any moment to drop the curtain.

The minder who showed up to collect me when I arrived at the small airport of Lumbo was a fellow by the name of João Braga Peres, the civil secretary of the district. We drove straight from the airport to the town's harbour, where we caught a launch for the short ride across to Ilha de Moçambique at the entrance to Mossuril Bay. The shallow waters were choppy. It took maybe twenty minutes to cross, spray blowing back into our faces. An invigorating ride. Nowadays there is a dead-straight causeway nearly four kilometres long connecting the mainland to a point at the southwestern tip of the tiny island. As I discovered, it would be possible to walk the entire length of the island in an hour – if one could feel so invigorated on a warm day. However, such strenuous exercise would be defeating the principal reason for going there. It is an ancient place with an intriguing history – the old capital (until 1898) of the country to which it gave its name; simultaneously laidback and stimulating, there is much to see on Moçambique Island.

Minder João was a quiet and rather studious man, a little older than me.

He was kindly, and without words gave off the impression his obligation to the *Estado Novo* – and PIDE as its most noticeable extension – was a distasteful necessity he preferred not to discuss. On the short drive through the town to the pier where the motor launch to the island was docked, I noticed how people would rise from positions where they might have been squatting by the side of the road – in order to doff their hats as we passed. Likewise, if they had been walking, they would stop, step back and come to attention so as to throw us a military-style salute. They would have recognized the official car in which we were riding; this alone was enough to propel them into such servile demonstrations of their subservience. How well they appeared to know their place! It was my commenting on these actions that tipped João into indicating he did not care for such attentions; his terse comment revealed a hidden and deeper sentiment concerning a regime that held such control over a cowering population.

The launch delivered us to a jetty at the north end of the island where we were met by the local administrator. There the saluting and kowtowing continued apace. It intrigued me. Even in the British colonies I had never witnessed such grovelling, and it was easy to tell that João was acutely embarrassed by it – especially at having a witness to his embarrassment. As for the administrator, his air was nonchalance but he lapped it up; he expected the adulation (if that is what it really was) to be no less than his due. It was a strange pantomime over which I had no control. Apart from a flabby handshake when first we were introduced, the fellow avoided any eye contact with me, ignoring me and deliberately turning his back in order to speak in Portuguese to João. His manner was overbearing and rude; his inability to speak to me in a language I could comprehend would have been perfectly understandable, but for him to turn his back the way he did, or in any way acknowledge the presence of the person to whom he had just been presented, was not the only thing that irritated. The man was boorish, imperial, and was quick to display a mean temperament. That was bad enough; but what brought me to an instant boil was the way in which he paid not the least attention to the common folk round about who had taken the trouble to greet him by their bowing, saluting or simply removing their hats. Strutting, pompous little schmuck that he was, he walked through their ranks as though they were no more to him than a nuisance cloud of buzzing flies.

Usually I would exercise a little control in such a scenario. On this occasion I did not feel like it. Calling out, and loudly, I made sure everyone around me could hear my voice:

"João!"

My voice was so loud and insistent that my minder stopped dead, and even the administrator looked up. My tone alone must have conveyed something to them both. Very deliberately I looked at João, not the administrator.

"Please inform the administrator that I note how the locals hereabouts are honoured and very attentive to his presence."

The word administrator is virtually the same in both English and Portuguese, so the man in question wanted to know what I had just said about him. João, who spoke very passable English and could hardly have mistaken my pique, was now doubly embarrassed for, without saying a word, the administrator was plainly seeking an explanation.

João was on the spot. Lowering his voice and glancing at me sideways, he spoke in Portuguese to his superior. I do not know what he said but, in just a few words, I assume he managed to convey my message without detailed reference to my sarcasm.

When he had finished, the administrator turned and looked at me. He shrugged his shoulders and raised his hands as one tends to when utterly blameless.

"Zay loff me!" he shrugged in broken English, and there was a short pause as he looked questioningly at the two of us.

There was nothing more to be said, so the administrator turned his back on me slowly, turning his nose to the air.

João summoned a couple of men at the side of the road. They came over, picked up our baggage and started walking with it. We followed them a short distance, presently arriving at a small hotel where we would be staying the night.

"The administrator was rude. I am sorry," João commented as we walked.

"It wasn't your fault," I told him. "I don't take his behavior towards me too much to heart … but yes – he was bloody rude. Without cause as far as I could see. There were a lot of people there, happy to see and greet him. He was rude to all of us, I reckon. Why, do you think?"

"Xenophobia. He's obsequious to those above him, the sort of person who can only speak in any way easily with people of his own kind and rank. People of lower rank – me, for instance – are truly beneath him, barely worth addressing."

"It goes hand-in-glove with racism," I said. "It's a shame that so many people – perhaps even good people – are invisible to him."

João, thoughtful, frowned and looked down. Instinctively he performed a shadow of the Latin shrug, pulling his mouth down at the corners. A man like that, he commented, has his circle of contacts and friends, and sees no need to expand it. It leaves him free to be miserable to lesser mortals. Like so many men raised in a fascist mould – Portugal, for instance – he probably snarls at his wife, browbeats his son, and locks up his daughter when her boyfriend comes calling. The closest he would ever come to an African is the prostitute who would have to haggle with him for the money he had originally agreed to pay her – but she would have to be careful not to push him too far, for fear of the beating he could give her.

"Good God …! You paint quite a picture."

"That's not the half of it," my companion said. "There is a strong psychological quotient involved. My observation of people like him is that they rise out of a rather low strata of society, obeying orders until they attain a rank they feel gives them status. They encourage their sons to behave as badly as they do – particularly with women and people of low rank. He's the kind of man who probably thinks it's his responsibility to introduce his son to prostitutes and claps him on the back as a 'chip off the old block' when the boy succeeds in being accepted by one of them. He locks away his daughter from her boyfriend either because he's jealous, or in fear of the young fellow eventually treating his daughter the way he himself treats the poor girl's mother. He feels ashamed and is in denial of a behavioural pattern within himself he doesn't seem able to control – so drinks excessively, ignores those he considers his juniors or, worse, shouts at those he suspects live nobler lives than he does, and perhaps will replace or pass him one day …"

João saw me wincing at his description and laughed.

"You probably don't know us very well, but I feel I should emphasize this with you: the Portuguese are a great and noble people, with deep and meaningful traditions that have been passed down to us over centuries. In all of Europe there exist no people more intensely one. We are a sturdy and hot-blooded people, but unlike many other Latins, we are not prone to fighting. We are stoic and accept immense hardship, avoiding a fight whenever there is an alternative.

"But, you know, all that enhances our bovine cruelty. We have always lived in a dictatorship of one kind or another. Our kings were dictators. We had a short republic early in the century, but we were not trained in handling it, and soon reverted to dictatorship again. We had no barons to ensure the signing of a Magna Carta for our benefit. *Habeas corpus* was definitely a sometime thing. We are not a racist people in the ways of the northern Europeans – but our dictatorship has led to fascism, and fascism inevitably to domination of the rich over the poor. Our social differences are economic, not racial – but those who are rich are generally white, and those who are the poorest are often black or *mestiço*, especially here in Africa. It is the emphasis on acquisition, and the defence of our acquisitions, that has tripped the worst of us into racism. That's not our nature, though. Look at Brasil – look at us! *Mestiço* is an idea as well as a fact – and it is a Portuguese word!

"Please don't judge us by the people you meet like the administrator. There are lots of them, especially in the colonies, but they are not the ones who will teach you about the Portuguese. They are the ones who will teach you about fascism and racism, and there are people like them all over the world."

My minder was nothing if not passionate. By now we had put our bags into our respective rooms and had reconvened under an umbrella at a small street-level café. João was proving himself an admirable instructor.

A World Heritage site, Ilha de Moçambique is one of several islands on the east coast of Africa that have been populated since long before recorded history. In the XIV century the Swahili-speaking people from Kilwa filtered south and brought Islam with them, arriving about the same time as a movement of Bantu peoples from the interior of the mainland. The name was derived from Ali Musa Mbiki – sultan of the island at the time of Vasco da Gama's visit on his way to India in 1498. In time the name hopped onto the mainland and was given to the entire stretch of hinterland south to Swaziland and north to Tanganyika. After da Gama's visit the island very quickly became an important stop for all ships of the Portuguese navy intent on setting out on the long trans-oceanic journey to the Indian subcontinent or returning home to Europe. A naval port was established on the island in 1507; in 1522 the chapel of *Nossa Senhora de Baluarte* was consecrated and is today recognized as the oldest building in the Southern Hemisphere.[40] Five hundred metres across at its widest, and three kilometres long, the island today is home to some fifteen thousand Moçambicanos. It remained the capital of Portuguese East Africa until 1898 when the country's administration was moved to Lourenço Marques (today's Maputo).

The whole island is a museum. After lunch João and I walked a short distance from our hotel to the fort of São Sebastião at the north end of the island; it was built in 1546. From its ramparts we could look down on the exquisite little white chapel dedicated to *Nossa Senhora de Baluarte* which, João told me, contains the human remains of the first bishop appointed to

---

[40] The Portuguese also claim the Cathedral of the Holy Saviour at M'banza-Congo, northern Angola (built in 1549) that stands on the exact site of an earlier small stone church built in 1491, to be the oldest church south of the Sahara. See note 35, above. The chapel of *Nossa Senhora de Baluarte* is also claimed to be the oldest building in the southern hemisphere.

serve a newly Christianized congregation in Japan. The poor fellow never arrived. He died on the island on his way there.

Canon on the rampart
of São Sebastião fort
overlooks tiny chapel
of *Nossa Senhora de Baluarte*,
in distance below

The island runs from southwest to northeast and is shaped like the slightly-crooked forefinger of the left hand – the gentle curve of it facing out over the ocean, the current causeway stretching like a taut umbilical cord connecting the island's southwestern tip to the mainland. We had started in the north, however, because that is where the launch docked and where our hotel was located. This was *Cidade de Pedra* – Stonetown – where the fort and most of the old Portuguese buildings are located to this day. The somewhat larger southern portion of the island is given over to Reedtown, known also as *Makuti*, where the majority of the island's inhabitants have built their homes of slathered mud dried onto woven wattle frames, topping them with roofs of thatch or zinc *chapa*. We walked south along a road arcing above Santo António's beach, almost all the way to the southern tip of the island, the brilliant blue of the sky overhead a mirror image of the deep waters of the Indian Ocean on our left. Now and then a gaff-rigged fishing skiff, taking advantage of light winds, would skim the small waves of a tranquil sea, scattering diamonds of spray in its wake. At the end of the beach, on a little spike of land that juts itself out into the water, is the tiny fort and church of Santo António – a XVI century whitewashed gem much in need, when we saw it then, of a loving refurbishing (which I am told it finally received in 1969). The entire island was declared a UNESCO World Heritage site in 1991.

As we passed the little fortification and church I couldn't help wondering how Camões, the national poet, had felt about this place – if, perhaps, he had stopped just as we had to steep in the quiet peace of the island. He had lived on the island for two years; I had to admit to my minder I did not know his work, nor in fact had ever taken particular notice of him ...

João was an educated man. He raised his eyebrows, studying me for a long moment.

"That is one terrible admission. You have some reading to catch up on!" he admonished. "If you wish to know us well, or take Portugal seriously, then you had better read Camões. Not knowing about him is worse than entering England and asking, 'Who's this guy Shakespeare?' Remember the name: Luís Vaz de Camões. You cannot write anything worth reading about Portugal if you have to admit you do not know the name of our most illustrious citizen. Our entire culture is built around him."

Right then and there I felt like the most ignorant of chumps. Yes, I'd come across Camões' name when I was in Toronto, convincing myself I was studying what I needed to know about Portugal – and I passed clean over the top of the one man who embodied the soul of the entire nation, ignoring him. João had every right to dress me down, to point a finger at my sheer crassness.

In time I did my best to correct such an error, making a point of reading Camões first in translation, and even attempting some of his work in its original language. Now, when people ask my counsel about the country in which I eventually settled and lived for the most significant portion of my working life, I have no hesitation in suggesting, if they are serious about the place, 'read Camões.'[41] And then there are some others ...

João and I made our way to the southern end of the island. The tide was out and for a time we watched the locals from Makuti Town, women and children mostly, picking the crustaceans from the hundreds of rock pools that stretch all the way out to the fortress of São Lourenço. At high tide the little fort is on an island of its own, and twice a day rejoins its bigger brother to form the very southeastern tip of Ilha de Moçambique.

---

[41] Portugal's national poet; see Appendix #12 – Camões.

We walked north to return to the hotel, through the narrow streets of Makuti. On the way we came across a Hindu temple, a mosque and various Christian churches: a small chapel dedicated to Saint Francis Xavier; *Igreja de Nossa Senhora da Saúde*; the former convent of São Dominic, now a courthouse; the church of *Misericórdia* and its hospital. As we approached Cidade de Pedra we passed a variety of houses dating to the XVII century, some of them with delightfully-shaded arcade walkways and gardens, to a small square where the city's *pelourinho* – pillory – had been installed; and finally, the governor's palace, with a statue of Vasco da Gama out front. Everywhere there had been an effort at maintenance and recovery, but it could not hide the preponderance of antique and chipped *reboco*, the overall level of *laissez-faire* poverty. Whitewash had been used to great effect to cover a multitude of decaying walls – many of which, I have been happy to learn, fifty years on, have been the object of UNESCO's recovery efforts.

Twice, as we were walking, we were offered rides in rickshaws. They were an idea unmistakably imported from Macau. We declined. I felt there was something uncomfortably un-Canadian about being toted about streets of poverty in a vehicle pulled by a barefoot human, one step from slavery, who uses '*Master*' as a form of polite address. But then, knowing very well how I would feel, I admit curiosity got the better of me. I needed to know what it would feel like – so on the morning we were to leave the island I hitched a ride in a rickshaw.

They had been banned on the island, but were brought back by 'popular demand,' João told me. The Africans themselves wanted them. It was a means of making a living.

I don't think I have ever felt more conspicuous or uncomfortable ... like a white lord sitting back while the poor beast performs his labour. I did not at all care for the 'beast' being human. It was a short ride. I eased my conscience somewhat by offering the 'beast' twenty escudos – which was a lot more than he had asked.

The houses of Makuti were small but welcoming, each with its thatched roof and very often a stone bench built on the street along the length of an outer wall offering a place to sit for anyone coming home laden with merchandise or food. I commented to João about some of the young women and girls we passed who had covered their faces with a white pack – a paste made from the crushed root of a local herb.

"A tradition of the girls on the island," João told me. "Not my taste, exactly, but they consider it beautiful. I'm told the custom exists elsewhere in Africa, too ..."

I asked one girl if I could take a photograph of her. She sat on the end of a bed she had brought from inside the house, then looked at me with a demure but confident curiosity. She gave every indication she knew what I wanted, which caused me embarrassment and made me think that perhaps she had been photographed before by other visitors to her island. It took a few minutes to set up the shot. There was a red blanket on the bed which I wanted removed; I wanted the woven matting of the bed itself to be seen in the photograph. I made signs for her to remove it, so she flipped it over a cord against the wall behind her then settled herself on the end of the bed, her eyes expressionless, her mouth pursed into a slight pout of toleration at my pernicketiness.

Makuti town girl

After I had taken the shot, I sat next to her on the stone bench that ran along the length of her house wall. João had moved a little way up the street and was not available for translation, so the girl and I were unable to talk. I peered into her face, behind the caked layers of white paste. She looked straight into my eyes, and there was no doubt about what I saw; she was, indeed, a most beautiful young girl. Absent the words to express myself, I smiled at her and gave my best rendering of a Latin shrug as I showed her the emptiness of my wallet after giving her the fifty-escudo note I had had inside it – a bit of street art mime, eyes heavenward. The smile she returned was instant, a burst of laughter as she plunged the offering down between her breasts. Laughter always works. It has a way of leaping generations and cultures faster than one can thumb through a thesaurus for the words that conjure the apt phrase. It breaks down all kinds of barriers and is far less imposing than the tinkling disharmony of coin or the dishonest crinkle of paper.

Road to Nampula

João and I travelled from Lumbo to Nampula by car. With us on this day-long journey was a man who introduced himself as Henrique Taradas, then aged in his mid-fifties. He told me he had been born in Lisboa, had come to central Moçambique 'a number of years ago,' and used to be the head of a major mining concern about one hundred and sixty kilometres from Lumbo. His company exported its base material to the United States. The mine faltered because of the developing uncertainty in Moçambique's political situation, so he resigned his position and began teaching at the commercial and industrial school on Ilha de Moçambique.

Taradas had travelled widely in Europe and South America. His two brothers and a son were living in Brasil. He himself was fluent in Spanish, French and English, all of which, he told me, he could speak almost as well as his native Portuguese. He came across as a confident and knowledgeable man of the world, and at first I was impressed. He made no effort to conceal an abiding dislike of America and Americans, and it was this little phobia that opened a useful channel for me to talk to him – chiefly by attempting to agree with him.

In his travels he spoke to many people who felt as he did, he told me – people like him who were gung-ho supporters of the Portuguese effort to continue their domination of Angola and Moçambique. His argument was generally in agreement with the dictatorship in Lisboa, though he laced this point of view with salty little asides of criticism the better to emphasize the reasonableness of his essential fascism. It was a rhetorical tactic I had encountered before – sweet reason to butter over burnt toast. In Europe it was a toss-up as to whether it was the Americans or the Germans who were the more disliked, he told me – but he reckoned, again with most gracious reasoning, the Americans won that sweepstake hands down. They were two-faced and vile, he said. He did not appreciate the idea of America mixing ham-fistedly in African affairs; he tended to see them as avariciously trying to milk the continent of its riches before anyone else could, paying lip service to the concept of human rights but, in their headlong rush for gold, actually trampling those rights and carelessly ignoring local sensibilities and culture. Taradas most certainly did not care for what he termed American duplicity towards an ally, selling arms to Portugal's enemies, criticizing the Portuguese and siding against them in the United Nations in order to take for themselves that which had 'belonged' to Portugal for five hundred years – and doing all this while claiming stalwart friendship through the NATO alliance.

I was growing adept at perceiving how those Portuguese who so wanted to 'set me straight' on matters colonial, would inadvertently slip into a blind psychological projection – their curses for the Americans a transparent articulation of the rest of the world's grievances with the Portuguese.

"To me they are like immature children," Taradas was shouting above the sound of the engine. "They do not understand the world they wish to grasp, the political savvy to know what their money has just bought. They are universally disliked because they are insensitive and bombastic. They are convinced of their correctness, and that they alone have found the key to democracy that best fits all doors that have been closed to them ..."

The Americans did not have the least idea about the problems of Africa, he claimed, and yet they insisted on dabbling in them, even creating problems by lending large sums of money to those who were only too anxious to cause trouble for – especially – benighted little Portugal. To process this projection I tried to imagine to what extent a Portuguese farmer, or a Portuguese soldier, knew (or cared) about the differences between, say, the Ovimbundu and the Macua when both the farmer and the soldier, with Lisboa's assistance, were busily evicting the indigenous African and settling onto his lands in Bie or the Limpopo. All were Portuguese but some fortunates, it appeared to Taradas, were more Portuguese than others.

"The Americans say, 'Let's do it!' – but it is the Europeans who hold their hands up in the air and take a mature look at what's really involved ..." Taradas exclaimed.

I did not want the man to stop talking, so led him on where I could by agreeing with him enthusiastically. He wanted someone to champion the Portuguese, so that's what I did – with a poke at the Americans (an easy exercise for Holier-than-Thou Canadians!)

"They make lots of mistakes," I told him, "and they're hasty and alarmist.

They are a notoriously poorly educated people, so their money is their God. Unlike you Portuguese, they have no creed other than money. Your Pope dresses himself in white; the Americans bathe themselves in green ..."

"Ha! Ha! That's a good one ...!" shouted my companion.

"They're corrupt, they believe God wants them to be rich. They mean well, and most are honest and democratic, really doing no more than trying to set for the whole world the same high standards their constitution has set for them. They truly believe in their constitution ..."

"I cannot agree with that!" huffed Taradas. "Yes, they believe in their constitution – but it's lip service. They do not live up to it. They believe in money. When they smell money, they'll fold up their constitution and stick it in their hip pocket where they keep their wallet ..."

"Well," I argued, "the American credo of justice is a high and honourable one, and I feel that as a country they do, quite genuinely, try to live up to it. But details for their programmes have to be worked out carefully, and on paper first – and it is in the implementation of what has been written into law that is proving to be so difficult for them to administer. America stumbles often, and there is no shortage of people who will be happy to point the finger and laugh at her for even trying ... Surely the nation is not to be blamed for making an effort ...?"

He didn't want to hear it, so I laid it on some more.

"Never has the American administration come right out and said that the Portuguese must leave Africa. On the other hand, America has stressed the need for the people of Portuguese Africa to be given the right to govern themselves – whites and blacks together. The US has fought for this principal at the United Nations. This is not the same as 'Get out!' It seems to me the Portuguese I'm meeting misinterpret America – they tell me America's real interest in Africa is economic, and I earnestly quarrel with that ..."

Taradas threw his hands in the air and guffawed with laughter at my naïvety.

"My point is this," I persisted. "As I see it, the American interest in Africa falls into three categories, and it is a gross mistake to insist on any one category too heavily. First there's the money, and I agree with you on that. They make no bones about their economic interest. But their interest in human rights is also vital, touching them in a very tender spot – Alabama, you know? Thirdly, they want Africa to join the western bloc of countries, to back the west in facing off against communism ..."

Taradas rolled his eyes.

"Communism! Ha! The Americans are children, and the communists know well how to play their hand. And do you think the Americans have faith in the effectiveness of the United Nations as a world-governing body?" he asked.

He did not believe it for one minute and was sniggering at me. I seriously wondered why he would want to continue conversation with such a booby.

"Are you thinking that the American faith in the UN is an evil thing?" I asked, wide-eyed.

By now he must have been exasperated with me, so he settled in to give me a lecture.

"You must give the Portuguese some credit," he began. "It is my belief that Portugal is the only country in Europe able, in its small and rather self-interested way, to make the Americans stop to re-examine their interests in Africa.

"At least as a nation and a culture, the Portuguese have more than survived; right now we lay claim to the world's most far-flung empire. And though we have done this by living off the backs of our colonies, we have been able to avoid the crassness of materialism the Americans think such important symbols of 'civilization.' American civilization – Ha!"

"Right or wrong, the Portuguese have so far stood their ground and forced America to have a new look at herself – no small achievement for one of the smallest nations in the so-called developed west. America has no respect for history – and even less for the cultures of peoples in nations all over the world, her own included ..."

It seemed about the right moment to sit back and allow Taradas' tirade against the Americans to continue uninterrupted. There was barely a thing he said with which I did not concur to some degree; and there was barely a criticism of America that could not in far greater measure apply to the fascist dictatorship of the Portuguese regime in Lisboa and the operation of their 'overseas provinces' in Africa. His arguments seemed far too important to him for me even to suggest that most Americans would be blithely ignorant of Portugal and her colonial problems; most would probably have to look up 'Portugal' on the map to see where it was. And as for Moçambique ... wasn't that an island somewhere off the coast of Florida?

So far in this conversation there had been plenty of talk about Portugal and America, and not much mention of the indigenous people over whose lands we were at that very moment travelling. I found consideration of that small point bizarre, to say the least. This man, long posing as a pillar of this community, and personable as he was, actually believed that Moçambique – all of it – belonged to Portugal (and maybe even a small part of it to him). And on the other side of Africa there was Angola which, likewise, 'belonged' to Portugal. In all this talk of Portugal and America there had been no mention so far of Portugal's great 'civilizing mission' – to 'raise' savages living in wretched conditions to be good, useful and well-polished Christian Portuguese citizens. Somehow I knew his view would be: 'It will take generations, but it will be done – eventually ..."

And, almost by extension, if this miracle soup-brewing were to be resisted, then those resisting would just have to be eliminated – with the help, of course, of such social brew masters as PIDE ...

None of us said as much. To have done so would have risked making the rest of the journey to Nampula intolerable. It was clear if Portuguese minds had been so determinedly set there would be no recourse to dialogue or negotiation; the pig-headedness of the dominant side would prevent any consideration of gracious bending, and so all entities involved might as well start to prepare to fight it out ...

From the outside, looking in, it was a sad prospect.

Mopeia Highland Whisky

I have bleak memories of Nampula. There were so many military people, and everyone talked the same way Taradas had talked – or in even harsher terms. I was among government and military people whose prime responsibility was to show their allegiance to the flag, so the arguments I was hearing were all the official government line, over and over the same level of intolerance and stupefying belligerence. Quite literally I had heard it all before and there was no reason for me to hear it again – except that I was among them and there would have been an unpleasant penalty for such rudeness as to not listen and pay the closest attention to what they had to say. Sooner rather than later I might have been taken for an *oposicionista*, and then the game would have been up; all channels of information would be closed to me and I would be prevented from seeing anything at all or, worse, I would be removed and hustled away ... The singular irritation was that whatever it was these people had to say to me, they thought they were saying – and I was hearing – for the first time. They simply did not realize that I had had the same message bellowed into my ear at every stop I had made throughout my entire journey, and I was sick of it. For two days I messed with these people, ate breakfast, lunch and dinner with them. At every meal I was pounded with the correctness of the Portuguese 'civilizing mission,' and the senselessness of the idea of independence – whether propounded by the Africans themselves or some – any – political opposition of any stripe or colour. I began to realize how good I was at smiling, at saying nothing as I offered up the Latin shrug.

Those with whom I talked and argued appeared to understand the shrug. Again I was witnessing how fascism is born of a lack of sensitivity, arrogance in face of a deep ignorance, even stupidity – turning itself into self-aggrandizement, and greed. Latin shrugs are nothing if not filled with accommodating acquiescence – thus affording the generous liberty of accepting the simplicity of its gesture to mean whatever one pleases. My interlocutors might well have concluded I agreed with them; by now I did not care.

I was quick to detect the presence of a class system among the Portuguese – especially pronounced in an officers' mess, but also extant outside the military – and I could easily tell how it manifested itself rather differently than the ghastly snobbishness I had observed in Britain and in a British army officers' mess. My inexpert observation was that Portugal's upper classes generally demonstrated a well-defined sense of *noblesse oblige* – the responsibility one assumes (visible in demeanour, dress and manners) as the bearer of an acceptable leadership over 'the masses.' At its worst (and most marked) it can come across as a ferocious lordliness, an air that carries one (the snob) through life at a fictional and lofty altitude that almost demands others – particularly the *hoi polloi* – to doff their caps, pull their forelocks, say 'sir' (or '*Master*') and generally agree to subservience as underling. It is revolting, and is recognized as revolting by Portuguese themselves at all levels of their society. While the snob is certainly seen clearly for what he/she is, it is definitely not inconceivable to discover, at the other end of this social spectrum, members of the upper and monied classes who scowl at the pretentiousness of their impolite peers. Displays of sincere and earnest graciousness on the part of the privileged – a notably sincere cordiality and civility – stand in extreme contrast to the boorishness of the snob. It was a quality that, in the British mess, I seldom discovered among the well-advantaged.

Upper class snobbishness is noxious in any form, British or Portuguese, but one conspicuous trait I consistently recognized in the latter (it was a gesture that amused me) is something I have not especially remarked in the former: a manner of lifting the chin at the same time as hooding the eyes, most often accompanied by a slight (and slow) turn of the head away from any individual being addressed. The gesture can be conspicuously magnified by carrying an overcoat on the shoulders rather than taking the trouble to slip one's arms through the sleeves (an unbuttoned camel hair coat seems to offer the best effect) and is yet more devastatingly amplified when the action is attended by the simultaneous (and very slow) pulling on of a pair of pig-leather gloves – the way I had been shown by the cavalry officer on the palace stairs in Lisboa. The British don't seem to do this any more, and in any case they are no match for such overt Portuguese panache.

The flight from Nampula to Quelimane near the mouth of the Rio dos Bons Sinais took just an hour; here I said goodbye to João, my minder from Ilha de Moçambique, who had flown down with me. Minder, maybe, but in no way had he been a heavy; I liked him. Now at Quelimane I was to meet my new minder, Artur Vila, second secretary to the local governor.

Anyone taking notes of my progress on this journey might be forgiven for thinking I was a most important guest of the Portuguese government. Had they stopped to ask me how I felt, I could have told them I was being courteously but meticulously escorted – through more schools than I cared to count, through industries and factories and land projects and water projects, and just about anything else the Portuguese thought might divert my attention, tweak me into believing the government was doing something useful for its people. To me it was quite clear I was being monitored – guided as well as curbed. I was their guest, but now they were having suspicions as to my usefulness to them, they did not know quite what to do with me. How to rid themselves of a guest they had already invited to dine?

Had I been just a little more on the ball concerning my hosts' vigilance it might have dawned on me earlier that I was already falling under suspicion. I had written a number of articles for the papers in Toronto, and there was no other way of despatching them than to use the Portuguese mail service. Similarly, I had written letters to numbers of friends and contacts and these, also, had to be shipped out by post. There was no other way of moving the written word from point A to point B. Subsequently I was to discover that all my material arrived safely at its destination, but there were signs of tampering. My correspondents later told me some of the envelopes they had received had been slit open, then brazenly taped shut again. In one or two instances, when steam might have been used to open an envelope, a brown-coloured glue had been used rather carelessly to reseal it. Such treatment was not unexpected; I had been careful not to name names but otherwise felt that, as a matter of conscience, I should not submit to being bullied into writing words with which I could not agree. It presented me with a dichotomy – I could have withheld all my writings until I was well clear of Portuguese territorial control; I was not writing news, after all. But in the end I felt satisfied that being open about what I was seeing and thinking was the correct way to go – even if it finally counted against me.

The result was that by the time I arrived in Nampula I could have been fairly certain that at least some of my writings were now in the hands of PIDE, that if my earlier material had not been caught on its way out of Angola, some of it might well have appeared in print back home in Canada – and if it had, it would most certainly have been monitored, copies being sent back to Lisboa for assessment.

As it happened, I was correct. Many years later I was to find out that as soon as the first of my stories appeared in Canadian papers, Jorge Ritto – the Portuguese consul back in Toronto who had organized this tour and had been so confident his nation's colonial policy 'had nothing to hide' – had clipped them from the papers and sent them (*a culpa é minha*) to his superiors. I was happy he had put his money on me; I would not have been able to enter Portuguese Africa without his initial invitation and support. However, he had greatly miscalculated. In choosing me for the job he had in mind, he had caused himself no end of trouble. I had warned him, and very clearly, that I would 'call it as I saw it' – that I would attempt to record what I saw, what I was told, and my commentary about it all. I had emphasized that I was not prepared to undertake a public relations junket to favour a dictatorial regime. As penalty for selecting me Jorge Ritto was blamed by his ministry for extreme poor judgement and for embarrassing his minister, his government and his country. He was not, however, summoned home to face a firing squad. Instead, as punishment, he was posted to Leopoldville for three years – a career move over which he had no control, and which I subsequently learned he disliked intensely.

I might have felt sorry for him, but I didn't. In 1974 the regime he had represented so faithfully was toppled from power, its leaders forced out in disgrace. But Jorge Ritto had an engaging personality. A trained diplomat, he possessed the sort of winning traits that could convince people of his liberal-minded sincerity. As the hullabaloo of the 1974 *Carnation Revolution* wound down, he himself managed to pop up again like the proverbial Portuguese cork – the consummate survivor who well understood class and charm and possessed the cunning sense of when to lie low and become invisible. He drew little attention to himself and refrained from broadcasting too loudly that he had previously served his nation's fascist regime willingly and with energy. When all the air had been sucked out of the revolution and Portugal was once more a compliant member of the western alliance, he again found his niche within the same diplomatic corps that had once welcomed him to exile in Congo DRC. In time he was appointed Portugal's ambassador to UNESCO based in Paris. His career soared. He was fast becoming one of the diplomatic darlings not just of Portugal, but of all Europe.

However, Jorge Ritto's comfortable life suddenly slipped sideways at the turn of the century. He was swept up as one of the principal defendants in a paedophilia ring that had been sexually abusing children at a number of orphanages in Lisboa and elsewhere since the 1970s. He and several other well-known members of Portuguese 'high society' and intelligentsia were duly arrested. Their trial lasted nearly six years. In 2010 Ritto himself was found guilty and sentenced to six years in prison.

The plane landed at Quelimane and I was whisked off to a comfortable room at the Hotel Vera Cruz. The area round about was renowned for its production of sisal and copra – sisal a sharp-pointed cactus-like plant used in the production, principally, of cords, ropes and matting; copra, a derivative of the coconut, is used in the extraction of coconut oil and cattle feed. Historically, the cultivation of both plants was an activity that could be carried on by smallholders, the extracts from the plants – leaves or nuts – being collected on site by the individual farmer and a minimum of workers – his family – and shipped off for processing at larger factories. The planting of sisal or copra made it possible for a small farm to pay for itself and produce a reasonable living for the land owner.

So, while in Quelimane I was duly taken out to investigate two or three sisal operations and several coconut plantations where copra was in production. In between I was taken to several schools and an orphanage and was shown water works and electrical installations until my head was hurting and my ears were buzzing. In every instance there had been a spic-and-span clean-up, walls washed, floors swept and gleaming, pipes polished – everything 'just-so,' and ready for inspection. All very impressive – and then in the evenings there were the usual conversations over dining tables about the Portuguese mission to civilize 'their' Africans. The routine had become extremely tedious.

Coconuts

Then early one morning Minder Artur came to my hotel room and said:

"Finally! I've been able to secure permission to visit a sugar plantation!"

This was hardly an offer of cake and ice cream, as I saw it, and I had to concentrate my sullen mindset before delivering my answer. I feared my face must have indicated disinterest, perhaps even displeasure.

"Come on!" he encouraged. "I've managed to secure a plane, and we can be there and back before supper. It'll be fun. We'll be flying over a portion of the Zambezi and I think you'll find it interesting."

I liked this fellow. Artur was about my own age, clearly had a schooling that permitted him to hold down a job in the local governor's office but equally did not appear to take it so seriously it had crimped his humour. He was quiet, alert, confident and interested in the role he had been obliged to play as my guide/companion for this leg of my journey. Minder, yes, but not intrusive, and not one to belabour me with political concepts he seemed instinctively to know had already been amply presented to me. The governor had asked him to do a job, and to me it seemed he genuinely wanted to present a picture of Zambezi district as he knew and understood it. He told me he had attended university at Coimbra and had returned to his home in Moçambique to wait until he would be called into the army.

"Everyone has to do military service, so I'll have to do mine, too. I'm not looking forward to it, but I don't have a choice," he had told me.

At one point he admitted to me:

"I'm not entirely comfortable with Portugal's position in the colonies. It's probably time for those of us who live here to take on the responsibility of our own destinies – but if ever you tell anyone I said that to you, I'll deny it!"

With only the pilot for company, the two of us flew in a twin-engine Cessna southwest from Quelimane to the town of Luabo on the banks of the Rio Zambezi. On either side of us a wide plain spread into the distance. The land was arable, but it was flat. It was only a few metres above sea level behind little more than the same series of sand dunes and low hills that ran along much of the coast – not unlike the dunes I had seen in the Limpopo area a few weeks earlier. The mean height of Quelimane itself was only one metre above sea level, which accounted for the extreme danger from high winds, high tides and, most of all, high river run-offs capable of bursting banks.

We flew low over Luabo, and then up-stream for several kilometres in a northwesterly direction, following the big river almost halfway to Mopeia. Artur explained that much of the land we could see below us was usually flooded in the rainy season. Banking to the north, we made a wide circle. The land began to rise in front of us as we swung around, then we headed back to the airstrip at Luabo. Flying at just a few hundred feet above the ground, we passed over enormous cane fields crossed north-to-south by a variety of substantial streams – tributaries of the Zambezi – canals and earthworks to contain them. No shortage of water in these parts. We landed on the supply strip for the famous Sena Sugar Estate.

Meeting us at the strip were three British men, all senior officers of the enterprise: Lieutenant Colonel J.D. Hornung was the director, John Kemball, the deputy general manager, and William Eyre, the company's field manager. A fourth man, Tibório Covas, a Portuguese, was introduced as the factory manager.

363

Tall, square-shouldered and erect as a flagpole, as one might expect a senior British army officer to be on the parade square, Hornung spoke in stentorian tones, but was not without humour. I would like to think our arrival contributed a rare dash of zing into his day. I had the notion that everyday at Luabo was inclined to be like the one before it, and any breach of the ordinary was welcome.

We were given a quick tour of the immediate surroundings of the plantation core and offices, with Col. Hornung filling us in on the history of the place. The estate at Luabo was started by his grandfather in 1893, but the very first crop of sugar cane had been harvested at nearby Mopeia. Other plantation estates followed – at Morromeu in 1902 and Caia in 1909. Luabo itself did not enter full production until 1923. Each estate was nestled close to the others, so that the entire Sena sugar operation was run as a unit – 'a colony within a colony' he explained ingenuously. I could see how the Portuguese in Artur winced, for military men are given readily to neither diplomacy nor tact. In 1930 both Caia and Mopeia were closed down, so that the company ran on the production of Luabo and Morromeu alone; even so, it was an extremely large operation. The easiest way of getting around was by air, so there were several different landing strips.

I noted some statistics: each of the two great surviving plantations ran to twenty-five thousand hectares, with a total of some nineteen thousand workers. There were eight workers' compounds at Luabo, and the same at Morromeu. The company had its own railway system, with one hundred miles of track on each of the two estates, and a further fifty-six miles of track to connect the Morromeu concern with the Trans-Zambezi Railway. In addition, the company operated nine paddle-wheel steamers on the Zambezi between Morromeu and the coastal port town of Vila do Chinde. The only river transport available, the journey downstream took six hours; back against the current, twelve hours. Hornung told us the fleet was somewhat bigger than just the nine boats, but that they were out of commission.

They were interesting craft. Rebuilt and refitted, some of them dated to the 1890s. Each one drew only three feet in order to navigate the river's treacherous waters and shifting sand bars but, because of this shallow draft they were inclined to tip over in a high wind without an ingenious stabilizing device: barges would be lashed to either side of a steamer. In addition to stability this increased the cargo space.

Sena was an extremely well-organized enterprise. For instance, the eight workers' compounds in Luabo were scattered about the estate in such a way that no single worker had too far to walk to the train that would take him to the cane fields. Some eight hundred workers and their families were housed in a new compound right next to the townsite. The houses comprising this compound were built of concrete, and appeared like rows of tents when viewed from the air.

"Actually, not very successful," Bill Eyre commented. "The old style round grass huts were far better – easier to keep clean. If they became too unhygienic, it was easy to burn them down and rebuild. We have found this can be done each year, and the Africans prefer them. The concrete houses get too hot; the grass ones are warmer in cold weather, cooler in the hot months."

Over lunch and a glass or two of good Portuguese red wine Hornung relaxed his military manner and recounted a few personal snippets that gave me an overview of this area of Moçambique when his grandfather first started the place. It happened that old Peter Hornung was the fifth son of a Yorkshire family. He saw no future for himself in England, so cast off for an adventurous life on the Zambezi. He brought a variety of seeds and cuttings with him to plant and determine which ones would best grow in the local climate and soil.

"Sugar survived when he planted it at Mopeia, sometime around 1883 – so sugar it was!" chuckled the colonel.

Cane cutter on the Sena sugar estate

The market for sugar at that time was very poor, so the young settler started distilling spirit from the crop, adding a whisky extract. He bottled it and took the load to Johannesburg – there selling it as 'Mopeia Highland Whisky.' The concoction proved a great success.

Hornung guffawed.

"Only a few years ago I was in Jo'burg and called in at Grandpapa's old club. One of the older members was introducing me around, and a few of the older chaps could remember my grandfather. One of them told me the club had 'gone to pot' – just wasn't the same after Grandpapa ceased brewing his whisky!"

Sena was strictly a family concern, but about eighty percent of the workforce was 'Portuguese.' He did not elaborate when I asked him if that number of workers was from Portugal, or whether perhaps they were African 'Portuguese' or *mestiços*. I could see efforts were being made, in a colonial way, to provide the necessities of life for the workers at Sena: there was a social club for the whites who worked there, another club for the Portuguese and yet a third for the Africans. Housing had been organized, again according to one's racial status; there were rudimentary medical facilities run by a qualified medical staff. There were schools for the children. There was a herd of cattle, twenty thousand head, that required tending, and which provided meat and protein. Mobile canteens had been set up in the fields. There was a pay scale – better than elsewhere, but hardly generous – designed to keep the workers content enough with their lot that they would continue working – and not complain too much. Loyalty – two-way loyalty – and everything was made available for the workers. And yet ...

I could not help but smell the noxious stench of advantage and gross disadvantage – paternalism. If the African workers were being supplied with 'all' they needed, then it was because it was basically good for the family business – not because it bolstered the Africans' yearning for anything like the dignity of upward mobility. The 'all' was definitely limited.

'Progress ...?' Not really.

A colony within a colony – absolutely. A private little empire where Hornung himself would pass half-a-year at a stretch before returning to Britain. It was plain to see – Hornung was providing, but he and his close associates were also taking. He was onto a very 'good thing,' thank you ... It would have been hard to criticize him at that particular historical time in southern Africa – because *every*body was doing it: the South Africans with their *apartheid* in their own land and an extension of it in Namibia, the British settlers in the Rhodesias, the Americans seemingly everywhere at once in order to introduce their concepts of freedom, democracy and the corporate grab – the Canadians with their vaunted 'mining skills.' It was the Great Scramble for Africa all over again – but the truth was, *it had never stopped*!

The colonel himself had started in the family business in 1948, and he had done very well for himself, thank you and thank you again ...

Only the evening before, Artur and I had been talking about the 'Portuguese abuse' of the indigenous people of Moçambique. It was bad, no question, but both of us had the same idea that the British had probably been as bad in their colonies – and very possibly worse. Artur had queried me on British attitudes, and British racism.

"It's hard for me to put into words," I had told him. "Man is a cruel animal, and any man is capable of atrocity. But they differ in their administration of cruelty. To me the Portuguese are an easygoing people – good merchants, good negotiators, but not overly given to harshness and overt brutality. I don't think so ... They are Latins, after all. Hot-blooded, true, but a Christian people capable of compassion – and the capacity to remember this before driving themselves to extremes. In the end, even in the worst of situations they seem to have a softness about them."

I was not entirely sure what I was talking about. I had been forming this point of view only since setting foot in the Portuguese world. The comparison I was attempting to make was likely based more heavily on my assessment of the far harsher Anglo-Saxon mentality – and on that subject I had strong convictions. Portuguese softness ...? Now and then I was sure I could detect a flash of fire.

What I imagined was the Latin way did not mesh with what I knew of the way of northern European tribes, I argued. Northern peoples – and particularly the English – were hard as granite, unbending, ruthless and vindictive. Throughout their history they had demonstrated this time and again. This was why the British Empire had spread so far and survived so long – cold-blooded abuse and merciless oppression hiding behind a set of laws drawn up to favour themselves, stamped by the seal of an unyielding monarchy and carried out to the letter.

Thus, as Hornung unravelled himself and his little empire before us, so I could detect a twinkle in Artur's eye. He was witnessing, in miniature, a precise example of my all-Canadian thesis, and I think he was thinking Canadians are pushovers at heart.

We had a plane to catch. Time to go.

Guerillas and Green Tea

Artur assured me the town of Vila Junqueiro was a 'must.'

"Tea plantations. Have you ever seen a hillside of tea? Moçambicano tea – the most vibrant green you've ever seen! Mountains, the most unusual geological formations – the entire landscape covered over with thick bushes of this extraordinary green colour. Tea …"

I was sceptical, but the sugar cane excursion had been more enlightening than I had at first thought, so now I reckoned it worthwhile to follow Artur's lead.

It was a day's drive by car to get there – three hundred kilometres on a winding and poorly-surfaced road. We could stay over a few nights, he said, return at our leisure. We would cross the floodplain of the Zambezi, head almost directly north into the hills and the mountains that lie beyond.

We made an early start, stopping for breakfast in a bustling town called Namacurra.

"Have you ever heard of this place before?" Artur asked me.

"Namacurra? Can't say I have …"

"This was as far south as the Germans managed to come during the First World War …" said my guide. "Do you know the name von Lettow-Vorbeck…?"

"Oh …?" The name was ringing a bell.

Artur was referring to the extraordinary war-time escapades of Col. Paul Emil von Lettow-Vorbeck, the leader of a small German army that played havoc with the allies from the very outset of the war until days after the armistice had been signed that concluded the war in 1918.

"Namacurra fell to the Germans in July 1918," Artur said. "They attacked a Portuguese military post here and managed to capture so many weapons they could replenish every man in their army with a new rifle and more ammunition than he could carry. They also captured machineguns and mortars, and enough food to sustain themselves for weeks."

The events of the distant African sidebar story to which Artur was referring, when stacked alongside the cataclysmic First World War being fought in Europe, reads like a surreal tale concocted by H. Rider Haggard, or perhaps an episode from some Boys' Own Adventure series. In fact, it was a bloody war within a war, and resulted in the deaths of over three hundred thousand men, women and children.

About two years prior to the outbreak of the First World War, the German government appointed Heinrich Schnee as governor of the territory of German East Africa. He was a lawyer and a judge as well as a civil servant in the Imperial German Foreign Office. By the end of the XIX century he had served his empire in such places as German New Guinea and German Samoa, and prior to the outbreak of war had held several senior appointments in Berlin and London.

As governor he was officially the commander of all military forces in German East Africa – but as soon as war was declared he found himself at odds with the newly-appointed commander of the fighting corps known as the *Schutztruppe* – by far the most effective native warriors in the territory. With German officers and senior non-commissioned officers, this force had been given over to the command of von Lettow-Vorbeck.

Schnee had neither von Lettow-Vorbeck's drive nor his foresight. He wanted to hold German East Africa in a state of neutrality until the war in Europe had drawn to a close. Von Lettow-Vorbeck, on the other hand, wanted to go on the attack – his plan being to harass the British and keep them occupied, drawing allied forces into a sideshow that would reduce the number of troops otherwise useful in Europe. Though there was a stiff rivalry between the two German commanders at first, eventually Schnee came around to backing von Lettow-Vorbeck's idea of training the *Schutztruppe* in the arts of guerilla warfare. Any doubts Schnee might have had vanished altogether following the November 1914 Battle of Tanga, in which a tiny army of German-trained soldiers led by von Lettow-Vorbeck routed a better-equipped British force of whites and Africans eight times greater in size. Just nine months later, after Britain's Royal Navy had compelled the Germans to scuttle their prized light cruiser, *Konigsberg*, in the Rufiji River delta, there was cause for further British alarm. The Germans had managed to salvage the best of the *Konigsberg's* guns and to give them to the *Schutztruppe,* who then used them most effectively as ground artillery against the British.

Von Lettow-Vorbeck was born into Pomeranian aristocracy in 1870. At the age of twenty he was commissioned as a lieutenant into the Imperial German Army and assigned to a staff position in Berlin. He was posted to China in 1900 as part of an international effort to put down the Boxer

Rebellion. In 1904 he was sent to German South-West Africa (Namibia), later fulfilling several home commands before being named in 1913 to a post in German Kamerun (Cameroon). His orders were changed, and he never got there. Four months prior to the outbreak of the First World War, and by now a Lieutenant Colonel, he was given command of the *Schutztruppe* throughout the territory that now forms the mainland of Tanzania. At the very outbreak of war von Lettow-Vorbeck's command was small. It comprised some two thousand seven hundred Germans, and slightly fewer African *askaris* – native soldiers divided into a number of operational companies – in total about five thousand men. None of them, except a handful of older and senior officers, was particularly well trained.

Action was started by the British the day after war had been declared. The British attacked German outposts near Lake Victoria, and German supply ships on the lake itself. The Germans retaliated by crossing the border into British East Africa (Kenya) at several points with small guerilla groups – and from then on, the events escalated. The British set up a naval blockade of the Tanganyika coast. After a fierce engagement in the delta of the River Rufigi, the German sailors scuttled their well-armed light cruiser, the *Königsberg,* managed to salvage the main battery of the ship's guns – and then joined the *Schutztruppe.* It was a boon to von Lettow-Vorbeck who now found himself armed with far heavier artillery than the British could field, and used it with devastating effect.

A map showing the lines of movements by all forces involved in the East African campaign resembles a bowl of worms. Both sides resorted to guerilla warfare – the main difference being that von Lettow-Vorbeck's *Schutztruppe* never amounted to more than sixteen thousand men – and on operations managed with far smaller units. This added greatly to their maneuverability, and the speed with which they could mount an attack. As the war progressed the allies were obliged to pour in more and more troops, eventually amounting to a full-blown force of more than three hundred thousand men. At peak, von Lettow-Vorbeck was holding off the combined armies of Britain, British India, Belgium, Portugal, South Africa and the Rhodesias – and no one could catch him. One day the *Schutztruppe* would be making lightning-fast raids along the railway system in Kenya; a day or two later they would be knocking out British shipping on Lake Tanganyika, or blowing up railway bridges and blocking supplies in any portion of the huge area of fighting. On the allied side were Generals Jacob van Deventer, Jan Smuts and Louis Botha.

Hugely outnumbered and under pressure from his enemies' combined armies, the *Schutztruppe* left German East Africa and crossed the Rio Rovuma into Moçambique in November 1917, capturing the town of Ngomano. Far more experienced by now than the forces arrayed against them, the Germans were nonetheless in desperate condition – but they refused to give up. However, the capture of this Portuguese military base provided them with new weapons and much needed supplies of food, so they continued south – about seven hundred kilometres to Namacurra. Here they again replenished their supplies of weapons and food before heading north again, all the time foraging, laying waste to the countryside and looking for a fight with the allies.

"They followed the same route north that we are travelling," Artur commented ... "except their road was nowhere as good as the one we are on right now. In fact, they had no road ...

"Like us, they were headed for the tea plantations of Vila Junqueiro and the rugged countryside we will encounter up there. A little further north they came to a place call Lioma, and here they very nearly came to an end. The British knew they were in the area and laid an ambush – encircling the *Schutztruppe* on three sides ... There was a fierce pitched battle."

But the Germans found a gap in the encirclement, fought their way out of the trap and made their way back into German East Africa. In their retreat across the Rio Rovuma many of von Lettow-Vorbeck's battle-weary column were brought down by a bronchial influenza. Numbers of them became so weak they could put up no resistance when they were attacked and carried away by the lions that roamed the nearby plains.

From German East Africa what was left of the force crossed into Northern Rhodesia – and took the country's northern provincial capital, Kasama. This was two days after the war had officially ended.

In his memoir of the occasion, von Lettow-Vorbeck recounts an amusing story:

From a hiding place in the bush a German marksman drew a bead on the Rhodesian regimental flag that fluttered above the stockade – and blew a hole in it.

Startled, the Rhodesians turned and stared as the invaders stepped quietly out of the forest to show themselves – the last of a crack column of German officers and the best-trained African *askaris* ever to fight in East Africa.

The Rhodesian troops ran for their guns, of course, and they did put up something of a fight. But when it became quite apparent they were losing, the Rhodesians abandoned their weapons and fell on the stores of liquor kept inside the stockade.

"By the time we were able to break into the stockade the entire post was thoroughly intoxicated," the German commander wrote years later.

It was here that he was first informed an armistice had been signed on 11 November, ending the war in Europe. At first the German commander suspected a trick and he was prepared to fight on. But eventually the allies were able to convince him. Undefeated and still bearing their weapons, von Lettow-Vorbeck's *Schutztruppe* marched north to Abercorn, and it was here he formally surrendered on 23 November – fully twelve days after the war had ended in Europe.

"Exciting stuff, a good part of it happening right around here," my guide commented. "We'll be cutting across the very same ground the *Schutztruppe* plundered fifty years ago. A snatch of living history for you …!"

Artur was immensely happy I had been so intrigued by his story.

"Unfortunately, these events triggered others we Portuguese are not so proud of. Our army suffered defeat at virtually every turn, so we have little to be proud of on the military side. Afterwards, many of these same troops behaved very badly in suppressing the rebellions in Tete province … massacres, and so on. Not our finest colonial period, and very likely the seed for many of the problems we can feel brewing today. I think we Portuguese have yet to learn a severe lesson."

"Do you believe Moçambique will go the same route as Angola …?" I asked him.

He thought for a moment.

"Well, I'm not supposed to say this – but maybe even worse."

It was getting late in the afternoon as we crossed the Zambezi plain and approached Vila Junqueiro from the south, the forested Namuli Mountains rising before us like a great blue-green *Adamastor* beyond the town. Mount Namuli itself is Moçambique's second highest mountain at a little over two thousand four hundred metres high (seven thousand nine hundred feet). It, and the mountains of Vila Junqueiro create an extensive tropical rainforest area, although much of the lush first growth has been cut away to make room for tea plantations in the valleys and up the lower slopes. The elevations just above the tea are cultivated by the locals to supplement both diet and incomes. There is a small production of coffee and a varied cultivation, potatoes, maize, millet, sorghum, cassava, cashew and macadamia nuts are also produced. The area has an unusually wet and temperate microclimate which is perfect for the cultivation of tea. The original rainforest is limited to the highest elevations and is also found blanketing the steep banks of the streams and small rivers that drain out onto the plain and eventually flow into the Rio Zambezi.

The town, originally named Gurúè, was re-christened Vila Junqueiro in 1959 to honour the chief tea producer in the region, Manuel Saraiva Junqueiro, who was killed in a plane crash. Following independence, however, the town reverted to its original name. At the time of our visit it had an estimated population of some forty-five thousand. In recent years this number increased considerably; today it stands at about one hundred and fifty thousand.

Some of the mountains before us had been thrust upwards by the flexing of an ancient tectonic heave-ho. They look randomly jagged, as if an angry god had thrown down his basketful of rocks in a tantrum, then kicked them into a heap on the surface of the great plain. Among these peaks, though, were other mountains of a totally different aspect. Clearly volcanic, the residue of their slopes worn away by time, they appeared like rugged and ungainly pillars – their hardened magma cores pinpointing where the fearsome fires of earth's innermost furnaces had blasted molten rock through the crust of Mother Earth. The slopes of the volcanoes had eroded over millennia, leaving behind these ungainly 'thumbs' sticking up into the air. Gradually everything settled down and these cousin mountains, brooding and weathering for an eternity, cloaked themselves in their vibrant green shroud. Now, as we drew near, the entire vista was blanketed by a mist and the smoke from scores of deliberately-set small brush fires.

We were to visit three different tea companies – by far the largest of which was the Plantações Manuel Saraiva Junqueiro. Arriving just after darkness had fallen it was impossible to see much, but I could sense there was a thrill in the air, a busy silence at the supper hour. I noticed dozens of small cooking fires burning – some close by, others tucked away semi-hidden in areas where the indigenous had built themselves grass huts among the trees. The canopies of the trees, still as sentries, drooped in the roadway, so poorly-lit the headlamps of our car could only intensify our insignificance under the mountains we knew were there but could not see. The forest, in the dark somewhere behind the fires, gave us an unannounced welcome. As the car pulled to a stop near some low buildings, people closed in around us and one of them, looking at me with curiosity, introduced himself to Artur. They spoke for a few moments in Portuguese.

"I think you must be hungry by now," Artur said, turning towards me. "We are being offered a supper by this gentleman, *Senhor* Magalhães. He is the Junqueiro company's manager."

"Something to eat would be very welcome," I replied as Magalhães stepped forward to shake my hand.

We dined by the flickering light of two oil-burning lamps in what appeared to be a company canteen. Magalhães apologized that the generator was currently being serviced. Everyone would have to go about after dark with flashlights for a day or so, he explained – but the condition was not entirely unusual.

"We keep repairing this old generator, when what we really need is a new one. But the world market in tea is low now, so we're being prudent and cutting back. It's a matter of budget. We'll be fine for a time once this cranky old thing is repaired."

The company maintained a guesthouse high on the slopes of one of the mountains. This is where we would be staying that night. We were tired and so were silent throughout most of the meal, and afterwards we followed in our vehicle behind Magalhães' car, up a steep and winding dirt road. It was no short distance; we were driving for quite some minutes. It was such a pitch-black night we could see nothing beyond the edge of the forest that flitted by on the periphery of the road in the beam of our headlamps, but at last we arrived at what looked like a turn-around closing off the end of our approach, although I had the distinct feeling there was ample more mountain just above us. There were no stars visible from here through the thick canopy of trees. Without the cars' lights or our flashlights, it was black. I could not remember ever before being outside in such an impenetrable darkness.

At the side of the road, a short distance into the forest, there was a large house of stone and wood, with a thatch roof and wide glass windows. Entering through the front door we found ourselves in a well-furnished lodge, its hallway comfortably simple with side tables and upright chairs. Oil lamps had been lighted, and there were several of them in the rooms we entered. As we came through, I noticed a well-equipped kitchen off to one side; beyond it, and through an archway, there was an enormous space that comprised, first, a voluminous dining area and then, down two shallow steps, a massive living room at a slightly lower level. From the outside it had been easy to misjudge the overall size of the house. Entering the dining area before the living room might have seemed at first to present a backwards configuration, except that the roominess of the whole place gave it a sense of benevolent welcoming.

The dining table was made of a darkened hardwood, long enough and wide enough to seat round about a score of people on both benches and high-backed chairs. A sideboard and serving table were set off against one end of the room, the same species of hardwood, but ornately-carved with human and animal figures in a variety of hunting scenes. The living room, open and in full view of the dining area, was a generously comfortable space, furnished with three cushioned rattan sofas and several easy chairs, also of woven wicker. There was a writing desk off in one corner, and a picture window that took up the entire far side wall of the living area – a darkened glass through which we could see nothing but the night. It was mysterious and enticing, concealing a vista to be revealed to us only with the first light of dawn. For the moment, facing into the blackness of night, there was nothing to be seen through this wall of glass except our own reflections thrown opaquely back at us by the dim light of the oil lamps.

We had been greeted at the entrance by a house servant and his wife. Magalhães spoke to them briefly.

"This is Entévio and his wife, Flávia. They take good care of this lodge, and I am sure they will take good care of you, too. If you need anything, just ask …"

He told us he would send up a company vehicle to collect us in the morning, then bid us goodnight and returned to his car.

"Have you been here before?" I asked Artur, returning to the living room after Flávia had shown us our bedrooms.

"Never," he replied. "I've heard of its existence from others who have come to Vila Junqueiro, and I have visited the plantation and factory before, but I've never been up here. I'm told it's very pretty in the daytime."

We sat for a while and talked over a nightcap. We were both exhausted from the long drive, and were more than happy to make it an early night.

The following morning I was awoken by the aroma of fresh-brewing coffee. For a moment I lay and tried to remember where I was. Outside the window was a curtain of the most vivid blue – far too piercing a blue for even a sunny sky. I rubbed my eyes and peered out. It was a sight and a colour startling enough that I sprang out of bed immediately, and approached the glass for a closer look. No – it was not sky. It was a colossal tree covered by a dazzle of luminous blue flowers overlying – virtually swamping – the thinnest filigree backdrop of wispy greenery. Jacaranda. I had heard about it, even seen it – but I had never encountered such a startling display of it. Washing and shaving quickly, I was eager to see more of this lodge's surroundings, and so came into the living room – to find it entirely transformed by the daylight that flooded in from outside. Artur was already sitting at a breakfast prepared for him by Flávia who, when she saw me, motioned for me to sit at the table while she went to fetch a pot of coffee. She poured a generous cup and pushed a sugar bowl and pitcher of cream towards my elbow.

"Have you been outside?" I asked Artur.

"Just onto the deck. Incredible view!" He had left the deck door open.

"Quite a spectacle!" he said. "Eat up quick, and let's take a look around."

There was no question of 'eating up quick.' The housekeeper-cum-cook in the kitchen followed up the coffee with a platter of scrambled eggs and toast, and something she called '*marmelada*' which was unlike any marmalade I had ever tasted.

"Delicious," I commented. "What is it?"

"We call it *marmelada* – quince. The English were most impressed with it when they came to Portugal during the Napoleonic wars, and they tried to make it for themselves. Instead of using quince they tried making it with oranges, but they called it marmalade anyway. A bit different, no?"

Artur saw me reaching for the butter and counselled me against it.

"Eat the *marmelada* by itself or put it directly onto the bread. You won't get the full taste if you mix it with butter …"

It was a bit like a jelly, so I took his advice. It did not have the same consistency as the marmalades and jams I was used to for breakfast. Instead of trying to mush and spread it, I cut it into slices and laid them down side-by-side atop my toast. It had a subtle but strong sweetness to it.

"Unusual …!"

Artur was amused.

"It's fun to see your reaction to something so new when it's so very commonplace to us. My mother raised me on the *marmelada* my grandmother used to make."

"This entire journey has been a schooling for me," I told him.

I enjoyed this man's simplicity. There was nothing strident about him. His grandmother was a practical reality at that moment.

After eating we both stepped out onto the deck beyond the great window. There was a balustrade around it, and I walked to the edge.

The house and the deck on which we were standing could not possibly have been built any closer to the face of the mountain's spur. We were on the very lip of space. Right below us there was a drop of several hundred feet. Close beside the balustrade to the right of the deck, a small mountain stream tumbled noiselessly over the edge of the spur into a secret place hidden by trees far below. Listening for it, the faint splash of the water hitting rocks was signaled back up to us – not quite drowned out by the sporadic whistles and voices of unseen field workers far below our level and across the valley. These voices came to us amplified, and with a shrill but distant echo, an accompaniment insufficient to smother the determined harmony, the constancy, of the brook's insistent splashing from somewhere deep in the greenery. Looking out across the valley I could make out neighbouring slopes, but they appeared to be disconnected from us by a combination of fog and the smoke of fires rising from the valley floor. The tops of these mountainous outcroppings were like floating islands, with our perch bobbing along beside them. Far above us the even blue of a bright-lit sky blanketed everything with an indescribable tranquility – the sweep of sky, the heights of the forested mountains, the distant water-splash and the labourers' voices as they called out their morning hurrahs.

I was intoxicated by it all, and could not dispel the sweet taste of quince from my mouth.

Two colours leap at me still when I recall that morning: the intensity of the green tea hills, and the blue of the jacaranda. The tea bushes of Vila Junqueiro – so vivid their colour has been indelibly stamped into my memory – defy the brilliance of every colour I have registered since; and jacaranda blue, combined with its scent, all of it set against that green, the carpets of blue petals on the roads and verges – the waterfall through the mist and smoke that I could only hear by its splashing against unseen rocks hundreds of feet below me ...

The gods may have been dancing through the night, but they were resting that morning ...

Then Magalhães arrived. For a time we all sat on the patio deck, talked tea and drank coffee. He wanted to show us his plantation. I would have preferred to stay behind to write a poem.

As with the sugar cane operations on the plantations at Luabo and Mopeia, the tea farms at Vila Junqueiro were exploitive. I took notes and wrote figures into my diary of the time. At least to my way of thinking the conclusions to be drawn are undeniable when reading it all again.

Picking tea

Although we were told the global tea market was faltering, this could not have been entirely true. Sizeable profits were yet being made by each of the companies operating in the area. Artur and I visited three of them, and it seemed very much as though the management in each case operated in cahoots with his colleagues and neighbours (and social buddies). These companies were offering the only work to be had for kilometres around and, in a take-it-or-leave-it situation of the kind, it is always easy to exploit. There was no question of laying the blame at the feet of any one man or one outfit; it was simply 'the system.' The system of milking the workers. Everyone was doing it. Although agreeable and sympathetic noises were made on all sides, nothing changed. Nothing could change.

In the case of the Manuel Saraiva Junqueiro plantation, I was told the operations were spread across two large areas, one of two thousand hectares, the other of five hundred. In the rainy season (November to April) one thousand eight hundred men were employed. In the dry season this was cut back to one thousand two hundred.

The basic wage was one hundred and fifty escudos per month – plus food, accommodation, a blanket, a shirt, a pair of shorts, a raincoat, a water bottle, firewood, transport to and from work, and 'required medical assistance.' During harvesting, an additional 'incentive bonus' of fifteen escudos was paid for each eighty kilos picked.

Figure approximately twenty-eight escudos to the American dollar. This relates to a 1963 calculation when financial matters were counted on a rather different scale than they are today. But even taking into account the fact the scale has changed, the word 'exploitation' is still applicable.

"We give them a low basic, and a good bonus," Magalhães was calculating ...

In my diary I made the note:

> *None of this looks bad on paper, or in list form. But the clothing is little enough; the accommodation squalid; the transport in the employer's best interest; the medical needs nothing more than the minimum any man or woman will get in any other district, whether working or not. I am not overly impressed ...*
>
> *Magalhães claims the price of tea is far too low on the world market ... Techniques are improving but costing more as the government strives for better working conditions for the Africans – all of which costs more. He claims no plantation in the Zambézia district is making a profit, and few subsidies are available to assist the industry ...*

We passed a group of men chipping stone at the side of a road. They were rebuilding a flume to carry water to a small hydro plant. I asked Artur to ask the pertinent question: chipping stone – four hundred to five hundred escudos per month – at the going rate, perhaps of fifteen escudos ...

Artur and I stayed three days before heading back to Quelimane. We set out at night, approaching the coast at daybreak.

"Good luck with your military service," I told him.

Artur pulled a wry face, then smiled broadly.

"As I told you, it's not my choice, but I don't want to do less than others..."

He shook my hand as I boarded the plane for the short flight south to Beira.

"Go to Gorongosa. It's close to Beira. The biggest lions in all of Africa!"

When war came to Moçambique the next year, the whole country suffered, but some of the worst of the fighting was over Zambézia, the very ground we travelled between Vila Junqueiro and Quelimane. Bombs fell in and around Vila Junqueiro, tanks and artillery dragged their metal carcasses across the landscape – and the tea plantations were torn apart and destroyed. Tea exports – mainly to Britain, the United States and Canada – evaporated. What had been a verdant Paradise before – enchained, but beautiful – would now lie dead. The loveliness that had been Vila Junqueiro at the time of my visit with Artur was turned into the hellish Gurúè war zone.

Beira and the Spanish Catamaran

I was looking forward to Beira. It was the jump-off spot for visiting the Gorongosa game park Artur insisted was 'a must.'

Yet at this point I noted in my diary:

> *Suddenly, just this evening in seems, I have wearied of Portuguese Africa, and want to get back to something I know. I'm tired, tired, tired of the perpetual arguments of the colonizers here, their explanations, excuses – their 'best behaviour' to a visiting foreigner. I suddenly feel very far away, and I'm sick of minders.*

That was written late at night in Beira – so it was after I had been met by my next minder at Beira airport and informed flight plans had been altered.

380

The new plan was that I would now be flying back to Canada out of Beira rather than Lourenço Marques – via Luanda and Lisboa.

I was, indeed, tired of minders. A man called Fernando David, presenting himself as a journalist, came to meet me when I landed, and almost immediately set about irritating me. I should not by now have been so surprised by this irritability, and I couldn't be bothered as to whether it was justified or unjustified, or in defining the way I felt. I found myself taking an almost instant dislike to this man – it didn't matter why, and I did not care. It was his manner at the instant of our meeting that teed me off. I have always found the need to be aware of strong likes and dislikes, how tumbling into a hurried opinion about someone can create havoc. More than once I have had occasion to regret hasty judgement, so will often deliberately try to temper my reactions when meeting people, to hold back feelings and avoid strong judgement – not so much until I am quite sure of the person just met, but until I can be sure of myself. This Fernando had a laugh that hissed and wasn't shy in employing a smutty mouth. We were out-of-sync right from the start, failed to connect in our small twists of conversation in a way that was definitively unfunny. I was much younger then, so was less practiced at maintaining my calm.

"So, you're the man who has come all the way from Canada to look at the animals in our wonderful zoo … I've been out to it so many times … a bore, really …! Wouldn't you prefer to have me escort you to one of our many houses of sexual pursuit …?"

"No, thank you. I'd prefer the animals …"

"Ah-ha! So you're one of *those*, are you? Sheep? Goats? A donkey, perhaps …? I know them all. The animals at Gorongosa might be a little too strong for you at first encounter … Ha! Ha!"

We had only just met. I was already irritated by him, but this exchange was just a little too strong for my taste – and we had not even managed to clear the airport concourse. It was not in the least difficult to tumble to a negative judgement of him right away, and I thought it best to set some parameters from the start.

"If you speak to me like that again, I'll break your legs," I told him.

Hardly a word more was spoken between us until we reached the hotel, at which point I told him I was tired and needed to rest, so he could go. He had followed me to the door of my room in some lame attempt to set things onto a better footing between us, but I felt nothing like the same sentiment. I closed the door as he was standing in the hall still trying to make light of his airport greeting. This was not the man with whom I wanted to spend any time at all discovering the delights of Gorongosa.

When I was sure he was no longer at the other side of my door, I ventured out and went down to the reception desk. I asked to see the manager.

"That guide who just brought me to the hotel – do you know him, and where he works?"

"You mean *Senhor* Fernando David? Yes, we know him. He's a journalist in the city, and he also does some work for the tourism office – meeting and guiding people like yourself ..."

"In that case, I wonder if you could connect me by telephone with the director of the tourism office?"

The manager was curious, but he did as I asked, and the connection was made almost right away. He spoke for a few moments with the tourism director, then handed me the telephone receiver.

"Dr. Falcão de Paiva ..." he said, explaining to whom I would be talking.

"Dr. Falcão de Paiva? I was met a short time ago at the airport by your representative, Fernando David. We have had some trouble, and I wonder if I might come to speak to you ...?"

Overhearing, the hotel manager looked surprised.

The director of tourism tried to elicit more information from me over the phone, but I told him I'd prefer to speak to him face-to-face. He suggested I come right away. His office was close and the hotel manager could explain to me how I might arrive there.

"You've had trouble? What kind of trouble?" asked the manager, taking the receiver from me and hanging it up. He then agreed to escort me himself to the tourism office – and off we went.

A few minutes later the two of us entered the office of the tourism director, and I had to explain myself in front of the pair of them.

"I've come to Beira to visit Gorongosa game reserve. I would like to spend at least a couple of days there, and I fully understand that as I am a journalist rather than a tourist, your office is required by the government to provide me with an escort ... Having to put up with an escort is not so much of a problem; it's the escort himself ..."

Dr. Falcão Paiva looked embarrassed.

Before he could say anything further, I told him how I had been greeted at the airport by his representative. His mouth opened and he scowled his concern. He was clearly mortified.

"Por 'mor de deus!" he exclaimed. "I can't believe the man would say such a thing ..."

"But he did, and that being the case, *Senhor Doutor*, you will understand why I do not wish to spend further time with Fernando David – let alone several days with him – in one of your country's most beautiful animal sanctuaries. I'd appreciate it if you would find me a more agreeable escort."

The hotel manager concurred. He, too, expressed shock and a distress I'm quite sure he genuinely felt.

"You may be sure, I'll not permit *Senhor* David to bother you any further while you are a guest at the hotel."

The happy outcome: Dr. Falcão Paiva declared he would call David off the trip to the Gorongosa reserve and he would do his best to find a substitute escort.

"You do understand, the escort is required on the orders of the government. I am obliged. Tourists also must enter the park with a guide – so in that matter there is no difference whether or not the government considers you as a tourist, or a visitor in some other capacity, *Senhor*. But I will see what I can do. It may take a little time – someone a little more mature ..."

"And less offensive ...?"

"And less offensive, certainly. Please accept my apologies, *Senhor* ..."

On my second morning in Beira word was sent up to my room that I had a guest waiting for me in the hotel lobby. When I went down, it was to discover my visitor was a young lady dressed in modest safari-style jacket and pants, a brightly-coloured kerchief tied nonchalantly about her neck. She was blonde and hatless.

"Senhor Jeremias? The tourism office has been in touch with me. They tell me you require an escort to go with you to Gorongosa ... When would you like to go?"

"How very kind of the tourism office," I replied.

And so it was; I was able to dump the one obnoxious spy who had been put on my tail – and have some discretion over the spy who would replace him. It was a small victory.

This unusual incident must have been instrumental in buying me some liberty in Beira, for I was not aware of a minder following behind me, and the young lady who had come to the hotel to introduce herself did not seem to be very interested in following me about. She had asked for a day or so to arrange some personal matters, and then we would go to Gorongosa together – no rush. I was able to poke about Beira's streets and spend time looking in shop windows; I was half-heartedly on the lookout for affordable wood carvings – aware that if I bought any of the fairly heavy ones I liked, I would have to pack them and nurse them as extra luggage on a variety of flights before finally arriving home. That limited me as to size; the prices were reasonable, but the cost of flying them would double whatever I spent, and there would have been the added hassle of having to carry them with me just to make sure they were not damaged. In the end I settled for two or three smaller pieces that could be wrapped in my clothing and stuffed into my travel bag.

The beaches of Beira, as with almost the entire Moçambique coastline, stretch out like a long ribbon, the purest sand gift-wrapping the edge of the continent, and permitting the waves to hold back and sing – sweet foot-tapping melody when the sun was shining, foot-stomping and crashing Wagner in the cyclone season. I had heard about a fine restaurant just behind the sands at *Clube Nautico*, so caught a cab and drove out the few kilometres. Today the area is residential, but at the time of my visit it was somewhat off the preferred pathways leading out of the centre of the city.

Three strange sailing craft, each the carbon copy of the other two, were pulled up at the head of the beach in front of one of the club buildings. One of them was ready with its lateen sail set for hoisting.

It was a catamaran, each of its two identical hulls finely tapered in the prow and, oddly, with neither rudder nor tiller of any description. Each pontoon had a shallow skid, but no keel. The twin hulls were battened together by cross-beams which left, in place of a deck, a cradle of tautly suspended strapping, the seawater able to slop up and run off instantly. Anyone sailing such a craft would be soaked in a flash, so it was definitely a warm-water boat. An older man, strong and bronzed by the sun, whitening hair, was tinkering about the craft, coiling sheets in preparation for taking her out. I stopped and watched for a few moments as he laid the gaff along one of the pontoons.

At that point the fellow saw me and signalled for a hand to help push the boat into the water. Thinking I might be tempted to take a dip, I had worn a bathing suit under my jeans, so kicked off shoes, shed jeans and shirt, and was ready for the beach in seconds.

Although the fibreglass hulls were each perhaps six metres in length, the whole structure – mast and sail included – was surprisingly light. Taking up a position in the stern where I could get some leverage, the two of us leaned in and it was no huge effort to shift the hulls across the sand. The older man began to talk to me in Portuguese. I had no idea what he was saying, but undoubtedly it was light commentary, banter on the joys of the day. As we heaved, he waved an arm out across the sky and back in a wide sweep across the sea, universal gesture at the breadth of ocean and the infinity of the skies. Both were an intense deep blue – each hue enormous and audacious, magnificently independent.

It was necessary to say something – my most oft-asked question on this trip:

"Do you speak English?"

"Of course I do!" he said, studying me. "Are you English?"

"I speak English. I'm Canadian."

"Then you speak French, too …"

"Not well. I'm from western Canada, and we speak English out there. I'd like to be able to speak better French. The two areas are a long way apart."

"That's a shame. My French is better than my English," he said in perfect English. "I am from Moçambique, so English is a necessity. In Beira we have many dealings with South Africans. We do business with them, they come here as visitors …"

"Is sailing popular here?" I asked.

"I am the president of our *Clube Nautico*, and we have a strong membership. Lots of young fellows like yourself – and a lot younger. School children. We teach them how to sail."

"Boats like these?"

"Yes – these are quite new, as you can see. We acquired them recently. This is a Spanish design. We have other craft, too, up in the boathouse – but these catamarans are great fun to play with. Even a beginner can learn to handle one quite quickly. We have other types, too … but I think these are the most fun."

The twin-prow of the boat bobbed at the edge of the light surf as its more substantial stern remained grounded in the sand. It would take no more than a nudge to have her fully afloat. My new acquaintance introduced himself as Caregal Ferreira. Bare-chested, bare-footed and wearing only a pair of cut-offs, he seemed so much at ease as a sailor there was no way to tell he was also, as he informed me when I asked, one of the directors of the local brewing company, *Fábrica de Cerveja da Beira*. He was curious about my interest, so he spent some moments explaining how the boat was operated.

"There's no rudder system," I queried. "How do you bring her about?"

"The best way to tell you is to show you. Jump aboard and we'll take her out."

The sea was shallow right there, the waters warm and seductive. A slight effort, and the stern came clear of the sands and we both jumped aboard.

"Sit on the strapping close under the mast – and keep your head clear of the boom," said Caregal.

I did as he ordered. It was a wet spot. In fact there was not a dry spot anywhere, and in no time the two of us were soaked by the spray that came over the prow, and the waters that surged up from beneath the strapping.

Deftly using his fingers and feeding the sheet controlling the sail, Caregal set a course at a right angle to the beach, straight out into the Indian Ocean. A light breeze blew at us from our port side.

"You maintain or alter direction by a combination of the placement of your weight on the pontoons, and the angle of the sail. A rudder is not necessary. When you do it right you can spin the craft like a top to almost any point of the compass, heading any direction you wish. She comes in pretty close to the wind, as you can see she is doing now ..."

He moved his weight forward on the port pontoon, ducking his head as the craft gybed and the boom came crashing over him from the starboard side. The rig immediately swung to starboard.

"And watch this ..." he said, again using careful placement of his weight, and feeding the sheet. With deft movements, he brought the little craft closer into the wind, and the port pontoon started to lift clear of the water. Simultaneously, we picked up speed until we were zipping across the waves faster than a gull fishing for his lunch – a thrilling chase after nothing but the fun of it.

Caregal was chuckling. He was more than a sailor – he was like a carefree bacchant, his wine the wind and sea.

"Want to take her on ...?" he shouted.

"Sure!"

"She's all yours!"

He dove overboard and started swimming for shore.

With the impetus of his leap and no tiller, the little craft shuddered and swung itself into the wind. Like a runaway pony suddenly brought to bridle, when I shifted into Caregal's place and took the sheet the whole rig – hull and sail – settled back to work as if they knew exactly what to do. For maybe an hour or more I played about, back and forth parallel with the beach. I was getting the hang of it quickly, and even experimented raising first one pontoon, then the other, each time feeling the instant swell of speed as fifty percent of the boat's drag was lifted clear of the water.

I watched Caregal walk up out of the surf and turn to see how I was doing. I was having so much fun I did not really want to end it, but eventually reckoned it was time to head in.

All was well until I could feel the first scrape of sand on the two hulls, then I lost control completely. In a second, like being on the flip-end of a schoolroom ruler, I flew like a spitball onto my backside in the shallows, the catamaran lying awkwardly over onto the side of its port pontoon, its sister pontoon high in the air and its sail flopping in the water just beside me. It happened right at the feet of my erstwhile instructor, who was standing ankle deep in the water, laughing at my antics. I was embarrassed.

"What the devil did I do wrong?" I asked Caregal.

"You did well! You did well! No matter! No damage done – you probably pulled the sheet in a little tight at the last moment, and she kicked back at you... You should have beached her full-on so both pontoons had equal drag as she ran aground. You came in at an angle, so your port pontoon dragged first ..."

We pulled the cat upright, and a few metres up onto the sand, then took the sail down and left her ready to go out again. Caregal suggested we take lunch at a beachside restaurant, so we walked up to the boathouse and the spot where I had left my clothes.

"Isn't she a little beauty? I'm trying to persuade the club to buy a few more of those. I'm pretty sure the plans are available from the builders in Barcelona, so perhaps it's possible we can build one or two ourselves ..."

Beira is a fine city with a current population today of over half-a-million. That's close to double what it was when I visited. I am told it now possesses the amenities and attractions of all great cities, so it must be very different from the place I knew – and very different from the wreckage to which the whole city was reduced during the country's civil war. My adventure aboard Caregal's catamaran seems to be even a remoter memory of Moçambique than others I have recounted here. It was during a carefree and sunshine playtime, before the gathering of dark clouds, the planting of mines and the terrible thunder of bombs and artillery, and the miseries of a population trying to find their road through it all so they could go on living. Knowing that the city was blown to smithereens, recollections of its streets and buildings are not so vivid any more. But recall of those blissful few hours playing out on the waters of the Indian Ocean in front of the *Clube Náutico* – Caregal's generosity and kind laughter, the simplicity and the fun – maybe this is why every detail of such an unusually blithe interlude should stick so tenaciously in my memory. I passed several days in Beira before and after my excursion to Gorongosa, but unfortunately never had opportunity to return to that end of the town.

Gorongosa

Happily, Maria Alves Amaral was more guide than spy. She knew and understood the traits of Africa's wild animals and turned out to be the best kind of minder I could have wished for. She was assigned to me because she knew the tourism director and, like Joaquim Lemos in Angola, now and then she had to submit to being co-opted by PIDE – on pain of the forfeiture of some aspect of the safari operation she ran with her husband. She knew all corners of Moçambique – but the game parks, and especially Gorongosa, best of all. She notified me she would be driving out there to meet up with her husband within the next day or so. With any luck we could all get together at the reserve village, Chitengo.

Among my papers I have an ancient map of Moçambique that marks the area of the Gorongosa game reserve as a *zona de caça* – a hunting zone. In 1960 the animal-rich area – until then left almost entirely to the wiles of nature – was declared a national game reserve. However, the colonial war against continued Portuguese rule flared in 1964; Moçambique was granted its independence in 1975 – and then, just two years later, came the terrible civil war that lasted through until 1992. During this extended period of warfare not many people gave a thought to the incredible throngs of the country's wild animals. Whole herds were virtually wiped out. For a few years Gorongosa had been counted one of the finest wild animal preserves in the world. The slaughter that came with the wars was nothing less than a war crime, although it is impossible to pin the blame on any one person or group. Every species in the park suffered devastation; the lion population, for instance, known to be a sub-species of the largest lions in the world prior to the war, were virtually exterminated. Likewise the elephants were killed, their ivory sold to pay for weapons, or to line the pockets of some warlord. Only a few of them escaped into the farthest reaches of bush and mountains. The rhino population was a special target of the killing spree, their horns being hacked off and exported to the Far East to raise funds for the 'war effort' of one side or the other. Powdered rhino horn, prized and costly, is considered an aphrodisiac by many throughout the Far East.

It was senseless and wanton butchery. I remember the reserve as it had been at its best. Spending time at Gorongosa with Maria and her husband, Tiago, was one of the most fulfilling experiences of that period of my life. I was indeed fortunate to see it as it had been – a natural haven for some of the most astonishing animals on the continent, the output of millennia of nature's creation prior to the idiocy of man. The war is a thing of the past, now, thank God; like the *zona de caça* marked on my map. With government funding and help from enlightened people who have vowed to restore it to its previous levels of excellence, many from organizations abroad, an effort is being made to bring the region back to its former state as a zone for wild animals. It is a project that is going to require close attention for generations.

The drive up was about four hours in duration. Maria took her small car, intending to park it at the camp in Chitengo. Tiago had driven the company's safari wagon to the park several days before, so we would have a decent mode of transport to use on the rough terrain inside the reserve.

"He'll have no idea I'm coming," I commented.

"Not important. There will be plenty of accommodation, and the group he has with him now is small, so there will be lots of room in the wagon …"

We were travelling a bush road about half-an-hour from the park village, and already I was spotting some animals. A wart hog and his mate scampered into the bush as we approached, and I had seen several species of buck poking about among the thorn trees.

"Do you think we could stop for a moment?" I asked. "I'd like to take a pee, and perhaps a shot or two of the countryside – maybe those buck we saw…?"

Maria cast about for an open space so that we could have a clear field of observation.

"Watch out for animals …" she said. "We're getting close to the park, and they don't know how to read boundary signs."

I took my pee behind the back of the car, then walked out in front where I could get a clearer view of the animals I had seen. But they had disappeared. I was looking through my camera's view-finder …

"Jeremy …!" Maria called frantically from inside the car.

Hearing a tone of alarm, I turned around just in time to see a lone lioness emerge from behind a bush about thirty metres away from the left side of the car. I froze. There was no question of running. The animal was headed slowly but quite deliberately at an angle to pass behind the rear of the car – where I had taken my pee just moments before. My mind was racing, but I was alert and felt almost serene – calm enough to calculate it was wiser to remain still than to make a dash for the car. Instinctively I knew I couldn't make it. Maria was seated behind the steering wheel on the right side of the car. I saw her lean across and unlatch the passenger door on the left, but hold it closed against the approaching lioness so that when I could move to get in the cat would already have passed by the car, left to right, at the rear. Unless she paused to sniff at my pee …

All of this took up milliseconds.

If my time's up, I remember thinking, I might as well see if I can get a good shot of the occasion … so raised the viewfinder once more to my eye.

The clicking of the camera sounded like an explosion. I remained holding my breath until I could see the lioness walking back into the bush at the far end of the car. Quick, quick like a mouse at the entrance to his hole in the wall, I hopped back into the car.

It was the only photograph I took on my Gorongosa excursion that did not pan out well. The focus was none too sharp and so it was blurred – but overall an accurate testament to the frailty of my 'steely-calm' nerves.

"Well, I wanted to see lions," I told Maria.

She rolled her eyes.

"Everybody wants to see lions," she mimicked. "That's the reason they come here. But not everyone sees them quite the way you do. No panache."

"I'm really sorry to have alarmed you," I told her earnestly. "I certainly didn't do that on purpose."

Passing lioness

"Well, let's not tell Tiago – at least not right away. He'd be furious – at both of us. The number one rule of the park is: *remain in your car at all times* – with the windows rolled up. Technically we weren't yet in the park, so you're not all that guilty …!"

We did not tell Tiago when we arrived at Chitengo, so were able to avoid his pique. In fact, I found him such an upbeat and warm personality it was hard to imagine him being 'furious.' For the past several days he had been showing the park's wildlife to two clients from South Africa – men whose safari kits were spanking new, and whose bush nous certified this was a major 'first' into the wild. It was not hard to imagine their natural avocations required polished shoes and brief cases.

"They'll be leaving in their own vehicle after lunch, so why don't we all spend a sociable few hours together. Later, before it gets too dark, we might go out to a waterhole I know, and tomorrow we can take our time to go a little further afield …?"

Agreed, and so we spent that afternoon in camp, with the two South Africans enthusiastically going over the high points of their own adventure. The lions had particularly impressed them.

"I've seen lions before, in Kruger, but these ones are huge ..."

His companion popped his eyes and nodded in agreement.

391

"Bloody enormous, man!"

The lioness with which Maria and I had crossed paths earlier in the day had not entered my consciousness because of its size, necessarily, but rather because of its proximity. In any case I was aware of the compact I had made with Maria not to raise the issue in front of Tiago. But later, thinking a little more cogently of the encounter, I remembered the back of the animal was near the same level as the sill of the car window – and that a lioness is a considerably smaller animal than her mate. It was a large lioness by any standard.

After the South Africans had left, and shortly before sundown, Tiago, Maria and I bundled into his safari wagon and drove to a waterhole a few kilometres from the camp. We parked on a low hill off to one side where we had a good view of the entire surface of the water – and waited. It was not long before several gazelles and zebras approached to drink. All the hoofed species seemed to congregate around one section of the edge of the hole, on the side farthest away from us. In a little while a clan of lions, eight or ten of them, ambled over with slow deliberation to drink as a group on our side of the hole. Hunters and quarry – truce.

The following day Tiago took me in his bush vehicle to see lions – more lions and bigger lions than I had ever seen before. By the end of the day I reckoned we had seen several families of them – maybe close to thirty in total.

On my return to Toronto I wrote an article for one of the local papers which I entitled '*A Vanishing Nobility.*' It was published in 1964 and is useful reading as the expression of what by now must be an historical viewpoint, for much has changed in all of Africa's parks since then – and likely in Gorongosa most of all:

The guide leaned across the front seat of the safari wagon. He was pointing to a small dark splotch in the distant sweep of the African plain that blended with a mirage on the horizon-line.

"Waterbuck," he said.

There was a stillness about the scene; a whole herd of waterbuck grazing peacefully on a green pasture slightly below where we sat in the vehicle observing them. A shallow lake spread out beside them, and some of the animals were up to their hocks in the water. The waterbuck is a large antelope an amateur naturalist might easily identify by the flashes of white on its rump. The animal has a habit of turning its back when it notices it has been noticed – which aids greatly in identification. A waterbuck is deep red-brown in colour, all over except when it turns around. Then it looks as though it had accidently sat itself down on a freshly-painted white toilet seat. The ring of white on its bum is startling.

Moçambique's Gorongosa Park, which I had come to visit for two days, is one of many protected areas for Africa's wild animals, and at three thousand two hundred square miles in size, is one of the biggest parks on the continent. On this occasion, at any rate, the herd's vanishing act was no more than a trick played on the eyes. One moment the herd was before us, the next it had vanished completely. Likely some predators had approached the pool to drink.

But Africa's herds of noble wildlife are vanishing from even the protected areas.

They are vanishing because of poachers; because of the lax administration of even laxer laws which are meant to control the slaughter of wild animals – and this laxity is continent-wide.

For me, it was particularly important to see game on this trip through Africa. Even if I should return one day, it would probably never again appear in such profusion. It is hard to imagine the African bush without its animals.

There's an economic value to Africa's game. It attracts tourists; the average for Kenya and Tanzania together in 1964: nearly forty million dollars. If systematically controlled, it would also be quite possible to 'farm' the vast gazelle herds in all parts of the continent, providing much-needed protein for millions of Africans.

Those who know and understand the rhythm of the bush will tell you there's yet another value – but to know it and benefit from it one has to be prepared to study and learn, observe and wait. It has to do with patience and finding value in the beauty of nature's wildlife; that although so many do not see it this way, its worth is infinitely greater than the price one pays at the bazaar for a zebra's or gazelle's hide, an elephant's foot, its ivory, or a rhinoceros horn. The monetary value of wildlife the world over, properly husbanded and managed, would far outstrip the sale of body parts, skins and furs as trophies, trinkets and curiosities. In Africa, so blessed with so much and such variety, there is an entire economy wrapped up in the enlightened oversight of the continent's wildlife.

Man should check himself and think:

Just to observe them – the lion, elephant, buffalo, rhino, the scores of different species of gazelle (and even the ugly little warthog) – the incredible numbers of birds (one hundred and thirty different species to be found in, or passing through, Gorongosa) man must rely on the material equipment of his ingenuity. He needs a rifle to defend himself; a car to provide himself with transportation and protection as he heads into the bush; he needs a camera, a pair of binoculars, the right food and the right clothing – and a thousand-and-one other things to give him comfort, security, sustenance and pleasure. Strip him of this paraphernalia and he is suddenly naked – physically inferior to every other creature in the bush.

The rhythm of the bush is the rhythm of life and death, survival not always of the fittest. It was a pattern of nature that existed long before man ever set his foot there. Seeking that pattern, feeling it, brings a man to earth. For this is a part of Life itself in which his participation is limited to what he can see at a distance through the lens of his binoculars or replicate through the deft manipulation of his camera.

We started to drive across the plain. Way on the left of the waterbuck herd a small yellow dot moved slowly under the hot afternoon sun. The guide said it was a lion. He'd know. We drew closer, and I could make out his shape as he moved away from us, loping along with his heavy shoulders heaving, his head sleepily low: a magnificent fur-collared male, the level of his back a full handspan higher than the level of the car's windowsill. He had set himself a course across the level plain; he had no intention of deviating, stopping or being distracted.

We pulled up beside him and he ignored us. We drove in tight circles around him and finally came to a stop, broadside on, about thirty feet in front of him.

His eyes were closed to narrow slits. Slobber dripped from his jowls. He had eaten well that day.

Not once did he falter or change his pace. He walked straight at us and, when no more than two or three metres from the car, it was us who gave way. Had we not done so and he had taken us as an impediment to his progress, he almost certainly would have attacked the car. He was proud.

We saw more lions and elephants that day than I could possibly count, to say nothing of the numerous other species – waterbuck, bushbuck, duiker, impala, springbok, sable.

Hippopotamuses by the score had gathered on the muddy shore of an expansive shallow lake. Timid creatures except when alarmed, they lumbered off awkwardly and took refuge in the water, snorting at us from a safe distance as we sat inside the car and watched them.

They amused me. Every one of them, even the youngsters, looked like fat English colonels wallowing in the warm pools of some fashionable spa.

Returning to the camp at Chitengo that evening, we rounded a corner and almost collided with a bull elephant. He was standing by the side of the track, feeding himself great clumps of leaves that he tore with his trunk from the top of a tree.

Elephants are considered one of the most dangerous species in the bush. They attack without warning and make an unholy mess of anything or anybody on the receiving-end of their rage. With other game, a man on foot can at least climb a tree to safety. But an elephant would pluck him out, or simply tear the tree out of the ground, roots and all.

Keeping the engine running, we sat and watched this sight for nearly fifteen minutes, finally sneaking away and feeling rather ashamed of ourselves for intruding on the fellow at his supper. Being ignored the way that old bull elephant ignored us can be a humbling experience.

When I was in Kenya several years ago, I heard a story about elephants and ivory poachers. I thought of it as we watched that fellow at his dinner.

A band of African poachers had crossed the old Belgian Congo frontier into Uganda. There they had managed to drive a herd of sixty elephants far enough into a swamp that they sank to their bellies. Had they been left alone at this stage they would doubtless have been able to make it safely to firmer land. Being relatively light in weight, the poachers had been able to walk across that portion of the swamp, stepping from one tuft of grass to another. Once in among the defenseless animals, they had systematically shot every one of them, and made off across the border with their precious ivory spoil. Nothing was known of the incident until the following dry season when a game warden chanced by. The vultures and scavengers had been at work and picked the bones clean. All that was left were the white skeletons held fast by the hard-cracked mud.

For years the people of the Congo have been renowned for their skill and determination as ivory poachers – albeit an ignoble fame. Even today, in the streets of Leopoldville, one will find more ivory being sold than in practically any other city in Africa.

Elephants are deliberate in their grace – a fact that belies their size and shape. There is something utterly meticulous about the motion of an elephant, the way he will pick up his feet to walk, or the way in which he will raise his trunk like a crane to rip the foliage off trees, then double it back under to his mouth to pack in a whole bale of shrubbery and let it rumble its way to his belly. His ears, when he flaps them, look like bedsheets hanging on the clothesline in a back yard.

We had felt privileged and humbled to watch one old bull at dinner – but the following day we skulked like children on some furtive escapade, hiding in the bushes to invade the privacy of another fellow taking a bath.

We were down wind of him, so he never knew we were there.

We had seen him coming and had a fair idea where he was headed. We were able to reach the water hole before him.

He came slowly through the bush, his regular route, and paused at the edge of the water to test the mud with his front feet. Then he slid forward, up to his knees in the brown muck, and splashed great trunks full of it over his back and sides. Then he lay down in it and seemed to hum to himself in contentment before getting awkwardly to his feet and ambling off, a good deal grubbier than when he had arrived. Elephants take baths to make themselves filthy, not to clean themselves up. It helps to keep flies and parasites at bay.

Hunting for sport or necessity is a far cry from indiscriminate killing, as is the necessary 'game-cropping' in areas where herds occasionally reach pest proportions. But Africa's poachers are indelicate men, and they will go after anything. The ivory tusks of elephants fetch a poacher about forty-five cents a pound; rhino horn, which is later powdered and sold in the Far East as an aphrodisiac (it is nothing of the kind; I'm told by those who claim to know that it does not work) is worth about one dollar and forty cents a pound.[42]

Middlemen jack up the prices, each of them taking considerable profits off the top. Final market prices can vary anywhere between ten and twelve dollars a pound for rhino horn, and one-and-a-quarter to three-and-a-quarter dollars per pound for ivory, depending on its quality.

Illegal meat sales (bush meat) are particularly profitable to a poacher, even though he will often not be able to get rid of the meat until it is rancid.

Hides are always marketable. The tails of wildebeest, used as fly-whisks, have been known to sell for as much as five dollars and fifty cents. In stores all over Africa, one will find hollowed elephant hooves being sold as doorstops and waste paper baskets.

Whips and walking sticks are made from strips of skin cut from the flanks of elephant, rhino and hippo. Ladies' handbags are made from gazelle, monkey skins and crocodiles.

In Kenya, in a single year (1960) somewhere between four thousand and five thousand elephants were killed illegally. Between seven hundred and nine hundred and fifty rhinos were slaughtered in the same way, and the proportions are no different in other regions of Africa.

And so the game herds are vanishing. Unfortunately teaching the world the value of its wildlife resources may take longer than the process of elimination mankind has so irresponsibly adopted.

If that happens then I have surely been privileged on this trip. I may never get to see these animals again – and likely nowhere ever again in such abundance.

---

[42] Game-cropping: culling large herds – killing selected numbers – was considered a necessity in the days before tranquilization and transportation were introduced, and when there were much larger herds of all animal species. Estimated prices are for 1963. That said, while at Gorongosa I was told by the director that about four hundred cape buffaloes were currently being transported from Gorongosa to the park at Maputo – a big move by any standard.

It was impossible not to compare the abundance of wildlife I had seen in Kenya during my military service there in the mid-fifties with what is now known to be the case. As young soldiers, we were spending every single day in the outdoors, patrolling the bush and forests, and so coming into contact with every sort of animal. There was an unbelievable profusion of rhinos, for instance – both black and white – that one simply cannot imagine today. They would wander into coffee plantations, trampling the crop and causing millions of dollars in damage, ultimately necessitating culling by the game department (no tranquilizing in those times). Rhino could wander into your aunt's back garden at tea time and scare the wits out of the ladies caught with their little fingers in the air. They could (and did!) appear at the kitchen window while supper was being prepared. And they were out there in the bush as we patrolled and tried our best to avoid them – and the buffalo, and the big cats, and the elephant ... On the road from Nyeri to Nairobi, I remember, we would find giraffe and ostrich and impala and Thomson's gazelle and zebra by the score, as well as many other and uncountable species of gazelle.

It is a very different story today. There are far fewer numbers, but one may take heart in the awareness of the various game departments involved, and in the laws of the lands where the animals may yet be found. Poaching is still a major problem, but after years of neglect, at last there are responsible entities attempting to come to grips with it. There is less and less legal hunting, too; it has been discovered sightseeing and photo safaris are a major source of taxable income that, over time, can eclipse funds engendered by permitting trophy hunting.

Maria, Tiago and I spent two full days at Gorongosa before heading back to Beira. The 'menu' of wildlife presented to us was spectacular:

Lions (extremely large and proud, and dozens of them) – elephants (not as big as those in the Maputo reserve, but impressive nonetheless, and plentiful). Uncountable were the bushbuck – duiker – buffalo – zebra – hyena – sable – hippo – baboon – waterbuck – wildebeest – wart hog – impala.

No rhinos. While we were there, in the southern portion of the park, the rhinos were located only in the northern mountainous region, closed to visitors at the time.

I have referred briefly to the slaughter of the animals in Gorongosa during the independence and civil wars in the territory. There are no easily accessible and accurate figures available for the number of animals, of all species, killed within the park. The latest word is that the poaching does continue in various Moçambique reserves, but that the hard-pressed government is determined to combat it.

Throughout Africa, the trade in 'bush meat,' body parts and skins has always been a clandestine and ugly business, and for many years prior to entering Moçambique I was interested to know how widespread the activity was. One UNESCO figure I unearthed in 1956, long before accurate reporting had been undertaken, indicated that over fifty thousand elephants had been killed that year alone. Just elephants – no other species included in the survey. The figure is particularly staggering when one considers that it was at a time when most of Africa's independence and civil wars had yet to be initiated; that the years of most widespread slaughter had yet to begin.

Just as this portion of this narrative was being prepared for publication, I was fortunate enough to make contact with staff working on the recuperation of the animals in Gorongosa National Park.

For the first time since the 1980s, reports indicate sightings of more than one hundred thousand of the larger mammals; these include more than six thousand impala, more than one thousand buffalo, more than six hundred wildebeest and more than five hundred hippos. They have counted nearly five hundred and fifty elephant. In a concerted helicopter aerial survey conducted at the close of 2018, numbers appeared to be up all around; a report of the survey claims these numbers applied only to certain species within a limited count block. Numbers outside the surveyed area show that although there is much progress yet to be made, the park is at last on the path to a healthy recovery.

Gorongosa had been decimated during the civil war, with the sad loss of virtually all of the park's famed lion population. Estimates were that well over ninety-five percent of the wildlife was slaughtered during the period 1977 to 1992.

Species	Total number counted
Blue wildebeest	627
Buffalo	1,021
Bushbuck	1,787
Bushpig	203
Common Reedbuck	10,821
Duiker grey	66
Duiker red	28
Eland	142
Elephant	544
Hartebeest	647
Hippo	546
Impala	6,274
Kudu	2,105
Nyala	2,269
Oribi	4,027
Sable	968
Warthog	11,274
Waterbuck	57,016
Zebra	44
Total	100,409

The results of the 2018 helicopter count of mammals at Gorongosa.

At first the park's recovery was slow; it could have been abandoned altogether, the lands turned over to agriculture or mining. However, a far-sighted approach on the part of the Moçambique government has drawn considerable interest from non-profit agencies and actively-interested philanthropists. In 2008, American philanthropist Gregory Carr, who had inaugurated the Carr Centre for Human Rights Policy at Harvard University, backed the idea of 'Peace Parks' presented to him by Moçambique's then-president, Joaquim Chissano. The Moçambicano leader had been working in tandem with his friend Nelson Mandela, then president of South Africa, to establish cross-border parks that would enhance employment and create cooperative areas of human rights. Animal husbandry, and working with local populations in an effort to teach them the benefits of preservation, was a major part of the concept. Carr was so taken with the idea that he put up twenty million dollars towards the project at Gorongosa. Working in conjunction with other non-profits, the programme at Gorongosa is widely considered a successful model on which to base other similar efforts at Africa's beleaguered game reserves.

The reader will note there are no big cats listed – no lions, no leopards, no cheetahs. Operatives at the park have explained the big cats are not successfully surveyed from the air, but that the current count of lions on the park's database is one hundred and forty six – and growing. This is a most hopeful sign, an indication that the enormous effort being made at Gorongosa to build the lion population seems to be working. Recent reports from other areas of the continent paint an Africa-wide picture of lion populations having been depleted by as much as seventy percent in just the past fifty years.

In March 2018 guests at the Chitengo lodge took photographs of the first leopard seen at Gorongosa in fourteen years.

Cheetahs are thought to have numbered around one hundred thousand in Africa in 1900. They are a particularly shy and delicate animal; today there are estimated to be, continent wide, fewer than nine thousand of them. Four cheetahs were introduced to Gorongosa in 2011, but none managed to survive in the wild.

Censorship and Arrest

My journey was nearing its completion. I was informed that rather than departing from Lourenço Marques, my flight would leave in a couple of days from Beira. The plane would be coming up from the capital and passing this way anyway, so there seemed little point in going south only to fly back to Beira, before crossing Africa on its westward leg to Luanda. I spent what time I could arranging my notes and photographs and writing a few last-minute letters. I was occupied with this one evening when there was a knock at my hotel room door.

Two Portuguese, both about my age, were standing on the threshold. I knew neither of them, but they were aware of my name, and they asked if they could speak to me. Rui Cartaxana, a reporter for the *Diário de Moçambique*, spoke very little English; his companion, Virgílio de Lemos, a poet and a pharmaceutical salesman, was able to speak for the two of them. They were both *oposicionistas*, they told me, and they had information for me.

It sounded dramatic, so I encouraged them to keep talking. I was wary. Operatives for PIDE had a way of presenting themselves as sympathetic to people they supposed might be *oposicionistas* – or worse, communists! 'Communist' to the skunky mind of a PIDE agent was anyone who disagreed with the government in Lisboa; once they were satisfied their prey had adequately revealed him- or herself, they could take great delight in getting nasty – and arresting – the person they had initially befriended. On the principle of 'shoot first and ask questions afterwards,' these goons had carte blanche. They could do, and did, a lot of damage before letting one of their prisoners go free for lack of evidence. I would be leaving in a day or so, and whatever viewpoint I might have expressed could not have amounted to much. But one could never tell; there seemed to be nothing more satisfying to a mean man than humiliating and making an example of someone he has the power to bully. I was pretty sure that by now at least some of the pieces or letters I had written from Angola, or even from Moçambique, must have been monitored – if, indeed, they had not been opened and read the moment I sent them off. My sympathies by then must have been well-understood by PIDE.

Virgílio and his companion talked exhaustively about all manner of politics, much of it the theoretical gas-bag excuses and whimperings I had heard before from others. But their performance had about it a driving sort of desperation to let me know how life really was in their world. There were dark things happening in this deceptively sunny corner of Africa, they told me – something I already understood. One thing they told me that lined-up with my own thinking was that the man who had met me at the airport when first I arrived, Fernando David – the man about whom I had complained so forcefully to the director of tourism — was a PIDE agent first and foremost, but whose front was to present himself as a journalist. Somehow their description fitted my own assessment, and I began to listen to them a little more carefully, to ask questions. Virgílio told me Rui worked at the newspaper with David, that he was himself a member of a local clandestine group collecting data on PIDE agents and fascist sympathizers. The group had certain knowledge of David's malevolence, he assured me.

Another piece of information that gave Virgílio some credence was the way in which he told me he had been imprisoned for his contrary political thinking – that the charge against him had not been so serious but had nonetheless warranted him being locked up for fifteen months. He had been released only the previous December and cautioned to be more circumspect in future about the opinions he expressed in his poetry and the public readings of his works. Since his release he had concentrated more on his pharmaceutical sales than in seeking the applause of the café audiences who frequented his soirées. He laughed, but it was the bitter laughter of a man denied the right to express himself creatively. The vitriol of his indignation at this suppression of his thoughts and words somehow rang true.

I might have thought the two of them communists but for the fact – and I knew it – that Portuguese communists are far too well-organized to send two of their own blundering into my hotel room. In the end I had to see these two fellows for what I believe they truly were – angry and disillusioned political opponents of the fascist regime that controlled their lives, and anxious to meet with a foreign journalist who might spread abroad details of the plight felt by many of their countrymen. For this they were prepared to take risks and make sacrifices.

We continued our talk for an hour or more in my room, then went downstairs to the hotel dining room to have something to eat.

"Are neither of you afraid of being seen with me?" I asked Virgílio.

He laughed.

"It could be a problem," he admitted – then added he would prefer to be open about the people to whom he spoke.

"PIDE expects me to hide. They want me to be afraid. I refuse to be bullied, and I shall continue to demand the right to be seen with anyone I like, and speak to anyone I like …"

"That could be hard on you," I commented.

"I have been in their jails. They know that I am known, that my poetry is honest, and I am known by my audience to speak truthfully. That is important to me. PIDE bothers me a great deal, but I will not allow their tactics to defeat me …"

Over dinner we relaxed and even managed to make light of their political predicament.

"In Portugal today there are ten million political viewpoints," said Virgílio. "Our problem has always been our inability to coalesce to defeat the fascists. They have the guns and the money; we simply have our voices. It will change in time. It always does – but it is a slow process. Those who hold the money are reluctant to let go of it …"

I had already figured it out, but these two young men reminded me anyway: there were two forms of opposition in Moçambique: those in favour of independence for the colonies, but with white Portuguese rule, and those in favour of independence no matter who rules – which would ensure black rule.

"And which are you two?" I asked.

They both laughed. Continued white rule of any kind was a sure recipe for war, they reasoned. It would not work. Black rule – or war. No other choice.

"There are competent Africans in Moçambique with whom the Portuguese could certainly work very well. The trouble is ..." here Virgílio laughed aloud, "... the Portuguese have been trying to rule this place for five hundred years and look where it has brought us ...! Maybe it's time to give it back to the Africans!"

Over dinner Rui suggested I go with them to the newspaper office to see how the *Diário de Moçambique* was operated – but, particularly, to examine the censorship routine for both news reports and photographs.

The office was empty except for cleaning staff, so we were able to poke about at will. Rui knew his way around very well. He showed me the office of the government censor and described how the process worked. The office was open to the newsroom, so we turned on the light and walked in. All incoming reports – foreign and domestic – were brought here to the censor before they were permitted to proceed to the editorial desk. The censor would decide what was news and what had to be kept from the public. I noted a pair of scissors on his desk – the most essential tool of his miserable trade. Everything that went out of his office had to be stamped: 'cut,' 'suspended' or 'approved.' It was a thorough process. Nothing considered fit to print escaped examination.

It was late when my two companions finally walked me back to my hotel. We stood for a few minutes on the pavement outside the main door, then they bid me goodnight and turned away. I entered the hotel alone and went straight to the reception desk to collect my key.

The receptionist looked nervous as he stood at his desk.

"Your flight is booked for tomorrow, *Senhor* Jeremias," he said, handing me my key and looking past my shoulder.

I turned to see two men walking quickly towards me across the foyer.

"What's going on?" I asked the receptionist. He did not answer.

Instead, the two men came to stand on either side of me, and one of them spoke to me in barely comprehensible English.

"Your room?" he said, at the same time putting his hand on my back and giving me a gentle push forward.

Their insistence had a momentum to it, so I led the two of them to my door, unlocked it and turned on the main light. Both entered the room, but to my relief did not close the door behind them.

The man who had spoken to me initially pulled out a wallet and showed me an identification card. It showed his photograph, and I could read quite clearly, among words that I could not read, *'Polícia Internacional e de Defesa do Estado'* – PIDE.

I understood right away, but neither of us could talk intelligibly to each other, so I went to the telephone and called down to reception.

"I have the police in my room and we are having trouble communicating... could you possibly have someone come up who can translate?"

The concierge arrived a few moments later.

"I understand he's an officer from PIDE," I said. "I don't understand what he wants me to do. Would you please talk to him and tell me what he says?"

The concierge spoke nervously to the PIDE agent for a minute or two. Then, with a sense of understanding the situation, turned back to me.

"You will be leaving Moçambique for Lisboa on a flight later today. Until the police arrive to take you to the airport, you are to remain in your room."

"Am I under arrest?" I asked.

The two men spoke again, and then the concierge said:

"No – you are not arrested. But you will be if you attempt to leave your room. I am sorry, *Senhor*, but there is nothing the hotel can do, except perhaps to make your final hours here as comfortable as possible. We can arrange to bring your meals to the room ..."

I looked at my watch. It was well after midnight.

"At what time does the flight leave?" I asked.

The concierge queried the PIDE agent.

"He doesn't know the exact time, but it will likely be the afternoon flight. There is a flight that leaves everyday at five o'clock for Luanda ..."

I had less than twenty-four hours to kill. Not being permitted to leave my hotel room was a tedious imposition, but at least it was comfortable. Members of the hotel staff were accommodating, inviting me to call down to the desk for anything they could provide me. The room itself had good lighting, a table and chairs, and the bed when I needed to stretch out. I was not short of work to keep me busy. I could write by hand into my notebooks or diary, or I could even set up my typewriter and get an article or two ready to send off to Toronto. In the end I decided not to do this last; I feared whatever story I wrote might be confiscated, but I was not so worried about my notebooks. Over the years I had developed a form of speed writing for taking notes – a series of blips and dashes filling my various notebooks, and was satisfied even PIDE would not bother with them. The scrawl would have been unintelligible to anyone trying to decipher them.

The two PIDE agents who had accosted me were not overt heavies; they had a job to do and as long as I was being co-operative, they would have had no reason to treat me badly. They knew I was an invited guest in their country and they had doubtless been instructed not to cause their government any further or unnecessary embarrassment. I had managed to travel throughout Angola as well as almost the entire schedule of my stay in Moçambique before the Portuguese authorities caught up with me, twigged to the idea that I favoured rather more an opposing viewpoint to the government's – and had probably come to that decision as a consequence of earnest journalistic investigation. As soon as the first of my writing from Angola started appearing in the Toronto papers, clippings had certainly found their way back to the ministry in Lisboa. I imagined a harried Jorge Ritto, in his consular office back in Toronto, scissors in hand as he clipped those of my articles that had appeared in the press, trying to explain to his superiors his inept choice of public relations representative. What capped my fate, I learned much later, was a piece that Arnold Edinburgh had published in *Saturday Night* magazine. He had taken a quote buried deep in the body of the text and used it for the title: '*These Portuguese Looked Like Africans to Me.*' As a guest of the government I had by now run my course and had already become an embarrassment; I felt the Portuguese authorities wanted nothing more, now, than to limit the damage, powder their red faces and get me the hell out of their hair by encouraging me to quit their country more or less voluntarily. However, I was still their guest, and reckoned they could not be too overt about their displeasure ...

By now, at the end of my journey through Moçambique, I was becoming increasingly irritated by the incessant surveillance and suspicion surrounding my every move and realized I had begun to feel that way while still in Angola. On several occasions I had gone out of my way to escape my minders, and at least a few times I had been able to set up meetings with people very clearly in opposition to the Lisboa regime. In Moçambique I had travelled from the very south to the Rio Rovuma that forms the frontier with Tanzania in the far north, then worked my way south again. And here in Beira, at the point of my intended departure, PIDE (like the cavalry late for its final charge) arrived on the doorstep of my hotel room to arrest me and escort me to the airport. It was hard not to smile at the futility.

The following day I was handcuffed, led from the hotel and, at the airport, loaded aboard a hump-backed Super Constellation to be shipped back to Lisboa – presumably in disgrace. Two different PIDE escorts, both stone-faced and less sympathetic than their companions of the night before, took their charge seriously. They sat on either side of me in silence, and I remained handcuffed even after we were airborne.

It was the longest airplane journey I have ever suffered – thirty-two hours in the air (plus two tedious layovers) aboard a lumbering airliner that reeked of cigarette smoke, howling babies competing the entire time with the loud drone of the engines. My two garlic-saturated captors, both looking like the heavies they were in fact, wore almost identical crumpled light khaki tropical suits – cheap, stained by sweat, both men wearing coloured socks that must surely have turned rancid in their scuffed and unpolished shoes – now slouched in their seats. One snored.

From Beira we were able to cross Southern and Northern Rhodesia and then the width of Angola without too much fear of attack. We sat inside the plane at Luanda while the fuel tanks were being filled, a new load of passengers packing the seating to capacity with homebound families. We then headed northwest in a wide arc far out over the Atlantic to avoid the hostile air space of the countries in Africa's continental western bump – Gabon, Camaroon, Nigeria, Mali, Algeria and Morocco. All of them were vociferously anti-Portuguese, had recently denied overflight or landing privileges, and any one of which would have delighted in causing us even greater troubles. Instead we were required to fly around West Africa to land at Bissau in Portuguese Guiné.

Despite the discomfort of our stopover in Luanda, I was lucky to be granted a significant reprieve.

An elderly gentleman I later learned was named Amándio Van der Kleij boarded the plane and was immediately recognized by both of my escorts. They paid the newcomer a regard bordering on servility. Clambering out of their seats, the three of them talked excitedly in Portuguese. Then the newcomer took his seat immediately behind the bank of seats we occupied.

He leaned forward and spoke to me in a precise but almost antique

407

accented English, clearly a man of some substance.

"These men tell me they're escorting you back to Lisboa," he said to me, anxious to chat.

I tried to turn and look at him.

"What have you done?" he asked.

"They haven't really told me," I replied. "But I think it has something to do with the fact I'm a journalist. They don't appear to care for what I have been writing ..."

"Oh – very bad! No good at all! Terrible crime, to be a journalist. Not many of you understand what we have been going through down here. But come and sit beside me, here. I'd like to know you a little better – and I can probably tell you a story you could put in your newspaper ..."

Once again, he leaned forward and spoke to my two captors.

"Clever fellows!" Van der Kleij confided, when my handcuffs had been removed and my captors allowed me to sit in the seat behind.

"They were with my regiment until earlier this year, but now they are members of the police."

The story he told me was both amusing and astonishing, but for some reason I never did manage to 'put it in my newspaper.' A Lisboa businessman of exceptional wealth and social standing, as well as the lord over vast estates – *latifúndios* – in the country's Alentejo province, Van der Kleij was a man already into his late sixties. Although his name was unmistakably Dutch – dating from the XIII century when Portugal traded salt and preserved fish with the people of the northern lowlands – the family was staunchly Portuguese. When war broke out in Angola van der Kleij's aristocratic pedigree and wealth was such that he was able to approach the country's dictator personally. At least in the manner he recounted the story (and, one might suppose, with grandiose ideas of chivalry and nationalistic fervor) he pleaded with his leader to be allowed a place of honour in the military – in the very centre of the action.

"Salazar told me not to be such a clown," Van der Kleij laughed. "He said I was already an old man, and that I would be of far more use to him if I'd just put my money to work."

And so he had done just that. At his own expense, he told me matter of factly, he had raised a battalion of one thousand men, equipped and trained them in Portugal, then sent them to fight in the north of Angola as his own private army. Now and then, as he was able to take time away from his

Alentejo farm, he would fly down to Luanda himself and take command of them in the bush.

"It was like a holiday for me ... gave me something to do when I needed to escape the rigors of family!"

He was immensely proud of his troops, and related how they, also, were enormously proud to be serving under him. Right now, he said, he was completing an especially sentimental visit to Angola – where, after two years, he had been attending a formal military ceremony to bequeath his beloved regiment to the ranks of the regular Portuguese army.

"Really, I've just been having a wonderful time – the greatest adventure of my life. But all good things come to an end. I must step aside. There are more professional commanders in the regular army," he admitted.

Our plane was due to make just one stop in West Africa – at Bissau in Portuguese Guiné.

"The governor there is a friend of mine. Vasco Rodrigues – former navy flyer. Wonderful fellow! He knows I'm arriving and will be coming to the airport to meet me. Would you like to have a chat with him? They're fighting a war in Guiné, too, you know. Perhaps he can also give your paper a good story ...?"

"I'd love to, but I'm in irons!" I pointed out.

"Yes, strictly speaking, but you're in my custody now, and these fellows will stand aside if I ask them. You don't need to worry about that. Besides, you can't really run off anywhere, can you? We don't even have to tell the governor – though if I know him, he'd immensely enjoy the humour of the situation."

The blinkered and nonsensical derring-do of this obscure and vicious little colonial war seemed to permit the occasional gesture of what passed for romantic chivalry. At last the Portuguese upper classes could trumpet the righteousness of their imperial fight, blithely immune to the reality of the horrors faced by the young men who were doing most of the dirty work for them.

The two police heavies had expressed their concern I might attempt a run for freedom, but they need not have bothered. Van der Kleij argued on my behalf with much shrugging and arm-waving assurance (plus appropriate facial contortions), all of it expressing his conviction that I would be safe in his custody. In the end he was obliged to make a spirited surrender when his two former regimental comrades insisted their jobs would be on the line if it was discovered they had removed my handcuffs while I was not actually inside the plane.

"I'm very sorry," he apologized. "But we must respect that they have their job to do," said Van der Kleij, and he smiled broadly as he offered me a delightful Latin shrug.

And so it was that even though I was cuffed and clearly under a most restrictive form of arrest, right there in the arrivals lounge of Bissau's international airport, I got to interview Vasco António Martins Rodrigues. Garrulous fellow, so happy he was to be meeting with his old friend Van der Kleij – and, it seemed by the attention he paid me, happy to treat as friend the friend of his friend. Till that moment his name had never been of significance to me, and I'm very sure he never paid attention to mine. Nor, surprisingly, did he appear to pay any great attention to the fact I was in custody at the time, and standing before him with my hands securely manacled. He was safe, he could have been sure of that with two policemen right there. But more than anything, he was just deliriously overjoyed to see his old friend once again. He glanced at my hands, then looked full into my face – but Van der Kleij was right there before him, and immediately this open and congenial man looked to his friend with a lively and generous smile. His eyes neither narrowed nor twitched as I sat beside him on an airport couch, pen and notepad in hand. His greeting was in Portuguese, but for my benefit alone he thereafter spoke to me in English.

It was awkward trying to take notes. I was shackled at the wrists by what amounted to a two-link chain. At one point, Governor Rodrigues obligingly reached over and helped steady the notepad I was holding in my lap with my left hand. I was having difficulty holding the pad at the same time as manipulating the contorted fingers of my right hand. Note taking required concentration, and no little dexterity.

The governor suppressed a smile, using Portuguese to make a comment I could only guess at. Van der Kleij responded in English:

"He's not a criminal, he's a journalist."

"Could be the same thing ..." said the governor with a degree of cordiality, and we all laughed.

The information the governor imparted during this artless interview was the usual standard fare: fighting a 'classical' guerilla war, Portuguese troops in this tiny West African territory had the situation 'entirely in hand,' the governor claimed. He attempted to describe the tactics employed by the nationalists trying to set Portuguese Guiné free from Lisboa. The governor explained the nationalists were infiltrating from across the borders of the Republic of Guinea (Conakry) and Senegal, hiding out in the jungles and swamps in a series of hit-and-run actions. The problem was always the 'outsiders!' It was a type of warfare little different from that then in progress in northern Angola, and was thought to be the form of warfare now being prepared for Moçambique by nationalist organizations headquartered in Tanganyika, he said.

However, he insisted, the Portuguese administration of all townships in Guiné was secure and under control ...

Commenting on a Portuguese government statement made in Lisboa just the previous July, that the rebels were in control of fifteen percent of the territory, the governor said:

"That is a misunderstanding. The terrorists are *operating* in about fifteen percent of the country, but they certainly do not control that much of it."

Most of the action was taking place in the swampy region south of the Rio Corobal, infiltration of men and supplies coming from Guinea (Conakry), he claimed.

"In the last few months we have been having some trouble in the north as well – with terrorists coming across from Senegal. The territory's entire population – six hundred and fifty thousand – is with us, loyal to Portugal. The trouble always comes from outside."

Rodrigues estimated the white population in Guiné numbered about twenty thousand, a figure which included the armed forces stationed there. The Portuguese army employed considerable numbers of African troops in the territory. I requested, but he was unable to give, any figures on the number of casualties suffered on either side in the crisis.

"Perhaps about fifty whites have been killed in total – and many innocent Africans, of course. But I cannot give you exact numbers." He was also unable (or unwilling) to be specific about the number of Portuguese troops employed in the territory.[43]

Flat, swampy land, with dense jungle, and crisscrossed by hundreds of streams and rivers, Portuguese Guiné's economy then rested almost entirely on the cultivation of rice, groundnuts and palm. Because of the harsh terrain,

---

[43] At war's end, in 1974, the statistics for Guiné Bissau's eleven-year independence war: Portuguese combatants – nearly two thousand one hundred killed; nearly four thousand left with permanent psychological or physical deficiencies. African combatants – more than six thousand confirmed killed; approximately four thousand unconfirmed; approximately five thousand civilian deaths.

poor communications and an unhealthy climate, many Portuguese considered the country virtually indefensible. Its economic value to Portugal had always been comparatively minor – but losing any portion of the territory for any reason after Portuguese occupation for five hundred years – well, that would have been a severe blow to Portugal's pride and morale ...

"We are trying to defend this country because it is Portuguese," Governor Rodrigues told me. "We are not merchants, counting our losses in cash. We defend Guiné just as we would defend the shores of Portugal itself. This *is* Portugal! Are your handcuffs perhaps a little too tight ...?"

He was a kind man, but not slated to remain very long in Portuguese Guiné. He was replaced by a military governor the following year.

The actuality of the independence war in Portuguese Guiné differed from the governor's almost benign description of it to me. It was not followed by the awful civil conflicts that devasted the other two larger African colonies following their independence, but on its own the colonial war of independence was considered so dreadful it was later, and often, referred to as 'Portugal's Vietnam.' The brutality of the war was generally conceded to have been far more extensive than in the other two theatres – although that is admittedly an opinion others would contest.

The war of independence in Guiné-Bissau lasted from 1961 to 1974. It involved a rebel army drawn from both Portuguese Guiné itself and from the off-shore Ilhas de Cabo Verde. This force, perhaps ten thousand fighters in total, was liberally supported from abroad (Russia, China, Cuba) and able to take full advantage of the fact the tiny territory was surrounded by sympathizers. Arms, equipment and military training, skimpy at first, became far more robust as the war progressed. At the peak of military operations, the rebels were confronted by a well-equipped Portuguese force combining ground troops, naval and air forces – a total deployment over the period of hostilities of more than thirty thousand men. When it was finally over and statistics could be collected, more than two thousand Portuguese military had been killed and nearly four thousand were left with permanent physical or psychological injuries. On the rebel side, more than six thousand combatants had been killed plus nearly four thousand unconfirmed deaths. In addition, more than five thousand civilians died.

After the close of hostilities with Portugal, the new rebel regime offered a choice to former native fighters who had served with the Portuguese forces: return to their families and receive full pay until the end of the year, or continue their service for and with the rebel political party. Nearly seven thousand five hundred of these troops declined to join the rebels, thinking they had made their contribution, and were now allowed to return to their homes. Instead, all of them were rounded-up and summarily executed.

PART V

Fim, and Then Some

Part V – *Fim*, and Then Some

Lisboa – Minders, Fascists, Communists 417

Van der Kleij's Dinner Party – and Rembrandt 419

Serrano Again, Explosively 425

Scholarly Afterthought 431

Lisboa – Minders, Fascists, Communists

As soon as we touched down in Lisboa, I was driven in a ministry car to the Hotel Embaixador and handed a letter that had been waiting for me at the reception desk from the *Ministério de Ultramar*. The letter, written in English, was firm, polite and brief: there were no restrictions on my remaining in Portugal for as long as I wished, but the validity of my air ticket to Toronto (via London) would expire one week after checking into the hotel. I was asked to contact a ministry operative on the working day following my arrival in the city.

"Thank you," I told the receptionist, tucking the letter into my pocket.

The clerk behind the desk handed me the key to my room, glancing past me over my shoulder as he did so.

"Do not look now," he whispered. "The man behind the newspaper in that chair across the lobby has been waiting for you since he came on duty at breakfast time this morning ... PIDE. Pay him no attention. Just go up to your room and I'll get rid of him."

An impersonal and sinister minder, this one. They would appear like mildew – not there until you realized they had been there all the time, germinating – beneath a damp rock, behind a news sheet, in an alley around the trash cans, stench, rats and mouldy cabbage.

"*Muito obrigado!*" I whispered back.

You're welcome, *Senhor* Jeremias. Sleep well ... It always amazed me, how many people *'just doing my job'* spend what could be the creative hours of a day dispensing misery to their fellow human beings.

I was tired and climbed into bed, only to be woken again at close to midday. The telephone went off next to my pillow, and a chirpy female voice on the other end asked:

"*Senhor* Jeremias ... do you want brown or white toast sent up with your eggs?"

"I beg your pardon ... I don't think I ordered ..."

"Thank you, *Senhor* Jeremias! I'll notify room service ..." She hung up before I could say anything more.

I lay still for a moment, gazing at the ceiling. The phone went off again moments later. Same voice.

"I'm sorry to trouble you, *Senhor*. Agents of the police entered the hotel telephone exchange just a few moments ago, as I was connecting with you. One of them was standing right behind me, so I had to say something. They have gone now ... They have asked that we note down and report to them all numbers you call from your room, so please go outside the hotel to a payphone for any important contacts you need to make. There's a policeman in the lobby at all times ready to follow wherever you go. Be careful!"

"Thank you," I said. "Please have the eggs sent up with brown toast."

I chuckled as I got out of bed, washed and dressed. John Buchan and Anthony Hope had written episodes like this, and I had always enjoyed reading them. I had the sudden urge to satisfy the wretched agent sitting on his fanny in the lobby. It was difficult to avoid comparing the example of efficiency shown me at the Overseas Ministry when I arrived in Lisboa earlier in the year, with the clumsiness of the agents who were now charged with overseeing my exit from their capital. Time and again over the next few days I was able to elude them, and the more I did it the more I fancy their suspicions were raised that I was up to no good. I did not care about their suspicions, but I was very attentive to seeing they had difficulty following me. It was not hard to spot them either waiting for me or tailing me.

After breakfast in my room, I grabbed a sheaf of papers, rolled them into a tube, and carried them with me as I galloped down two flights of stairs into the lobby deliberately making a bit of a commotion as I did so. Striding to the front entrance and throwing it open before the doorman could get to it, I started walking briskly up the street. As I had passed through the lobby a character slouched into a comfy chair with a newspaper (I imagined he had cut small holes through it so he could watch any comings and goings) suddenly gathered the sheets together, leaped out of the chair and made for the door right behind me. I got a good look at him before setting off up the road. Athletic fellow, but I was also in good physical shape, and I walked very fast.

I turned left and crossed the road at the top of Avenida Duque de Loulé, then threaded my way through back streets to Avenida Almirante Reis. At a good clip I headed northeast, past Arroios and Areeiro and onto Avenida Almirante Gago Coutinho. I walked the full length of it, as far as the rotunda before the entrance to the airport – and then around the rotunda to head back down the way I had come.

The poor fellow had followed me at a respectable distance, but by now was clearly perplexed as well as puffed. He stopped and watched me as I circled the rotunda, trying to look nonchalantly into the distance. He fumbled in his pocket for a packet of cigarettes and stuck one in his mouth just as I came around and drew up beside him. Taking out my Zippo, I offered him a light – and he took it.

"*Vamos embora*! – Let's go!" I said to him, heading back to my hotel.

He threw his newly lit cigarette onto the ground, glowering at me.

"*Bolas*!"

I did some reckoning later. We must have paced out close to six kilometres of hard pavement.

Van der Kleij's Dinner Party – and Rembrandt

"Ah-ha! You're a communist!"

"I'm probably less a communist than you're a fascist!"

Amândio Van der Kleij was driving me in his very fast sportscar at about seventy kilometres an hour down Lisboa's Avenida de Liberdade. He was taking me to dinner at his family home, a three-floor palace on the edge of the Alfama district. He was in a hurry to get there and paid no attention to traffic lights, green or red. Luckily there was no gridlock.

My retort was a silly one, accurate in only the narrowest aspect. Van der Kleij was a highly privileged aristocrat, and such people tend to see themselves in a league all by themselves, far above (and impervious to) the politics of the day. They are the ones for whom God created the world, anointing them custodians of all the good things on earth, with the rest of humanity – the minions – to keep it all running smoothly for them. Fascists, in fact, but also quite able to turn against the idiocy of fascism and express a viewpoint way out in left field.

"Me, fascist? I spit on them!" spat Van der Kleij screeching up to the gate of his palace and sitting on the horn till one of his minions came out and opened it for him, obsequiously bowing and tugging his forelock as we raced into the parking compound.

A total of seventeen cars – I counted them – had been pulled up in lines. A couple of Mercedes, an old Bentley, an assortment of sports cars; the accumulated playthings of a family at ease with itself, their friends and houseguests. It was 1963, but the scene was more reminiscent of the Gatsby '20s.

The palace was divided into three floors, each the separate – and large – apartment of a senior member of the family. Amândio and his family were at the very top of the grand interior staircase. His sister lived on the floor below, and a cousin lived behind big doors giving off the ground-floor entrance hallway. Tonight the family was assembled on the third floor for a magnificent dinner – in honour of the special guest from Canada. Amândio swooped into the living room of his home where everyone was waiting for us, his arm about my shoulder ushering me forward so that his progeny and entourage could examine me. They all rolled their eyes in my direction as if studying a new species of bug. Fellini might have immortalized the moment.

"This is my Canadian friend, Jeremias," said Amândio. "He says he's not a communist, but that I'm a fascist."

It was most unfortunate. I had chosen to wear a bright red Canadian lumber jacket that evening. Denials of my communist affiliations got me nowhere.

Everyone roared with laughter, my host louder than anyone else, and a couple of the more curious ambled over to examine me a little closer. One old thing, smiling broadly, tottered forward to rub the back of her hand on the red fabric of my lapels.

"Amândio? Fascist? Ha! Ha! Ha! He's far too loose a canon to be a good fascist. They wouldn't have him! Fascists are supposed to be tight, disciplined, ready to stand in line. Our Amândio has never stood in a line in his life!"

Van der Kleij beamed at my bemused embarrassment, and another little old cousin of the family patted the sofa cushion beside her. She wanted me to sit with her so as to question me about this communist business I was involved in …

"It gets awfully cold in Canada, doesn't it? They tell me you all have to drink a lot of alcohol to stay alive with all that snow …"

"Anti-freeze …" I muttered, and she nodded her understanding.

Everyone in the room around me had switched into English, presumably for my convenience. They all spoke with the same delightful intonation I had first heard in Toronto months before, but with such ease and fluency that I felt awkward and cumbersome in not being able to meet them in their own idiom, or any other. There is something infinitely sad about a Canadian anglophile dangling in francophonia ...

"Do you speak French?" someone will invariably ask innocently enough, because French is the language of the cultivated and educated, and absolutely *every*one knows it is spoken in Canada – where the people who matter are educated and cultivated.

"Er, no," the Canadian anglophile is too often forced to reply, feeling he might as well make a joke of his ignorance by adding: "Because I come from the west, and we only speak Bear in those parts ..."

"Ah-h-h ...!" The joke confuses everyone.

When the skewered anglophile admits 'no' – he does not speak French, the confusion is about the same as for the bear joke. The silence in the ensuing empty space is awkward, a terrible *faux pas* on the part of the questioner for unwittingly rolling back the blanket of ignorance revealing an embarrassing hole in the anglophile's schooling. Among linguists like the Portuguese – for a Portuguese with an education will likely speak four languages with commendable fluency – the word *gauche* takes on special significance.

A maid dressed in black, with white apron and bonnet, entered to announce in undertones to our hostess that dinner was now ready to be served. There were twenty-two of us. We all rose, drinks in hand, and headed towards the dining room.

A lugubrious woman, lanky like a rope, pale of face and with black hair, black brows and dressed in the blackest black, pulled up alongside me.

"I speak English perfectly," she announced in perfect English. "And Spanish, of course, because I am Portuguese and Portuguese like to speak better Spanish than the Spanish themselves. And Italian. And German. A little Swedish, quite good Russian. And French, of course. It's the language of diplomacy, after all ..."

And then, taking my arm, she asked the one question I was dreading.

"And you speak French, of course ...?"

Shit! I thought.

"Ach! Don't ask him that! Communists can't speak French!"

Van der Kleij, bless him, was walking just behind me. He pounced exuberantly into the conversation I was having with *Senhora* Dona Black and rescued me, really not knowing or giving a damn whether I spoke French or not. At that moment he became the most charming fascist I thought I would ever be likely to meet. In certain circles it is acutely embarrassing to pass oneself off for an educated Canadian when one does not readily speak the nation's alternate tongue.

Towards the end of dinner the dark woman, now sitting directly across from me, leaned forward and drooled onto her plate as she fumbled with a bunch of grapes.

She had imbibed a fair quantity of Van der Kleij's cocktail before dinner, and during the meal I noticed she had been pouring herself liberal portions from the jugs of red wine placed strategically along the length of the table. She was crying silently, her mascara streaking her cheeks. Nobody paid any attention to her, so she looked up at me with the mournful eyes of the bereaved and announced:

"I'm bereaved. My husband died in Washington last month. Diplomat, you know, but the doctors couldn't save him ..."

Later Van der Kleij whispered in my ear:

"Last month, *uma ova*! The *cabrão* has been dead more than two years. Drank himself to death. I would, too, if I'd been bridled by such a mule."

Much later, as the party was breaking up, he pulled me aside.

"There's a little club I know ... We could drop in there and mix with the clientele before I take you back to your hotel ..."

Wink-wink, nudge-nudge.

At the club a goodly portion of both attendants and clientele wore net stockings and little else, and all of them treated my host as the grandpappy rooster of the establishment. We dallied in the garish luxury of this dubious haunt of human frailties till the sun was coming up over the Lisboa rooftops, bathing the early city in translucent pink.

Truly I have yet to see the soft light of an early day to equal the subtlety of Lisboa awakening at five o'clock on a summer morning.

"Bath? Shower? Waste of water!" Amândio roared. "I could show you. I can take a perfectly adequate bath – or shower – using no more than a single glass of water. No need for a drop more to clean myself head-to-toe!"

"Yes!" interjected his wife, acerbically. "So clean I can smell you arriving when you're still out on the stairwell landing!"

There was a certain volatility to the interaction between Amândio and his wife, but I think the fact I was party to it from time-to-time was indication they accepted me quite openly. I saw them many times in following years, and the rancour between them appeared to be a feature of their household – sad, but not altogether surprising; they had been married many, many years – almost since the first blush of their exploratory youth – and in spite of her grumbling and his macho posturing, there was something beautiful in their relationship, and it was a privilege for me to witness it. The entire family was always gracious and kind towards me, and I cannot imagine it was merely because they found me something of a curiosity. They were generous people – and provided an insight into the quality of their lives I would not have discovered had they not deliberately invited me to enter in and accept them. I knew they were judged, by their own countrymen, to be fascists – and we talked about it. My own political opinions were gradually crystalizing by now, but being called even jokingly a communist might have been closer to the truth than I was prepared to admit at that stage of my life. I was not a communist. I was socially conscious, but not especially politically versed. My life to that point had been as a journalist, and I deliberately attempted to remain dispassionate and non-judgemental. ('Objective' is the journalist's word for it.) However, such perfection was already *areia demais para a minha camioneta* – too much sand for my truck. I found myself championing, out of a most earnest conscience, broad socialistic concepts that, inevitably, defined the gap between the sultans and the slaves, the honchos and the hobos.

Amândio and his long-suffering wife maintained a volatile affection for one another, and I thought the world of them.

"What is this painting in the living room?" I enquired. It was a tactic to divert them from their bickering.

"That's the only Rembrandt we have in the house," Amândio said.

I perked up.

"A Rembrandt? What ...?"

"Rembrandt nothing," snapped his wife. "It's not a Rembrandt at all. It's not a bad painting, but it's unsigned, and there is no indication at all Rembrandt painted it ..."

"It is so ..." huffed Amândio, as if trying to start up the quarrel again.

I did not have a camera to take a photograph, so I took out my notebook and did a reasonable ballpoint sketch of the painting on the wall – a fine framed portrait, perhaps eighty by sixty centimetres, darkened by years of cigarette smoke and inattention: a bearded man wears a wide hat and holds in his hand a *cabaça* – or gourd – of wine.

Rembrandt

"Jeremias – come! Let me take you for lunch and a good bottle of house wine," Amândio invited.

"Yes!" barked his wife. "Take Jeremias for a good lunch and leave me in peace!"

Fascist, communist – makes little difference. When they flare, the cruel harangues of hearth and home reduce all political notions to meer sweepings of human self-indulgence. Even with a Rembrandt on the wall, the man who has everything has less than nothing when an angry wife tells him she can smell him on the landing.

Serrano Again, Explosively

It was a surprise to learn at Serrano's office that he no longer worked there.

"Any idea where I might find him?" I asked, thinking perhaps he had been moved upstairs, or into another department.

In response I received the Latin shrug. No idea. Smiles. He was just not there any more. No one knew what had become of him. He appeared to have garnered no friends while employed in the ministry. There was also the distinct aura around my simple query suggesting no one was particularly interested in making enquiries or helping me out. The man had vanished. More smiles.

"That's strange!" I commented to the office worker who attended me. "He seemed to be so much a part of this office when I passed through Lisboa a few months ago ..."

"So sorry ..." Again, the shrug.

I recalled a small 'Café X' near Restauradores; Serrano had taken me there a few times, and one of the waiters spoke a little English. I went there and asked about my former minder. The waiter remembered me, showed me to a table set off against a back wall, and left me to stew for a few minutes. Presently he returned with a small *bica* of black coffee and set it down in front of me. He kept his back to the activity of the café, and refrained from bending down to talk to me.

"Where can Serrano contact you?" he asked.

"I'm staying at the Hotel Embaixador – I've a week before I have to leave. Do you know where I can reach him ...?"

"Not possible. I'll contact him, and he can contact you."

With that the waiter returned to his station near the bar and continued serving customers at other tables. Presently he returned to my table and presented me with a slip of paper – the bill for my coffee. Pulling my wallet from my pocket, I paid him what I owed.

"*Obrigado, Senhor!*" he said. Leaning in ever so slightly, he added under his breath: "Do not come here again."

Clued-in by several months of clandestine cloak-and-dagger hide-and-seek in Portugal's colonies, I thanked him, turned my back and walked out into the crowded street. It was almost impossible not to notice a gentleman in a well-tailored suit who had been sitting at another table, get to his feet and follow me out the door. I smiled at him and gave him a shallow bow. Likewise, he smiled, tipped his head almost imperceptibly in acknowledgement, folded his newspaper into his jacket pocket and walked stiffly away from me. At the same moment, yet another man who had been sitting alone at a sidewalk table rose, studiously avoided eye contact with the first man as he left – and fell into stride twenty metres behind me as I walked up the boulevard. 'Not again!' I thought and quickened my pace.

From Restauradores to Parque Eduardo VII the avenida rises at a steady incline, and it is a fit man who can manage the distance at a fast walk (two stops on the subway) and not arrive puffed. At the top, close to the statue of the Marquês de Pombal, there was a small kiosk which I managed to use to block the vision of the man following me. I sat down on a bench and waited. Sure enough, in a matter of seconds, the poor fellow steamed around the corner of the kiosk – and stopped dead when he caught sight of me, as though the soles of his shoes had suddenly become glued to the *calcário* cobble stones. He moved over and sat on the bench next to me, so I got up immediately and headed up Avenida Duque de Loulé to my hotel. As the doorman greeted me, I looked back the way I had come. My shadow was a good two blocks back, standing in the middle of the sidewalk and no doubt ready to quaff a cool beer.

Not unexpected, another gum-shoed spook was huddled behind his newspaper in one of the foyer's comfortable chairs. I wondered if these minions of nefarious law got to compare notes at the end of a day …

I kept my room at the hotel, but for three days I was the guest of Van der Kleij and his family. In one or other of the cars he kept in his courtyard, Amândio would whisk me away to the beaches of Costa da Caparica, or south to Setubal, or even further afield to his farm in the Alentejo. I enjoyed these outings – the exceptional opportunities they afforded me to see the Portuguese countryside, the sandy-floored forests along the southern Atlantic coastline of the Alentejo, and the numerous rural villages through which we passed. On one all-day excursion we headed south and took lunch at a small restaurant in Grândola, afterwards driving into the heat of the vast interior granary that is this southern province – to Beja, then north through Cuba to the ancient walled city of Évora. We arrived back at the palace in Lisboa to take a late snack at the table in Van der Kleij's kitchen. At the end of a long day, I was delivered to the front door of my hotel at close to four o'clock in the morning. Van der Kleij suggested a nightcap; exhausted, I declined.

I knew who this man was. His hairbrained views, political or otherwise, were tossed out in boastful synapses, but I liked him and his effervescence; and he clearly enjoyed trying to impress me, showing me those aspects of his bailiwick that gave heft to his up. In the rural expanse of southern Portugal, he was a farmer and I dare say a good one; in the city he was a businessman, and he seemed to have no trouble increasing his fortune. Bravado trumped certain elements of decorum, but he did not appear to give a damn – and in the end I had to admit Amándio Van der Kleij was no true fascist at all. More accurately I saw him as an outrageously (and amusingly) opinionated aristocrat who considered himself so far above and beyond the level of mere political thinkers and others of similar persuasion, that whatever he had to say on anything relating to the social mores of ordinary men, spun out of him like the pronouncements of a lesser God sorting things out for the rest of us.

Yet he was not at all incapable of acknowledging the comforts that unremarkable mortals have quite cleverly forged for themselves. His vulnerabilities were legion and visible. His energy immense. He was so far beyond the capacity to muster a political correctness that he and his pals (and a man like that must have had a few similarly effervescent aristocrat friends to pump him along) would have formed a totally disconnected class all by themselves. Such people lived in a throwback not to fascism, but to constructs of feudalism and the sycophantic loyalties more commonly associated with an age of human bondage. He was curious about people and, highborn or lowborn, seemed to revere them, their conversation and opinions. No side-stepper, he was not one to offer up justifications. Van der Kleij possessed an innate understanding of people, high and low. He had no need to excuse himself when wrestling with impartiality.

There was a knock on my door about nine o'clock one morning.

"Who is it?" I demanded without opening. It was only moments ago that I had fallen asleep, and I was far too groggy to talk to anyone.

"Maria Alícia from the telephone switchboard. I have a message for you..."

I opened the door a crack to allow her to pass through a slip of paper. There was writing: 'Ceuta, Avenida República – lunch.' It was signed with the letter S.

Serrano.

Ceuta was the name of a popular restaurant, pastry shop and café at the southern end of the avenida close by Saldanha, a stop on the metro. No hour had been marked, but 'lunch' would have likely been around noon – so by that time I was comfortably seated at an outdoor table perusing the menu and leafing my way through a pamphlet concerning experiments in literacy by the famous Brasilian professor, Dr. Paulo Freire. At some point in my recent travels someone had pushed the paper into my hands for my comment, and with the suggestion that Dr. Freire's methods might be put to practical use in Portuguese Africa. I was none too sure of the depth of my interest in the subject; in the past months I had enjoyed a heady bout of physical adventuring and was of a mind I would like to keep that sort of thing going for as long as I could. Somewhere buried deep within the psyche of a discernibly tremulous soul there lay severe self-doubts concerning my ability to concentrate on anything resembling the *parada intelectual*.

"I shall witness; someone else can make sense of my witness." I was having trouble reading Dr. Freire's ideas.

"How was your adventure in Portuguese Africa?" Serrano had come around a corner and surprised me from behind.

"Fantastic!" I almost bellowed, rising to offer him my *abraço*. "I've been trying to find you ..."

"You've been looking in the wrong places. I am no longer employed by our Ministry of Lies. I learned you were back – from the waiter at Café X – and I left a message for you with Maria Alícia at your hotel ... You received it, of course ..."

He sat, and we ordered food.

"Did anyone follow you here?" asked Serrano.

"I think not. I came up on the metro. It was crowded, and I took the precaution of going south before coming north. I've been here a few minutes, and I haven't noticed anyone ..."

When we had finished and paid our bill, Serrano delved into a backpack he had brought with him and pulled out an old raincoat and a cloth cap.

"Put these on, and we'll walk south. I want to show you something."

Avenida Fontes Pereira de Melo, like Avenida República, is a broad thoroughfare that runs northeast from Praça do Marquês de Pombal and finishes at Praça Duque de Saldanha, just a few steps away from where we had eaten our lunch. In a sense the two avenidas are extensions of each other, and in an earlier day both of them had been lined by gracefully ornate neo-Gothic homes, most in grey stone, some in white, their porticos and windows in the most intricately-carved stonework. Each house was a mini palace, the overarching effect a spectacular display of old-world charm and wealth. These houses stood on some of the city's prime patches of real estate, and so became targets for developers. For years there was resistance from owners and the wider public which identified them as historical. However, in time the developers began to win, and construction started on a variety of enormous edifices – now hotels, offices and apartment buildings. But in 1963 many of the ancient mansions were still standing.

Wrapped in Serrano's raincoat and cap, I walked with him back towards Marquês de Pombal, to the door of one of these ornate houses. He went first up the stairs, opened the door seemingly without a latchkey, and beckoned me to enter quickly.

The very first thing I saw as we came inside was a larger-than-life poster of Che Guevara plastered onto the wall at the foot of the stairs.

"That has to be a bit risky, no?" I commented.

Serrano chuckled.

"Not as risky as what's going on upstairs," he said. "By now I don't think any of us care very much about what the authorities might think. For us Che is important – much more important than the narrow little minds that would forbid us to hang a picture of him on our walls."

"But why take the chance? Anyone coming through your unlocked door and seeing that would know in an instant the political sympathies of those living here. It seems incautious ..."

"PIDE will have a nasty shock if ever they come knocking on this door," was all he said, and he bounded up the ornate hall stairway two steps at a time.

"Come on!" he called. "You've been asking questions about our opposition for months, so now I can show you ..."

I followed him to a door leading into a large room on the upper floor. I did not count, but there must have been ten or twelve people in the room – all of them sitting on the floor in front of a large low table, working in a circle then passing their handiwork to the person on their right – a sort of assembly line. No one got up as we entered, but they acknowledged Serrano, and a couple of them nodded to me and smiled. They seemed a friendly bunch, but the conversation between themselves was low in tone and interspersed with long silences. Each of them was being very diligent with his or her hands – wires and short pieces of what looked like metal piping. It appeared to be repetitive work, each person doing the same task over and over before passing the work on to the person at his or her side. One of the workers was Maria Alícia from the hotel switchboard. She smiled and lifted her hand in greeting when she saw I had recognized her, then her head bent down again as she concentrated on the work on the table in front of her.

"Serrano ...? What the hell ...?"

He nodded.

"We have a little munitions factory going here. You are free to write about it in your paper if you wish – just don't publish the address ..." And he laughed at the alarm I'm sure my face expressed.

"This whole bloody house could go up ..." I started to say.

"And it will, if PIDE comes to our door," he said. Then he added: "Don't worry. A couple of these fellows are military bomb experts, and they know what they are doing. We are not so much manufacturing little bombs as we are manufacturing a revolution ... It had to start sometime, and in fact it has been going on for quite a time ... This is just one part of it."

Within ten minutes, and at my insistence, we were back on the street, and I had shed Serrano's hat and coat.

"I am not at all sure I should have seen that," I told my companion earnestly. "I'm glad I know about it and thank you for trusting me enough to bring me here – but it is not the sort of story I can use without serious implications, most probably for all of you. You are taking a terrible risk ..."

"You've been through Africa," he replied. "You've seen what is happening. I am sure you had a great adventure – an exciting holiday. But we are Portuguese, and this is something we must now do for ourselves, and our country. It is a serious thing. Some of us are likely to die. Many have already died. But it is past the time for negotiation, and we must act on our beliefs. You are now in a position to know us and understand our story, so now we count on you to tell it …"

"I leave for London and Toronto tomorrow," I told him. "Yes, I have seen a lot – and I do understand that all Portuguese have been forced into a trap – a corner not entirely of your own making. This has to be your war. I can only be a spectator."

"And commentator …?"

Scholarly Afterthought

On my final day in the capital a package was delivered to me at my hotel from the *Secretariado Nacional da Informação*. It was, at last, an attempt to answer the written questions concerning Portuguese education I had submitted at the outset of my journey to the director of foreign press, Manuel Rino. After several months of trekking about in Africa I had almost forgotten I had ever asked, so was at first surprised and delighted these concerns were receiving some attention. However, when digging into the document more thoroughly I was dismayed. There was much in it of political and self-serving puffery. Someone clearly had gone to considerable effort to assemble a high-minded profile – but I could hardly view it as a satisfactory answer to the many questions I had asked.

Well-educated societies tend to think twice about sending their armies off to war. Prior to leaving for Africa I had heard disconcerting stories about Portuguese illiteracy, and the recruitment by the military of young men from the remote villages of the country's hinterland. The figure bandied about was that as much as forty percent of the population of Portugal was illiterate – whole families of a largely peasant population who might have had difficulties knowing much more than their favourite football team's latest triumph on the scoreboard, and were surely unacquainted with the intricacies of their government's delicate involvements in Africa. In a country of such enormously wide-spread illiteracy, primary education was compulsory for only four years between the ages of seven and twelve. When the war fronts opened up, this strata of society proved a useful recruitment pool.

There was no admission in the document of that forty percent, but considerable space was devoted to explaining what amounted to a most dismal record.

It was an exhaustive thirty-page Gestetnered public relations effort, single-spaced on large legal-sized foolscap – so obviously someone had given a healthy second-thought to a catch-up type-script (in cumbersome English), possibly attempting to fill a gap in a legitimate area of enquiry that had so plainly been overlooked, or deliberately suppressed, for years. In attempting to defend itself and its shadowy record in the colonies, the Portuguese government had of late been issuing series of pamphlets relating to all manner of its policies – foreign relations pamphlets, explanations of public works being carried out at home and in the 'Overseas Provinces,' leaflets and whole essays concerning everything from farm production to shipping and rail transport, and the building of dams. There was a glossy little booklet concerning just about every aspect of Portuguese life and industry – but until this envelope was pushed into my hand, never so much as a line that I had read in relation to any level of Portuguese education. Now, for the first time, I was examining a laboriously long-winded written explanation that dipped into, yet evaded, as many aspects of the existing Portuguese educational system as the author could think of that might present a cheerful picture for the current year, 1963. Its language was cluttered with highfalutin English-isms, but with errors in spelling, grammar and punctuation, giving me the impression it had been hurriedly thrown together to 'cover' this most important field. There was nothing about the document I could take personally, yet I began to think maybe, as a result of my questioning, there had been a frenzied meeting of some government response team to cope with the embarrassing void of information concerning the country's lower levels of education. Perhaps someone had woken up to the realization this gap should be closed in case some other snooping journalist should ever come asking embarrassing questions ...

The document did explain the 'Centenaries Plan' of 1940 – how there had been an attempt to blitz the country with a building programme of more than seven thousand schools containing twelve-and-a-half thousand classrooms. But then it went on to explain how this grandiose plan had to be trimmed right back – how it had failed – because little old neutral Portugal had had to face extreme 'difficulties' brought about by the Second World War. There was considerable explanation as to the necessity of emphasizing Christian morality – along with instruction in 'the native tongue,' Portugal's history, arithmetic, geometry, geography and natural sciences. None of this, however, extended beyond the four years of schooling mandated in 1952 and reaffirmed in 1960. The most notable comment concerning secondary education was that all school books, even those in private colleges, were necessarily approved by the Ministry of Education to ensure a 'finer moral education.'

For all its length and density, the document was cursory in the way it dealt with the history of the country's educational system, brushing over matters that must have been uncomfortably probed in the past – by government or, possibly, even outsiders. It seemed very clear levels of basic education that had to involve an area of major administrative responsibility had been largely neglected in the past – perhaps deliberately – a situation that must have been made even more acute, put off and then put off again, as the country's government turned its full attention to the build-up for war while at the same time trying to fend off mounting international criticism.

Portugal had been a quiet and isolated country, largely ignored by a world that had so much else on its international plate – and yet the world's most far-flung empire now that the British lion had slunk off into relative obscurity – at least for the time being. But with the war in Africa and the clamour for decolonization, the world was now looking askance at this little empire in the sun. There was something about this education document that presented a government's catch-up effort to present itself as clean, like a small boy holding out his hands to assure his father he had washed them before dinner. For some unstated reason the Portuguese government apparently understood, it was essential to show a tidy copy book for outsiders who were now knocking on the republic's door making disconcerting comments and queries about the country's education system.

The leaders of nations can keep their people down and doing their bidding by keeping them dumb, but only to a certain point, and only for a limited time. Oppression has a way of rolling over, stretching itself out and knocking things akimbo. Portuguese history is chock-full of periods of gross hardship and oppression – at home in the European *Metropole*, but especially in the colonies – and there can be no serious doubt much of this was brought about deliberately so that the power of the society's upper echelons would not be challenged, shunted aside or in any way diminished by the masses. Education, generally, was a useful area to mess around.

This kind of control can be hard to measure accurately in a large society like pre-war Germany, or Italy, or Spain. It can be disguised altogether in super large societies such as in America and its English-speaking largely Commonwealth sidekick, or throughout the Russian landmass. The Great White Mass, throughout history, has been very sure it has got it right – so sure it has been prepared to fight bitter wars of attrition, and to slaughter millions, in an effort to 'preserve' what it has convinced its surfs is a 'sacred' way of life.

Sanctimoniously the leaders of these great nations have proclaimed warfare necessary, calling it variously the 'sacred fight for freedom' – of a way of life, a religion, or whatever else might have seemed apt at the time. What they were actually talking about was their own intolerance, greed and stupidity – their own top-down control of people and the value of the wealth they embodied – the labour of the masses, or (most often) the mineral wealth on which the masses sat merely poking about with their digging sticks and twiddling their thumbs. In modern times white man has shown time and again he is terrified of being recognized in the uniform identifying the minority he actually represents when he steps into a wider world, and he has spent much effort in trying to convince his own masses.

But in a country the size of Portugal – and, maybe more importantly, within a culture as uniquely isolated and identifiable as is the Portuguese – things tend to be more visible. It can be difficult to disguise overt corruption for very long.

For centuries, Portugal had been a nation proud of its higher education. There were universities in Lisboa and Porto, and one of the oldest in Europe at Coimbra. They had existed for an elite, and they were all fine institutions with impeccable credentials. But getting into them in order to take advantage of what they had on offer – this was the game, and it was largely controlled by withholding the fundamentals of early scholarship that would have permitted a boy (and certainly a girl) from almost any village from making the grade. He or she would be needed on the land; he was needed as a soldier or a sailor, she was needed as a servant to the elite.

They are a tough people, the Portuguese. The impression I had gathered during that extraordinary summer was that the elites of Portuguese society tended to be foppishly over-privileged, unaware and selfish as is the higher strata of any society. But it is the so-called lower classes – the rank and file of the military, the people who work the land, those dealing every day with the intricacies of making a living and feeding their families – these people are as tough as old leather boots. And it is they today, forty and fifty years after being tested by an unjust war in the colonies and revolution in the streets of their homeland, who are now claiming the benefits of education and proving themselves the backbone of a new and stronger society. It is a magnificent improvement on any overture ever attempted by Salazar's *Estado Novo* and the band of fascist thugs it encouraged.

PART VI

Envoi

Part VI – Envoi

New Start A-Brew 439

Buccaneers, Thieves, Colonists –
    Thoughts in Closing 453

New Start A-Brew

I flew to London the following day and was happy to have Peter Pinsway come on the line when I telephoned him at *The London Daily Register.* Our paths had last crossed earlier that year – a lifetime ago – in Birmingham, Alabama. Whenever in London, call and we would go for a beer, he had said...

We met again in the foyer of his office building – Peter looking every bit as dapper as he had in Birmingham, but now not quite such a stand-out. His black bowler hat, an anachronism in Alabama, was identical to those worn by thousands of other men coming to work in The City. Likewise his black patent leather shoes, his black pin-striped and immaculately-pressed trousers, his brushed lint-free black jacket, the white handkerchief peeping from his breast pocket and the tiny rose bud in its button-hole. The tightly-rolled umbrella was *de rigeur* owing to the caprice of English weather no matter the season. As soon as we stepped out of his building Peter Pinsway as I remembered him in Alabama vanished, and suddenly he looked just like everyone else on a 1960s City of London street.

We snuggled into a well-worn wooden booth at a crowded inner-city pub, ordered up some warm English beer, and over the next hour I filled his ear with an abbreviated run-down of the book in your hands.

"The world spins a little faster than either you or me, old son! It's hard to keep up – but you seem to be on your way. You have all you need to tell a good story, if ever you can bring yourself to write it out," he said.

Over time I have written segments of it for various publications, but it has taken me a bit longer to set down the itinerary in any sequence that might make sense of the whole. Fifty-six years.

Within a week I was back in Toronto. The newspaper editor to whom I had sent my reports and stories from Africa received me politely enough. The paper had published two or three vignettes, colourful anecdotes allowing a reader to glean background to a much larger story – but they had not published any of the longer pieces I had written, stories I considered had been insightfully conceived explaining what was going on in the entirety of the Portuguese Empire. At several junctures during the journey I had suffered monstrous self-doubts, my capacity (in terms of green years and worldly wisdom) to grasp the significance of all that was going on around me – and interpret these findings for a wide (and I assumed sophisticated) readership. From my standpoint on the ground the full story was immensely complex, convoluted and yet so personal for so many, that I often felt like a nosey intruder rummaging about right through the middle of it – and very capable of misinforming, misinterpreting and confusing the details of major issues. I feared misunderstanding. Far better to avoid presenting myself as the master chef of the entire kitchen operation when I felt barely capable of peeling the onions intended for the day's soup. But I was not stand-offish; I was determined to make every effort to comprehend all within my range of witnessing and hearing.

My youth, my gullibility – but most of all my inability to comprehend or speak Portuguese – were weaknesses that were only superficially relieved by what I have always believed was a well-developed sense of Canadian fair play. Even in pinpointing clear shortcomings within myself, it was not beyond my capacity to recognize how clever Portuguese were eager to exploit such a *mark*. My naïvety, my lack of confidence in front of hard-bitten propagandists were easy bait; but easily detected, too, by an astute editor in Toronto who demanded whiz-bang, and something more than mere nuance.

But then a compelling thing happened. One newspaper editor who had asked for a single-page memo outlining my journey, tossed my earnest effort back at me with a second sheet pinned to it – a memo to the same editor from his preferred fact-checker. That second-opinion on my findings:

> *Limited fare. Seems your man failed to find the front, or even enter the war zone. I note he mislabelled Roberto Holden's name. If he can't get that right, how much else of his story will likewise be fed to us backwards? Who is this Hespeler-Boultbee?*

The note was signed *Marcus* – the newspaper's hotshot foreign correspondent.

Inwardly I burned, and sent both memos back to the editor – with a third:

> *The correct name is Holden Roberto. Who is this Marcus?*

A pinch of snidery too much for those concerned – and my good name never more graced the sheets of that particular paper.

Arnold Edinborough laughed at my discomfort, but he was kindly and supportive.

"That's the adamantine news world, Jeremy – perhaps it's not for you, ... On the other hand, as a contributor to *Saturday Night* magazine, I can surely tell you I have no complaint ..."

Arnold laughed even harder when I told him how difficult it had been to cash his personal cheque in Lourenço Marques. When I told him how one of the stories I had written for his magazine was likely responsible for my arrest in Beira, I was fearful his mirth might topple him out of his chair.

"Never mind! Never mind! You did well," he told me when his laughter had subsided. To prove his sincerity, he cut me another cheque for which I was grateful indeed.

Maclean's Magazine eventually commissioned and published a major piece on the overall subject, and in time I was able to peddle pieces here and there to a variety of outlets – the *Economist, Independent TV* and the *BBC* in Britain, and several papers in Toronto and across Canada. All-in-all the trip had not been a magnificent financial success and, as time wore on, I began to think my witness to Portugal's struggles was little more than a brief scenario, an introductory peek at a much greater and slower-moving history, the momentum of which very quickly eclipsed my privileged but circumscribed view of what was going on.

Portuguese Africa was a long way away from matters Canadian. It was difficult to drum up interest in the subject area. Strong memories for me, for sure, but after a time its fuller significance withered while I got on with other matters in my life – one of which was to relocate from Toronto to Vancouver Island – and nowhere, apart from Pitcairn or South Georgia, could possibly induce the feeling of remoteness from the rest of the world than Vancouver Island with its wide Pacific vistas that stop at not much else until they come to rest on Tokyo ... Distance and the warm and woolly contentment of a virtuous oblivion will work wonders for those able to croon *Haul up the ladder, Jack, I'm aboard.*

I had never lost a deep sentiment for Portugal; the simple honesty of the people appealed to me as well as the country's landscape and exceptional history. My singular encounter with the place and its extant empire had proven a strong educational reality for me. It was easy to separate the land and its people from the grotesque mismanagement of the selfish overlords who had controlled them for decades, and I was anxious to return. My mother, on her own by the close of the '60s and a sunbird by nature, had decided she wanted to live in the south of Spain and, through a combination of curious circumstances and deft juggling, by 1971 I also was able to return to Iberia. Portugal had intrigued me more than Spain, and I reckoned one of the advantages of living there would be my ability to visit with my mother relatively easily, keep in close touch with her without too burdensome a commitment to either one of us. We got along well together over short bursts of time, but neither possessed an easy temperament, so a little distance between us seemed the wisest way to head off any problems before they developed. It worked, and by the beginning of 1972 I had arranged to move into a tiny apartment in Lisboa, earning a crust by finding work as a language teacher at a school on Avenida República – not far from where Serrano and his friends had set up their bomb-making operation nine years earlier. I would study Portuguese, I thought, and in time would set myself up as a correspondent for any one of several journals with which I had maintained contact.

However, I had been working at the school no more than a few weeks when officers from PIDE arrived one morning and interrupted my class. The name of the force had been changed (it was now *Direcção Geral de Segurança* – DGS) but it was still generally known and called PIDE by the populace, and the brutish tactics of the force had not changed. They bundled me into a car and took me to their headquarters building on Rua António Maria Cardoso, not far from the Chiado, sat me on a wooden chair in an empty room, and nine officers – I counted them – proceeded to ask me if I was the same contrary-minded newspaper reporter who had visited Portugal and the 'overseas provinces' in 1963.[44]

None of them could speak English very well, and my Portuguese was still non-existent, so it took a few minutes for us to connect. One or two of the men referred to the leader of the pack as 'Capitão Coutinho.' The more we failed to understand one another, the louder my interrogators shouted their anger and frustration, but in the end my visit of 1963 was hardly something I could deny. For sure they must have known the correct answer anyway, otherwise I would not be sitting on that wooden chair …

"Yes," I said, when finally I understood what it was they wanted to know – whereupon one of the officers standing behind me used his fist to level a back-handed blow to the side of my head. The force of it knocked me from the chair onto the floor. His companions then set about kicking me – chest,

---

[44] State police. PVDE (*Polícia de Vigilância e de Defesa do Estado*) – PIDE (*Polícia Internacional e de Defesa do Estado*) – DGS – (*Direcção-Geral de Segurança*) – These, in succession, were the acronyms for Portugal's secret police. The origin of their more notorious activities follows the *coup d'état* and military dictatorship of 1926. In turn, and over time, they relied on the models of Britain's MI6 and the Gestapo of Germany's Third Reich. A civilian organization of Portugal's intelligence services, SIRP, (*Sistema de Informações da Republica Portuguesa*) was established in 1984.

stomach, back, buttocks and legs. There was no big fish in the net here; but there was that sadistic need on their part to inflict punishment for contrary words and thoughts expressed almost a decade before.

After what I estimated to be an hour in their delightful company, I was again pushed into the police car and driven to the residence I had been renting on Avenida António Augusto de Aguiar. I was in dreadful pain, and sick, but had suffered no broken bones and, apart from a few slaps and punches, they had left my face pretty much untouched.

"Pack your bags," I was told. "We shall return for you in one hour ..." presumably to hustle me to the frontier, and they left.

I was shaken and felt weak but managed to make a phone call to a friend. He already knew that I had had previous encounters with PIDE, so there was no need to explain my situation in detail.

"I'd better come and get you right away. If they indicated they'd be driving you to the frontier, it's very possible you'll never get there. Far better you be gone by the time they come to fetch you ..."

Within minutes my friend arrived in his car at the front of my building, and we drove away from the city – south to Setúbal.

I needed rest and sleep. We drove to a small *pensão* and my friend spoke to the proprietor. The two of them knew one another. The police required operators of all hotels and guesthouses to provide a list containing the name and passport number of everyone staying with them. In this case, though, with the exchange of conspiratorial understanding and a few bank notes, this intrusive formality was waived. The following morning the owner fed me a full breakfast, some strong coffee, and tucked a bag of Portuguese bread under my arm – patting me on the back and wishing me *boa sorte* as I left his shelter. From Setúbal I caught a bus to Serpa in southern Alentejo, and from there hitchhiked a ride to Vila Verde de Ficalho. I was picked up by a group of six Dutch university students in a VW van. They elected to stay overnight on the farm of a friend on the Portuguese side of the frontier, and invited me to go along with them. By now I reckoned it would be pushing my luck to remain longer in Portugal, and was anxious to get myself across the border into fascist Spain. The Spanish police had nothing on me – and I was pretty sure my mother's record was unstained.

The road from Vila Verde de Ficalho to the frontier at Rosal de la Frontera can be a lonely stretch, even today, but it was even lonelier in 1971. I walked for several hours, and not a single vehicle passed until late in the afternoon when a donkey cart appeared out of a field and turned in the direction of the border.

I stuck my thumb out and the plodding donkey turned his mournful expression upon me and stopped. On the bench of the *carroça* sat an elderly farmer and his wife, all smiles and suntan, boots and mud-stained clothing. There was no room for a third person on the bench, so the farmer's wife, waving her arms and chattering like a cartoon squirrel, indicated I should shove the cargo over a bit and make space on the deck of the cart so I could sit facing backwards, my feet dangling near the road. The sole cargo was a mountainous pile of oranges. The old man shook the reins, and we moved off with a jerk – a clip-clopping only marginally faster than I could walk. It saved my legs, though, and I was grateful for the ride. All the while the farmer's wife kept up her unintelligible monologue, peeling orange after orange for me to eat until my shirt fair stank from the juices.

Today much of Europe enjoys open borders and it would be an easy matter to cross from Portugal into Spain without interruption. But at that time the borders were manned by guards who, because virtually no one crossed at that point, tended to be extra zealous when they had the opportunity to put their mundane profession into practice. I was fearful that I could be discovered – but there was not much else I could do. I lay back among the oranges hoping (as I was certain I would be spotted) that at least I would be taken for the farmhand I am certain I appeared to be. I felt for my passport in my shirt pocket, and exercised my wildest imaginings to concoct a story that would pass muster with surly border guards – first the Portuguese, then the Spanish …

I need not have bothered. My friend the donkey did not falter a single step but clipped and clopped his way right through both border posts without stopping. And my new friends (I chose to christen them *Senhor* and *Senhora Laranjo*), border people who passed this way every day of their lives, called cheerfully to their friends the guards, who called back and waved and wished us a good evening and God speed us on a safe journey …

A day or two later I was welcomed by my mother in Málaga. She washed my shirt, but it retained an orange tinge thereafter. One day it was ripped into rags so I could polish my shoes.

*

Salazar who had left office in 1968 after suffering a stroke, was never told by his colleagues that he was no longer in charge. He died in 1970 and nothing changed; his legacy of dictatorship was continued by his close protégé, Marcelo Caetano. I was still very much enamoured of Portugal. The people were not representative of their government any more than their government represented them. Many Portuguese by now had informed me they were utterly sick of their leaders, that they had become fossilized and unable to march with the times. Knowing who these leaders were, how they thought and what they feared, I could understand very well why I had been treated so roughly at the hands of PIDE. That knowledge fostered a stroppy contempt that could boil into anger quickly and that harboured not-so-secret feelings of revenge for clear injustice; but thankfully it was tempered by a mixture of lip-trembling humiliation and the realization, in the end, that more positive results are almost always attained by presenting the other cheek – or just walking away.

It was not difficult to convince myself I now held a legitimate stake in the toppling of the country's fascist regime. That was an emotional reaction. More realistic was the knowledge there would be no peace for me in Portugal – that it would be necessary to wait, perhaps for a long time, before I could return to meet again with the good friends I had made there. A long bout of Málaga, its sunshine and my mother's scatty frolickings, served me well before I finally decided to move up to France. Living in the centre of Paris I was again able to make a living for myself by teaching English – at the factory near Fresnes just south of the city where the seating for the Concorde was made. I remained in France for six months before returning to North America by ship at the start of 1973. I boarded it in Lisboa so that my last visual aspects of that chapter of Europe were from the ship's stern – the wide vista of the mouth of the Rio Tejo, the surf breaking on the shores of Costa da Caparica and the distant high cliffs of Cabo da Roca.

*

The Portuguese military staged their *Carnation Revolution* on 25 April 1974. Considering the general unpopularity of the dictatorial *Estado Novo* and its war on three fronts in Africa, it can hardly be claimed it was unexpected. The wonder is that it went off as evenly as it did, and that more people were not harmed. I was living in Victoria, British Columbia, at the time, and on the morning of that revolutionary day I dropped into the Market Square printing workshop of my friend Steve Wachtin. We would often get together for a coffee and a chat at that hour of the day, and I enjoyed watching him work so skillfully on his XIX century letterpress.

"Hey, what's the name of that place you like so much in Europe ...?

Portugal is it?" there were newspapers old and new scattered across the floor of his shop to soak up spilled ink and grease, and he started pushing them about with his foot.

"Yeah – here it is!"

He bent down and picked up the front page of the local newspaper to show me the day's banner headline: revolution in Portugal, tanks in the streets of the capital, ceasefires on all fronts in the colonies.

"I've got to be there ...!"

"I'll help you!" Steve said, and he gave me a cheque for one thousand dollars.

I was back in Lisboa by May Day, celebrating with the millions of Portuguese civilians and military who had been dancing in the streets night and day for nearly a week, happily stuffing red carnations into the spouts of the soldiers' rifles.

Even with a party as grand as that one, there was a limit as to what one could write about it in the newspapers. The capital city, in which the entire citizenry appeared to be bubble-headed with hysteria, was awash with political parties, political hucksters, committees claiming to represent every man, woman, child and the family *burro*. The military marched in the streets, the people's heroes, and armoured cars and jeeps zoomed about town with flags poking out of windows and turrets – just everybody shouting and wearing the most beguiling smiles on their faces.

This time I remained in the city a month before returning to Canada, determined at this juncture to wrap up my personal affairs and move to Portugal. Only this way would it ever be possible to immerse myself so thoroughly in Portuguese culture that I could hope to come to grips with who these extraordinary people were, and how they had, after so many years, so ably managed to shuck off one of the world's heavier yokes of oppression.

It took nearly a year to resolve issues in Canada; I arrived once more in Lisboa in the summer of 1975, this time to stay. The revolution was still in full swing, but its tone had changed. Now there was a multitude of political parties vying for the support of a democratically-minded largely left-leaning population – and there, too, were all the components of the Western Alliance – particularly the USA, ready to steer Portugal in the 'correct' way. There was a strong possibility the communists, under the leadership of Álvaro Cunhal, or the young 'independent' leader of the revolution, Otelo Saraiva de Carvlho, might gain the ascendency. At one point it was possible to count sixteen different political parties clamouring for votes – most of them left of centre, some of them even further left than the one pronouncing itself the official communist party. It was a mess. Trying to explain it all in a telephone call to a distraught foreign editor at *Maclean's Magazine* (then in the midst of transforming itself into a bona fide weekly news magazine), I heard his plaintive voice squeal:

"My God, man! Can't you try to keep it simple ...?"

There was nothing simple about it. The revolution was ultimately to last nineteen months, during which time there were nightly manifestations, sufficient Latin intrigue to keep all rumour mongers happy, and dangerous divisions developing between different units of the armed forces. Bombs would go off in various parts of the capital and often no one knew who had ignited them, or why. Military vehicles crammed with troops wearing their helmets and bristling with weaponry raced about with earnest intent, always stimulating suspense and alarm. At first they had been heroes, now they were sinister. There was talk – we never took it too seriously – the country was on the brink of civil war, but we really did not know. There were two or three major alarming moments every day, a mass of excitement that kept newsmen on an adrenalin high night and day. Angry dry dock workers took exception to a story published in *The Guardian*, so took hold of the paper's Lisboa correspondent and beat him so ferociously he seldom ventured into the streets thereafter (he would send out his Japanese-born wife to gather essential data). Violence always appeared to be a threat but was seldom seen.

*

One of the more dramatic events to close out those chaotic revolutionary nineteen months, occurred at the end of the summer – the sacking of both the Spanish chancellery and embassy by a mob of very angry *alfacinhas*. Depending on one's point of view, the double-deed was done – by the unwashed left, the fanatic right, or the contemptable anarchists. At this distance in time it doesn't much matter, and in any case, I never stopped to ask. Seeing the fires, I ran around the ones that had been lit – first at the Chancellery, then the embassy – into each of the two buildings, and attempted to photograph whatever I could. My best efforts were hampered by people getting in the way, showing their faces on camera. Three times I was ordered by supposed organizers to remove the film from the camera and toss it onto one of the fires. In the end the only decent shot I obtained of the unfolding drama was the one accompanying this description. Though I perused the following day's newspapers as best I could, the absence of action photographs of the fire was a surprise, so I was quite happy to have obtained at least this one.

A few days previously, across the border in Spain, Generalissimo Francisco Franco was still the leader of an intolerant and highly unpopular fascist dictatorship. He was to die shortly himself (20 November 1975) but, right to the end, he stubbornly hung onto his self-righteous political views. Needless to say, there was little love lost between the revolutionary left-wing regime that had just thrown out a fascist dictatorship in Portugal, and the fascist right-wing regime to be found still prepared to draw blood next door in Spain ...

But the train of Destiny was already in movement. Franco must have been fearful of what had happened in Portugal, no doubt imagining much the same fate for his own miserable life's work. The long-suffering Spanish people, sickened by the loathsome police-state control over them, looked to Portugal as an example of how they could be rid of their dictator.

But Franco was not to give in so easily. Not at all, in fact. Earlier that year his cohorts had caught two Basque 'terrorists' who had been responsible for the assassination of Franco's puppet Prime Minister, Don Luis Carrero Blanco, first Duke of Carrero Blanco. By committing this assassination these men had unleashed within the country an unstoppable movement towards democracy. They had learned the prime minister's route to and from his church and had burrowed a tunnel under the roadway where he customarily passed. They packed it with more than one hundred kilos of explosives, and on 20 December 1973, they blew Carrero Branco's car so high into the sky – over the top of a Jesuit monastery – it landed upside-down on a second-floor balcony located on the other side of the main monastery building.

There was a mock trial held in mid-September 1975, the outcome of which was never in doubt: the two Basques were found guilty and condemned to death.

The whole world spoke up in their defense – the President of the USA, the Pope, and practically every senior government minister everywhere else. All of them pleaded with Franco not to carry out the executions. The Portuguese, particularly, were horrified. Franco's regime was the very antithesis of the new thinking in Portugal. So, the Portuguese rallied in the streets of their capital and chanted – to no avail. Franco did not wish to listen.

On the morning of 26 September 1975, the two Basques and three other young revolutionaries were executed in the forest outside Madrid.

The streets of Lisbon erupted. This was a direct affront to the ideals of the Portuguese revolution. The people rallied, a million strong, on Lisbon's Avenida de Liberdade and began marching and chanting. The chant that went up was:

"Arriba Franco! Mais alto que Carrero Branco!" – "Up with Franco! Higher than Carrero Branco!"

As the horde passed the Spanish Chancellery on the avenida, they battered their way through the heavy doors, mobbed whatever security there was inside (no one, miraculously, was injured), and threw the entire contents of the building onto fires that had been lit in the street below. They then marched up the avenida and on to Praça d'Espanha where was located the magnificent palace of the Spanish Embassy – a virtual museum of antique Spanish works of art dating back over a period of more than three hundred years. Again, the members of the crowd smashed their way into the embassy, putting the ambassador, his family, and the entire staff to flight. In fury, they tore from the walls beautiful paintings and tapestries; they went through the offices and destroyed every document they could lay their hands on, they passed treasures of silver and gold out among themselves and hurled every stick of furniture onto fires that had been lit just outside the building. Though the walls remained standing the palace was gutted.

I was busy with my camera. Again I was caught by members of the mob who obliged me to tear rolls of film from the camera and pitch them onto the fires. A fourth and last roll I managed to save – this picture, and perhaps one or two others not as clear. I watched as a collection of Lucas Jordan paintings was thrown into the flames, and I saw unique seventeenth century tapestries in silk receive a similar fate. Beautifully-carved antique furniture was burned and reduced to ash.

At one point, as I was at an open upstairs window trying to take pictures of what was going on outside, I heard a voice behind me.

"Camarada!" a sturdy young man was shouting to me. He was struggling with a large wooden filing cabinet. "Help me load this onto the fires!"

"I can't!" I called back to him. "I'm supposed to be taking photographs!"

"No faces!" he shouted in alarm.

He had balanced one end of the cabinet on the window sill, and was about to shove the whole thing out onto the fires below. But he hesitated, and I thought for a moment he might drop the cabinet and rush me and my offending camera.

"No faces! No faces!" I shouted back. And then: *"A luta continua!"*

That somehow reassured him of my political stripe.

"A luta continua!" he bellowed back and, with a final almighty heave, he managed to shove the cabinet through the window. It fell two stories and

smashed to matchwood, its contents – scores of files – spilling onto the ground. People outside picked everything up and fed the flames.

"*Viva!*" he cried.

"*Sempre!*" I called back over my shoulder, for by that time I was hightailing it out of the building to be sure to save my film.

On my way I noticed a small empty ledger lying on the floor. I picked it up and made my way onto the grass of the praça outside. There I sat down and began to write in it. I filled several pages of the notebook describing what I had just witnessed. I still have it. Then soldiers appeared and started shooting – into the air, but close enough to put everyone to flight. I lived only a block or two away, on Avenida Elias Garcia, so walked home without further incident.

Two or three years later, when an embarrassed Portugal was attempting to apologize to a newly-liberated Spain, and pay the bill for the damage to the embassy palace, my friend, Inocencío Arias, who was then a functionary at the Spanish Embassy, gave me a partial inventory of the artworks destroyed that night. It is pasted into the ledger I had salvaged.

*

Frank Carlucci was appointed ambassador to Portugal by Gerald Ford in January 1975 and worked closely with Eanes to 'stabilize' the country. For years Portugal had been a stalwart member of NATO – and clearly it would never do for a nation so bound to the Western Alliance to be allowed to vote a hard-left government into power. Commies in NATO ...? Ridiculous! Besides, America wanted to continue using the air base at Lajes in the Açores. Carlucci was on hand to prod and guide until February 1978, by which time he had completed his handiwork. He returned to his country to take up the position for which his qualifications were so appropriate: number two man under Stansfield Turner at the Central Intelligence Agency.

A free election ran the risk of voting into power a leftist bloc of one stripe or another – but the watchful and wily Portuguese had kept an eye on how things had panned out for the Chilenos when Gen. Augusto Pinochet came to power in 1973 with the blessings of America's CIA. They did not relish a repeat performance – which daily throughout the summer months had seemed more and more likely. By November Gen. António Ramalho Eanes, an un-smiling no-nonsense veteran of the colonial war in Angola and the leader of a moderate faction of the *Movimento das Forças Armadas*, succeeded in gaining an upper hand, and immediately went to work – with the assistance of the CIA – in quelling the hot spots within the revolution. A presidential election was called for the summer of 1976 in which Eanes gained more than sixty percent of the vote. (He won again in1980 with more than fifty-six percent.)

*

The Americans were successful; they succeeded in the collapsing of the revolution and helped set up free elections – 'free' but for the preponderance of propaganda, the sort of hype Americans are good at but that tended to swamp and confuse the Portuguese. General Ramalho Eanes was elected president. The election headquarters was at the Gulbenkian Foundation. The place was packed with people when Eanes entered in triumph.

I was standing with a group of foreign journalists. The Canadian Broadcasting Corporation's Joe Schlessinger had set up his camera in the lobby, a perfect location to catch footage of the general and his entourage as they entered the building and close to a dais set up for the inevitable victory speeches. Suddenly, through the main hall there marched a small group of secret service heavies – Gen. Eanes' bodyguards. In the lead was none other than my acquaintance of several years earlier – Capitão Coutinho, the senior police operative who had given me a thrashing at PIDE headquarters in 1972. It now appeared he was a senior security chief for his country's new president.

"Hey! That man!" I said to Schlessinger, and quickly I recounted my meeting a few years earlier with the *capitão*.

"Are you sure it's him?" he queried.

"I'm not likely to forget!"

Schlessinger spoke to his chief cameraman, and in an instant the CBC camera lights were beamed on the *capitão* as I walked over to re-introduce myself to him.

"Capitão Coutinho, do you not recognize me?" I greeted him.

He looked puzzled, but smiled, obviously pleased to be meeting again with an old acquaintance – even though it was clear there was not so much as a spark of recognition.

"I have a beard now that I didn't have during our last meeting ..."

His smile broadened as he tried to look beneath my whiskers, but still he did not know me.

"How's your English now?" I asked him, keeping him dangling as long as I could. He was confused, but appeared to be quite pleased to be singled out by the television lights while an old friend remembered him. For a moment I tried to make small talk, but I could not keep it up.

"You and your fellow PIDE operatives gave me a beating in 1972 ... down there at your headquarters on Rua António Maria Cardoso." I smiled at him.

He knew. He understood immediately. For an instant he recognized, and then his eyes hooded, his face changed.

"I not remember you ... I dunno nothing PIDE ... you are make mistake..."

He looked alarmed and started backing away, trying to get out of the lights.

"I very busy. Election, you understand ... excuse me ..." and in an instant he had managed to disappear into the crowd.

Buccaneers, Thieves, Colonists – Thoughts in Closing

In the summer of 1592, just four years after the Spanish Armada's attempted invasion of England, Sir Walter Raleigh, with six warships and a gang of English buccaneers (Martin Frobisher among them) captured the Portuguese carrack, *Madre de Deus,* in a fierce day-long battle off Flores Island in the Açores. Queen Elizabeth I herself had given the expedition her blessing.

The entire engagement – it is known as the Second Battle of Flores – lasted almost three months and involved many more ships than just the *Madre de Deus*. It was at that awkward point of Portugal's history, nearly four and a half centuries ago, when Spanish kings sat on the Portuguese throne, and felt at liberty to take fullest advantage of the Iberian Union that had joined the crowns of Spain and Portugal in 1580. The old king of Portugal, Cardinal

Dom Henrique, had only been on the throne for two years when he died without an heir. The closest relative to succeed him was half-Spanish and half-Portuguese, King Felipe II of Spain, who was son of Isabella of Portugal and Charles V, the Holy Roman Emperor. He came to the throne of Portugal as Filipe I. Spain was at war with Britain (1585-1604) and, despite the *Anglo-Portuguese Treaty* signed in 1373 as a guarantee of friendship and non-aggression between them, Filipe calculated he could use Portuguese warships and transport galleons to advance his own interests – as he had done by launching the formidable Spanish Armada in 1588. That ill-fated fleet had consisted of many Portuguese vessels sailing under the flag of their Spanish king.

However, sensitive to the degree of Portuguese cultural sovereignty, and the undercurrent of Portuguese public discomfort at having a series of Spanish kings on their throne, the Spanish crown – (each of the three Filipes, I, II, and III in Portugal, Felipe II, III and IV in Spain who reigned between 1580 and 1640) – had promised not to interfere in Portugal's commercial activity with her holdings overseas – possessions that were to be left intact to the mercantile administration of Portugal.[45] The *Madre de Deus* was part of a purely Portuguese overseas commercial enterprise, and thus sailed under the guarantee of non-interference by the Spanish. She was now headed home, north through the Atlantic to Lisbon, escorted by a flotilla of Portuguese ships returning with their holds laden with trade goods from the Far East.

The British, however, were not so especially inclined to consider the fine details of whatever arrangements had been made between the Spanish and the Portuguese. Their sentiment was contemptuous and aggressive. In these same waters one year earlier, in the First Battle of Flores, the Spanish had inflicted a severe defeat on English vessels; two hundred and fifty English seamen had been killed or captured. Itching for blood and booty by the summer of 1592, the British considered the entire flotilla sailing up the Atlantic was fair pickings.

---

[45] Filipe I [II of Spain] – 1580-1598; Filipe II [III of Spain] – 1598-1621; Filipe III [IV of Spain] – 1621-1640. At the time Filipe I ascended the throne of Portugal, he was already King Felipe II of Spain (note slight difference in spelling). Son of King Charles V, Holy Roman Emperor, and Queen Isabella of Portugal, he acquired a number of titles during his lifetime (1527-1598). He was King of Spain from 1527; King of Portugal (as Filipe I) from 1581; King of Naples and Sicily from 1554; *jure uxoris* King of England and Ireland during the period of his marriage to Queen Mary I, 1554-1558 (half-sister to Queen Elizabeth I [1558-1603] who succeeded Mary on the throne of England). *Restauração* – the restoration of Portugal's full independence from Spain – commenced the Fourth Dynasty, the House of Bragança, with the reign of Dom João IV – 1640-1656.

The second Battle of Flores had been joined in the closing weeks of May, and lasted through until mid-August of that year. It involved a number of excellent ships on both sides – some of the Spanish/Portuguese craft measuring burthens of eight hundred and nine hundred tons. They were mercantile vessels equipped with armaments, but nowhere near as formidable as the English ships that had both canons and soldiers with musketry who had been well-trained in boarding techniques. Engagement with the *Madre de Deus* did not occur until the first days of August. It was sighted and chased by the crew of the *Dainty*, which was soon joined in its attack by several other British ships. These sailors could hardly believe their eyes when they manoeuvred closer in order to attack the *Madre de Deus*, and saw the enormous size of the Portuguese vessel.

Of all the trading vessels involved in this three-month battle, the *Madre de Deus*, built in 1589, was by far the biggest ship ever constructed in Europe. She measured one hundred and sixty-five feet long (fifty metres) and had a beam of forty-seven feet (fourteen metres). Crewed by as many as seven hundred men, she had seven decks, thirty-two guns and burthen of one thousand six hundred tons.

The engagement with *Madre de Deus* lasted a full day. She fought gamely, but her size meant that her guns were too high, shooting over the tops of the smaller ships that were able to come in close to her. When she was finally cornered, rammed and boarded, the English discovered that the holds and every deck were laden with chests of the finest gems and gold and silver coinage. There were fabrics of the best silks and taffeta, carpets and tapestries, sculpture and artwork, and quantities of ornate furnishings and exotic woods – fifteen tons of ebony. There were also tons of spices, oils and perfumes. The take was massive, and in addition there was the vessel itself. Wanting to preserve everything from determined on-board thieves, the commander of the boarding party stationed guards at key points throughout the ship and, on the long voyage home to Britain, managed to take an inventory.

However, when the *Madre de Deus* was brought into harbour at Dartmouth, the townspeople mobbed both it and the crew members. Marauding thieves and vagabonds from all over southern England descended on the port to grab what they could for themselves, in the end chalking up what turned out to be one of the greatest robberies ever recorded. The theft totaled approximately half the value of the English treasury.

Much as Queen Elizabeth I and her assorted officers were appalled at the sheer size of the theft, the capture of the *Madre de Deus* and realization of just how much booty she carried on her decks and in her holds, stoked Britain's awareness of the riches to be acquired by trading in the Orient – especially with India – which they began almost immediately. Queen Elizabeth I awarded the British East India Company its Royal Charter in 1600. It was the start of a lucrative and ongoing interest in the subcontinent that was bolstered mightily seventy years later when King Charles II of England married Princess Catherine of Bragança, daughter of Dom João IV, King of Portugal. Dom João's widow, acting as regent over a kingdom that stretched far beyond India, bestowed on King Charles II as a wedding gift a small group of islands and a stretch of mosquito-infested lowland at the entrance to the Gulf of Cambay, on India's northern Malabar coast. She calculated the area was no longer of great value to the Portuguese. Charles, in turn, awarded these lands to the British East India Company with the idea that they might prove useful as a base of expanded company operations. It was a move that effectively slid the predatory British Empire into gear; these were the very lands on which the city of Mumbai stands today.[46]

Strange story, full of the ironies that have confounded and fascinated historians since mankind first started searching for origins and explanations – but in this case the ramifications were enormous, for India was to become the central cog of the most substantial colonial empire ever devised.

A gift that turned to abuse that turned to domination, then to war and humiliation. Colonialism.

One constantly hears comments of comparison, such as "… the British were arrogant, yes, but at least they were better than the French …," or "… the German colonies were not as cruel as the Spanish …," or "… the Portuguese were much more easy-going than the Belgians." The fact is that all colonies – the central idea of colonialism, intended or otherwise – is the deprivation of local indigenous; long-settled populations have their land and liberty taken away from them. Just that level of invasion and abuse would be bad enough; when it involves culture to boot, and invariably it does (how can it not?) all hell can break loose – and invariably it does.

The very definition of colonialism entails the grinding down of locals in order that the colonizers may flourish. It is a repugnant concept by any measure; no one colonial administration was ever 'better' than any other. They were all vile.

There is a bibliography still growing on colonies and colonialism, but one

---

[46] Dom João IV ushered in the dynasty of the Braganças when he came to the throne in 1640. The last of the Bragança dynasty to reign was Dom Manuel II who abdicated in 1910 when the country became a republic. The current pretender to Portugal's throne is Duarte Pio de Bragança.

of the most comprehensive and succinct is a study written by Jürgen Osterhammel of the University of Konstanz, entitled *Colonialism,* that casts an especially keen eye on (mostly) the variations of European-style colonialism. Right at the start of his work, explaining some of the basics, he freely admits that 'Colonization is ... a phenomenon of colossal vagueness.' Later he goes on to divide the concept of colonies and colonization into three basic categories: a) exploitative colonies, b) maritime enclaves, and c) settlement colonies.

The first, he claims, is usually the result of military conquest, which customarily involves exploitation of wealth and/or minerals, and a 'relatively insignificant' occupier presence – usually in the guise of soldiers, civil servants and businessmen, all of them enforcing an autocratic government on the part of the 'mother country' – and often with a deal of 'paternalistic solicitude.' He cites examples: British India and Egypt, French Indochina, German Togo, the Americans in the Philippines and the Japanese in Taiwan. A close variation of this type would be Spanish America, which ultimately led to heavy European immigration and the development of a strong creole minority.

The second category was the result of 'fleet action' to pressure a formerly autonomous entity in order to establish hinterland penetration, and thus assist the support of a military foothold. Describing this as classic 'gunboat diplomacy,' he cited: Hong Kong, Singapore and Aden for the British, Batavia for the Dutch and Malacca for the Portuguese. Shanghai, he said, became an example of international colonial control.

Settlement colonies, Osterhammel's third category, came about as the result of strong military support and policing. The aim behind this action would have been to benefit from cheap land and/or labour, and to encourage the cultivation of new forms of social, religious and cultural participation. Meanwhile this would lead into a permanent colonial agricultural presence overlooking the interests of the indigenous population that ultimately demanded its own self-government. This would very often involve the displacement, even eventual extinction, of unwanted or unnecessary indigenous lifestyles. In Africa, particularly, this involved a dependence on an indigenous workforce akin to slavery; in the Americas it promoted imported slavery.

(North America's displacement of First Nations – their 'Indian wars' – would fall inside this last category.)

On my journey through Portuguese Africa, I came across many examples outlined in Osterhammel's pithy book. And closer to home, it has caused me to note, after one hundred and fifty years of nationhood, how Canadians have become adept at seeing clean through the nation's large indigenous minority – almost as if they were invisible. Apart from the annihilation of the Beothuk indigenous of Newfoundland, a *fait accompli*, various Canadian administrations have wrestled ceaselessly since colonial times with the problems of conscience arising from the colonization of the nation's native peoples. Government throws millions of dollars into indigenous laps in an attempt to right such a terrible string of wrongs. All indications are that the nation's colonizers have never adequately explained themselves to those they continue to dominate. I have heard the rather lame rejoinder that Newfoundland was not a part of Canada at the time and, as a *fait accompli,* the massacre of the Beothuk is not a legitimate contemporary Canadian problem. This can hardly satisfy the remaining (and growing) numbers of Canada's indigenous champing at their continued position around the bottom of the ladder, despite whatever efforts are being made through various channels of government. There is certainly no single easy response to all those earlier *faits accomplis*. Not in Canada; not anywhere.

The Portuguese Empire was some two centuries older than the British Empire. It was never as big, even when Brasil was a part of it, but it was just as far-flung and lasted quite a number of years longer. The rapaciousness of the Portuguese was never quite the match for British rapaciousness – as that of the British, horrendous as it was, never quite matched the unseemliness of American greed and sense of entitlement. Since the close of the Second World War a localized hunger for riches has developed into a great global gluttony – and the concept of a full-blown American colonization has not extended beyond the scope of imagining.

It has taken mankind millennia to discover the wheel, a blink in time since the advent of civilizations in the Fertile Crescent – and now, suddenly, we are able to blow ourselves to kingdom come or hurl ourselves into outer space, riding the digital age of communication, travel and commerce. But we have also, finally, developed the capability of looking after every man-Jack in this world – and his wife and children to boot – and, who knows, in time the universe (adding the cautionary hope: that if we can take on such a daunting assignment 'out there,' we apply to our efforts a little more enlightenment and common sense than we have shown 'down here'). To date, our universal struggle has only managed to raise our species to a childlike level of greed – wanting, demanding and taking *all* the contents of the pot just for ourselves. We are dazzled by a collection of bright marbles in their glass jam jar, and rather than play with them with our neighbours, we smash the glass, leave the shards on the ground to cut our neighbours' feet, and walk away with all the marbles in our own pockets to play with by ourselves. That way we get to write all the rules, come out 'on top' – winner every time!

The world has never been ready for enslavement, but it is clear we have to learn the lesson over and over.

For five hundred years the people of Portugal's 'overseas provinces' had no doubt about the connection between colonialism and enslavement, that colonialism is only another word for slavery. The suppression was great, and it took years to summon the courage to face into it, to collect the resistance. And then it took a war and revolution to drive the point home to their oppressors ...

India's Red Fort Trials in 1945/6 were a stupendous audacity, Indian warriors in their own land being charged with 'treason' for daring to accept Japan's offer to help rid their country of British Imperialism during the Second World War. Millions of Indians were outraged, particularly in the military. The Indian Navy mutinied, and the Indian Army threatened the same. Suddenly there were red British faces in the halls of the Red Fort, and the trials were speedily called off.

The Mau Mau rebellion in Kenya was a desperate attempt by dirt poor people to hold onto their own homelands – territories close to, even on, acreage the British thought would be suitable for themselves and their capital city. Just outside the city, British farms were established on lands taken from the Kikuyu. After years of failed negotiations, the Africans reckoned to take matters into their own hands – 'illegally,' claimed the British, who then shot them down by the thousands, and threw thousands more into concentration camps. Compensation for such historic arrogance was paid to only a few of the camp survivors, and only many years later (2013) – far too little and far too late.

The stories and incidences of British Empire building are heroic when recounted by Rudyard Kipling et al. But then there are those – especially among people whose lives were buggered up 'out there' (and not just grumblers, naysayers and misfits) who believe Kitchener himself, and even Britain's monarchy, were responsible for, and committed, war crimes. (The Geneva Convention did not exist at the time of the East India Company, but does that fact give the nod to colonialism?)

Absurdities abound!

As for the Portuguese Empire – 1415 to 1975 – its history has been well-documented, and there is still much to discover and write about it. The nation was caught, by the myopia of its own dictatorial leaders, and forced to learn a severe lesson. Whatever it is that man carries with him when he ventures abroad – everything about him that is virtuous and all that is rotten and corrupt – was carried all over the world by this extraordinarily adventurous people. In the beginning the ships in which they sailed were no bigger than the lifeboats of the ferries that ply the harbours and near coastal waters of many of our cities today; over the centuries they educated themselves about the seas, their ships and the weather, the landfalls they made and the societies that peopled them; they grew rich through the use of their wits, and corrupt through heartless exploitation. They were noble and they were venal – though probably not much better or worse, for all that, than the saints and martyrs or brigands and cutthroats of other nations. It was the epoch of eye-boggling, adventurous and dangerous discovery, after all, and the newness of such findings brought them all to the feast, and for any number of reasons. Portuguese is one of the world's great languages, its varied cadences and dialects as beautiful and mysterious and subtle as any other anywhere, and all of it expressed in a boundless literature, prose and poetry. Reviewing their recent African trauma, their historical brush with the faces of fascism, my feeling is that there would be few Portuguese today who seriously believe it was not yet high time to chuck the imperial pose. For a small country the Portuguese have created a mammoth history, and no one could ever take that from them.

For all that my own initial experience of the Portuguese was coloured by the harsh events of the epoch of my journey, it was never sufficient to blanket or hide the essential goodness and humanity of the culture and the people. I am grateful I came to discover my love for the country was – and remains – every bit as great as my love for my own homeland. I chose to live there for twenty-five years of my working life; it was a productive and healthy time for me as a younger man, and the life I lived brought me an abundance of joy and know-how and wisdom and understanding I almost certainly would never have achieved had I remained anchored those years to North America. Looking out my window at Portugal today, I see only a garden – the exquisite array of a nation that decided, collectively, on re-birth.

How about all the other players – the French, the Spanish, the Italians, Germans or Dutch? And the Chinese in their big and not-so-subtle way?

How about America …?

Times and expectations have changed greatly, and quickly, and it is legitimate to question the rise of corporate banking and industrialization on a global scale, for at what point will it merely amount to an alternate and intolerable imperialist abuse?

Is the constant repetition of this question, perchance, a part of the human condition? A dream? A nightmare? A madness?

It is appropriate, at both the opening and the closing of this work, to quote the fractured humour of Fernando Pessoa. He has much to say about dreams:

'I have dreamed more than Napoleon ...' he wrote in his most famous of poems, *'Tabacaria.'*

And madness? He dealt with that one, too. Pessoa might have been contemplating any number of white-collar, red-necked, imperialistic-minded western con men – tricksters, all, for sure – when he wrote:

'Em todos os manicómios há doidos malucos com tantas certezas!'

Which is to say in English:

'In all the insane asylums there are nut-heads who have many certainties!'

He makes a salient point. On all sides we strive to set free zippy-minded madmen – *and we harken to them.* Our democratic principles are so honed we have managed to convince ourselves out-and-out wackos deserve a place at the table when they can prove themselves able to outwit us – which, being so diabolically far out, routinely they do. Something's wrong. While we have done away with the safely enclosed coops (we used to call them *asylums*, but any euphemism would serve) where we might quietly and comfortably put away such noisome creatures to roost for the duration – hood or hibernate them, so to say, in order to bring them out for an airing and a reassuring cuddle next spring – we fail to loosen the string that has hitherto bound them to a solid perch. It becomes difficult to maintain our purchase on them, to turn them about and wring their wretched necks when it is clearly time to do so. Instead we seek relief from their discordant battiness and give them rein to reign ...

That is crazy!

It seems drastic, but sometimes Rooster squawks too loudly, too incessantly, too inanely. The distraction so rattles and disturbs the mind that offing his silly head would barely shadow the conscience, and would in any case seem small vexation in exchange for tranquility.

The sun comes up; the sun goes down ...

461

Dichotomy: we do not seem able to learn fast enough that some of us may be evolving faster than others, so the exhausting cycle continues.

Damned bird!

APPENDIXES

Appendixes

1. United Nations Working Paper,
   A/AC.109/L.126 – 9 June 1964 465

2. Ethnic Appelations 504

3. Racism 506

4. Forced Labour 507

5. Torture 508

6. Song 510

7. Portuguese Toleration of Protestants 511

8. Holden Roberto 513

9. Jonas Savimbi 518

10. Dondi – Growing Centre of Education 521

11. Camões 523

12. American Duplicity and Medling 527

Appendix 1 – United Nations Working Paper, A/AC.109/L.126 – 9 June 1964

(JJH-B) – *The following is an extract from a 'working paper' prepared by the Secretariat of the UN General Assembly with regard to the granting of independence to 'colonial countries and peoples/territories under Portuguese administration.' For space reasons the original document has been edited to include details for only those territories relevant to this memoir. References to unavailable documentation not greatly concerned with this work has likewise been removed. Access to the full paper, reference code listed above, has been made available through the offices of UN Publications.*

I. ACTION TAKEN BY THE SPECIAL COMMITTEE IN 1963, BY THE SECURITY COUNCIL AND BY THE GENERAL ASSEMBLY DURING ITS EIGHTEENTH SESSION

1. Following the adoption by the General Assembly at its seventeenth session of resolution 1807 (XVII) on 14 December 1962 and resolution 1819 (XVII) on 18 December 1962, the Special Committee again considered the Territories under Portuguese administration at its meetings in March and April 1963.

2. In accordance with the decision of the Special Committee, the Chairman, on 6 March 1963, addressed a letter to the Permanent Representative of Portugal, inviting the participation of Portugal at the Committee's meetings. This invitation was not accepted.

3. After considering the developments in the Territories under Portuguese administration, the Special Committee, on 4 April 1963, adopted a resolution by which it decided to draw the immediate attention of the Security Council to the situation in the Territories under Portuguese administration, with a view to the Council taking appropriate measures, including sanctions to secure the compliance by Portugal of the relevant resolutions of the General Assembly and of the Security Council.

4. The Secretary-General transmitted the text of this resolution on 5 April 1963 to the President of the Security Council, and on 19 July 1963 the Chairman of the Special Committee transmitted to the President of the Security Council the Committee's report on the Territories under Portuguese administration.

5. In May, the Heads of African States and Governments, meeting at Addis Ababa, decided to send a delegation composed of the Foreign Ministers of Liberia, Tunisia, Madagascar and Sierra Leone to represent the African States at the meeting of the Security Council called to consider the question of the Territories under Portuguese administration.

6. On 11 July 1963 the President of the Security Council received a request from thirty-two African States to convene a meeting of the Council, at the earliest possible date.

7. On 22 July 1963, the Security Council started discussions on the question of the Territories under Portuguese administration and, on 31 July 1963, the Council adopted resolution S/5380 by eight votes to none, with three abstentions.

8. By this resolution, the Security Council determined that 'the situation in the Territories under Portuguese administration is seriously disturbing peace and security in Africa.' The Council urgently called on Portugal to implement the following:

(a) The immediate recognition of the right of the peoples of the Territories under its administration to self-determination and independence;

(b) The immediate cessation of all acts of repression and the withdrawal of all military and other forces at present employed for that purpose;

(c) The promulgation of an unconditional political amnesty and the establishment of conditions that will allow the free functioning of political parties;

(d) Negotiations, on the basis of the recognition of the right to self-determination, with the authorized reprsentatives of the political parties within and outside the Territories with a view to the transfer of power to political institutions freely elected and representative of the peoples, in accordance with resolution 1514 (XV);

(e) The granting of independence immediately thereafter to all the Territories under its administration in accordance with the aspirations of the peoples.

9. In the same resolution the Security Council urged that 'all States should refrain from offering the Portuguese Government any assistance which would enable it to continue its repression of the peoples of the Portuguese Territories and to take all measures to prevent the sale and supply of arms and military equipment to the Portuguese Government.' The Council also asked the Secretary-General to furnish assistance to ensure the implementation of the resolution and to report to the Security Council by 31 October 1963.

10. In his report the Secretary-General informed the Security Council that in accordance with its resolution of 31 July 1963 he had, after preliminary consultations, initiated conversations between representatives of the African States and Portugal and set out a brief account of the discussions on the concept of self-determination.

11. On 6 November 1963, the African Group at the United Nations issued a statement setting out the position of the African States regarding any further conversations with Portugal.

12. On the recommendation of the Fourth Committee, the General Assembly, on 3 December 1963, adopted resolution 1913 (XVIII). In this resolution, the General Assembly recalled the measures which the Security Council had called on Portugal to implement; noted with deep regret and great concern the continued refusal of the

Government of Portugal to take any steps to implement the resolutions of the General Assembly and the Security Council; and requested the Security Council to consider immediately the question of the Territories under Portuguese administration. The President of the General Assembly transmitted the text of resolution 1913 (XVIII) to the Security Council on the same day.

13. In a letter dated 13 November 1963, twenty-nine African States requested the President of the Security Council to convene a meeting at an early date to consider the report of the Secretary-General.

14. On 6 December 1963, the Security Council started discussions on the question of the Territories under Portuguese administration and, on 11 December 1963 adopted resolution S/5481 by a vote of 10 to none with one abstention. By this resolution, the Security Council, recalling its resolution of 31 July 1963 and General Assembly resolution 1541 (XV), noting with appreciation the efforts of the Secretary-General in establishing contact between representatives of Portugal and representatives of African States, expressed regret that the contacts had not achieved the desired results because of 'failure to reach agreement on the United Nations interpretation of self-determination.' It again called on all States to refrain forthwith from offering the Portuguese Government any assistance which would enable it to continue its repression of the peoples of the Territories under Portuguese administration, and to take all measures to prevent the sale and supply of arms and military equipment for this purpose to the Portuguese Government.

15. In the same resolution, the Security Council referred to General Assembly resolution 1542 (XV) and reaffirmed the interpretation of self-determination as laid down in General Assembly resolution 1514 (XV) as follows:

'All peoples have the right to self-determination; by virtue of that right they freely determine their political status and freely pursue their economic, social and cultural development.'

It expressed the belief that action by the Government of Portugal to grant an amnesty to all persons imprisoned or exiled for advocating self-determination in these Territories would be an evidence of its good faith. The Security Council again requested the Secretary-General to continue with his efforts and report to it not later than 1 June 1964.

II. INFORMATION ON THE TERRITORIES – GENERAL

Introduction

16. Information on the Territories is already contained in the Report of the Special Committee on Territories under Portuguese administration and the reports of the Special Committee to the General Assembly at its seventeenth and eighteenth sessions. Supplementary information on recent developments is set out below.

1. Political and constitutional developments

17. At its meetings in 1963, the Special Committee was informed of the proposed revision of the Overseas Organic Law of 1953). The revised Overseas Organic Law was approved by the National Assembly and published on 24 June 1963.

18. In explaining the changes which had been made, the Prime Minister, Dr. Oliveira Salazar, said on 12 August 1963:

'The Overseas Organic Law has been reformed in accordance with the tendencies or aspirations revealed by the Provinces and with what seemed to be required for the present moment. The points of view of the Provinces were expressed in the Overseas Council, among others, by their direct representatives – the governors and the elected members of the local Legislative Councils and indirectly also by the representatives of economic activities. The main lines of orientation revealed in the discussions which took place in the Overseas Council, in the Corporative Chamber and in the National Assembly may be, notwithstanding the complexity of the matter, enunciated as follows:

'greater representation in the local organs; more powers for these organs in the sphere of local administration; greater intervention of the Provinces in the direction of national policy.'

19. Since the publication of the 1963 Overseas Organic Law, other relevant legislation has also been revised to give effect to the changes introduced. These include amendments to the legislation establishing the Overseas Council, new political and administrative Statutes for each of the seven Territories, and a new overseas electoral law. The changes introduced in the central, territorial and local organs of government are summarized below.

20. Elections to the legislative councils took place in the last part of March 1964, and information relating to these developments is given in Section (e) below.

(a) Central administration

21. The Overseas Organic Law of 1963 does not make any substantial changes in the powers of the organs of the Portuguese Government to legislate for the Territories which have been described previously.[47] The principal changes introduced affect the participation of representatives of the Territories in the central advisory bodies, namely the Overseas Council, the Corporative Chamber, and the Conference of Overseas Governors. No changes have been made in the composition of the National Assembly.

---

[47] The Overseas Organic Law of 1963 introduces slight changes in the powers of the Overseas Minister. One change relates to his right to legislate on the composition, recruitment, etc., of the private and complementary staff of the provincial public services which is transferred to the Governors. The other change concerns the authorization of changes in the allocation of funds within the approved territorial budget; this is to be governed by a special law.

(i) **Corporative Chamber**

22. Under article 102 of the Political Constitution of Portugal, the Corporative Chamber is a general advisory body composed of representatives of 'local autonomous bodies and social interests'[48] and it is consulted by the Government on proposals, draft bills and treaties that are to be submitted to the National Assembly for approval. The Government is at liberty to consult the Corporative Chamber on decrees to be published or on bills to be submitted to the National Assembly when they apply to the Territories.

23. The Overseas Organic Law of 1963 provides that the Territories shall be adequately represented 'through their local authorities and social interests in the Corporative Chamber.' Under the new political and administrative statutes of Angola and Mozambique, the Economic and Social Council is responsible for electing the territorial representatives to the Corporative Chamber, and in the other five Territories, it is the Government Council that does so. The respective Council is specially convened for this purpose and voting is by secret ballot.

24. There is no information on the actual number of representatives each Territory is to have in the Corporative Chamber. In Angola and Mozambique one half of the number of representatives are to be chosen from members of the Economic and Social Council, in order to ensure representation of moral, social and economic interests, and the other half are to be chosen from members of the administrative bodies and legally recognized public bodies performing administrative functions.[49] In Cape Verde, Portuguese Guinea, São Tomé and Príncipe, Macau and Timor, representatives in the Corporative Chamber are to be chosen from present or former members of the Government Council, and present or former members of the Public Service or other bodies performing administrative functions.

(ii) **The Overseas Council**

25. The Overseas Council is the highest permanent consultative organ for the Overseas Ministry on matters relating to policy and administration for the Territories. The Overseas Minister must consult the Council on certain matters, including the political and administrative statutes of the Territories. The Overseas Council is also the supreme tribunal on administrative, fiscal and customs matters, and the tribunal on questions of constitutionality, as well as on questions of conflict of powers and functions. It is also the superior judicial council of the overseas Territories. The Overseas Council meets in plenary sessions at least once a month and it also meets in committees. There is a disputed claims committee comprising six members who are especially appointed by the Overseas Minister, and there are two advisory committees which sit on matters brought before the Council for its opinion.

---

[48] Most of the representatives in the Corporative Chamber are appointed by the Corporations in which there is equal representation of capital and labour.

[49] These apparently include local government bodies, such as municipal councils and parish boards.

26. As set up in 1954, the Council is composed of *ex officio* members, regular members and alternate members. The governors of the Territories are *ex officio* members when in Lisbon. Of the regular members, some are appointed by the Overseas Minister and some by the Council of Ministers on the proposal of the Minister.[50] In accordance with the provisions of the Overseas Organic Law of 1963, new legislation was published in August 1963 providing for the first time for the addition to the membership of the Overseas Council of nine regular members elected by the Legislative councils of the Territories.[51] Angola and Mozambique are to elect two representatives each and the other Territories one each. These representatives are to be elected from among persons who have held high posts in the fields of education or administration, or who have been distinguished in economic, social or cultural activities. Each Territory is also to elect an alternate representative who is resident in Lisbon.

27. Although each of the five smaller Territories are to have an elected member on the Overseas Council, it appears that all these members are not to attend the meetings at the same time: Macau and Timor are to be represented by one of their elected members, while Cape Verde, Portuguese Guinea, and Sao Tome and Principe together are to be represented by one member in the same way. In the day-to-day work of the Overseas Council, seven Territories are, in effect, to participate through four representatives who may be assigned to either of the two advisory committees, which now comprise ten members each.

28. It therefore appears that the newly introduced 'representation' of the Territories in the Overseas Council does little more than to give former administrators in the Territories and other high government officials some voice in the consultative machinery. That this is the case is seen from the results of the elections for the Legislative Council of Angola; an administrative inspector and the former governor, General Deslandes, are two of the three members representing the Territory in the Overseas Council.

(iii) **Other central advisory organs**

29. In addition to the Corporative Chamber and the Overseas Council the two other important central advisory bodies are the Conference of Overseas Governors and the Overseas Economic Conference. Both meet from time to time when considered necessary by the Overseas Minister and are presided over by him. Under

---

[50] The regular members are appointed as follows: six by the Overseas Minister to the disputed claims committee; eight by the Council of Ministers on the proposal of the Overseas Minister for an unrenewable term of five years; three by the Overseas Minister on the proposal of the Overseas Council, adopted in a secret ballot; two freely appointed by the Overseas Minister from directors and inspectors-general or senior inspectors of the Ministry, such members being subject to removal, depending upon the requirements of the service.

[51] Mr. (Franco) Nogueira (Overseas Minister) is quoted as stating that the territorial representatives in the Corporative Chamber and the Overseas Council would be increased from 27 to nearly 100.

the Overseas Organic Law of 1963, the composition of the Conference of Overseas Governors has been widened. As before, the Secretary-General of the Overseas Ministry and the heads of the departments of the Ministry may participate in the work of the Conference and have voting rights. Under the new provision, the Provincial Secretaries of Angola and Mozambique, and the Secretaries General of the other Territories may, also participate, at the discretion of the Minister, but without the right to vote. This change appears to do little more than enable the Conference, if it so desires, to hear the views of senior Portuguese administrators from the Territories.

(b) **Territorial administration**

30. The Overseas Organic Law of 1963 introduces a number of changes in the territorial Governments. In the Territories with a Governor-General, namely Angola and Mozambique, the membership of the legislative councils has been widened and the former government councils abolished and replaced by economic and social councils. The administrative services have also been reorganized to give them more responsibility. In Angola and Mozambique, departmental services are to be grouped into six provincial secretariats, each under a provincial secretary. The provincial secretariats are to have the role of embryo local ministries under the Governor-General. In the Territories with a Governor, namely Cape Verde, Portuguese Guinea, São Tomé and Príncipe, Macau and Timor, legislative councils are to be created for the first time; the Government Councils are to be retained, however, with modified membership and functions. In all Territories financial control remains the responsibility of the Governor or the Governor General.[52] This power may not be delegated.

(i) **The legislative councils**

31. In all Territories, as before, the legislative organs have power to legislate on all matters which exclusively concern their respective Territories, other than those which are the responsibility of the National Assembly, the Government, or the Overseas Minister. Under the Overseas Organic Law of 1963, the Governor is now precluded from legislating on certain matters when the Legislative Council is in session.[53]

32. Both the Governor and the members of the Legislative Council may initiate legislation. The latter may not, however, propose legislation involving any increase in expenditure or decrease in revenue as established by earlier decrees. Under the political and administrative statutes of 1963, this power is reserved to the Legislative Council when in session: (a) to approve the budget of the Territory; (b) to authorize the contracting of loans; (c) to evaluate the annual report of the Technical

---

[52] In the succeeding paragraphs of this section, the term 'Governor' should be taken as also referring to 'Governor General,' unless otherwise stated.

[53] The Legislative Councils sit for two ordinary sessions of 30 days' duration each year. These sessions may be extended by the Governor but the total duration of the two sessions may not exceed three months. The Councils may also be convened by the Governor in extraordinary sessions at which only the special items for which the Council was convened may be discussed.

Commission on planning and economic integration; and (d) to elect the territorial representatives to the Overseas Council.

33. The Governor has the right to refuse to enact legislation passed by the Council. If the measure is one which the Governor himself initiated he is only required to inform the Legislative Council of his decision. If, however, the legislation has been initiated by the Council, the Governor must either submit the matter to the Overseas Minister, or 'request' reconsideration by the Legislative Council. If, after reconsidering the measure, the Council approves it by a two-thirds majority, it becomes mandatory for the Governor to enact it. Although this provision makes it possible for the Legislative Council to over-ride the Governor's refusal to enact legislation passed by it, recourse to this procedure is at the discretion of the Governor.

34. The Overseas Organic Law of 1963 describes the Legislative Council as 'an assembly of representation suited to the social environment of the province.' Accordingly, the composition of the membership of the Council varies from one Territory to another. In all Territories, however, the Legislative Council is composed of a majority of elected members, some elected by direct suffrage and some by special 'organic' groups. There are also two or three *ex officio* members, except in Macau, which no longer has any nominated members.

35. Although the majority of the members of the legislative councils are to be elected, not all are to be elected by direct suffrage. In Angola, less than half of the membership is to be elected by direct suffrage, less than one third in Mozambique, Cape Verde and Macau, and less than one-quarter in Guinea, São Tomé and Príncipe and Timor. Moreover, there appears to be no direct relationship between the size of the population and the number of representatives elected by direct franchise. In Angola, there is to be one directly elected representative per 320,000 inhabitants, in Mozambique, one per 711,000 inhabitants, and in Cape Verde, one per 37,000. In the remaining four Territories, with total populations ranging from 67,000 in São Tomé to 500,000 in Timor, there are to be, uniformly, three directly elected representatives.

36. In all Territories, the majority of the members are to be indirectly elected by special 'organic' groups (which previously in Angola and Mozambique had been represented by both elected and nominated members). These special 'organic' groups are: (a) taxpayers paying a certain minimum tax which varies from 15,000 escudos per annum (approximately US$525) in Angola and Mozambique, to 2,000 escudos in Macau (approximately US$70) and to 1,000 escudos (US$35) in all the other Territories; (b) bodies representing employers and associations of economic interests; (c) bodies representing workers; (d) bodies representing cultural and moral (religious) interests, (in Angola and Mozambique, one member must be a Catholic missionary); (e) administrative and other legally recognized bodies performing administrative functions in the public service[54] and (f) indigenous authorities. Both the type of interests which are to be represented in the legislative councils and the number of

---

[54] These apparently include local administrative bodies such as municipal councils and parish boards, etc.

representatives these groups are to have also vary from one Territory to another. Details of the membership of the legislative councils are given in the sections relating to individual Territories.

37. As recorded in the Secretary-General's report (S/5448), in the explanation given by the Portuguese Minister for Foreign Affairs of the way Portugal was bringing about a greater degree of self-government, emphasis was placed on the enlarged membership of the legislative councils in Angola and Mozambique. The information available shows, however, that the enlarged membership has not increased the participation of all the inhabitants equally, but has favoured certain groups. For instance, the influence of the direct voter has not been increased to the same extent as that of the indirect voter. In Angola, although the total number of elected members has now been doubled, those to be elected by direct franchise still represent only about two-fifths of the membership. In Mozambique, the influence of the direct voter has actually decreased, as there the number of members elected by direct franchise remains at nine which is less than one third of the total membership.

38. Among the special 'organic' groups, tax payers and public and private economic interests now have a greater influence in the legislative councils than they had before. The indigenous authorities, known as *regedorias*, now have three representatives elected from among themselves, instead of two nominated to represent them; it should be borne in mind, however, that the indigenous inhabitants make up over 95 percent of the population. Administrative and public bodies remain well represented, with five out of 34 members in Angola and five out of 29 members in Mozambique. Since it is well known that, in these two Territories, the members of these groups, the tax payers, the public and private economic interests and the administrative personnel, are mainly Portuguese, it is evident that the increased participation has not really broadened the basis of government, but strengthens the representation of certain special interests. This trend is also evident from the new electoral law (see paragraphs 54-73 below) which was enacted in December 1963 and to which the Minister for Foreign Affairs has also drawn attention.

39. Under the new political and administrative statutes, the qualifications for candidates standing for election to the legislative councils remain substantially the same as before. A candidate must: (a) be an 'original' Portuguese citizen (*cidadão português originário*); (b) be of age (21 years); (c) read and write Portuguese; (d) fulfil a residence qualification; and (e) not be a government official or a member of the administrative service of active status. The residence requirement is three years in all Territories, except in Macau, where it is one year. Teachers in government service may not stand for election in Angola and Mozambique, though they may do so in the five other Territories.

40. It is not clear from the information available who are considered to be 'original' Portuguese citizens. Before the repeal of the Native Statute in 1961, the term was used to distinguish citizenship acquired by birth from citizenship acquired through 'assimilation,' which could be revoked. Further information is needed to clarify the interpretation of (*cidadão português originário*). If it is interpreted so as to

473

restrict eligibility to the legislative councils to those who acquired Portuguese citizenship by birth, this could exclude almost all indigenous persons in Angola, Mozambique and Portuguese Guinea. In this connexion it is to be noted that the Electoral Law of 1963 does not include the word '*originário*' in the qualifications of those entitled to vote.

(ii) **Territorial advisory councils**

41. In the five smaller Territories the Government Councils are retained as permanent advisory bodies, but in Angola and Mozambique they have been replaced by newly created economic and social councils. In addition to their advisory functions, government councils and the economic and social councils also assist the Governor in the exercise of his executive functions and are responsible for the election of territorial representatives to the Corporative Chamber (see paras. 22-24).

42. Under the Overseas Organic Law of 1963, the Governor must consult the advisory council in his Territory in the exercise of his legislative functions. He must also consult the council on decrees he proposes to submit to the legislative council.

43. In Angola and Mozambique, as provided by the political and administrative statutes, the economic and social councils are presided over by the Governor-General and comprise eight elected members (with eight alternates), four members nominated by the Governor-General, and the following *ex officio* members: (a) the highest ranking officer of the three armed forces; (b) the Rector of the *Escudos Gerais Universitarios*; and (c) the directors, of the departments of political and civil administration, education, and economy. Of the eight elected members, two are to be elected by the administrative bodies from among their members; two by organizations representing cultural and moral (religious) interests, one of whom must be a Catholic missionary; two by representatives of bodies representing economic associations or interests; and two by organizations representing workers. The four nominated members are to be chosen from among persons especially experienced in administrative, economic, social or cultural matters and may be officials of senior rank.

44. The membership of government councils in the smaller Territories has been changed slightly. Each council comprises, as before, the Secretary-General, the highest-ranking officer of the armed forces, the representative of the Attorney-General in the Territory and the head of the financial services. In addition, instead of directly elected members, it now has three members elected by the legislative council from among its members.[55]

45. As in the case of the legislative councils, the membership of these advisory councils now enables high officials and special, interest groups to make their views known through a formally constituted body. In Angola and Mozambique there is no

---

[55] In Cape Verde, one of these three must be a representative of the administrative services; in São Tomé one must be a representative of the *freguesias*; in Portuguese Guinea and Timor one must be a representative of the *regedorias*.

representative of the *regedorias* in the economic and social councils. Thus instead of extending participation to the indigenous inhabitants, the new measures appear to be designed mainly to offset criticisms from Portuguese officials, business interests and settlers in the Territories by giving them some say.

(c) **Local administration**

46. The Overseas Organic Law of 1963 retains the concept that the division of each Territory 'shall accompany its economic and social progress.' Each Territory is divided into districts headed by district governors appointed by the Governor. The sub-division of the districts varies and may change to reflect its development. The basic unit of a division is stated to be the *concelho* (municipality) with further sub-divisions into *freguesias* (parishes) along the pattern of metropolitan Portugal. However, in regions 'where the economic and social development deemed necessary has not been reached,' *concelhos* are replaced 'temporarily' by *circumscricões*.

47. In accordance with this concept, local administrative authorities may take either of two forms: *regedorias*, or elected boards and councils. In Angola, Mozambique and Portuguese Guinea, in rural areas inhabited predominantly by indigenous inhabitants living in traditional societies, the basic unit of administration is the traditional *regedoria*, with a *regedor* who carries out the functions delegated to him 'by his administrative superiors.'[56]

48. In urban and other areas, the law provides that where there are enough persons who qualify as electors, the local administrative bodies take the form of boards or councils with an elected membership. Under the 1963 Overseas Organic Law, district boards were established for the first time. These boards have deliberative and advisory functions. In addition, there are municipal councils (in *concelhos*), municipal commissions (in *circumscricões*) and parish and local boards, which were all reinstituted in 1961. Administrative and financial authority is to be devolved from the centre to these bodies by law[57]; executive authority remains, however, in the hands of centrally appointed officials at each level.

49. Municipal councils are composed of a president, who as a rule is the administrator, and four members, two of whom are elected by direct suffrage and two by representatives of public or private economic interests, moral (religious) or professional interests or, in their absence, by 'individual tax-payers of Portuguese nationality whose direct tax liability is assessed at 1,000 escudos or more.'[58] Parish boards, which in Portugal axe elected by 'heads of family' are also elected by direct

---

[56] After the repeal of the Native Statute in 1961 the system of *regedorias* was given legal recognition.

[57] The law is not yet available in the Secretariat.

[58] As an exception the municipal councils of Luanda and Lourenço Marques each comprise six members, with two members elected by direct suffrage, two by corporate bodies and associations representing economic interests, and two by representatives of moral (religious) interests.

suffrage.[59] Qualifications for direct suffrage in local elections are the same as those for direct suffrage in elections to the legislative councils. Elections to the various local administrative bodies are to take place towards the end of 1964.

50. According to the Overseas Organic Law of 1963, 'relations between the organs of general administration and those of local administration shall be so arranged as to guarantee effective decentralization of the management of the interests of the respective aggregates, but without detriment to the efficiency of administration and public services.' However, the administrative life of the local authorities is subject to control by the Government of the Territory. Furthermore, decisions by the respective administrative bodies may, in some cases, be, made dependent on authorization or approval by other bodies or authorities.

51. Although the form of local administration is determined by the nature of the particular community, in areas where one form of local administration predominates, there may be communities or groups coming under another form. Thus parishes are to be formed 'corresponding to groups of families developing a common social activity.' On the other hand, the law organizing *regedorias* provides that where 'agglomerations of population' come into existence which do not constitute traditional *regedorias* and which do not constitute parishes, *regedores* may be appointed with police and auxiliary administrative functions. It appears from this provision that although indigenous persons living on the outskirts of urban areas automatically come under Portuguese civil law, they do not necessarily participate in the local councils or boards, but may be administered by an appointed *regedor*.

52. In his conversation with the representatives of African States, the Portuguese Minister for Foreign Affairs pointed out that as a means of developing self-government in the overseas Territories, the number of local government bodies had been increased. It may be noted that this increase had already been made possible by the legislation enacted in 1961 which changed the requirements for the establishment of such bodies. Whereas previously municipal councils had been established only in territorial capitals or in areas where there were more than 2,000 Europeans or *assimilados*, under the 1961 legislation such councils are to be established where there are 500 electors in a concelho and 300 electors in a *circumscricão*. Parish boards or local boards are to be established in areas with at least 20 electors.

53. The foregoing paragraphs show that neither the 1963 Overseas Organic Law nor the new political and administrative statutes of the Territories have made any substantial changes in the dual form of local administration existing in Angola, Mozambique and Portuguese Guinea, which in 1962 led the Special Committee on Territories under Portuguese administration to observe that 'the great majority of the African population living in rural areas continue to be ruled as before by administrators approved by Portuguese authorities; their actual participation in the conduct of their own affairs remains limited.'

---

[59] See paras. 54-64 below.

(d) **The Electoral Law of 6 December 1963**

54. In September 1961 Portugal repealed the Native Statute which, among other things, had laid down the principle that 'indigenous persons shall not be granted political rights with respect to non-indigenous institutions.' Since then, official spokesmen for Portugal have emphasized that henceforth, whatever their status in private law, all Portuguese citizens would have the same political status. It was also stated that the right to vote would be extended to all citizens on the same basis. The new electoral law governing elections to the territorial legislative councils was finally published on 6 December 1963.

55. This law governs the election of members to the legislative and advisory councils in the Territories and supplements the provisions contained in the new political and administrative statutes. It provides that the election of representatives of employers' and workers' associations, cultural and moral (religious) groups, economic interests, and administrative bodies shall be governed by regulations promulgated by the territorial Governments[60]; it sets out procedures for the elections by the tax-payers and representatives of indigenous authorities, and enumerates the suffrage qualifications of those who may take part in the direct election of representatives to the legislative councils.

56. Persons entitled to vote in the direct election of members to the legislative councils are as follows:

1. Male Portuguese citizens of full age (over 21) or *emancipados*[61] who can read and write Portuguese;

2. Female Portuguese citizens of full age or *emancipadas* having completed the first cycle of secondary school or equivalent ability;

3. Male and female Portuguese citizens of full age, or *emancipados* who, though unable to read and write, are heads of families;

4. Female Portuguese citizens who are married, can read and write Portuguese, and pay, either in their own right or jointly with their husbands, property taxes amounting to not less than the minimum set by the territorial Governments.

57. Some of the qualifications differ from those governing elections to the National Assembly.[62] For instance, in the elections to the National Assembly, persons who cannot read and write may vote if they contribute to the State and administrative bodies a sum not less than 100 escudos in payment of one or more of the following taxes: property tax, industrial tax, professional tax, or tax on the use of capital. In the new electoral law governing elections in the Territories, male and female citizens who are unable to read and write may vote only if they are also 'heads of family.'

---

[60] Not yet available in the Secretariat.
[61] Under Article 305 of the Civil Code, a minor who is *emancipado* has the same rights regarding his person and his property as if he were of age.
[62] The qualifications governing elections to the National Assembly are set out in A/5160, paragraph 113.

58. As specially defined in the new electoral law a 'head of a family' is:

1. Any Portuguese citizen with a legitimately (*legitimamente*) constituted family living with him under his authority and sharing his board, who pays taxes amounting to at least the minimum set by the provincial Governments;

2. Any Portuguese woman, whether widowed, divorced, judicially separated or a spinster, of full age, or *emancipada* who, being a person of good character, is entirely self-supporting and has ascendants or dependants to maintain and pays property taxes amounting to at least the minimum set by the provincial Governments;

3. Any Portuguese citizen of full age, or *emancipado*, who owns and occupies a house and pays property taxes amounting to at least the minimum set by the provincial Governments.

59. In Portugal, 'heads of family' vote in elections to parish boards (*juntas de freguesias*). Under the Portuguese Constitution (Article 19) every family has the right to participate in these elections through the head of the family. The definition of a head of family in the Civil Code (Article 200)[63] differs from that in the new electoral law in that the Civil Code definition does not contain a property ownership or a property tax requirement. *A priori*, the additional qualifications appear to make it impossible for the majority of the indigenous inhabitants in Angola, Mozambique and Portuguese Guinea to qualify to vote.

60. Firstly, the law requires that a person who cannot read and write must have a 'legitimately constituted' family living with him and sharing his board. It is not clear from the text of the electoral law alone whether this implies a marriage recognized by civil law; if it does, it would automatically exclude Africans living in traditional societies, who are governed by 'custom and usage.'

61. Secondly, the special law governing the *regedorias*, in Angola, Mozambique and Portuguese Guinea, implies that persons living in traditional societies do not generally own property individually. Thus, the property ownership requirement would probably exclude the great majority of the indigenous population.

62. Thirdly, whereas the qualifications for voting in elections to the National Assembly require that the minimum amount of tax to be paid has been set at 100 escudos, which may be paid in the form of various taxes, under the new electoral law governing elections in the Territories the qualifying tax payment is limited solely to a property tax. Further the minimum amount is to be set by each territorial Government which may establish levels that would tend to exclude even those who might meet all the other qualifications.

63. Finally, there is the question of status and its relation to electoral registration. The electoral law provides that: 'A person's status shall be determined in accordance

---

[63] Manuel Baptista Dias da Fonseca, Portugal: *Legislação electoral actualizada e anotada*, Coimbra Editora, 1949, page 163.

with the law or local custom and usage, except that only one spouse, whether married, widowed or divorced or judicially separated, may be enrolled in the electoral register in respect of the same man. The regulations for establishing and proving such status are to be promulgated by the territorial Governments, having regard to the legislation on civil registration.' Under the civil registration reorganization decree (No. 43,899 of 6 September 1961) registration is obligatory for persons coming under Portuguese civil law. The stated goal is to register all inhabitants but, as yet, adequate facilities do not appear to have been established to register all persons living in *regedorias*. Thus, the linking of electoral registration to the process of civil registration raises a doubt as to how many persons who do not come under Portuguese civil law have been placed on the electoral registers.

64. It appears from the foregoing that although all may now vote on the same basis, in practice, direct franchise can be exercised only by those who come under Portuguese civil law thus excluding the vast majority of the population.[64] The information on the results of the recent elections summarized below tends to confirm this conclusion.

(e) **Elections in the Territories held in March 1964**

65. In the last part of March 1964, elections to the legislative and advisory councils in all Territories were held under the new electoral law. Although a number of reports have appeared in Portuguese language papers, the information is incomplete, so that it is not possible to determine how many voters were registered. In most cases the newspapers merely report the percentages of the qualified electors who voted, and the names of the candidates elected. The way in which voting took place is described below.

(i) **Indirect elections**

66. 'Organic' groups. Each of the 'organic' groups was organized into an 'assembly' or 'section' for the purpose of electing members. These sections comprised persons listed as being qualified under rules established by the territorial Governments. Each section elected from among its members the required number of representatives to the legislative council and to the economic and social council or the government council, as relevant.

67. From the information available, it appears that some of the sections were very small. In Portuguese Guinea, for instance, the section for the representatives of administrative and public bodies was composed of 17 members, while that for the tax payers (paying a minimum of 1,000 escudos) consisted of some 240 persons.

68. Indigenous representation. The indigenous inhabitants of Angola, Mozambique, Portuguese Guinea and Timor who live in *regedorias* are represented in

---

[64] It was reported from Mozambique last year that only those who choose to live under Portuguese law can exercise the vote because 'it is said, the others are not registered in Mozambique records and are therefore unidentifiable. Why they cannot be registered is not explained.'

the legislative councils through three representatives elected by an electoral college. Under the electoral law, in Angola and Mozambique, some time before the elections, each district governor published a list of the indigenous authorities (*regedores*) who were to take part in the elections to this electoral college. On the Sunday before the elections, the listed *regedores* met in an appointed place and elected two members from among themselves to the electoral college. In the smaller Territories the lists were drawn up by the administrators for their own areas. On the day of the elections, the electoral college met to elect the three members to the legislative council. Reports from the Territories do not give details of the size of the electoral colleges or the number of indigenous inhabitants so represented in the legislative councils.

(ii) **Direct elections**

69. The two larger Territories, Angola and Mozambique, are divided into electoral districts, each returning one member to the Legislative Council. Cape Verde is divided into two districts, each returning three members, while the, remaining four Territories each comprise a single district returning three members.

70. Voting took place at appointed voting centres. Reports from Angola give incomplete figures of the number of registered voters and the number of votes cast at different centres. Incomplete though the figures are, it would appear that, in Angola, probably not more than five percent of the total population took part in the direct vote. In Cape Verde, which in the past has always had the highest percentage of voters, probably not more than 10 per cent of the population took part in the direct voting.[65]

71. In most cases, there appears to have been one list of candidates, but no information is available on the number of votes received by individual candidates.

72. Under the electoral law, candidates for election to the legislative councils must be 'original' Portuguese citizens and they may be from Portugal or from any of the other Territories provided only that they have resided in the Territory for a minimum of three years. In Angola, Mozambique, São Tomé and Príncipe more than half of the elected members are from Portugal. In Portuguese Guinea, of the eleven directly elected members, only four are 'naturals' of the Territory[66], four are from Portugal, two are from Cape Verde and one is from São Tomé and Príncipe.

73. From the published results of the recent elections, there does not appear to have been any significant transfer of power to the indigenous inhabitants. Even though the Native Statute has been repealed, the right to vote and to participate in the legislative councils and in the administration of the Territories still appears to be related to the attainment of a degree of 'social Progress' which, in effect, means the assimilation of Portuguese culture and the attainment of a Portuguese way of life.

---

[65] See section on Angola (paras. 111-147).

[66] Natives of the Territory in the sense that they were born there, including both Europeans and indigenous inhabitants.

2. Other developments

(a) Military activities

74. According to regularly issued Portuguese military bulletins, fighting continues in the north of Angola and in Portuguese Guinea. At intervals, troops are being sent overseas with a bare six months' training, to relieve those on active service. Both the departure and the return of troops on the completion of what are described as 'missions of sovereignty' are attended by well-publicized ceremonies and exhortations to those not at the front to greater patriotic efforts.

75. In his speech of 12 August 1963, Prime Minister Salazar declared that Portugal would defend its territories to 'the limit of its human and other resources.' In keeping with this statement, Portugal, in the past year, has increased the special police and military units overseas. Portugal's 70,000 to 80,000 troops now constitute the largest foreign army in Africa. In October 1963, the overseas armed forces were placed under war-time discipline. War-time penalties, including the death penalty, have been introduced for crimes committed by armed forces serving in the overseas territories in actions threatening public order or the integrity of national territory. However, the death penalty may be commuted to life imprisonment in cases where the military action is not against a foreign country.

76. Although there are some 40,000 to 55,000 Portuguese troops in Angola, over half of whom are in the northern region, Portugal claims that only some two percent of the territory is involved in fighting. However, Portugal's army, navy and air force, as well as paratrooper units, have all been engaged in operations. It is also reported that guerrillas have become better organized. Furthermore, a Portuguese military bulletin (for the period 26 February-4 March 1964, for instance) has reported fighting as far south as Dembos and Ucua, both of which lie within a radius of some 200 kilometres from Luanda. Fighting has also been reported in various parts of Cabinda.

77. Since the fighting broke out in Portuguese Guinea in 1963, the number of Portuguese troops in the territory has been increased to an estimated 10,000, which is twice the number stationed there in 1961. In July 1963, the Portuguese Minister of Defence was reported to have said that some 2,000 square miles (approx. 5,200 square kilometres) were involved. Other sources report that about one-fifth of the total area (33,125 square kilometres) is involved. The fighting appears to be fairly wide-spread. For instance, a Portuguese military bulletin (for the period 2-8 March 1964) has also reported action in the northern region of the territory in Farim, Mansoa, Susana and Mansaba. Early in April 1964, the *Patride Africano da Independência da Guiné e Cabo Verde* (PAIGC) reported that Portuguese aircraft had dropped napalm bombs in villages in the 'liberated' region in the south.[67] Early in May 1964, Portuguese Guinea was placed under a military Governor. It will be

---

[67] Telegram dated 8 April 1964 addressed to the Secretary-General from PAIGC, Conakry. According to PAIGC communiques, its guerrillas have successfully isolated the Portuguese in the towns of Cacine, Como, Catio, Buba and Falacunda which have been cut off from economic and other activities (Afrique, 1 February 1964).

recalled that a similar action was taken in Angola in l961.

78. In February 1964, the situation on the northern border of Mozambique was reported to be tense and the Portuguese were said to be anticipating disturbances after the rainy season ended. These reports, however, were denied by the Portuguese Authorities.[68] Portuguese troops in Mozambique are variously reported between 20,000 and 35,000.[69] Additional troops are reported to have been sent to the border to reinforce the existing 'well-armed solid cordon.' Other reports indicate that a new network of airfields has been completed in Mozambique to facilitate troop movements, that a military base is being built at Beira where the airfield has also been enlarged to accommodate heavy transport planes, and that a number of new naval radio stations have been built along the coast.

(b) **Financing defence and development**

79. Since 1961, Portugal has mobilized its own resources as well as those of the overseas territories and given priority to expenditures for 'national defence.' Among other measures, various taxes have been increased and a new overseas defence and development tax has been introduced. Tax modifications introduced in Portugal in l963 are to come into operation in 1964. The territories also pay a share from their ordinary budgets towards the costs of 'national defence' and, under a new provision enacted in l963, will contribute a minimum of 10 percent of the revenue from each of the autonomous services which have self-balancing budgets.[70]

80. The mounting costs of the military operations overseas are reflected in Portugal's budgets for 1963 and 1964. In addition to the cost of troops in Angola and Mozambique, 100 million escudos was allocated in 1963 for the armed forces assigned to the five other territories, as follows: Cape Verde, 10 million escudos; Portuguese Guinea, 36.6 million escudos, São Tomé and Príncipe, 5.6 million escudos; Macau, 18.6 million escudos; and Timor, 28.9 million escudos.

81. In the first eight months of 1963, defence expenditure was reported at 3,865 million escudos (US\$135 million) out of a total budget expenditure of 8,688 million escudos for that period. The 1964 budget provides for an ordinary expenditure totalling 9,596 million escudos (US\$335 million), and an extraordinary expenditure

---

[68] It was reported in April 1964 that the Portuguese Defence Ministry had issued a communique categorically denying a Nairobi radio broadcast that guerrilla warfare had broken out in northern Mozambique. The radio quoted 'Mozambique sources' that guerrillas had made raids against several border ports and that the Portuguese had declared a state of emergency. The communique said that the radio reports were false and that 'there had not been the slightest incident.'

[69] Press reports estimate the troops at 20,000; Frelimo estimates the number at 35,000.

[70] The autonomous services in Angola, for instance, include those of the ports and harbours, post and telegraph, national press, roads, electricity and the Settlement Board. According to published figures (*0 Comercio do Porto*, 8 February 1964) the revenue of these services is expected to amount to some 956 million escudos in 1964. Similarly, funds are made available for the other branches of the armed forces. See also section on Mozambique.

of 5,187 million escudos (US$182 million). Of the extraordinary expenditure, 50 percent (2,609 million escudos, US$92 million) is to be used for national defence. Defence expenditures include an initial allocation of 1,750 million escudos for the forces overseas, but it is noted that this may have to be supplemented, as was done in 1963 when the original allocation was raised by an additional 1,663 million, bringing the total for this defence item alone to 3,413 million escudos. Together with other defence expenditure included in the ordinary budget, it is reported that Portugal's initial defence budget for 1964 will be approximately 5,200 million escudos (US$180 million). In March 1964, the Ministry of the Army was authorized to acquire immediately war materials and other equipment valued at up to 1,500 million escudos against the 1964 budget and the anticipated allocations for 1965 and 1966. All defence expenditures are considered to be financed by 'national' efforts. Extraordinary expenditure is to be financed partly from ordinary receipts and budgetary surpluses from the previous year, from the special overseas defence and development tax (estimated to yield 120 million escudos), and from the internal sale of treasury bills and bonds (*empréstimos e produto da venda de títulos, mercado interno*). In addition, approximately 1,726 million escudos (US$60 million) is to be raised by external borrowing.

82. To meet its increased expenditures, Portugal has had to raise loans internally and to borrow both on the international market and in Angola and Mozambique. Internal loans have included one in 1962 of 1,000 million escudos (US$35 million) under the title of 'Treasury notes - Second Development Plan,' and a second one of a similar amount issued in 1963 under the title 'Treasury obligations – 3.5 percent, 1963.' In May 1962, Portugal received a loan US$20 million through a group of American banks, and later in the year a loan of 150 million German marks through the *Kreditanstalt fur Wiederaufbau*. In 1963, it received a further loan of US$15 million from the group of American banks bringing the total to US$35 million which was converted into a long-term loan. In November 1963 the *Banco de Fomento Nacional* floated a loan which was managed by a group of banks led by the *Societe Belge de Banque*, the *Kredietbank* and the *Banque Lambert* (Brussels). The loan was for 13 million European payment units of account (each equivalent to US$1.00). In 1963, Portugal received its first assistance from the International Bank for Reconstruction and Development (IBRD) when it was granted two loans totalling US$12.5 million for hydro-electric power projects. In April 1964, France was also reported to have granted Portugal a long-term loan amounting to US$125 million for the construction of 20 naval vessels, two escort ships and seven submarines.

83. Large sums have been raised in Angola and Mozambique mainly for development. Since, however, priority is given to national defence, most of the development projects undertaken have been ones which facilitate defence and troop movements, including such works as the construction of ports, harbours, airfields, roads and other means of communication. Between June 1962 and June 1963, over 1,200 million escudos (US$44 million) was raised in Angola, and from mid-1962 to the end of 1963, some 550 million escudos (US$20 million) was raised in

Mozambique. Of the money raised in Angola, 150 million escudos was lent by the Angola Diamond Company, 60 million escudos by the Benguela Railway and 1,000 million escudos of an internal bond issue were taken up by the Bank of Angola. In Mozambique, 500 million escudos was raised for development through an internal loan. In addition, part of the 50 million escudos raised for defence expenditures came from budgetary surpluses (7.6 million escudos) and from *lucro de amoedação* (profits from monetary operations) – 32.4 million escudos.

84. To provide Portugal with much needed capital in the industrial sector, four Portuguese banks are reported to have established a *Sociedade de Estudos Financeiros* (LUSAFINA). Ten banks, six of which are Spanish, are said to be associated in this project, which will have an initial capital of about US$12 million. This capital will be used for buying shares of various industrial concerns. Another group which will finance Portuguese industry is called the *Social-Sociedade de Investimentos e Administracões* which is supported, among others, by the London Rhodesian Mining and Land Co. A Brazilian group is reported to be interested in investing 'many millions of dollars' for tourists and other development in Angola and Mozambique.

85. In spite of all the measures that have been taken, it is reported that the chronic shortage of finance continues to be of serious concern to Portugal in its efforts to continue its military operations, and that unless Portugal can produce more, trade more and cut down imports, which are now running at almost twice the value of exports, it cannot afford to maintain its military strength in Africa.

86. In the past year, Portugal has strengthened its economic ties with the countries and territories neighbouring Angola and Mozambique. According to a statement to the Press by the Portuguese Minister for Foreign Affairs in April 1964, the negotiations between Portugal and South Africa, which have been continuing for some time have led recently to the conclusion of several treaties. Matters covered by these treaties include the sharing of the waters of the Cunene River between Angola and South West Africa and the sharing of hydro-electric power between the two territories; general questions of commercial exchange, economic planning and investment; civil aviation and the development of the airports; and the use by South Africa of the rail and post facilities in Mozambique.

87. In April 1964, Portugal also concluded an agreement with the United Kingdom concerning the construction of a short rail link in Mozambique to provide Swaziland with access to the port facilities of Lourenço Marques. To the existing transport and communications links between Mozambique and Southern Rhodesia, there is being added a new 300-kilometre oil pipe line (between Beira and Umtali) which is expected to come into operation early in 1965.

(c) **Reports on visits to Angola and Mozambique**

88. In 1963, some 400 public figures and writers from various countries were invited to visit Angola and Mozambique. Visitors have included members of the United Kingdom Parliament; members of the Brazilian Legislature, state governors

and government officials from Brazil; British, Canadian, French, German, Swedish, Swiss and United States newspapermen and writers. More recent visitors have included the President of the Federal Republic of Germany, Dr. Richard Jaeger, and 15 deputies of the German Parliament, a group of 24 United States newspapermen and the United States Ambassador to Lisbon, Admiral (George W.) Anderson. According to an official Portuguese report, Ambassador Anderson said that his visit as a local observer to Angola and Mozambique had been made by agreement between the Portuguese and United States Governments and was considered to be of great interest by the United States Department of State and the Secretary of State. Other foreign envoys to Portugal who have recently visited or plan to visit the two territories include those of Austria, Belgium, Canada, the Netherlands and Sweden.

89. Speeches made by the visitors and interviews with them have been reported in the Portuguese Press. There have also been a number of articles in the international Press describing economic conditions in Angola, as well as a small number of articles on Mozambique. It is reported that overseas newspapermen are able to send out news uncensored. Few visitors, it appears, have been invited to visit either Portuguese Guinea or São Tomé and Príncipe. There have been no reports that any foreign visitors were invited to observe the elections which took place in the last part of March 1964.

90. Most of the articles in the international Press give accounts of the economic development in the two territories and discuss Portugal's policy of building a multi-racial society in Africa. In Angola, where there are only some 220,000 Europeans out of a total population of almost five million, it is reported that a 'multi-racial' society is to be achieved by 'large immigration from Portugal, Cape Verde and the Azores.' A recent article reports also that 'Half of the 40,000 Portuguese troops now in Angola have settled or are expected to settle there, a leaven in the social mass. They may also serve as a stabilizing influence, a sort of permanent civil defence corps.'

91. Visitors to Angola and Mozambique are shown hydro-electric dams, ports and harbours, rail and road development, airports, factories, agricultural settlements and housing projects. In the past year some schools and hospitals have been included in the itineraries. Some have noted that in the field of education emphasis is still mainly on future plans. However, in spite of the developments, as it was stated in a recent article: 'The Africans themselves of course, are still for the most part on the circumference rather than at the centre of the over-all political development, and the prosperous urban centres are plainly the white man's show, although the African lives there with him.'[71]

92. Towards the end of March 1964, the Portuguese Government agreed to permit some Protestant missionary personnel to return to Angola.

(d) **Education**

93. In 1961, the Special Committee on Territories under Portuguese

---

[71] Hugh Kay, 'The Portuguese Way in Africa' – Fortune, January 1964.

administration observed that, with the exception of some improvements, mainly in the field of primary education, 'the over-all educational situation (in the territories) remains wholly unsatisfactory.' Noting the existence of a special system of *ensino de adaptação* in some of the territories under Portuguese administration, the Committee considered that reforms to unify primary education were indispensable and that strenuous efforts were needed to establish universal, free and compulsory primary education. It emphasized that it was not only necessary to establish systems of primary, secondary and higher education, but that even more important, as stated by the General Assembly in resolution 743 (VIII), education provided in the non-self-Governing Territories must take into account the basic cultural values and the aspirations of the peoples concerned.

94. The legislation governing primary education in Portugal is 'national' in scope.[72] However, due to the 'special circumstances' in the territories, these provisions continue to be extended to the Territories with certain modifications. Before the repeal of the Native Statute, there had been a special system of rudimentary education for the indigenous inhabitants in Angola, Mozambique and Portuguese Guinea. When the system of primary education was reorganized in 1960, the special education for indigenous children was renamed *'ensino de adaptação.'* This course covered in three years the normal first two years of the primary course, the first year being devoted mainly to the teaching of the Portuguese language.

95. Under the changes introduced in February 1964, for the first time primary education has become obligatory for all children between the ages of six and 12 in the Territories. Primary education is to consist of a single cycle of four classes with an additional special preparatory class.

96. The preparatory year, which is a special feature of primary education in the Territories, is intended to familiarize the pupils with the use of the 'national language' and school activities. However, the preparatory class may be omitted, at the request of the parents or guardian, for children who will be seven years old by the end of December of the entrance year, and who speak Portuguese fluently and have the required maturity. As in Portugal, children up to the age of 14 may attend primary schools.

97. The new legislation which is to come into force at the beginning of the next school year sets out in great detail the primary education syllabus for all the courses to be covered in the Territories. For the Portuguese language course, arithmetic, geometry and natural sciences, only approved text books may be used. Furthermore, the only teachers' handbooks to be used in the overseas primary schools are those prepared in Angola, for rural education. Although the 1963 overseas Organic Law provides that in primary schools 'the use of the local language is authorized as an

---

[72] Decree Law 42,994 of 28 May 1960. Under this decree primary education in Portugal comprises one single cycle of four classes. Previously, primary education had been divided in two cycles, the first cycle comprising three years (known as the elementary stage) and the second cycle comprising one year, known as the complementary stage.

instrument for teaching the Portuguese language,' the syllabus does not make any reference to such use. In the preparatory class, which is to be devoted mainly to teaching the Portuguese language detailed instructions have to be followed. This language is to be taught by the direct observation method, starting with names, familiar objects which are to be pointed to, such as parts of the body, passing on to pictures, short phrases and teachers' instructions.

98. In order to proceed to the next class, pupils must successfully pass an examination. This rule applies also to the preparatory class. Thus, although indigenous children may now enter the regular primary school system earlier than under the previous *ensino de adaptação*, it appears that only those who have successfully acquired an adequate facility in the Portuguese language can enter the first grade.

99. It appears from the information available that in the last year particularly, more educational facilities have been established, and there are more children at school. This is especially true in Angola and Mozambique where the greatest increase has been in the establishment, of *postos de ensino* (corresponding to 'one-room schools') in the rural areas.[73] In these schools, most of the African children are in special classes where they learn to speak Portuguese. Although the emphasis on the Portuguese language is not new[74], greater urgency is now being given to expanding schools and inculcating Portuguese language in the rural areas as a means of strengthening 'national unity.'[75]

100. There are no recent statistics relating to education, the latest being for 1961. However, according to an official statement made in April 1964, in Mozambique, only approximately one-third of the pupils completing the fourth primary year proceed to academic or technical and professional secondary schools and, of these, only 16 per cent take advantage of opportunities for higher education.[76]

---

[73] In June 1963, 10 million escudos was made available in Angola from budgetary surpluses especially for rural education.

[74] For instance, in an article published in 1958 in the *Estudos de Ciencias Politicas e Sociais*, Luis C. Lupi writes 'If the national language in all Portuguese territory is without exception Portuguese ... our national unity will only be attained when all, or an overwhelming majority, of our fellow citizens, speak, read, sing and think in this common language.'

[75] This point was made in a speech by the Governor-General of Angola at the swearing in of the new Provincial Secretary for Education, as reported in the *Diário de Noticias*, 29 March 1963.

[76] Speech by the Rector of the University of Coimbra, Professor Dr. António Jorge Andrade de Gouveia, in Lourenço Marques, at a conference on 'Education and the Universities,' as reported by the *Diário de Notícias*, 14 April 1964. It is also significant that only a small number of the children enrolled in primary schools have been able to pass the fourth grade examination. For instance, in Angola, according to official statistics, out of a total of 37,627 students in government and private primary schools, 4,564 students passed the fourth grade exam at the end of the school year 1960/1961 (Portugal, Provincia de Angola: *Repartição de Estatistica Geral, Anuário Estatistico,* 1961, Luanda 1963, page 59).

101. Among measures taken to improve education are the establishment of primary teacher-training schools in the Territories, including special rural teacher-training schools (*magistério rural*) in Angola, and the authorization of the governors to establish institutes for the training of social welfare workers of various types within the framework of the government school system.

102. In 1963, in both Angola and Mozambique, provision was made to increase the teaching staff in the academic and technical secondary schools and additional technical, commercial and industrial schools were authorized. The *Estudos Gerais Uhiversitarios* for both Territories authorized in 1961 did not start to function until 1963. In these institutions, there are courses in pedagogical science, civil, mining, mechanical, electrical, industrial and chemical engineering, and advanced courses in agriculture, silviculture and veterinary sciences. With the exception of the course in pedagogical science, the courses are to be set up jointly by the Overseas Minister and the Minister for National Education. New courses in natural sciences were recently reported to have been started in Mozambique but no courses appear to be available in either Angola or Mozambique in the liberal arts, humanities, or the social sciences. It is reported that in November 1963 there were 280 pupils taking 'university studies' in Mozambique. No figures are available for Angola.

103. School facilities in the other Territories have received less attention. Under legislation enacted in 1963, some new scholarships were made available for students in the overseas Territories especially for those from Territories without higher education facilities. Under a decree enacted in 1963, as a means of facilitating applications, all scholarships irrespective of their source, whether government or private, are to be centrally co-ordinated and standardized as to the qualifications and the amount of the awards.

104. To create better understanding between young people from 'different parts of the national Territory' holiday study courses for overseas students (*Curso de Férias para Estudantes Ultramarinos*) have been established. One of the first groups to visit Portugal from Angola were students from a primary teacher-training school. Visits by Portuguese students to the Territories will also be authorized.

(e) **Public Health**

105. In June 1962, at the request of the Portuguese Government, a three-man team of health experts was assigned by the World Health Organization to make an over-all survey of the health and sanitary conditions in Angola, Mozambique and Portuguese Guinea. The WHO Report was submitted to the Portuguese Government and although there have been many references to this report, the text is not available.

106. On the basis of the information available to it, the Special Committee on Territories under Portuguese administration, in 1962, drew attention in its report to the serious lack of public health facilities in those Territories and expressed the hope that the WHO surveys would lead to much needed integrated, over-all long-term planning to improve health conditions.

107. The official Portuguese position on the WHO recommendations was set out in an article in a government publication in June 1963, which indicated that new measures were envisaged that would take into account most of the suggestions.

108. The new legislation reorganizing the overseas public health service, was published early 1964.[77] Under the new legislation, government services are to be expanded and in each Territory there is to be a network of hospitals, sanitary posts and special services. There are to be central, regional, sub-regional and rural hospitals.[78] Together with each rural hospital there is to be a rural health centre which will be the basic unit for all health activities. At administrative posts and, where necessary, there are to be established health posts and rural maternity posts. Mobile units are to be increased. Medical, surgical and therapeutic services are to be free to all 'who because of their social or economic situation need the assistance of the State.' The Governments of the Territories are to establish regulations prescribing the conditions under which medical care will be free.

109. Existing services established by administrative bodies, or missions, are to be integrated in the over-all network, and will be required to collaborate with the territorial services. As already provided in the 1962 Labour Code, employers remain responsible for the provision of medical care for their employees, although these facilities will be subject to inspection and regulation.

110. Training facilities for nurses and auxiliary public health personnel are to be established in the central hospital in the capital of each Territory. Local legislation is to be enacted for this purpose. It is expected that some time will be needed to put all the provisions of the new legislation into effect.

ANGOLA

General

111. At the 1960 census, the total population of the Territory was 4,830,449 of whom 172,529 were, listed as '*branco*;' 53,392 were listed as '*mestiço*,' and 4,604,362 as '*preto*.'

Government

112. As provided in the Overseas Organic Law of 1963, a new basic law of the Territory, provisions relating to the powers and functions of the Governor, the Legislative and 'advisory Councils,' which are similar for all the Portuguese Territories have been described above. The following paragraphs set out some additional details.

---

[77] The overseas health services were last reorganized in 1945.
[78] Decree No. 45,541, of 23 January 1964: Central hospitals will have a minimum of 300 beds, regional hospitals 200, and sub-regional hospitals, 100 beds.

(a) **Legislative Council**

113. The Legislative Council of Angola which is presided over by the Governor-General, comprises thirty-six members, of whom two are *ex officio* (the Attorney-General and the Director of Public Finance), and thirty-four are elected as follows: three by individual taxpayers registered. as paying direct taxes amounting to a minimum of 15,000 escudos; three by corporative bodies representative of employers and associations of economic interests; three by corporative bodies representative of workers' interests; three by bodies representative of moral (religious) and cultural interests, one of whom must always be a Catholic missionary; three by Native authorities (*regedorias*) from among their own members; four by administrative bodies and legally recognized collective bodies performing administrative functions of public interest; fifteen by direct franchise of citizens, whose names are inscribed in the general books of the electoral register.

114. Previously the Legislative Council of Angola comprised 29 members, of whom eight were nominated and 21 elected.[79] Of the eight nominated members, six were nominated by the Governor-General, and at least three had to be chosen from directors of departments or senior members of the public service. The other two members were nominated by the Government Council from a list of three members submitted by the Governor-General to represent the interests of the indigenous population. These representatives did not, however, have to be indigenous inhabitants. Of the 21 elected members, the Statute provided for seven to be elected by the five 'organic' groups[80], and the balance by direct vote.

(b) **The Economic and Social Council**

115. The Economic and Social Council, which replaces the former Government Council as an advisory body, has a widened membership which now includes members elected by various 'organic' groups. Previously, the Government Council had been composed almost entirely of government officials.[81] The armed forces continue to be represented in the new advisory council, either by the commander-in-chief or, if his functions are exercised by the Governor-General, by the most senior officer of either the army, navy or air force. As noted previously, there is no special representation in this Council of the interests of the indigenous inhabitants.

Local administration

116. Under the Political and Administrative Statute of Angola, 1963, the Territory is divided into 15 administrative districts. These correspond to the electoral districts,

---

[79] The former Statute of Angola enacted in 1955 (Decree No. 40,225) provided for a Legislative Council of 26 members of whom 18 were elected. This was subsequently amended.

[80] These seven were elected on the same basis in Angola and Mozambique.

[81] Under the 1955 Statute, the Government Council was composed of the provincial Secretaries, the Secretary General, the Military Commander, the Attorney General, the Director of Public Finance, and two members of the Legislative Council chosen from the elected members by the Governor-General.

and each returns one directly-elected member to the Legislative Council. The sub-divisional boundaries of the districts have been altered and the number of *concelhos* has been increased. This, together with the reduction in the number of electors required to form the various councils, has brought about an increase in the number of local government bodies.[82]

Results of the elections

117. In the direct elections to the Legislative Council, almost all of the 15 districts had only one candidate. It is reported that in one district there were two candidates for the one seat, and that in another there were three candidates. Portuguese press reports stress that the number of voting centres in Angola increased by 20 to 100 percent in the various districts. There are no comprehensive figures for the total number of voters registered and voting in each of the districts. Some figures were given in the Portuguese Press of the number of voters registered at some of the voting centres in Angola; in most cases there were less than 2,000 voters registered. At one centre, Villa Henrique de Carvalho, in the Lunda District, there were 7,281 voters registered, of whom 6,508 voted. It appears, however, that although a high percentage of those registered did vote, the total number of persons voting did not exceed 10 percent and was probably not much more than 5 percent of the total adult population.[83] It also appears that only a small proportion of those voting were Africans.

118. The Portuguese Press has drawn attention to the fact that many of the candidates in Angola were 'naturals' of the Territory – persons born in Angola. The results of the elections show, however, that of the 34 elected members to the Legislative Council only 15 *naturais* are from Angola, 18 are from Portugal and one is from Cape Verde.

119. Portuguese sources generally do not give the actual number of voters but only the percentages of the registered voters taking part in the vote. The information also shows that of the 19 members elected by the 'organic' groups, eight are resident in Luanda. Of the three members elected by and representing indigenous authorities, not one is from the southern part of the Territory (which Portugal has always claimed as being most loyal); two of the three are from Cuanza-Norte District (an important coffee growing district and one of the main areas of the 1961 uprising); and one is from the Malange District.

The war in Angola

120. On 15 March 1964, Angola entered its fourth year of war, and from reports, it appears that the end is not yet in sight. Portugal is said to have 55,000 troops in Angola, over half of whom are in the north. Volunteer Corps were established on a

---

[82] See paras. 46-53 above.

[83] At the 1957 elections to the National Assembly under the previous electoral law, the elected candidates each received fewer than 50,000 votes. This was less than 2 percent of the total population of the Territory.

permanent basis in 1962 to assist the regular armed forces.[84] These are now widely used to perform police, guard and patrol duties.

121. In April 1964, it was reported that the number of refugees crossing the border into the Congo (Leopoldville) had sharply increased in recent weeks. This was attributed to increased attacks by the Portuguese Army against civilians who had resisted resettlement plans and had remained in hiding. The report stated that from 1 March 1964 a medical post 20 miles from the border of Angola had assisted 12,492 refugees, as compared with 819 in the month of January. In a press release dated 13 April 1964, the Permanent Mission of Portugal to the United Nations denied the reports 'about the alleged flight of people' from Angola into the Republic of the Congo (Leopoldville). The press release went on to say that 'It is absolutely false that any crossing was made by Angolan inhabitants into the Congo, beyond the usual transit, legally authorized by the local authorities.'

'Psycho-social measures'

122. In Angola, military action is being supplemented by 'psycho-social measures' which are sometimes referred to in the English language press as 'psycho-welfare war.' This term is used for activities by Portuguese troops to win over the local population and to convince them 'that they have more to gain' with Portugal than with the guerrillas.

123. The 'psycho-social measures' are designed to encourage the return and resettlement of refugees and persons in hiding, as well as to improve the living conditions of those who have been uprooted since 1961. The Portuguese military bulletins frequently announce the number of refugees who have returned, or who 'have given themselves up to the authorities.'

124. The total number of refugees who have returned or surrendered is difficult to ascertain. A Portuguese source states that 200,000 Africans have been resettled, while other sources indicate that there are still over 300,000 Angolan refugees in the Congo (Leopoldville).

125. The resettlement of the local population into planned villages makes it possible to provide schools, clinics and services not existing previously; it also makes it easier to isolate the local population from guerrilla activities. There are various accounts of the new villages which have been built with the help of the army to resettle the local population. In general, each village has a school, a church and a medical dispensary; the resettled inhabitants are given free land and assistance in planting crops; and the administrators try to ensure that they receive fair prices for their crops.

Settlement projects

126. Settlement projects under the development plan, have been promoted

---

[84] Formed on 2 March 1962, the duty of the Volunteer Corps is to collaborate in the defence of the national integrity and sovereignty.

through immigration from Portugal arranged by the Provincial Settlement Board, established in 1961, and through the settlement of soldiers who have completed their tour of duty in Angola. Soldiers are considered especially desirable settlers since they add to the defence strength of the Territory.

127. Under one plan, for instance, each soldier settler receives free of cost, a piece of land, between 10 and 35 hectares in area which the Government also undertakes to prepare free of cost. The settlers also receive 1,500 escudos a month in the first year, and a maximum of 1,000 escudos a month in the second year. These payments, which are in the nature of long-term repayable loans, are to be made partly in cash, the main part being in kind. There are similar soldier settlement schemes for cattle-raising projects. No recent figures on the total number of soldier settlers are available.

128. In 1962, in addition to its normal expenses, the Settlement Board was given a government guarantee for special credit amounting to 200 million escudos (US$7 million) for the purchase of agricultural equipment and for other goods and services. In 1963, the Settlement Board adopted measures to facilitate the acquisition of agricultural land (with safeguards to existing rights) and to increase credit concessions to settlers, who were not able to finance the charges on farms of 100 to 200 hectares in size.

129. The settlement of families from Portugal continues and appears to be gaining momentum. In 1963 there was a net gain of some 6,000 immigrants, including 3,000 settlers. In April 1964, it was reported that over 700 persons had left Portugal to settle in Angola. In addition, another 400 families from Cape Verde were reported to be going to Angola under the sponsorship of the Settlement Board. These families are being settled in the Cela project, where other Cape Verdian families are already established.

Economic conditions

130. Since the latter part of 1963, reports from Angola have emphasized the Territory's return to economic prosperity and a strengthening of the determination of the Portuguese to remain, whatever the cost. The economic picture is not, however, completely favourable. On the one hand, business is reported to be thriving partly as a result of accelerated development spending and partly because of the presence of the large numbers of troops from Portugal. On the other hand, imports have been cut and taxes and customs duties have been raised, especially on imports of luxury goods (including wine from Portugal). Furthermore, although preparatory legislation to implement the escudo zone programme went into effect in March 1963, exchange controls remained in effect, and during the year transfers of escudos from Angola to Portugal were still reported to be subject to losses of up to 25 per cent. These difficulties have hampered business transactions with Angola, which at one time, were said to have come to a standstill and even affected Macau.

131. In March 1964, it was reported that, following the discovery of irregularities in exchange transactions by which over US$15 million escaped control, new

measures were being introduced to tighten control both of the imports and of exchange. In April 1964, Mozambique was reported to have made available to Angola a loan of 60 million escudos (approximately US$2 million) to help solve Angola's exchange problem.

132. Increased attention is being focussed on the coffee crop in Angola, which is sometimes referred to in Portuguese official publications and the Press as a major source of 'National wealth.'[85] Most of the coffee exported from Angola goes to the United States (for use in making instant coffee) and in 1962 amounted to over US$35 million. The figure is expected to be even higher in 1963. In addition, coffee exports to the Netherlands amounted to some 400 million escudos (US$14 million) in 1962. Output of diamonds also rose in 1963. In spite of the fact that diamonds are sold under world prices to a monopoly[86], in 1962 exports were valued at 556 million escudos (US$19 million), all of which went to the United Kingdom.

133. A major effort has been made to increase the areas planted to coffee. In the northern region, where much of the best coffee land is located, large numbers of troops are stationed and are supplemented by Volunteer Corps to guard the roads and plantations. Areas planted to sugar and sisal are also being increased, since these are also important exports. There appears to have been little growth outside the exchange sector, and it was reported that the production of several food staples, including maize, beans and manioc had decreased in 1963. The fishing industry remained depressed.

134. In the industrial sector, the most rapid growth has been in petroleum production, which rose, from 198,000 tons in 1961 to 337,000 tons in 1962, and was still increasing in 1963. Output in 1963 was reported to have exceeded the local refinery capacity and a new refinery was being built in Portugal to handle the excess. In 1964, the discovery of new oil deposits was announced. Asphalt and cement also registered some increases in output.

135. Foreign investments are reported to have increased, though no figures are available. New industries are being established, among which the more important are reported to be an iron-alloy industry with a capital of 125 million escudos (US$4.3 million), a margarine processing plant and a cellulose factory. Krupp, which has already granted a loan of US$50 million for mining iron was reported in 1963 to be interested in establishing a steel mill. Iron reserves in Angola are estimated at over 400 million tons. In 1964, it was reported that a manganese mining company financed by Portuguese, German and French capital had been set up to work a 500,000 acre concession in Cabinda in a region where there is an estimated 80-100 million tons of manganese. An Anglo-American group representing capital amounting to some

---

[85] Speech by the Under-Secretary of State for Overseas development, Dr. Mario de Oliveira, 1963.

[86] *Diário de Notícias*, 12 Oct. 1963 quoted an article published in Angola that while South West African diamonds were sold at over 1,000 escudos per carat, Angolan diamonds were sold to the monopoly at just over half that price.

US$10 million was recently reported to be interested in the establishment of a canning factory and a cattle-breeding centre.

136. There is little information on the participation of the indigenous inhabitants in the economic life of the Territory, apart from their role as wage earners. While there are indications that wage rates have risen, there are also reports that, with the influx of artisans from Portugal, some Africans are being displaced from their jobs. This is probably more evident in Luanda where it is reported that the majority of waiters and taxi drivers are Portuguese.

137. The Territory's 1964 budget has been trimmed to reduce expenditures, and the total revenue of 3,357 million escudos (including extraordinary revenue) stands at almost the same level as that for 1961 (3,232 million escudos). Following the abolition of the Native Statute in 1961, a minimum general (personal) tax was introduced which applies to all persons. The revenue from this source more than doubled between 1961 and 1962 (from 117 to 271 million escudos) but taxes paid by industries rose by only 10 per cent. The increased recourse to loans in financing various projects is reflected in the charges for servicing the public debt which increased from 87.5 million escudos in 1961 to 160 million escudos in 1964.

138. The largest single item of expenditure is for 'development,' which amounts to almost one-third of the total. Under the heading 'National defence - armed forces,' 474 million escudos are allocated, which represents approximately 15 per cent of the total expenditure.

139. As reported above, large loans have been raised in Angola to finance projects envisaged under the Second National Development Plan. In December 1963, the expenditure of some 350 million escudos on various projects was authorized. Of this total, some 120 million escudos will be used towards development and distribution of electric power; 40 million escudos for roads; 30 million escudos for improvement and expansion of the ports, including those of Luanda, Lobito and Moçâmedes; 50 million escudos for airports and telecommunications; 43 million escudos for construction and equipment of schools; and 20 million escudos for 'local improvements.'

140. It is reported that, both in Angola and outside, many people feel that only foreign capital and time are needed to develop Angola. However, some Portuguese have questioned the wisdom of the economic course now being followed. It has been pointed out that the large loans which were raised in the Territory are being used for projects that do not earn revenue and that the cost of servicing these internal loans is an increasing burden.

Education

141. There are several sources of education statistics. In a press release issued by the Permanent Mission of Portugal to the United Nations, dated 1 August 1962, school statistics for Angola at 1 January 1962 were given. According to this source, there were 14,607 educational institutions and the total school enrolment was

709,705. Of the primary schools, 2,250 were government schools; 11,933 schools with 387,050 students were maintained by Roman Catholic missions; and 3,000 schools with 160,000 students were maintained by Protestant missions.

142. According to another source, as of 31 December 1961 there was a total of 2,947 educational institutions in Angola, with 4,988 teachers and an enrolment of 141,222 students. Total primary enrolment was 122,628 pupils, of whom 89,142 were in government schools and 33,486 in private schools.

143. A third set of statistics shows that for the school year 1960/1961 (i.e., the school year before the one referred to above) there were 2,133 educational institutions with 3,875 teachers and a total enrolment of 119,380. There were 37,627 students enrolled in primary schools and 68,000 enrolled in adaptation courses. Of those in primary schools, 17,362 passed the first three grade examinations; 5,579 passed the first grade; 5,143 passed the second grade; and 6,640 the third grade. Only 4,564 pupils completed and passed the fourth primary grade, and of these, 2,367 were in government schools and 2,197 in private schools. There were 7,486 pupils enrolled in academic and 5,033 in professional secondary schools. There were 227 pupils in the last year of secondary school and 119 in higher education.

144. By comparing the date in the third source with those of the second, it appears that there was a 20 per cent over-all increase in enrolment between 1960 and 1961. Furthermore, it is evident that the figures for primary enrolments given in the second source include those enrolled in adaptation courses. This practice apparently anticipates the provisions of the 1964 education law, under which the preparatory year is considered to be an integral part of the primary course that is to come into effect with the next school year.

Public health

145. According to a press release issued by the Permanent Mission of Portugal on 7 May 1964, the public health facilities in Angola are as follows: '... there are presently 96 public and private hospitals, 68 district clinics, 782 local clinics, 57 maternity clinics, 12 child welfare dispensaries, 9 anti-tuberculosis dispensaries, 19 anti-leprosy centres. The personnel in all these institutions consists of 593 doctors, 1,467 nurses (male as well as female), 89 chemists, 116 assistant chemists, 129 laboratory and radiology assistants and 107 midwives, drawn from all races. There is one hospital bed per 322 inhabitants, one Public Health Officer per 3,000, one clinic per 4,381 and one doctor per 10,000.'

146. In 1961, for public health purposes, the Territory was divided into 81 *delegacias*, four *sub-delegacias* and 207 sanitary posts. Facilities for treatment and in-patients were: two central hospitals, 13 regional hospitals and 62 private hospitals; 67 health centres, 35 maternity clinics and some special dispensaries. There were 234 medical doctors, three analysts, 18 pharmacists, 577 nurses and auxiliary nurses, 48 midwives and 529 other personnel. In addition, there were 890 health centres of which 423 were government, 418 were private and 49 others. In 1961, 240 of these health centres had beds.

147. There were 48,978 patients treated in the hospitals, and 8,842 maternity cases in the maternity centres and special dispensaries, with 5,409 live births during the year.

MOZAMBIQUE

General

148. According to the 1960 census figures, the population of Mozambique was 6,592,994. No racial breakdown is given. According to previous official estimates, the total population in 1959 was 6,371,430, of which 169,380 were *'civilizado'* and 6,202,050 were *'não civilizado.'*

Government

149. Under the Overseas Organic Law of 1963, a new basic law for the Territory, the Political and Administrative Statute of Mozambique, was published in November 1963. The main provisions relating to the powers and functions of the Governor, the Legislative and Advisory Councils, which are similar for all Territories, have been outlined above. The following paragraphs set out some additional details.

(a) **Legislative Council**

150. The Legislative Council of Mozambique, which is presided over by the Governor-General, comprises 29 persons. There are two *ex officio* members, the Attorney-General and the Director of Public Finance, and 27 members elected as follows: three by individual taxpayers registered as paying direct taxes amounting to a minimum of 15,000 escudos; three by corporative bodies representing employers and associations of economic interests; three by corporative bodies representing workers interests; three elected by bodies representing moral (religious) and cultural interests, one of whom must always be a Catholic missionary; three by Native authorities (*regedorias*) from among their own members; three by administrative bodies and legally recognized collective bodies performing administrative functions of public interest; and nine by direct franchise of citizens whose names are inscribed in the general books of the electoral register.

151. Previously the Legislative Council of Mozambique comprised twenty-four members, of whom eight were nominated, as in Angola, and 16 were elected. Seven of the elected members were elected by 'organic' groups and nine were elected directly. There has been no increase in the number of directly elected members.

(b) **Economic and Social Council**

152. The composition of the Economic and Social Council in Mozambique is similar to that in Angola, and the Governor-General is also the Commander-in-Chief of the armed forces.

(c) **Local administration**

Individuals or concerns. Although the law also requires buyers to purchase all grades of cotton (not only selected grades).

153. Under the new Statute, Mozambique is divided into nine districts for the purpose of local administration. These districts are also the electoral districts, each returning one directly elected member to the Legislative Council. The subdivisions, however, have been changed. Whereas the previous Statute divided the Territory into some 25 *concelhos* and 63 *circunscricões*, there are now 32 *concelhos* and 60 *circunscrições*. Since the Overseas Organic Law of 1963 provides that the basic unit of local administration is the *concelho*, it appears that in the greater part of Mozambique 'the economic and social development deemed necessary' has not been reached for the establishment of the regular municipal councils.

Results of elections

154. The official statement on the results of the elections issued by the Overseas Minister gives only the percentages of the registered voters who voted. There is no information on the number of registered voters or the actual number of persons who voted. Of the 27 members elected to the Legislative Council by direct and 'organic' votes, 11 are *naturais* of Mozambique, 15 are from Portugal, and one is from Angola. Of the sixteen members elected to the Economic and Social Council, eleven are *naturais* of Mozambique and five are from Portugal.

Economic conditions

155. Mozambique's share in defence costs has risen with the increased number of troops in the Territory which has been described above. In 1963, 14.4 million escudos was allocated for the naval forces and 347.4 million escudos for the army in the Territory. Of the amount allocated for the naval forces, eight million escudos was to come from Mozambique's ordinary receipts and 6.4 million escudos from the autonomous revenue-producing services. Of the amount allocated for the army, 149 million escudos was to come from the Territory's ordinary receipts, five million escudos from the extraordinary receipts, 54.6 million escudos from the autonomous services, 65.5 million escudos from the receipts assigned to the Overseas Military Defence Fund, and 82.2 million from 'other receipts' which are not specified. The cost of the armed forces alone, which is only part of the total defence expenditure, was thus more than 10 percent of the ordinary receipts of the Territory for 1963, which was reported at 3,635.7 million escudos.

156. Investments under the Second National Development have concentrated on ports, harbours and railways. Almost all of an allocation of 144 million escudos received from the *Banco de Fomento* in 1962 is reported to have been spent on public works, and an additional 37.5 million escudos was allocated in 1963 for other projects, which included agricultural development, 10 million escudos; Revué settlement scheme, 10 million escudos, including five million escudos for irrigation; construction of hospitals and maternity clinics (*congeneres*), nine million escudos; and three million escudos for 'local improvements.'

157. In January 1964, another allocation of 90.9 million escudos was made for

railways and ports projects under the Development Plan, divided as follows: the 'Mozambique' railway, 15.4 million escudos; the port of Lourenço Marques, 52.7 million escudos; the port of Beira, 17.3 million escudos, and Nacala and other works, 5.5 million escudos. The airport at Beira is being expanded to accommodate jet planes, at an estimated cost of 48 million escudos. A dredging scheme estimated to cost 60 million escudos (over US$2 million) will be completed in 1964 and will enable vessels of heavy tonnage to dock for loading minerals and other products.

158. Cotton remains Mozambique's most important single export. In recent years it has generally accounted for 600 million escudos each year, or approximately one-third of the total value of exports. Various efforts have been made in the past to increase the production of cotton in Mozambique and large concessions were granted for this purpose. Although the system of 'forced cultivation' was abolished in 1961, reports indicate that the small producer is, as yet, no better off. New legislation introduced in 1963 abolishes the cotton concessions in all Territories, makes the local cotton institutes responsible for co-ordinating, regulating and encouraging cotton growing activities, and establishes conditions for the trading in seed and raw cotton and for ginning and processing by specially-licenced operatives – and at fixed prices, the small producer thus remaining at the mercy of the local licenced buyer.

159. The legislation envisages that within a maximum period of five years there will be free trading in cotton. In the meantime, export to foreign countries of cotton grown in the Overseas Territories is prohibited, unless national industries have been adequately supplied.

160. In May 1964, the *Banco Nacional Ultramarina* was reported to have made a loan of 30 million escudos to the Cotton Institute of Mozambique.

161. New measures are being taken to expand sugar output. In May 1964, it was reported that a Portuguese sugar refinery was to be established in the southern part of the Territory at Manhica. The refinery will cost some 430 million escudos (US$15 million) and is expected to begin production in June 1965, with an initial capacity of 40,000 tons a year. As part of this project the area planted with sugar will be increased by 6,000 hectares, of which 2,800 hectares will be the property of the refinery and 3,200 hectares are to be cultivated under a settlement scheme under its direction by the refinery.

162. Some improvement in the economic and business outlook in Mozambique was reported in 1963. Production of cotton, cashew nuts and sisal increased over 1962. Owing to bad weather however, large quantities of maize were imported from South Africa. Towards the end of the year the general food situation was said to have improved. The balance of trade deteriorated however, due apparently to increased imports of a wide variety, including textiles and other consumer goods. Over the period January-July 1963, the adverse balance of trade was 871 million escudos, compared with 803 million escudos for the same period in the previous year.

163. In the industrial sector, increased production was reported in petroleum refining. The output of fuel oil, gasoline and gas-oil increased by 37.4 percent in the

first six months of 1963, compared with the same period of the previous year. New industries established include a cement factory at Nacala, with an investment of over 150 million escudos (over US$5 million) which is expected to increase cement production by 100,000 tons a year.

164. Economic relations with South Africa have been strengthened through several formally negotiated agreements, as reported above. For South Africa, Mozambique is important as an export market and convenient outlet to the sea. For Mozambique, on the other hand, South Africa is a source of foreign exchange. A revision has been negotiated of the 1928 Convention under which some 100,000 workers from Mozambique were recruited for work in South Africa and a guaranteed tonnage was exported from South Africa through Lourenço Marques. No details are available as to the new terms of agreement.

165. Some new investments of South African capital in Mozambique were made in 1963. In November, a South African company, the Mozambique Development Corporation, was formed with the backing of the Anglo-American Corporation. The share issue is reported at 2 million Rand (US$2.8 million) and will be used to equip a fisheries enterprise, including a freezing plant at Port Amelia. The South African Government is also one of the financial guarantors for the 187-mile Beira-Umtali oil pipe line which is reported to cost US$10.5 million and which is being built by a South African company. In early 1964, a Luso-South African Economic Institute was set up in Johannesburg to interest investors in Mozambique and facilitate commerce.

166. With over 1,500 miles of coast-line, Mozambique is an important means of access to the sea for its several land-locked neighbours. The most important ports are Lourenço Marques in the south, and Beira, Quelimane and Mozambique to the north. In April 1964, as reported above an agreement was signed between the Governments of the United Kingdom and Portugal to improve communications between Swaziland and Mozambique. A new rail link will be built in Mozambique between Lourenço Marques and Goba on the Swaziland border. A new contract has also been signed by Swaziland cattle owners for a new meat export project. Capital will be provided by the cattle owners to increase the facilities of the Lourenço Marques municipal slaughterhouse which will be used for freezing and packing meat for the European market. The city of Lourenço Marques is expected to receive an income of 8 million escudos (US$280,000) per year from this operation.

167. Following the dissolution of the Central African Federation, Southern Rhodesia, Northern Rhodesia and Nyasaland are expected to review the former agreement under which they used the port facilities in Mozambique. According to reports, Nyasaland has already initiated some preliminary steps to discuss the use of port facilities.

168. In spite of these developments, the heavy defence and public expenditure are reported to be creating serious strains in Mozambique's finances. One such indication is reflected in the fact that in November 1963, the Overseas Ministry had to make available an extra sum of 427,000 escudos (US$14,000) for the payment of

the interest due on a 1960 loan.

169. Investments are being sought by Mozambique not only from international and regional sources but also from Portugal. During a recent visit to Lisbon, the Governor-General of Mozambique appealed to industries and to those with technical skills or capital to establish or transfer their operations to Mozambique so as to assist its economic development and 'to increase the links of national unity.'

PORTUGUESE GUINEA

General

170. According to the 1960 census, the population of Portuguese Guinea was 544,184. This compared with 510,777 at the 1950 census when the population was distributed as follows: 2,263 Europeans, 4,568 *mestiços*, 11 Indians, and 1,478 assimilated Africans. In 1963, the total population was estimated at 650,000, including 2,500 Europeans and 5,000 *mestiços*, most of whom are from Cape Verde.

Government

172. The new basic law of the Territory, the Political and Administrative Statute of Portuguese Guinea, was published in November 1963. The main provisions relating to the powers and functions of the Governor, the Legislative Council and the Advisory Council, which are similar for all Territories, have been outlined above.

The following paragraphs set out some additional details.

(a) **Legislative Council**

173. The Overseas Organic Law of 1963 established a Legislative Council in the Territory for the first time, with the same powers and functions as those in the other Territories. As set out in the Statute, the Legislative Council in Portuguese Guinea, which is presided over by the Governor, comprises 14 members. The balance of the composition among representatives of various interests is similar to that of the former Government Council established under the 1955 Statute. There are three *ex officio* members, the Secretary-General, the representative of the Attorney General, and the Director of Public Finance, and 11 members elected as follows: two by individual tax payers registered as paying a minimum of 1,000 escudos in direct taxes; two by administrative bodies and legally recognized collective bodies performing administrative functions; three by indigenous authorities of the *regedorias* from among their own members; one by bodies representative of moral (religious) and cultural interests; and three by direct suffrage of citizens inscribed in the general books of the electoral register.

174. It may be noted that there are no representatives of workers or employers or other economic interests. As the Legislative Council is an assembly of representatives suited to its economic and social environment, the omission of these representatives give recognition to the fact that economic interests and workers organizations do not yet play a significant role in the life of the Territory. On the other hand, even though

the indigenous population is about one-eighth of that in Angola and one-twelfth of that in Mozambique, the indigenous authorities in Portuguese Guinea are also represented by three out of a total of 14 members.

(b) **The Government Council**

175. Under the 1963 Statute, the Government Council is established on a permanent basis to assist the Governor in the exercise of his legislative functions, to advise on matters on which it is consulted by the Governor, and to approve items laid down in the development plan prepared by the Technical Commission of Planning and Economic Integration.

176. The Government Council, which is presided over by the Governor, comprises the Commander-in-chief of the armed forces (or in his absence, or when this function is exercised by the Governor, by the most senior ranking officer of one of the three branches of the armed forces), the representative of the Attorney-General, the Director of Public Finance, and three members elected by the Legislative Council, one of whom must represent the *regedorias*.

(c) **Local administration**

177. For the purpose of local administration, the Territory is divided into *concelhos* and *circunscricões* which are subdivided respectively into *frequesias* (parishes) and *postos administrativos* (administrative posts). The administrative posts are divided into *regedorias* and groups of villages. For the purpose of the direct elections to the Legislative Council, the Territory is one electoral district.

Results of elections

178. As in the other Territories, there is no information on the number of voters registered and the number of votes cast in the direct elections of the three members of the Legislative Council. It is officially reported that candidates were elected by 97 per cent of the registered voters.

179. According to an article in the Portuguese Press in the election of the representative of tax payers, 233 votes were cast representing 99.5 per cent of the registered voters; in the election of the two representatives of administrative groups, 17 votes were cast, representing 100 per cent of the votes; and the representatives of the *regedorias* were elected by an electoral college comprising 24 *regedores*.

180. Of the 11 members elected to the Legislative Council, four are *naturais* of the Territory, four are from Portugal, two from Cape Verde and one is from São Tomé and Príncipe. There is no similar information concerning the three members elected by the Legislative Council to the Government Council.

Recent developments

181. Since 1963 most of the news on Portuguese Guinea has been concerned with the fighting. In July 1963, one of the political parties, the Union of Portuguese Guinea Nationals (URGP) sought and was granted conversations with Prime Minister Salazar with a view to obtaining 'autonomy' for the Territory. The results of the

conversations were not disclosed. This move has had no support from other parties.

182. According to various reports, although most of the fighting is in the south, with Catio as one of the main centres, areas within forty miles of Bissau, the capital, have also been affected. Some reports suggest that Portuguese troops control only the main towns, but official reports emphasize that the local population is loyal to Portugal and look to Portuguese troops for protection from the 'terrorists.' The information services of the Portuguese armed forces regularly issue communiques on the fighting. The Partido *Africano da Independencia da Guiné e Cabo Verde* (PAIGC) which claims to be the main party organizing the fighting in the southern part, also issues information bulletins.

183. In the 1963 military budget for Portuguese Guinea, of the 26.6 million escudos allocated for the territorial armed forces, 19.4 million escudos was for the army, 5.8 million escudos was for the navy and 11.4 million escudos for the air force. In October 1963, a new company of public security police was added, and in 1964 a special allocation of five million escudos was made for this purpose.

184. Since the beginning of 1964, fighting in Portuguese Guinea has intensified. In May 1964, Brigadier Arnaldo Schulz was appointed as Governor and Commander-in-chief of the armed forces in the Territory. Other changes in the Territorial Government are also expected. There are also indications that the military budget for Portuguese Guinea is rising. In January this year, for instance, the special measure under which autonomous services contribute towards defence expenditures was, put into effect in Portuguese Guinea.

185. There is little information on the economic development of the Territory. The ordinary revenue for 1963 was officially reported at 134 million escudos (US$6 million) and the extraordinary revenue at 33 million escudos. The ordinary revenue was lower than in any single year over the period 1957-60. Expenditures on development in 1963 included five million escudos for agricultural development, two million escudos for fisheries, five million escudos for highways and roads, eight million escudos for river transport, three million escudos for air ports and three million escudos for schools. The total was only slightly above the 1960 development expenditure.

Appendix 2 – Ethnic Appelations

(JJH-B) – *Dr. Ian Gilchrist and his wife, Joyce, feature prominently in the portion of this work that deals with the author's contact with Protestant missionaries in southern Angola.*

Canada is a big place, and more than fifty years have elapsed since the events described. However, quite by chance, we managed to reconnect across many kilometres and numerous time and climactic zones, and have had the opportunity to review some of the events surrounding the period when our paths crossed in Leopoldville. They were traumatic times for so many, and not least the Protestant missionaries, their families and co-workers who were often considered fifth-columnists by the fascist Portuguese regime.

Not unnaturally the author invited Joyce and Dr. Gilchrist to contribute their counsel and years of experience to the mix of material to be found in these pages – and gratefully acknowledges their investment in those portions of their story woven into the text.

As a journalist travelling through Angola during the period of a single summer, the author can in no way lay claim to the breadth of experience gathered by Dr. and Mrs. Gilchrist who were residents there over a number of years. These additional appendixes, therefore, composed in great part by the Gilchrists and keyed to elements within the text, will provide useful additional background information, and contribute to a broader understanding of events within the narrative.

(IG) – 1. The Ovimbundu (singular *Ocimbundu*) whose language and culture are *Umbundu*, are a totally different ethno-linguistic group from the *Kimbundu*, whose language is also Kimbundu despite their apparently similar appellations, reflecting root words derived from the great Bantu protolanguage of most of the diverse peoples of the southern part of the African continent. The distinction between Kimbundu and Umbundu is of fundamental importance because of the colonial effectiveness of the practice of "Divide and Rule" and the problematic adoption of a similar approach by the foreign Protestant missionaries. The latter made an arrangement among themselves with the laudable aspiration of avoiding religious division and sectarianism, so that members of any one mission church would join a single indigenous united Protestant church. Thus, religious competition would be avoided by each foreign group accepting a dedicated ethno-geographic assignment. But alas, when ethnic rivalry broke out in the frustration of the too-difficult revolution, the ethnic-affiliated missions reinforced a growing geo-cultural divide, where the Bakongo were largely served by British/Canadian Baptists, the Kimbundu by American/Scandinavian Methodists, and the Ovimbundu by United Americans/ Canadians.

2. Geographically the Bakongo Kingdom occupied northern Angola (where the traditional capital lies), south-western Democratic Republic of the Congo, southern Congo (Brazzaville), and Cabinda.

The Kimbundu homeland lies around Luanda, and although the Bakongo were the *first* Angolanos to be colonized by the Portuguese, it was the Luanda area that was most intensely affected by colonization and the subsequent development of a sizeable population of Luso-centric *mesticos* and language-losing Kimbundu. This was a key factor in the origin of the MPLA and in its orientation towards Euro-Communism (the late Christine Messiant traced this carefully in her 2008 *L'Angola post-colonial*), and a key source of rejection by GRAE and UNITA.

Then we come to the Umbundu country, which was the central part of Angola, although its people were great travellers and traders so that Umbundu became something of a *lingua franca* through the diversity of Central African peoples. It was from here that Savimbi came and from where he attempted to achieve Angola liberation.

Not mentioned anywhere, because no strong leader came forth from this relatively neglected (but highly repressed) part of Angola, were the Chokwe people, the fourth largest group, occupying the northeast of the country, where conflict continues today with the Angolano Government.

When the European explorers arrived at the great river flowing out of central Africa it became known as *the Congo,* the actual name of the people whose land surrounded the terminal portion of the flow. Progressively as the lands became colonized by the various European powers, they continued to apply this name to the bits that they took over. Thus, the *Belgian Congo,* the *French Congo*, and the northern province of Angola became the *Portuguese Congo.* In later years the International Africa Institute (in London) worked to achieve a standard spelling for African languages, and the spelling for the Congo people became *Kongo.* As to the term *Bakongo*, this is a reflection again of the Bantu prototype language, where affixing *Ba, Va,* or *Wa,* to the name of a given people simply means "of those people."

505

Appendix 3 –Racism

(IG) – The Portuguese were not seen to be 'colour racists,' necessarily – until after the close of the Second World War. As the Salazar government began to consider the masses of homeland Portuguese living in extreme poverty (40% illiteracy) and concerned by the aspirations of all societies coming out of such a calamitous war, there arose the notion of granting lands to an impoverished homeland peasantry in the vast spaces available in Africa. It was an attractive solution to a mammoth problem. It was hoped that an increased Portuguese population in Africa might also help to calm 'restless natives' also showing signs of post-war muscle flexing, and that it would eventually assert some form of control over a visibly growing colonial problem. Land was promised to soldiers completing their service, something they would never be able to afford in the homeland – and in this way *'colonatos'* were established. With these, almost as a matter of course, there arose colour racism.

Appendix 4 – Forced Labour

(IG) – Until the end of the Second World War – and well beyond – the Portuguese were not so much engaged in 'colonization' as they were in continuing a form of 'plantation slavery' – forced labour – justifying the system by arranging a concordat with the Vatican approving a Portuguese 'civilizing mission' through the 'dignity of labour' (forced or otherwise). The term used was 'contract labour,' but those obliged to provide the 'labour' had no say whatsoever concerning the conditions of the 'contract,' and they feared it because it could last for months at a time, even years.

(JJH-B) – The system was operative at the time of the author's visit, but when enquiries about it were made, invariably the response was that they were 'prisoners' released from their usual cells to perform civic work (sweeping streets, unloading trucks, carrying cargo, etc. – pretty well anything for which a team of workers might be needed) – and under the supervision of guards, of course. It was a part of their 'punishment,' and all 'prisoners' (including innocents doing forced labour) were treated the same way.

Appendix 5 - Torture

(IG) – 'Storing vegetables ...?' São Nicolau certainly had the reputation for torture and suffering ... when my father's nursing staff were arrested and taken away '... Twelve intimate African friends and fellow workers were tortured to death, or committed suicide to cheat their sadistic captors when human flesh and spirit could stand no more.'

It was always our understanding that most of these people perished at São Nicolau.

Just one person being tortured in a small facility is enough to intimidate the whole community. Travelling to a village outside the mission on Sunday trips, my siblings and I were obliged to stop to make the obligatory visit to our *chef do posto* and wait for his permission to continue on our way. We would hear screams as we waited.

One night, Joyce told me somebody had been looking in the bathroom window at her. A few nights later she wakened me to say there had been somebody beside our bed, with a flashlight. I woke my parents up and we searched the house, which was never locked. Found missing was a cash fund of donations local people had made for building a better treatment centre. Because there was a fresh team of *Policia Movel* in Bailundo, I naïvely suggested to my father that he advise them of the robbery. He was reluctant, saying they would just choose a victim to accuse, but I persuaded him by claiming that because the stolen monies had come from people who were already poor, it would be important to register a claim in case a robber should be caught.

Both these events seemed strange, however, as my parents employed a watchman. But trusting me, the watchman said he could not say it, but that the person who had come to the house on both occasions was not dark-skinned. He knew if he ever made the claim, he would immediately be killed.

A couple of days later a jeep arrived at the house with the police chief and a number of armed officers. They said they had come because they had solved the case; they had arrested a man who had told them he was the watchman's partner in crime.

The watchman was placed in the jeep and I saw on his face the terror of a man who knew he was already dead.

I knew I had to do something quickly, so told the police chief I would go along with them too, as I had also seen the intruder. When we got to the police station I demanded to meet with the accuser of our watchman – but of course there was no such person. So, I told the police chief there must have been a 'mistake,' that I would return to the mission with the watchman and we would initiate our own investigation.

Clearly there was nothing to incriminate the poor man – but even so, we urged him to flee the district because he had witnessed the behavior of the police.

Appendix 6 - Song

(IG) – One of the principal characteristics of all the great Bantu peoples of southern Africa is the central role of music and song in their societies. In Angola this cultural trait is so strong that books have been written about '*njimbasilili*' – which, translated, means 'I sing so that I do not cry.' (Its ultimate reflection is its transmission to the Americas in the form of 'negro spiritual' music and song.)

Song arising from the São Nicolau prisoners could have as easily represented pain and fear as it might have seemed to show joy and satisfaction. In the given scenario, I would suggest the first of these is more likely!

Imprinted on my childhood memory are the trucks arranged by the police going by our house, stuffed with unlucky men caught in *rusgas* sent to collect quotas of forced labourers for the plantations. They passed by singing, knowing that many would never come home again, and nearly all would never find their families intact if they did return.

Appendix 7 – Portuguese Toleration of Protestants

(IG) – In correspondence, Dr. Ian Gilchrist contributed the following thoughtful and nostalgic comments concerning the mission at Dondi as it was during the dangerous time he and his family were so closely associated with it:

"One reason for the Portuguese Government *allowing* Dondi Mission to function for so long as it did, was because it was almost the only place in Angola where *Angolans* were receiving post-primary education in a number of fields, with the mission following faithfully and obediently the rules set down by Government, producing graduates who not only then had important technical skills, but who were fluent in Portuguese and entirely familiar with Portuguese culture and history. It served the Government well for the running of technical services under a cadre of Portuguese Government administrative officials.

"But this did not mean that the Dondi graduates necessarily became quite what the missionary teachers might have hoped they would become. For those Angolan students accepted into the Dondi programs, there was the incredible opportunity of graduating with all the qualifications to become "*Assimilados*," a path out of profound poverty and into a world of much more limited oppression.

"But the result too was that there was a student body that was also learning *privilege,* and I well remember the frustration of Dr. Allen Knight, Dondi's Director of the Agriculture program, when a truckload of supplies would arrive and had to be unloaded, and *no* student would agree to help him do it – because they desperately desired to become *Assimilados* (Portuguese of African origin), and no Portuguese of any consequence did manual labour. A student so doing could be seen as still not ready for the elevated status of a Portuguese citizen.

"One other vivid example of this dilemma was seen when my father was making a trip to one of the rural villages in the area that he covered. As always there were people who were originally from the community who sought to take advantage of a vehicle going there to head home for a short visit. On this occasion it was a student from one of the mission schools who asked my father for such a lift. When they arrived, as always, there were many people excited to see them, and the youth's mother came forward joyfully clapping her hands and greeting him in their Umbundu language. But now he turned on her angrily, saying, '*Olha mulher, eu não falo a lingua dos cães*!' To speak Umbundu, even to his mother, was to threaten that coveted educational glimpse of escape to Lusitanian assimilation ...

"... How much is Angola an appropriate site for the training of leaders for peaceful development with its so recent bad past? It is the reason I have urged those who labour in love for Angola to consider, rather, key leadership training for a few Angolans – yeast for the constitution of a new world, like that offered by the complex of United World Colleges (Pearson College, for instance). It should be remembered, of course, that all three leaders of the main revolutionary parties in Angola were the prize products of different Protestant missions there; and during the subsequent devastatingly cruel *civil* war between them, *none* appeared to have adopted the model of Christ …"

Appendix 8 - Holden Roberto

(IG) – As so happens in oppressed societies, those who undertake to lead rebellion tend to be bright, perceptive and to have been exposed to schooling and a literacy level that has revealed the potential for reversal of inequities and injustice.

This was well-exemplified by the nascent Angolan revolution against a centuries-old, dictator-driven and religiously conservative Portuguese colonialism: all the principal leaders of the rebel groups –i) MPLA's Agostinho Neto (American Methodism); ii) UNITA's Jonas Savimbi (American/Canadian united Protestant churches); iii) UPA's Holden Roberto (British Baptist); iv) PDA's Emanuel Kunzika (Baptist/Salvation Army) represented small minorities of the overall Angolan population and were products of those foreign religious educational programs barely tolerated by the Portuguese colonial authorities.

But although these leaders' scholarship and temerity greatly heartened those from whom they had sprung in longing for release from generations of Portuguese oppression, their mission education and simple motivation did not actually equip any of them individually for the task of undertaking the total struggle for revolutionary emancipation. After decades of strife (often internal as well as external) it was the awakened Portuguese themselves, following their own home-grown revolution in 1974, who used their by now well-experienced military to bring a definitive resolution to the struggle.

Holden Roberto was a young man at the time he accepted leadership of UPNA. He was devoted to his Bakongo people both in their Congo exile, and in their Portuguese-controlled northern Angola. He was astute enough, after his horizons had been expanded by other African leaders like Kwame Nkrumah, to organize deletion of the 'N' (North) from the original name of the party.

PDA – *Parti Democratique Angolaise*. A large percentage of PDA adherents were from families finding refuge in the old Belgian Congo for decades before the war for independence began. In spite of the tough Belgian regime these displaced Angolans were deeply involved with the Francophone educational and commercial systems of *Congo Belge.*

He perceived correctly that the Bakongo shared a common fate with other Angolan ethnolinguistic groups, and that union of *all* the people of Angola was an imperative. Hence the new name, 'UPA,' for his party. The sincerity and enhanced vision of this move was manifest by a second move: the creation of a government-in-exile, the GRAE – *Governo Revolucionário de Angola no Exílio* (Revolutionary Government of Angola in Exile). This incorporated, along with other smaller groups, the PDA – the leaders of which, centred in Leopoldville, felt a French name more appropriate than Portuguese. The formation of the GRAE created a structure and cabinet that included a diversity of the territory's population. This move inevitably induced greater organizational, technical and political complexity, demanding greater leadership skills, a particular necessity in the context of waging war – a highly technical enterprise indeed.

Roberto was considerably compromised by the fact that the locus and focus of the UPA and the PDA was very clearly (and in one sense *had* to be) in the geographic northern homeland of the Bakongo. Ethnic cleansing by the Portuguese was well recognized by revolutionaries throughout the territory, but resources were so limited it was a virtual impossibility to do anything about it. The military and the police were the chief instruments of repression, but a '*colonato*' policy, whereby Angolans would be forcibly removed to make way for the new settlement of immigrant farmers from Portugal itself, seemed to give clear indication of the intensity and direction the repression would take. (A 'successful' *colonato* was set up in 1961.) This cruel policy did not distinguish between ethno-cultural groups, some of which were overtly rebellious while many others remained passive. The Portuguese greatly feared 'educated primitives' whom they saw as potential rebel communicators and leaders; a man could be arrested, imprisoned or even shot for possession of a pencil. Ironically, only twenty-five years earlier, the Portuguese themselves had been victims of the controlling power of literacy/illiteracy in their Iberian homeland; about forty percent had themselves been illiterate. New arrivals in Angola from Portugal were surprised – even terrified – to discover there were some literate Angolans throughout almost all areas of the territory.

I arrived in Leopoldville (Kinshasa) in early 1963, supported by The American Committee on Africa. My wife followed a little later with the children, and Roberto installed us in the centre of the refugee compound adjacent to the clinic for the *Serviço de Assistência aos Refugiados de Angola* – SARA. His own office and that of the GRAE headquarters was nearby. We met often, and he was warm and supportive, always kindly and courageous. We talked a lot as he struggled to get the new multi-ethnic GRAE going – my own presence indicative of the no color, language, religious, gender or resource exclusions within the new entity. Not infrequently he begged me to help find funds to extend operations into the southern and central regions of Angola; all the new non-Bakongo in his cabinet were insisting the struggle was not helping their people at all. That was most definitely not my role, and in a relatively short period of time his ideal cabinet gradually started to fall apart. Notably Savimbi left to form his own new liberation movement in southern and central Angola. Alexandre Taty (Savimbi's former housemate who overtly attempted an overthrow of Roberto) headed for his homeland of Cabinda. Many others of the Kimbundu leadership, cabinet members and others in leadership roles, also left – many of them to Agostinho Neto's already powerful MPLA. One of the Ovimbundu leaders who quit (but did not follow Savimbi) was my much-loved immediate director and medical colleague, Dr. José Liahuca, who fled to Congo-Brazzaville (where the MPLA was based), and later committed suicide after attending a failed peace conference among the rival Angolan parties.

With Liahuca gone, I stayed for another year with the Relief Service, but ultimately there were further revolts within the GRAE ranks, and one night this involved some of the nurses. By then I had moved with my family from the GRAE compound to the British Baptist residential grounds; the missionaries there felt it was becoming unsafe for us at the compound, so offered us accommodation. On that crucial night one of the nurses arrived at our door telling me that GRAE and Congolese military police had come looking for him at his own house, but not finding him had taken his young brother away, and he begged me to do something.

I went directly to the GRAE compound and on my way saw a Relief Service vehicle driving by stuffed with Angolan and Congolese soldiers. I had been sent to the home of Roberto's uncle the charismatic, kindly, and highly esteemed Eduardo Pinock, which was on the GRAE compound. He was a member of Roberto's cabinet. While waiting there for Roberto's arrival, Pinock told me Roberto was very angry – which proved to be true when he got there. But I was also very disturbed with the abuse of the relief equipment, and I told Roberto the vehicles could not be used for political or military purposes – the same position taken by Dr. Liahuca that had obliged him to depart. Roberto replied to me that the vehicles were not my property and belonged to the GRAE relief service. This was correct, but it was also the case that I had fund-raised for the equipment in the United States and Canada, and at the United Nations, and knew very well such usage of the vehicles would have been unacceptable to the donors – as it was also to those of us who were the relief workers. Roberto said he was not going to allow me to destroy the friendships he had established with the donors to the Relief Service – and demanded I surrender my keys to the vehicles forthwith.

I did as he bid, walked back to the Baptist compound (witnesses along the way whispering sorrow at this turn of events) and told the missionaries what had transpired. I told them I believed my work with the Relief Service was over, and that we would have to leave the Congo.

I was amazed at how quickly I received incredible kindness from the many groups then working in the Congo for Angolan refugees, and who undertook without hesitation to protect myself and my family – and to achieve our extraction from a scenario gone bad. These included the British Baptists who had so generously accommodated us already, officials of the Congo Protestant Relief Agency, the Mennonite Travel Agency, the Conseil Protestant du Congo, personnel of the United States and Canadian embassies and many others who immediately coordinated a plan to get me out of the Congo – along with a separate plan to get Joyce and the children out. All of this was on a weekend. I was astounded that one of them went to the home of a Congolese authority and immediately acquired exit visas for us, and the Mennonites booked a flight out for the next day.

On the morrow, as we prepared to leave, one of the Relief Service vehicles of the SARA came into the driveway of the Baptist compound full of soldiers and police under the leadership of Roberto's Chief of Security, Manuel Peterson, who had a warrant for my arrest. Fortunately, the driveway had a separate exit, and a missionary placed his vehicle to block the driveway while another took myself and my family out the exit. We were driven directly to the home of the Canadian ambassador, where I remained until flight time while Joyce and the children returned to the mission house to pack up. We were then driven to the airport.

The exit itself is another chapter, but as it is not relevant to my observations about Roberto. I will just say here that I got out on a flight that went to Nigeria and Holland and proceeded from there to New York. I arrived three days later, and within hours Joyce and the children were there too.

So, do I have a profoundly negative sentiment about Holden Roberto? Not at all. Unlike Savimbi, Holden never became a warlord – and nor did the GRAE's Vice-President, Emmanuel Kunzika. Both Roberto and Kunzika, although representing different elements of it, were really the cream of the Bakongo nation. And although politically close to American liberals they did not develop a rigid copying of their benefactors, as Neto and the MPLA did with the Russian and Cuban communists.

Roberto was personally warm and I remember when, not long after I had arrived to work at SARA, I developed a serious fever and was hospitalized at a Belgian hospital – where the only available physician was a gynecologist! Roberto worried that by inviting me to work for the Relief Service he might have caused my death. Living on the GRAE compound I saw a lot of him and, having a short-wave radio, I remember the night I heard on the Voice of America that President Kennedy had been assassinated. I hastened to Roberto's office to tell him, and once again I saw his distress. He had been a great admirer of the US President. Showing concern for my safety, Roberto had early on given me an old French military helmet to wear when I was travelling on my refugee work along the Angolan border, where Portuguese troops and air patrols were active.

What went wrong? As I have indicated, none of the original Angolan leaders were military tacticians or organizational experts. As the war went badly for the GRAE, competition grew with the MPLA (and later with UNITA) and there was a flight of non-Bakongo from Roberto's government. More and more he had to exercise recourse to readily available family and clan members, until the GRAE began to look like a 'family affair.' They were not all people bent on returning to UPNA status, but inevitably it tended to include some who were thugs and brutes, and this contributed to Roberto's progressive loss of control. In his writings Chinua Achebe has brilliantly illustrated how those who escape long oppression begin to show what they have learned from the oppressor by adopting the same practices that were once directed at them. There is a surfeit of such examples. It is a sad reality in many socio-cultural sites on our old globe today.

Holden Roberto has passed away now, but I remember him as a bright and decent person who was unable, because of the time and place in which he lived, to achieve his original goals and who saw good intent deteriorate into broad tragedy. I regret that when I visited Angola in 1992 I was unable to meet him, but was very happy to be hosted by Emmanuel Kunzika, who now has also died.

As a long-time civil servant in Canada I have repeatedly seen the divide between visionary elected officials who are often technically naïve, and technically dominant bureaucrats who are politically naïve. It is a scenario that leads too often to unrealized progress, so it is easy to understand the worthiness and failures of a man like Holden Roberto.

Appendix 9 – Jonas Savimbi

(JJH-B) – *Eulogy written shortly after Savimbi had been killed on the battlefield in 2002.*

(IG) – Jonas Savimbi and I were the same age when we met for the first time, although his father, a Church leader in the Chilesso area of Angola, was known to me from childhood. Both of us arrived in the Congo fresh from our university studies, he to be Foreign Minister in Holden Roberto's Angolan Government in Exile, and I to work in the Relief Service for Angolan Refugees (SARA – *Serviço de Assistência aos Refugiados de Angola*).

Both of us had grown up in Angola and had known from our beginnings the cruelty of the Portuguese colonial regime. We came with the energy and determination of youth, prepared to give our all to changing that terrible way of life for the masses of the Angolan people.

The Congo was clearly the most promising place for the initiation of such change, because not only was it now independent itself, and had received thousands of refugees who had poured across the border from early 1961, when there were spontaneous desperate eruptions in Angola but because, for decades already, Angolans had fled to all the neighboring countries. This was to escape what Henry Nevinson had called, in 1906, *A Modern Slavery.* Nevinson had investigated the Portuguese colonies for *Harper's Monthly Magazine*, at the urging of the Aborigines Protection Society and the British and Foreign Anti-Slavery Society. Fifty-five years later much had changed, but it was not better.

The issue of routes of escape was important. Holden Roberto had worked hard (partly because of urging by Ghana's Kwame Nkrumah) to evolve his Union of the Peoples of Northern Angola into a union of all Angolan peoples. But it was still Roberto's northern Kongo populations who could most easily get out of Angola (although they also paid terrible prices in lives lost to Portuguese bombardment and starvation).

Roberto's efforts were reflected in the choice of Savimbi (a central Angolan) to a cabinet position of the exiled government; and further reflected by Savimbi sharing accommodations with Alexandre Taty, who was from the Cabinda Enclave and had been similarly appointed – and, indeed, by my own acceptance into the Relief Service.

But it was not enough, because the consequences of the northern rebellion were being felt through Portuguese repression and cruelty throughout Angola. In Savimbi's home area people were even being shot for being found in the possession of pencils (because of the risk of rebellion that the colonial authorities thought lay in literacy).

Savimbi felt it was urgent that routes of escape also be created for central, eastern, and southern Angolans on the other borders of the country. When that didn't happen, it was only a few months later that he left Roberto to set up UNITA, right within south-central Angola itself.

Whatever else may be said, Savimbi had organizational genius. Along with his long military campaigns against the Portuguese army, and then against the Marxist MPLA that replaced it, he insisted on educational and health services, which were always impressive and highly effective. (Some of these are detailed by Maria Chela Chikueka in her book *Angola Torchbearers*, which she wrote in Toronto shortly before her death there in 1999.)

But nothing succeeds like success, and maybe nothing fails like failure, and Savimbi never quite made the breakthrough for which he always strived, although for years UNITA controlled a major portion of the Angolan countryside. Colleagues and friends began to desert him, and he became more heavy-handed. Among the new dissidents was George Chikoti, who also came to Canada, and who now represents the Angolan Ministry of Foreign Affairs.

The Canadian Government and other groups of Canadians had variable interests and activities during the Angolan conflicts. During colonial times the NATO alliance (it included both Canada and Portugal) presented an impediment to Canadian objection to the ethnic cleansing being pursued by the Salazar government of Portugal. Later, a curious connection developed when members of the FLQ (*Front de Libération du Québec*) went to Cuba just as Cuba was supplying large numbers of troops and civilian cadres to the new fellow Marxist MPLA government of Angola, and Canadians surfaced who were connected to the MPLA.

In 1988, requested to meet with staff of the Department of External Affairs, in Ottawa, I was asked what I would feel about the 'removal' of Savimbi.

A telling strike against the UNITA founder and leader was his resort to *apartheid* South African military support even though, often ignored, was the massive support being provided to Angola's MPLA by Cuba at the same time. This was ill-perceived by nearly everybody.

Undoubtedly Savimbi became a warlord, and when I met with him for the last time (in Luanda, in 1992), he was surrounded by such trappings. Maybe they were essential for his survival, because just four months after our meeting, he was driven back into the bush. Present with us when we saw each other was the gentle mining engineer Jeremias Chitunda, who had been working in British Columbia in 1970 when my own parents and sister died (Globe and Mail editorial of June 17, 1970). Chitunda was assassinated before he could leave Luanda with Savimbi.

What must be said of Savimbi, regardless of what he became, is that he was unlike any other. He remained always with the people he saw himself serving. He did not command war from the sanctuary of exile. Although 'blood diamonds' were a significant source of his revenue, the funds obtained went not into personal foreign bank accounts, but entirely for the cause in which he believed.

My wife, Joyce, wrote a poem in 1965 while we lived and worked with Savimbi in an Angolan refugee compound. I was reminded of it when I learned of my friend's death:

And yesterday I saw a man who cried

An aging man, whose shoulders drooped beneath his too-large clothes

His head between his knees, he sat upon the fallen tree and sobbed

Around him children ran, people passed by and he sat unnoticed in his sadness.

Why did he cry, this brown-skinned man with greying hair?

Was it in hunger, or in pain?

Or was it from some trivial thing grown out of size in midst of both of these?

Or was it from a noble cause, gone sour?

~

I did not know, but I too in my heart shed tears with him.

Three weeks ago another remarkable Angolan who has settled in Canada, João Samuel Matwawana, was on a peace mission to the rebels of Burundi. He e-mailed me from South Africa, asking if, at the conclusion of his current work, I would join him to once again approach Savimbi. That door has suddenly been closed. *Lalapo an Jonas.*

Appendix 10 – Dondi – Growing Centre of Education

(JJH-B) – Rev. Michael Solberg, of Hinsdale, Illinois, pastor of the United Church of Christ (USA), has been a member for more than fifteen years of the Illinois Conference, Angola Partnership Team, and thus in close contact with the Igreja Evangelica Congregacional de Angola (IECA). He is a member of the Board of Trustees for the Superior Polytechnic Institute of Dondi (or ISP Dondi). He was asked to comment on Dondi as a rising centre of education in southern Angola.

(MS) – Luís Samacumbi formerly led IECA's Department of Education and Social Programs, currently works for the United Nations in Angola, and is also IECA's national director of external relations and development there. He has been extremely active in the re-development of ISP Dondi.

An 'ISP' is a university level school, but with fewer courses of study. In short, IECA has done extensive preparation to receive the government approval needed to open ISP Dondi, a three-year process so far. They have one remaining requirement: the construction and reconstruction of the necessary buildings and infrastructure – at the moment about seventy percent complete. The final government inspection will be in May or June (2019) and the establishment will then be ready to begin classes when the school year begins in early 2020. In addition to IECA's own resources, the German branch of Bread for the World is providing a grant of funds, and the Illinois Conference of the United Church of Christ has supported the work as well. ISP Dondi will focus on theology, agriculture, medical sciences (including nursing and dentistry), and eventually education and teacher training.

Dondi again has a functioning hospital (with just about all services except surgery so far). There are two doctors, several nurses and other staff assistants. The hospital is already providing critical service to the area's population and is expanding its reach as resources and capability increase.

Part of the ISP Dondi program will also be a language institute in Huambo (approximately one hundred kilometres away) where there will be instruction in English to prepare students for advanced study and global interaction. That program will begin in June 2019.

Many of Dondi's original buildings were bombed to rubble during the civil war, but many have been rehabilitated, including the main (two spire) gathering and sanctuary building that was part of the well-known Currie Institute. It is once again a beautiful gathering and worship space, used regularly by Emmanuel Seminary (which is also back on the Dondi site, in restored buildings). It will be a central part of ISP Dondi.

It may have been less expensive to erect new buildings, but with IECA's strong and beloved connection to Dondi's history and its people, local residents have felt it important to restore as many of the old sites as possible rather than tear down and build anew.

"A tree cut off from its roots cannot grow," the locals have said.

Although delayed by Portuguese colonial oppression and then by civil war the dream first articulated at the founding of Dondi Mission Station in 1914 – having university level education for Angolans at the Dondi Mission Station – will soon be a reality due to the hard work and leadership of the current General Secretary, Rev. André Cangovi Eurico, and his many helpers.

Appendix 11 – Camões

(JJH-B) – Strangely enough, not a great deal is known about the man other than what can be deduced from his writings. The stories about him I eventually learned left me enthralled, and I came to realize what an exceptional human being he must have been. I had heard of other great Portuguese, why never Camões if he had been as important as everyone assured me he was?

I think the answer probably lies somewhere hidden in the fact that an encultured people will revere and defend the poet who writes lyrically of their culture, looking on him as they might the grandparent of their own cultural family. However, they do not necessarily read him, know him intimately, understand him. It is a rare scholar who can quote accurately, and at length, the words of his nation's literary hero, comprehending and knowing him so well that he can assume the hero's mindset, or his fitting response, to any given accumulation of contemporary events. To me, what makes any national poet truly great is his ability to take his nation's most noble characteristics or attributes and zoom so far out in front of the common herd that his own people (and maybe some who are not) can refocus, see themselves anew and in clear perspective.

It was not hard to become enthralled by the scant details of Camões' raucous personal story. Always blessed (sometimes cursed!) by a romantic sense of discovery and adventure, I have derived a vicarious thrill from 'the search,' allowing it to cause me great pain and heartache - and Camões' story certainly fit that bill as he came to life before me. Perhaps (thanks to João's admonishment!) I had come to love him before I had actually read him, before I had determined for myself the need to know him more intimately. When the opportunity finally did present itself, there was a natural inclination to compare his greatest work with what I had read of Shakespeare; the Englishman had been a major portion of my literary upbringing, after all. It soon became evident, even though never having been previously aware of Camões, that I would never comprehend the Portuguese psyche until I had made a serious effort to come to grips with what he had written about his people.

I reckoned he would have been on Ilha de Moçambique just about three hundred years ago, when the little church João and I were looking at would have been somewhat less than one hundred years old. I wondered if he was as completely charmed by St. António's as I was – whether, in fact, he would have been as charmed by Ilha de Moçambique in its entirety – as was I – after being marooned here for two years, unable to raise the funds to get home ...? (Eventually friends came to his assistance.)

Luís Vaz de Camões is indeed Portugal's national poet and, by any standard remains the literary entity to Portugal that Shakespeare remains to England – unparalleled leader of a poetic culture. Both men were preeminent in the world of letters – poets and playwrights. Both towered above all comers within his own surroundings and spoke louder and clearer than any single writer of his time or any time before or since. Every culture has at least one who rises to a pinnacle. In Portugal it was Camões. Stand the great ones beside each other and of course incomparable differences emerge – the principal point any one of them would have in common with the others being the quality of greatness.

(It is curious to note their dates: Camões, born in 1522 or 1524, dying aged fifty-six or fifty-eight in 1580; Shakespeare born in 1564, dying three days short of his fifty-second birthday in 1616. Shakespeare would have been sixteen at the time of Camões' death. While both men would have been writing at a time of historical overlap, it is virtually certain Camões would have come to Shakespeare's wide-ranging attention, but probably just as unlikely Camões would ever have known or heard about Shakespeare.)

In a most peculiar way, though, Camões appears to stand above Portugal even higher than Shakespeare stands above England, and I believe it is for this reason: Shakespeare wrote of universal themes – great men and their lives, their deepest fears and twists of psyche, their loves and hatreds, their nobleness and their base failures. He wrote of Everyman, in fact – and as a result, his works translate into every language of the world and speak to all men of what they know and recognize of their own humanity within themselves. He has become universal, speaking for all of mankind.

Camões was different in that he spoke especially (in his most celebrated epic, *Os Lusíadas*) of the Portuguese, attempted to rally them to the pinnacle of their greatness – sadly, perhaps, a late call in the last moments of Portugal's historic glory. He identified the Portuguese to the Portuguese, told them who they were, and that what they really had to accomplish was to steady and secure the ship of state, to continue doing as they had been doing – maintain their noble drive.

But tragically, perhaps inevitably, by the time this message reached his people, Portugal had simply run out of steam, the energy to maintain its place in the global pecking order of the day. History was busy logging itself, and the great events of the epoch were leaping ahead of such a small country's capacity to maintain the pace. (At the apex of her powers Portugal's population never amounted to more than one-and-a-quarter million souls.) In just eight years of the 1540s, Dom João III had been obliged to abandon four of Portugal's battle-won strongholds in wars against the Moors of the North African Maghreb; by 1578 his successor, the zealous religious dreamer boy-king, Dom Sebastião, was to lead the cream of Portugal's elite on one last great crusade to reclaim fading glories – and he lost all in the decimation of the Battle of Alcácer Quibir. The king and the best of Portugal lay dead upon the field, and from that point forward there was nothing to rally, too few men of calibre to pick up the pieces and re-start that which had ground to a halt.

Sebastião was succeeded by his aging uncle, Cardinal Dom Henrique and, when he died just two years after accepting the crown, it was a Spanish king, Filipe I, who stepped forward to claim Portugal and unify Iberia. Filipe I was followed by two more – Filipe II and III – for a total of sixty years of Spanish domination. By the time the Portuguese had thrown the Spaniards out and put their own king back on their throne (Dom João IV, 1640-56) the country was in the process of being outstripped by other European powers – Spain, Holland, France, Britain – and the contours of the Portuguese Empire were being greatly altered.

Camões was born into a family of lesser nobility in Lisboa. Through his grandfather there was a connection to the family of Vasco da Gama, who had died a national hero about the time of Camões' birth. Through his family and court connections, and his studies at the University of Coimbra, the young Camões would have been familiar with the thrilling stories of Portugal's era of The Discoveries. It was a period when the whole country was in the middle of its glorious days of Renaissance, a breathtaking time to be a student and at the epicentre of a monumental European surge in knowledge and discovery in every field – and with Portugal, superpower of its day, very much in the forefront of global learning, awareness and expansion. Camões was a romantic; he studied the humanities and had a strong interest in the classics, so applied himself to all the ancient histories available to him, spoke Latin, Italian and Spanish, and wrote his first poems during his carefree time as a student. There is no record that he ever graduated, however, and by about 1544 he had left Coimbra and was back in Lisboa where he frequented Court, consorted with aristocratic friends – wrote poetry and tried his hand at comedy.

A love affair went hopelessly wrong, Camões was banished from Lisboa, and in 1548 was exiled to the Ribatejo. The following year he joined the Portuguese militia expedition fighting in Ceuta, lost his right eye in a skirmish and was returned to Lisboa a hardened, abrasive and more assertive man. He was involved in a street fight in 1552, wounded a Court official, and so was arrested and imprisoned for nine months. Eventually he was granted a King's pardon on the condition that he serve three years in Portugal eastern colonies.

There are records showing Camões arrived in Goa in May 1553, which most likely means he had arrived there by way of the Ilha de Moçambique. This was the route Portuguese sailing ships normally travelled at that time after rounding *Cabo de Boa Esperança* – the Cape of Good Hope. They would stock up and rest up at the port facility established on the tiny island before sailing on to the Malabar Coast – Goa and beyond, as far as the island of Ternate. It occurred to me that perhaps the Ilha de Moçambique was the first tropical island Camões would ever have known intimately; there are other islands at which the ship that transported him here, the *São Bento*, may have called – Cabo Verde, São Tomé – but this would have been the first in the Indian Ocean. For certain, the Ilha de Moçambique, with its widely differing demographic and religious strands, would have been unlike any others on which he might have landed. It is only probable he stopped at the island on his way out to India; on his way home years later he certainly came to know it well.

In all he spent fifteen years in the Far East. He saw service in Goa, Macau (where it appears he began to accumulate some wealth); he visited Malacca and the Moluccas Islands (then known as the Spice Islands) – but then disaster struck anew. A ship he was on foundered off the Mekong Delta, and Camões had to swim for it.

Legend has it that he swam with his manuscript for *Os Lusíadas* held aloft from the waves, but his fortune to this day somewhere at the bottom of the South China Sea.

He managed to get back to Goa, but in those days if a soldier was sent out to the colonies on the king's purse, it was understood his return must be at his own expense. Camões was stuck until a friendly captain appointed to Sofala agreed to take him as far as Moçambique – and so dropped him, penniless, on Ilha de Moçambique. For two years he lived among the islanders, unable to pay for his passage home. He used the time to work on a book of poems which he called *Parnaso de Luís de Camões*. Friends finally came through for him, fronting him his fare – but somehow, between the island and Lisboa (which he reached in April 1570) the *Parnaso* was lost and has never been found. *Os Lusíadas* was published in 1571, for which he received a small pension over a period of three years.

While Camões certainly understood the ignominy of the defeat at Alcácer Quibir in 1578, thankfully he did not live to see a Spaniard assume the crown of Portugal in 1580. He lived his last days in the room of a house next to the church of Santa Ana, begging for food on the streets of Lisboa and attended by his faithful slave, Jau, who had accompanied him from India. He died on June 10th of that year, a date that has been celebrated ever since as Portugal's national day. His tomb is at Mosteiro de Jerónimos in Belem, next to his hero, Vasco da Gama.

Appendix 12 – American Duplicity and Meddling

(JJH-B) – This short paper, by military historian Dr. Chandar Sundaram, is included as commentary on the unwanted intrusion of the United States of America into the affairs of a sovereign nation whose people, culture and internal divisions are unknown and deeply misunderstood – and the devastation caused by its armed (ultimately unsuccessful) blundering attempt at 'persuasion.' The theme of Dr. Sundaram's short paper complements themes found in several areas of this work, but is especially apt in regard to the section headlined 'Antagonists – a colonial survey' (p.245) through to the end of that section (p.265).

(CS) – Since 1945, the US has seen itself as the centre of a 'Pax Americana,' a pre-eminence in international affairs. Yet, paradoxically, to maintain this 'peaceful' position, America has engaged in almost permanent warfare. Since the end of World War II, the US has undertaken either a major military operation or a covert paramilitary intervention (usually by the CIA) an average of once every 18 months.

It would be shocking enough if this all happened within its borders, but what is really scandalous is that this bellicosity has been carried on in supposedly sovereign nations, especially the former colonial, or dependent, countries of Africa. Asia, the Middle East, Latin America, and Europe have not been spared, and in recent years the fighting in Iraq and Afghanistan has dragged the US into protracted warfare.

The military-political meddling of the Americans in Angola, which long predated the territory's independence and lasted for years, was only one of its more notable and unhelpful incursions into post-World War II Africa. As the colonial power in Angola, Portugal was important to the Americans because of the enormous oil resources in the northern Angolan province of Cabinda. In addition, Angola possesses exceptional mineral wealth (gold, copper, diamonds, etc.) which US mining corporations have long been anxious to exploit. Finally, as allies in the Cold War, Portugal and the US were bound by an ongoing agreement which had been signed during World War II for the establishment of a strategic military and air base at Lajes Field on Terceira, one of the Atlantic islands in the Portuguese self-governing province of the Azores. This gave the US a leg-up on the Soviet Union in the Atlantic – an advantage which has since been cut back, leaving the islanders with a $35,000,000 deficit in the local economy, and a toxic waste problem which has caused considerable health issues among the local islanders.

Although Washington provided military aid to Lisbon, ostensibly intended to bolster Portugal's anti-Soviet efforts, much of it was in fact redirected to support Portugal's colonial wars in Africa – America basically turning a blind eye to the Portuguese misallocation.

Here, however, the US played more than a double-game: in order to make certain its interests would be safeguarded whichever way the wind blew, and that their access to Angola's considerable oil and mineral wealth were secured to their benefit, the US additionally funded and provided political support to Holden Roberto's right-wing FNLA in its struggle against Agostinho Neto's left-wing MPLA. All of this was going on as the US continued to fund the Portuguese – throughout the 1960s.

Sources on the ground at that time reported the existence of this formalized, though covert, conduit supplying Roberto. US Hercules and Starlifter military transports, flying under the aegis of the CIA, were known to be landing at Kinshasa in Zaire. Here, their cargoes, comprising a variety of military hardware – rifles, machine guns, light artillery, and mortars, along with the necessary ammunition – would then be dispersed among smaller bush-planes. These would then fly to Ambriz, on the coast of Angola just north of the capital, Luanda, and to other strategic bush locations, to be unloaded. In addition to this, American reconnaissance, and artillery spotter planes, piloted by US nationals, regularly overflew combat areas. The US also trained and financed large numbers of mercenaries.

In the late 1960s the Nixon administration, wanting to bolster relations with the then white-ruled South Africa, decided on a drastic reduction of its covert funding to Roberto, giving him only a nominal sum to allay his costs for supplying intelligence – an activity for which they had been paying him since 1950. However, in early 1975, on the eve of Angolan independence, the US decided to re-activate the account they had previously reduced so drastically, and they handed him $300,000. This was intended to cover the cost of 'bicycles and non-military supplies' – euphemism, of course, for military aid.

Despite this, the FNLA now suffered repeated defeats at the hands of the MPLA. By the end of September 1975, the MPLA controlled Luanda, Angola's Capital, the strategic Benguela railway, and all the country's major ports. More significantly, only two of Angola's sixteen provinces, Zaire and Uige, remained in FNLA hands – and these were hard pressed by MPLA forces.

However, by this time the US was supporting yet another Angolan independence organization. This was the National Union for the Total Independence of Angola (UNITA), formed in 1966 by Jonas Savimbi, Roberto's break-away former Foreign Minister. US policy makers, led by Henry Kissinger, decided to fund Savimbi to the tune of $300,000 – a magic number seemingly pulled from the hat – in an effort to prevent Angola from succumbing to left-wing MPLA control. In this effort the Americans enlisted South Africa's support, even though the country's white minority rule was facing growing and violent unpopularity at home.

However, this was game-changing. In late October 1975, South African military units invaded Angola from their bases in Namibia. By 11 November, UNITA and FNLA fighters, commanded by South Africans, had wrested control of most of the Angolan coast and its southern provinces from the MPLA, whose claim to be the legitimate leadership of Angola was now in serious danger.

While initially successful militarily, this US-sponsored intervention was a political disaster. Many African nations such as Nigeria, Ghana, and Tanzania, were sympathetic to the MPLA. That these states would organize a formal condemnation at the Organization of African Unity's upcoming annual conference in early 1976 worried US policy makers, who now engaged in some furious lobbying. This bore fruit, in that the vote on Angola resulted in a deadlock.

Meanwhile, all three Angolan nationalist bodies had declared independence, each proclaiming itself as the legitimate government of Angola. The stage was set for a civil war that roiled the country, brought the Cuban military into the fray onto the side of Agostinho Neto, and resulted in death and destabilization for millions of Angolans – a slaughter that continued until 2002. Far from presenting itself as an effective and responsible 'international policeman,' the US, with its *realpolitik* meddling in the region, stood, and still stands, largely to blame for fomenting one of the African continent's bloodiest conflicts.

LIST OF ACRONYMS,
SOME UNUSUAL
WORDS AND PHRASES

Below is a list of acroynms, some unusual words and phrases used in this text:

a luta continua	the fight continues
abraço	hug, embrace
Adamastor	sea monster (in Camões' *Os Lusíadas*)
alfacinha	a person from Lisboa (lettuce-face)
apartheid	racial segregation in South Africa
askari	African soldier
azulejo	glaze-decorated wall tile (*azul*=blue)
bairros de lata	slum housing
BDS	*Bloc Démocratique Senégalais*
bica	espresso coffee
boite	nightclub
calçada portuguesa	small sidewalk paving stones
carimbo	stamp, or seal of approval
catana	machete (see also *panga*)
chá	tea
chapa	sheet of corrugated iron
CIA	Central Intelligence Agency
circumscricão	municipal commission
conselho	municipality
CT	communist terrorist (Malaya)
CTT	*Correios Telégrafos e Telefones* (Portuguese post office and telephone organization)
dama-da-noite	strong-scented night-blooming jasmine
DGS	*Direcção-Geral de Segurança*
ditado	saying or expression
DRC	*Democratic Republic of the Congo*
duka	shebeen, small store
emancipado (a)	emancipated person, able to read & write
escolher	to choose
escudo	unit of Portuguese currency, ancient navigational instrument depicted on Portuguese flag
Estado Novo	Concept of government introduced by Salazar
estrangeiro	foreigner
festa	party, festival
FLQ	*Front de Libération du Québec*
FNLA	*Frente Nacional de Libertação de Angola*
Force Publique	Congolese army under Belgian Gen. Émile Janssens
fragata	river sailing barge (see also *varino*)

freguesia	parish
galão	coffee with milk
golpista	coup leader (Spanish)
GRAE	*Governo Revolucionário de Angola no Exílio*
latifúndio	large land holding, farm
Linha de Cascais	Lisboa-Cascais commuter rail line
LUSO	Lusitânia news agency
Maridadi	chic, beautiful (Swahili)
Mau Mau	1950-61, Kenya independence and terror organization
mestiço (a)	mixed-race
minifúndio	small land holding, farm
MNC	*Mouvement National Congolais* (Belgian)
mordomo	butler, steward
MPLA	*Movimento Popular de Libertação de Angola*
MUD	(see UMA below)
mulato (a)	mixed race
MUNAF	(see UMA below)
NATO	North Atlantic Treaty Organization
o povo	the people
oposicionista	political oppositionist
Os Lusíadas	Portugal's national epic poem by Luís Vaz de Camões
padrão	plinth, a stone marker
PAIGC	*Partido Africano para a Independéncia da Guiné e Cabo Verde*
panga	machete (Swahili)
pântano	swampland, bog
PDA	*Partido Democrático de Angola* (Portuguese-speaking)
PDA	*Parti Democratique Angolaise* (French-speaking)
pelourinho	pillory or whipping post
pensão	small hotel, bed & breakfast
PIDE	*Polícia Internacional e de Defesa do Estado*
pombe	home brew beer
povo	(the common) people, citizenry
pulga	flea
puta	*prostitute*
PVDE	*Polícia de Vigilância e de Defesa do Estado*
reboco	rendering in cement or plaster
regedoria	area of indigenous authority

saloio	market farmer in vicinity of Lisboa
SARA	*Serviço de Assisténcia aos Refugiados de Angola*
Schutztruppe	German East African army under von Lettow-Vorbeck
seguro	secure, reliable
serra	ridge of mountains
SNI	*Secretariado Nacional de Informação*
SIRP	*Sistema de Informações da Republica Portuguesa*
TAP	*Transportes Aéreos Portugueses* – Portugal's national air carrier
terra cotta	cooked earth - ceramic
UMA	United Movement of Antifascism – later MUD, *Movimento de Unidade Democrática*, founder organization of MUNAF, *Movimento de Unidade Nacional Antifascista*
UN	United Nations
UNESCO	United Nations Educational, Scientific and Cultural Organization
UNITA	*União Nacional para a Independência Total de Angola*
UPA	*União das Populações de Angola*
usofruto	bounty of the land
varino	river sailing barge (see also *fragata*)

CPSIA information can be obtained
at www.ICGtesting.com
Printed in the USA
LVHW110826260722
724417LV00001B/14